T0391294

CHINESE MUSIC IN PRINT

Chinese Music in Print

From the Great Sage to the Lady Literata

Yang Yuanzheng

with contributions by Fong Sing Ha and Colin Huehns

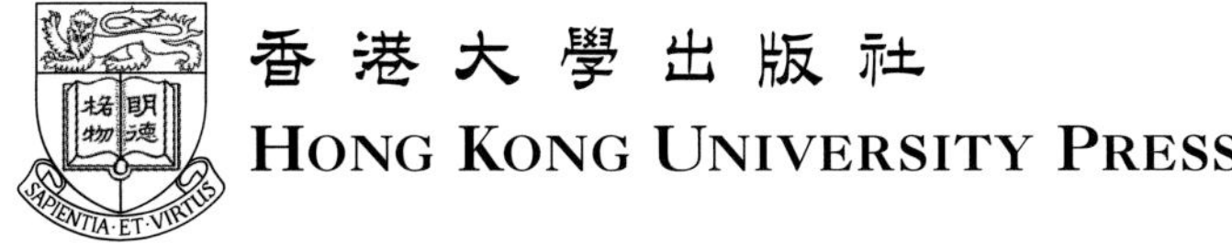
香港大學出版社
Hong Kong University Press

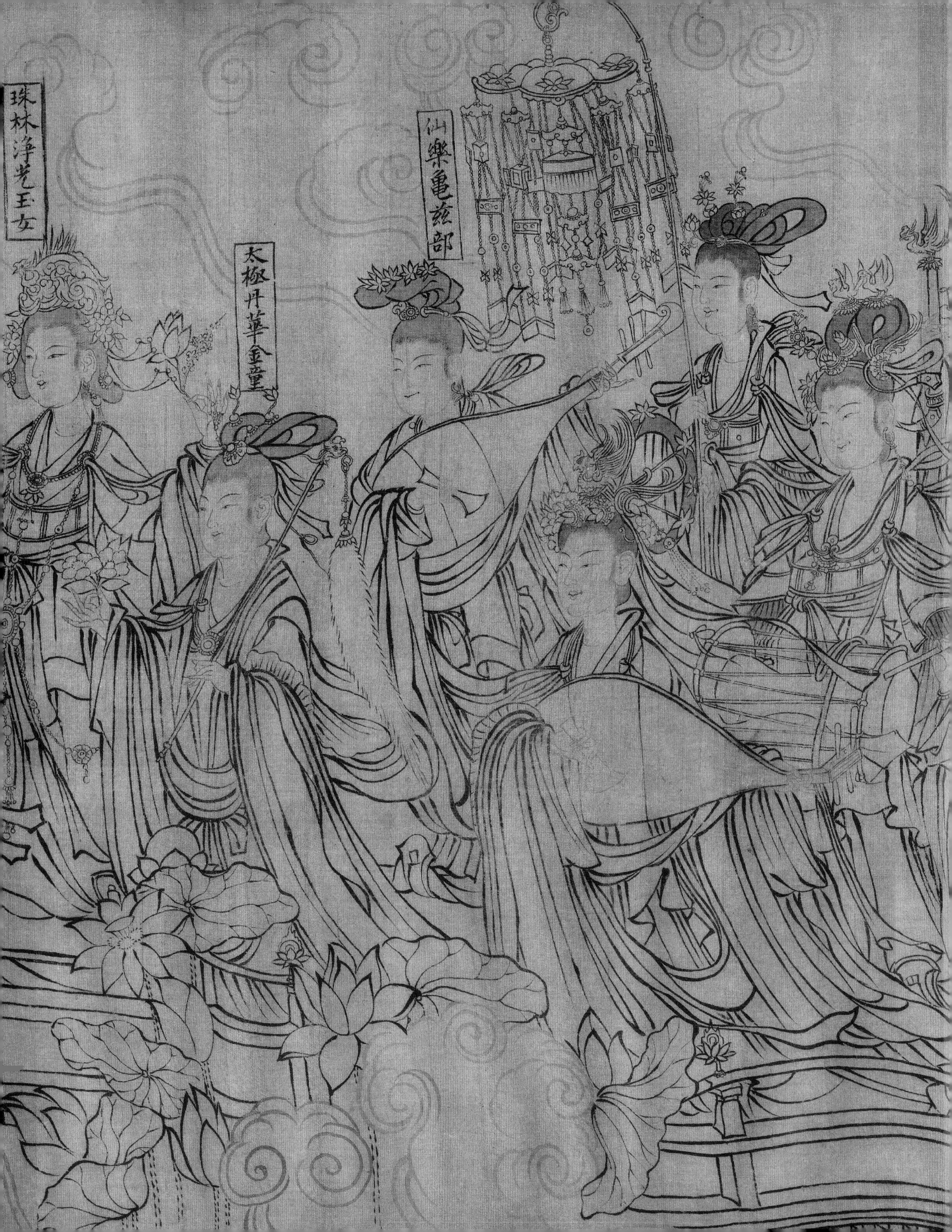

珠林淨光玉女
太極丹華金童
仙樂龜茲部

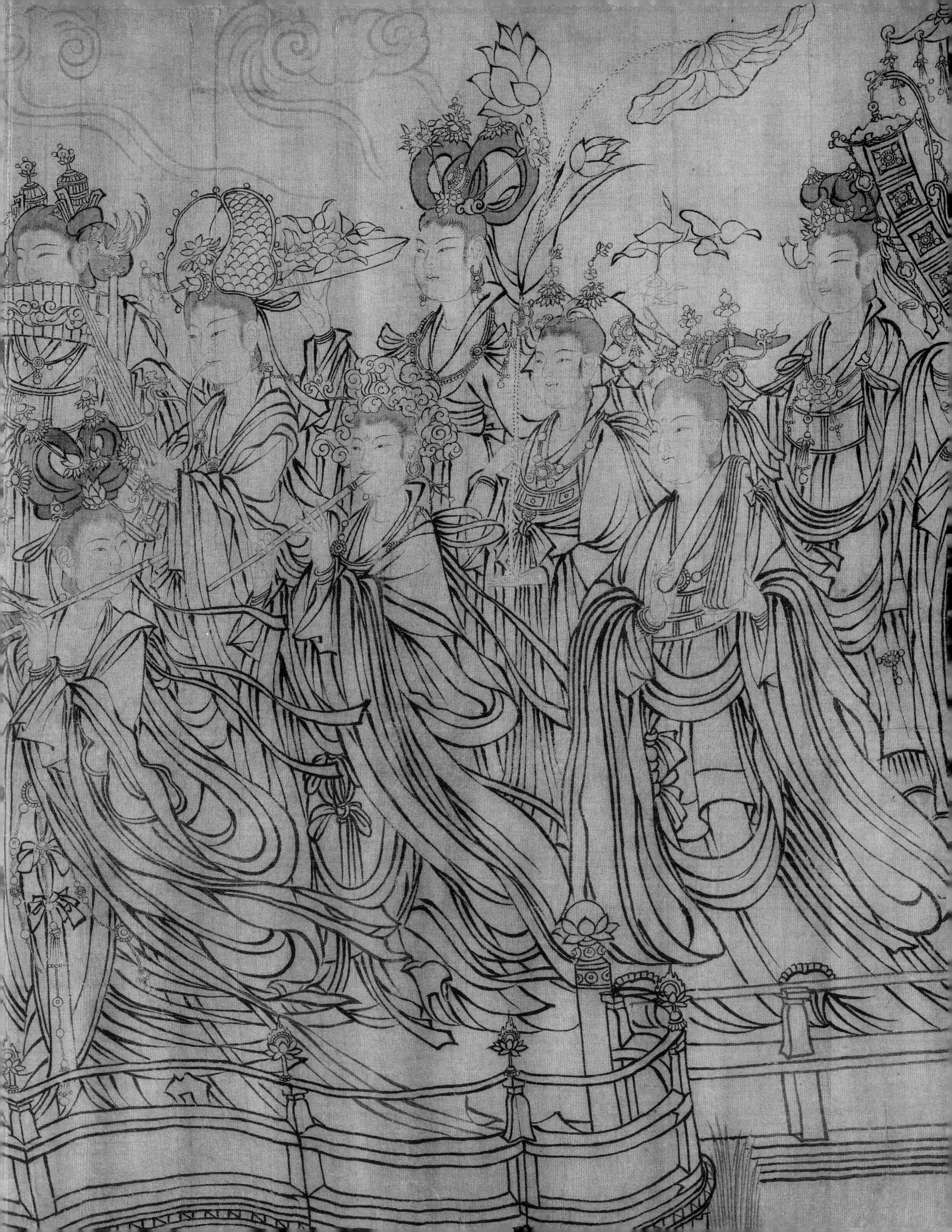

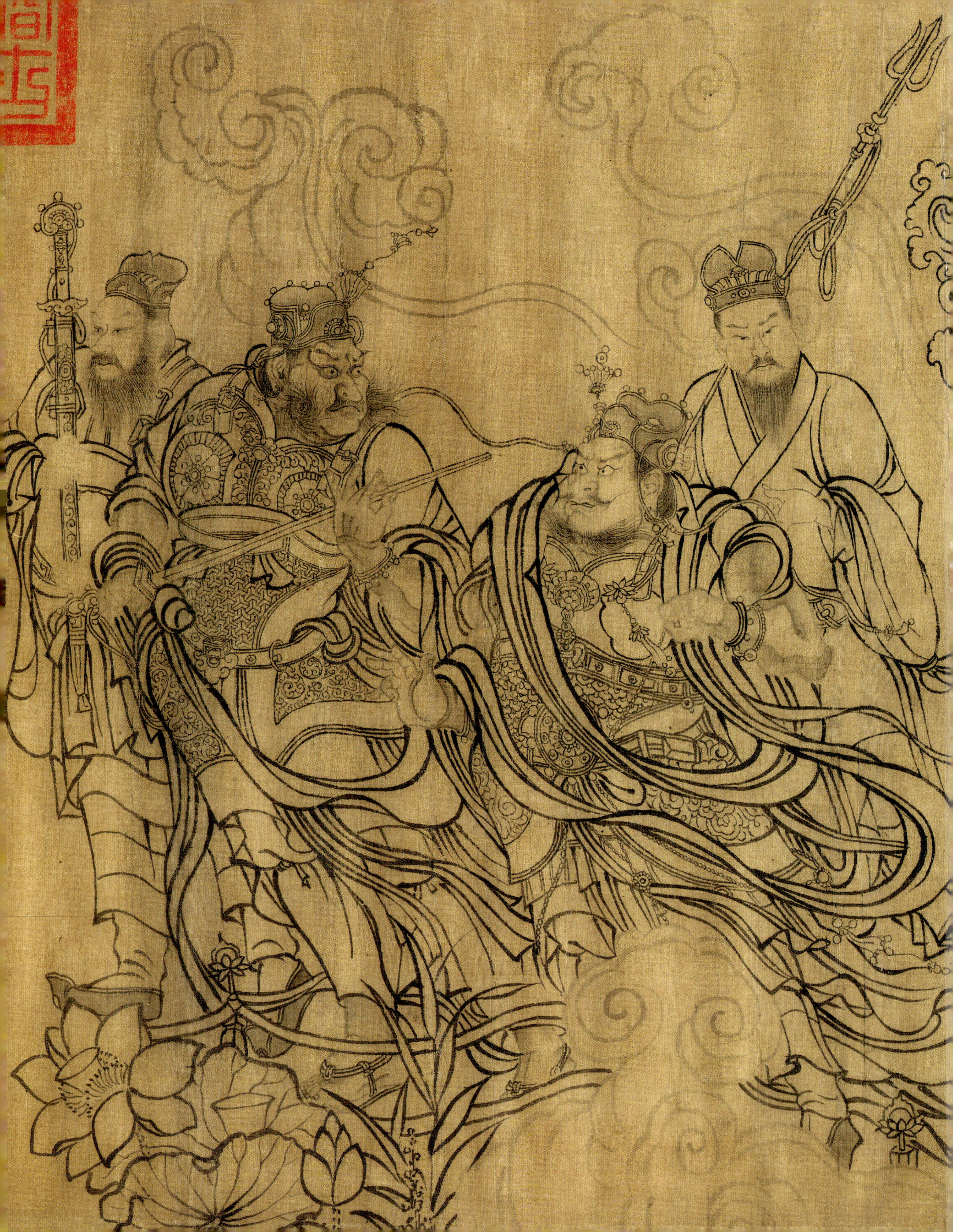

Contents

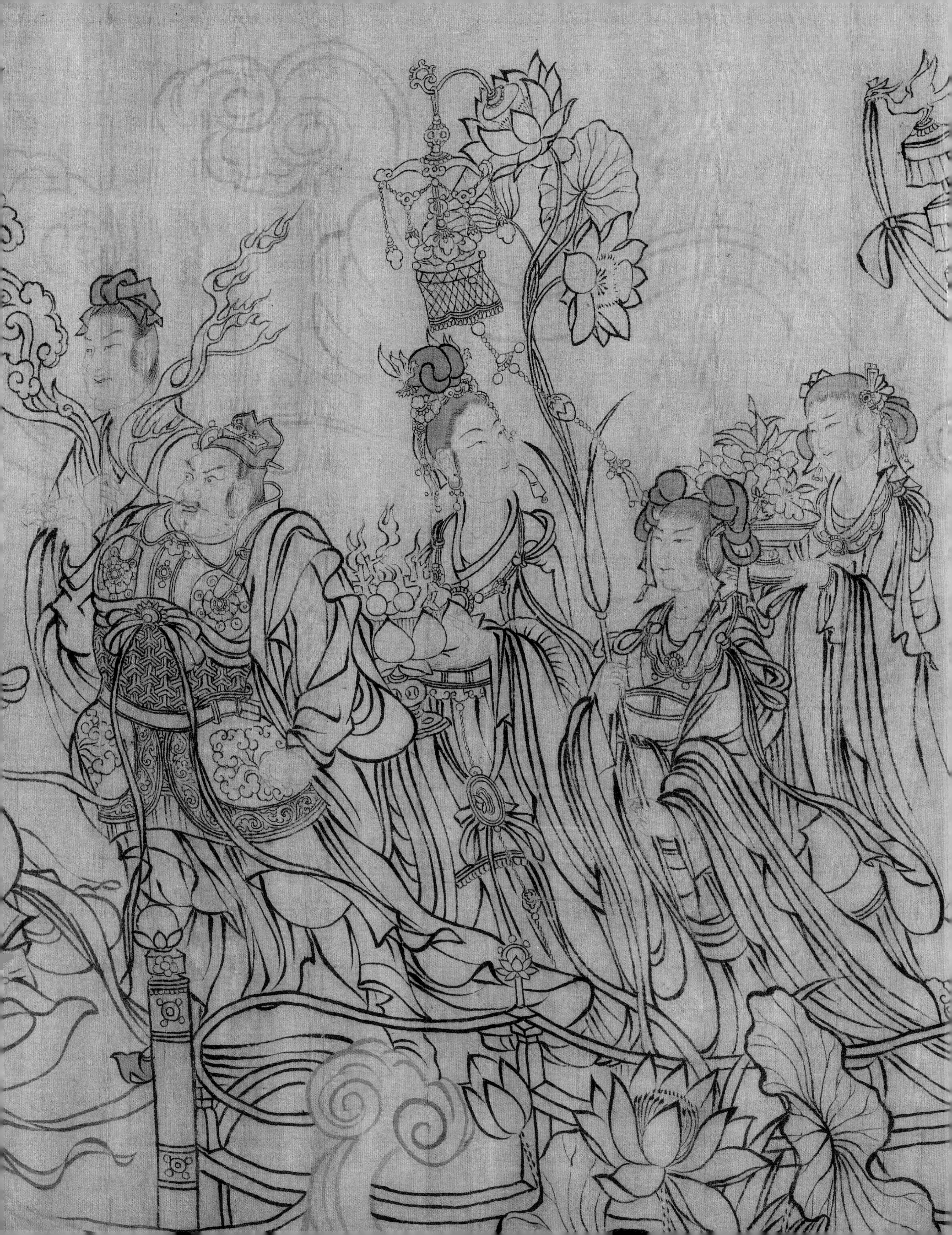

Acknowledgements

The writing of this book resulted from an invitation from the University of Hong Kong Libraries to guest-curate an exhibition "Music in Print: Selections from the Fung Ping Shan Library and the Western Rare Book Collection" from January 26 to March 11, 2021. The preparation of the exhibition offered me a rare opportunity to search for an appropriate framework to scaffold the entire viewing of these particular but significant exhibits so that I could offer viewers a highlighted scholarly trip through the history of Chinese music in print. It also triggered me to think about how to insert the dissemination and transmission of music into the discussion of manuscript and printed culture in China. This book emerges out of the exhibition and retains its spirit of guided revelation.

The foundation for studies in this field was established by three distinguished scholars: Jao Tsung-i of the University of Hong Kong, and Wang Shixiang and Yuan Quanyou of the Music Research Institute, the Chinese Academy of Arts, Beijing. Jao, with assistance of He Peixiong, Ma Youhuan, Huang Zhaohan, etc., published the first bibliographical records of the Fung Ping Shan Library's Chinese rare books, *Xianggang daxue Feng Pingshan tushuguan cang shanben shulu* [*An Annotated Bibliography of Chinese Rare Books in the Fung Ping Shan Library*] (Hong Kong: Longmen shudian, 1970), and an enlarged edition of this book, including new entries written by bibliographers Li Zhifang and Zhang Lijuan, was published in 2003. In the field of Chinese music bibliography, Wang Shixiang's *Zhongguo gudai yinyue shumu chugao* [*A Preliminary Catalog of ancient Chinese Musical Books*] (Beijing: Yinyue chubanshe, 1961) is the benchmark modern study. Yuan Quanyou, in collaboration with Wang Shixiang, compiled and published in ten installments the *Zhongguo yinyueshi cankao tupian* [*Reference Illustrations on Chinese Music History*] (Shanghai / Beijing: Xinyinyue chubanshe / Renmin yinyue chubanshe, 1954–1987). In tandem with Liu Dongsheng, Yuan's magnum opus *Zhongguo yinyue shi tujian* [*A Pictorial Guide to the History of Chinese Music*] (Beijing: Renmin yinyue chubanshe, 1988) contains extensive illustrations of printed Chinese music. Without the research of these three individuals, we would have had few clues as to the quality of the rare books housed in the Fung Ping Shan Library and the relationship of these items to Chinese music.

To the co-authors, Fong Sing Ha and Colin Huehns, I would like to express my deep gratitude for their scholarly contributions and years of commitment. The compilation of this book is the culmination of decades of research conducted by us in the fields of Chinese music literature and iconography. Our hope is that the combined expertise of our trio has assisted in contextualising individual artifacts into their long and varied historical and cultural environments, in examining the mixed social milieux of the figures who created and remade them, and in assessing the readers who made use of them over and over again as the centuries passed. It is our collaboration that has rendered the whole into a coherent narrative.

From the outset, the project has received support from Peter Sidorko, the former University Librarian, and his successor Flora Ng, the Chief Information Officer. In 2019, Esther Woo, the Deputy University Librarian and Fung Ping Shan Librarian, was instrumental in securing a Knowledge Exchange grant from the University Knowledge Exchange Office, which made the related exhibition possible. Financial support for the preparation and manufacture of the book was provided by the Hsu Long Sing Research Fund, the T. H. Chan Publication Fund, and the Hong Kong Arts Development Council.

I owe much to the friends and colleagues who supported the writing of this book: Karl Kügle (University of Oxford), Benjamin A. Elman (Princeton University), Rembrandt Wolpert and Elizabeth Markham (University of Arkansas), Yu Siu-wah (Lingnan University), Bell Yung (University of Pittsburgh), Helen Rees (University of California, Los Angeles), Frank Kouwenhoven (European Foundation for Chinese Music Research), Robert C. Provine (University of Maryland, College Park), Joseph P. McDermott (University of Cambridge), Shigehisa Kuriyama (Harvard University), Christopher Pak (The Hong Kong Academy for Performing Arts), Terauchi Naoko (Kobe University), and Tsuchida Eizaburō (Tokyo University of the Arts). Support and encouragement have also come from my colleagues at the University of Hong Kong: Daniel Chua, Chan Hing-yan, Giorgio Biancorosso, Joshua Chan, Youn Kim, José Vicente Neglia, and Deborah Waugh.

For their support of my examination of source materials on-site, I am grateful to the following librarians and private collectors: James Cheng and Ma Xiaohe (Harvard-Yenching Library), Charles Aylmer and Koyama Noboru (Cambridge University Library), Koos Kuiper (Leiden University Library), Martin Heijdra (Gest Library, Princeton University), Chen Xianxing and Liang Ying (Shanghai Library), and Edith Chan (University of Hong Kong Libraries); and Georges Goormaghtigh, Sören Edgren, Howard C. Yang, and Christopher Bruckner, who have assisted this project with access to their valuable collections.

This book was produced as a cooperative effort of many individuals. Thanks are due to: Michael Duckworth and Peter Daniell (Publishers), Kenneth Yung (Acquisitions Editor), Serina Poon (Senior Production Coordinator), and Clara Ho (Managing Editor) at the Hong Kong University Press for their trust in the scholarly efficacy of this research; Christopher Mattison at the Hong Kong University Museum and Art Gallery for skillfully editing the manuscript; William Furniss for photographing the images; and Stephy Tsui for realizing such an elegant design. At the University of Hong Kong Libraries, the management of the exhibition was entrusted to the capable hands of Jody Beenk and Lesley Liu, former and current Head of the Preservation and Conservation Division, who were assisted by Xiaoping Cai, Carmen Chan, and staff at the Main Library and the Music Library. To these friends and colleagues, I offer my gratitude for your unstinting support.

Yang Yuanzheng
The University of Hong Kong

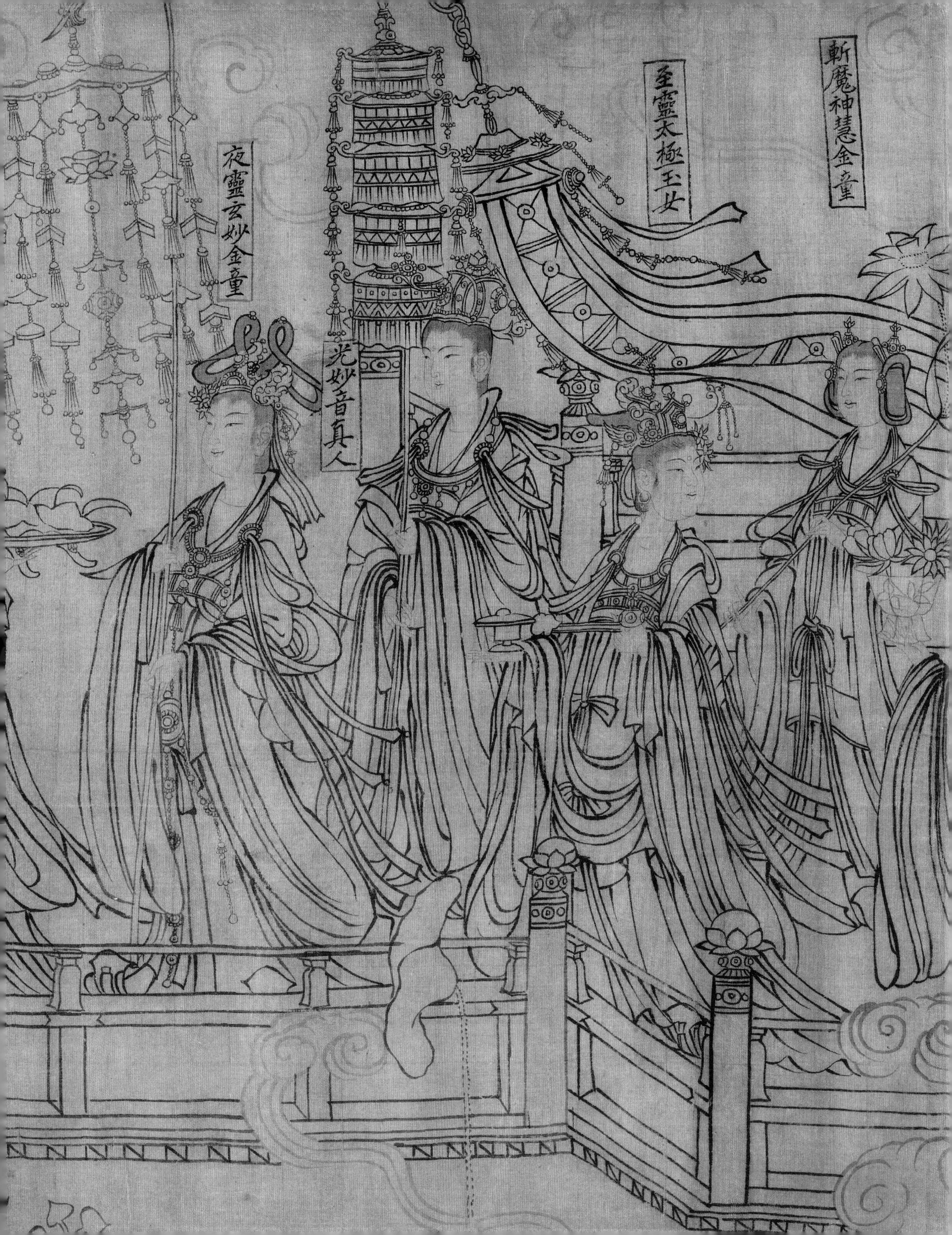
夜靈玄妙金童
光妙音真人
至靈太極玉女
斬魔神慧金童

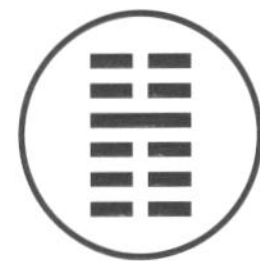

Thunder arising from the earth symbolizes Happiness. The ancestral ruler, in accordance with this, created music in honor of virtuous morality. He presented it ardently to the Supreme Emperor, and to his ancestors.
雷出地奮，豫。先王以作樂崇德，殷薦之上帝，以配祖考。

The Book of Changes 易經

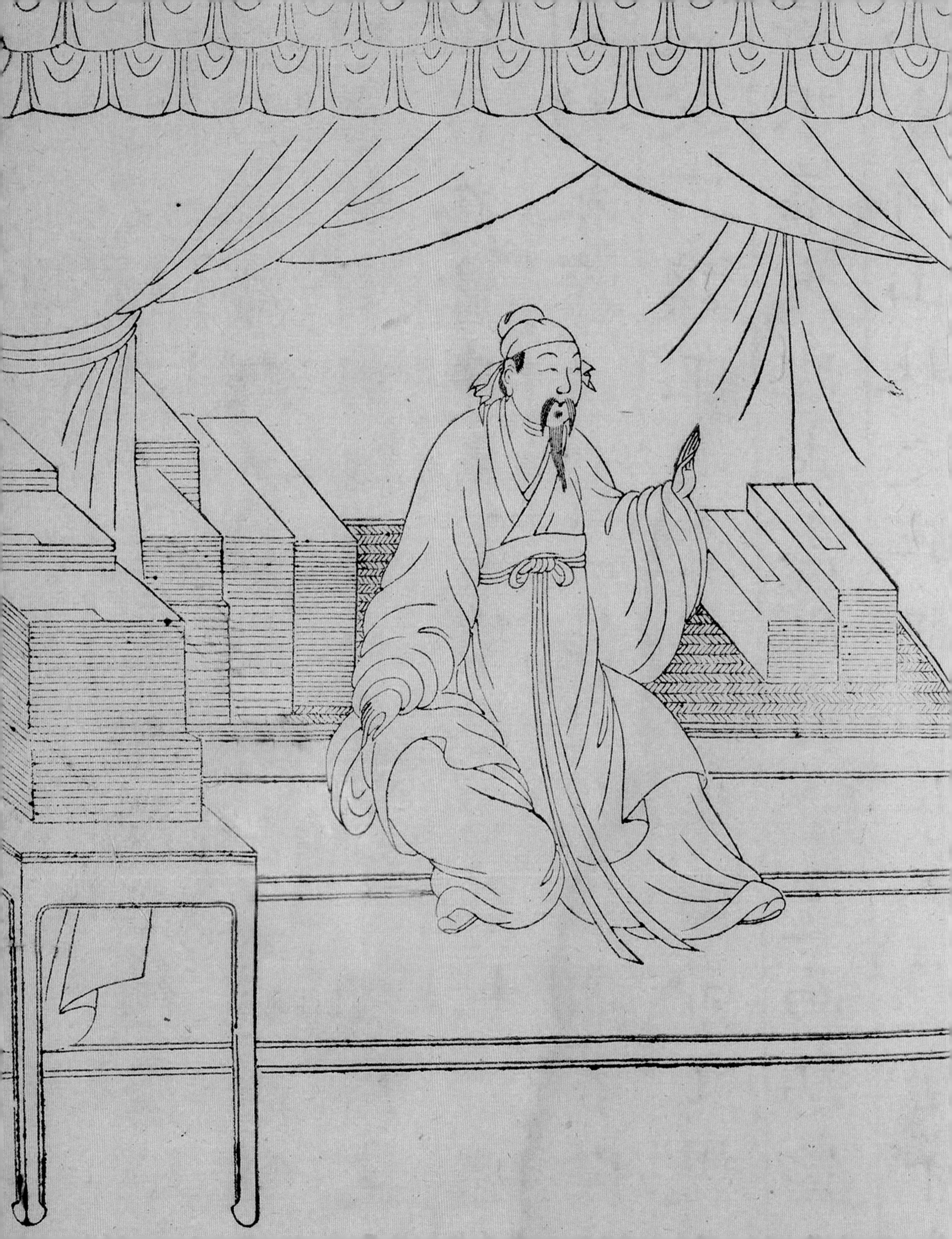

Introduction

Locating Books on Music Using Traditional Classification Systems

Yang Yuanzheng

The publication of *Chinese Music in Print: From the Great Sage to the Lady Literata* was inspired by the extraordinary response to an exhibition on the same subject prepared in collaboration with the Department of Music, University of Hong Kong, and the Preservation and Conservation Division, University of Hong Kong Libraries.[1] The exhibition focused on the presentation of music's material culture in pre-modern China as told through books and bound manuscripts held in the University's Fung Ping Shan Library and Western Rare Book Collection. The starting point of the present volume is a scholarly desire to bring back to life these rare collection items that are entwined within the world of music. It views the library as a repository not of information but of artifacts, and engages with those artifacts as a means for generating a scholarly narrative.

For the three contributors to the current manuscript, a shared passion for rare and historic books is our primary link. Not only are books—as their authors intended—a source of information and enlightenment, but they exist to tell a story. Thus, we are interested not simply in the exegetical power of books, but also in layers of redactions and draft layouts, printings, introductions, colophons, marginalia, library stamps, typefaces, bindings, condition, and provenance. In short—how has information come to be presented in this particular manner? In this way, the overall volume is concerned both with Chinese music and a particular form of bibliophilic fervor. Specimens found in American, British, and Asian repositories are provided for an international context, while books from the Fung Ping Shan Library (Fig. I.1) hold pride of place, appropriately given its 90th anniversary in 2022.

Fig. I.1: *Renjing yangqiu (Mirror of Morality)*, *juan* 12, fol. 48r, woodblock engraving of Ma Shu (522–581) with his books (detail).
Author: Wang Tingne (1573–1619).
Date: 1600.
Woodblock: 24.4 × 16.5 cm.
Fung Ping Shan Library.

Another emphasis of the present study is that although the evolution of manuscript and printed culture in China has become more frequently discussed,[2] its dynamic interaction with the dissemination and transmission of music remains largely ignored.[3] This book seeks to address this lacuna. The selection of materials gets to the heart of how Chinese music history has been constructed: When were the works created and

1. Yang Yuanzheng, *Music in Print: Selections from the Fung Ping Shan Library and Western Rare Book Collection* (Hong Kong: University of Hong Kong Libraries, 2021).

2. See, for example, K. T. Wu, "Ming Printing and Printers," *Harvard Journal of Asiatic Studies* 7.3 (1943): 203–260; Thomas Carter and L. C. Goodrich, *The Invention of Printing in China and its Spread Westward* (New York: Ronald Press, 1955); Sören Edgren, *Chinese Rare Books in American Collections* (New York: China Institute in America, 1984); Tsien Tsuen-hsuin, *Chemistry and Chemical Technology: Paper and Printing*, in *Science and Civilisation in China*, ed. Joseph Needham, vol. 5, pt. 1 (Cambridge: Cambridge University Press, 1985); Sören Edgren, "Southern Song Printing at Hangzhou," *Museum of Far Eastern Antiquities Bulletin* 61 (1989): 1–212; Frederick W. Mote and Hung-lam Chu, *Calligraphy and the East Asian Book* (Boston: Shambhala, 1989); Susan Cherniak, "Book Culture and Textual Transmission in Song China," *Harvard Journal of Asiatic Studies* 54.1 (1994): 5–125; Ellen Widmer, "The Huanduzhai of Hangzhou and Suzhou: A Study in Seventeenth-Century Publishing," *Harvard Journal of Asiatic Studies* 56.1 (1996): 77–122; Lucille Chia, *Printing for Profit: The Commercial Publishers of Jianyang, Fujian (11th–17th Centuries)*, Harvard-Yenching Institute Monograph Series No. 56 (Cambridge, Mass.: Harvard University Asia Center, 2002); Inoue Susumu 井上進, *Chūgoku shuppan bunka shi* 中国出版文化史 (Nagoya: Nagoya University Press, 2002); Kai-wing Chow, *Publishing, Culture, and Power in Early Modern China* (Stanford: Stanford University Press, 2004); Ōki Yasushi 大木康, *Minmatsu Kōnan no shuppan bunka* 明末江南の出版文化 (Tokyo: Kenbun shuppan, 2004); Christopher Reed, *Gutenberg in Shanghai: Chinese Print Capitalism, 1876–1937* (Honolulu: University of Hawai'i Press, 2004); Tsien Tsuen-Hsuin, *Written on Bamboo and Silk* (Chicago: University of Chicago Press, 2004); Cynthia Brokaw and Kai-wing Chow, *Printing and Book Culture in Late Imperial China* (Berkeley and Los Angeles: University of California Press, 2005); Joseph McDermott, *A Social History of the Chinese Book: Books and Literati Culture in Late Imperial China* (Hong Kong: Hong Kong University Press, 2006); Cynthia Brokaw, *Commerce in Culture: The Sibao Book Trade in the Qing and Republican Periods* (Cambridge, Mass.: Harvard University Asia Center, 2007); and Tobie Meyer-Fong, "The Printed World: Books, Publishing Culture, and Society in Late Imperial China," *The Journal of Asian Studies* 66.3 (2007): 787–817.

3. Musicologists and cultural historians working on European historical sources have started to take charge of this new scholarly field. See, for example, Roger Chartier, "Music in Print," in *Music and the Cultures of Print*, ed. Kate van Orden (New York: Garland Publishing, 2000), 325–341; Kate van Orden, *Music, Authorship, and the Book in the First Century of Print* (Berkeley: University of California Press, 2014); and Kate van Orden, *Materialities: Books, Readers, and the Chanson in Sixteenth-Century Europe* (New York: Oxford University Press, 2015).

published? Who wrote them and why? Are the sources and their interpretations trustworthy? Studying these rare books about music brings one closer to understanding their authors, compilers, backers, printers, players, audiences, and sellers. Beyond these established lines of inquiry, it is possible to delve into the depiction of music in the visual arts—including the numerous woodcuts and engravings—and to consider how these representations have played into the development of instrumental technique, ensemble formation, and social context.

Before moving into a detailed analysis of raw materials, it would be wise to briefly introduce the traditional Chinese book classification system, in which the structure of the present volume is embodied.

The surviving records of Chinese book classification schemes begin with the father-and-son team of Liu Xiang 劉向 (77–6 BCE) and Liu Xin 劉歆 (46 BCE–23 CE) and their *Qilüe* 七略 (*The Seven Summaries*, 5 BCE, see Table I.1).[4] This text divides the totality of the Western Han (206 BCE–25 CE) imperial library into six categories or "summaries" 略. In addition to these six, which comprise summaries two to seven, the first acts as an explanatory introduction that details the significance and scholarly wellspring of each of the other categories, as well as outlining their relationship and the potential usage of the books classified therein. The first section is best regarded as an overarching "abstract" to the entire cataloged collection.

The six summaries are then subdivided into thirty-eight subcategories, making for two levels of classification. The first summary "Liuyi lüe" 六藝略 ("Six Arts") is divided into the nine subcategories given in the second line of the table; music is the fifth of these, placing it directly within the Confucian educational model.

The total number of titles represented in *The Seven Summaries* is 603, in which are 13,219 essays, and of these, music comprises 6 titles and 172 essays. When Ban Gu 班固 (32–92) compiled *Han shu* 漢書 (*The Official History of the Former Han Dynasty*), he took over Liu Xiang and Liu Xin's classification system with only minor alterations and reproduced it in *juan* 卷 30, "Yiwen zhi" 藝文志 ("Monograph on Arts and Literature").[5] The six items on music that are listed by both texts are as follows:

[1] *Records of Music* 樂記: 23 essays
[2] *Wang Yu's Records [of Music]* 王禹記: 24 essays
[3] *Elegant Songs and Poems* 雅歌詩: 4 essays
[4] *Master Zhao's Elegant Qin Music* 雅琴趙氏: 7 essays
[5] *Master Shi's Elegant Qin Music* 雅琴師氏: 8 essays
[6] *Master Long's Elegant Qin Music* 雅琴龍氏: 106 essays[6]

As an illustration of *The Seven Summaries* template as a direct precursor to Ban Gu's version, the only discrepancy to report in respect of these six texts is the number 99 instead of 106, which he provides for the number of essays in *Master Long's Elegant Qin Music*. Liu Xiang and Liu Xin's commentary to this selection and categorization, which is reproduced intact by Ban Gu, reads:

> *The Book of Changes* states: "The ancestral ruler created music in honor of virtuous morality; ardently, he presented it to the Supreme Emperor and to his ancestors." Therefore, from the Yellow Emperor through to the three dynasties of Xia, Shang [c. 1600–1046 BCE], and Zhou [1046–256 BCE], in each, music was called by specific names. Confucius writes: "For keeping the emperor at peace and governing the common people, nothing is more efficacious than the rites; for adjusting social mores and transforming customs, nothing is more efficacious than music;" the two are mutually compatible and march in step. When the Zhou dynasty declined, both the rites and music degenerated, and of these, music dwindled most palpably, almost to a state of non-existence; such discipline as had been required by the system of modes and melody was also disordered by the styles of the states of Zheng and Wei, and thus nothing now survives of its practice.
>
> 《易》曰：「先王作樂崇德，殷薦之上帝，以享祖考。」故自黃帝下至三代，樂各有名。孔子曰：「安上治民，莫善於禮；移風易俗，莫善於樂。」二者相與並行。周衰俱壞，樂尤微眇；以音律為節，又為鄭、衛所亂，故無遺法。[7]

Liu Xiang offers an account as to why nothing had survived of ancient ritual music. In the following section, he outlines two attempts to reconstruct the canon:

With the establishment of the Han dynasty [206 BCE–220 CE], the Zhi clan, because they were musicians and proficient in the elegant music of Confucian ritual and its mode and melody, as had been transmitted through generations of professional court musicians, and though they could recall and reproduce the percussive sounds of drums and dances, they could not recount their inner meaning. Of the rulers of the Six States, Marquis Wen of Wei [472–396 BCE, r. 446–396 BCE] was fondest of ancient practices. At the time of the Han dynasty, Emperor Xiaowendi [Liu Heng 劉恆, 203–157 BCE, r. 180–157 BCE], the musician Dou Gong came into his service and offered him a book, namely a tract entitled "The Director of Music" from the chapter "The Supreme Minister" of *Zhou guan* [*Zhou Officers*, i.e., *Zhou li* 周禮, *The Zhou Rites*].

漢興，制氏以雅樂聲律，世在樂官，頗能紀其鏗鏘鼓舞，而不能言其義。六國之君，魏文侯最為好古，孝文時得其樂人竇公，獻其書，乃《周官．大宗伯》之《大司樂》章也。[8]

In the time of Han dynasty Emperor Wudi [Liu Che 劉徹, 156–87 BCE, r. 141–87 BCE], the Prince of Hejian, Liu De 劉德 [160–129 BCE], had a deep admiration for Confucianism, and together with a scholar named Mao they extracted all of the passages from *The Zhou Rites* and the writings of various philosophers that discussed music, and used them to compose *The Records of Music*. They presented [to Emperor Wudi] the results of their research, including the performance of an eight-row-by-eight-column, sixty-four-person dance, which was nearly identical to the same dance as transmitted by the Zhi clan. Liu De's chamberlain Wang Ding was then charged with disseminating their findings and presented them to Wang Yu of Changshan. In the time of the Han dynasty Emperor Chengdi [Liu Ao 劉驁, 51–7 BCE, r. 33–7 BCE], Wang Yu was an official envoy and spoke loquaciously on their significance, presenting the Emperor with these *Records* organized into twenty-four *juan*.

武帝時，河間獻王好儒，與毛生等共采《周官》及諸子言樂事者，以作《樂記》，獻八佾之舞，與制氏不相遠。其內史丞王定傳之，以授常山王禹。禹，成帝時為謁者，數言其義，獻二十四卷《記》。[9]

Finally, Liu Xiang explains why the urtext of the *Records of Music* that he has provided (item 1) is different from the version transmitted by Wang Yu (item 2):

> I, your humble servant, Liu Xiang, have collated and edited the text of this book, and upon obtaining *Records of Music* in twenty-three *juan*, found that it differs from Wang Yu's version; scholarship in this field is gradually becoming scarcer.
>
> 臣向校書，得《樂記》二十三篇，與禹不同，其道寖以益微。[10]

Liu Xiang's text focuses entirely on justifying the presence and provenance of only the first two of the six items on music—the two *Records of Music* that outline its role in Confucian ritual—presumably to accentuate his catalog's compliance with official ideology, but the six items themselves fall naturally into three subdivisions, though this is not made explicit: (1) *Records of Music* (nos. 1–2); (2) songs and poems (no. 3); and (3) *qin* 琴 zither music (nos. 4–6). Of these, only (1) is dependent on pre-Qin dynasty textual sources, (2) stems principally from the early Han dynasty poet-musician Yu Gong 虞公 and his lyrical oeuvre,[11] while Zhao Ding 趙定, Shi Zhong 師中, and Long De 龍德 whose repertoires comprise (3) all lived at the time of the Emperor Xuandi (Liu Xun 劉詢, 91–48 BCE, r. 74–48 BCE) and were contemporary musicians playing the *qin* music of their own times.[12] In order to legitimize situating nos. 3–6 alongside the first two and their weightier Confucian affiliations, Liu Xiang conceived the ploy of prefixing them with "*ya*" 雅 or "elegant" so as to imply their higher status and proximity to the

4. Liu Xiang 劉向 and Liu Xin 劉歆, *Qilüe yiwen* 七略佚文 (Aomen: Aomen daxue, 2007).

5. Ban Gu 班固, *Han shu* 漢書 (Beijing: Zhonghua shuju, 1962), vol. 6, 1701–1784.

6. Liu Xiang and Liu Xin, *Qilüe yiwen*, 99–100.

7. Ibid., 80; and Ban Gu, *Han shu*, vol. 6, 1711–1712.

8. Liu Xiang and Liu Xin, *Qilüe yiwen*, 80; and Ban Gu, *Han shu*, vol. 6, 1712.

9. Ibid.

10. Ibid.

11. Ibid., 99. Liu Xiang 劉向 and Liu Xin 劉歆, *Qilüe bielu yiwen* 七略別錄佚文 (Aomen: Aomen daxue, 2007), 26.

12. Liu Xiang and Liu Xin, *Qilüe yiwen*, 99–100. Liu Xiang and Liu Xin, *Qilüe bielu yiwen*, 26–27; and Yang Yuanzheng 楊元錚 and Yang Jun 楊軍, "Haihun hou Liu He mu chutu de qixian qin yu Xihan qinzhi 海昏侯劉賀墓出土的七弦琴與西漢琴制," *Wenwu* 文物 (2022): forthcoming.

Table I.1: The Book Classification Scheme in *The Seven Summaries*

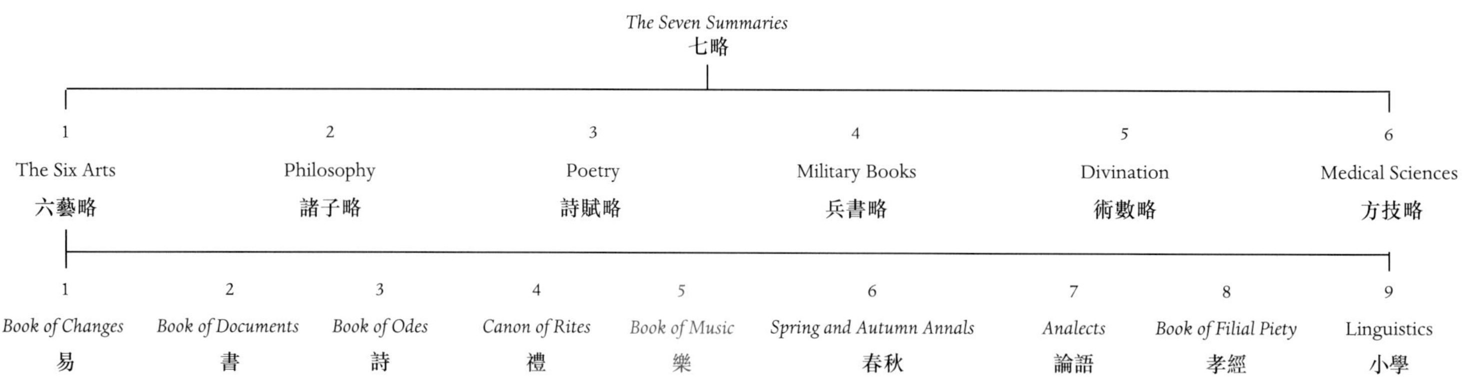

Table I.2: The Book Classification Scheme in "Monograph on Books," *The Official History of the Sui Dynasty*

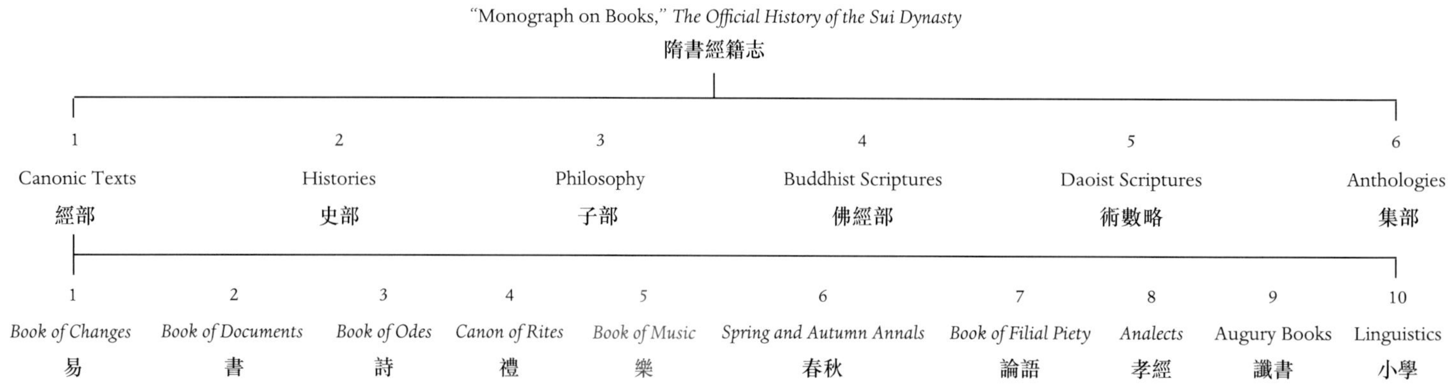

Table I.3: The Book Classification Scheme in "Monograph on Books," *The Old Official History of the Tang Dynasty*

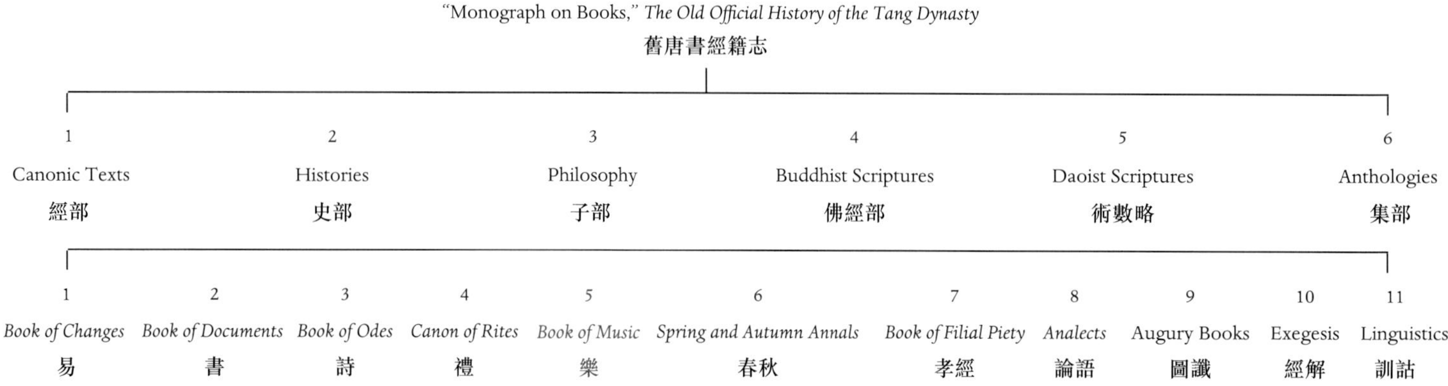

Table I.4: The Book Classification Scheme in *General Catalog of the Academy for the Veneration of Literature*

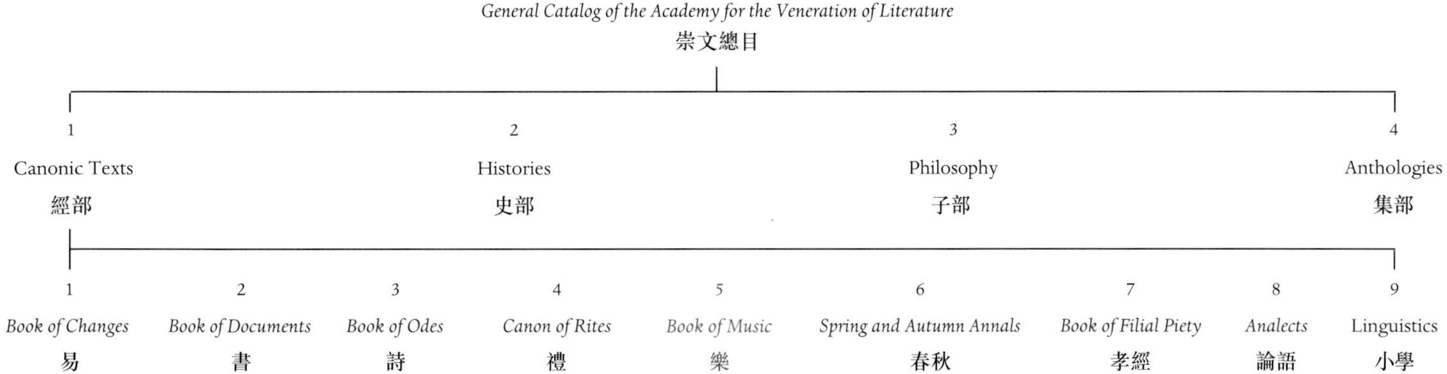

Table I.5: The Book Classification Scheme in *Descriptive Catalog of the Zhizhai Studio*

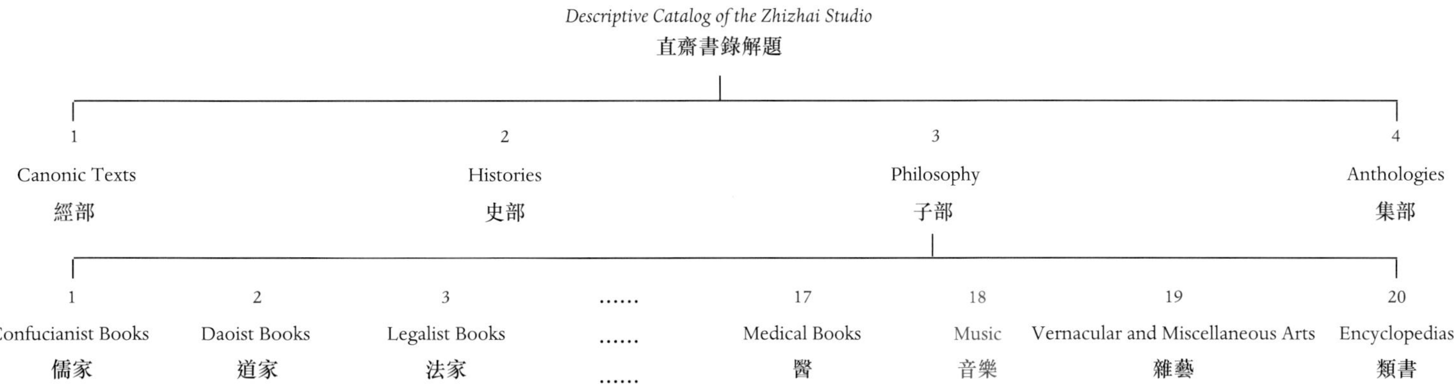

Table I.6: The Book Classification Scheme in *Catalog to the Complete Books of the Four Repositories*

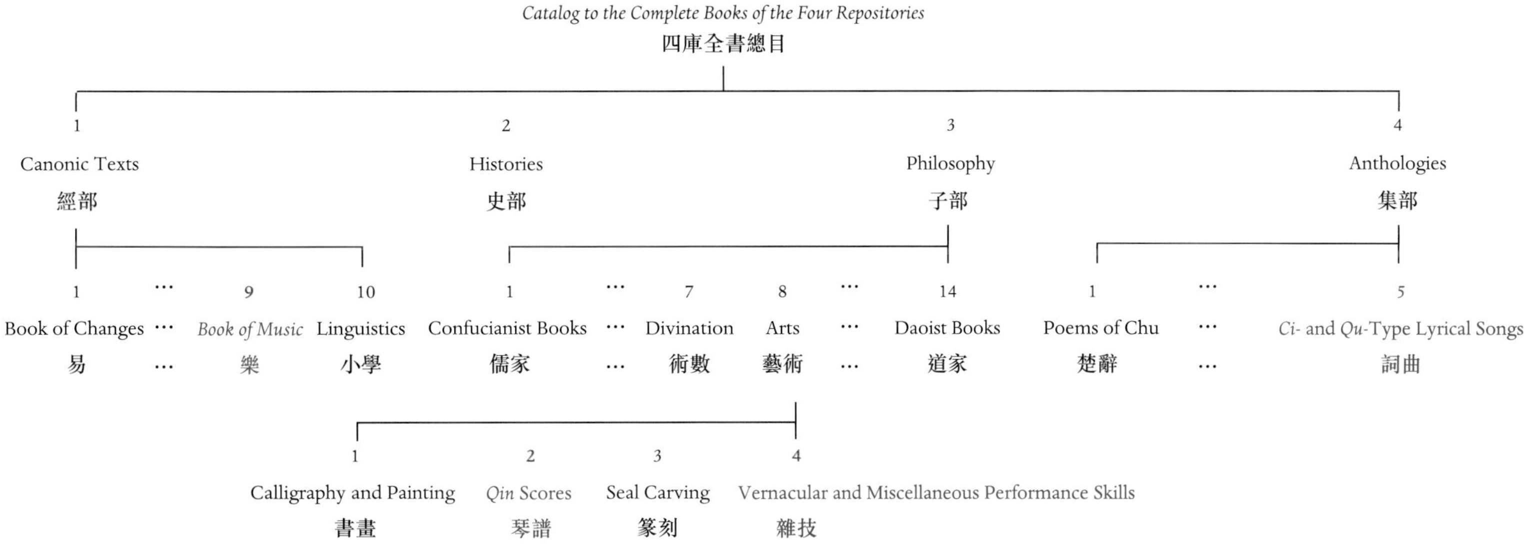

official ideology of Confucianism. The promotion of this school of thought as the orthodoxy of the Chinese imperial state is a feature of the Western Han dynasty and has traditionally been associated with the philosopher-politician Dong Zhongshu 董仲舒 (c. 198–c. 107 BCE).[13]

In a later generation of classification, that of *Sui shu* 隋書 (*The Official History of the Sui Dynasty*, dated 629–636), the equivalent bibliographic section comprises *juan* 32–35 and is called "Jingji zhi" 經籍志 ("Monograph on Books," see Table I.2).[14] More extensive than its Western Han dynasty predecessor, it lists a total of 3,212 books comprising 36,708 *juan*; the total increases to 4,757 with the inclusion of titles of lost items listed and the *juan* count to 49,467. Of these, the section on music consists of 44 surviving books in 142 *juan*, 47 if lost books are included, for a total of 263 *juan*.

Like Liu Xiang and Liu Xin's *Seven Summaries*, the Sui dynasty (581–618) "Monograph on Books" is also divided into six sections (as given in the first line of Table I.2), but the configuration is now radically different. "The Six Arts" of *The Seven Summaries* has been renamed "Canonic Texts," though the overall second-level categorization inside the Sui dynasty equivalent, as given in the second line of Table I.2, is broadly similar. "Poetry" of *The Seven Summaries* has been renamed "Anthologies." "Philosophy" remains a discrete section, though books on military sciences, divination, and medical techniques have been scattered into it because separate sections on these have disappeared. New arrivals are "Histories" and sections on Buddhist and Daoist works, the latter two reflecting traditions that flourished at the time. In fact, "Daoist Works" was formerly a subcategory of the section "Philosophy" in *The Seven Summaries* that was upgraded.

Each of the six sections is further subdivided at a second level and music again finds its place within the first section as the fifth of ten subcategories. Of these, only the ninth, "Augury Texts," is without precedent.

A further hypothetical third layer of subdivision is available to the music section with items therein falling into three categories: (1) the theory of elegant music (nos. 1–16); (2) *qin* music (nos. 17–23); and (3) practical treatises on elegant music and banquet music (nos. 24–47).[15] Of these, (3) was further divided by the late Qing dynasty (1644–1911) bibliographer Yao Zhenzong 姚振宗 (1842–1906) into historical records (nos. 24–35), repertoire lists (nos. 36–40), music of suspended instruments (nos. 41–43), and pitch standards (nos. 44–47).[16] Apart from the spurious *Yue jing* 樂經 (*The Book of Music*) in four *juan* (no. 16), which was afforded the status of a Confucian canonic text in 4 CE by the notorious usurper Wang Mang 王莽 (45 BCE–23 CE), all other books are either contemporary (i.e., Sui dynasty) or from the relatively recent Jin dynasty (265–420) or Northern and Southern dynasties (420–589). Their presence continues the precedent set by Liu Xiang of including texts on music of much less ancient provenance and parallels the Sui dynasty addition to the first level of organization of the third to sixth categories that are more strongly grounded in recent writing.

Jiu Tang shu 舊唐書 (*The Old Official History of the Tang Dynasty*, dated 941–945) records the total number of items in the "Monograph on Books" 經籍志 (*juan* 46–47) as 3,060, comprising 51,852 *juan*, of which music contributes 29 items of 195 *juan*. Table I.3 sets out the overall classification; its four-part division at the first level—Canonic Texts 經部, Histories 史部, Philosophy 子部, and Anthologies 集部—is the familiar categorization of more recent times.

The Buddhist section present in the Sui dynasty equivalent has been removed entirely. During the interim, ever-more-numerous Buddhist tomes had, by necessity, acquired their own independent three-layer system, and driven by concerns that its resultant complexity would overburden an already congested classification, it was simply excised.[17] The section on Daoist works has been downgraded and once again becomes a subcategory of "Philosophy." Reorganization at the second level of "Canonic Texts" is less radical: the first nine sections are identical and the tenth is simply divided into "Canonical Exegesis" and "Etymological Origins," both exemplars of a rise in exegetical scholarship; *The Book of Music* remains fifth on the list.

The music subsection can again be subjectively divided into three further subdivisions, though no such categorization is explicitly indicated: the first two (1) the theory of elegant music (nos. 1–15) and (2) *qin* music (nos. 16–21) are identical to those of *The Official History of the Sui Dynasty*, but (3) vernacular and Central Asian music (nos. 22–29) is a new departure and an indication of a rise in textual records of vernacular sources, as well as a byproduct of growing cultural interaction between China and Central Asian neighbors.[18]

Chongwen zongmu 崇文總目 (*General Catalog of the Academy for the Veneration of Literature*, dated 1034–1041) is the principal contribution of the Northern Song dynasty (960–1127) to book classification.[19] Produced on imperial command by scholars of the *Hanlin* 翰林 Academy spearheaded by Wang Yaochen 王堯臣 (1003–1058), the book total is now 3,445, comprising 30,669 *juan*, of which music contributes 49 books in 302 *juan*. As given in Table I.4, the overall structure of the index has changed little from its Tang dynasty predecessor and employs the same four-part division at the first classification level. *The Book of Music* remains the fifth of nine subdivisions of the "Canonic Texts," and other than the omission of "Augury Books" these nine are an identical series to that found in the Sui dynasty classification. Again, the music subsection can be divided into three hypothetical categories, with the familiar elegant/banquet music (nos. 1–13) and *qin* music (nos. 14–44) comprising the first two, while the third is another new arrival, music for the *ruan* 阮 lute (nos. 45–49).[20]

The introductory preamble to the music section is written by no less of a luminary than the celebrated Northern Song scholar-official Ouyang Xiu 歐陽修 (1007–1072). In a similar fashion to Liu Xiang, he first outlines a rationale for the paucity of surviving pre-Qin dynasty writings on music:

> The rites and music of the three ancient dynasties [Xia, Shang, and Zhou] have, since the latter years of the Zhou dynasty, for the most part been lost, and likewise suffered the Qin dynasty's [221–206 BCE] violent extirpation of scholarship; however, *The Book of Documents*, *The Analects*, and *The Book of Filial Piety* were preserved in the ancestral dwellings of Confucius' family, and *The Book of Changes* as a divination text was not burnt along with the others, while *The Book of Odes* was grounded in recitation and not just written on bamboo slips and silk sheets, but instead transmitted by oral tradition; thus, of the Six Classics, *The Canon of Rites* was the one whose degradation was the most serious, and *The Book of Music*, as it was passed on by singing and the playing of instruments, was naturally the easiest to suffer loss. On the establishment of the Han dynasty when research into classical texts was instigated, *The Book of Music* was found to be the most glaring lacuna. Scholars realized that it could no longer stand on its own, and it was thereupon combined with *The Canon of Rites*. Thus, the texts of only Five Classics survived and their scholarship remained classified in the Six Arts.
>
> 三代禮樂，自周之末，其失已多，又經秦世滅學之暴，然《書》及《論語》、《孝經》得藏孔氏之家，《易》以卜筮不焚，而《詩》本諷誦，不專在于竹帛，人得口以傳之，故獨《禮》之于六經，其亡最甚，而《樂》又有聲器，尤易為壞失。及漢興，考求典籍，而《樂》最缺絕。學者不能自立，遂並其說于禮家。書為五經，流別為六藝。[21]

The Sui and Tang (618–906) dynasties follow Liu Xiang's lead regarding tacit inclusion of more items of contemporary music, but make no attempt to justify their choice. It fell to Ouyang Xiu to attempt to address this issue, one that Liu Xiang had managed to avoid, and as a historian and musician to offer for the first time a convincing rationale for the inclusion of contemporary musical items:

> The reason that music can connect to the harmoniousness of heaven and earth, and effect governance on the myriad things, lies principally in its ability to transform mankind

13. According to *Han shu*, Liu Xiang was an important figure who excessively admired Dong Zhongshu's views. See Michael Loewe, *Dong Zhongshu, a "Confucian" Heritage and the Chunqiu Fanlu* (Leiden: Brill, 2011), 337.

14. Piet van der Loon, *Taoist Books in the Libraries of the Sung Period: A Critical Study and Index* (London: Ithaca, 1984), 1–2.

15. Yao Zhenzong 姚振宗, *Sui shu jingji zhi kaozheng* 隋書經籍志考證, in *Xuxiu siku quanshu* 續修四庫全書, ed. Xuxiu siku quanshu bianzuan weiyuanhui 續修四庫全書編纂委員會, vol. 915 (Shanghai: Shanghai guji chubanshe, 1995), 83–90.

16. Ibid., 86–90.

17. Wang Zhongmin 王重民, *Zhongguo muluxue shi luncong* 中國目錄學史論叢 (Beijing: Zhonghua shuju, 1984), 71–74. Su Bai 宿白, *Hanwen foji mulu* 漢文佛籍目錄 (Beijing: Wenwu chubanshe, 2009), 42–78.

18. Liu Xu 劉昫, *Jiu Tang shu* 舊唐書 (Beijing: Zhonghua shuju, 1975), vol. 6, 1975–1976.

19. Piet van der Loon, *Taoist Books in the Libraries of the Sung Period: A Critical Study and Index*, 6–8; and Yves Hervouet, ed., *A Sung Bibliography* (Hong Kong: Chinese University Press, 1978), 195.

20. Qian Tong 錢侗, *Chongwen zongmu jishi* 崇文總目輯釋, in *Xuxiu siku quanshu* 續修四庫全書, ed. Xuxiu siku quanshu bianzuan weiyuanhui 續修四庫全書編纂委員會, vol. 916 (Shanghai: Shanghai guji chubanshe, 1995), 619–624.

21. Qian Tong, *Chongwen zongmu jishi*, 624; and Ouyang Xiu 歐陽修, *Ouyang Xiu ji biannian jianzhu* 歐陽修集編年箋注 (Chengdu: Bashu shushe, 2007), vol. 7, 77.

and the spirits and to manifest itself in worthy deeds and virtuous morality. *The Records of Music* gives: "After each of the Five Emperors had abdicated, because they lived in different periods, their music faded with them, and subsequent styles were fashioned afresh by new regimes;" later sage kings have therefore sanctioned a wealth of musical creation in response to the times they lived in; what need is there to painstakingly seek out the remnants of the ancients? As for modes and melodies once performed and the construction of musical instruments that played them, the practice of the sages, though having undergone changes through the generations, can still be investigated. From the Han dynasty [until the Wei and Jin dynasties, 220–420], explanation of the evolution of music can only be found in the musical monographs of official historiographers because no relevant book of this period has survived. The remaining books on the music of the Sui and Tang dynasties are thus recorded here.

夫樂所以達天地之和而飭化萬物，要之感格人神，象見功德，《記》曰：「五帝殊時，不相沿樂」，所以王者有因時製作之盛，何必區區求古遺缺？至于律呂鐘石，聖人之法，雖更萬世，可以考也。自漢以來，樂之沿革，惟見史官之志，其書不備。隋唐所錄，今著其存者云。[22]

For Ouyang Xiu, because sage kings had achieved sagehood, they could create anew the music of their own time according to the principles of their innate virtuous morality. The purpose of music was to "transform mankind and the spirits" and not to "seek out the remnant deficiencies of the ancients." This innovative philosophy rendered legitimate the inclusion of new materials.

After an interim of nearly a century, the next important catalog to appear was Chao Gongwu's 晁公武 (c. 1105–1180) *Junzhai dushu zhi* 郡齋讀書志 (*Records of Reading at the Prefectural Studio*; preface written in 1151).[23] During the Southern Song dynasty (1127–1279), the advent of printing stimulated a revolution in the dissemination of texts, and private library catalogs assumed a new importance. The oldest surviving of these, it lists 1,461 books comprising 24,500 *juan*, of which only 6 were books on music that contained 17 *juan*. The Chao family was originally from northern China, but owing to the invasion of the Jurchen Jin dynasty (1115–1234), Chao Gongwu's father, Chao Yuezhi 晁説之 (1059–1129), had led the family to settle in Sichuan.[24] After obtaining the *jinshi* degree in the 1130s, Chao Gongwu acted as an official for many years in the province and it was at this time that he acquired the complete private library of Jing Du 井度 (act. 1141) as the basis for his own collection. The comment of these *Records* on the value of books on music is far from appreciative:

> From the Han dynasty onwards, a point is often made that music is in fact no more than an empty vessel owing to a polluting admixture of sounds from the states of Zheng and Wei and barbarians from beyond the frontiers, and even if fashionable for a while, it is swiftly abandoned, lost, and can never be recovered, to say nothing of any relevant books. Here, a few paltry tomes are assembled simply to make up numbers in the index.
>
> 自漢以來，指樂為虛器，雜以鄭、衛、夷狄之音，雖或用於一時，旋即放失，無復存者，況其書哉！今裒集數種，姑以補書目之闕爾。[25]

Chao Gongwu's rasping tone expresses something deeper than mere disparagement, as at its core is dissatisfaction with the location of music within the "Canonic Texts" section of the traditional cataloging system, a status that nonetheless he retained. If music is not of sufficient Confucian gravity to be placed there, then where? Once more, after nearly a century had passed, the next book classification milestone emerged that did offer a solution. It was the *Zhizhai shulu jieti* 直齋書錄解題 (*Descriptive Catalog of the Zhizhai Studio*) of the private collection of Chen Zhensun 陳振孫 (1179–1262).[26] By this time, neo-Confucianism was becoming increasingly influential, as epitomized by Zhu Xi 朱熹 (1130–1200), and to some extent the new classification scheme reflects its ethos. When compared with Ouyang Xiu and earlier Confucian bibliographers' more humanistic view on the location of literature on music within the classification system, Zhu Xi's attitude is much more rigid. Whereas they had regarded the Five Classics (*The Book of Odes*, *The Book of Documents*, *The Book of Changes*, *The Book of Rites*, and *The Spring and Autumn Annals*) as canonic texts, Zhu Xi made it his life's work to replace them with the Four Books (*The Great Learning*, *The Doctrine of the Mean* from *The Book of Rites*, *The Confucian Analects*, and *The Mencius*). His chief toolkit in this process of formulating his own systematic philosophical framework was his *Sishu zhangju jizhu* 四書章句集注 (*Interlinear Analysis of and Collected Commentaries on the Four Books*). The central pillar of its essential rationalism was to regard the Confucian–Mencian lineage as the repository which "upheld heavenly principles and eliminated human desires." In his own words:

> Confucius talks of "curbing one's self and returning to propriety," *The Doctrine of the Mean* speaks of "achieving the state of Mean and Harmony," "respecting the nature of virtuous morality," and "using the Way to enquire into scholarship;" *The Great Learning* talks of the "manifesting of one's bright virtue;" *The Book of Documents* gives: "The mind of man is restless—prone to err; its affinity to what is right is small. Be discriminating, be uniform [in the pursuit of what is right], that you may sincerely hold fast the Mean." The sages' multiplicity of admonition simply teaches humankind to "uphold heavenly principles and eliminate human desires."
>
> 孔子所謂「克己復禮」，《中庸》所謂「致中和」、「尊德性」、「道問學」，《大學》所謂「明明德」，《書》曰「人心惟危，道心惟微，惟精惟一，允執厥中」，聖人千言萬言，只是教人「存天理、 滅人欲」。[27]

In the field of music, Zhu Xi advocated an admiration of "elegance" and the elimination of "crudity," and that this was a fundamental prerequisite for the establishment of order in society. Under the guidance of this train of thought, Zhu Xi and his disciples took vernacular opera performances and other appreciative musical activities and classified them as "vagrant desires," frequently seeking to "prohibit opera" as public policy. Zhu Xi himself penned *Qin shuo* 琴説 (*On the Qin*), a text on music theory, and furnished his disciple Cai Yuanding's 蔡元定 (1135–1198) *Lülü xinshu* 律呂新書 (*New Book on Pitch-Pipes*) with an introduction.

Curiously, the next important book collector, new-Confucianist Chen Zhensun, was born into and raised by a family of Confucians in Yongjia (now Wenzhou) opposed to the Zhu Xi School and was himself a grandson of Zhou Xingji 周行己 (*jinshi* degree 1091),[28] the main propagator of the Yongjia School of Thought.[29] The latter emerged in response to social and political crises in the Southern Song dynasty, more specifically the attempt on the part of Zhu Xi and Lu Jiuyuan 陸九淵 (1139–1192) to establish authority over the Confucian Classics, while at the same time the overall political situation was aggravated by military threats from the north and corruption in the government. Its wellspring was a need to contend with the changing intellectual climate's lurch towards neo-Confucianism, and in addition to Zhou Xingji, it included the materialist thinkers Ye Shi 葉適 (1150–1223) and Chen Fuliang 陳傅良 (1137–1203), who advocated elevating the social status of those engaged in commercial and mercantile activities. Ye Shi is noted for amending mainstream Confucian ideology by focusing more on the pursuit of profit, and he rejected ideas such as giving a high priority to justice and a low priority to the accumulation of wealth, such as had been suggested by the neo-Confucianists. Regarding music, Ye Shi, in his *Xixue jiyan* 習學記言 (*Learning Notes*), written in the twilight of his career, cunningly expresses his suspicion of Zhu Xi's narrow-minded value judgements by criticizing Dong Zhongshu, who had lived fourteen centuries earlier:

> To evaluate the level of governing of a state by means of listening to and observing its music is entirely possible. In seeking to govern, however, [one should not only] rely on the primacy of music. How can the mere performance of bells, drums, pipes, and stringed instruments rescue the degeneration of virtuous morality? [Dong] Zhongshu also [seeks to govern] by advocating the primacy of music, [but he is confined to this superficial level] and disregards the practice of good governance. In addition, [Dong's superficial enterprise] concludes in interpreting

22. Qian Tong, *Chongwen zongmu jishi*, 624; and Ouyang Xiu, *Ouyang Xiu ji biannian jianzhu*, vol. 7, 77.

23. Piet van der Loon, *Taoist Books in the Libraries of the Sung Period: A Critical Study and Index*, 25–27; and Yves Hervouet, ed., *A Sung Bibliography*, 196–197.

24. Peter K. Bol, *"This Culture of Ours": Intellectual Transitions in T'ang and Sung China* (Stanford: Stanford University Press, 1992), 60–75 and 345–352, especially 67 and 74–75; and Thomas H. C. Lee, *Government Education and Examinations in Sung China* (Hong Kong: Chinese University Press, 1985), 293–299.

25. Chao Gongwu 晁公武, *Junzhai dushu zhi jiaozheng* 郡齋讀書志校證 (Shanghai: Shanghai guji chubanshe, 1990), vol. 1, 91–92.

26. Piet van der Loon, *Taoist Books in the Libraries of the Sung Period: A Critical Study and Index*, 27–28; and Yves Hervouet, ed., *A Sung Bibliography*, 198.

27. Zhu Xi 朱熹, *Zhuzi yulei* 朱子語類 (Beijing: Zhonghua shuju, 1986), vol. 1, 365.

28. Chen Zhensun's grandmother was Zhou Xingji's third daughter. See Hou Wailu 侯外廬, *Zhongguo sixiang tongshi* 中國思想通史, vol. 4, pt. 2 (Beijing: Renmin chubanshe, 1960), 741.

29. Huang Zongxi 黃宗羲 et al., *Song Yuan xue'an* 宋元學案 (Beijing: Zhonghua shuju, 1986), 1127–1133.

omens of auspiciousness. This is particularly eschewed by those who truly wish to promote good governance through personal practice.

以樂論治可也，求治而以樂為先，鐘鼓管弦之存，何救于德之敗乎？而仲舒亦以樂為先，躬行之實廢矣。又終于祥瑞，尤躬行者之諱也。[30]

Chen Zhensun, however, regarded the Yongjia School of Thought as "insufficiently commensurate with anything that is pure and noble" 未得為純明正大 and admired Zhu Xi most.[31] Even larger than Chao Gongwu's collection, Chen Zhensun's contained 3,096 books in 51,180 *juan*, of which music comprised 26 books in 289 *juan*. As shown in Table I.5, the same first level division into four categories has been retained, but music is now shunted into the third of these ("Philosophy") as the eighteenth of twenty subcategories and no longer occupies a prime spot in the first category "Canonic Texts." The titles to these subcategories have themselves lost direct reference to the titles of the classic texts that form their basis and are now more generic in flavor. Daoist and Legalist works constitute the second and third subsections of "Philosophy," and encyclopedias are now so numerous and extensive as to make up a subcategory in their own right (the twentieth).

As before, texts on music readily lend themselves to subjective subdivision, here into *qin* music (nos. 1–15), vernacular and Central Asian music (nos. 16–17), and elegant music (nos. 18–26). The introduction to the music section in *juan* 14 justifies the overall re-positioning, first by criticizing the unsustainable position of retaining a subcategory in the "Canonic Texts" when no single appropriate text remained to fill it:

> Although Liu Xin and Ban Gu took *The Canon of Rites* and *The Book of Music* and categorized them as belonging to the "Summary of the Six Arts," neither of these texts is as ancient as Master Confucius [551–479 BCE] himself; however, the *Three Rites* [*Li ji* 禮記 (*The Book of Rites*), *Zhou li* 周禮 (*The Zhou Rites*), and *Yi li* 儀禮 (*The Book of Etiquette and Ceremonial*)] remain in circulation entirely as if they were still in their older pre-Qin dynasty's format, whereas influence of the six texts on music [as listed by Liu Xin in *The Seven Summaries* and Ban Gu in *The Official History of the Former Han Dynasty*] is no longer apparent. Dou Gong's tract "The Director of Music" can already be found in *The Zhou Rites*; the Prince of Hejian's *Records of Music* is already reproduced in Dai Sheng's 戴聖 [fl. first century] redaction of *The Book of Rites*; thus, ancient music is already bereft of the possibility of presenting itself as a complete book. Bibliographical monographs in the various official histories, as have existed hitherto, take from each other as their sources, however, the two institutions that provide music for entertainment, the Bureau of Music and the Imperial Music Academy, and barbarian music played on the *pipa* lute and Central Asian drum, are also tapped to supplement the genres of music available; placing these alongside the Canonical Texts of the sages—is this not an affront to reason!
>
> 劉歆、班固雖以《禮》、《樂》著之六藝略，要皆非孔氏之舊也，然《三禮》至今行於世，猶是先秦舊傳。而所謂《樂》六家者，影響不復存矣。竇公之《大司樂章》既已見於《周禮》，河間獻王之《樂記》亦已錄於《小戴》，則古樂已不復有書。而前志相承，乃取樂府、教坊、琵琶、羯鼓之類，以充樂類，與聖經並列，不亦悖乎！[32]

Texts culled from other sources are then vilified as entirely inappropriate companions to Confucian canonic volumes. This view is diametrically opposed to that of Ouyang Xiu, who saw books on music as evolving according to the sagehood of successive rulers. Perhaps that is why he was only admired by the neo-Confucianists for his literary skills and not as a Confucianist. Furthermore, Chen Zhensun suggested following the book classification system of a Fujianese scholar-official Zheng Yin 鄭寅 (d. 1237), who adamantly insisted on the exclusion of books on music from the category of the Confucian canons:

> Later, I obtained Zheng Zijing's [i.e., Zheng Yin] *Book Catalog*; it alone is not like this, and its argument in this respect runs: "'State rituals' and 'Chronologies' are categories in their own right and should not be attached to *The Canon of Rites* or *The Spring and Autumn Annals*; similarly, later books on music should also not be packaged among the Six Arts." Here, this dictum is followed, and books on music are placed in the "Philosophy" section, immediately before "Vernacular and Miscellaneous Arts."
>
> 晚得鄭子敬氏《書目》獨不然，其為說曰：「儀注、編年各自為類，不得附於《禮》、《春秋》，則後之樂書固不得列於六藝。」今從之，而著於子錄雜藝之前。[33]

In Zheng Yin's original classification, music books are not squeezed into the already fulsome "Philosophy" section, as Chen Zhensun did in his own catalog; instead, Zheng Yin creates three new sections, namely, "Arts," "Divination," and "Encyclopaedias,"[34] and books on music are regarded as a subsection of "Arts."

The most majestic book classification scheme of imperial China was the *Siku quanshu zongmu* 四庫全書總目 (*Catalog to the Complete Books of the Four Repositories*),[35] the index to a project that came to fruition in 1773 during the reign of the Qing dynasty (1644–1912) Emperor Qianlong 乾隆 (1711–1799, r. 1735–1796). In all, 3,461 books comprising 79,309 *juan* were reproduced. As well as texts duplicated in their entirety, a larger amount had only their titles given, and these represent 6,793 books in 93,551 *juan*. Table I.6 summarizes the classification system. The first level has retained its now-familiar four-part division, but the location of music books has been divided in an unprecedented manner; they are not simply concentrated in a music subsection of the "Canonic Texts," or the "Philosophy" section as implemented by the neo-Confucianist Chen Zhensun, but can instead be found in four different sections in a radically modified classification scheme.[36]

Of the four locations, the most prestigious is still the music subsection of the "Canonic Texts," and its title and those of many of the other subsections have resumed direct reference to the classical book that forms their foundation. The section on music includes 22 books of 483 *juan*; those with only their titles listed account for a further 42 books and 291 *juan*. There are fourteen subsections to the "Philosophy" section, and their titles are more practical in feel, with a section on agriculture, as well as less esoteric, with one on "Novels and Stories" and another on "Arts," which is where other texts on music are placed. The latter subsection is divided into four subdivisions with musical items found in the second "*Qin* Scores" (4 books comprising 29 *juan*; titles only: 12 books and 49 *juan*) and fourth "Vernacular and Miscellaneous Performance Skills" (2 books comprising 2 *juan*; none with only titles). Musical notation and lyrics of various vocal music genres, such as the twelfth-century poet-musician Jiang Kui's 姜夔 (1155–1221) *Baishi daoren gequ* 白石道人歌曲 (*Songs of the Whitestone Daoist*), are placed in the "Anthologies" subsection "*Ci*- and *Qu*-Type Lyrical Songs."

Justifications for this more elaborate arrangement abound. In *juan* 38, regarding the distribution music books into the three subcategories "Canonic Texts," "Philosophy," and "Anthologies":

> It can be observed that since the Han dynasty both the elegant and the vernacular were displayed [in the classification system] side by side; whether love songs in a lewd mode, they too were categorized as *yayue* ["Elegant Music"]. Thus, successive official histories are so written that even if music is as insignificant as that for *zheng* zither or *pipa* lute, it is still attached as an appendage to the section on canonic texts. Taking this process and moving it further to its logical conclusion, is this not taking the no-holds-barred gossipy language and plots of colloquial novels and setting them alongside *The Book of Documents* and *The Spring and Autumn Annals*?—thereby subverting reason and wounding sound moral tenets to an extraordinary degree. Here, all books on music are differentiated from one another so that those that discuss music theory and illuminate *yayue* are still listed in the section on canonic texts, while song genres, the performance skills of theatrical entertainers, and the multifarious sounds of instrumental music of string and pipe are relegated to the two subcategories of

30. Huang Zongxi et al., *Song Yuan xue'an*, 1774. The text has here been abridged and modified by the compilers of *Song Yuan xue'an*. For the original text, see Ye Shi 葉適, *Xixue jiyan xumu* 習學記言序目 (Beijing: Zhonghua shuju, 1977), vol. 1, 323.

31. Chen Zhensun 陳振孫, *Zhizhai shulu jieti* 直齋書錄解題 (Shanghai: Shanghai guji chubanshe, 1987), 313; and Wang Zhongmin, *Zhongguo muluxue shi luncong*, 121–123.

32. Chen Zhensun, *Zhizhai shulu jieti*, 399.

33. Ibid., 399.

34. Ibid., 236–237.

35. For information on the compilation of *The Complete Books of the Four Repositories*, see R. Kent Guy, *The Emperor's Four Treasuries: Scholars and the State in the Late Ch'ien-Lung Period* (Cambridge, Mass.: Council on East Asian Studies, Harvard University, 1987).

36. This does not mean that apart from these four locations no literature on music is to be found. Other places, such as the "Statecraft and Administration" subsection of "Histories" and the "Miscellaneous Skills" and "Encyclopedias" subsections of "Philosophy" also contain books related to music. Some of these, such as *Zhongxing lishu* 中興禮書, *Mengxi bitan* 夢溪筆談, and *Shilin guangji* 事林廣記, are crucial to the study of Chinese music history. Furthermore, the Chinese invention of equal temperament was transmitted to Tokugawa Japan through one of the appendices of Ming dynasty doctor of Chinese medicine Zhang Jiebin's 張介賓 (1563–1640) medical treatise *Lei jing* 類經. In considering their primary affiliation, these books have been classified into categories other than music.

> "Vernacular and Miscellaneous Arts" and "*Ci*- and *Qu*-Type Lyrical Songs." This formula has been adopted because it can be employed to reveal the original sound of the greater music of the ancients and is of a wisdom equivalent in power to that of heaven and earth, as well as being entirely devoid of the debauched music of the state of Zheng.
>
> 顧自漢氏以來，兼陳雅俗，豔歌側調，並隸《雲》、《韶》。於是諸史所登，雖細至箏、琶，亦附於經末。循是以往，將小説稗官未嘗不記言記事，亦附之《書》與《春秋》乎？悖理傷教，於斯為甚。今區別諸書，惟以辨律呂、明雅樂者仍列于經，其謳歌末技，弦管繁聲，均退列雜藝、詞曲兩類中。用以見大樂元音，道侔天地，非鄭聲所得而奸也。[37]

Here, the compilers of Emperor Qianlong's *Catalog to the Complete Books of the Four Repositories* have made explicit the same ideas that the Southern Song neo-Confucianist bibliographers Chen Zhensun and Zheng Yin had proposed some five hundred years earlier. They object to the placement of "love songs in a lewd mode" and "music . . . as insignificant as that for *zheng* zither or *pipa* lute" in the "Canonic Texts," just as Chen Zhensun had taken exception to music of "the two institutions that provide music for entertainment, the Bureau of Music and the Imperial Music Academy, and barbarian music played on the *pipa* lute and Central Asian drum." The language justifying their criticism is equally pointed: Qianlong's compilers regarded inclusion of these lower forms of music as "subverting reason and wounding sound moral tenets to an extraordinary degree," while to Chen Zhensun the situation is "an affront to reason;" indeed, the Emperor's catalog goes so far as to say: "Is this not taking the no-holds-barred gossipy language and plots of colloquial novels and setting them alongside *The Book of Documents* and *The Spring and Autumn Annals*?" The inspiration here is an equivalent remark by Zheng Yin. Although his tone is more measured, the message remains the same: "Later books on music should not be packaged among the Six Arts."

In fact, despite similarities in their rhetoric, Emperor Qianlong's *Catalog* makes only partial reference to Chen Zhensun's classification and does not copy it. There are two major differences: (1) the subsection on music has been preserved in the "Canonic Texts;" and (2) to accommodate sources of non-Confucian music, instead of a single subsection on music under "Philosophy," Qianlong's *Catalog* creates two, namely "*Qin* Scores" and "Vernacular and Miscellaneous Performance Skills," both situated in the "Arts" subsection of the "Philosophy" section.

Regarding reasons for preserving the subsection on music of the "Canonic Texts," the initial justification is given in *juan* 38:

> Shen Yue (441–513) claimed that *The Book of Music* was destroyed in the Qin dynasty. . . . For the most part, the performance formats of *The Book of Music* can be found in *The Canon of Rites* and its song lyrics in *The Book of Odes*. The mere percussive sounds of drums and dances were transmitted through generations of professional musicians. At the start of the Han dynasty, other than the records of the Zhi clan and their remnant music notation, no other canonic text had passed through the hands of a sage and thus bore his stamp of legitimacy. Only because music has the function to spread happiness and guide towards harmoniousness, to mold spirits and mankind, and to connect to heaven and earth, is its use so great and its meaning so refined that, in respect of its teachings, it in itself is sufficient to serve as equivalent to a canonic text. Books on music theory of later generations were thus also recorded in the section on canonic texts and not regarded as belonging to the genre "Arts."
>
> 沈約稱《樂經》亡於秦。……大抵《樂》之綱目具於《禮》，其歌詞具於《詩》，其鏗鏘鼓舞則傳在伶官。漢初制氏所記，蓋其遺譜，非別有一經為聖人手定也。特以宣豫導和，感神人而通天地，厥用至大，厥義至精，故尊其教得配於經。而後代鐘律之書亦遂得著錄於經部，不與藝術同科。[38]

Chen Zhensun's catalog listed only the contents of a private library, and his motivations for devising its system were philosophical, practical, and not political. By contrast, the Manchu emperors were keen to legitimize their regime by assuming the trappings of Confucian sagehood, so for them retaining a music section in "Canonic Texts" was vital. An important step towards establishing Confucian musical legitimacy had already been taken by the Emperor Kangxi 康熙 (1654–1722, r. 1661–1722) and his *Lülü zhengyi* 律呂正義 (*The Orthodox Meaning of Pitch Standards*) in 5 *juan*, a direction of travel that the Emperor Qianlong had continued and greatly expanded with his

Lülü zhengyi houbian 律呂正義後編 (*Sequel to the Orthodox Meaning of Pitch Standards*) in 120 *juan*. A solution had to be devised that removed the polluting musical texts so decried by earlier commentators from the "Canonical Texts" and retained the legitimizing Confucian divisions, but that also had the elbow room to place other books on music elsewhere. The introductory remarks 凡例, entry 5, give:

> "Monograph on Books" in *The National History of the Ming Dynasty* by Jiao Hong (1540–1620) categorizes its books into many more sections and a three-layer system throughout, but this arrangement has come to be regarded as excessively elaborate. Here, a happy medium between the two is sought by which the system is neither entirely two- or three-layered but a combination of both. Only in . . . four subsections in "Philosophy"—namely, Divination, Arts, Scientific and Practical Treatises, and Miscellaneous Books—and the "Anthologies" subsection of *Ci*- and *Qu*-Type Songs—are the different scholarly schools of thought represented so numerous and the separate strands so easily indistinct that a cautious and approximate further subdivision . . . of Arts . . . is made into four further subcategories . . . and the subsection *Ci*- and *Qu*-Type Lyrical Songs further subdivided into four subcategories in order to render the overall organization more orderly.
>
> 焦竑《國史・經籍志》多分子目，頗以餖飣為嫌。今酌乎其中，惟……子部之術數、藝術、譜錄、雜家四類，集部之詞曲類，流派至為繁夥，端緒易至茫如。謹約分……藝術……為四子目，……詞曲為四子目，使條理秩然。[39]

From a Manchu perspective, the beauty of the system is that it avoided the need for two separate music sections that carried the word "Music" in their title, which would have been both intellectually embarrassing and politically untenable since it undermined the Confucian legitimacy of music's re-categorization under "Canonic Texts." Musical items that had been shifted into the "Philosophy" section were thus disguised in locations not explicitly afforded the appellation "Music" and placed only in a third level subdivision of the subcategory "Arts"—and then merely as its second and fourth members, respectively, "*Qin* Scores" and "Vernacular and Miscellaneous Performance Skills."

On the face of it, the rationale was for books on elegant music to be placed in the "Music" subsection of "Canonic Texts," and those on vernacular music in "Vernacular and Miscellaneous Performance Skills" in the "Arts" subsection of "Philosophy." Both types of literature on music could be satisfactorily recorded and preserved, and simply situated in different regions of the classification scheme. Introductory remarks, entry 6:

> In the past, books like *Jiegu lu* (*Records of the Jie Barbarian's Drum*) were categorized under "Music" but now only discussion of music theory is entered there. Practical treatises that discuss the music of pipes and strings are written in *gongche* notation, and do not rise above the vernacular or secular, so that their categorization has been altered and is now subsumed under "Arts."
>
> 《羯鼓錄》之屬，舊入樂類，今惟以論律呂者入樂。其論管弦工尺者，不過世俗之音，亦改隸藝術。[40]

In *juan* 113, that is, *juan* 23 of the "Philosophy" section and *juan* 2 of the subsection "Arts," here pertaining to "Vernacular and Miscellaneous Performance Skills":

> Regarding the "Monograph [on Arts and Literature]" [i.e., *juan* 57–60] of *Xin Tang shu* (*The New Official History of the Tang Dynasty*), inserting *Records of the Jie Barbarian's Drum* and *Yuefu zalu* (*Vernacular and Miscellaneous Records on Songs from the Music Bureau*) into the music subsection of the section on canonic texts simply does not differentiate between elegant music and the degenerate music of the state of Zheng, and has absolutely no logic. Here, these two items are categorized into the subsection on "Arts," and in that way both genres achieve their rightful role.
>
> 《羯鼓錄》、《樂府雜錄》，《新唐書・[藝文]志》皆入經部樂類，雅鄭不分，殊無條理。今以類入之於藝術，庶各得其倫。[41]

37. Ji Yun 紀昀 et al., *Siku quanshu zongmu* 四庫全書總目 (Beijing: Zhonghua shuju, 1965), vol.1, 320.

38. Ibid., vol.1, 320.

39. Ibid., vol.1, 17.

40. Ibid., vol.1, 17.

41. Ibid., vol.1, 972.

The actual situation tells an entirely different story. The third-level subdivision "Vernacular and Miscellaneous Performance Skills" contains 15 books in 52 *juan*, but of these, only two books in two *juan*, both Tang dynasty books, i.e., *Records of the Jie Barbarian's Drum* and *Vernacular and Miscellaneous Records on Songs from the Music Bureau* (as mentioned previously) concern music. As they are allowed to suffice as the totality of the examples of books on the music of non-Confucian contexts, there was evidently no real intention to absorb anything of this type into the category.

The other thirteen books in this subdivision refer to non-musical pastimes, for example, *weiqi* 圍棋 (board games) or *shejian* 射箭 (archery); texts on various types of gambling are common, such as *touhu* 投壺 (pitch-pot), *shupu* 樗蒲 (chaupar), *chuiwan* 捶丸 (ball-hitting), and *shuanglu* 雙陸 ("double six" backgammon).[42] The intention is clear: any music that does not measure up to Confucian standards and merit inclusion in "Canonic Texts" is regarded as mixing with the dregs: it is "bad" music. Compared to official catalogs from the Western Han dynasty's *The Seven Summaries* to the Northern Song's *General Catalog of the Academy for the Veneration of Literature*, Qianlong's *Catalog* has almost entirely lost the function of recording contemporary and vernacular music. It has become a political statement.

In respect to the culture of the elite's *qin* music, the compilers of Qianlong's *Catalog* had observed and responded to tensions between Confucianism and Naturalism. Generations of literati *qin* players, such as Ji Kang 嵇康 (223–262) and Yuan Jue 袁桷 (1266–1327), had attempted to free *qin* music from the straitjacket of Confucian ideology,[43] while in the opposite direction, scholar-officials, such as Fan Zhongyan 范仲淹 (989–1052) and Zhu Changwen 朱長文 (1038–1098), had worked to confine the interpretation of *qin* music within this ideology.[44] Faced with this dilemma, instead of regarding it as an indispensable component of Confucian music, and therefore placing it in the music subsection of "Canonic Texts," Emperor Qianlong's *Catalog* splits sources of *qin* and *se* 瑟 (another type of zither) music into two types. All 16 handbooks of *qin* music in 78 *juan* are in fact squeezed into the newly invented subdivision "Vernacular and Miscellaneous Performance Skills" (*juan* 112, that is, *juan* 22 of the "Philosophy" section, *juan* 1 of the subsection "Arts"), where the following is recorded:

> The *qin* is grounded in elegant music and was once listed in the section on music. Later generations of vernacular musicians began playing with new plucking and strumming techniques, leading the way to creating new sounds; these were not performances that replicated the ancient styles of poems from *The Book of Odes*, for example, *The Primal Ancestor of the Zhou Dynasty Royal Clan* and *The Clear and Bright Temple*, but a special and different skill.
>
> 琴本雅音，舊列樂部，後世俗工撥捩，率造新聲，非復清廟生民之奏，是特一技耳。[45]

In *juan* 113, that is, *juan* 23 of the "Philosophy" section, *juan* 2 of the subsection "Arts" titled "*Qin* Scores":

> The items listed represent the skills of hermits living in the mountains or the literati, that is, those who are cognizant of musical compositions and appreciate musical sound. Others, for example, of the manner of Xiong Penglai's [fl. thirteenth century] *Se pu hou lu* (*Postscript to Se Zither Scores*) or Wang Haoran's [fl. Ming dynasty] *Qin se pu* (*Qin and Se Scores*) are for performance in elegant settings and thus remain categorized in the "Canonic Texts" section on music and are not included among the ranks of compositions listed here.
>
> 以上所錄，皆山人墨客之技，識曲賞音之事也。若熊朋來《瑟譜後錄》、汪浩然《琴瑟譜》之類，則全為雅奏，仍隸經部樂類中，不與此為伍矣。[46]

Se Zither Scores by Xiong Penglai was fabricated by the composer during the Yuan dynasty (1271–1368). He relied entirely on his own imaginings of what he considered Confucian music would have been like; this text was subsequently lost. It was reconstructed together with two other Yuan dynasty companion anthologies with a neo-Confucian leaning, Yu Zai's 余載 (fl. 1328–1330) *Shaowu jiucheng yuebu* 韶舞九成樂補 and Liu Jin's 劉瑾 (c. 1245–c. 1315) *Lülü chengshu* 律呂成書, during Qianlong's reign by assembling surviving quotations preserved in the *Yongle dadian* 永樂大典 (*Emperor Yongle's Grand Encyclopedia*). Other than this, the only monograph on *qin* music to merit categorization in the "Canonic Texts" section of Qianlong's *Catalog* is *Qin zhi* 琴旨 (*The Gist of the Qin*) by Wang Tan 王坦 (fl. eighteenth century). According to Qianlong's *Catalog*, the reason for this work's inclusion in the "Canonic Texts" section was:

> Up until now, those who discuss *qin* melodies are prone to five errors. . . . only the book *The Orthodox Meaning of Pitch Standards* compiled under imperial orders makes detailed and clear investigation of the issue and sets forth those matters that were not set forth by the ancients. The book that Wang Tan has written is systematically grounded in the principles of *The Orthodox Meaning of Pitch Standards* and makes a thorough explanation of them. It takes all the illustrations of the latter book and furnishes them and their text with precise and copious exegesis, and alone of those in recent times that have discussed the *qin* cannot be said to have lost sight of its purpose.
>
> 自來言琴律者，其誤有五。……惟《御制律呂正義》一書，考定詳明，發古人之所未發。坦作是書，一一本《正義》之旨，而反復推闡。於《正義》諸圖說尤能精思闡發。在近時言琴諸家，可謂不失其宗者矣。[47]

A comparison, however, between the imperial manuscript edition (1781) of *The Gist of the Qin* in *The Complete Books of the Four Repositories*[48] and the first printed edition of the book (1746)[49] reveals that: (1) Wang Tan's own Preface outlines that he had first learned the *qin* from his father and that the experience had nothing to do with the Emperor Kangxi's *The Orthodox Meaning of Pitch Standards*. In the imperial manuscript edition that followed, this Preface was discarded. (2) The text in the imperial manuscript edition has been thoroughly "corrected" by the imperial compilers of Emperor Qianlong's *The Complete Books of the Four Repositories* to give the impression that Wang Tan was an enthusiastic admirer of Kangxi's theoretical writings on music. (3) In the most extreme case, the text of the chapter "Discussion of when there are Lyrics and when there not" 有詞無詞說 has been entirely re-written by the imperial compilers and Wang's opinions altered to the exact opposite of their original stance.

The result was that no individual *qin* handbook in *The Complete Books of the Four Repositories* matched the new standards of the Manchu court. In addition, any juxtaposition of *qin* music based on Confucian ideology with that "of hermits living in the mountains or the literati" was moreover no more than an illusion forged by the catalogers. In this sense, Emperor Qianlong's *Catalog* was no longer a classification system, but rather a manipulation of music's intellectual history.

Since the turn of the twentieth century, the classification of Chinese modern publications has been largely westernized, and several specialised catalogs devoted to the historical souces of Chinese music have themselves been compiled.[50] In terms of rare books, however, the most popular classification system remains the model refined in the high Qing.[51]

The present publication follows the Qing classification system, and the first four chapters replicate the relevant sections through a discussion of books held in the Hong Kong University Libraries and elsewhere. Taking inspiration from *The Old Official Book of the Tang Dynasty*, which incorporated music from outside China, the fifth chapter presents views on Chinese music of foreign visitors.

Chapter 1 discusses ritual music in the Confucian Classics and takes a journey through the sacred territory of the Confucian rites, beginning with *Yi li* 儀禮 (*The Book of Etiquette and Ceremonial*)

42. Ji Yun et al., *Siku quanshu zongmu*, vol.1, 971–972 and 980–981.

43. See Chapter 4.

44. Ibid.

45. Ji Yun et al., *Siku quanshu zongmu*, vol.1, 952.

46. Ibid., vol.1, 971.

47. Ibid., vol.1, 329–330.

48. Wang Tan 王坦, *Qin zhi* 琴旨, in *Siku quanshu zhenben 5 ji* 四庫全書珍本五集, ed. Zhongyang tushuguan choubeichu 中央圖書館籌備處 (Taipei: Taiwan shangwu yinshuguan, 1974), vol. 59.

49. Wang Tan 王坦, *Qin zhi* 琴旨. S.l.: Su tang, 1746. Shanghai Library (call number: 線善772816-17).

50. For example, Zhou Qingyun 周慶雲, ed., *Qinshu cunmu* 琴書存目 (Shanghai: Mengpo shi, 1914); Zhou Qingyun 周慶雲, ed., *Qinshu bielu* 琴書別錄 (Shanghai: Mengpo shi, 1914); Yuan Tongli 袁同禮, "Zhongguo yinyue shu juyao 中國音樂書舉要," *Zhonghua tushuguan xiehui huibao* 中華圖書館協會會報 3.4 (1928): 6–17; Guoli Beiping tushuguan 國立北平圖書館, ed., *Guoli Beiping tushuguan xiqu yinyue zhanlanhui mulu* 國立北平圖書館戲曲音樂展覽會目錄 (Beiping: Guoli Beiping tushuguan, 1934); Zhongyang yinyue xueyuan minzu yinyue yanjiusuo 中央音樂學院民族音樂研究所, ed., *Zhongguo yinyue shiliao chenlieshi shuoming* 中國音樂史料陳列室說明 (Beijing: Zhongyang yinyue xueyuan minzu yinyue yanjiusuo, 1956); Wang Shixiang 王世襄, ed., *Zhongguo gudai yinyue shumu chugao* 中國古代音樂書目初稿 (Beijing: Yinyue chubanshe, 1961); and Zhongguo yishu yanjiuyuan yinyue yanjiusuo ziliaoshi 中國藝朮研究院音樂研究所資料室, *Zhongguo yinyue shupuzhi* 中國音樂書譜志 (Beijing: Renmin yinyue chubanshe, 1994).

51. For example, Zhongguo guji shanben shumu bianji weiyuanhui 中國古籍善本書目編輯委員會, ed., *Zhongguo guji shanben shumu* 中國古籍善本書目, 9 vols. (Shanghai: Shanghai guji chubanshe, 1986–1996); and Zhongguo guji zongmu bianzuan weiyuanhui 中國古籍總目編纂委員會, ed., *Zhongguo guji zongmu* 中國古籍總目, 26 vols. (Beijing and Shanghai: Zhonghua shuju and Shanghai guji chubanshe, 2009).

and its detailed description of ceremonies. This is followed by various interpretations of these texts, especially Zhu Zaiyu's 朱載堉 (1536–1611) Ming dynasty series *Yuelü quanshu* 樂律全書 (*Collected Works on Music and Pitch-Pipes*, 1595–1607) along with his detailed choreographic diagrams. Set against his earnest scholarship is Shen Cai's 沈彩 (c. 1748–?) exquisite calligraphy of her husband Lu Xuan's 陸烜 (1737–1799) treatise *Shang shu yi* 尚書義 (*Meanings in the Book of Documents*) and the heartfelt poems she included in the margins of the manuscript after copying out each section. Although the carping preaching of neo-Confucianism can become irksome, a humble spirit of scientific discovery and quest for truth is sometimes also self-evident, for example, in Zhu Zaiyu's experiments in equal temperament and Shen Cai and Lu Xuan's joint construction of their *jian* 簡 pentachord device.

The second section of Qianlong's book classification scheme comprises "Histories," and Chapter 2 thus deals with historical records of court music. As is stated by Ouyang Xiu: "From the Han dynasty [until the Wei and Jin dynasties], explanation of the evolution of music can only be found in the bibliographical monographs of official historiographers."[52] With the advent of historiography in the Spring and Autumn period (770–476 BCE), and its espousal by the Confucian orthodoxy, new resources emerged for the study of musical practice at court, in particular, *Chunqiu* 春秋 (*The Annals of the State of Lu*). As is recorded in this text, on a diplomatic mission to the state of Lu 魯, the son of the ruler of Wu 吳, Ji Zha 季札 (576–484 BCE), was privileged to witness a complete performance of the entire 305 poems in *The Book of Odes*. He left an account of the experience that explicitly connected their aesthetic effect with aspects of statecraft.[53] After the establishment of the Han dynasty and Confucianism as its official ideology, music came to occupy a vital role in the official histories of successive dynasties. Included in the oldest of these—Sima Qian's 司馬遷 (c. 145–c. 86 BCE) *Shi ji* 史記 (*Records of the Grand Historian*, completed in 91 BCE)—are two related works: "Yue shu" 樂書 ("Monograph on Music") and "Lü shu" 律書 ("Monograph on Pitch Standards"). Monographs on pitch standards remain common items in successive official histories, consistently proving to be an arena where the great minds of the day chose to flex their intellectual muscles.
In the Song dynasty, imperial antiquarian interest in artifacts had become a driving force, as is illustrated in *Xuanhe bogu tulu* 宣和博古圖錄 (*The Xuanhe Era Illustrated Catalog of Ancient Bronzes*). Later in the Qing dynasty, the forces of antiquarianism, and a desire to clarify pitch relationships, combined forces to produce a series of works that sought to assert consistency in these areas. The first of these was Emperor Kangxi's *Orthodox Meaning of Pitch Standards*, which itself also absorbed music from an entirely new non-Han source, that of Jesuits active in China, principally the work of Thomas Pereira (1645–1708) and Theodorico Pedrini (1671–1746).

Chapter 3 deals with vocal music, that is, opera and song. *Catalog to the Complete Books of the Four Repositories* gives: "Song genres and the performance skills of theatrical entertainers are all relegated to the subcategory "*Ci*- and *Qu*-Type Lyrical Songs.""[54] The advent of printing in the Song dynasty meant that lyric song began to achieve a much broader circulation. At the heart of this enterprise were poets and musicians such as Jiang Kui, whose *Songs of the Whitestone Daoist* (1202) retains the only surviving samples of musical notation of that era. This text was later reissued by eighteenth-century enthusiasts. In contrast to this genre's refinement, the *Yue'ou* 粵謳 (*Yue Ballads*) of the Qing dynasty was a narrative song form of the Pearl River Delta whose text was both classical and vernacular. An anthology of these compiled by Zhao Ziyong 招子庸 (1786–1847) and published in Guangzhou in 1828 includes pedagogic diagrams of a *pipa* 琵琶 together with the finger positions used for *gongche* 工尺 notation indicated on the frets.

The dynamic between Confucianism and naturalism is the focus of Chapter 4, exploring *qin* music played by the literati. Confucius and the Confucians who followed claimed the *qin* as their cultural preserve. After the end of the Han dynasty, the scholar-official Ji Kang in his "Qin fu" 琴賦 ("Rhapsody on the *Qin*"), which is included in *Liujia Wenxuan* 六家文選 (*Six Commentaries on Selections of Refined Literature*), attempted to redefine *qin* music more as an aspect of personal expression, and as a result, the *qin* evolved into a literati instrument. Conversely, in the Song dynasty, Fan Zhongyan sought to reverse this process and to return the *qin* to its ancient roots as an aspect of statecraft, as is discussed in his essays preserved in *Fan Wenzheng gong ji* 范文正公集 (*The Literary Collection of Duke Fan Wenzheng*). The dynamic between these two opposing schools of thought became a hallmark of subsequent discourse, for example, Zhu Changwen famously sided with Fan, while Yuan Jue was more practical and appreciative of the *qin*.

Taking an entirely different view of Chinese music in print, Chapter 5 considers the subject through European eyes. Given that the writer is an *erhu* 二胡 performer, he employs depictions in the visual arts found in printed books as a rich source for investigating historical performance practice. Initially considered an instrument of the rural poor, theatrical entertainers, prostitutes, or beggars, the *erhu* is rarely depicted in indigenous sources, especially not in texts with Confucian connections. It does routinely appear, however, in illustrations produced by European visitors to China who were unrestricted by Chinese conventions. Two eighteenth-century books are selected for their particular interest in this regard: Isadore Stanislas Helman's *Conquêtes des Chinois* and George Staunton's *An Authentic Account of an Embassy from the King of Great Britain to the Emperor of China*. This chapter assesses the extent to which, as cultural outsiders, these interlopers were in fact faithful observers, and discusses the value of their depictions as documentary evidence.

China's relationship with the outside world has at times been delicate and problematic, and at others engaged and accepting. So too, how music from outside China has been viewed. In the Middle Ages, the indigenous and foreign sat comfortably side by side, and both were performed and appreciated, while in the early modern period, a tendency grew to place anything distant from the Confucian psychological heartlands in positions of ever greater obscurity, at least in official records. Chapter 5 is grounded in a desire to express a reverse process by which those very outsiders sought to increase their engagement with the musical riches of the Middle Kingdom. The journey starts, however, with the Great Sage himself and the music that evolved around his lineage.

52. See above.

53. *The Annals of the State of Lu* was regarded as having been edited by Confucius himself and so was placed in the "Canonic Texts" section of the catalogs of imperial times. In our volume, based on content rather than editorial process, it is discussed in Chapter 2.

54. See above.

後其節目及其久也相說以解不善問者反此善待問者如撞鐘叩之以小者則小鳴叩之以大者則大鳴待其從容然後盡其聲不善荅問者反此此皆進學之道也記問之學不足以為人師必也其聽語乎力不能問然後語之語之而不知雖舍之可也良冶之子必學為裘良弓之子必學為箕始駕馬者反之車在馬前君子察於此三者可以有志於學矣古之學者比物醜類鼓無當於五聲五聲弗得不和水無當於五色五色弗得不章學無當於五官五官弗得不治師無當於五服五服弗得不親君子曰大德不官大道不器大信不約大時不齊察於此四者可以有志於本矣三王之祭川也皆先河而後海或源也或委也此之謂務本

樂記第十九

鄭氏注

凡音之起由人心生也人心之動物使之然也感於物而動故形於聲聲相應故生變變成方謂之音比音而樂之及干戚羽旄謂之樂樂者音之所由生也其本在人心之感於物也是故其哀心感者其聲噍以殺其樂心感者其聲嘽以緩其喜心感者其聲發

民平好惡而反人道之正也人生而靜天之性也感於物而動性之欲也物至知知然後好惡形焉好惡無節於內知誘於外不能反躬天理滅矣夫物之感人無窮而人之好惡無節則是物至而人化物也人化物也者滅天理而窮人欲者也於是有悖逆詐僞之心有淫泆作亂之事是故強者脅弱衆者暴寡知者詐愚勇者苦怯疾病不養老幼孤獨不得其所此大亂之道也是故先王之制禮樂人為之節衰麻哭泣所以節喪紀也鐘鼓干戚所以和安樂也昏姻冠笄所以別男女也射鄉食饗所以正交接也禮節民心樂和民聲政以行之刑以防之禮樂刑政四達而不悖則王道備矣樂者為同禮者為異同則相親異則相敬樂勝則流禮勝則離合情飾貌者禮樂之事也禮義立則貴賤等矣樂文同則上下和矣好惡著則賢不肖別矣刑禁暴爵舉賢則政均矣仁以愛之義以正之如此則民治行矣樂由中出禮自外作樂由中出故靜禮自外作故文大樂必易大禮必簡樂至則無怨禮至則不爭揖讓而治天下者禮樂之謂也暴民不作

敦和率神而從天禮者別宜居鬼而從地故聖人作樂以應天制禮以配地禮樂明備天地官矣天尊地卑君臣定矣卑高已陳貴賤位矣動靜有常小大殊矣方以類聚物以群分則性命不同矣在天成象在地成形如此則禮者天地之別也地氣上齊天氣下降陰陽相摩天地相蕩鼓之以雷霆奮之以風雨動之以四時煖之以日月而百化興焉如此則樂者天地之和也化不時則不生男女無辨則亂升天地之情也及夫禮樂之極乎天而蟠乎地行乎陰陽而通乎鬼神窮高極遠而測深厚樂著大始而禮居成物著不息者天也著不動者地也一動一靜者天地之間也故聖人曰禮樂云昔者舜作五弦之琴以歌南風夔始制樂以賞諸侯故天子之為樂也以賞諸侯之有德者也德盛而教尊五穀時孰然後賞之以樂故其治民勞者其舞行綴遠其治民逸者其舞行綴短故觀其舞知其德聞其謚知其行也大章章之也咸池備矣韶繼也夏大也殷周之樂盡矣天地之道寒暑不時則疾風雨不節則饑教者民之寒暑也教

感條暢之氣而滅平和之德是以君子賤之也凡姦聲感人而逆氣應之逆氣成象而淫樂興焉正聲感人而順氣應之順氣成象而和樂興焉倡和有應回邪曲直各歸其分而萬物之理各以類相動也是故君子反情以和其志比類以成其行姦聲亂色不留聰明淫樂慝禮不接心術惰慢邪辟之氣不設於身體使耳目鼻口心知百體皆由順正以行其義然後發以聲音而文以琴瑟動以干戚飾以羽旄從以簫管奮至德之光動四氣之和以著萬物之理是故清明象天廣大象地終始象四時周還象風雨五色成文而不亂八風從律而不姦百度得數而有常小大相成終始相生倡和清濁迭相為經故樂行而倫清耳目聰明血氣和平移風易俗天下皆寧故曰樂者樂也君子樂得其道小人樂得其欲以道制欲則樂而不亂以欲忘道則惑而不樂是故君子反情以和其志廣樂以成其教樂行而民鄉方可以觀德矣德者性之端也樂者德之華也金石絲竹樂之器也詩言其志也歌詠其聲也舞動其容也三者本於心然後

成而後下有先有制於天下子夏曰吾則唯恐臥不知倦敢何也新樂夏對曰今旅和正以守拊鼓始武治亂以子於是語及家平均發也今夫姦聲以濫侏儒獶雜樂終不可古此新樂所問者樂夫樂者與文侯曰敢曰夫古者當民有德不作而無當然後聖臣以為紀下大定天六律和五之謂德音云莫其德明克類克邦克順克德靡悔既子此之謂者其溺音溺音何鄭音

Chapter 1

Ritual Music in the Confucian Classics

Yang Yuanzheng

As Confucianists have traditionally regarded music as a fundamental tool for educating and edifying, music has historically maintained an intimate relationship with Confucian thought and the ruling classes, both as a means of personal enlightenment and as a key aspect of statecraft. In the earliest Confucian texts, music and rites were inextricably linked. At the heart of this connection are the Six Classics, said to have been edited by Confucius (551–479 BCE) himself: *The Book of Odes*, *The Book of Documents*, *The Canon of Rites*, *The Book of Music*, *The Book of Changes*, and *The Spring and Autumn Annals*. Complementing these canonical texts are the physical exercises known as the Six Arts: Rites, Music, Archery, Charioteering, Calligraphy, and Mathematics.

The Book of Music would then be a natural starting point for any discussion concerning the nexus of music and Confucianism, but no definitive copies of this work have survived. Scholars have posited that the chapter on music called "Yue ji" 樂記 ("Records of Music") contained in the *Li ji* 禮記 (*The Book of Rites*, Fig. 1.1) is in fact *The Book of Music*;[1] others have proposed that *The Book of Music* was never actually a physical text, but rather a musical artifact passed on by aural tradition.[2] In either scenario, modern historians do not have access to a reliable textual source concerning the Confucian musical canon from the Age of Confucius. Even so, a discussion of music through *The Canon of Rites* does allow for the development of an initial framework.

Later, in the Eastern Han dynasty (25–220 CE) in respect to *The Canon of Rites*, three books became integral: *The Book of Rites*, *Zhou li* 周禮 (*The Zhou Rites*), and *Yi li* 儀禮 (*The Book of Etiquette and Ceremonial*). Together these came to be regarded as "The Three Rites,"[3] but when considering the Western Han dynasty (206 BCE–8 CE) and the Age of Confucius, *The Book of Etiquette and Ceremonial* was the only one of these three to be afforded the status of "*jing* 經," meaning a canonical text; so, any discussion of music and Confucian rites must use this work as a starting point.

Many ancient texts suffer from issues of canonicity, and *The Book of Etiquette and Ceremonial* is no exception. Originally, it consisted of an "Old Text" of fifty-six chapters, but only a "New Text" of seventeen chapters has survived from the Han dynasty. Subsequently, two of the most important layers of exegesis are by the second-century scholar Zheng Xuan 鄭玄 (127–200), who compiled an edition and wrote a commentary, and Jia Gongyan 賈公彥 (fl. 651–655) of the Tang dynasty (618–907), who added an additional layer of notes. *The Book of Etiquette and Ceremonial* was first printed in a woodblock edition between 932 and 953,[4] but it was not until 1521 that the original text, Zheng Xuan's commentary, and Jia Gongyan's notes were combined and published as a discrete book entitled *Yi li zhu shu* 儀禮註疏 (*Notes to the Commentary on the Book of Etiquette and Ceremonial*, Fig. 1.2).[5] The instigator of this project was the Provincial Governor of Shandong, Chen Fengwu 陳鳳梧 (1475–1541), who in 1526 sent the edition's plates to the Imperial College in Nanjing to be archived. As there were two

Fig. 1.1: *Li ji* (*The Book of Rites*), "Yue ji" ("Records of Music"), rubbing of *The Stone Classics of the Kaicheng Era of the Tang Dynasty* (detail).
Date: 834–837.
Dimensions: c. 180 × c. 80 cm.
Private collection.

1. Liu Xiang 劉向, and Liu Xin 劉歆, *Qilüe bielu yiwen* 七略別錄佚文 (Aomen: Aomen daxue, 2007), 13; Zhang Shunhui 張舜徽, *Han shu yiwen zhi tongshi* 漢書藝文志通釋 (Wuhan: Hubei jiaoyu chubanshe, 1990), 55 and 59; and Li Guangdi 李光地, *Guyuejing zhuan* 古樂經傳 (Taipei: Shangwu yinshuguan, 1980). For an English translation of "Yue ji," see Scott Cook, "'Yue Ji' 樂記 — Record of Music: Introduction, Translation, Notes, and Commentary," *Asian Music* 26.2 (1995): 1–96.

2. Ouyang Xiu 歐陽修, *Ouyang Xiu quanji* 歐陽修全集 (Beijing: Zhongguo shudian, 1986), vol. 2, 998; Shao Yichen 邵懿辰, *Lijing tonglun* 禮經通論, as printed in Ruan Yuan 阮元 and Wang Xianqian 王先謙, eds., *Qing jingjie* 清經解, vol. 13 (Nanjing: Fenghuang chubanshe, 2005), 6351.

3. Pi Xirui 皮錫瑞, *Jingxue tonglun* 經學通論 (Shanghai: Shangwu yinshuguan, 1930), vol. 3, 1.

4. William G. Boltz, "*I-li*," in *Early Chinese Texts: A Bibliographical Guide*, ed. Michael Loewe (Berkeley: Society for the Study of Early China, 1993), 234–244, especially 240; and Wang Guowei 王國維, *Wudai liang Song jianben kao* 五代兩宋監本考, in *Wang Guowei quanji* 王國維全集, ed. Xie Weiyang 謝維揚 and Fang Xinliang 房鑫亮 (Hangzhou: Zhejiang jiaoyu chubanshe, 2009), vol. 7, 195–201.

5. Li Kaisheng 李開升, "*Yi li zhu shu* Chen Fengwu ben, Wang Wensheng ben bukao《儀禮注疏》陳鳳梧本、汪文盛本補考," *Wenshi* 文史 (2015) 2: 277–280.

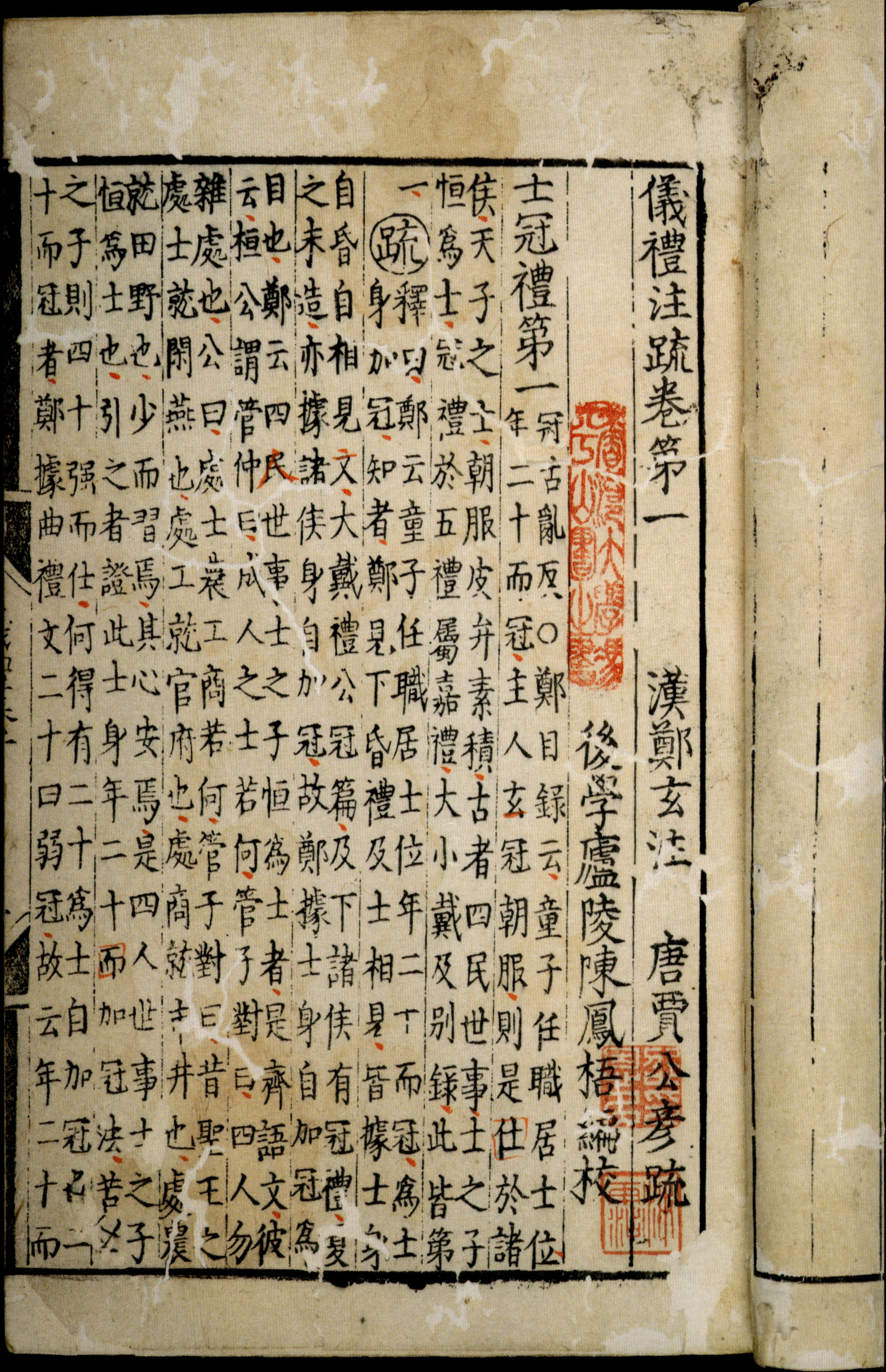

儀禮注疏卷第一

漢鄭玄注　唐賈公彥疏

後學盧陵陳鳳梧編校

士冠禮第一冠古亂反○鄭目録云童子任職居士位年二十而冠主人玄冠朝服則是仕於諸侯天子之士朝服皮弁素積古者四民世事士之子恒爲士冠禮於五禮屬嘉禮大小戴及別録此皆第一

疏釋曰鄭云童子任職居士位年二十而冠爲士身加冠知者鄭見下昏禮及士相見皆據士身自昏自相見文大戴禮公冠篇及下諸侯有冠禮夏之末造亦據諸侯身自加冠故鄭據士身自加冠爲目也鄭云四民世事士之子恒爲士者是齊語文彼云桓公謂管仲曰成人之士若何管子對曰四人勿雜處也公曰處士農工商若何管子對曰昔聖王之處士就閑燕也處工就官府也處商就市井也處農就田野也少而習焉其心安焉是四人世事士之子恒爲士也引之者證此士身年二十而加冠法若父之子則四十強而仕何得有二十爲士自加冠名一十而冠者鄭據曲禮文二十曰弱冠故云自年二十而

Fig. 1.2: *Yi li zhu shu* (*Notes to the Commentary on the Book of Etiquette and Ceremonial*), *juan* 1, fol. 1r.
Editor: Chen Fengwu (1475–1541).
Date: 1526.
Woodblock: 21.2 × 13.7 cm.
Fung Ping Shan Library.

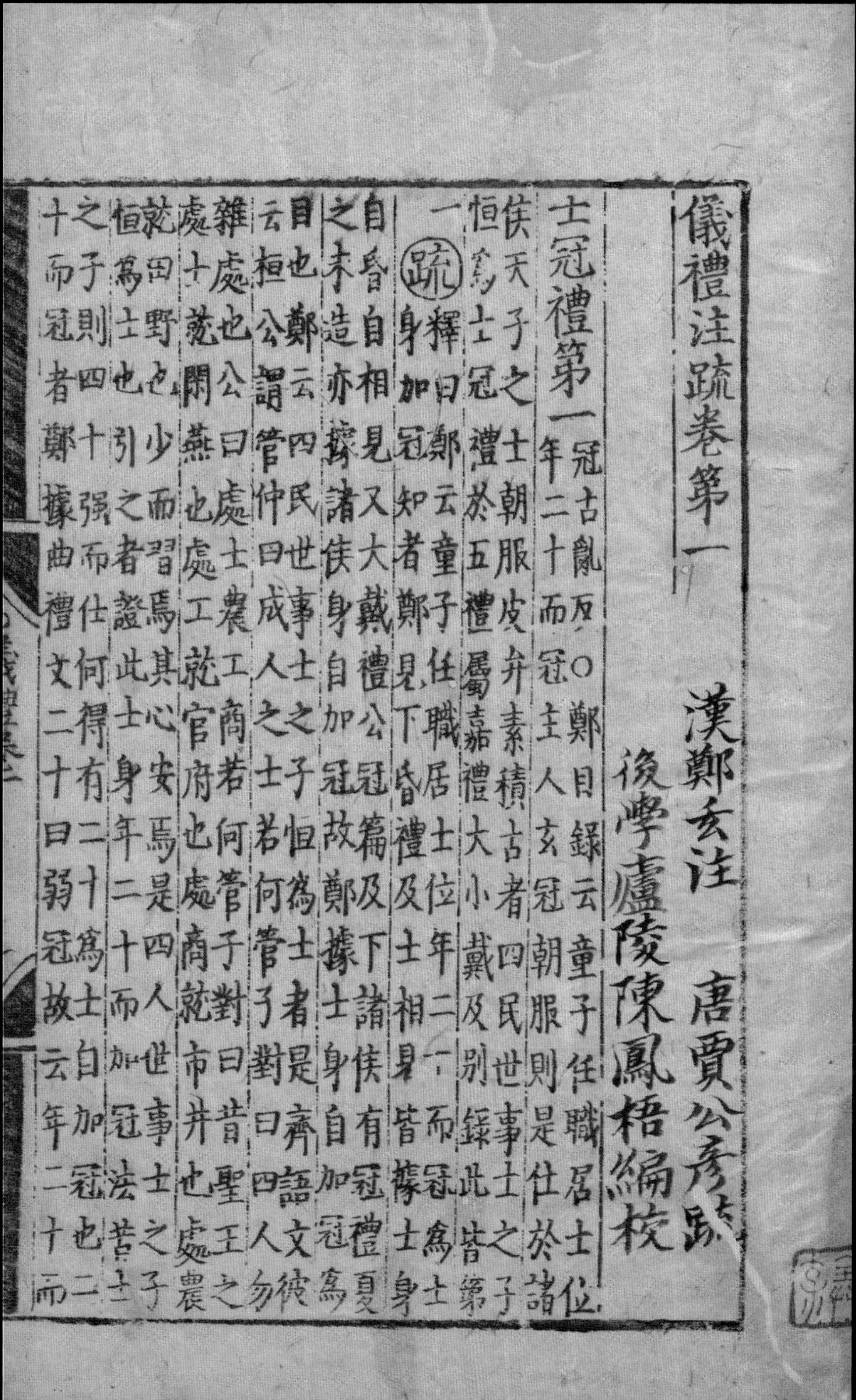

儀禮注疏卷第一

漢鄭玄注　唐賈公彥疏

後學盧陵陳鳳梧編校

士冠禮第一冠古亂反○鄭目錄云童子任職居士位年二十而冠主人玄冠朝服則是仕於諸侯天子之士朝服皮弁素積古者四民世事士之子恒爲士冠禮於五禮屬嘉禮大小戴及別錄此皆第一

疏釋曰鄭云童子任職居士位年二十而冠爲士身加冠知者鄭見下昏禮及士相見皆據士身自昏自相見又大戴禮公冠篇及下諸侯有冠禮夏之末造亦據諸侯身自加冠故鄭據士身自加冠爲目也鄭云四民世事士之子恒爲士者是齊語文彼云桓公謂管仲曰成人之士若何管子對曰四人勿雜處處也公曰處士農工商若何管子對曰昔聖王之處士就閑燕也處工就官府也處商就市井也處農就田野也少而習焉其心安焉是四人世事士之子恒爲士也引之者證此士身年二十而加冠法昔之子則四十強而仕何得有二十爲士自加冠也二十而冠者鄭據曲禮文二十曰弱冠故云年二十而

Fig. 1.3: *Yi li zhu shu* (*Notes to the Commentary on the Book of Etiquette and Ceremonial*), *juan* 1, fol. 1r.
Editor: Chen Fengwu (1475–1541).
Date: 1526.
Woodblock: 21.2 × 13.7 cm.
Harvard-Yenching Library (T 554 1880c).

Imperial Colleges at the time, one in Beijing (the "northern") and another in Nanjing (the "southern"), this version came to be known as the *nanyong ben* 南雍本 "Southern Imperial College Edition."[6] Subsequently in the Jiajing era (1522–1566), its text was reprinted at least three times, by Wang Wensheng 汪文盛 (?–1543), Ying Jia 應檟 (1493–1553), and Li Yuanyang 李元陽 (1497–1580) respectively.

Regarding this edition, Japanese sinologist Nagasawa Kikuya 長澤規矩也 (1902–1980) proposed a novel theory: Chen Fengwu did not in fact print it himself and instead simply reused the same printing plates that Wang Wensheng had employed, scraping off Wang's name from the woodblocks and replacing it with his own.[7] Modern scholarship has since demonstrated that Nagasawa was mistaken: the Wang Wensheng edition is actually a re-cut that closely imitates a later impression of the Southern Imperial College Edition;[8] but why did Nagasawa dare to offer such a bold interpretation? The reason, I believe, is because early impressions with Chen's ascriptions are extremely rare, and all the copies that Nagasawa consulted are later impressions that had Chen's original ascriptions either deleted or altered.[9] The copy kept at the Harvard-Yenching Library (Fig. 1.3) is one such version, and the ascription at the opening of *juan* 1 has been completely excised from the woodblock.

The University of Hong Kong's Fung Ping Shan Library holds a copy of a rare early impression of the Chen Fengwu edition.[10] Soon after its printing, it came into the collection of the bibliophile and publisher Mao Jin 毛晉 (1599–1659) of Changshu, as is indicated by his two square seals in the bottom right corner of the recto of the preface's first folio (Fig. 1.4, left). The seals read respectively: "Mao Jin siyin" 毛晉私印 ("Mao Jin's Private Seal") and "Zijin" 子晉 (his *zi* 字 soubriquet). On the verso of the final blank page before the first printed folio is a handwritten *ba* 跋 colophon (Fig. 1.4, right) by Shao Enduo 邵恩多 (fl. late eighteenth–early nineteenth centuries). Shao Enduo came from the same region as Mao Jin, which allowed him to make a comparison between a separate Southern Song dynasty (1127–1279) edition of *The Book of Etiquette and Ceremonial* and this copy. The colophon reads:

> Ma Tingluan (1222–1289) states: "Although I have already lived for fifty-eight years, I have yet to read a copy of *The Book of Etiquette and Ceremonial*. One day, I happened to find in an old chest a copy in four cases of an official version of a Jingde era (1004–1007) *Notes to the Book of Etiquette and Ceremonial*; the original text and commentary were laid out and recorded one after the other in the main text, with accompanying notes placed below." This means that the Song dynasty (960–1279) edition did not contain Zheng Xuan's commentary and was divided into fifty *juan*, which is identical to the version mentioned in the *Wenxian tongkao* (*Comprehensive Examination of Literature*).[11] Once, while in the library of Huang Pilie (1763–1825) in Suzhou, I came across just such a Song edition. It is one of the most treasured items in the repository.
>
> 馬廷鸞曰：「余生五十八年未嘗讀《儀禮》之書。一日從敗篋中得景德官本《儀禮疏》四袟，正經、注語皆標起止，而疏文列其下。」蓋宋槧本不載鄭注，分卷五十，與《文獻通考》之說合。余曾於吳門士禮居一見之，實鎮庫物也。
>
> This version is an imprint of the early Ming dynasty (1368–1644) edition and is closest to the ancient original. I abide by Wei Ti's (act. 1226) words: "[Jia] Gongyan, together with Li Yuanzhi, wrote *Notes to the Book of Etiquette and Ceremonial*," and the character "deng" ["etc."] at the close of the author column at the head of the text is there so as to include [Li] Yuanzhi in the editorship; the modern Imperial College edition and the Jiguge edition [published by Mao Jin] have both eliminated it; is this not preposterous?
>
> 是書為明初槧本，最為近古。余按衛湜云：「公彥同李元植編《儀禮疏》」，則結銜中「等」字，是統元植而言；今監本及汲古閣本悉去之，其謬何如？
>
> In addition, according to Chao Gongwu's (c.1105–1180) *[Junzhai] dushu zhi* (*Records of Reading at the Prefectural Studio*): "Huang Qing of the Northern Qi dynasty (479–502) and Li Mengzhe of the Sui dynasty (581–618) both wrote *Notes to the Book of Etiquette and Ceremonial*, and [Jia] Gongyan cut and merged the notes of both authors to make his own book. The Song dynasty court had at one time invited Xing Bing (932–1010) to organize and edit it." Among the notes in the modern edition are none that have Xing Bing as their provenance, and only at the end of the Jingde era edition is it noted in an endnote column

that "Xing Bing proofread this;" from this it can be ascertained that "organize and edit it" refers simply to proofreading, and no contribution was made by him to the supplementary notes. When reading books, the oldest edition should be sought, and doing so is the most reliable.

又按晁公武《讀書志》云：「齊黃慶、隋李孟悊各有《疏義》，公彥刪二疏為此書，國朝嘗詔邢昺是正之」，今疏中絕無邢氏說；惟景德本末有「邢昺校題」銜一條，是可知「正之」在校之也，固無與于疏也。讀書必求古本，信然。

Below this passage is stamped: "A twenty-fourth generation descendent of [Shao] Kangjie [Shao Yong 邵雍, 1011–1077], 'Resounding Immortal,' His Seal" 康節二十四世孫朗仙圖章. At the bottom right corner of the recto of the first page of the first *juan* (Fig. 1.2) are two square seals: "Shao Enduo Yin" 邵恩多印 ("Shao Enduo, His Seal") and "Peizhan" 沛霑 (his *zi* soubriquet). In the early Republican period, the book found its way into the library known as Jiaye tang 嘉業堂 (The Hall of Magnificent Achievement) of Liu Chenggan 劉承幹 (1881–1963) in Nanxun, as is verified by his stamp on the recto of the first page of the preface, placed directly above the two stamps of Mao Jin (Fig. 1.4, left). After the Second World War, it came to Hong Kong, and eventually into the collection of the Fung Ping Shan Library (est. 1932). Interestingly, apparently representing a calligraphic style of the late Yuan and early Ming, the book has been mistakenly regarded as a Yuan dynasty (1206–1368) imprint, and a lithograph photograph of the book's first folio was included in an illustrated catalog of the Song and Yuan editions in Liu's collection that was published in Shanghai in 1929.[12]

Focusing now on the seventeen chapters of the "New Text" of *The Book of Etiquette and Ceremonial*, chapters 4–7 contain plentiful and detailed references to music. The titles of these four chapters are:

4. District Rites for Drinking Wine 鄉飲酒禮
5. District Rites for Archery Contests 鄉射禮
6. Banquet Rites 燕禮
7. Rites for Imperial Archery Contests 大射

The chapter "District Rites for Drinking Wine" is taken here as a case study, as it offers an account of the role of music in societal functions. It includes descriptions of selecting guests, welcoming them, offering them food and wine, and providing them with musical entertainment—outlining as many as ten different routines as part of the ceremonies. The overarching event is that of a district head throwing a banquet for local dignitaries as a means for selecting the most able and virtuous for recommendation to superiors for government office. Music was a crucial part of these occasions, and the *yuezheng* 樂正 (music master) and *yuegong* 樂工 (ordinary musicians) were closely involved in the ritual. Before the musical performances took place, elaborate ceremonies were enacted that

6. During his lifetime, Chen Fengwu published *The Book of Etiquette and Ceremonial* twice. Five years earlier, in 1521, Chen had already published an annotated edition based on Zheng Xuan's exegesis. Liu Chenggan also owned a copy of this edition. In the bibliographical record of Liu Chenggan's library, the entry for the 1521 edition is written by Miao Quancun 繆荃孫 (1844–1919), who died in 1919, so the book must have come into Liu Chenggan's collection prior to this date. See Miao Quansun, Wu Changshou 吳昌綬, and Dong Kang 董康, *Jiaye tang cangshu zhi* 嘉業堂藏書志 (Shanghai: Fudan daxue chubanshe, 1997), 146. Liu Chenggan's diary entry for the ninth lunar month, the fourth day, 1913, records that the renowned scholar Miao Quansun sold him five books, of which four concerned *The Book of Etiquette and Ceremonial*; the total price was 480 silver dollars. One of these was the 1521 edition published by Chen Fengwu. See Liu Chenggan 劉承幹, *Jiaye tang cangshu riji chao* 嘉業堂藏書日記抄 (Nanjing: Fenghuang chubanshe, 2016), 114; and Liu Chenggan 劉承幹, *Qiushu zhai riji* 求恕齋日記 (Beijing: Guojia tushuguan chubanshe, 2016), vol. 3, 254. Currently, Liu's copy of the 1521 edition is kept at the National Central Library in Taipei. See Guojia tushuguan 國家圖書館, *Guojia tushuguan shanben shuzhi chugao: Jingbu* 國家圖書館善本書志初稿: 經部 (Taipei: Guojia tushuguan, 1996), 105.

7. Nagasawa Kikuya 長澤規矩也, *Jūsankyō chūso eifu* 十三經注疏影譜 (Tokyo: Nihon Shoshi Gakkai, 1934), 6–7 and pls. 35–37; Nagasawa Kikuya 長澤規矩也, *Shoshigaku ronkō* 書誌學論考 (Tokyo: Shōundō shoten, 1937), 9; and Nagasawa Kikuya 長澤規矩也, *Nagasawa Kikuya chosakushū* 長澤規矩也著作集, vol. 1 (Tokyo: Kyūko Shoin, 1982), 16.

8. Li Kaisheng, "*Yi li zhu shu* Chen Fengwu ben, Wang Wensheng ben bukao," 279–280. Liao Mingfei 廖明飛, "*Yi li* zhu shu heke kao《儀禮》注疏合刻考," *Wenshi* 文史 (2014) 1: 185–207, especially 204–206.

9. Nagasawa Kikuya, *Jūsankyō chūso eifu*, pls. 35–36.

10. Jao Tsung-i 饒宗頤, *Xianggang daxue Feng Pingshan tushuguan cang shanben shulu* 香港大學馮平山圖書館藏善本書錄 (Hong Kong: Longmen shudian, 1970), 27–28; and Jao Tsung-i 饒宗頤, Li Zhifang 李直方, and Zhang Lijuan 張麗娟, *Xianggang daxue Feng Pingshan tushuguan cang shanben shulu* 香港大學馮平山圖書館藏善本書錄, enlarged ed. (Hong Kong: Hong Kong University Press, 2003), 15. For more bibliographical information on this edition, see Qu Yong 瞿鏞, *Tieqin tongjian lou cangshu mulu* 鐵琴銅劍樓藏書目錄 (Beijing: Zhonghua shuju, 1990), 56; Fu Zengxiang 傅增湘, *Cangyuan qunshu jingyan lu* 藏園羣書經眼錄 (Beijing: Zhonghua shuju, 1983), 49; and Liao Mingfei, "*Yi li* zhu shu heke kao," 185–207.

11. *Wenxian tongkao* was compiled by Ma Tingluan's son, Ma Duanlin 馬端臨 (1254–1323), in 1307.

12. Liu Chenggan 劉承幹, *Wuxing Liushi Jiaye tang shanben shuying* 吳興劉氏嘉業堂善本書景 (Shanghai: Jiaye tang, 1929), vol. 1, fols. 24r–v.

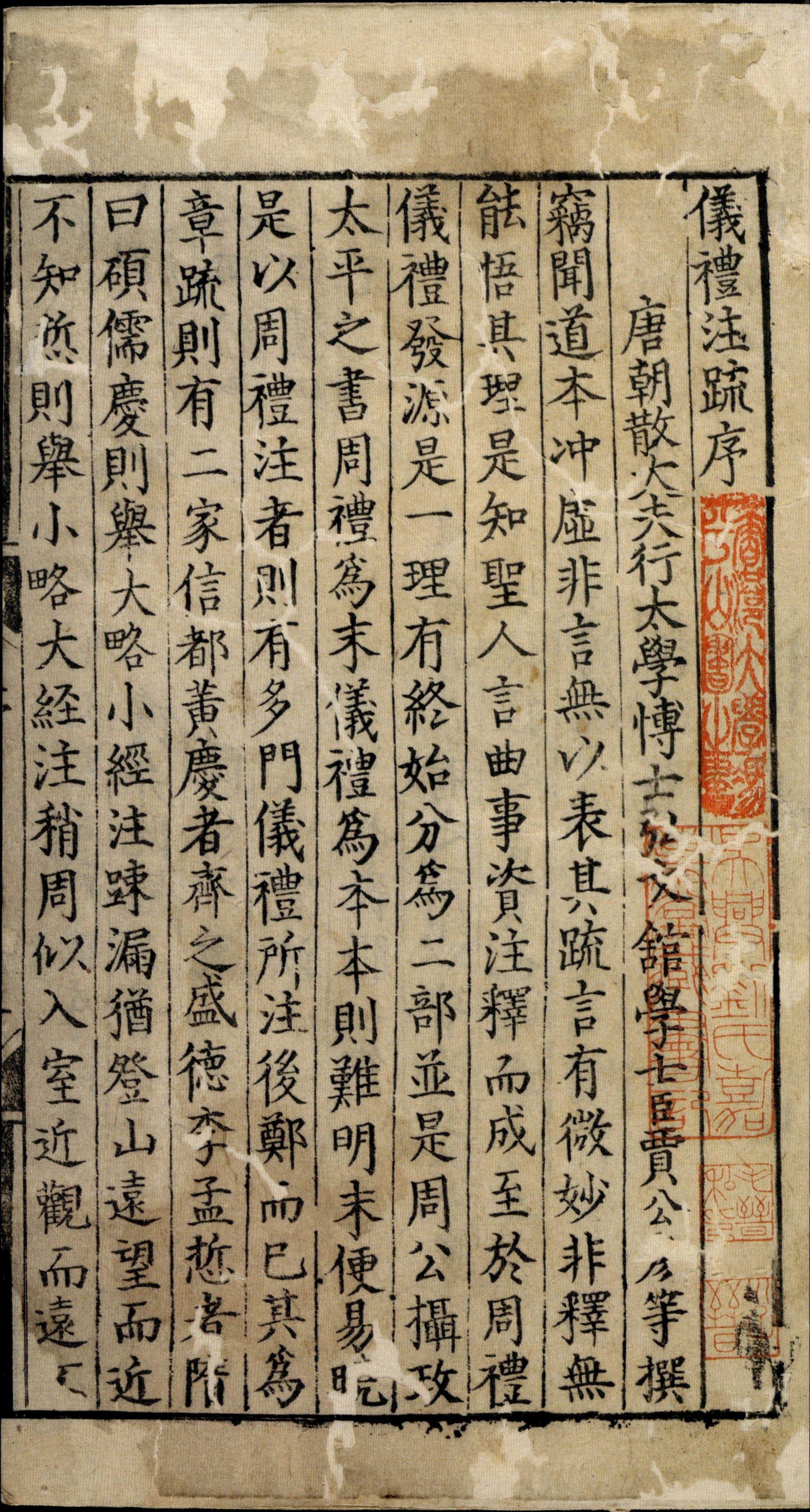

儀禮注疏序

唐朝散大夫行太學博士弘文館學士臣賈公彥等撰

竊聞道本沖虛非言無以表其疏言有微妙非釋無能悟其理是知聖人言曲事資注釋而成至於周禮儀禮發源是一理有終始分為二部並是周公攝致太平之書周禮為末儀禮為本本則難明末便易曉是以周禮注者則有多門儀禮所注後鄭而已其為章疏則有二家信都黃慶者齊之盛德李孟悊者隋曰碩儒慶則舉大略小經注疎漏猶登山遠望而近不知悊則舉小略大經注稍周似入室近觀而遠不

Fig. 1.4: *Yi li zhu shu* (*Notes to the Commentary on the Book of Etiquette and Ceremonial*), preface, fol. 1r, and Shao Enduo's handwritten colophon.
Editor: Chen Fengwu (1475–1541).
Date: 1526.
Woodblock: 21.2 × 13.7 cm.
Fung Ping Shan Library.

馬廷鸞曰余生五十八年未嘗讀儀禮之書一日從敗篋中得景德官本儀禮疏四袟正經注語皆標起止而疏文列其下蓋宋槧本不載鄭注分卷五十與文獻通考之說合余曾於吳門士禮居一見之實鎮庫物也是書為明初槧本最古為近古余按衛湜云公彥同李元植編儀禮疏則結銜中等字是銳元杖而言今監本及汲古閣本悉去之其謬何如又按晁公武讀書志云齊黃慶隋李孟悊各有疏義公彥刪二疏為此書國朝嘗詔邢昺等是正之今疏中絕無邢氏說惟景德本末有邢昺等校題銜一條是可知正之云校之也固無與于疏也讀書必求古本

信述

included the "Ascending Processional Song" and "Offering Wine to the Musicians."

Opening the book to the verso of the eighteenth folio of the fourth *juan* (Fig. 1.5), the text as translated below is found; Zheng Xuan's commentary and Jia Gongyan's notes are also present and clearly differentiated. Both the recto and verso of each folio have ten ruled columns, and the original text occupies one vertical line of twenty characters down each of these columns, as can be seen in the second and third columns (from the right); following the original text is Zheng Xuan's commentary with two lines of text in each ruled column, though still with twenty characters to each line; in the second character space of the eighth column a circled character ㊄疏 indicates that this is where Jia Gongyan's notes begin, and they too are written two lines to a ruled column with twenty characters to each line. The section of text beginning on this page marks the introduction of musical involvement into the ritual:

> Mats should be set along the edge of the hall, with the eastern as the most honored side. Of the four musicians, two are *se* players [and two are singers]; upon entering, the *se* players lead the way. Supporting them are two attendants who hold the *se* in their left hand with the head of the *se* pointing backwards, their left hand inserted into the sound-hole on the underside of the instrument, the strings facing inwards, and their right hand supporting the player. The music master is the first to ascend and take his place, and stands to the east of the western steps. As the four musicians enter, they ascend and take their places via the western steps, and then seat themselves facing north. Their supporting attendants seat themselves facing east, pass their *se* to the musicians, and then descend and depart. The musicians perform *The Deer Call*, *The Four Stallions*, and *Many-Hued are the Flowers*. After the songs have finished, the host offers wine to the musicians. The musicians place their *se* to the left, and the master musician pays obeisance to the host, and without rising receives a goblet of wine. The host, on the eastern stairway, pays his respects to the receiver of the goblet. A servant presents cured meats and pâté. The host bids a servant to assist the master musician with an offering of food. The master musician partakes of the wine, and having drunk his fill, with no requirement to pay obeisance, passes the goblet back to the host. The assembled musicians are not required to pay obeisance to the host and can receive the goblet and then a sacrifice is made. Having drunk, they receive the cured meats and pâté, and then no sacrifice is made. If there is a distinguished music master to whom wine is offered, the goblet must be washed for him. When the guests are ready to descend and depart, the host bids them farewell. When the goblet is washed, no thanks are offered by the musicians.
>
> 設席於堂廉，東上。工四人，二瑟，瑟先。相者二人，皆左何瑟，後首，挎越，內弦，右手相。樂正先升，立於西階東。工入，升自西階。北面坐。相者東面坐，遂授瑟，乃降。工歌《鹿鳴》、《四牡》、《皇皇者華》。卒歌，主人獻工。工左瑟，一人拜，不興，受爵。主人阼階上拜送爵。薦脯醢。使人相祭。工飲，不拜既爵，授主人爵。衆工則不拜，受爵，祭，飲辯有脯醢，不祭。大師則為之洗。賓、介降，主人辭降。工不辭洗。

The Book of Etiquette and Ceremonial is often regarded as being one of the most complex ancient Confucian texts, primarily because it describes elaborately choreographed ritual in such abundant detail. In the collection of the Fung Ping Shan Library, Zhu Zaiyu's 朱載堉 (1536–1611) Ming dynasty book series *Yuelü quanshu* 樂律全書 (*Collected Works on Music and Pitch-Pipes*, 1595–1607)[13] in the volume *Xiangyin shiyue pu* 鄉飲詩樂譜 (*District Rites for Drinking Wine: Poetical and Musical Scores*) solves this problem by providing a series of images that match the text; for example, where the text reads:

> [Supporting them are two attendants who] hold the *se* in their left hand with the head of the *se* pointing backwards, their right hand supporting the player 左何瑟，後首，右手相工 (Fig. 1.6, right).

13. Jao Tsung-i, *Xianggang daxue Feng Pingshan tushuguan cang shanben shulu*, 29–30; and Jao Tsung-i, Li Zhifang, and Zhang Lijuan, *Xianggang daxue Feng Pingshan tushuguan cang shanben shulu*, 19–20. For more bibliographical information on this edition, see, for example, Lucille Chia, "The Uses of Print in Ming Dynasty China: A Very Brief Survey," in *Books in Numbers*, ed. Wilt L. Idema (Cambridge, Mass.: Harvard-Yenching Library, Harvard University, 2007), 183 and 185; Wang Chung-min, *A Descriptive Catalog of Rare Chinese Books in the Library of Congress* (Washington, DC.: Library of Congress, 1957), 54–56; and Lu Zugu 陸祖穀, *Zhejiang shengli tushuguan shanben shumu tizhi* 浙江省立圖書館善本書目題識 (Hangzhou: Zhejiang shengli tushuguan, 1932), 17–19.

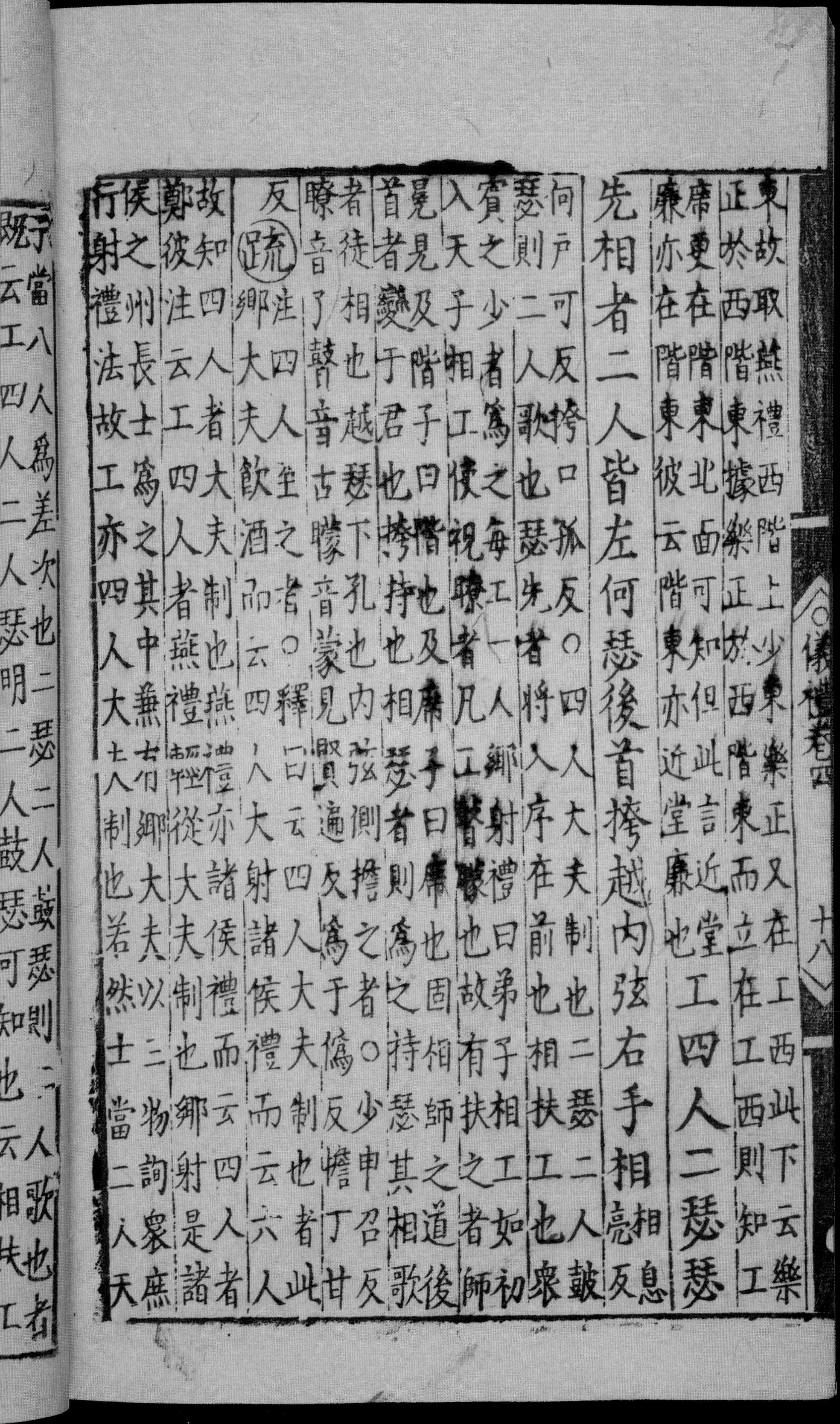

東故取燕禮西階上少東樂正又在工西此下云樂正於西階東據樂正於西階東而立在工西則知工席更在階東北面可知但此言近堂廉亦在階東彼云階東亦近堂廉也

工四人二瑟瑟先相者二人皆左何瑟後首挎越内弦右手相相息亮反

向戶可反挎口孤反○四人大夫制也二瑟二人鼓瑟則二人歌也瑟先者將入序在前也相扶工也衆賓之少者爲之每工一人鄉射禮曰弟子相工如初入天子相工使視瞭者凡工瞽矇也故有扶之者師冕見及階子曰階也及席子曰席也固相師之道後首者變于君也挎持也相瑟者則爲之持瑟其相歌者徒相也越瑟下孔也内弦側擔之者○少申召反瞭音了瞽音古矇音蒙見賢遍反爲于僞反擔丁甘反

疏 注四人至之者○釋曰云四人大夫制也者此鄉大夫飲酒而云四人大射諸侯禮而云六人故知四人者大夫制也燕禮亦諸侯禮而云四人者鄭彼注云工四人者燕禮輕從大夫制也鄉射是諸侯之州長士爲之其中兼有鄉大夫以三物詢衆庶行射禮法故工亦四人大夫制也若然士當二人天

Fig. 1.5: *Yi li zhu shu* (*Notes to the Commentary on the Book of Etiquette and Ceremonial*), *juan* 4, fol. 18v.
Editor: Chen Fengwu (1475–1541).
Date: 1526.
Woodblock: 21.2 × 13.7 cm.
Fung Ping Shan Library.

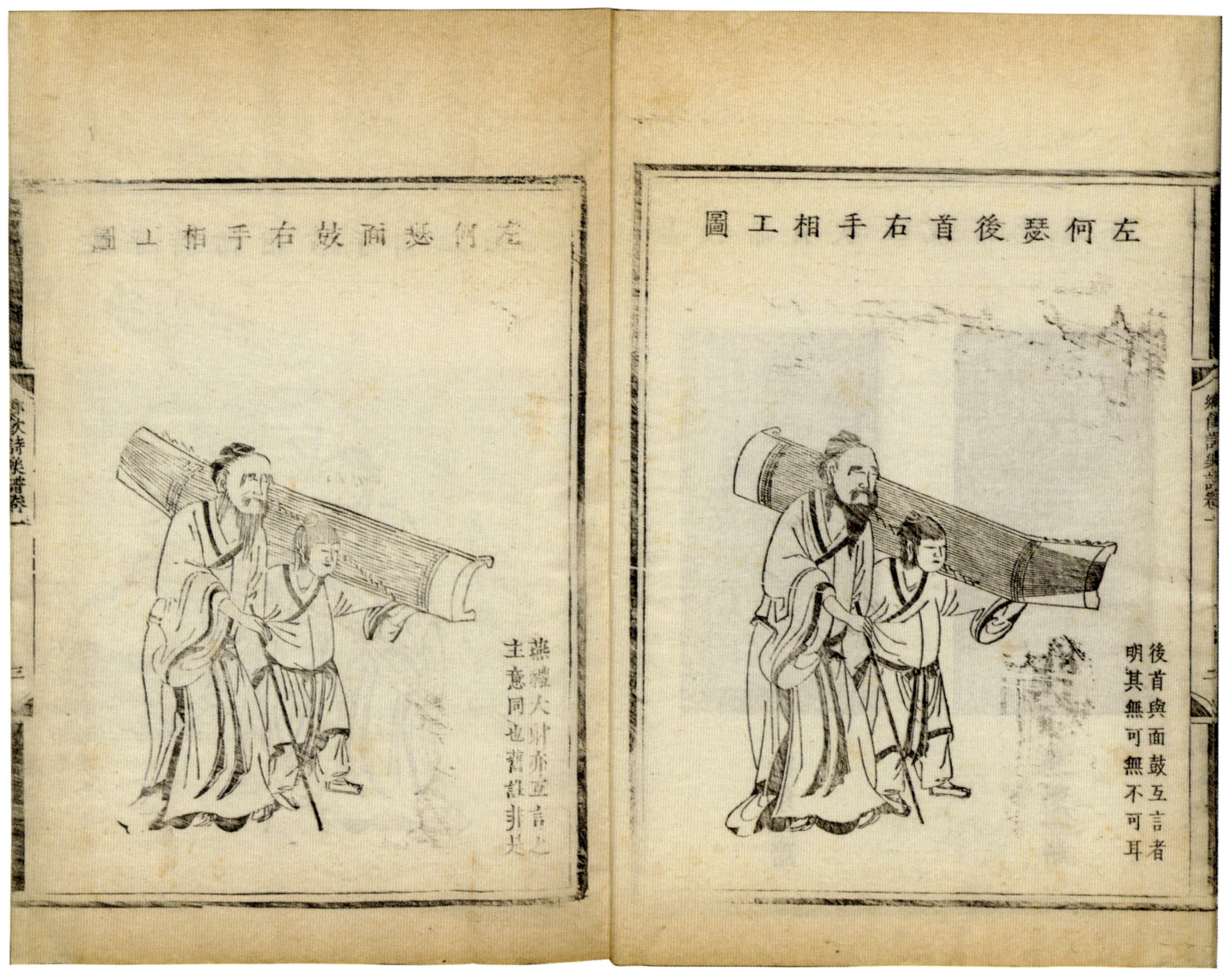

Fig. 1.6: *Yuelü quanshu* (*Collected Works on Music and Pitch-Pipes*), *Xiangyin shiyue pu* (*District Rites for Drinking Wine: Poetical and Musical Scores*), *juan* 1, fols. 2v–3r.
Author: Zhu Zaiyu (1536–1611).
Date: 1595–1606.
Woodblock: 25.0 × 16.6 cm.
Harvard-Yenching Library (T 6730 2944).

> The supporting attendants seat themselves facing east and pass their *se* to the musicians 相者向東坐，以瑟授工 (Fig. 1.7, right).

Set against the annotations of the various commentators, Zhu Zaiyu's pictorial interpretations are vastly more powerful explanatory tools; they stress the importance of the precise arrangement of each movement, which is especially significant given that the musicians would have been blind. For all the pieces mentioned in chapters four and five of *The Book of Etiquette and Ceremonial*, in an effort to illustrate the original performance, he has also reconstructed musical pieces in full score.[14] In a wider context, Zhu Zaiyu's contribution to musical knowledge and understanding goes far beyond this, as he was responsible for the Chinese discovery of "equal temperament."[15]

Later in *District Rites for Drinking Wine* there appears the following passage concerning a performance on the *sheng* 笙 mouth organ and the offering of wine to those who play the instrument:

> Those who play the *sheng* are assembled in formation outside the hall and the chimes are erected to the south, facing north. The musicians play *The Southern Stairwell*, *White Flowers*, and *Flowering Millet*. The host offers wine to them on the western steps, and the senior member of the ensemble pays obeisance in return, approaching the steps without ascending to the hall. He receives a goblet of wine and the host pays his respects to the receiver of the goblet. In front of the steps, the senior member of the ensemble seats himself and offers an oblation of wine, and then stands to drink his fill; with no need to pay obeisance,

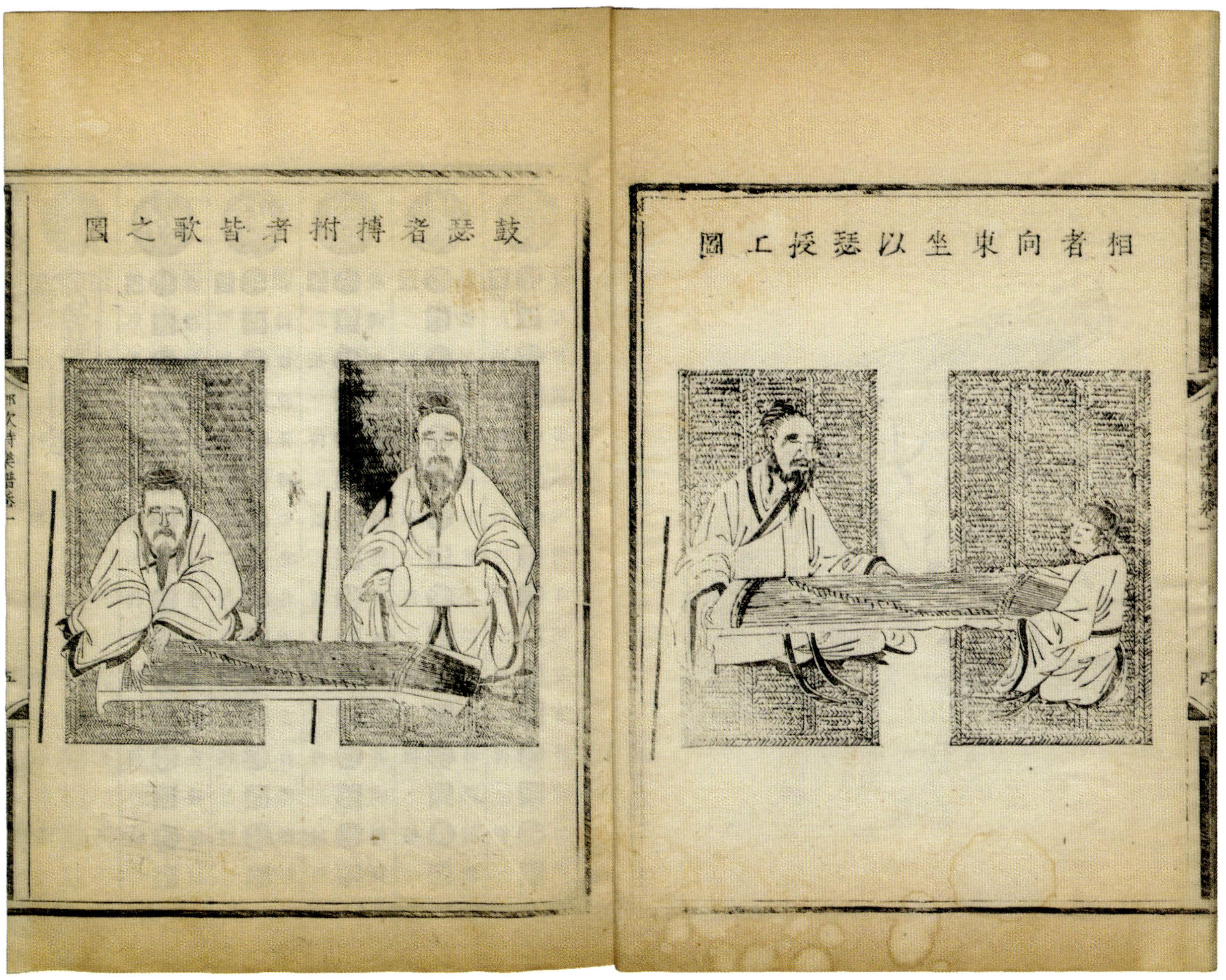

Fig. 1.7: *Yuelü quanshu* (*Collected Works on Music and Pitch-Pipes*), *Xiangyin shiyue pu* (*District Rites for Drinking Wine: Poetical and Musical Scores*), *juan* 1, fols. 4v–5r.
Author: Zhu Zaiyu (1536–1611).
Date: 1595–1606.
Woodblock: 25.0 × 16.6 cm.
Harvard-Yenching Library (T 6730 2944).

he ascends the steps and passes the goblet back to the host. The assembled *sheng* players are not required to pay obeisance to the host, and having received the goblet, seat themselves to make the food offering, and stand to drink their fill; when this is done, cured meats and pâté are made ready, and no offering is made.

笙入堂下，磬南，北面立，樂《南陔》、《白華》、《華黍》。主人獻之於西階上。一人拜，盡階，不升堂，受爵，主人拜送爵。階前坐祭，立飲，不拜既爵，升授主人爵。衆笙則不拜，受爵，坐祭，立飲；辯有脯醢，不祭。

In Zhu Zaiyu's book, matching the first two phrases of this passage are two illustrations of relevant ensembles and instruments. "The chimes are erected to the south, facing north" is depicted

14. The earliest surviving musical score of the songs in *The Book of Odes* is that of the twelve ritual songs said to have been transmitted via Zhao Yansu 趙彥肅 (1148–1196). See Laurence Picken, "Twelve Ritual Melodies of the T'ang Dynasty," in *Studia memoriae Belae Bartók sacra*, ed. Benjámin Rajeczky and Lajos Vargyas (Budapest: Aedes Academiae Scientiarum Hungaricae, 1956), 147–173.

15. Liu Fu 劉復, "Shier denglü de famingzhe Zhu Zaiyu 十二等律的發明者朱載堉," in *Qingzhu Cai Yuanpei xiansheng liushiwu sui lunwenji* 慶祝蔡元培先生六十五歲論文集 (Beiping: Guoli zhongyang yanjiuyuan, 1933), 279–310; Yang Yinliu 楊蔭瀏, "Pingjun lü suanjie 平均律算解," *Yenching Journal of Chinese Studies* 燕京學報 21 (1937): 2–60; Kenneth Robinson and Joseph Needham, "Sound (Acoustics)," in *Science and Civilisation in China*, vol. 4, pt. 1, ed. Joseph Needham (Cambridge: Cambridge University Press, 1962), 221; Fritz A. Kuttner, "Prince Chu Tsai-Yü's Life and Work," *Ethnomusicology* 19.2 (1975): 163–206; Gene Jinsiong Cho, *The Discovery of Musical Equal Temperament in China and Europe in the Sixteenth Century* (Lewiston, NY: Edwin Mellen Press, 2003); and Woo Shingkwan, "The Ceremonial Music of Zhu Zaiyu" (PhD diss., Rutgers, The State University of New Jersey, 2017).

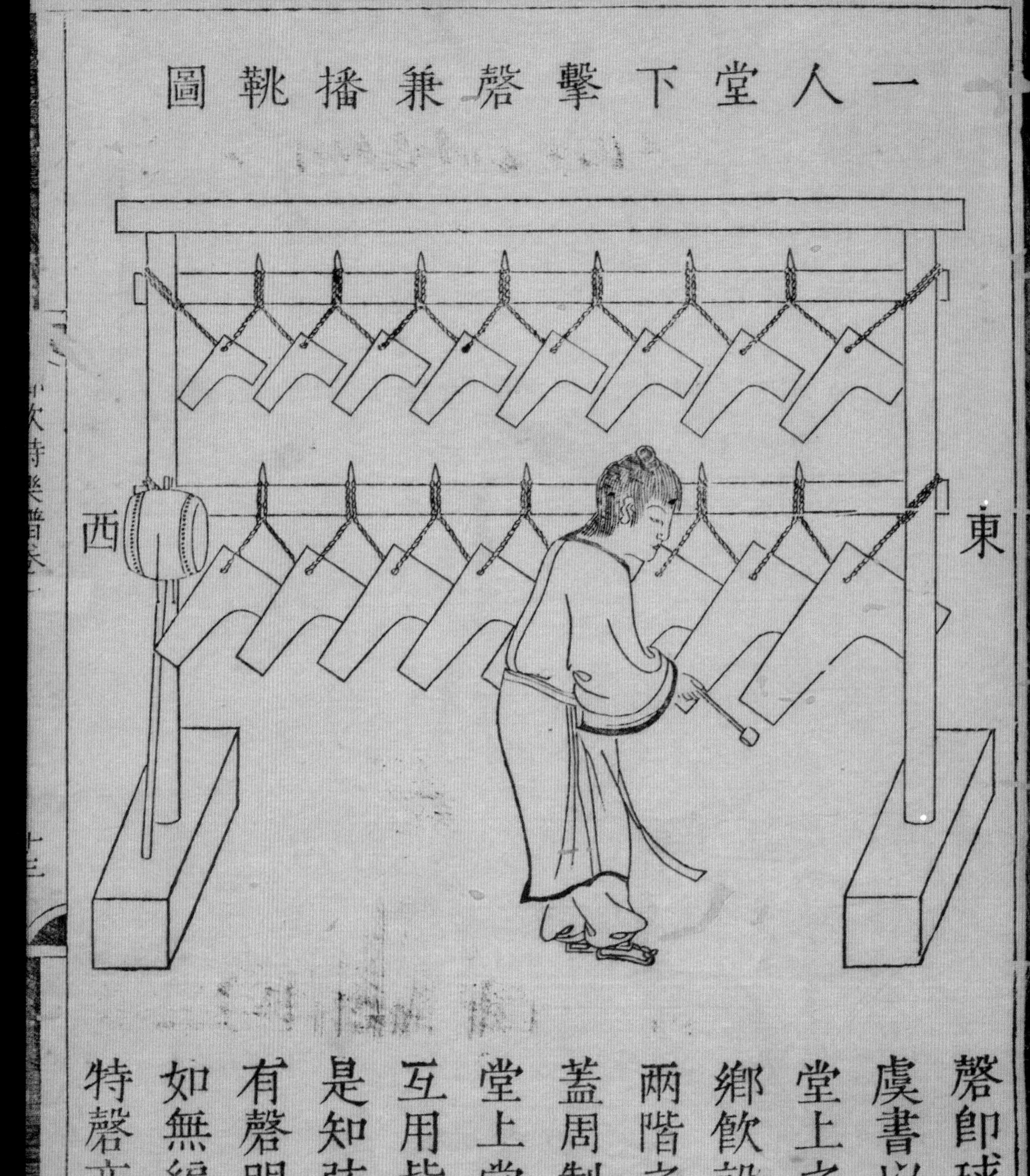

Fig. 1.8: *Yuelü quanshu (Collected Works on Music and Pitch-Pipes), Xiangyin shiyue pu (District Rites for Drinking Wine: Poetical and Musical Scores), juan* 1, fol. 13r.
Author: Zhu Zaiyu (1536–1611).
Date: 1595–1606.
Woodblock: 25.0 × 16.6 cm.
Fung Ping Shan Library.

Fig. 1.9 (opposite): *Mémoire sur la Musique des Chinois, tant anciens que modernes (Dissertation on Chinese Music, both ancient and modern)*, Figs. 36 (top) and 38 (bottom).
Author: Joseph-Marie Amiot (1718–1793).
Date: 1780.
Dimensions: 26.0 × 20.3 cm.
Hong Kong University Libraries

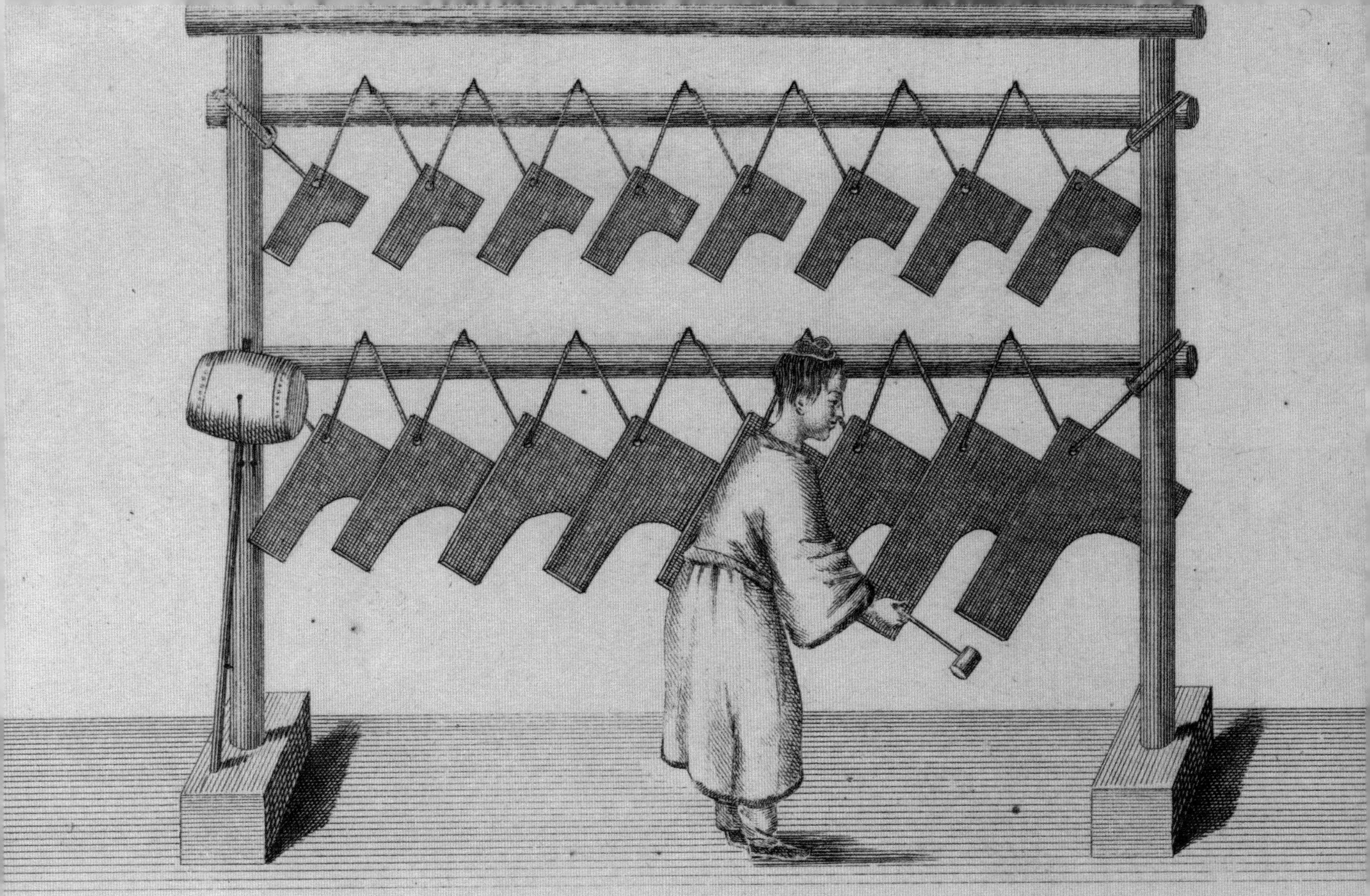

Fig. 38.

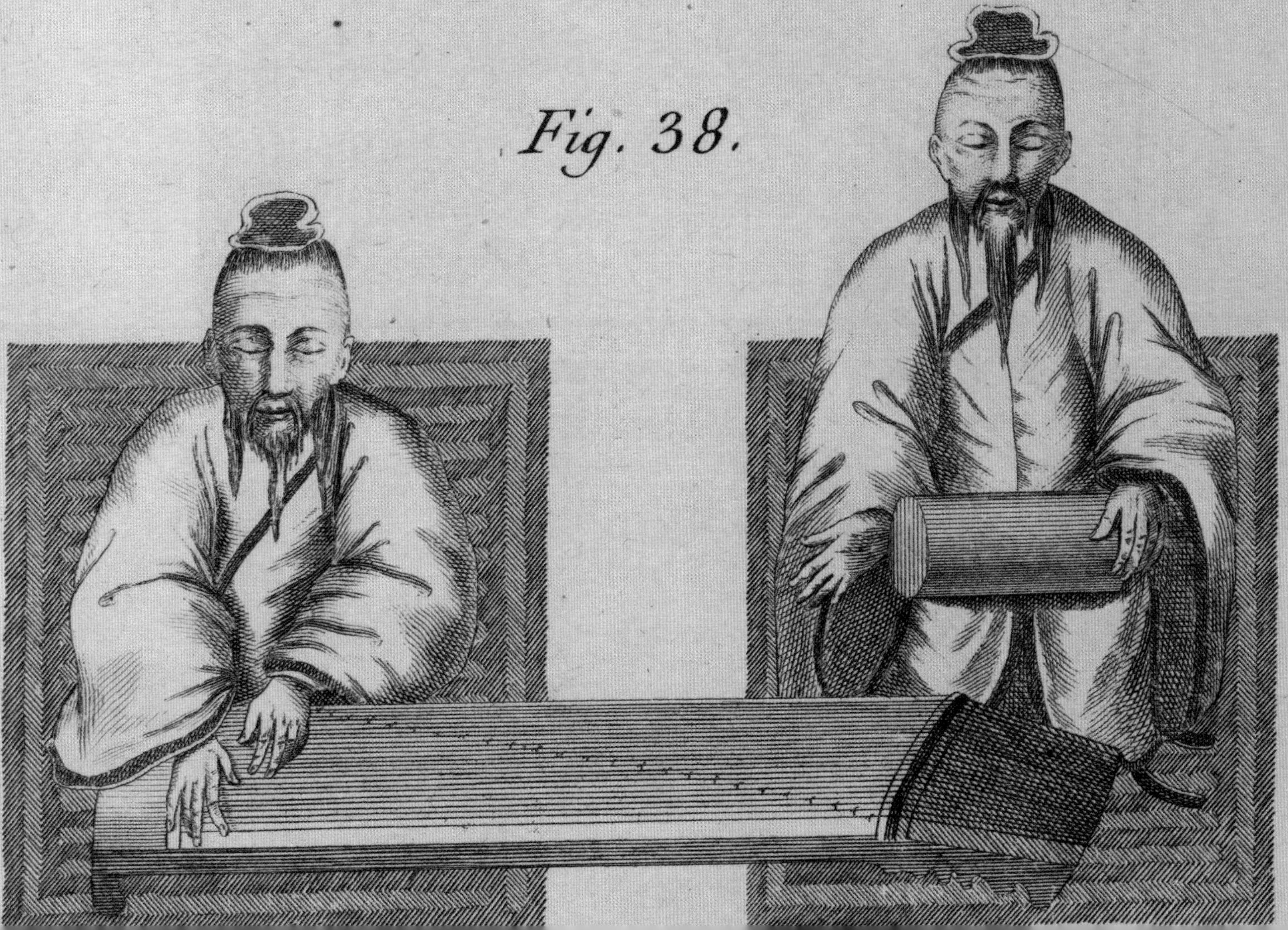

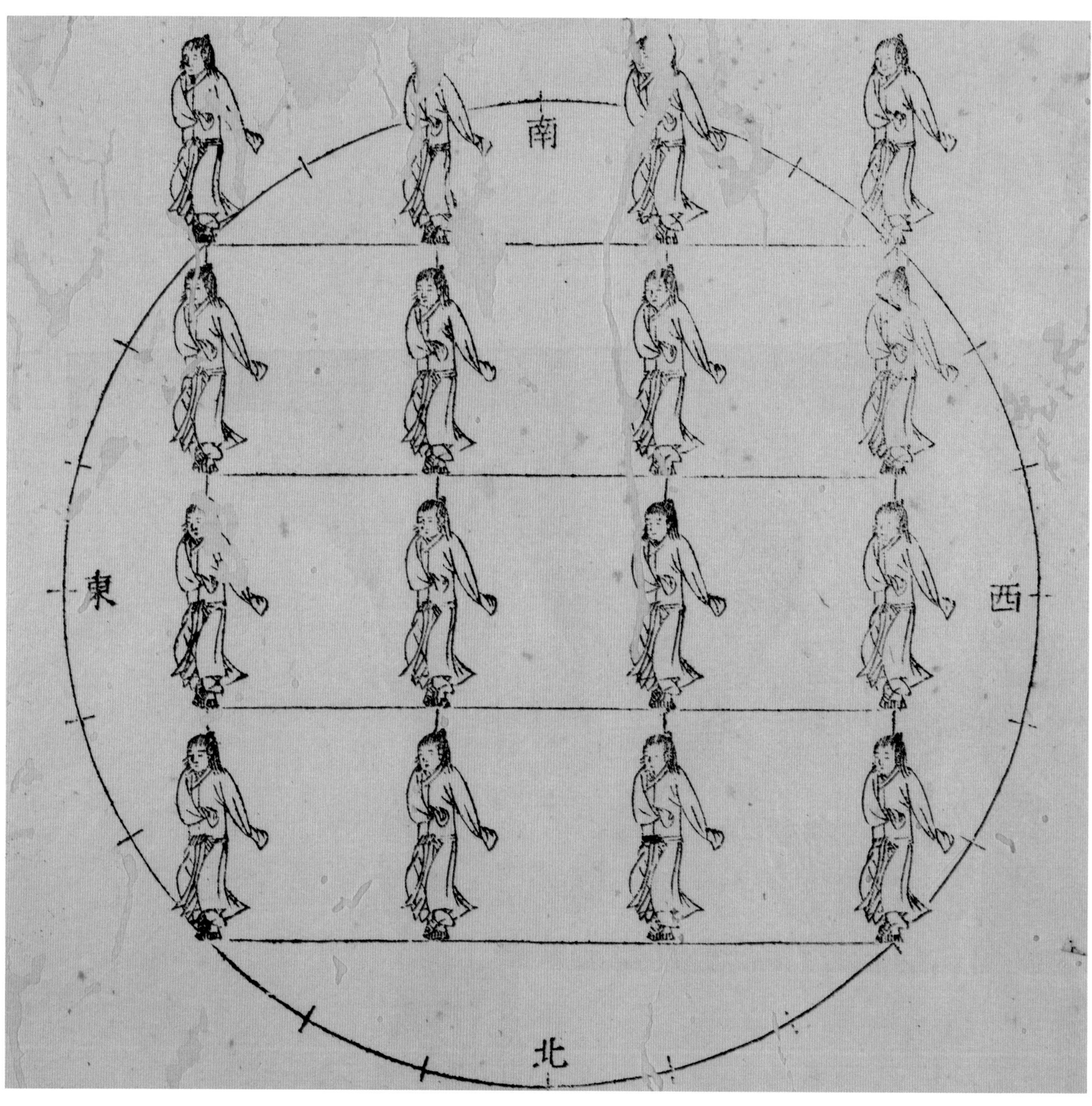

by an impressive two-rack set of chimes (Fig. 1.8), with the characters for "east" and "west" printed helpfully at either end to confirm that it faces north. Matching the phrase "Those who play the *sheng* are assembled in formation outside the hall" is a line of four players, three with a *sheng* and one with clappers, with the characters for "north" and "south" printed at either end. Alongside the illustration, Zhu Zaiyu notes: "All of those

Fig. 1.10: *Yuelü quanshu (Collected Works on Music and Pitch-Pipes), Lingxing xiaowu pu (Sacrifice to Agricultural Deities: Notation of Dance of the Adolescents), juan* 1, fols. 157v–158r (detail).
Author: Zhu Zaiyu (1536–1611).
Date: 1595–1606.
Woodblock: 25.0 × 16.6 cm.
Fung Ping Shan Library.

Fig. 1.11 (opposite): *Mémoire sur la Musique des Chinois, tant anciens que modernes (Dissertation on Chinese Music, both ancient and modern)*, Fig. 40 (detail).
Author: Joseph-Marie Amiot (1718–1793).
Date: 1780.
Dimensions: 26.0 × 20.3 cm.
Hong Kong University Libraries.

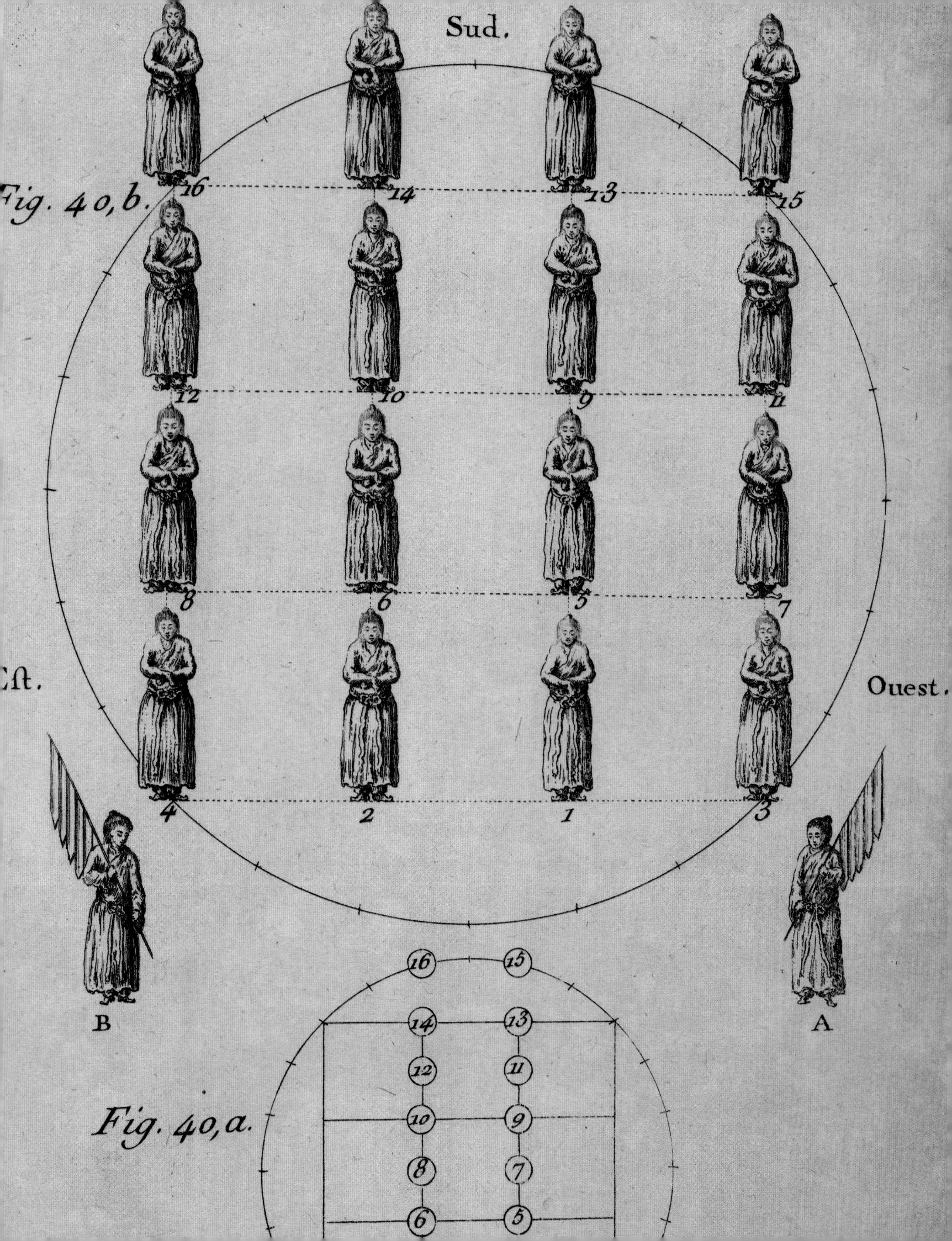

Sud.
Fig. 40, b.
16
14
13
15
12
10
9
11
8
6
5
7
Est.
Ouest.
4
2
1
3
B
A
16
15
14
13
12
11
Fig. 40, a.
10
9
8
7
6
5

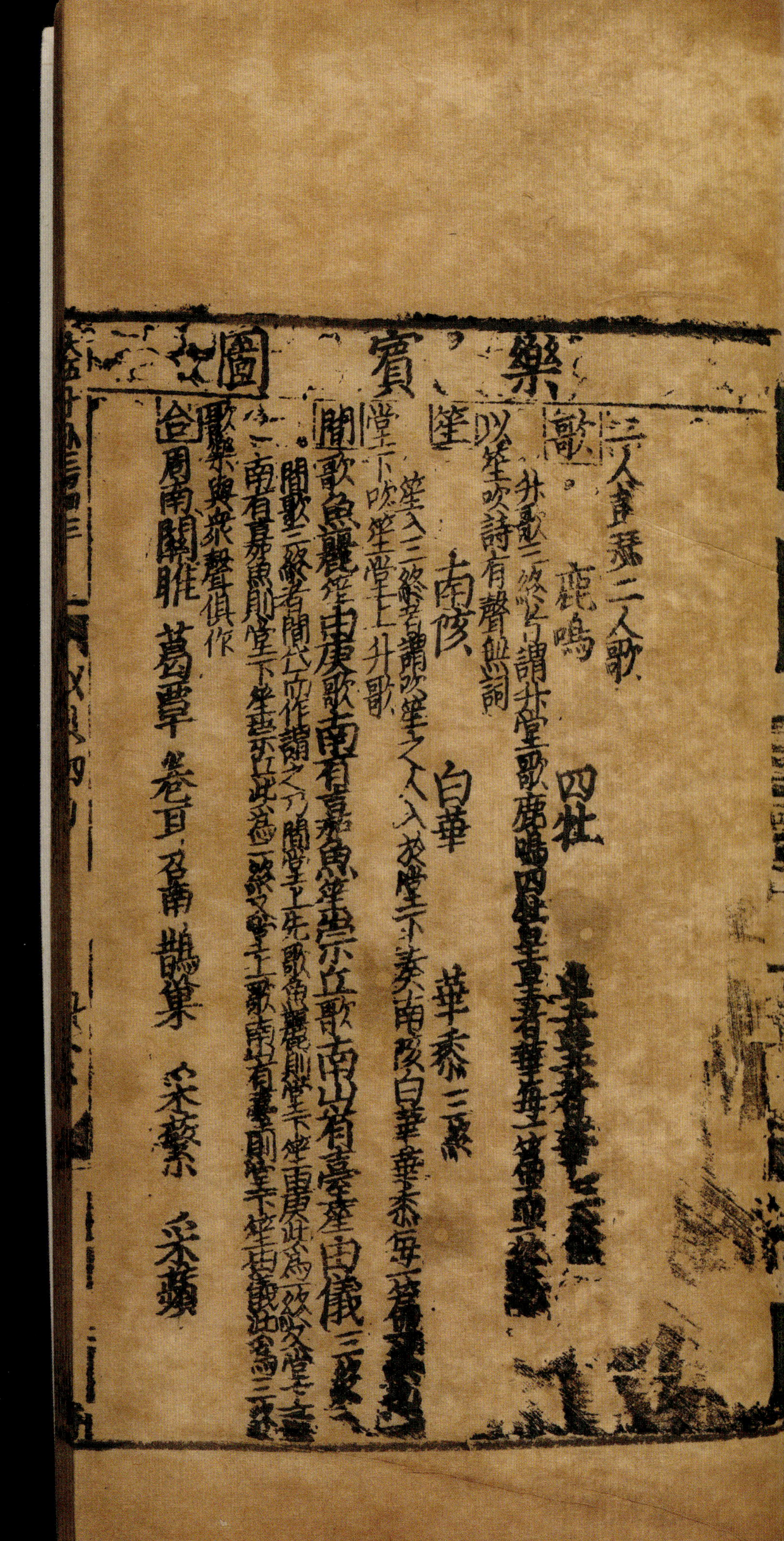

樂賓圖

工四人二瑟二人歌

歌 鹿鳴 四牡 皇皇者華

升歌三終者謂升堂歌鹿鳴四牡皇皇者華每一篇而一終也

以笙吹詩有聲無詞

笙 南陔 白華 華黍 三終

笙入三終者謂吹笙之人入立於堂下奏南陔白華華黍每一篇而一終也

堂下吹笙堂上升歌

間 歌魚麗 笙由庚 歌南有嘉魚 笙崇丘 歌南山有臺 笙由儀 三終

間歌三終者間代而作謂之乃間也堂上先歌魚麗則堂下笙由庚此為一終又堂上歌南有嘉魚則堂下笙崇丘此為一終又堂上歌南山有臺則堂下笙由儀此為三終

歌樂與眾聲俱作

合 周南 關雎 葛覃 卷耳 召南 鵲巢 采蘩 采蘋

Fig. 1.12: *Yi li tu* (*Diagrams for the Book of Etiquette and Ceremonial*), *juan* 4, fols. 22v–23r.
Author: Yang Fu (act. 1228).
Date: 1281–1380.
Woodblock: 18.4 × 12.4 cm.
Fung Ping Shan Library.

之詩謂列國諸侯大夫之室家者曰召南此爲得之謂之南者言其化自岐雍之間被于江漢之域自北而南也詩曰以雅以南即謂此也工告于樂正曰正歌備樂正告于賓乃降樂正降者以正歌備無事也降立西階東北面○記磬階間縮霤北面鼓之○獻工與笙取爵于上篚既獻奠于下篚明其異器敬也如是則獻大夫亦然上篚三爵○疏曰獻賓獻衆賓訖降奠于篚是其上篚一爵也獻工與笙既獻奠于下篚是上篚二爵也又鄉射禮云主人以爵降洗獻大夫此篇亦有大夫故知上篚有三爵也其笙則獻諸西階上謂主人拜送爵也於工拜于阼階上者以其笙于西階東也

右樂賓

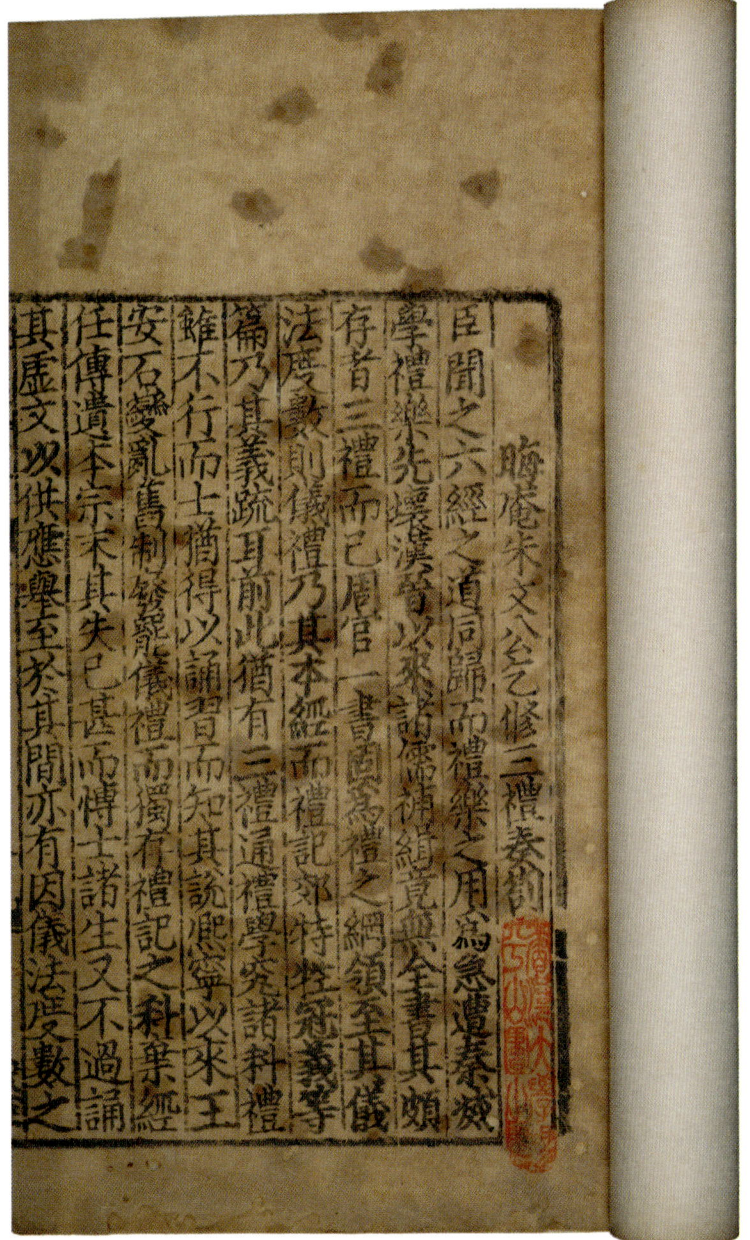

Fig. 1.13

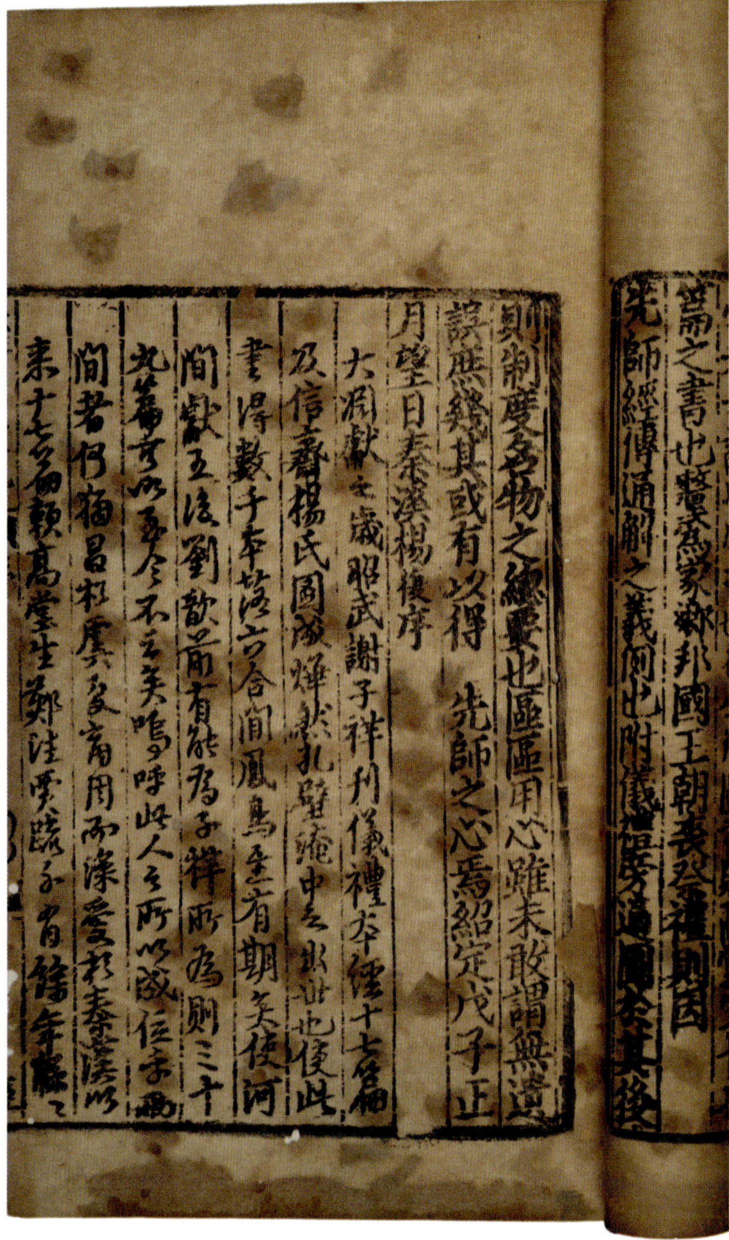

Fig. 1.14

who are outside the hall play while standing, as the canonical text does not mention mats, and must not be blind, as the canonical text does not mention attendants" 凡堂下樂皆立，故經文不言席；皆非無目之人，故經文不言相. Next in his book come musical scores of all the pieces listed on which are indicated individual sections highlighting particular instruments, that is, the *sheng* and chimes.

Zhu Zaiyu's marriage of ancient text to woodcut illustrations proved so persuasive that these pictures (Figs. 1.7, left, and 1.8) were re-used by the French Jesuit Joseph-Marie Amiot 錢德明 (1718–1793) as figures 38 and 36 respectively (Fig. 1.9) of his seminal book *Mémoire sur la Musique des Chinois* (1780).[16] Amiot's admiration for Zhu Zaiyu did not end with musical instruments, and he also included one of the latter's many diagrams of dance formations, which Zhu had employed for *Lingxing xiaowu pu* 靈星小舞譜 (*Sacrifice to Agricultural Deities: Notation of Dance of the Adolescents*, Fig. 1.10), as his own figure 40 (Fig. 1.11).[17] In both its Chinese original and French redaction, this illustration comprises eighteen individuals, sixteen of them organized in a 4 × 4 square, with the other two situated on either side of the formation holding banners. In total, Zhu Zaiyu employs 176 similar images that provide a "notation" of the required choreography.

Fig. 1.13: *Yi li tu* (*Diagrams for the Book of Etiquette and Ceremonial*), "Memorial Pleading for Rationalization and Editing of the Commentaries on 'The Three Rites,'" by Zhu Xi, fol. 1r.
Author: Yang Fu (act. 1228).
Date: 1281–1380.
Woodblock: 18.4 × 12.4 cm.
Fung Ping Shan Library.

Fig. 1.14: *Yi li tu* (*Diagrams for the Book of Etiquette and Ceremonial*), Preface by Yang Fu, fol. 4r.
Author: Yang Fu (act. 1228).
Date: 1281–1380.
Woodblock: 18.4 × 12.4 cm.
Fung Ping Shan Library.

Indeed, flicking quickly though the book gives the impression that the figures are actually moving on the page.

After the wine-drinking ceremony has come to a close, there follows a description of antiphonal singing and ensemble music performed for the guests' pleasure, as is noted in the following section:

> From both inside and outside the hall, songs are alternately performed. From inside comes a *se* song *The Fish's Doom*; then from outside a *sheng* piece *Of Origins*; from inside the hall a *se* song *The South has Splendid Fish*; from outside a *sheng* piece *Lofty Fells*; from inside a *se* song *The Southern Mountains have Sedge*; from outside a *sheng* piece *Of Flourishing*. Next are ensemble pieces from "The State of Zhou's Southern Region" section of *The Book of Odes*: *Quacking Waterfowl*, *Gorse Growing*, and *Juan Er Grasses*; and from "The State of Zhao's Southern Region" section of *The Book of Odes*: *Magpie Nest*, *Picking Mugwort*, and *Picking Water Clover*. After the performance has concluded, the musicians report to the music master, saying: "The requisite music has been performed." The master musician then reports to the guests and thereupon the musicians descend and depart.
>
> 乃間歌《魚麗》，笙《由庚》；歌《南有嘉魚》，笙《崇丘》；歌《南山有台》，笙《由儀》。乃合樂〈周南〉：《關雎》、《葛覃》、《卷耳》，〈召南〉：《鵲巢》、《采蘩》、《采蘋》。工告於樂正曰：「正歌備。」樂正告於賓，乃降。

Once more, Zhu Zaiyu includes musical scores for all of the pieces mentioned. Prior to Zhu Zaiyu, as early as the Song dynasty, the musical performances described in these texts were organized by Yang Fu 楊復 (act. 1228) in his book entitled *Yi li tu* 儀禮圖 (*Diagrams for the Book of Etiquette and Ceremonial*) into what can best be described as a concert program, though it contains no pictorial illustrations and, as its title suggests, is merely furnished with diagrams. As a student of the neo-Confucianist Zhu Xi 朱熹 (1130–1200), Yang Fu's pedigree for publishing such a volume is beyond dispute, and it contains no less than 205 diagrams. While first published by Xie Zixiang 謝子祥 (fl. late thirteenth century) in the Yuan dynasty (1271–1368), the specimen in the Fung Ping Shan Library, although it still uses Yuan dynasty woodblocks, was actually printed in the Ming dynasty.[18] Evidence for this can be gleaned from the outer margins of each page where they are folded in order to form both a recto and verso. On a Yuan dynasty imprint, the top portion of these margins often gives the number of large- and small-type characters found on the page; the middle portion indicates the *juan* and page numbers; and the bottom portion names the craftsman who carried out the work. An example of such a page is one that includes the program for the texts that are translated here (Fig. 1.12).

By the mid-Ming dynasty, some of the original Yuan dynasty woodblock printing plates for this book would have been so worn that they could

16. Two versions of Amiot's treatise on Chinese music appeared in Paris. In 1780, it was published in *Mémoires concernant l'histoire, les arts, les sciences, les moeurs, les usages des Chinois*, ed. Charles Batteux and Louis Georges Oudard Feudrix de Bréquigny (Paris: Nyon, 1776–1814), vol. 6 (1780). One year earlier, this treatise had, however, already been published as a monograph. See Joseph-Marie Amiot, *Mémoire sur la Musique des Chinois, tant anciens que modernes*, ed. Philipp-Joseph Roussier (Paris: Nyon, 1779). The main text of the 1780 version is identical to that of the 1779 version, except that the former includes additional introductory material, for example, "Essai sur les pierres sonores du Chine" by Pierre-Martial Cibot, a Jesuit missionary in Beijing and associate of Amiot, and an extract from a letter by Amiot, dated 28 September 1777. See Stewart Carter, "The Editor from Hell: Information and Misinformation on Chinese Music in Late Eighteenth-Century France," in *Music in Eighteenth-Century Culture*, ed. Mary Sue Morrow (Ann Arbor: Steglein Publishing, 2016), 23–47. For further information about Joseph-Marie Amiot and his studies on Chinese music, see Tchen Ysia, *La musique chinoise en France au XVIIIe siècle* (Paris: Publications orientalistes de France, 1974).

17. Amiot also wrote a book on Chinese dance, which remained unpublished at his death. Two surviving manuscripts of this work are Madrid, Real Biblioteca du Palacio Real, II/2010, and Paris, Bibliothèque nationale, Bréquigny 2, fols. 251–259; a modern edition of the work can be found in Yves Lenoir and Nicolas Standaert, eds., *Les Danses rituelles chinoises d'après Joseph-Marie Amiot: Aux sources de l'ethnochorégraphie* (Namur: Éditions Lessius and Presses Univérsitaires de Namur, 2005).

18. Liu Chenggan, *Wuxing Liushi Jiaye tang shanben shuying*, vol. 1, fols. 21r–22v; Jao Tsung-i, *Xianggang daxue Feng Pingshan tushuguan cang shanben shulu*, 3 4; and Jao Tsung-i, Li Zhifang, and Zhang Lijuan, *Xianggang daxue Feng Pingshan tushuguan cang shanben shulu*, 15–16. For more bibliographical information on this edition, see, for example, Qu Yong, *Tieqin tongjian lou cangshu mulu* (Beijing: Zhonghua shuju, 1990), 56; Fu Zengxiang, *Cangyuan qunshu jingyan lu*, 50; Wang Wenjin 王文進, *Wenlu tang fangshu ji* 文祿堂訪書記 (Beiping: Wenlu tang, 1942), *juan* 1, fols. 12v–13r; Luo Zhenchang 羅振常, *Shanbenshu suojian lu* 善本書所見錄 (Shanghai: Shangwu yinshuguan, 1958), 10–11; Guoli zhongyang tushuguan 國立中央圖書館, *Guoli zhongyang tushuguan Jin Yuan ben tulu* 國立中央圖書館金元本圖錄 (Taipei: Zhonghua congshu bianshen weiyuanhui, 1961), 33–36; Guoli zhongyang tushuguan 國立中央圖書館, *Guoli zhongyang tushuguan shanben shumu* 國立中央圖書館善本書目, enlarged ed. (Taipei: Guoli zhongyang tushuguan, 1967), vol. 1, 19; Guojia tushuguan, *Guojia tushuguan shanben shuzhi chugao: Jingbu*, 104; and Wang Zhongmin 王重民, *Zhongguo shanbenshu tiyao* 中國善本書提要 (Shanghai: Shanghai guji chubanshe, 1983), 18.

儀禮卷第一

敖繼公集說

士冠禮第一

鄭注曰童子年二十而冠主人玄冠朝服則是諸侯之士天子之士朝服皮弁素積古者四民世事士之子恒爲士冠於五禮屬嘉禮

繼公謂此篇主言士冠其適子之禮然此士云者據其子而言文也下篇放此冠者加冠之稱凡經言士禮者皆謂諸侯之士其言大夫禮者亦然蓋此經乃天子爲諸侯制之以爲其國之典籍者也故不及王朝大夫士之禮

Fig. 1.15: *Yi li jishuo* (*Collected Opinions on the Book of Etiquette and Ceremonial*), *juan* 1, fol. 1r.
Author: Ao Jigong (act. 1301).
Date: 1297–1307.
Woodblock: 22.7 × 17.6 cm.
Fung Ping Shan Library.

no longer be used, so new plates for these pages were cut to the same format, though some of the less eroded originals were retained. For the new plates, the upper portion of the extreme margin no longer records the number of characters on the page, but instead indicates the year in which the work was carried out. Re-cut pages of copies of this book typically give dates of 1511, 1517, or 1521, all from the Zhengde era (1506–1522). The Fung Ping Shan Library specimen has had all of these date records deliberately excised and blank slips of paper of a slightly different shade inserted between the folded sheets. These slips were then dyed to resemble the color of the original, and in some instances a few characters jotted down on them to make the whole effect look similar to the pages printed from the Yuan dynasty blocks. This is clearly a forgery, but why? At the opening of the book is an introduction by Zhu Xi titled "Qixiu sanli zha" 乞修三禮劄 ("Memorial Pleading for Rationalization and Editing of the Commentaries on 'The Three Rites,'" Fig. 1.13) then another (Fig. 1.14) by Yang Fu himself dated to 1228. With these essays and the Yuan dynasty plates giving the impression that the book might be a Song dynasty edition, the temptation was likely too great, and a later dealer, perhaps during the latter years of the Qing dynasty (1644–1911) and simply to increase its asking price, attempted, relatively effectively, to expunge all evidence that it is in fact a Ming dynasty imprint.

While Zheng Xuan's and Jia Gongyan's dual exegesis remained the mainstream interpretation of *The Book of Etiquette and Ceremonial*, in the Yuan dynasty a siren voice emerged to challenge the orthodoxy, that of Ao Jigong 敖繼公 (act. 1301), whose text is called *Yi li jishuo* 儀禮集說 (*Collected Opinions on the Book of Etiquette and Ceremonial*, Figs. 1.15 and 1.16). His starting point was that Zheng Xuan's urtext of the original was fatally flawed, and that the accompanying commentary was also deficient. He took it upon himself to argue against both. Ao Jigong was so persuasive that from the Yuan to the early Qing dynasty, he came to be regarded as an authority on research into *The Book of Etiquette and Ceremonial.* Indeed, in the fiftieth year of Qianlong's reign (1785), when the official versions of the three Confucian books on "the rites" were promulgated, and requisite editorial work on *The Book of Etiquette and Ceremonial* carried out, many of his interpretations took precedence and became standardized. By the end of the Qing dynasty, however, the pendulum had swung back, and Zheng Xuan's text and exegesis reasserted their erstwhile supremacy. The Fung Ping Shan Library specimen of Ao Jigong's book is in fact the original Yuan dynasty edition.[19]

On the cusp of the Ming and Qing dynasties, the book found its way into the collection of Ye Shulian 葉樹廉 (1619–1685) of Changshu. A later owner was Tiebao 鐵保 (1752–1824), a Manchu scholar-official, followed by the Lu brothers of Suzhou—Lu Zhuan 陸僎 and Lu Hang 陸沆—and then Wu Tang 吳棠 (1813–1876), another senior official. Like other books discussed here, it was eventually received into Liu Chenggan's library, The Hall of Magnificent Achievement in Nanxun. Evidence for its accession can be garnered from an entry in the diary of Liu Chenggan's friend Ye Changchi 葉昌熾 (1849–1917), dated to the twenty-sixth day of the second lunar month of 1915:

> Dropping by on Hanyi's [Liu Chenggan's *zi* soubriquet] literary studio, I saw, brought by a bookseller of Yangzhou who was surnamed Wang . . . the first two volumes of Ao Jigong's *Collected Opinions on the Book of Etiquette and Ceremonial*, at the front of which was an introduction dated to the [fifth year of the] Dade era [1301], and whose character strokes were cut cleanly and crisply, so it can be reliably regarded as the original edition, or a Ming dynasty imprint made using the same printing blocks; the asking price was five hundred silver dollars.
>
> 過翰怡齋，見揚州書估王姓持……敖繼公《儀禮集説》首二冊，前有大德序，刻畫清勁，原刻可信，或明印耳，索五百元。[20]

19. Jao Tsung-i, *Xianggang daxue Feng Pingshan tushuguan cang shanben shulu*, 4–5; and Jao Tsung-i, Li Zhifang, and Zhang Lijuan, *Xianggang daxue Feng Pingshan tushuguan cang shanben shulu*, 16–17. For more bibliographical information on this edition, see, for example, Lu Xinyuan 陸心源, *Bisong lou cangshu zhi* 皕宋樓藏書志 (Beijing: Zhonghua shuju, 1990), 71–72; Fu Zengxiang, *Cangyuan qunshu jingyan lu*, 50; Wang Wenjin, *Wenlu tang fangshu ji*, *juan* 1, fol. 13r; Mo Boji 莫伯驥, *Wushiwanjuan lou qunshu bawen* 五十萬卷樓群書跋文 (Guangzhou: s.n., 1947), *juan* 2, fols. 53r–55v; and Guoli zhongyang tushuguan, *Guoli zhongyang tushuguan shanben shumu*, enlarged ed., vol. 1, 29.

20. Wang Jilie 王季烈, ed., *Ye Changchi Yuandu lu rijichao* 葉昌熾緣督廬日記鈔 (Shanghai: Yinyinlu, 1933), *juan* 15, fol. 60v; and Ye Changchi 葉昌熾, *Yuandu lu riji* 緣督廬日記 (Taipei: Taiwan xuesheng shuju, 1964), 549.

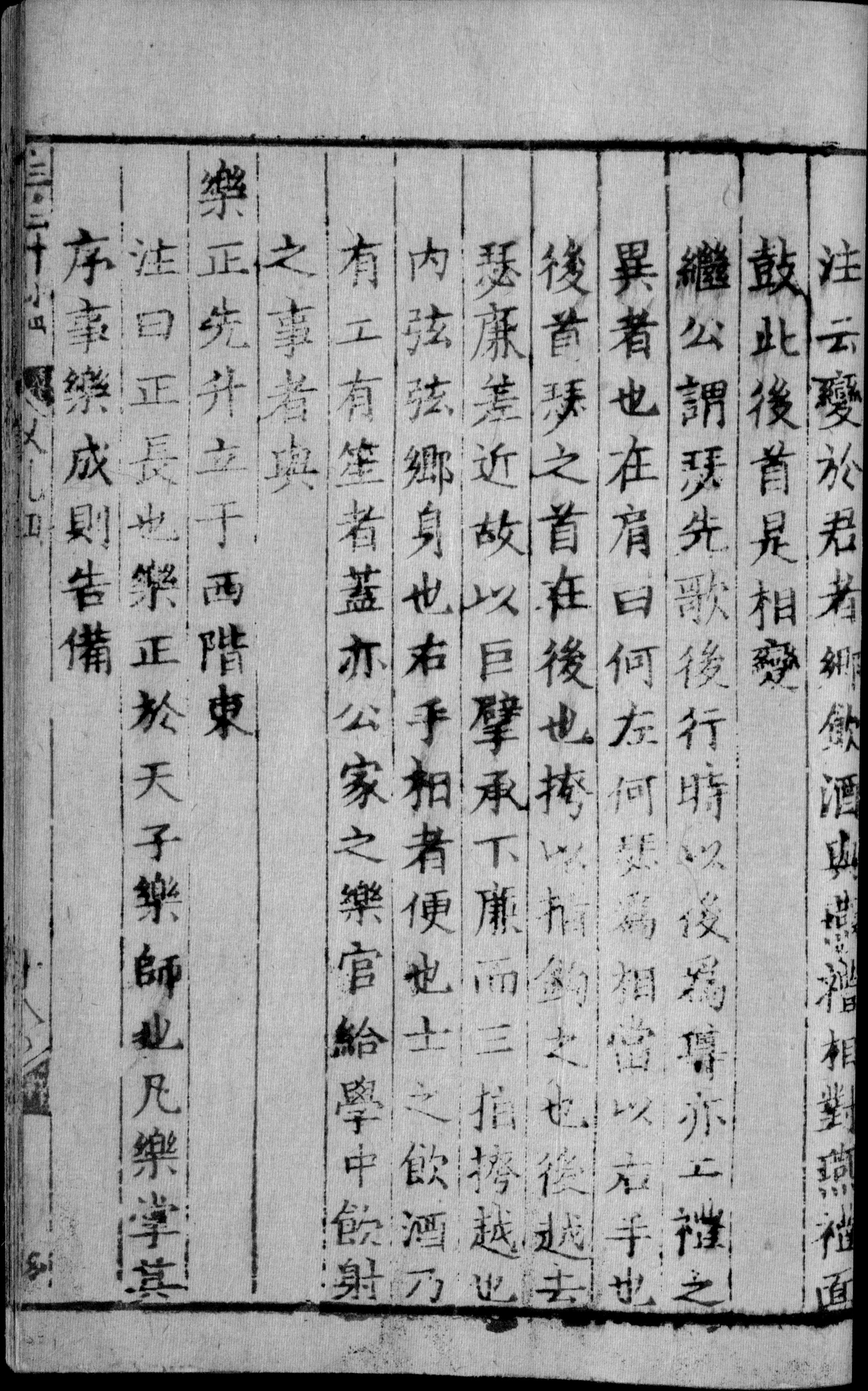

注云變於君者鄉飲酒與燕禮相對燕禮直

鼓此後首是相變

繼公謂瑟先歌後行時以後爲尊亦士禮之異者也在肩曰何左何瑟爲相當以左手也後首瑟之首在後也挎以指鉤之也後越去瑟廉差近故以巨擘承下廉而三指挎越也内弦弦鄉身也右手相者便也士之飲酒乃有工有笙者蓋亦公家之樂官給學中飲射之事者與

樂正先升立于西階東

注曰正長也樂正於天子樂師也凡樂掌其序事樂成則告備

Fig. 1.16: *Yi li jishuo (Collected Opinions on the Book of Etiquette and Ceremonial), juan* 4, fols. 17v–18r.
Author: Ao Jigong (act. 1301).
Date: 1297–1307.
Woodblock: 22.7 × 17.6 cm.
Fung Ping Shan Library.

繼公謂此云設席于堂廉言其南北節也鄉射云席工于西階上少東言其東西節也文互見耳席東上而下者當西階上少東

工四人二瑟瑟先相者二人皆左何瑟後首挎越内弦右手相（相並息亮反何胡我反挎苦孤反）

注曰二瑟二人鼓瑟則二人歌也相扶工也衆賓之少者爲之每工一人鄉射禮曰弟子相工如初入天子相工使視瞭者工瞽矇也故有扶之者從首者變於君也挎持也相瑟者則爲之持瑟其相歌者徒相也越瑟下孔所以發越其聲也内弦側擔之

疏曰相歌者亦二人以空手無事故不言

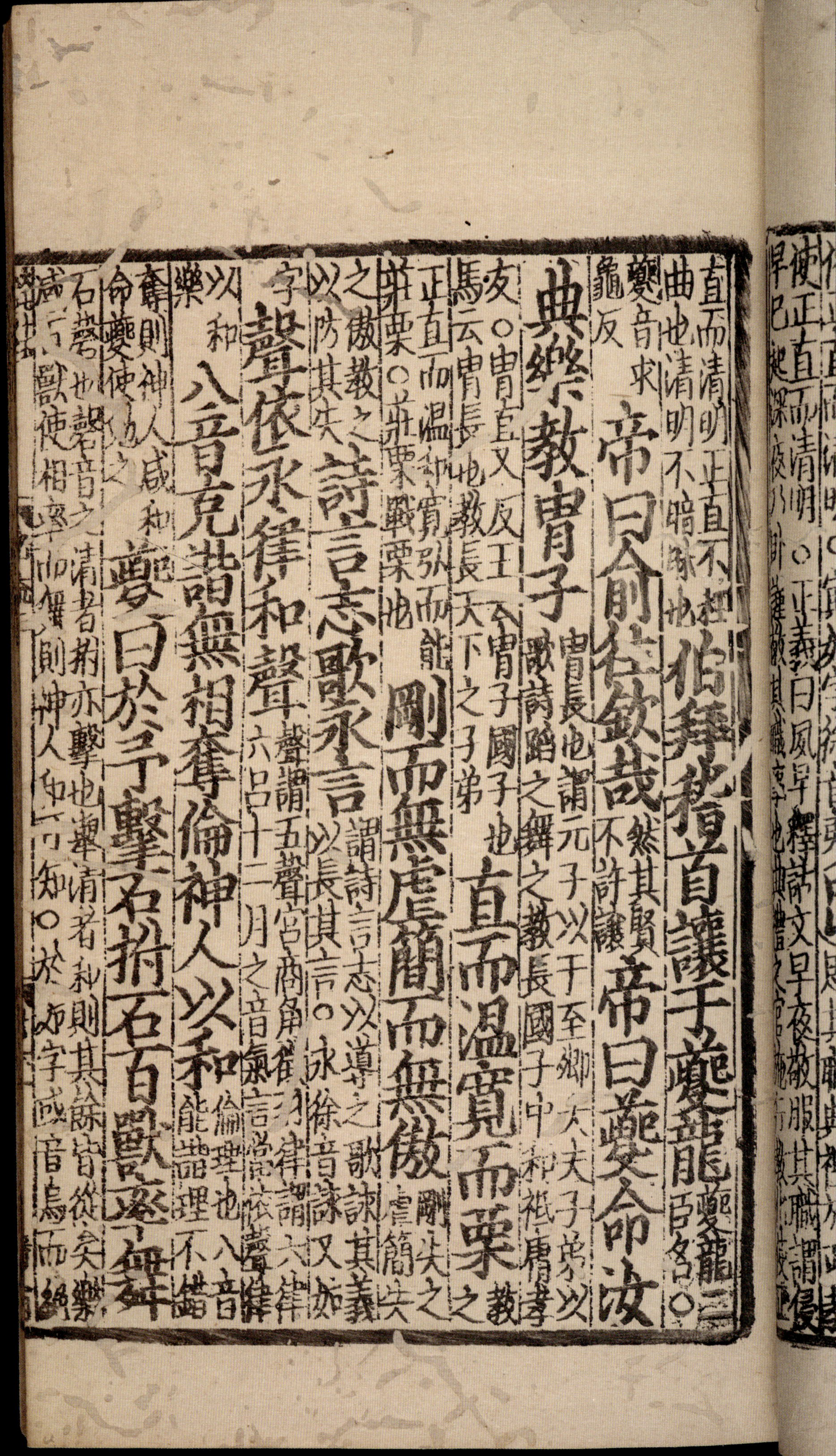

直而清明正直不枉曲也清明不暗昧也伯拜稽首讓于夔龍夔龍二臣名○夔音求龜反帝曰俞往欽哉然其賢不許讓帝曰夔命汝典樂教胄子胄長也謂元子以下至卿大夫子弟以歌詩蹈之舞之教長國子中和祗庸孝友○胄直又反王云胄子國子也馬云胄長也教長天下之子弟直而溫寬而栗教之正直而溫和寬弘而能莊栗○莊栗戰栗也剛而無虐簡而無傲剛失之虐簡失之傲教之以防其失詩言志歌永言謂詩言志以導之歌詠其義以長其言○永徐音詠又如字聲依永律和聲聲謂五聲宮商角徵羽律謂六律六呂十二月之音氣言當依聲律以和樂八音克諧無相奪倫神人以和倫理也八音能諧理不錯奪則神人咸和命夔使勑之夔曰於予擊石拊石百獸率舞石磬也磬音之清者拊亦擊也舉清者和則其餘皆從矣樂感百獸使相率而舞則神人和可知○於如字或音烏

Fig. 1.17: *Fu shiyin Shang shu zhushu* (*Supplementary Explanation and Pronunciation of the Book of Documents including Commentary and Additional Notes*), *juan* 3, fol. 26r.
Annotator: Kong Yingda (574–648).
Date: c. 1323–1328.
Woodblock: 19.4 × 13.3 cm.
Fung Ping Shan Library.

According to Liu Chenggan's diary entry of the same day, a bookseller called Wang Xisheng 王錫生 had called.[21]

From *The Book of Etiquette and Ceremonial* much can be learnt regarding the role music played in ancient ritual practice, not only from an organizational perspective, but also how music was imbued with as much emotional content as possible. Its persuasive power could not be overlooked by the ruling classes, and thus the invention of music was "reverse-engineered" into the epoch normally credited as representing the epitome of Confucian rectitude, that of the ancient mystical Emperors Yao and Shun. It is to these luminaries, as revealed by the *Shang shu* 尚書 (*The Book of Documents*), that the discussion now turns. Two quotations from the chapter of the latter text "Shun dian" 舜典 ("The Classic of the Emperor Shun," Fig. 1.18) that detail this august personage's life, deeds, and ethical conduct are cited below;[22] the first reads:

> After twenty-eight years, the emperor [Yao] died, and the ordinary people acted as if they had lost their mother and father; and for three years across the whole empire, it was forbidden to play any instrumental music. On the first day of the following year, the Emperor Shun came to the ancestral temple, consulted with the tribal elders, and threw open all the doors to his palaces so as to promulgate policy effectively, so all could see clearly, and so all could hear clearly.
>
> 二十有八載，帝乃殂落。百姓如喪考妣，三載，四海遏密八音。月正元日，舜格于文祖，詢于四岳，闢四門，明四目，達四聰。

The second details the emperor's instructions concerning the more precise organization of music and ritual (Fig. 1.17):

> The Emperor said: "Kui! You are ordered to act as the supervisor of the musical officials to educate the younger generations as upright yet gentle, broad-spirited yet steadfast, strong-willed yet not violent, and thrifty yet not arrogant. Poems are to make words of emotions, songs make words melodious, the five-note modes are arranged according to the melodies, and the *lü* tunings make the five-note modes harmonious. Musical instruments of the eight categories [according to the material from which they are made] should be properly tuned and not allowed to run amuck; thus, the spirits and the people will be harmonious." Kui said: "Ah! I will strike the stone chimes, beat the stone chimes, and let the myriad youths dressed as animals lead the dances."
>
> 帝曰：「夔！命汝典樂，教冑子，直而溫，寬而栗，剛而無虐，簡而無傲。詩言志，歌永言，聲依永，律和聲。八音克諧，無相奪倫，神人以和。」夔曰：「於！予擊石拊石，百獸率舞。」

Thankfully, both these quotations are found in a surviving *juan* of a partial copy held in the Fung Ping Shan Library of a 20-*juan* original entitled *Fu shiyin Shang shu zhushu* 附釋音尚書注疏 (*Supplementary Explanation and Pronunciation of the Book of Documents including Commentary and Additional Notes*) by Kong Yingda 孔穎達 (574–648), printed on Yuan dynasty blocks supplemented by Ming dynasty replacements. This specimen (Fig. 1.19) had earlier been housed in the library of the scholar-official Zhou Xingyi 周星詒 (1833–1904) known as Ruigua tang 瑞瓜堂 (The Hall of the Auspicious Gourd). Subsequently, it came into the possession of the ubiquitous Liu Chenggan, whose diary entry for the tenth day of the first lunar month of 1915 reads:

> Qian Changmei [a book dealer] came, and from him I purchased an edition printed from Song dynasty woodblocks repaired in the Ming dynasty of *Supplementary Explanation and Pronunciation of the Book of Documents including Commentary and Additional Notes* in ten volumes, paying one hundred and fifty silver dollars.
>
> 錢長美來，與購宋槧明修《附音釋尚書注疏》，計十冊，洋壹百五十元。[23]

The entry for this book in Liu Chenggan's bibliographical record was again written by Miao Quansun 繆荃孫 (1844–1919). The latter's opinion was that it was a Song dynasty edition with some Yuan and Ming dynasty replacement pages, though these were few in number as only a

21. Liu Chenggan, *Jiaye tang cangshu rijichao*, 224; Liu Chenggan, *Qiushu zhai riji* (Beijing: Beijing tushuguan chubanshe, 2016), vol. 4, 207; and Liu Chenggan, *Wuxing Liushi Jiaye tang shanben shuying*, vol. 1, fols. 23r–v.

22. For other passages in *The Book of Documents* related to music, see Walter Kaufmann, *Musical References in the Chinese Classics* (Detroit: Information Coordinators, 1976), 22–24.

23. Liu Chenggan, *Jiaye tang cangshu rijichao*, 235; Liu Chenggan, *Qiushu zhai riji*, vol. 4, 257.

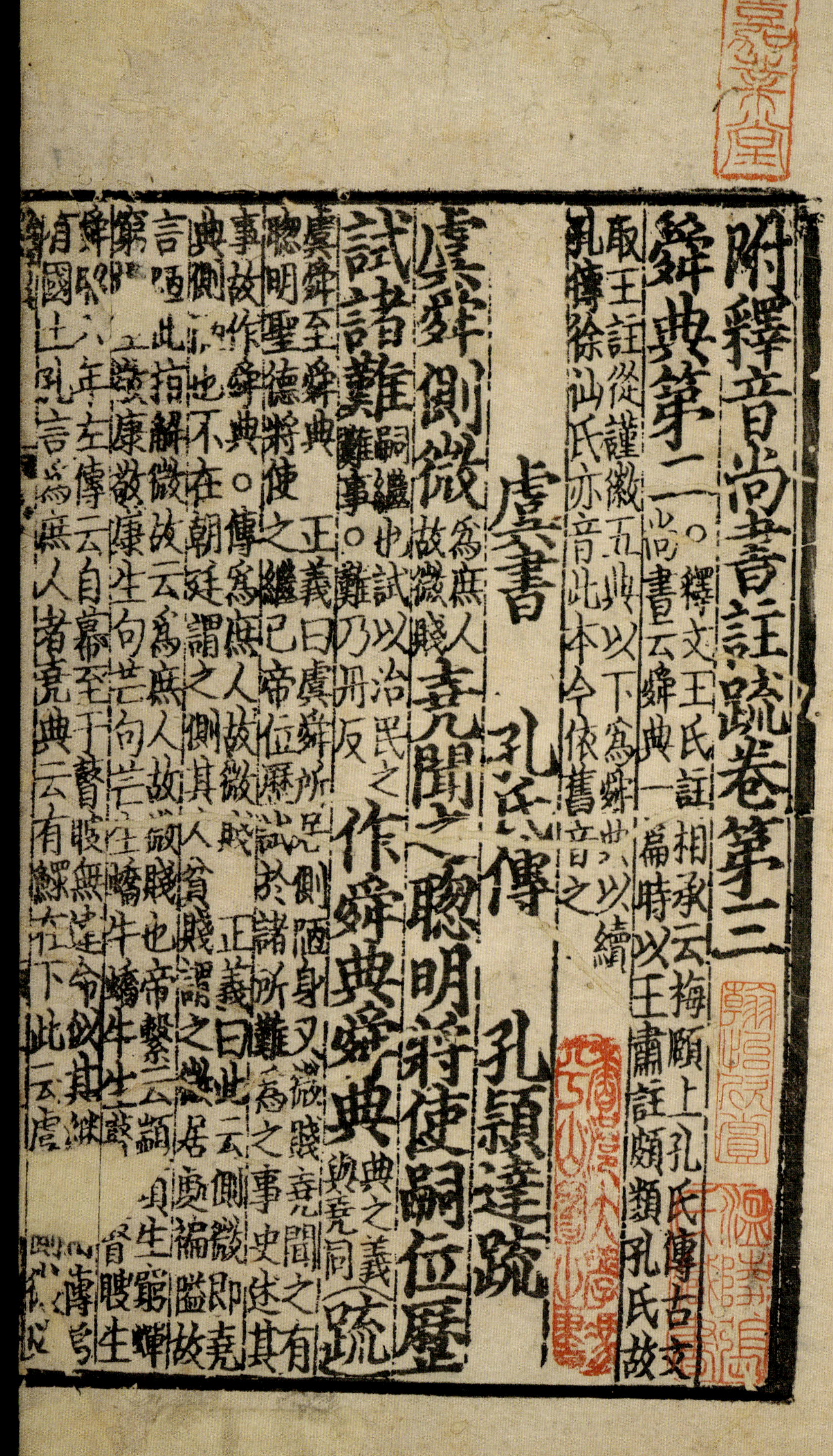

Fig. 1.18: *Fu shiyin Shang shu zhushu (Supplementary Explanation and Pronunciation of the Book of Documents including Commentary and Additional Notes), juan 3*, fol. 1r.
Annotator: Kong Yingda (574–648).
Date: c. 1323–1328.
Woodblock: 19.4 × 13.3 cm.
Fung Ping Shan Library.

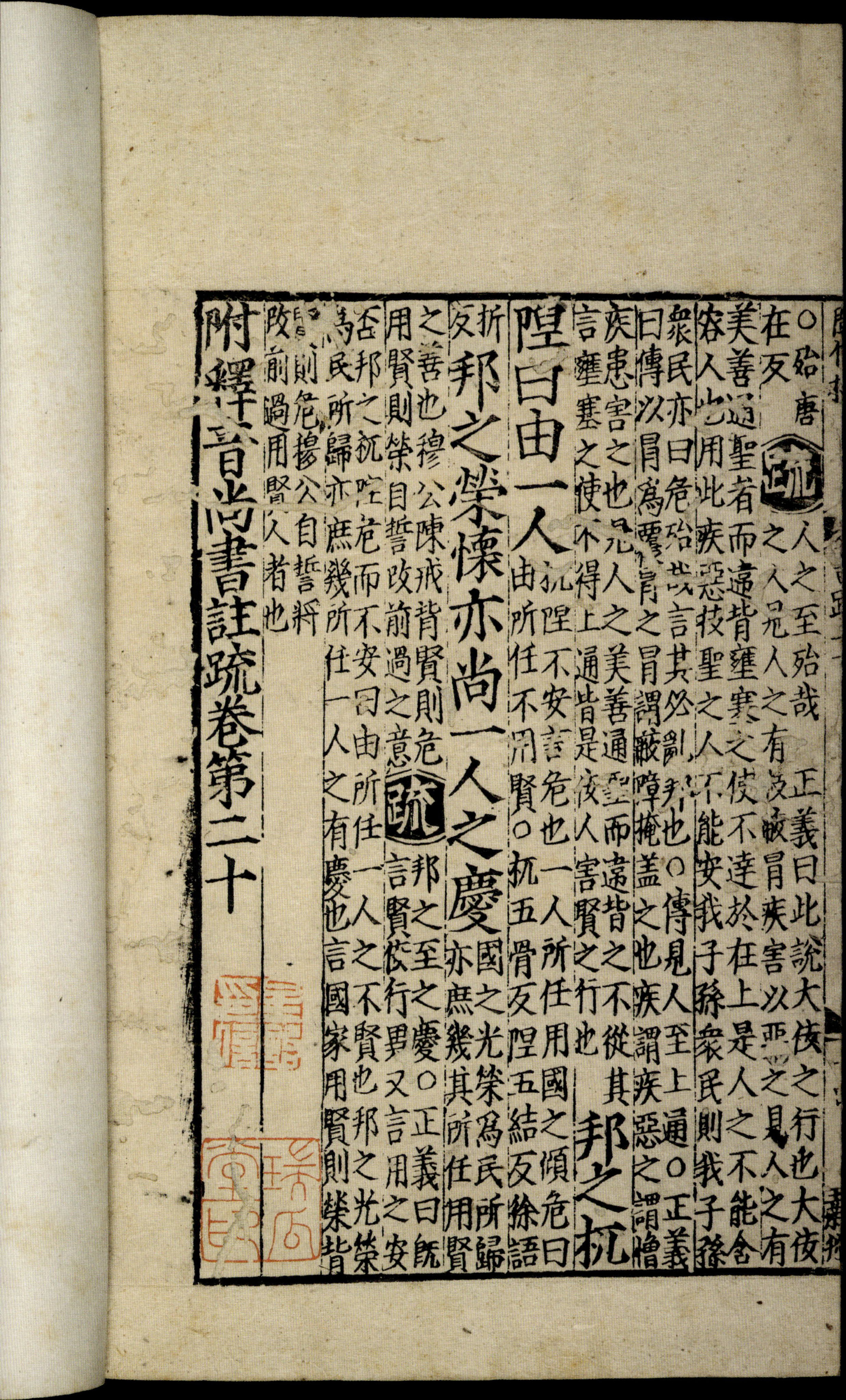

○殆唐疏人之至殆哉正義曰此說大佞之行也大佞
在反之人見人之有技蔽冒疾害以惡之見人之有
美善通聖者而違背壅塞之使不達於在上是人之不能含
容人也用此疾惡技聖之人不能安我子孫衆民則我子孫
衆民亦曰危殆哉言其必亂邦也○傳見人至上通○正義
曰傳以冒爲覆冒之冒謂蔽障掩蓋之也疾謂疾惡之謂憎
疾患害之也見人之美善通聖而違背之不從其邦之杌
言壅塞之使不得上通皆是傷人害賢之行也
隉曰由一人杌隉不安言危也一人所任用國之傾危曰
由所任不用賢○杌五骨反隉五結反徐語
折反邦之榮懷亦尚一人之慶國之光榮爲民所歸
亦庶幾其所任用賢
之善也穆公陳戒背賢則危疏邦之至之慶○正義曰既
用賢則榮自誓改前過之意言賢佞行畢又言用之安
否邦之杌隉危而不安曰由所任一人之不賢也邦之光榮
爲民所歸亦庶幾所任一人之有慶也言國家用賢則榮背
賢則危穆公自誓將
改前過用賢人者也

附釋音尚書註疏卷第二十

Fig. 1.19: *Fu shiyin Shang shu zhushu* (*Supplementary Explanation and Pronunciation of the Book of Documents including Commentary and Additional Notes*), *juan* 20, fol. 14v.
Annotator: Kong Yingda (574–648).
Date: c. 1323–1328.
Woodblock: 19.4 × 13.3 cm.
Fung Ping Shan Library.

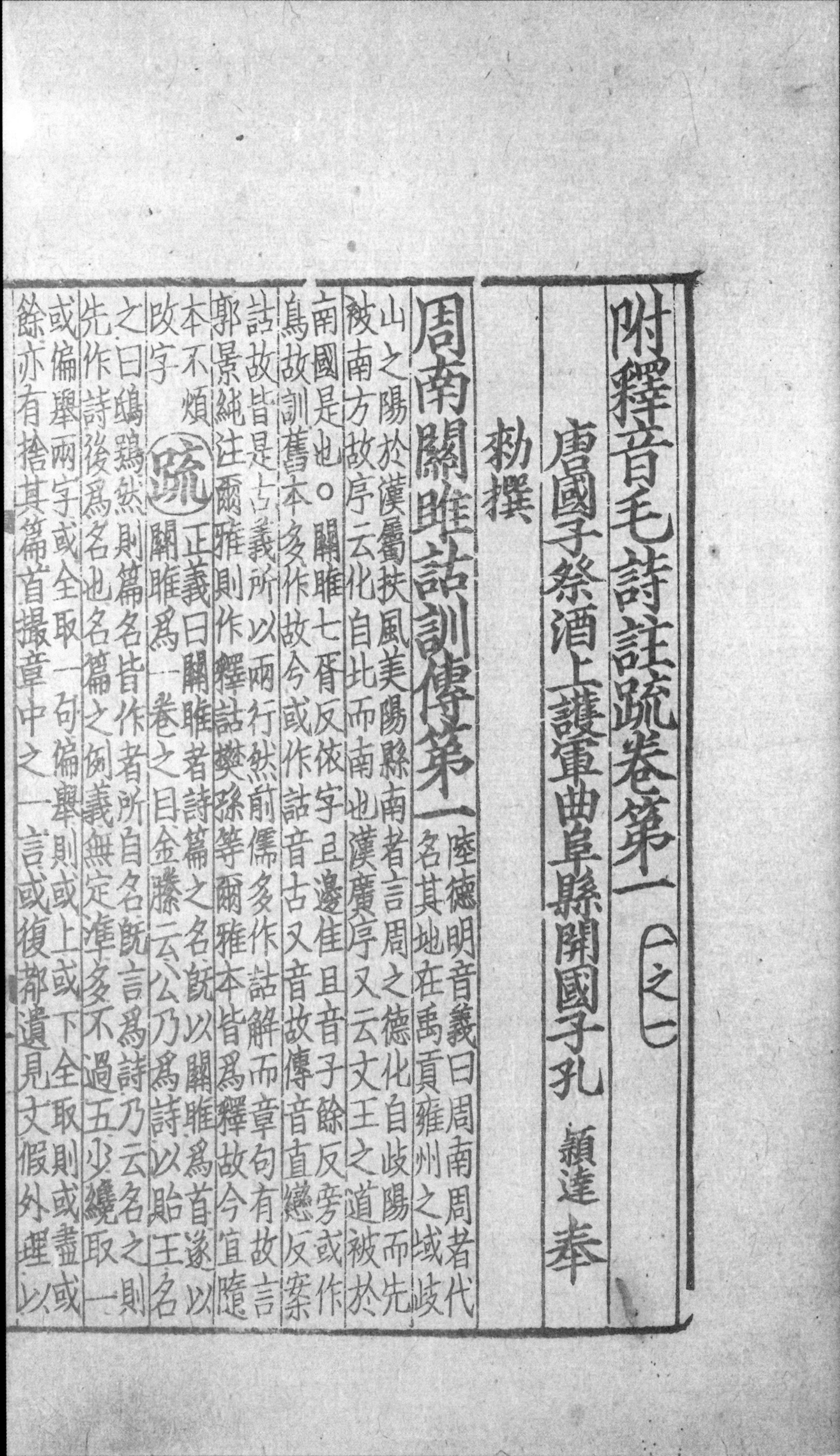

附釋音毛詩註疏卷第一（一之一）

唐國子祭酒上護軍曲阜縣開國子孔穎達奉

勑撰

周南關雎詁訓傳第一 陸德明音義曰周南周者代名其地在禹貢雍州之域岐山之陽於漢屬扶風美陽縣南者言周之德化自岐陽而先被南方故序云化自北而南也漢廣序又云文王之道被於南國是也○關雎七胥反依字且邊佳且音子餘反旁或作鳥故訓舊本多作故今或作詁音古又音故傳音直戀反案詁故皆是古義所以兩行然前儒多作詁解而章句有故言郭景純注爾雅則作釋詁樊孫等爾雅本皆爲釋故今宜隨本不煩改字【疏】正義曰關雎者詩篇之名既以關雎爲首遂以關雎爲一卷之目金縢云公乃爲詩以貽王名之曰鴟鴞然則篇名皆作者所自名既言爲詩乃云名之則先作詩後爲名也名篇之例義無定準多不過五少纔取一或偏舉兩字或全取一句偏舉則或上或下全取則或盡或餘亦有捨其篇首撮章中之一言或復都遺見文假外理以

Fig. 1.20: *Fu shiyin Mao shi zhushu* (*Supplementary Explanation and Pronunciation of the Book of Odes including Commentary and Additional Notes*), *juan* 1, fol. 1r.
Annotator: Kong Yingda (574–648).
Date: c. 1127–1279.
Woodblock: 6.3 × 4.1 inches.
Ashikaga Gakkō.
After Nagasawa Kikuya, ed., *Ashikaga Gakkō zenpon zuroku* (Ashikaga: Ashika Gagakkō Iseki Toshokan Kōenkai, 1973), pl. 20.

small percentage of the printing blocks had been re-cut (for example, the last folio of the book, as shown in Fig. 1.19).[24] In this respect, Miao was not the only scholar to be so mistaken, and was following in a tradition of many decades that had come to regard all Yuan dynasty commentaries to Confucian classics printed with ten-columns to each page face as having a provenance similar to Southern Song dynasty Imperial College reprints of classical texts.[25] This unfortunate scholarly tendency, namely that of heaping books of different origins into the same basket, was subsequently and comprehensively refuted by Nagasawa Kikuya using a collection of Song dynasty reprints of Confucian classics stored in the library of the Ashikaga Gakkō 足立學校 college that comprises Southern Song dynasty Imperial College originals (for example, *Fu shiyin Mao shi zhushu* 附釋音毛詩注疏 kept at Ashikaga Gakkō, see Fig. 1.20); his research conclusively demonstrated that Yuan dynasty commentaries on Confucian classics were undoubtedly of a different and separate provenance.[26] Fortunately, Jao Tsung-i 饒宗頤 (1917–2018), the Hong Kong scholar who prepared the descriptive bibliographic catalog of the Fung Ping Shan Library's historic Chinese book collection, took Nagasawa's research as his starting point and reaffirmed a Yuan dynasty origin for the Fung Ping Shan Library copy of Kong Yingda's work.[27]

Of the twenty *juan* that would have formed this book had it been whole, the Fung Ping Shan Library possesses only the third to twentieth *juan*, grouped together in pairs to form nine volumes. The first volume is missing, so the copy begins with the chapter "The Classic of the Emperor Shun" from which the citations have been extracted. In fact, the first volume, and presumably the one required to make the book complete, came up for auction in Shanghai in 2005, selling for a modest price.[28]

Regarding versions of *The Book of Documents*, the University of Hong Kong's Fung Ping Shan Library also possesses another uniquely important item that demands inclusion here, namely a clean manuscript copy of Lu Xuan's 陸烜 (1737–1799) *Shang shu yi* 尚書義 (*Meanings in the Book of Documents*) handwritten in 1787 by his amanuensis and concubine Shen Cai 沈彩 (c. 1748–?).[29] Lu Xuan was a native of Pinghu (modern Jiaxing) in Zhejiang and a scion of an illustrious family that had come to prominence in the Ming dynasty along with Lu Bing 陸炳 (1510–1560) who, directly under the Emperor and unique to all senior ministers throughout the dynasty, had successively held the posts of the Three Ducal Ministers, including the deputizing role in each case. This tradition of official service continued into the Qing dynasty, and a series of senior ministers of the Lu family worked for Emperor Kangxi 康熙 (1654–1722, r. 1661–1722). Lu Xuan's pathway into the civil bureaucracy was far from smooth, and after initial success in his late teens in the first stage of the *xiucai* 秀才 examinations, he proved unsuccessful in the subsequent *juren* 舉人 examinations in Hangzhou. At this juncture, he chose to abandon his aspirations to follow the well-trodden route of sitting the imperial examinations and turned instead to living in a retreat on Xu 胥 Mountain near present-day Wuxi. Taking inspiration from the Eastern Jin dynasty (317–420) poet Tao Yuanming 陶淵明 (365–427), who was born in Chaisang 柴桑 and spent most of his days in a rural idyll there, and the Tang dynasty's Wang Wei 王維 (699–759), who lived in similar seclusion at Lantian 藍田, Lu Xuan planted orchards of plum trees around his isolated residence, and thus took for himself the *hao* 號 soubriquet "Meigu 梅谷," which means "plum valley." There he assembled a large collection of old books; as well as specializing in editorial work, he was also a connoisseur of paintings and calligraphy; two of his many other areas of expertise were book-binding and scroll mounting.

24. Miao Quansun, Wu Changshou, and Dong Kang, *Jiaye tang cangshu zhi*, 134. Miao Quansun 繆荃孫, *Yifeng cangshu ji* 藝風藏書記 (Shanghai: Shanghai guji chubanshe, 2007), 213–214; and Liu Chenggan, *Wuxing Liushi Jiaye tang shanben shuying*, vol. 1, fols. 3r–v.

25. For similar opinions to Miao's, see Qu Yong, *Tieqin tongjian lou cangshu mulu*, 32–33; Fu Zengxiang, *Cangyuan qunshu jingyan lu*, 28; Lu Xinyuan, *Bisong lou cangshu zhi*, 44; Wang Wenjin, *Wenlu tang fangshu ji*, *juan* 1, fols. 20r–v; Guoli zhongyang tushuguan, *Guoli zhongyang tushuguan shanben shumu*, enlarged ed., vol. 1, 12; and Guoli zhongyang tushuguan 國立中央圖書館, *Guoli zhongyang tushuguan songben tulu* 國立中央圖書館宋本圖錄 (Taipei: Zhonghua congshu weiyuanhui, 1958), 13–14.

26. Nagasawa Kikuya, *Jūsankyō chūso eifu*, 5–6, and pls. 15–30.

27. Jao Tsung-i, *Xianggang daxue Feng Pingshan tushuguan shanben shulu*, 1–3; and Jao Tsung-i, Li Zhifang, and Zhang Lijuan, *Xianggang daxue Feng Pingshan tushuguan cang shanben shulu*, 8–9.

28. It was sold at Jianghua Auction on 22 December 2005, lot 1894, for US$3,321.

29. Jao Tsung-i, *Xianggang daxue Feng Pingshan tushuguan shanben shulu*, 114–116; and Jao Tsung-i, Li Zhifang, and Zhang Lijuan, *Xianggang daxue Feng Pingshan tushuguan cang shanben shulu*, 11–12.

尚書義

虞書第一

昔在帝堯聰明文思光宅天下將遜于位讓于虞舜作堯典

此孔子删述史傳撮其大要為羣書之序也聰明者一陰一陽之謂道繼之者善也成之者性也故人性固有之誠好善而惡不善也人性自然之明皆知好善而惡不善也欽承天命者誠好善而大明善克寄耳目于人乃善無不知不

律五音而不斲琴瑟宫㣲柱雖堯舜不能奏功

也均天下之道如理亂書歸于插架四部井然

乃得徐徐卒業也 烜于抱殘守闕之餘亦既粗

陳其理之之道道不亾則亦猶之不亡也故天

下國家可均也要惟率性之中道庸德不可能

也吾儕小人勉焉而已

大清乾隆五十一年正月吉日平湖陸烜製

侍史沈彩書

Fig. 1.21: *Shang shu yi* (*Meanings in the Book of Documents*), preface, fol. 2v (right), and *juan* 1, fol. 1r (left).
Author: Lu Xuan (1737–1799).
Scribe: Shen Cai (c. 1748–?).
Date: 1787.
Border: 17.1 × 12.2 cm.
Fung Ping Shan Library.

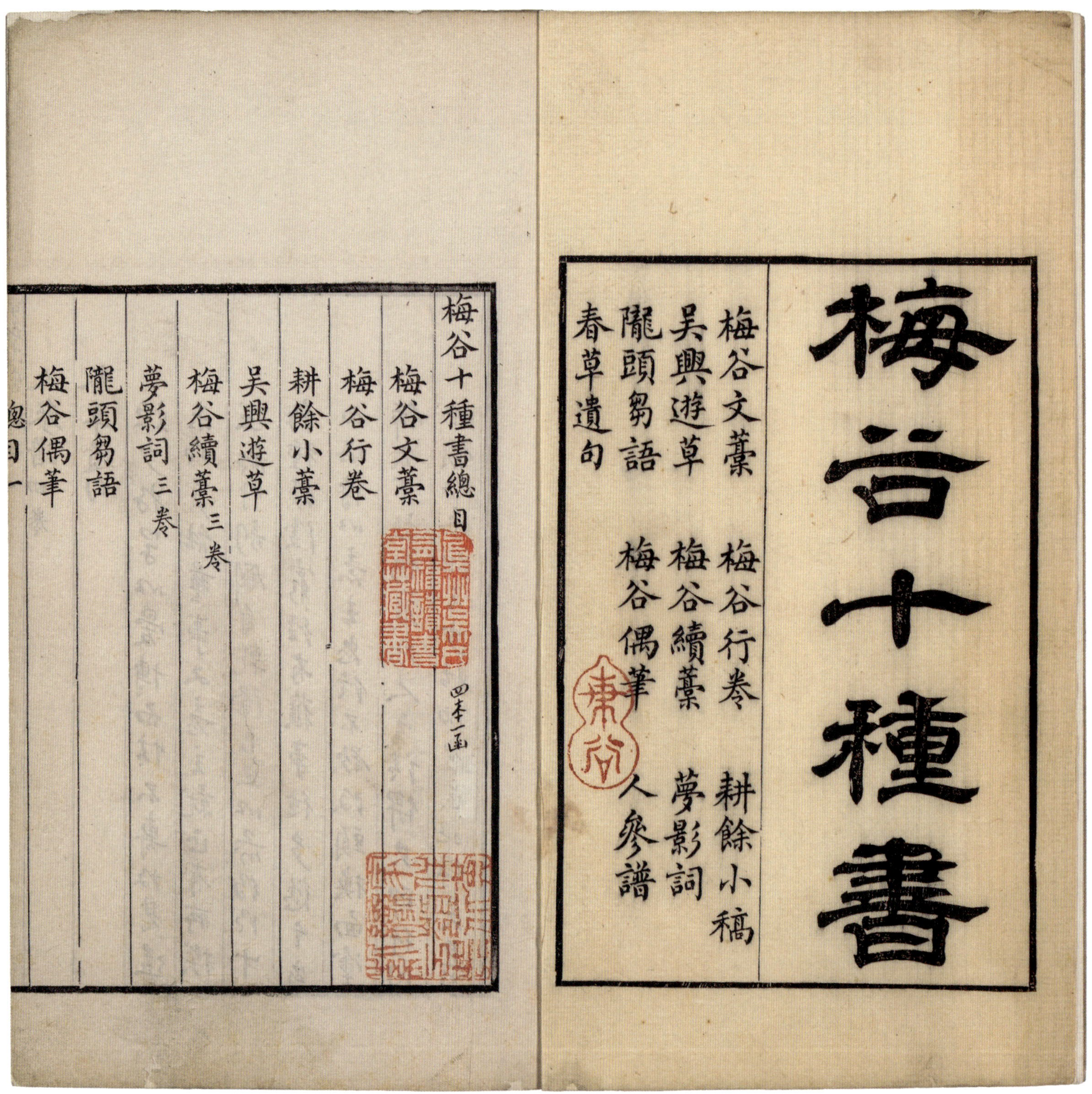
梅谷十種書總目
四本一函
梅谷文藁
梅谷行卷
耕餘小藁
吳興遊草
梅谷續藁 三卷
夢影詞 三卷
隴頭芻語
梅谷偶筆
總目 一

梅谷十種書
梅谷文藁 梅谷行卷 耕餘小稿
吳興遊草 梅谷續藁 夢影詞
隴頭芻語 梅谷偶筆 人參譜
春草遺句

Fig. 1.22: *Meigu shizhong shu* (*The Plum Valley: Ten Books*), title page and table of contents, fol. 1r. Author: Lu Xuan (1737–1799). Date: 1766–1768. Woodblock: 16.8 × 11.7 cm. Harvard-Yenching Library (T 9118 7191).

The preface to *Meanings in the Book of Documents* records that the book itself was finished in the first lunar month of 1786 (Fig. 1.21) and that copying began in 1787, taking about one year to complete. Despite all this work, the book was never published. As its starting point, it took the "New Text" format of *The Book of Documents*, so it is divided into the fifty-eight chapters of that tradition; in terms of exegesis, Lu Xuan's preference was for the older styles of the Han dynasty onwards, rather than the neo-Confucian Song dynasty school of Zhu Xi, as exemplified by the seminal commentary of his pupil Cai Shen 蔡沈 (1167–1230). Partly for this reason, in 1916 upon reading *Meanings in the Book of Documents*, the distinguished literatus Ye Changchi remarked:

> In terms of scholarship of Confucian canonical texts, it has no scholarly lineage and is not worth discussing; however, the book's entire

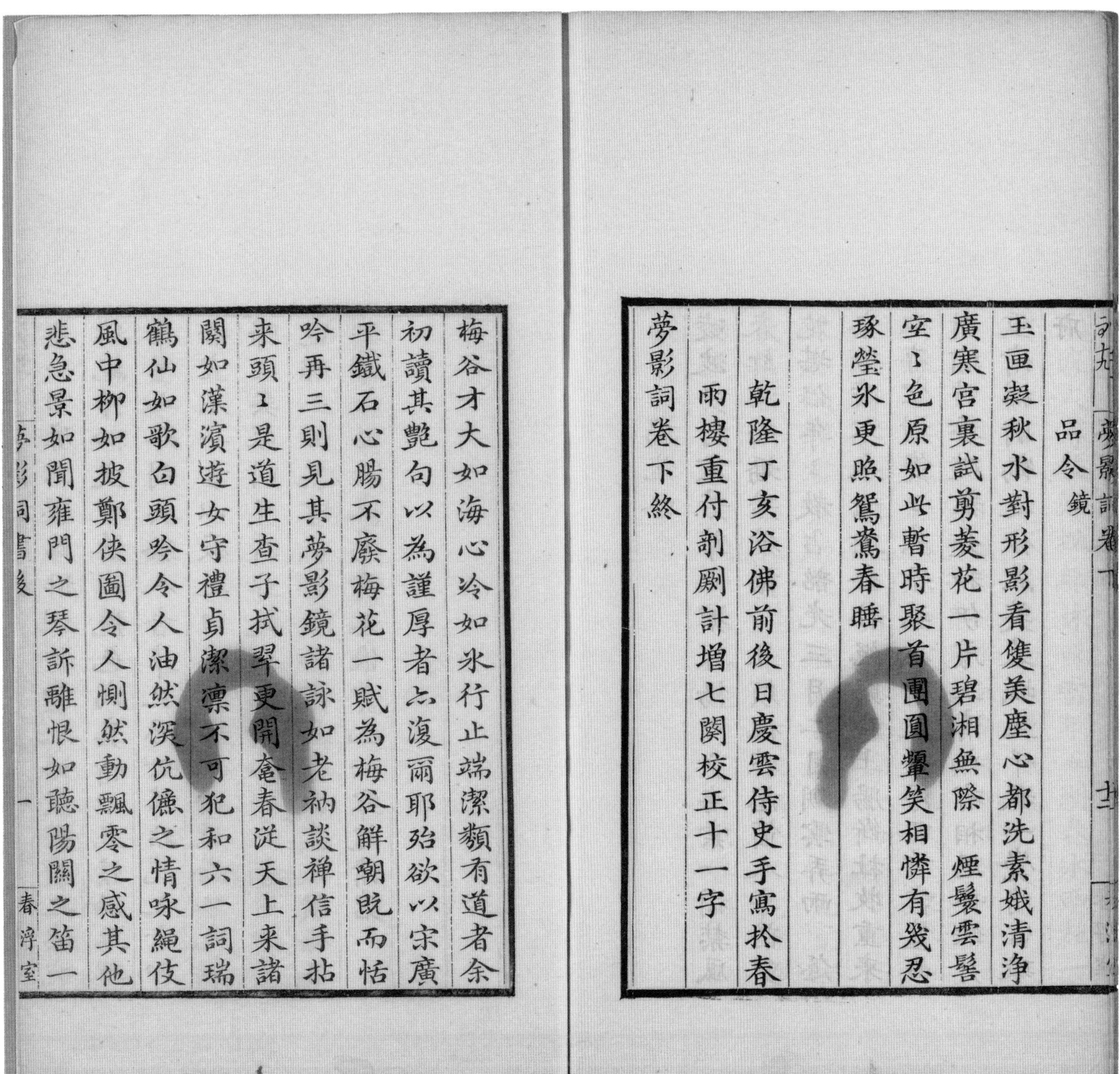

品令　鏡
玉匣凝秋水對形影看雙美塵心都洗素娥清淨
廣寒宮裏試剪菱花一片碧湘無際　烟鬟雲髻
空ㄡ色原如此暫時聚首團圓顰笑相憐有幾忍
琢瑩冰更照鴛鴦春睡

乾隆丁亥浴佛前後日慶雲侍史手寫於春
雨樓重付剞劂計增七闋校正十一字
夢影詞卷下終

梅谷才大如海心泠如冰行止端潔頗有道者余
初讀其艷句以為謹厚者亦復爾耶殆欲以宋廣
平鐵石心腸不廢梅花一賦為梅谷解嘲既而恬
吟再三則見其夢影鏡諸詠如老衲談禪信手拈
來頭ㄡ是道生查子拭翠更開奩春從天上來諸
闋如漢濱遊女守禮貞潔凜不可犯和六一詞瑞
鶴仙如歌白頭吟令人油然深伉儷之情咏繩伎
風中柳如披鄭俠圖令人惻然動飄零之感其他
悲急景如聞雍門之琴訴離恨如聽陽關之笛一
夢影詞書後　一　春浮室

Fig. 1.23: *Meigu shizhong shu* (*The Plum Valley: Ten Books*), *Mengying ci* (*Dreamed Reflections: A Song Lyric Anthology*), the scribe Shen Cai's note on *juan* 3, fol. 12v (right), and postscript, fol. 1r (left).
Author: Lu Xuan (1737–1799).
Date: 1766–1768.
Woodblock: 16.8 × 11.7 cm.
Harvard-Yenching Library (T 9118 7191).

contents are written out by the concubine Shen Hongping in a diminutive *kai* script, and very neatly and elegantly at that. Judging from whoever mounted the book, and also looking at the small seal placed on it, these are clearly the work of a lady and not a man, and as such an oft-repeated tale among literati, it is a precious deposit of the innermost treasury; so, I advised Hanyi to add it to his collection.

經學無師法不足論，其書全帙皆侍妾沈虹屏所書，小楷娟秀，裝池者觀其小印亦釵而非弁，誠為玉臺之佳話，鎮庫之尤物。既勸翰怡藏之。[30]

30. Wang Jilie, ed., *Ye Changchi Yuandu lu rijichao*, *juan* 16, fols. 28v–30v; Ye Changchi, *Yuandu lu riji*, 573.

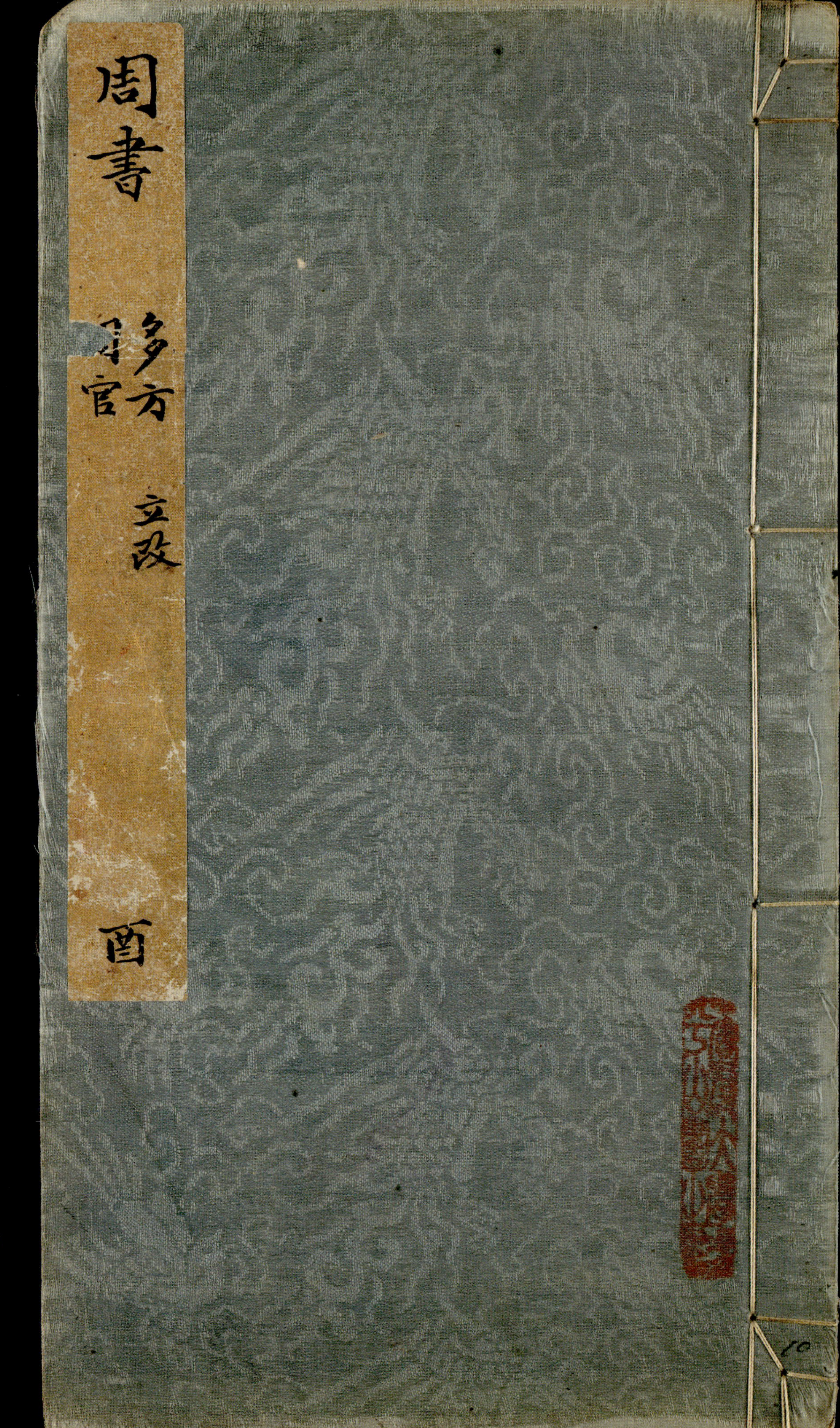

Fig. 1.24: *Shang shu yi* (*Meanings in the Book of Documents*), the original blue silk cover of fascicle 10.
Author: Lu Xuan (1737–1799).
Scribe: Shen Cai (c. 1748–?).
Date: 1787.
Dimensions: 27.2 × 15.4 cm.
Fung Ping Shan Library.

Miao Quansun echoes some of these views, and his bibliographical entry for Liu Chenggan's catalog includes the phrase: "In respect of its copying, it is fine, fastidious, and most delightful, and certainly worthy of preservation" 繕寫精妙可愛，尤足傳耳.[31]

Shen Cai, *zi* soubriquet Hongping 虹屏 ("Hongping" means "Rainbow Screen"), was originally a daughter of a gentry family of Pinghu in Zhejiang. As her family had fallen upon hard times, she entered the Peng household in Haiyan—descendants of the poet-scholar-official Peng Sunyu 彭孫遹 (1631–1700)—as a maid and became the personal servant of Peng Zhenyin 彭貞隱 (*zi* soubriquet Yuqian 玉嵌 which means "Jade Inlay"), of whom Peng Sunyu was a grand-uncle.[32] Later, when Peng Zhenyin was given in marriage to Lu Xuan, Shen Cai also moved with her mistress into his household, at which time she was thirteen years old. She subsequently became Lu Xuan's concubine and was entrusted with the task of organizing his collection of books, paintings, and calligraphy.[33] Lu Xuan's collected works were published towards the end of Qianlong's reign as *Meigu shizhong shu* 梅谷十種書 (*The Plum Valley: Ten Books*, Figs. 1.22 and 1.23) and Shen Cai's as *Chunyu lou ji* 春雨樓集 (*The Spring Rain Cottage Collection*); in both cases, her handwriting was used by the craftsmen cutting the woodblocks as their model,[34] as can be recognized immediately when comparing it to her work on *Meanings in the Book of Documents.*

The manuscript itself comprises twelve volumes. Originally each bound in blue silk, all but two of them have had mottled paper wrappings whose colored patterns resemble tiger-skin stuck over the silk, and only one of these two retains its original appearance (Fig. 1.24), while the other volume has the blue silk on one side only. The stitching along the binding edge of all the volumes has six holes through which the strings pass, which is more than the usual four and indicates the degree of care taken in respect of the overall presentation. White silk slips were originally placed over the binding corners to protect them, but they suffered removal when the manuscript was restored. The front cover of each volume has a strip of gold paper stuck to its left edge that records the book's title and the chapters contained therein.

At the end of each *juan*, Lu Xuan's name is recorded as the author and Shen Cai's as the copyist together with their seals. The wording of the seals employed by Shen Cai varies, for example, "Xu-shan canqie" 胥山蠶妾 ("The Silkworm Cultivating Concubine of Xu Mountain"); "Meigu shishi" 梅谷侍史 ("The Plum Valley Clerk"); "Pinghong nüshi" 虹屏女史 ("The Rainbow Screen Lady Literata"); and "Qingyao shanren" 青要山人 ("The Hermit of Qingyao Mountain"). It is as if each *juan* of exquisite calligraphy is given a perfectly fashioned and bespoke jewel to mark its close. In the late eighteenth century, such a sensitive and elegant gesture would have been regarded as completely inappropriate given that these were the holiest of holies, the Confucian classics, and she a mere woman. The most prominent exponent of this opposition was Lu Xuan's wife Peng Zhenyin, as is audaciously recorded by Shen Cai herself in an epilogue to the final and fifty-eighth chapter "Qin shi" 秦誓("[Duke Mu of] Qin's Vow"), after having completed copying the entire book (Figs. 1.25 and 1.26):

> [Shen] Cai, on receiving the order from her Master, has proofread and edited *Meanings in the Book of Documents*. Yet one day, Lady Jade Inlay [Peng Zhenyin] voiced her thoughts, saying: "A woman's role is to refine the five grains, cover [sieve] wines, and sew clothes, and that is all. Now, look at what you have become; although perhaps admirable, in the end, you have ruined your vocation. And besides, given the incandescent brilliance of *The Book of Documents*, for this to emerge from hands that have had contact with the hairgrip, skirt, and hair oil, does that not besmirch it?"
>
> 彩受主人命校謄〈尚書義〉。一日，玉嵌夫人謂曰：「婦人之事精五飯，幕酒漿，縫衣裳而已。今爾乃如此，雖屬難得，終為廢業。且煌煌大典，出簪裾膏沐手，毋乃近褻乎？」

31. Miao Quansun, Wu Changshou, and Dong Kang, *Jiaye tang cangshu zhi*, 138; Luo Zhenchang, *Shanbenshu suojian lu*, 5.

32. Lu Xuan 陸烜, *Meigu oubi* 梅谷偶筆, in Lu Xuan 陸烜, *Meigu shizhong shu* 梅谷十種書 (Pinghu: Lushi, 1766–1768), fol. 16r.

33. For more information on Shen Cai, see Yang Zhishui 揚之水, *Zhima tongjian* 脂麻通鑒 (Shenyang: Liaoning jiaoyu chubanshe, 1995), 126–134; Grace S. Fong, *Herself an Author: Gender, Agency, and Writing in Late Imperial China* (Honolulu: University of Hawai'i Press, 2008), 69–84; Zhou Xiaoying 周小英, "Nüxing huaxue zhuzuo de di yi bu shu *Chunyu lou shuhua mu* (shang) 女性畫學著作的第一部書《春雨樓書畫目》(上)," *Xin meishu* 新美術 (2009) 6: 42–53; and Grace Fong, Emily Goedde, Jeanne Larsen, Geoffrey Waters, and Michael Farman, *Jade Mirror: Women Poets of China* (Buffalo, New York: White Pine, 2013), 207–215.

34. Lu Xuan 陸烜, *Mengying ci* 夢影詞, in Lu Xuan 陸烜, *Meigu shizhong shu* 梅谷十種書 (Pinghu: Lushi, 1766–1768), *juan* 3, fol. 12v.

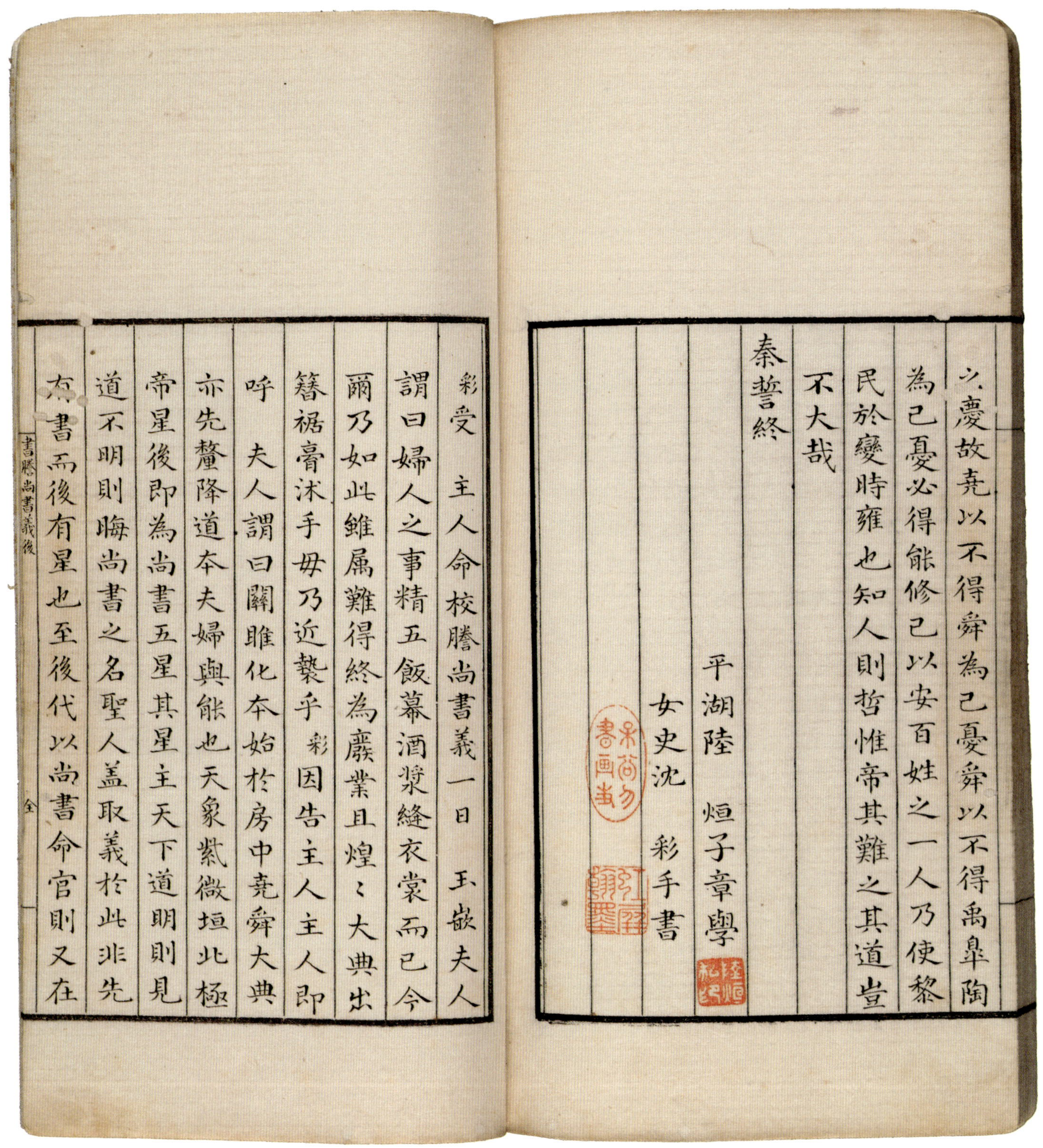
之慶故堯以不得舜為己憂舜以不得禹皋陶為己憂必得能修己以安百姓之一人乃使黎民於變時雍也知人則哲惟帝其難之其道豈不大哉

秦誓終

平湖陸烜子章學
女史沈彩手書

彩受主人命校謄尚書義一日玉嵌夫人謂曰婦人之事精五飯冪酒漿縫衣裳而已今爾乃如此雖屬難得終為曠業且煌煌大典出簪裾膏沐手毋乃近褻乎彩因告主人主人即呼夫人謂曰關雎化本始於房中堯舜大典亦先釐降道本夫婦與能也天象紫微垣北極帝星後即為尚書五星其星主天下道明則見道不明則晦尚書之名聖人蓋取義於此非先有書而後有星也至後代以尚書命官則又在

書謄尚書義後　全

[Shen] Cai, in response to this, informed her Master. The Master called for his lady wife and addressed her, saying: "*Quacking Waterfowl* is the essence of edification and has its origins in the chamber; before Yao abdicated in favor of Shun, he first married off his daughters to him, and this tells of husbands and wives, and their abilities and roles. Of the heavenly spheres in their prescribed orbits, after the Purple Enclosure Wall, North Pole, and Emperor Star constellations come the 'Imperial Secretary (*Shang Shu*)' five stars, who govern the world under heaven; and when the Way is enlightened they look on, and when the Way is unenlightened they are dimmed. *The Book of Documents* (*Shang Shu*) is titled in this way,

Fig. 1.25: *Shang shu yi* (*Meanings in the Book of Documents*), *juan* 58, fol. 4v (right), and postscript by Shen Cai, fol. 1r (left).
Author: Lu Xuan (1737–1799).
Scribe: Shen Cai (c. 1748–?).
Date: 1787.
Border: 17.1 × 12.2 cm.
Fung Ping Shan Library.

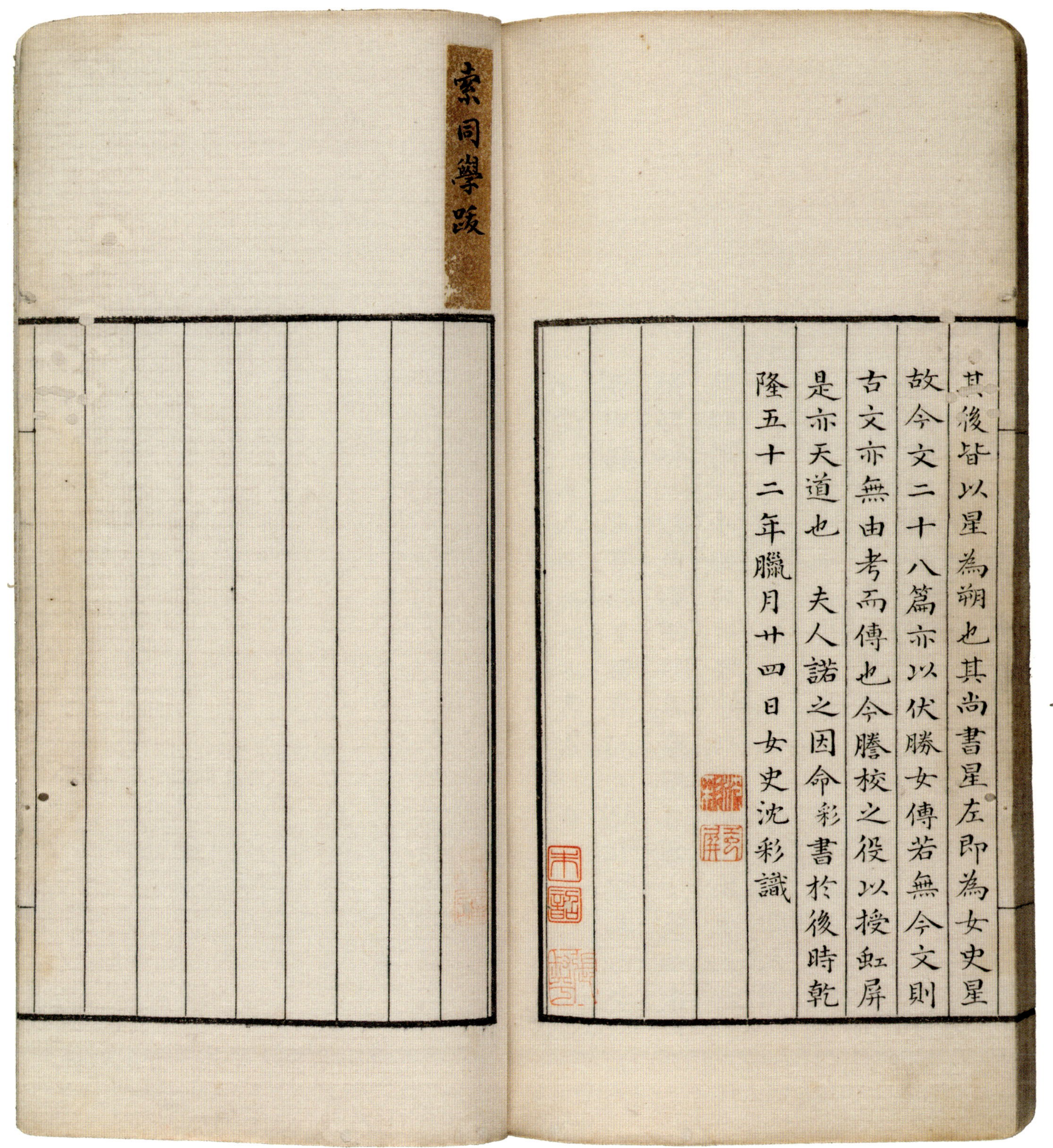
索同學跋

其後皆以星為朔也其尚書星左即為女史星
故今文二十八篇亦以伏勝女傳若無今文則
古文亦無由考而傳也今謄校之役以授虹屏
是亦天道也　夫人諾之因命彩書於後時乾
隆五十二年臘月廿四日女史沈彩識

Fig. 1.26: *Shang shu yi* (*Meanings in the Book of Documents*), postscript by Shen Cai, fol. 1v.
Author: Lu Xuan (1737–1799).
Scribe: Shen Cai (c. 1748–?).
Date: 1787.
Border: 17.1 × 12.2 cm.
Fung Ping Shan Library.

the sages took its meaning from this, and it was not so that first there was the book and then the stars. Later, the appellation 'Imperial Secretary' was used to mean 'an official,' and this also happened subsequently, with the star so-named always coming first. Leftwards from the 'Imperial Secretary' star is the 'Lady Literata' star. For this reason, the 'New Text' has twenty-eight chapters, and these were also transmitted by Fu Sheng's daughter;[35] were there no 'New Text,' there would be no means

35. Fu Sheng 伏生 (dates uncertain, but perhaps 268–178 BCE). As the only surviving record of *The Book of Documents* to survive Qin Shihuang's burning of books, Fu Sheng's memorized text was spoken on his behalf by his daughter to those chosen to record it; at this time he was ninety years of age and his voice too feeble to understand.

to investigate the 'Old' and 'New' Texts and their transmission. In our present time, the task of editing and proofreading has been entrusted to Hongping, and this is also Heaven's Way."

彩因告主人。主人即呼夫人，謂曰：「〈關雎〉化本，始於房中，堯舜大典，亦先釐降，道本夫婦與能也。天象紫微垣北極帝星後，即為尚書五星，其星主天下，道明則見，道不明則晦。尚書之名，聖人蓋取義於此，非先有書而後有星也。至後代以尚書命官，則又在其後，皆以星為朔也。其尚書星左即為女史星，故今文二十八篇，亦以伏勝女傳，若無今文，則古文亦無由考而傳也。今謄校之役以授虹屏，是亦天道也。」

His lady wife affirmed her assent, and thus ordered [Shen] Cai to record the matter at the end of the book. On the fifty-second year of the Emperor Qianlong's reign, the last month, the twenty-fourth day [31 January 1788], recorded by the Lady Literata Shen Cai.

夫人諾之，因命彩書於後。時乾隆五十二年臘月廿四日女史沈彩識。

At the end of various passages throughout the book, after the labor of copying was over and perhaps in a moment of leisure, Shen Cai often adds her own brief literary creations. In total there are sixteen places where these are found, comprising twelve *shi* poems, two *ci* poems, and four prose passages overall. Often simple in construction and language, they describe the natural world around her as the seasons pass, and draw the reader inexorably into the universe of her inner thoughts and her interaction with that world; for example, in the first volume, after "Yao dian" 堯典 ("The Classic of the Emperor Yao"), the first chapter of *The Book of Documents*, are notes that record (Fig. 1.27):

When my Lord [husband] drafted *Meanings in the Book of Documents*, he consistently ordered me, [Shen] Cai, to make a handwritten fair-copy, and for this reason presented me with a poem that contains the following lines: "In transmitting scripture, do you have as resplendently a flowered mouth; that even when winding words tangle teeth, you still transmit as well as she who spoke for Fu Sheng?"[36] And also: "An ingenious pen and a hairgrip flower are not mere playthings.[37] Through them, absolutist imperial governance transmits to the common people." This is the third draft of *Meanings in the Book of Documents* and was written beginning in the *bingwu* year of the Emperor Qianlong's reign, the twelfth month, the seventeenth day [4 February 1787]; by the first day of the Start of Spring [the first of the twenty-four solar terms], the weather was, morning after morning, unremitting rain and snow, and the river-plum trees were putting forth their first buds, the sky was cold, and hands trembled, yet there was just enough warmth to avoid the need to breathe on the inkstone to warm and thaw it. The Silkworm Cultivating Concubine of Xu Mountain Shen Cai records this.

主君作〈書義〉，皆命彩手鈔，故嘗贈彩詩有「傳經可有粲花口，詰屈聱牙記伏生」，又「妙筆簪花非玩物，藉傳皇極答蒼生」之句。此三易稿也，始寫於乾隆丙午十二月十七日，為立春日，時連朝雨雪，江梅初苞，天寒手顫，僅免呵凍云。胥山蠶妾沈彩識。

As icy winter turned into a gentle early spring, in the second volume after the third chapter is a poem that reads:

Do not laugh that my gold hairpins are crude
Only in having no jade scales am I ashamed
The two princesses assisted the ancient
  Emperor Yu[38]
The Ten Counsellors and Yi Jiang took part[39]
Sweet rain moistens the fountain plants
A warming wind reaches the photinia roses
As if inside the painting of teaching scripture
And receiving Fu Sheng's words

莫笑金釵陋，惟無玉秤慙。
二妃虞帝助，十亂邑姜參。
甘雨滋書帶，薰風到石楠。
授經圖畫裏，恍接伏生談。

36. The complete text of Lu Xuan's poem consisting of four lines can be found in: Shen Cai 沈彩, *Chunyu lou ji* 春雨樓集, in *Qingdai shi wen ji huibian* 清代詩文集彙編, ed. Qingdai shi wen ji huibian bianzuan weiyuanhui 清代詩文集彙編編纂委員會 (Shanghai: Shanghai guji chubanshe, 2010), vol. 379, 31; and Shen Cai 沈彩, *Chunyu lou ji* 春雨樓集, in *Jiangnan nüxing bieji san bian* 江南女性別集三編, ed. Hu Xiaoming 胡曉明 and Peng Guozhong 彭國忠 (Hefei: Huangshan shushe, 2011), vol. 1, 60.

37. The epithet "hairgrip flower" is also used by Shen Cai to refer to herself and appears several times in the text.

38. The two princesses and the Emperor Yu are mythological ancient characters. The princesses are Ehuang 娥皇 and Nüying 女英, daughters of Yao 堯, (the fourth of the Five Emperors), who later became wives of Shun 舜 (the fifth Emperor), also known as Yu 虞.

39. The Ten Counsellors are luminaries who assisted the Zhou dynasty's founding emperor Wu Wang 武王 (?–1043 BCE; r. 1046–1043 BCE); Yi Jiang 邑姜 was Wu Wang's empress.

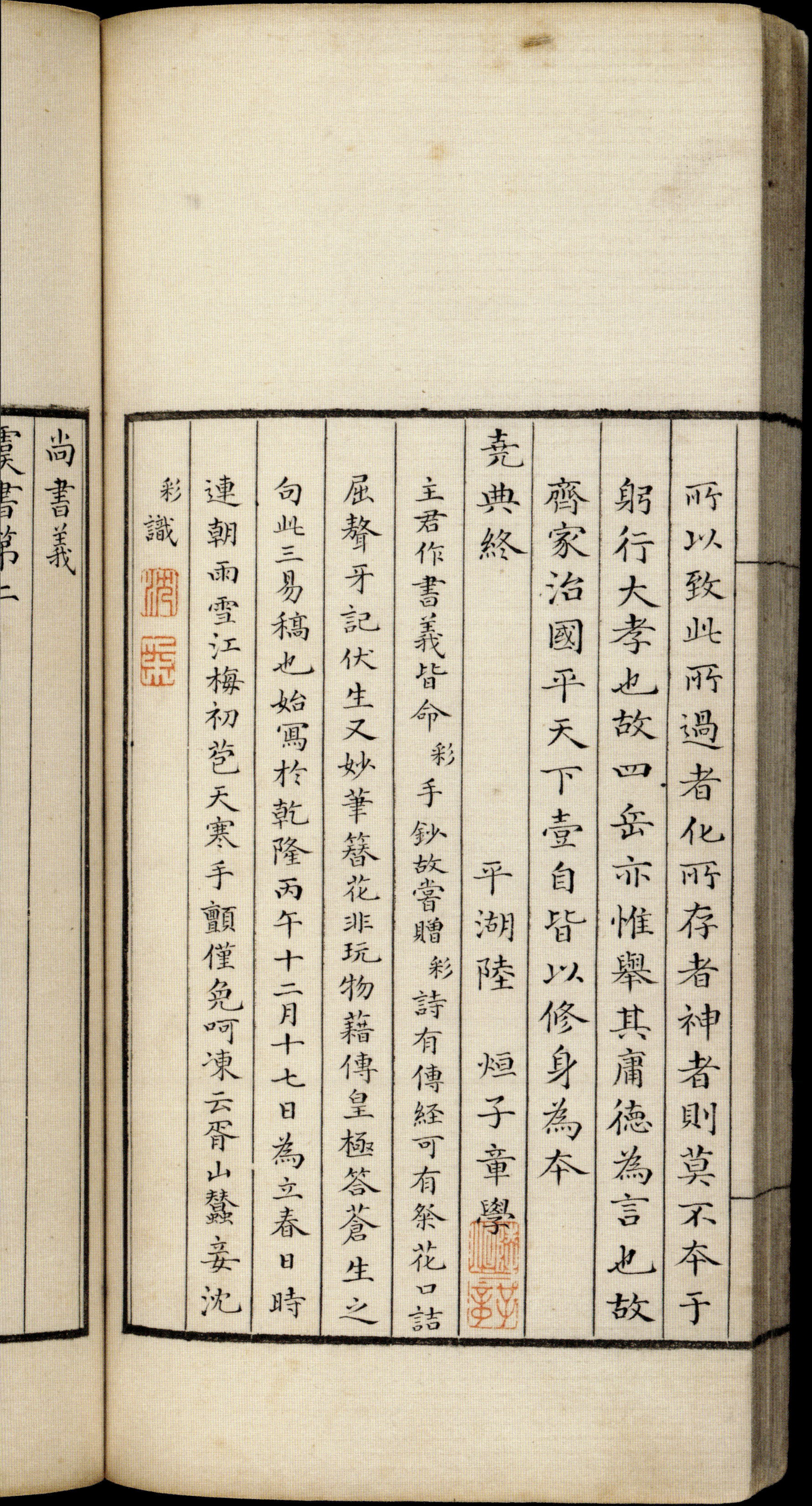

所以致此所過者化所存者神者則莫不本于躬行大孝也故四岳亦惟舉其庸德為言也故齊家治國平天下壹自皆以修身為本

堯典終

平湖陸烜子章學

主君作書義皆命彩手鈔故嘗贈彩詩有傳經可有粲花口詰屈聱牙記伏生又妙筆簪花非玩物藉傳皇極答蒼生之句此三易稿也始寫於乾隆丙午十二月十七日為立春日時連朝雨雪江梅初苞天寒手顫僅免呵凍云胥山蠶妾沈彩識

Fig. 1.27: *Shang shu yi* (*Meanings in the Book of Documents*), *juan* 1, fol. 14v.
Author: Lu Xuan (1737–1799).
Scribe: Shen Cai (c. 1748–?).
Date: 1787.
Border: 17.1 × 12.2 cm.
Fung Ping Shan Library.

In the *dingwei* year of the reign of the Emperor Qianlong, the first month, the fifteenth day [4 March 1787], having copied the chapter "The Counsels of Emperor Yu the Great," I therefore composed a poem in the five-character-per-line *lü* format, hoping that my Master might smile beneficently on me. [Written by] the hermit of Qingyao Mountain.

乾隆丁未正月上元日鈔〈大禹謨〉畢，因成五律一章，冀博主人莞爾一粲也。青要山人

A gentle spring had turned into a more vibrant growing season, and in the fourth volume, after the seventeenth chapter "Xian you yi de" 咸有一德 ("Common Possession of Pure Virtue") are two *ci* poems that read:

Having put on my morning make-up
Seated upright spreading out the treasury of book-boxes
A red sun half through the drapes, the wind softly soughing
Purple vines on the trellis, swallows singing "ni-nan"
The sky's hue a deep azure blue

晨粧罷，
端坐展瑤函。
紅日半簾風旖旎，
紫藤一架燕呢喃。
天色正蔚藍。

A chapter having been written
Carefully proofreading, thrice, still not dismissing
Already knowing that not a single character is a scribal error
When the characters are carved, it ought to be added that I too took part
Tentatively, I note a poem according to the rhythm and rhyme "Gazing at South of the River"

書寫畢，
細校不辭三。
筆誤已知無一字。
鐫時應附我同參，
聊識望江南。

In the fifth volume, together with a profusion of flowers in early summer, the following poems appear at the end of the nineteenth chapter "Pan Geng zhong" 盤庚中("Pan Geng, Part Two"):

An incense burner of musky fragrance, a cup of tea
The pure pleasure of editing text can be exaggerated
Unknowingly, the solar term Grain-Moistening Rain has suddenly passed
Their flowers open unto the halls, such are the poppies

一炷幽香一盞茶，謄書清韻亦堪誇。
不知穀雨匆匆過，開到庭前御米花。

The third month, the eleventh day [28 April 1787], having finished writing, proofreading done, playing for pleasure, so writing some lines of *jue* poetry.

三月十一日書畢校訖，戲題絕句。

After the twenty-third chapter "Yue ming xia" 說命下 ("Charge to Yue [of Fuxian], Part Three," Fig. 1.28):

"Salt-plum," "ferment-sprout,"[40] in the kitchen, I have delved
"Smiling, snapping the blossomed branch,"[41] in the orchard, I am not stupid
"How can it be said I have no clothes;"[42] I can abandon pen and ink
And with the sprouting mulberry for a month feed the newly-emerged silkworms

鹽梅麴蘗我曾探，笑折花枝不是憨。
豈曰無衣拋筆墨，青桑一月飼紅蠶。

The Silkworm Cultivating Concubine of Xu Mountain Shen Cai extemporizes.

胥山蠶妾沈彩口占。

Having reached high summer and to the sound of screeching crickets, at the end of the twenty-fifth chapter "Xibo kan li" 西伯戡黎 ("The Chieftain of the West [King Wen]'s Conquest of [the State of] Li"):

40. "Salt-plum" 鹽梅 and "ferment-sprout" 麴蘗 are unusual words found in historic texts whose etymological origins are obscure. Both occur in close proximity in the same passage of *The Book of Documents*, chapter 23 說命下, whose title is translated by James Legge (1865 and 1879) as "The Charge to Yüeh."

41. The original source of this citation is hard to determine, but the *ci* poem *Divination and Prophecy* 卜算子 by the Song dynasty poet Lu Zugao 盧祖皋 (1174–1224) is an early usage.

42. This is a quotation from *The Book of Odes*.

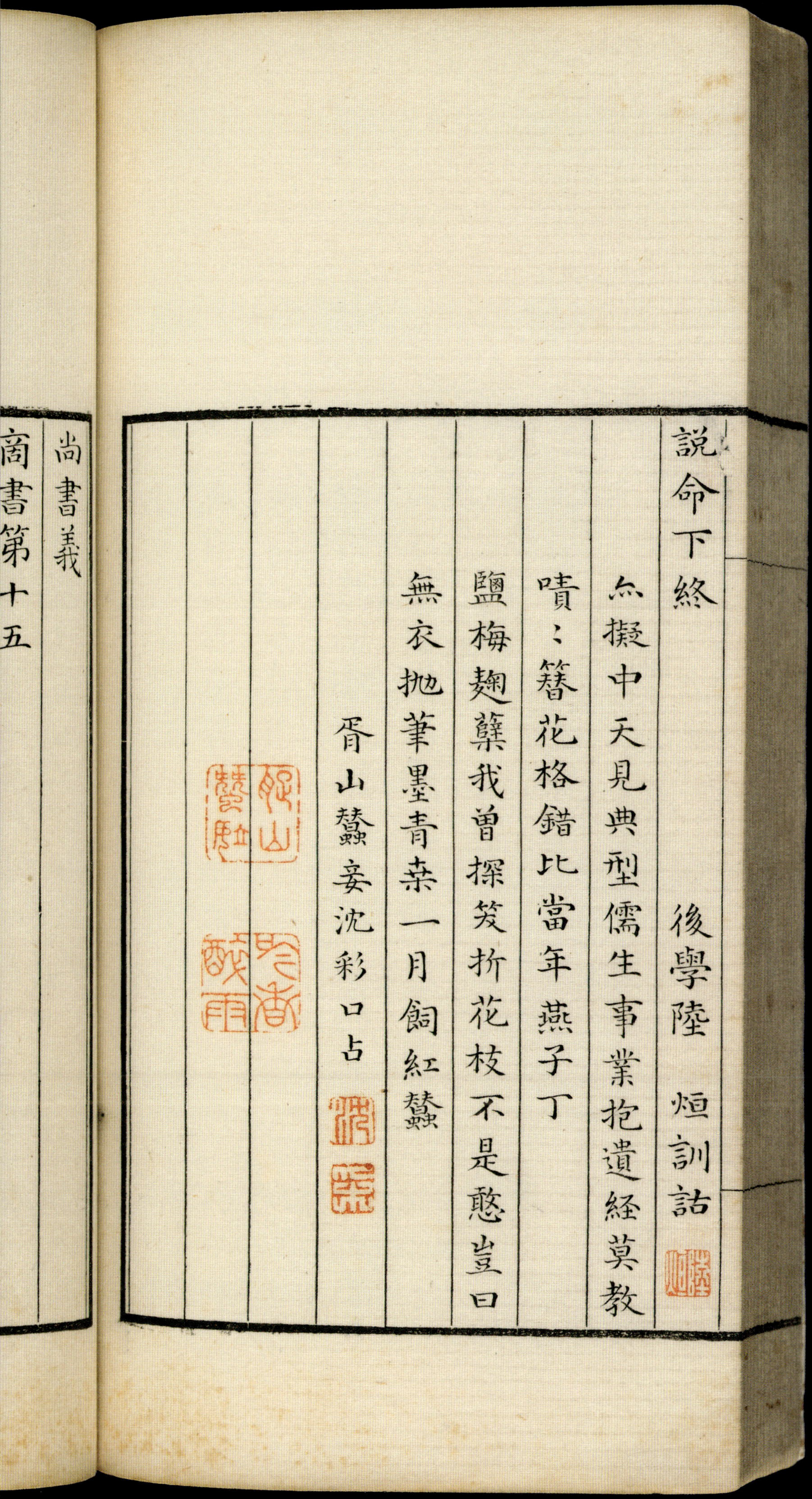

說命下終　　　　後學陸　烜訓詁

亦擬中天見典型儒生事業抱遺経莫教

嘖〻簪花格錯比當年燕子丁

鹽梅麴糵我曾探笈折花枝不是憨豈曰

無衣拋筆墨青桒一月飼紅蠶

胥山蠶妾沈彩口占

尚書義

商書第十五

Fig. 1.28: *Shang shu yi* (*Meanings*
Book of Documents), *juan* 23, fol. 8
Author: Lu Xuan (1737–1799).
Scribe: Shen Cai (c. 1748–?).
Date: 1787.
Border: 17.1 × 12.2 cm.
Fung Ping Shan Library.

Remembering my first taste of Yu Shen broth[43]
On paper drawn with squares, copying out the "Pan Geng" chapters[44]
From *The Book of the Yin Dynasty*, having reached the end of "The Conquest of Li"[45]
The purple beans' flowers open and the crickets sing[46]
記得初嘗玉糝羹，烏絲畫就寫盤庚。
殷書甫到戡黎畢，紫豆花開蟋蟀鳴。

The Plum Valley clerk Shen Cai writes this at the South of the Flowers, North of the Waters Pavilion and records it with a *jue* poem.
梅谷侍史沈彩書於花南水北亭中幷識一絕。

High summer had passed and the darker, sultrier days of early autumn had arrived; in the seventh volume, at the end of the thirty-third chapter (Fig.1.29):

A bronze lamp, tall as its antique chicken's feet stand
A gold inlaid inkstone box, purple-tipped lion mane's pen
Amidst the night-cooled osmanthus bushes' flowery fragrance
In *kai* script in word-columns, writing the chapter "The Lü Barbarians' Ao Hound"
一盞銅燈雞足高，鎗金硯匣紫猊毫。
夜涼叢桂花香裏，小字烏闌寫旅獒。

The eighth month, the seventh day [18 September 1787], in the evening, having finished writing, nonetheless penning these lines of *jue* poetry. Written by The Rainbow Screen Lady Literata Shen Cai.
八月初七夜寫畢，却題絕句，虹屏女史沈彩。

As autumn deepened, the shadows lengthened, the frost came, and a year had almost passed; and so, in the ninth volume, after the forty-third chapter:

The sun and moon are like revolving axles
Heaven and earth cannot stop
Moving my pen, writing on the tiers of bamboo slips
Suddenly again feeling I should add a thicker layer of clothing
A chill frost covers the late chrysanthemums
From the north, the wind blows the cold evening sunbeams
In the courtyard, leaves fall from the trees
Amidst the clouds, migrating geese fly past
日月如轉轂，天地無停機。
載筆親書策，忽復當授衣。
清霜蔽晚菊，朔吹冷夕暉。
庭際木葉脱，雲中征雁飛。

Having written the chapter "Against Luxurious Ease," jotting a poem; Shen Cai.
書〈無逸〉畢偶題，沈彩。

These beautiful literary creations by Shen Cai that are handwritten in her own delicate calligraphy are both illuminating and visually appealing. For bibliophiles and book collectors, they are highlights of the manuscript; however, her husband Lu Xuan's study on *The Book of Documents*, which demonstrates a new level of evidential scholarship based on empirical idea, is certainly not worthless, as was proposed by the Confucian literati Ye Changchi and Miao Quansun. From a musicological perspective, the most innovative contribution Lu Xuan made to interpreting *The Book of Documents* was his invention of a pentachord called a *jian* 簡. The pentachord has five strings, with a vibrating string length of two *chi* 尺 feet and two *cun* 寸 inches (70.4 cm). Composed of twelve frets and three half-frets, its five strings are tuned to the pentatonic scale: *gong* 宫, *zhi* 徵, *shang* 商, *yu* 羽, and *jue* 角. Astonishingly, Lu Xuan does not mention this laboratory instrument in his commentaries; for example, in *juan* 2 of *Meanings in the Book of Documents*, when annotating text on Emperor Shun's regulation of pitch-pipes, his three-page explanation is entirely confined to more conventional exegesis.[47] It was only in Shen Cai's *The Spring Rain Cottage Collection* that I came across a detailed account of it entitled "*Jian shuo*" 簡説

43. Yu Shen broth 玉糝羹. Another literary citation, this time from a poem by Su Shi 蘇軾 (1037–1101) called *The Day when my Son Guo suddenly had the New Idea to make Yu Shen Broth from Sweet Potatoes, whose Color, Fragrance, and Taste were all peculiarly wonderful* 過子忽出新意以山芋作玉糝羹色香味皆奇絕天.

44. The "Pan Geng" chapters of *The Book of Documents* (chapters 18–20).

45. *The Book of the Yin Dynasty* is presumably the later chapters of *The Book of the Shang Dynasty* 商書 (*The Book of the Shang Dynasty: The Book of Documents*, chapters 10–26).

46. This citation is from a poem entitled *At the Fourth Hour, the Happiness of Reading* 四時讀書樂 by the late Song dynasty poet Weng Sen 翁森 (dates uncertain).

47. Lu Xuan 陸烜, *Shang shu yi* 尚書義, manuscript copy prepared by Shen Cai 沈彩, Fung Ping Shan Library (善 093.2/74), *juan* 2, fols. 7r–8r.

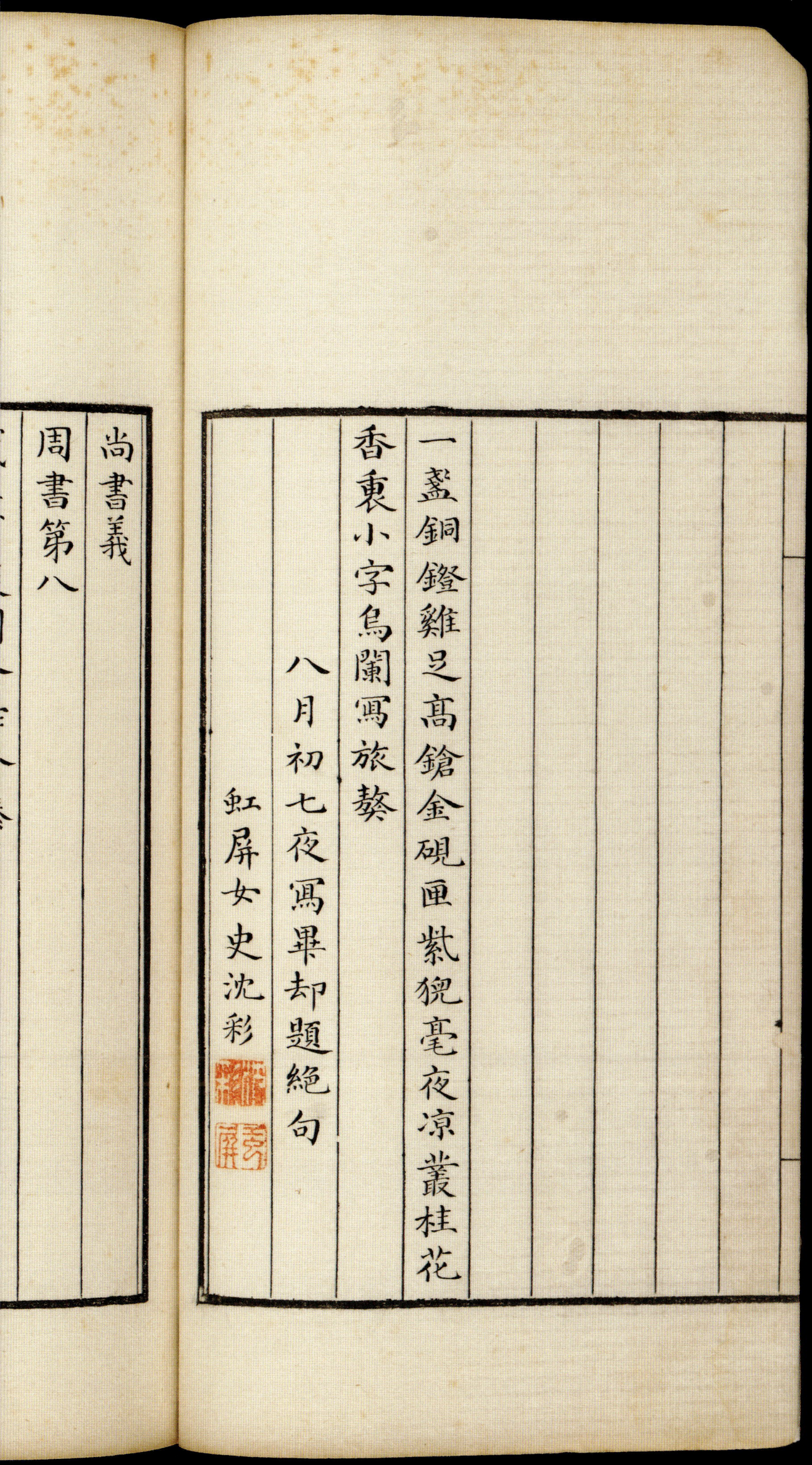

尚書義

周書第八

一盞銅鐙雞足高鎗金硯匣紫猊毫夜凉叢桂花

香裹小字烏闌寫旅獒

八月初七夜寫畢却題絶句

虹屏女史沈彩

Fig. 1.29: *Shang shu yi* (*Meanings in the Book of Documents*), *juan* 33, fol. 9
Author: Lu Xuan (1737–1799).
Scribe: Shen Cai (c. 1748–?).
Date: 1787.
Border: 17.1 × 12.2 cm.
Fung Ping Shan Library.

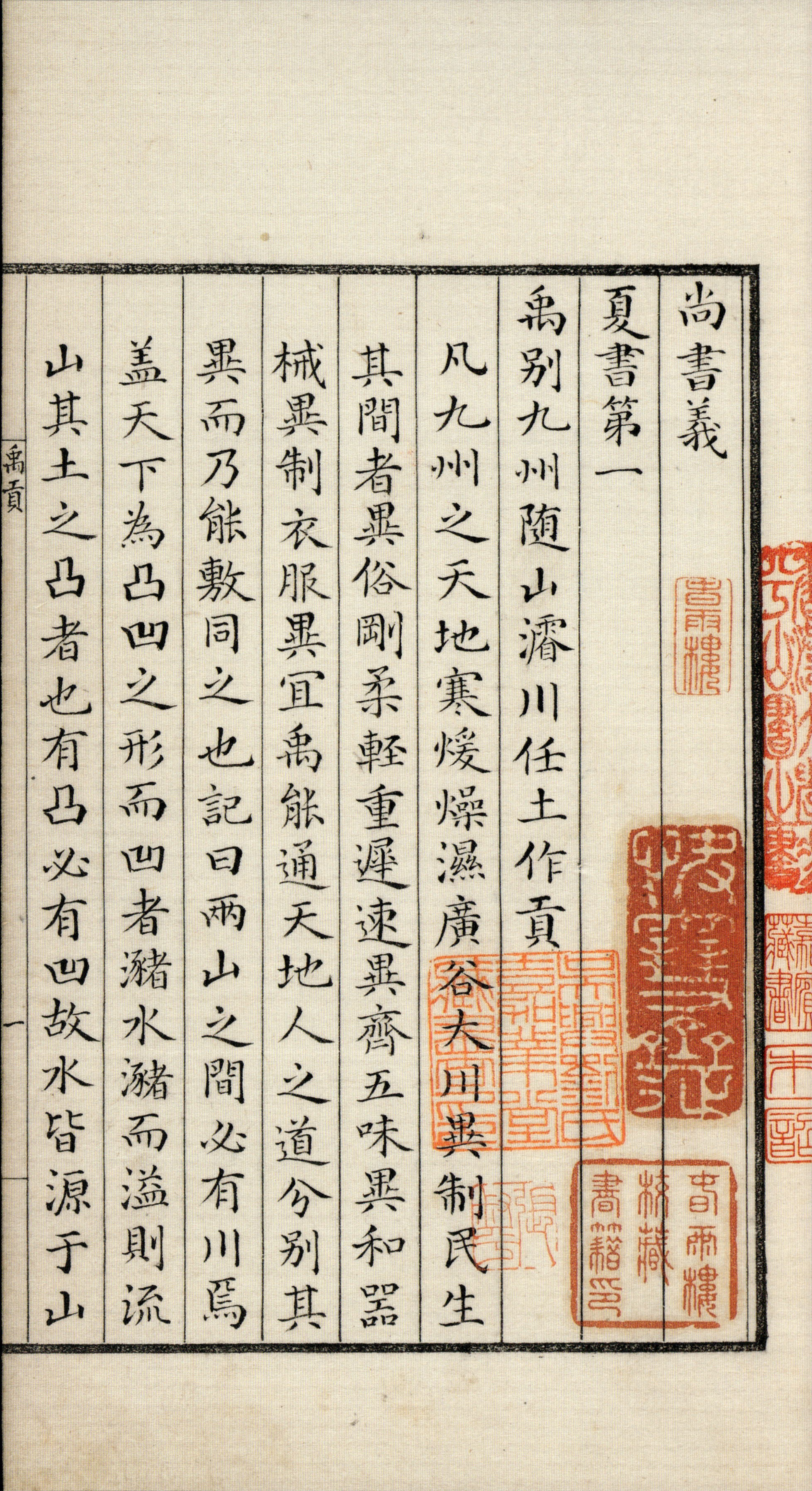

尚書義

夏書第一

禹別九州隨山濬川任土作貢

凡九州之天地寒煖燥濕廣谷大川異制民生其間者異俗剛柔輕重遲速異齊五味異和器械異制衣服異宜禹能通天地人之道分別其異而乃能敷同之也記曰兩山之間必有川焉蓋天下為凸凹之形而凹者瀦水瀦而溢則流山其土之凸者也有凸必有凹故水皆源于山

Fig. 1.30: *Shang shu yi* (*Meanings in the Book of Documents*), *juan* 6, fol. 1r.
Author: Lu Xuan (1737–1799).
Scribe: Shen Cai (c. 1748–?).
Date: 1787.
Border: 17.1 × 12.2 cm.
Fung Ping Shan Library.

("On the *Jian* Pentachord"). Here, Shen Cai lucidly renders Lu Xuan's propositions in respect to music theory by correlating the ancient Confucian musical nomenclature with later vernacular *sol-fa* terms. On the rationale for constructing the *jian*, Shen Cai states:

> The *jian* pentachord was made by my Lord and owing to the multiplicity of ancient music is therefore rendered as simply as possible. Not born from a desire for oversimplification, rather it attempts from the simple to gain understanding of the multiplicity. . . . People nowadays do not know whether contemporary music is like ancient music, and do not know whether the Five Notes and Six Pitches are the same. The *jian* acts as a raft for traveling along the river of understanding, and upstream can harmonize with the ancient *qin* and *se* zithers, and downstream commune with the subsequent *zheng* zither and *ruan* lute, and after this engenders the understanding that music nowadays is the same as ancient music. . . . This wisdom is known by all of today's downtrodden professional musicians. All those who manufacture *pipa*, *sheng*, and *ruan* know it, and yet the Confucianists are ignorant. The Confucianists use empty words to express their wisdom, and do not implement them in practice. Conversely, professional musicians who make instruments abide by practice but cannot annunciate the wisdom it embodies. The two are mutually incompatible, and therefore the practice of ancient times remains as shrouded as a long night. . . . Therefore, my Lord made the *jian*, which is thus positioned on the boundary of the modern and the ancient, and practiced this instrument in order to understand the wisdom thereof, and perhaps also to bring about a renaissance of ancient music. I imbibed these teachings, and grounded in the words that my Lord used to convey them, wrote this essay "On the *Jian* Pentachord."
> 簡者，主君所造，以古樂為繁，故從簡也。非欲其從簡也，欲其由簡以知繁也。……人不知今樂即古樂也，不知五音同也，六律同也。簡為之筏，上可以和琴、瑟，下可以合箏、阮，而後使人曉然知今之樂猶古之樂也。……其道今賤樂工皆知之。凡造琵琶、笙、阮者，皆知之。而儒者不知。以儒者空言其道，而不習其法。樂工造器者，守其法而不能明其道。兩不相值，故萬古如長夜也。……乃作簡，以界今古之間，俾習其器，知其道，庶幾古樂可興也。余受而學焉，因次主君傳授之語，作《簡說》。[48]

Capable of playing the *qin* 琴 zither, the *tiqin* 提琴 fiddle, and the *sheng* mouth organ,[49] Shen Cai even confesses that Lu Xuan's practical knowledge of music theory came from the wisdom of musicians instead of classical Confucian texts:

> Simply relying on the words of the Confucianists will not render music harmonious, and if music is not harmonious it is simply a theoretical practice of pen and paper, and not a living music of pipe and string. . . . As a distinguished Confucianist, my Lord practiced the techniques of the vernacular theatrical entertainer, and thereupon achieved a thorough understanding of musical theory.
> 依儒者之言，則多不和。不和，則紙筆之樂，非管弦之樂。……吾主君以大儒而習優伶之技，遂洞徹樂理。[50]

On the opening folios of the third volume (Fig. 1.30), the following stamps can be found: "Kuai-xue zhai" 快雪齋 ("The Studio of Swiftly-Melting Snows"), "Qi Jin zhai" 奇晉齋 ("The Studio of Rare Jin Dynasty Calligraphy"), and "Chunyu lou" 春雨樓 ("The Spring Rain Cottage"). The first two refer to Lu Xuan's own repositories for his collection, and the third to Shen Cai's literary studio. Other than these references to the two creators of the manuscript, no other seals that belong to the period prior to the fall of the Qing dynasty are to be found on any of its volumes, which most likely means that it remained in the possession of Lu Xuan's descendants until that time. Once again, Liu Chenggan's diary is the source for information as to its subsequent whereabouts, and his entry for the eleventh day of the eighth lunar month of 1916 records a Shanghai book dealer Luo Zhenchang 羅振常 (1875–1942) selling the manuscript and three other books to him for a price of 487 silver dollars.[51]

Other than *Meanings in the Book of Documents* copied by Shen Cai, the only specimens of her handwritten manuscripts that survive are two

48. Shen Cai, *Chunyu lou ji*, in *Qingdai shi wen ji huibian*, vol. 379, 41–42; and Shen Cai, *Chunyu lou ji*, in *Jiangnan nüxing bieji san bian*, vol. 1, 79–80.

49. Shen Cai, *Chunyu lou ji*, in *Qingdai shi wen ji huibian*, vol. 379, 12, 14, 24, and 26; and Shen Cai, *Chunyu lou ji*, in *Jiangnan nüxing bieji san bian*, vol. 1, 23, 27, 47, and 52.

50. Ibid.

51. Liu Chenggan, *Jiaye tang cangshu rijichao*, 287–288; Liu Chenggan, *Qiushu zhai riji*, vol. 5, 19. See also Zhou Zimei 周子美, *Jiaye tang chaojiaoben mulu* 嘉業堂鈔校本目錄 (Shanghai: Huadong shifan daxue chubanshe, 1986), 2.

陸師字子章，一字椒谷，又號紫雲子，平湖人，隱居胥山，藏書極富，工詩畫，有椒谷集、

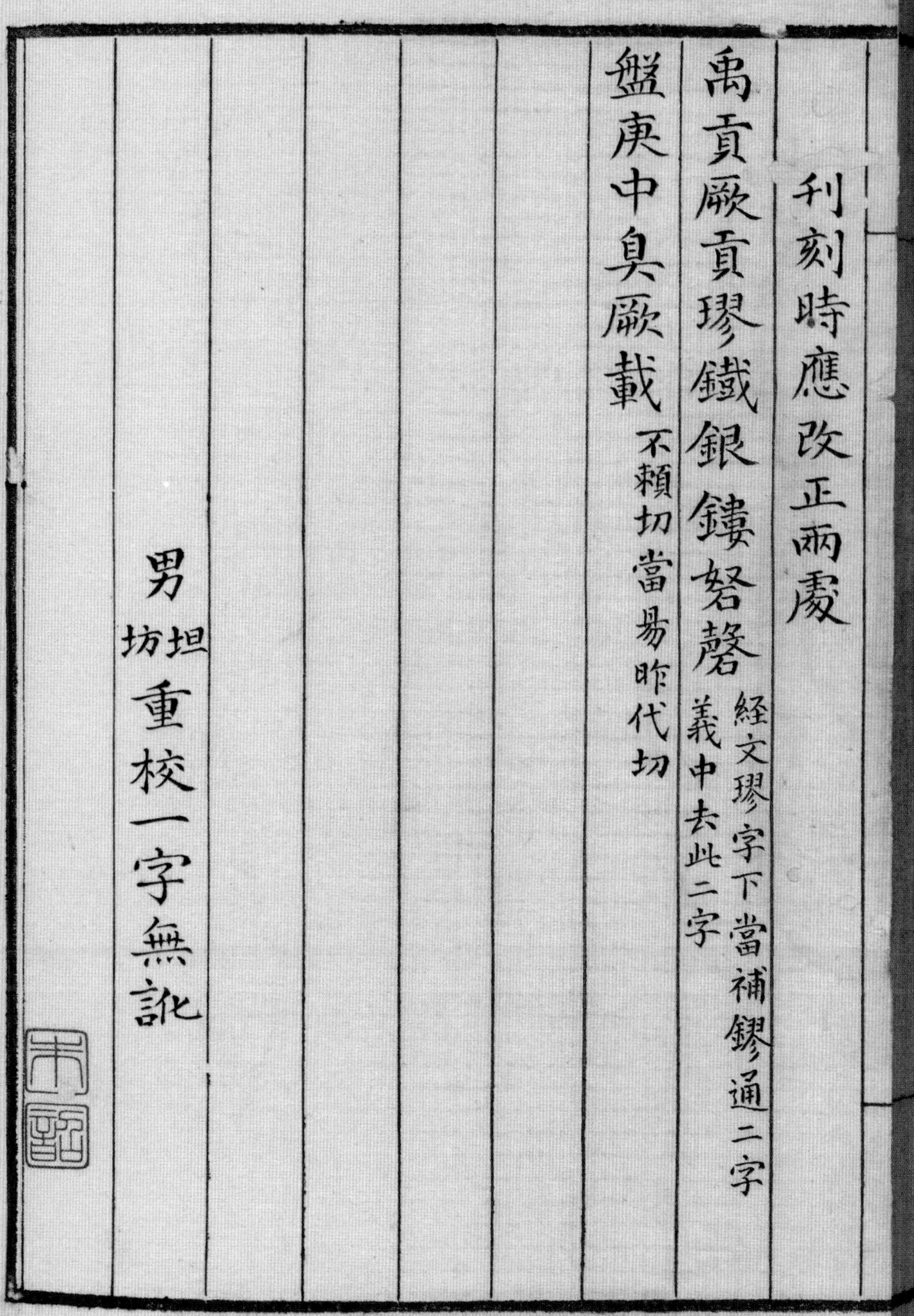

利刻時應改正兩處

禹貢厥貢璆鐵銀鏤砮磬 経文璆字下當補鏐通二字義中去此二字

盤庚中臭厥載 不賴切當易昨代切

男 坦 坊 重校一字無訛

Fig. 1.31 *Shang shu yi* (*Meanings in the Book of Documents*), a list of errata compiled by Lu Xuan's two sons, Lu Tan and Lu Fang, bound into the back of volume 12 (right), and modern collector Zhu Hongyi's handwritten colophon (left).
Author: Lu Xuan (1737–1799).
Scribe: Shen Cai (c. 1748–?).
Date: 1787.
Border: 17.1 × 12.2 cm.
Fung Ping Shan Library.

drafts of her opus *The Spring Rain Cottage Collection*, though these are much smaller in size and scope.[52] They too were sold by Luo Zhenchang, this time to the collector and literatus Zheng Zhenduo 鄭振鐸 (1898–1958) in the 1940s.[53] The latter died in an airplane crash in 1958, and both manuscripts then passed into the collection of the Peking Library where they reside to this day.

On the first page of the first *juan* of the first volume on the bottom right of the recto (Fig. 1.21, left; see also Fig. 1.30), two large square seals belonging to Liu Chenggan can be found. Above them in the extreme right-hand column are two smaller oblong seals: the top seal reads "Jiabin cang shu" 嘉賓藏書 ("Jiabin Ex Libris") and the bottom "Zhu Shao" 朱韶, which is a person's name. Both seals belong to the same individual Zhu Hongyi 朱鴻儀 (1902–1973), also known as Zhu Shao or Zhu Jiabin 朱嘉賓, a banker and book collector. In 1942, Liu Chenggan sold some of his Ming dynasty printed books to the Central Library of Republican China and the other portion of his library to Zhang Shuping 張叔平 (1898–1970). The latter then sold some of the most precious books to Zhu Hongyi. As the current owner, Zhu Hongyi affixed his seals, and on the back page of the twelfth volume also pasted in a piece of paper on which are written his collector's notes (Fig. 1.31, left). Zhang Shuping attempted to take advantage of the runaway inflation of the time, but the deal between him and Liu Chenggan quickly foundered. So, in order to squeeze the maximum profit from his nefarious enterprise, Zhang Shuping sought assistance from the Japanese occupying authorities.[54] Eventually in 1945, Liu Chenggan lost his remaining books to Zhang, and Zhu Hongyi was thrown into prison and forced to return the books he had purchased. This is how the book finally found its way back to Zhang Shuping, whose subsequent seal is found in the second column from the right on the first page of the first *juan* of the first volume, directly above those of Liu Chenggan, and to the left of Zhu Hongyi's (Fig. 1.21, left; see also Figs. 1.26 and 1.30). It was from Zhang Shuping that the manuscript then passed to the Fung Ping Shan Library.

So far, we have revisited the Confucianists' exploration of *The Book of Music* over the last two millennia. The narrative began with the second-century scholar Zheng Xuan's textual commentary, followed by a diagram created through the inductive reasoning of the Southern Song dynasty neo-Confucianist Yang Fu. In the early modern period, Zhu Zaiyu's marriage of canonical text with woodcut illustrations proved so persuasive that these pictures were re-used by the Jesuit Joseph-Marie Amiot in his publication in Paris in 1780 to introduce Confucian music and rites to eighteenth-century Europe. Contemporaneous with Amiot's seminal publication, in the lower Yangtze region, Shen Cai and Lu Xuan developed a pentachord to correlate the ancient Confucian musical nomenclature with later vernacular *sol-fa* terms. By then, discussion of the Confucian musical canon had developed from the original philological domain to experiments in musical laboratories. All of these proved that the first century BCE polymath and bibliographer of the imperial library Liu Xiang's 劉向 (77–6 BCE) observation on the loss of the canonical text of *The Book of Music* is correct: in Confucianism, the canon of music is entrancing. It is more than a definitive text, so its transmission and study can be both textual and aural.

52. For a facsimile edition of one of these two drafts, see Shen Cai 沈彩, *Chunyu lou gao* 春雨樓稾 (Shanghai: Tanyin lu, 1924).

53. Chen Fukang 陳福康, "Zheng Zhenduo *Qiushu riji* yigao 鄭振鐸《求書日錄》佚稿," *Wenxian* 文獻 (2005) 1: 175.

54. Liu Chenggan 劉承幹, "Renwu rangshu jishi 壬午讓書紀事," *Lishi wenxian* (di ba ji) 歷史文獻（第八輯）, ed. Shanghai tushuguan lishi wenxian yanjiusuo 上海圖書館歷史文獻研究所 (Shanghai: Shanghai guji chubanshe, 2004), 241–271; and Wu Ge 吳格, "Wuxing Liushi Jiaye tang cangshu jusan kaolue 吳興劉氏嘉業堂藏書聚散考略," *Shumu jikan* 書目季刊 37.4 (2004): 17–44.

樂書第二　史記二十四

正義曰天有日月星辰地有山陵河海歲有萬物成熟國有聖賢宮觀周域官僚人有言語衣服體貌端脩咸謂之樂樂書者猶樂記也鄭玄云以其記樂之義也按別録目屬樂記蓋十一篇合爲一篇十一篇者有樂本有樂論有樂施有樂言有樂禮有樂情有樂化有象法有賓牟有師乙有魏文侯今雖合之亦略有分焉劉向校書得書樂二十三篇著於別録今樂記雖有十一篇其名猶存也

太史公曰余每讀虞書至於君臣相敕維是幾安而股肱不良萬事墮壞未甞不流涕也成王作頌推己懲艾正義音刈悲彼家難正義曰乃憚反家難謂文王囚羑里武王伐紂可不謂戰戰恐懼善守善終正義曰言成王作頌悲文

Chapter 2

Historical Records of Court Music

Yang Yuanzheng

Though the early chapters of *The Book of Documents* deal with the legendary deeds of mythical emperors, this volume of the Six Classics continued to form an essential component of Confucian ideology. In the Spring and Autumn period (770–476 BCE), the seminal text *The Annals of the State of Lu* was recognized as having been edited by Confucius himself. These records provide a year-by-year account of historical events ranging from 722 to 481 BCE. Starting in the Han dynasty, successive official histories were later written (Fig. 2.1), often in subsequent dynasties as a tool for legitimizing the current political hegemony.

Rich descriptions of music are to be found in these texts, together with multi-layered interpretations. It is important to note there was much more at stake here than the mere recording of elaborate rituals. The coupling of musical performances at court with an analysis of the psychological role of music, along with an explanation of pitch relationships, were all equally crucial aspects of statecraft.

Three scholars in particular made early exegeses of *The Annals of the State of Lu*: Zuo Qiuming 左丘明 (556–452 BCE), Gongyang Gao 公羊高 (act. Warring States Period), and Guliang Chi 穀梁赤 (act. Warring States Period). Of these, *Zuo zhuan* 左傳 (*The Zuo Commentary*) pays most attention to musical features and is by far the superior work in this respect. Exegetical notes to *The Zuo Commentary* were written by Du Yu 杜預 (222–285) in the Jin dynasty, with a further layer of explanation added by Kong Yingda 孔穎達 (574–648) in the Tang dynasty. The latter's text is thus titled *Chunqiu Zuoshi zhuan zhushu* 春秋左氏傳注疏 (*Explanatory Material on Exegetical Notes to the Zuo Commentary on the Spring and Autumn Annals*). In the Tang dynasty, another scholar, Lu Deming 陸德明 (556–627), produced *Jingdian shiwen* 經典釋文 (*Textual Explanation of Classics and Canons*, c. 582–589), essentially a dictionary of the works it discusses. Later, in the Southern Song dynasty, both of these Tang dynasty traditions were brought together and combined in *Fu shiyin Chunqiu Zuo zhuan zhushu* 附釋音春秋左傳注疏 (*Supplementary Explanation and Pronunciation of Explanatory Material on Exegetical Notes to the Zuo Commentary on the Spring and Autumn Annals*). The Fung Ping Shan Library holds three versions of a Yuan dynasty imprint of this final book, whose worn woodblocks were supplemented at different stages of the Ming dynasty.[1]

Fig. 2.1: *Shi ji* (*Records of the Grand Historian*), *juan* 24, fol. 1r (detail). Author: Sima Qian (c. 145–c. 86 BCE). Date: 1194–1196. Woodblock: 19.9 × 12.6 cm. Kokuritsu Rekishi Minzoku Hakubutsukan (H-172).

One of these copies stands out not just for the finesse of its printing, but also because of the evidence it provides regarding the China-Japan book trade.[2] The first record of ownership appears in a large seal in the bottom right corner of the recto of the first page (Fig. 2.2), identifying it as the property of Mōri Takasue 毛利高標 (1755–1801), the eighth Edo period Lord of Saiki Han in Bungo province. A scholar-*daimyō* 大名, in 1781 he established the Saiki Bunko 佐伯文庫, a library comprising some 80,000 *juan* of books, within the grounds of Saiki castle, and this book, 60 *juan* in length, was one of those in the collection. In 1828, Mōri Takasue's grandson Mōri Takanaka 毛利高翰 (1795–1852) presented a significant percentage of the library, including this book, to *Shōgun* 將軍 Tokugawa Ienari 德川家齊 (1773–1841). Along with one third of Mōri's donation, the book then passed to the Shōhei-zaka Gakumonjo 昌平坂學問所, a state-run neo-Confucianist institution directly under the control of the Tokugawa Shogunate since 1797; the

1. Jao Tsung-i 饒宗頤, *Xianggang daxue Feng Pingshan tushuguan cang shanben shulu* 香港大學馮平山圖書館藏善本書錄 (Hong Kong: Longmen shudian, 1970), 6–9; and Jao Tsung-i 饒宗頤, Li Zhifang 李直方, and Zhang Lijuan 張麗娟, *Xianggang daxue Feng Pingshan tushuguan cang shanben shulu* 香港大學馮平山圖書館藏善本書錄, enlarged ed. (Hong Kong: Hong Kong University Press, 2003), 21–22.

2. For the Sino-Japanese book trade during the Tokugawa period, see Ōba Osamu 大庭脩, *Edo jidai ni okeru tōsen mochiwatarisho no kenkyū* 江戸時代における唐船持渡書の研究 (Suita: Kansai daigaku shuppanbu, 1967); and Ōba Osamu 大庭脩, ed., *Hakusai shomoku* 舶載書目 (Suita: Kansai daigaku tōzai gakujutsu kenkyūjo, 1972).

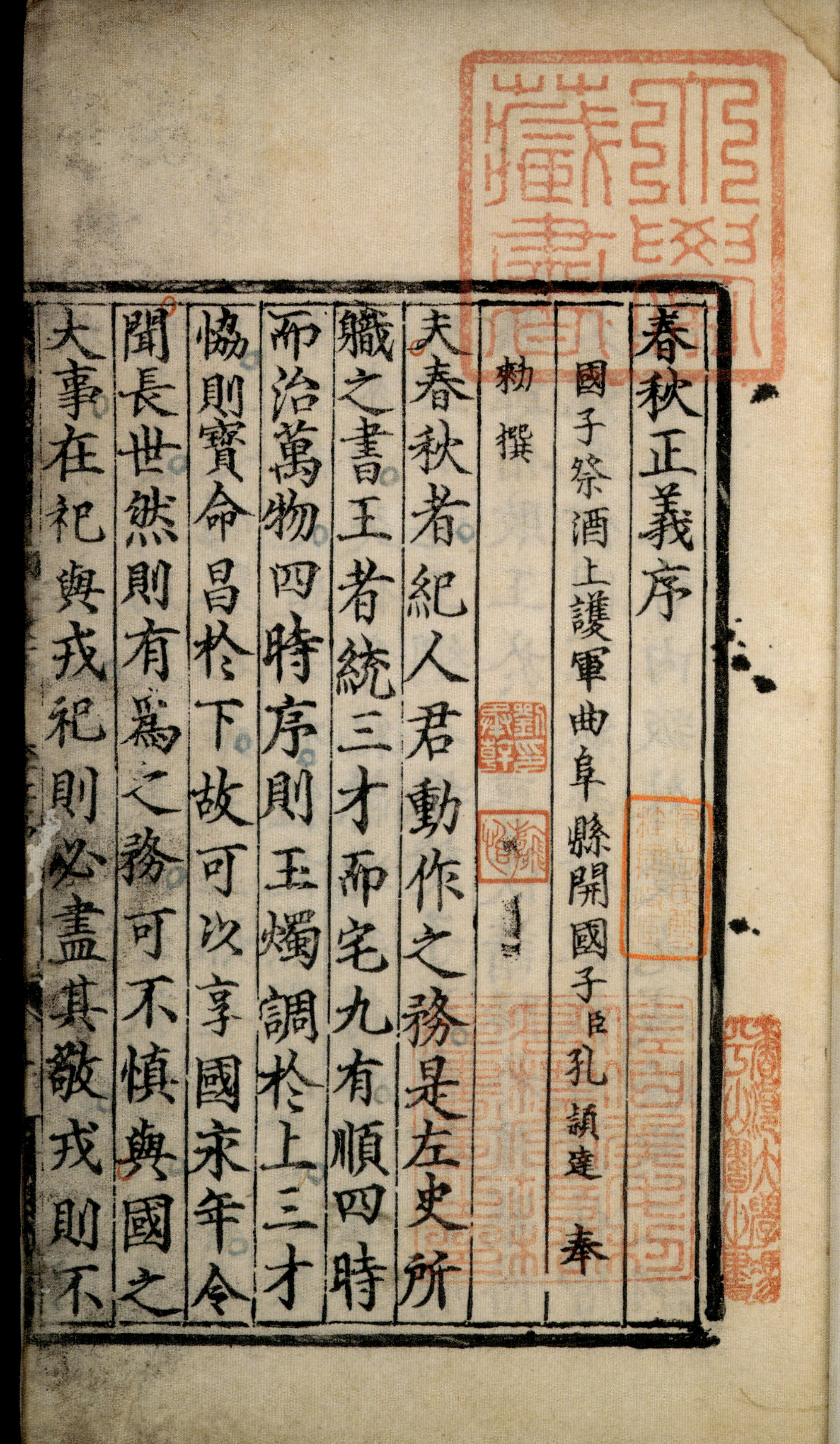
春秋正義序
國子祭酒上護軍曲阜縣開國子臣孔穎達奉
勑撰
夫春秋者紀人君動作之務是左史所
職之書王者統三才而宅九有順四時
而治萬物四時序則玉燭調於上三才
協則寶命昌於下故可以享國永年令
聞長世然則有爲之務可不慎與國之
大事在祀與戎祀則必盡其敬戎則不

Fig. 2.2: *Fu shiyin Chunqiu Zuo zhuan zhushu* (*Supplementary Explanation and Pronunciation of Explanatory Material on Exegetical Notes to the Zuo Commentary on the Spring and Autumn Annals*), preface, fol. 1r.
Annotator: Kong Yingda (574–648).
Date: c. 1323–1328.
Woodblock: 19.0 × 13.2 cm.
Fung Ping Shan Library.

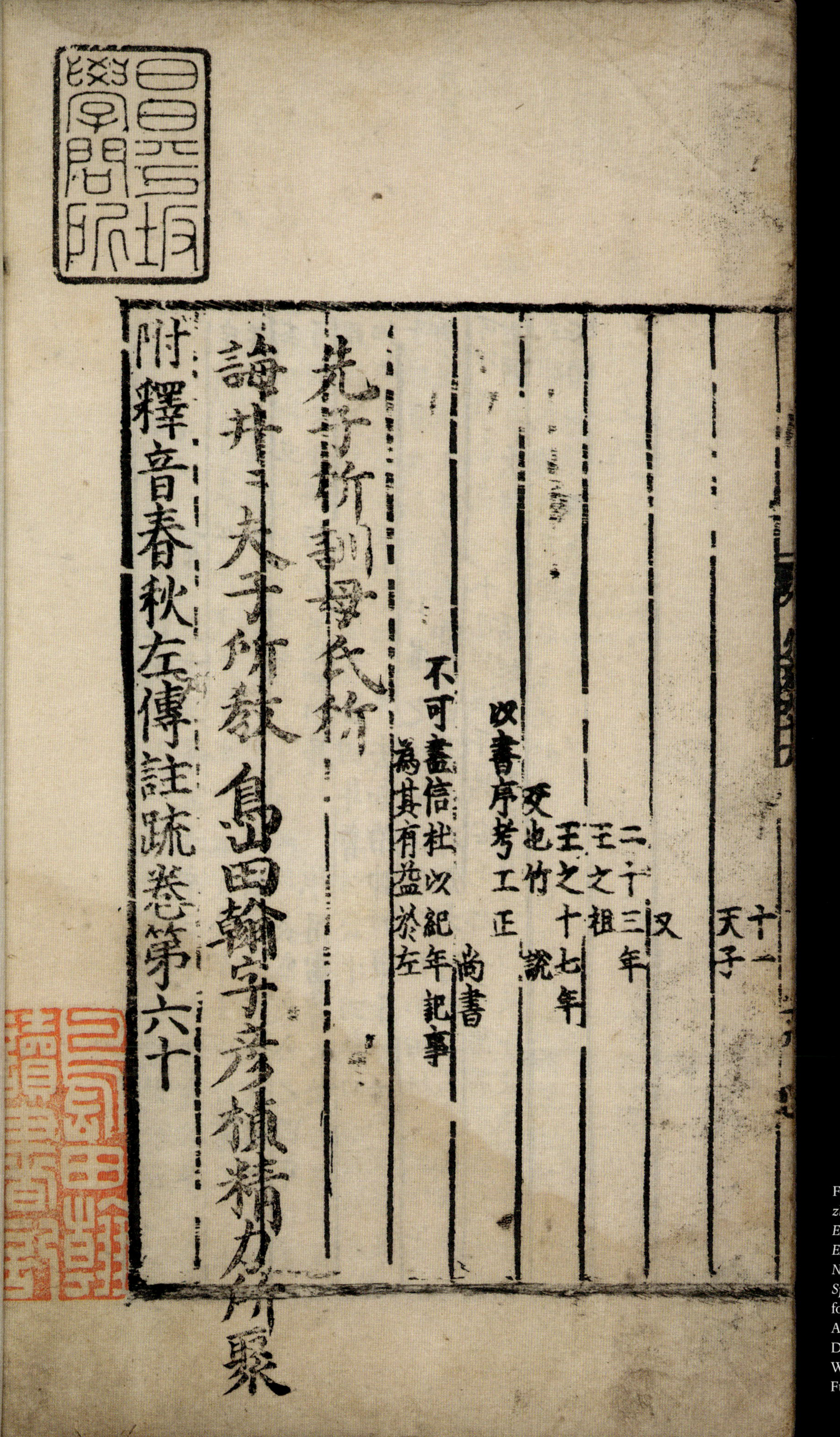

Fig. 2.3: *Fu shiyin Chunqiu Zuo zhuan zhushu (Supplementary Explanation and Pronunciation of Explanatory Material on Exegetical Notes to the Zuo Commentary on the Spring and Autumn Annals), juan 26*, fol. 29v.
Annotator: Kong Yingda (574–648).
Date: c. 1323–1328.
Woodblock: 19.0 × 13.2 cm.
Fung Ping Shan Library.

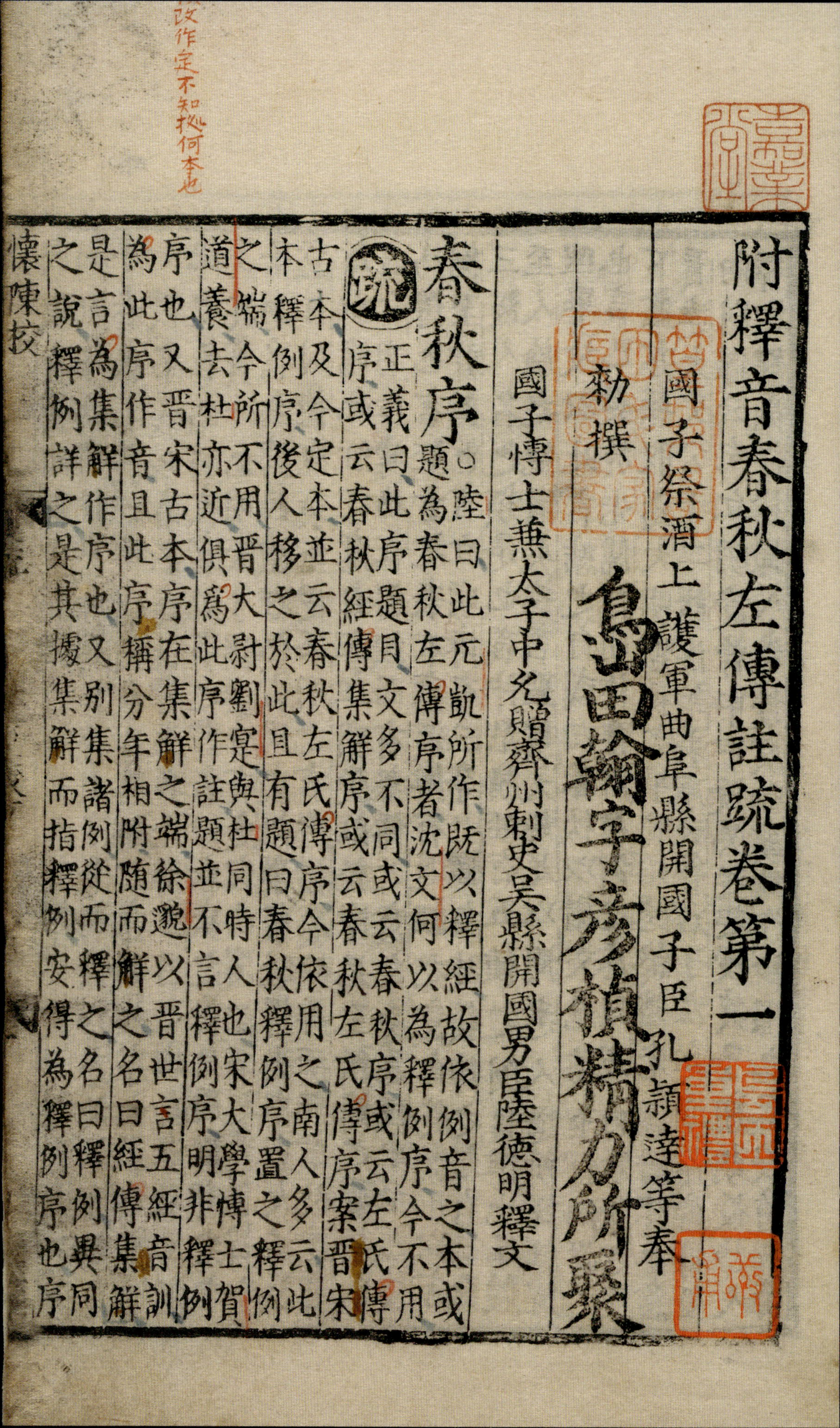

附釋音春秋左傳註疏卷第一

國子祭酒上護軍曲阜縣開國子臣孔穎達等奉勑撰

國子博士兼太子中允贈齊州刺史吳縣開國男臣陸德明釋文

春秋序 題。陸曰此元凱所作既以釋經故依例音之本或為春秋左傳序者沈文何以為釋例序今不用

疏 正義曰此序題目文多不同或云春秋序或云左氏傳序或云春秋經傳集解序或云春秋左氏傳序案晉宋古本及今定本並云春秋左氏傳序今依用之南人多云此本釋例序後人移之於此且有題曰春秋釋例序置之釋例之端今所不用晉大尉劉寔與杜同時人也宋大學博士賀道養去杜亦近俱爲此序作註題並不言釋例序明非釋例序也又晉宋古本序在集解之端徐邈以晉世言五經音訓為此序作音且此序稱分年相附隨而解之名曰經傳集解是言為集解作序也又別集諸例從而釋之名曰釋例異同之說釋例詳之是其據集解而指釋例安得為釋例序也序

Fig. 2.4: *Fu shiyin Chunqiu Zuo zhuan zhushu* (*Supplementary Explanation and Pronunciation of Explanatory Material on Exegetical Notes to the Zuo Commentary on the Spring and Autumn Annals*), *juan* 1, fol. 1r (detail).
Annotator: Kong Yingda (574–648).
Date: c. 1323–1328.
Woodblock: 19.0 × 13.2 cm.
Fung Ping Shan Library.

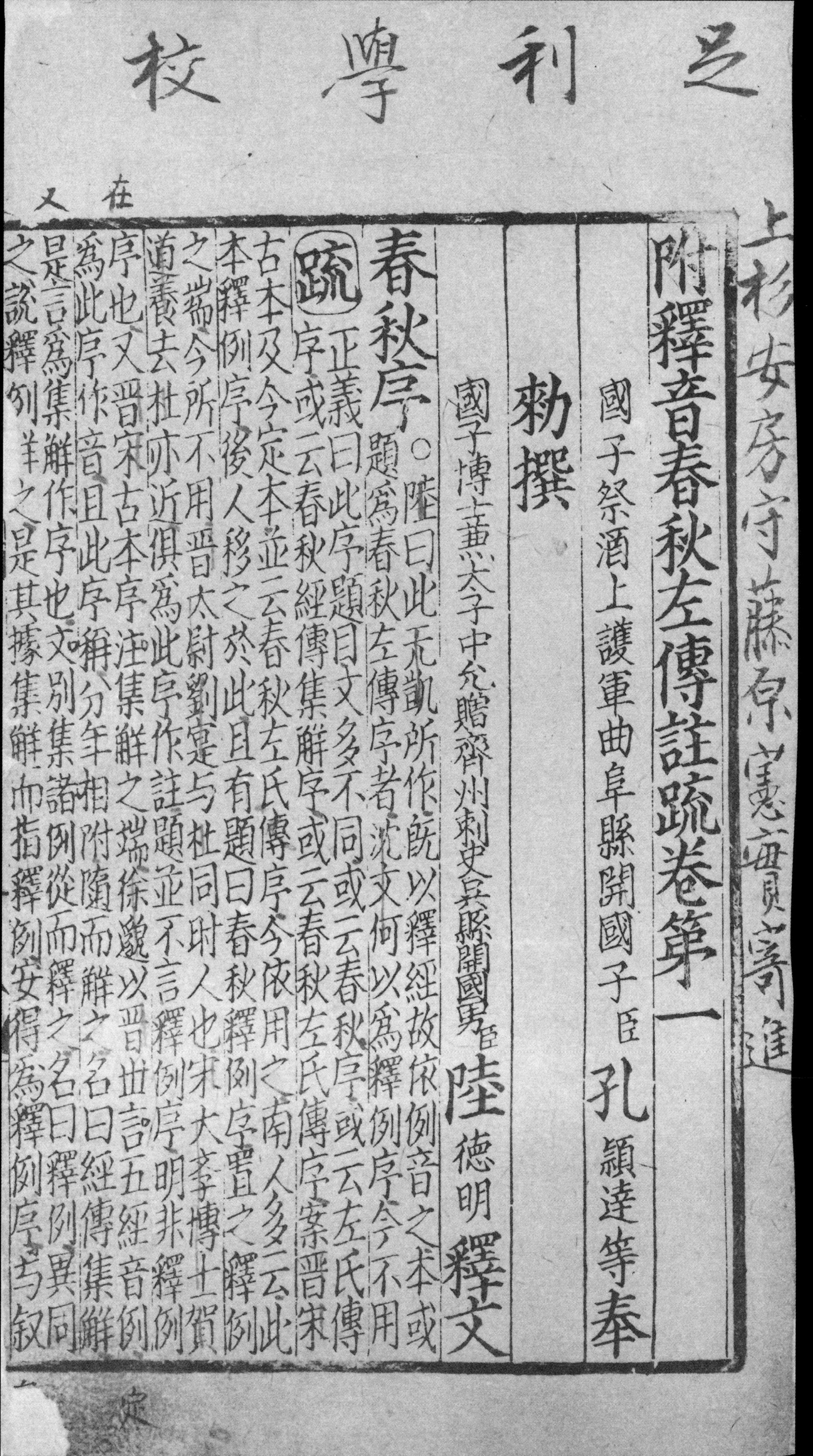

足利學校

上杉安房守藤原憲實寄進

附釋音春秋左傳註疏卷第一

國子祭酒上護軍曲阜縣開國子臣孔穎達等奉

勑撰

國子博士兼太子中允贈齊州刺史吳縣開國男臣陸德明釋文

春秋序 ○陸曰此元凱所作既以釋經故依例音之本或題爲春秋左傳序者沈文何以爲釋例序今不用

【疏】正義曰此序題目文多不同或云春秋序或云左氏傳序或云春秋經傳集解序或云春秋左氏傳序案晉宋古本及今定本並云春秋左氏傳序今依用之南人多云此本釋例序後人移之於此且有題曰春秋釋例序置之釋例之端今所不用晉太尉劉寔与杜同時人也宋大學博士賀道養去杜亦近俱爲此序作註題並不言釋例序明非釋例序也又晉宋古本序注集解之端徐邈以晉世言五經音例爲此序作音且此序稱分年相附隨而解之名曰經傳集解是言爲集解作序也又別集諸例從而釋之名曰釋例異同之說釋例詳之是其據集解而指釋例安得爲釋例序与叙

Fig. 2.5: *Fu shiyin Chunqiu Zuo zhuan zhushu (Supplementary Explanation and Pronunciation of Explanatory Material on Exegetical Notes to the Zuo Commentary on the Spring and Autumn Annals), juan* 1, fol. 1r.
Annotator: Kong Yingda (574–648).
Date: c. 1127–1279.
Woodblock: 6.3 × 4.05 inches.
Ashikaga Gakkō.
After Nagasawa Kikuya, ed., *Ashikaga Gakkō zenpon zuroku* (Ashikaga: Ashika Gagakkō Iseki Toshokan Kōenkai, 1973), pl. 39.

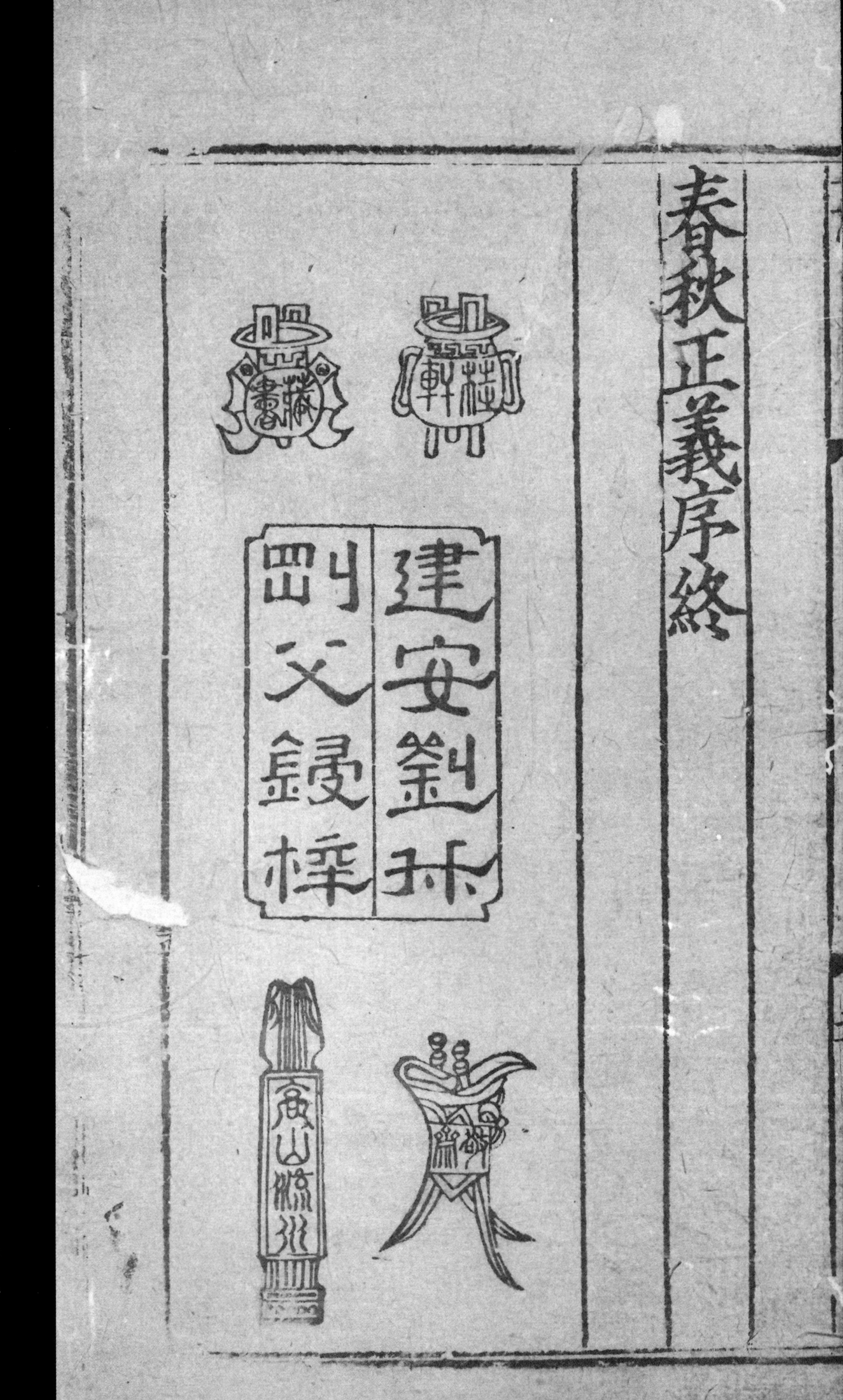

Fig. 2.6: *Fu shiyin Chunqiu Zuo zhuan zhushu (Supplementary Explanation and Pronunciation of Explanatory Material on Exegetical Notes to the Zuo Commentary on the Spring and Autumn Annals)*, preface, fol. 5v, publisher's note.
Annotator: Kong Yingda (574–648).
Date: c. 1127–1279.
Woodblock: 6.3 × 4.05 inches.
Ashikaga Gakkō.
After Nagasawa Kikuya, ed., *Ashikaga Gakkō zenpon zuroku* (Ashikaga: Ashika Gagakkō Iseki Toshokan Kōenkai, 1973), pl. 40.

relevant black institutional seal can be found at the top left of the back page of the last volume (Fig. 2.3). On the top right of the front page is a red seal of ownership of the same institution. On the Meiji restoration of 1871, the Shōhei-zaka Gakumonjo was closed, and the book came into the ownership of Shimada Shigenori 島田重禮 (1838–1898, also called Kōson 篁村), a professor of literature at Tokyo Imperial University; his seal is found on the far right column of the first page (Fig. 2.2), directly above the large seal of Mōri Takasue. Shimada Shigenori's repository was known as the "Double Osmanthus Studio" 雙桂樓.

Upon Shimada Shigenori's death, his third son Shimada Kan 島田翰 (1879–1915) inherited the book.[3] Shimada Kan is most remembered for his partnership with Yanosuke Iwasaki 岩崎彌之助 (1851–1908) in procuring the book collection of the scholar-official Lu Xinyuan 陸心源 (1838–1894) in 1907, including more than two hundred Song and Yuan dynasty rare editions that now form the basis of the Seikadō Bunko 靜嘉堂文庫.[4] The first page of the book was by this time already filled with seals, so Shimada Kan's seals can be found on the opening page of the first *juan* (Fig. 2.4) as well as the book's last page (Fig. 2.3). Both are unusual in that they are printed in black and not surrounded by a border. The seal on the opening page is situated in the third column and reads: "Shimada Kan, *zi* soubriquet Sadahiko, exerts his purest effort in concentration" 島田翰字彥楨精力所聚; the same seal can also be found in the bottom half of the ninth column of the last page, above which, spanning the seventh to ninth columns, is another expressing filial piety: "On the instructions of my late father, from the lessons of my mother, and through the teaching of Master Seisei" 先子所訓母氏所誨井井夫子所教. "Master Seisei" refers here to the Japanese diplomat and sinologist Takezoe Shinichiro 竹添進一郎 (1842–1917).[5] All of these seals were imprinted in black as a sign of respect for his recently deceased father. The period of mourning over, in the bottom left corner of the same page, his more customary seal of ownership is stamped in red. Accused and convicted of theft and the illicit sale of national art treasures, he was thrown into prison where he committed suicide in 1915. The next record of ownership comes from Ye Changchi 葉昌熾 (1849–1917), who notes in his diary, dated the twenty-sixth day of the eighth lunar month of 1916, that Liu Chenggan 劉承幹 (1881–1963) bought the book soon afterwards.[6] Significantly, not only Ye Changchi, but also Miao Quansun 繆荃孫 (1844–1919), Wu Changshou 吳昌綬 (1867–1924), and Dong Kang 董康(1867–1947), that is, all the specialists that Liu had consulted,[7] regarded the book as a genuine Song dynasty imprint, when in fact only two copies of the Southern Song Imperial College edition survive: one is now kept at Ashikaga Gakkō 足立學校 (Figs. 2.5 and 2.6),[8] while volumes of the other are split between the Peking Library and the National Palace Museum in Taipei.

In the thirty-ninth *juan*, the text discusses Lu Xianggong 魯襄公 (Duke Xiang of Lu, 575–542 BCE, r. 572–542 BCE), and the annals for the twenty-ninth year of his reign (544 BCE) contain a crucial description of music (Fig. 2.7). The backbone of this account is what appears to be a complete musical performance of the 305 poems in *The Book of Odes*, category by category, starting with the various regions represented in the "Guo Feng" 國風 ("Poetical Styles of the Different States") section that comprises the first 160 poems of the sequence, followed by the "Xiao Ya" 小雅 ("Lesser Songs of the Court"), then the "Da Ya" 大雅 ("Greater Songs of the Court"), and finally the concluding "Song" 頌 ("Praise-Songs"):

> In the twenty-ninth year of the reign of Duke Xiang . . . the ruler of the state of Wu's son [Ji] Zha [576–484 BCE] went on a diplomatic mission to the state of Lu and requested to view the music of the Zhou court.
>
> 襄公二十九年……吳公子札來聘，請觀於周樂。

3. For his principal contribution to historical bibliography, see Shimada Kan 島田翰, *Kobun kyūsho kō; tsuketari Kokon shokoku* 古文舊書考; 附古今書刻 (Tokyo: Min'yūsha, 1905).

4. For a list of these rare books, see Kawada Higuma 河田羆, *Seikadō hisekishi* 靜嘉堂祕籍志 (Tokyo: Seikadō, 1917–1919).

5. Takezoe was himself a classical sinologist and specialist in the study of *Zuo zhuan*, see Takezoe Kōkō 竹添光鴻, *Sa shi kaisen* 左氏會箋 (Tokyo: Fuzanbō, 1911).

6. Wang Jilie 王季烈, ed., *Ye Changchi Yuandu lu rijichao* 葉昌熾緣督廬日記鈔 (Shanghai: Yinyin lu, 1933), *juan* 16, fol. 33r; Ye Changchi 葉昌熾, *Yuandu lu riji* 緣督廬日記 (Taipei: Taiwan xuesheng shuju, 1964), 576.

7. Miao Quansun 繆荃孫, Wu Changshou 吳昌綬, and Dong Kang 董康, *Jiaye tang cangshu zhi* 嘉業堂藏書志 (Shanghai: Fudan daxue chubanshe, 1997), 153–154; Liu Chenggan 劉承幹, *Wuxing Liushi Jiaye tang shanben shuying* 吳興劉氏嘉業堂善本書景 (Shanghai: Jiaye tang, 1929), vol. 1, fols. 6r–7v.

8. Nagasawa Kikuya 長澤規矩也, ed., *Ashikaga Gakkō zenpon zuroku* 足利學校善本圖錄 (Ashikaga: Ashika Gagakkō Iseki Toshokan Kōenkai, 1973), 2.

疏注魯以至禮樂○正義曰明堂位云成王以周公爲有勳勞於天下是以封周公於曲阜命魯公世世祀周公以天子之禮樂又曰凡四代之服器官魯兼用之是魯以周公故有天子之禮樂也

使工爲之歌

周南召南

此皆各依其本國歌所常用聲曲○召上照反本或作邵

疏歌周南召南正義曰歌周南召南之詩而以樂音爲之節也周南召南皆文王之詩也周召者岐山之陽地名周之先公曰大王者自豳始遷焉而脩德建王業大王生王季王季生文王於時雍梁荊豫徐揚之民皆歸文王文王三分天下有其二以服事殷文王改都於豐乃分岐邦周召之地賜周公旦召公奭以爲采邑使此二公施政於已所職之國爲文王行先公賢化與已聖化使二公雜而施行之但南土感化有深有淺其作詩也或感聖化或感賢化及武王伐紂定天下巡守述職陳諸國之詩以觀民風俗其六州所作詩其得聖人之化者謂之周南其得仁賢之化者謂之召南其實皆是文王之化而分繫周召二公耳必分繫者文王以諸侯之身行王者之化詩人述其本志爲作聖賢之風此詩體實是風不可以雅名之文王身有王號不可以風繫之多無所繫詩不可棄因二公爲王行化是故繫之二公周公聖以聖化繫之召公賢以賢化

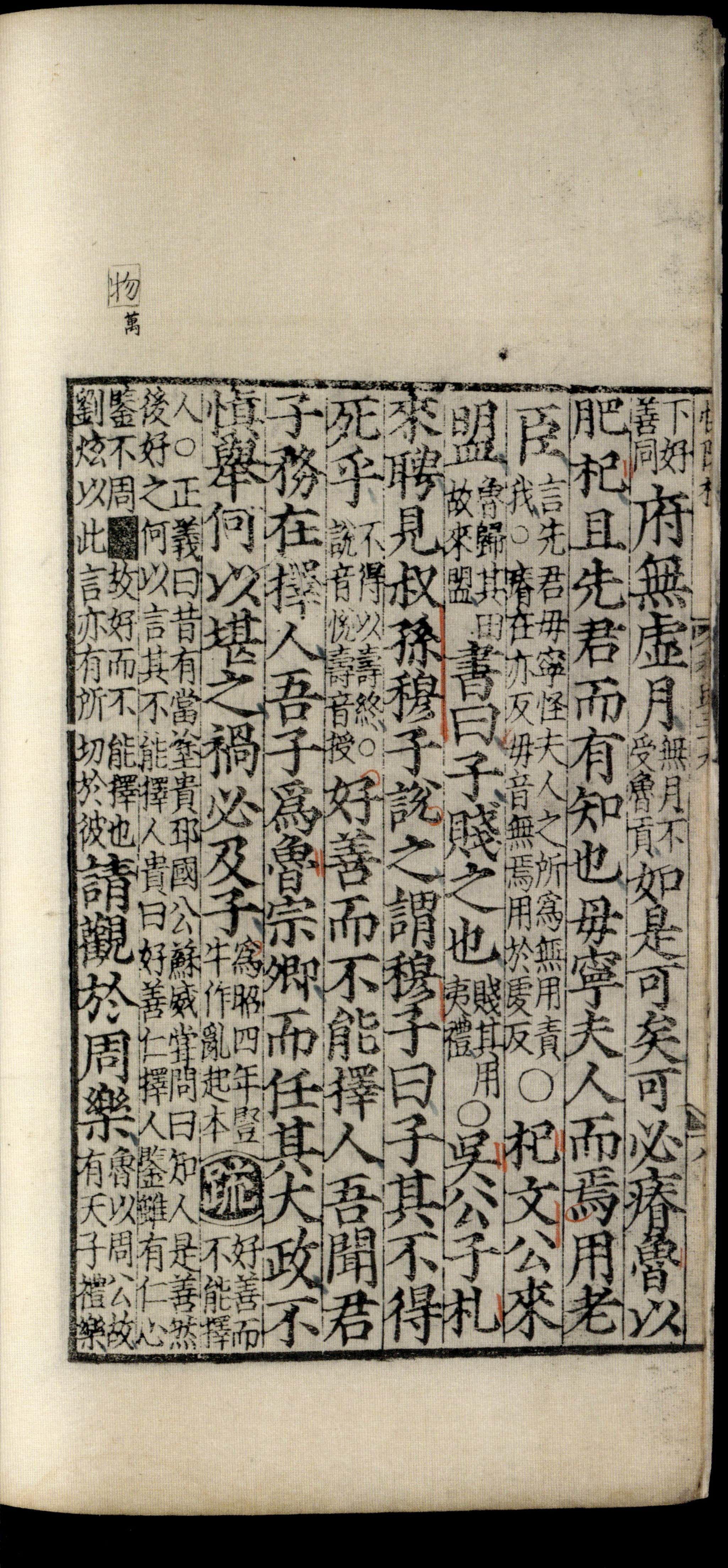

物
萬

下好善同府無虛月無月不受魯貢如是可矣可必瘠魯以
肥杞且先君而有知也毋寧夫人而焉用老
臣言先君毋寧怪夫人之所為無用責我○瘠在亦反毋音無焉用於虔反○杞文公來
盟魯歸其田故來盟書曰子賤之也賤其用夷禮○吳公子札
來聘見叔孫穆子說之謂穆子曰子其不得
死乎不得以壽終○說音悅壽音授好善而不能擇人吾聞君
子務在擇人吾子為魯宗卿而任其大政不
慎舉何以堪之禍必及子為昭四年豎牛作亂起本【疏】好善而不能擇
人○正義曰昔有當塗貴邳國公蘇威嘗問曰知人是善然後好之何以言其不能擇人貴曰好善仁擇人鑒雖有仁心
鑒不周■故好而不能擇也劉炫以此言亦有所切於彼請觀於周樂魯以周公故有天子禮樂

Fig. 2.7: *Fu shiyin Chunqiu Zuo zhuan zhushu (Supplementary Explanation and Pronunciation of Explanatory Material on Exegetical Notes to the Zuo Commentary on the Spring and Autumn Annals), juan 39, fols. 8v–9r.*
Annotator: Kong Yingda (574–648).
Date: c. 1323–1328.
Woodblock: 19.0 × 13.2 cm.
Fung Ping Shan Library.

The ruler of the state of Lu had the musicians sing "The Music of the State of Zhou's Southern Region" and "The Music of the State of Zhao's Southern Region." Ji Zha exclaimed: "Truly wonderful! The beginnings of a foundation have been laid, even if all is not yet perfect and complete, and besides, the common people are both assiduous and accommodating."

使工為之歌〈周南〉〈召南〉。曰：「美哉！始基之矣。猶未也，然勤而不怨矣。」

And he had them sing "The Poetical Style of the State of Bei," "The Poetical Style of the State of Yong," and "The Poetical Style of the State of Wei." Ji Zha exclaimed: "Truly wonderful! Such profundity! Tragic yet not embittered. I have heard that the founder of the state of Wei, Kangshu [act. 1042 BCE], and the eleventh ruler of the state, Duke Wu [852–758 BCE], personify virtuous morality of a like manner. Is this not the essence of 'The Poetical Style of the State of Wei'?"

為之歌〈邶〉〈鄘〉〈衛〉。曰：「美哉！淵乎！憂而不困者也。吾聞衛康叔、武公之德如是，是其〈衛風〉乎？」

And he had them sing "The Royal Demesne's Poetical Style." Ji Zha exclaimed: "Truly wonderful! Thoughtful yet not fearful. This must certainly be music subsequent to the migration eastwards of the Zhou royal house?"

為之歌〈王〉。曰：「美哉！思而不懼。其周之東乎？」

And he had them sing "The Poetical Style of the State of Zheng." Ji Zha exclaimed: "Truly wonderful! Yet they are so finely-wrought as to be too complex, and the common people would have been unable to absorb them. Is this why Zheng was the first state to collapse?"

為之歌〈鄭〉。曰：「美哉！其細已甚，民弗堪也。是其先亡乎？」

And he had them sing "The Poetical Style of the State of Qi." Ji Zha exclaimed: "Truly wonderful! Resoundingly magnificent, the resplendent style of a powerful state! Surely a model state of the eastern seaboard, is this not where the Great Duke [Taigong, c. 1128–c. 1015 BCE], the founder of the state of Qi, was lord? The meteoric rise of the state's future fortune is immeasurable."

為之歌〈齊〉。曰：「美哉！泱泱乎大風也哉！表東海者，其太公乎？國未可量也。」

And he had them sing "The Poetical Style of the State of Bin." Ji Zha exclaimed: "Truly wonderful! Generously moving! Joyful yet not extravagant. Surely this is the music of Duke Zhou's exodus to the east?"

為之歌〈豳〉。曰：「美哉！蕩乎！樂而不淫。其周公之東乎！」

And he had them sing "The Poetical Style of the State of Qin." Ji Zha exclaimed: "Truly wonderful! This is known as the voice of the Xia dynasty. And to be so named, like the Xia dynasty, it is also a manifestation of greatness, and the greatness of the Xia dynasty is greatness to the utmost. Is this not the music of the Zhou royal house's ancient homeland?"

為之歌〈秦〉。曰：「此之謂夏聲。夫能夏則大，大之至也。其周之舊乎？」

And he had them sing "The Poetical Style of the State of Wei." Ji Zha exclaimed: "Truly wonderful! Melodic and mellifluous! Both grand and tender, and also impetuous and flowing in meter. Through the assistance of virtuous morality an enlightened sovereign can truly be molded!"

為之歌〈魏〉。曰：「美哉！渢渢乎！大而婉，險而易行。以德輔此，則明主也！」

And he had them sing "The Poetical Style of the State of Tang." Ji Zha exclaimed: "Deeply pensive! Surely the music of a remnant people of the Tao Tang clan [to which the ancient mystical Emperor Yao belonged]! Otherwise, how could the music be so imbued with distant soulfulness? Other than descendants of an ancestor of virtuous morality, who else could this be?"

為之歌〈唐〉。曰：「思深哉！其有陶唐氏之遺民乎！不然，何憂之遠也？非令德之後，誰能若是？」

And he had them sing "The Poetical Style of the State of Chen." Ji Zha said: "This state had no virtuous ruler, so how could it survive?"

為之歌〈陳〉。曰：「國無主，其能久乎？」

From "The Poetical Style of the State of Kuai" onwards, Ji Zha ceased to pass judgment.

自〈鄶〉以下無譏焉。

The Confucian connection between successful music and successful statehood is made explicit in these passages. Those regions or states whose music Ji Zha praises (Southern Zhou, Southern Zhao, Yong, Wei, Wang, Qi, Bin, Qin, Wei, and Tang) were powerful and vibrant contributors to the Zhou tribe's aspirations for ascendancy, and important satellites during their subsequent dynastic rule. Those whose music he regards as degenerate (Zheng and Chen) were ancient China's "failed states." Kuai and Cao 曹 come so low in his estimation that neither their music nor their political ineptitude was worth reviewing. For the Confucianists, proper musical practice was evidently inseparable from virtuous governance.

The "Lesser" and "Greater Songs of the Court" tend to be longer, more courtly, and less vernacular in style, and comprise respectively poems 161–234 and 235–265 of *The Book of Odes*:

> And he had them sing the poems in "The Lesser Songs of the Court." Ji Zha exclaimed: "Truly wonderful! Brooding yet not divergent. Making complaint yet silent. Does this music not embody the demise of the Zhou dynasty? It is as if the music is from a remnant people of the founding dynastic rulers."
>
> 為之歌〈小雅〉。曰：「美哉！思而不貳，怨而不言，其周德之衰乎？猶有先王之遺民焉！」

> And he had them sing "The Greater Songs of the Court." Ji Zha exclaimed: "Truly magnificent! Boldly beautiful! Their winding melodies remain skeletally stern. This is the virtuous morality of the Zhou dynasty founder King Wen [1112–1050 BCE, r. 1100–1050 BCE]."
>
> 為之歌〈大雅〉。曰：「廣哉！熙熙乎！曲而有直體，其文王之德乎！」

Scholarship has generally regarded the "Praise-Songs" at the end of *The Book of Odes* as the oldest stratum of the compilation, and they often contain descriptions of sacrificial ceremonies. The "Praise-Songs" comprise three subsections, Zhou (poems 266–296), Shang (poems 297–300), and Lu (poems 301–305); that is, the Zhou and Shang dynasties and the state of Lu. Although the lion's share of these songs belongs to the Zhou category, the deposed Shang dynasty and subordinate state of Lu are still recognized; thus, it is the Confucian notion of upholding statehood that is at the heart of their meaning, rather than loyalty to any specific political entity:

> And he had them sing the "Praise-Songs." Ji Zha exclaimed: "Utter perfection! Strict yet not arrogant; obedient yet not submissive; intimate yet not threatening; distant yet not disowned; decorated yet not excessive; strophic yet not irksome; sorrowful yet not anxious; joyful yet not degenerate; re-worked yet not exhausted; grand yet not grandiloquent; deployed yet not marred; sought yet not greedy; static yet not staid; flowing yet not flooded. Their five voices harmonious, their eight sounds stylistic, their rhythm metric, and their performance orderly: identical to the epitome of virtuous morality."
>
> 為之歌《頌》。曰：「至矣哉！直而不倨，曲而不屈。邇而不偪，遠而不攜。遷而不淫，復而不厭。哀而不愁，樂而不荒。用而不匱，廣而不宣。施而不費，取而不貪。處而不底，行而不流。五聲和，八風平。節有度，守有序。盛德之所同也！」

At this point, the performance of *The Book of Odes* reached its conclusion and the dances began. All of these have an explicit connection with various generations of imperial control, and as such are at the heart of the Confucianists' espousal of dynastic orthodoxy:

> On seeing the dances *Xiang Shuo* and *Nan Yue*, Ji Zha exclaimed: "Truly wonderful! Though there are flaws."
>
> 見舞《象箾》《南籥》者。曰：「美哉！猶有憾！」

> On seeing the dance *Da Wu*, Ji Zha exclaimed: "Truly wonderful! The Zhou dynasty's prosperity was probably of a like kind."
>
> 見舞《大武》者。曰：「美哉！周之盛也，其若此乎！」

> On seeing the dance *Shao Huo*, Ji Zha exclaimed: "This has the mightiness of the great sage, yet it is as if there are deficiencies in its virtuous morality that would render the great sage ashamed."
>
> 見舞《韶濩》者。曰：「聖人之弘也，而猶有慚德！聖人之難也。」

> On seeing the dance *Da Xia*, Ji Zha exclaimed: "Truly wonderful! Assiduous yet unassuming; other than the Xia dynasty founding emperor Yu, who else could have fashioned this?"
>
> 見舞《大夏》者。曰：「美哉！勤而不德，非禹其誰能修之！」

樂書第二　史記卷之二十四

正義曰天有日月星辰地有山陵河海歲有萬物成孰國有聖賢宮觀周域官僚人有言語衣服體貌端脩咸謂之樂樂書者猶樂記也鄭玄云以其記樂之義也按別録目屬樂記蓋十一篇合爲一篇十一篇者有樂本有樂論有樂施有樂言有樂禮有樂情有樂化有象法有賓牟有師乙有魏文侯今雖合之亦略有分焉劉向校書得書樂二十二篇著於別録今樂記雖有十一篇其名猶存也

太史公曰余每讀虞書至於君臣相勑維是幾安而股肱不良萬事墮壞未嘗不流涕也成王作頌推己懲艾（正義音刈）悲彼家難（正義曰乃憚反家難謂文王因羑里）（武王伐紂）可不謂戰戰恐懼善守善終（正義曰言成王作頌悲文）

Fig. 2.8: *Shi ji* (*Records of the Grand Historian*), *juan* 24, fol. 1r.
Author: Sima Qian (c. 145–c. 86 BCE).
Date: 1525.
Woodblock: 20.1 × 12.8 cm.
Fung Ping Shan Library.

> On seeing the dance *Shao Xiao*, Ji Zha exclaimed: "The epitome of virtuous morality! Greatness! Like the sky, there is nothing it does not cover; like the earth, there is nothing it does not support. Even though the epitome of virtuous morality, there is none superior to this, and once seen, nothing more is required. If there were other music, I would not dare to request the opportunity to appreciate it."
>
> 見舞《韶箾》者。曰：「德至矣哉！大矣，如天之無不幬也，如地之無不載也！雖甚盛德，其蔑以加於此矣，觀止矣！若有他樂，吾不敢請已。」

Xiang Shuo is a masculine military dance, while *Nan Yue*, by contrast, is a civilian dance, and both were performed in praise of King Wen of Zhou. *Da Wu* is an adulation of King Wu of Zhou (?–1043 BCE, r. 1046–1043 BCE), while *Shao Huo* praises Cheng Tang 成湯 (c. 1675–1646 BCE), the founder of the Shang dynasty; *Da Xia* is directed at Yu, the founder of the Xia dynasty, and *Shao Xiao* aimed at the ancient Emperor Shun. Thus, the complete cycle represents a journey back in time marking out the key historical milestones exactly as the Confucianists understood them.

With the establishment of the Han dynasty and Confucianism as the official ideology, music came to occupy an important place in the histories of successive dynasties. In the oldest of these, Sima Qian's 司馬遷 (c. 145–c. 86 BCE) *Shi ji* 史記 (*Records of the Grand Historian*, completed in 91 BCE), are two books on the subject: "Yue shu" 樂書 ("Monograph on Music") and "Lü shu" 律書 ("Monograph on Pitch Standards"). According to Martin Kern's research, the "Monograph on Music" is in fact a product of the late Western or early Eastern Han dynasty, several decades after *Records of the Grand Historian* was completed.[9] As Sima Qian's "Monograph on Music" is largely identical to "Yue ji" 樂記 ("Records of Music") in *The Book of Rites*, the latter may also be no earlier than the same date range.

The Fung Ping Shan Library copy of *Records of the Grand Historian* was published in Beijing in 1525 by Wang Liang 汪諒 in his own publishing house (Fig. 2.8).[10] Of the Ming dynasty editions of *Records of the Grand Historian*, this imprint is regarded as being of extremely high quality because it is a "woodblock facsimile" of a Qingyuan 慶元 era (1195–1200) original first printed by Huang Shanfu 黃善夫 in Jianyang in Fujian province (Fig. 2.1). Creating "woodblock facsimiles" was Wang Liang's forte, and another of his masterpieces re-works the *qin* anthology *Shenqi mipu* 神奇秘譜 (*Mysterious and Secret Scores*) first issued in 1425, which is the first printed collection of compositions for the instrument. A hallmark of his publications is the inclusion of a page that advertises other volumes that he had printed; for example, in his edition of *Wenxuan zhu* 文選注 (*Commentary on the Selections of Refined Literature*) published in 1523, immediately after the contents page is just such an advertisement (Fig. 2.9).

In the first three columns on the right is the name of the shop and the proprietor, its address, and a statement of the bookselling part of the business:

> The current premises of Wang Liang, owner of the Golden Terrace Bookshop, are located inside the Zhengyang Gate, opposite the first watchtower to the west. Herewith on the left is presented a list of all our re-cut historic books. The old and new books kept in our shop cannot all be listed here, and customers are invited to browse our stock in person.
>
> 金臺書鋪汪諒見居正陽門內西第一巡警更鋪對門。今將所刻古書目錄列于左。及家藏今古書籍不能悉載，願市者覽焉。

The next eight columns list fourteen books. The seven on the top row are all re-cuts of Song and Yuan dynasty editions 俱宋元板, the first of which is *Records of the Grand Historian*; the seven on the bottom row are all re-cuts of earlier Ming dynasty editions 俱古板, of which the fourth is a *qin* treatise *Taigu yiyin* 太古遺音 (*Resonating Fragments of the Music of Extreme Antiquity*) and the fifth *Quxian Shenqi mipu* 臞仙神奇秘譜 (*The Emaciated Immortal's Mysterious and Secret Scores*) a volume of *qin* scores that will be encountered in Chapter 4.

The characters in the extreme left column in large type represent the "copyright page" of the book itself:

9. Martin Kern, "A Note on the Authenticity and Ideology of *Shih-Chi* 24, 'The Book on Music'," *Journal of the American Oriental Society* 119.4 (1999): 673–677.

10. Jao Tsung-i, Li Zhifang, and Zhang Lijuan, *Xianggang daxue Feng Pingshan tushuguan cang shanben shulu*, enlarged ed., 47–48.

文選卷第一

梁昭明太子選

唐文林郎守太子右内率府録事參軍事崇賢館直學士臣李善注上

奉政大夫同知池州路總管府事張伯顔　助率重刊

賦甲　賦甲者舊題甲乙所以紀卷先後今卷既改故甲乙並除存其首題以明舊式

京都上

班孟堅兩都賦二首　自光武至和帝都洛陽西京父老有怨班固恐帝去洛陽故上此詞以諫和帝大悅也

兩都賦序

班孟堅　范曄後漢書曰班固字孟堅北地人也年九歲能屬文長遂博貫載籍顯宗時除蘭臺令

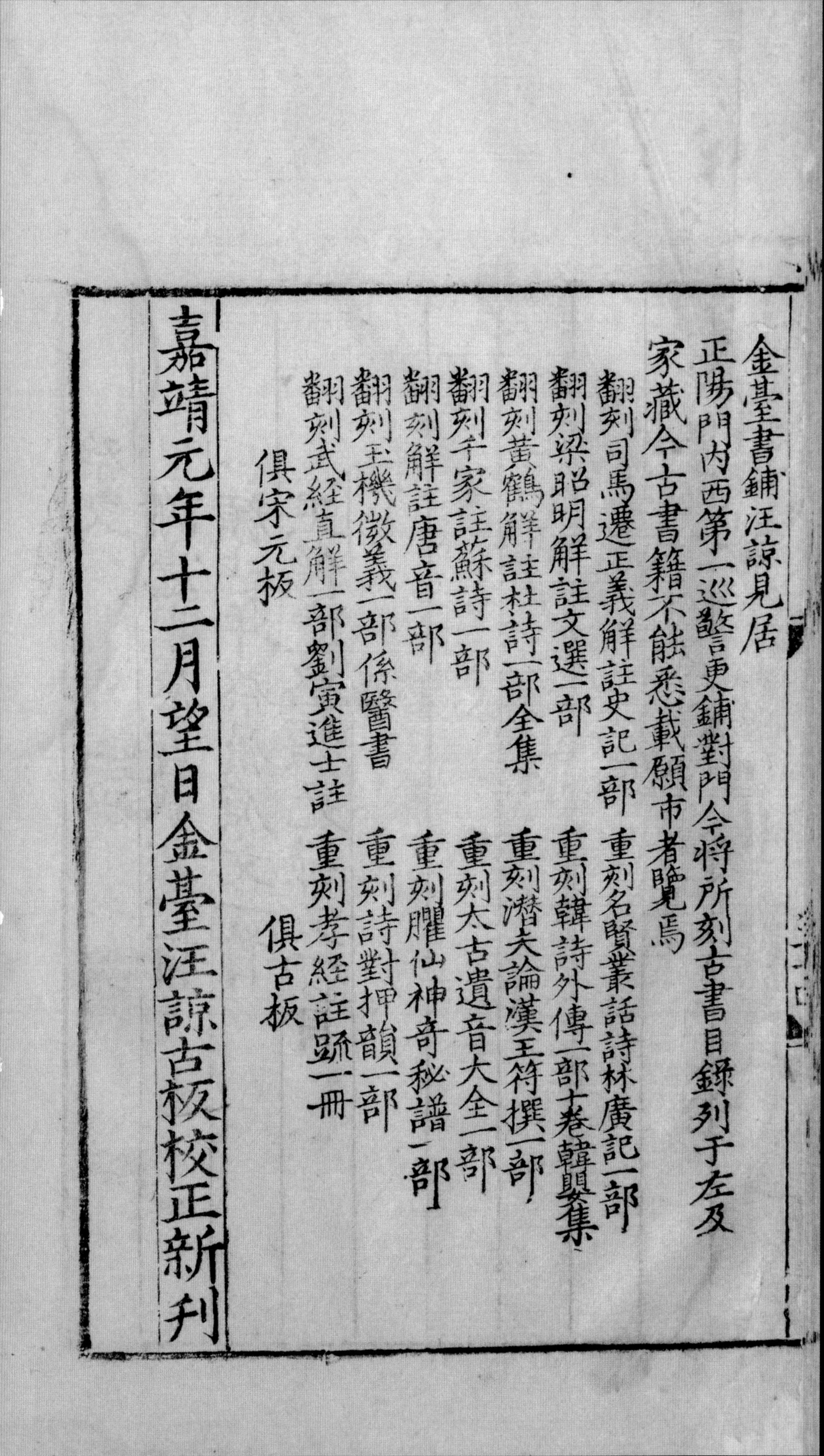

金臺書鋪汪諒見居
正陽門內西第一巡警更鋪對門今將所刻古書目錄列于左及
家藏今古書籍不能悉載願市者覽焉

翻刻司馬遷正義解註史記一部
翻刻梁昭明解註文選一部
翻刻黃鶴解註杜詩一部全集
翻刻千家註蘇詩一部
翻刻解註唐音一部
翻刻玉機微義一部係醫書
翻刻武經直解一部劉寅進士註
俱宋元板

重刻名賢叢話詩林廣記一部
重刻韓詩外傳一部十卷韓嬰集
重刻潛夫論漢王符撰一部
重刻太古遺音大全一部
重刻臞仙神奇秘譜一部
重刻詩對押韻一部
重刻孝經註疏一冊
俱古板

嘉靖元年十二月望日金臺汪諒古板校正新刊

Fig. 2.9: *Wenxuan zhu* (*Commentary on the Selections of Refined Literature*), table of contents, fol. 34v, publisher's advertisement (right), and *juan* 1, fol. 1r (left). Author: Xiao Tong (501–531). Date: 1523. Woodblock: 20.4 × 13.6 cm. The Chinese University of Hong Kong Library (PL2450.H7 1522).

史記正義序

諸王侍讀宣義郎守右清道率府長史張守節上

史記者漢太史公司馬遷作遷生龍門耕牧河山之陽南遊江淮講學齊魯之郡紹太史繼春秋括文魯史而包左氏國語采世本戰國策而摭楚漢春秋貫穿經傳旁搜史子上起軒轅下暨天漢作十二本紀帝王興廢悉詳三十系家君國存亡畢著八書贊陰陽禮樂十表定代系年封七十列傳忠臣孝子之誠備矣筆削冠於史籍題目足以經邦裴駰服其善序事理辯而

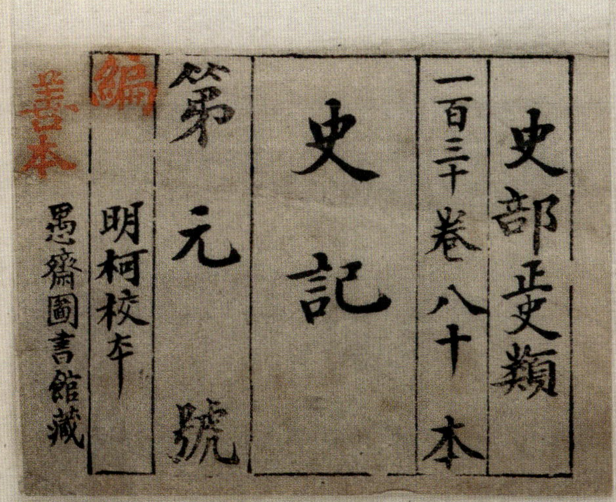

Fig. 2.10: *Shi ji* (*Records of the Grand Historian*), preface, fol. 1r.
Author: Sima Qian (c. 145–c. 86 BCE).
Date: 1525.
Woodblock: 20.1 × 12.8 cm.
Fung Ping Shan Library.

後漢書

卷一之二

律曆上中

志

Fig. 2.11: *Hou Han shu buzhi* (*The Official History of the Later Han Dynasty: Supplementary Monographs*), book cover. Author: Sima Biao (240–306). Date: 1131–1163. Woodblock: 21.4 × 17.3 cm. Library of Congress, Asian Division, Chinese Rare Books (B275.5.L75 China LM547).

> The first year of the Jiajing era, the twelfth month, the fifteenth day [1 January 1523], the Golden Terrace, Wang Liang, based on historic editions, proofread and newly published.
> 嘉靖元年十二月望日金臺汪諒古板校正新刊

In the Fung Ping Shan Library copy of *Records of the Grand Historian*, so as to pass the book off as a Song dynasty original, the equivalent text representing the "copyright page" has been scoured away, but in copies of the same book in other collections it reads:

> Ming dynasty, Jiajing era, fourth year, *yiyou* year [1525], Golden Terrace, published by Mr. Wang.
> 明嘉靖四年乙酉金臺汪氏刊行

For the same reason, in the Fung Ping Shan Library version, the preface and colophon that give the proofreader as Ke Weixiong 柯維熊 (*jinshi* 進士 degree 1517) have also been excised. On some of the first pages of various *juan*, relevant evidence of his participation survives at the bottom of the first column, where "of Putian, Ke Weixing proofread this" 莆田柯維熊校正 can still be read.

Three possible owners of the book can be identified from seals. The oldest belongs to the scholar-official Li Yangong 李言恭 (1541–1599), who is identified by three different stamps that appear in various places, though as they are often situated half-concealed by the binding edge and their color does not seem to match their age, they may be forgeries. The next identifiable owner was Fang Ruiyi 方濬益 (?–1899), an antiquarian and paleographer, and there is no reason to doubt the authenticity of his seals. Likewise, the third owner, Sheng Xuanhuai 盛宣懷 (1844–1916), a fabulously wealthy tycoon, leading light of the Westernization Reform Movement, and a Qing dynasty Minister of Transport. In 1910, he founded the Yu zhai 愚齋 (Studio of the Fool) Library in Shanghai, which was open to the public, and this book was in its collection. A library label (Fig. 2.10) and a seal recording a shelf-check in 1916 can also be found.

Fig. 2.12 (next spread): *Hou Han shu buzhi* (*The Official History of the Later Han Dynasty: Supplementary Monographs*), "Lüli zhi" ("Monograph on Pitch-Pipes and the Calendar"), *juan* 1, fols. 6r–v. Author: Sima Biao (240–306). Date: 1131–1163. Woodblock: 21.4 × 17.3 cm. Library of Congress, Asian Division, Chinese Rare Books (B275.5.L75 China LM547).

In official histories, two standard models existed for the "precedence" of monographs relevant to music. The first, originating with *Records of the Grand Historian*, consists of a separate "Monograph on Ritual" and then a "Monograph on Music," followed by a separate "Monograph on Pitch-Pipes" and then a "Monograph on the Calendar." The Fung Ping Shan specimen conforms to this model. The second, which began with *Han shu* 漢書 (*The Official History of the Former Han Dynasty*), combines the two monographs on ritual and music into a single essay called "Liyue zhi" 禮樂志, and those on pitch-pipes and the calendar into "Lüli zhi" 律曆志, placing the resultant "Monograph on Pitch-Pipes and the Calendar" first (Table 2.1).[11] Following the model of *The Official History of the Former Han Dynasty*, the monograph section of *Hou Han shu* 後漢書 (*The Official History of the Later Han Dynasty*) begins with the "Monograph on Pitch-Pipes and the Calendar."[12] It consists of three *juan*. Of these, only the first (numbered 91) deals with pitch standards and music theory.[13] The Library of Congress possesses a complete copy of the monograph section of *The Official History of the Later Han Dynasty* printed in the early Southern Song dynasty by the Transport Office of Lianghuai and Jiangdong provinces 兩淮江東轉運司.[14] It is preserved in a butterfly binding, by which the printed sheets are folded inwards and pasted together at the fold (Figs. 2.11 and 2.12).

Later official histories are also represented in the historic book collection of the Fung Ping Shan Library; for example, *Jin shu* 晉書 (*The Official History of the Jin Dynasty*, Table 2.1), which was compiled in 648 in the Tang dynasty with the Chancellor Fang Xuanling 房玄齡 (579–648) as its lead editor and the Emperor Taizong 太宗 (598–649, r. 626–649) contributing sections. A Yuan dynasty woodcut of this book that comprises 130 *juan* in total is represented in the Fung Ping Shan Library by four volumes that respectively contain *juan* 23–24, 25–26, 61–63, and 64–65.[15] Large in size, the writing block for each page face measures 22.4 × 17.4 cm set inside a page face of 30.4 × 20.4 cm. Fortuitously, *juan* 23, one of those that

11. Denis Twitchett, *The Writing of Official History under the T'ang* (Cambridge: Cambridge University Press, 1992), 207, footnote 3.

12. All the monographs in *The Official History of the Former Han Dynasty* were written by Sima Biao 司馬彪 (?–306).

13. A critical edition of this chapter can be found in Qiu Qiongsun 丘瓊蓀, *Lidai yue zhi lü zhi jiaoshi* 歷代樂志律志校釋 (Beijing: Zhonghua shuju 1964), vol. 1, 225–249.

14. For more information on this edition, see Zhao Wanli 趙萬里, *Zhongguo banke tulu* 中國版刻圖錄 (Beijing: Wenwu chubanshe, 1961), vol. 1, 26, and vol. 2, pl. 108; Ozaki Yasushi 尾崎康, *Seishi Sōgen-ban no kenkyū* 正史宋元版の研究 (Tokyo: Kyūko shoin, 1989), 288–293.

15. Jao Tsung-i, Li Zhifang, and Zhang Lijuan, *Xianggang daxue Feng Pingshan tushuguan cang shanben shulu*, enlarged ed., 51.

和聲此之謂也房又曰竹聲不可以度調故作準以定數準之狀如瑟長丈而十三弦隱閒九尺以應黃鍾之律九寸中央一弦下有畫分寸以爲六十律清濁之節房言律詳於歆所奏其術施行於史官候部用之文多不悉載故揔其本要以續前志

律術曰陽以圓爲形其性動陰以方爲節其性靜動者數三靜者數二以陽生陰倍之以陰生陽四之皆三而一陽生陰曰下

禮運篇曰五聲六律十二管還相爲宮此之謂也鄭玄曰宮數八十一黃鍾長九寸九九八十一也三分宮去一生徵徵數五十四林鍾長六寸六九五十四也三分徵益一生商商數七十二太蔟長八寸八九七十二也三分商去一生羽羽數四十八南呂長五寸三分寸之一五九四十五又三分寸之一爲四十八也三分羽益一生角角數六十四姑洗長七寸九分寸之一七九六十三又九分寸之一爲六十四也三分角去一生變宮三分变宮益一生變徵自此已後則隨月而變所謂還相爲宮以六十律分朞之日黃鍾自冬至始及冬至而復陰陽寒燠風雨之占生焉於以檢攝羣音考其高下苟非草木之聲則無不有所合虞書曰律

Table 2.1: Monographs on Music and Pitch-Pipes in the Official Histories

No.	Title	Author(s)	Publication Date	Period Covered	Total No. of Years	Total No. of Chapters	Location of Monographs on Music/Music and the Rites		Location of Monographs on Pitch-Pipes/Pitch-Pipes and the Calendar	
							Chapter Nos.	No. of Chapters	Chapter Nos.	No. of Chapters
1	*Shi ji* 史記	Sima Qian 司馬遷	c. 91 BCE	c. 2600 BCE –c. 90 BCE	c. 2500	130	24	1	25	1
2	*Han shu* 漢書	Ban Gu 班固	c. 80 CE	206 BCE–23 CE	229	100	22	1	21	1
3	*Hou Han shu* 後漢書	Fan Ye 范曄	c. 430 CE	25 CE–220 CE	195	120	--	--	91–93/91	3/1
4	*Sanguo zhi* 三國志	Chen Shou 陳壽	3rd century	184–280	96	65	--	--	--	--
5	*Jin shu* 晉書	Fang Xuanling 房玄齡 et al.	648	265–420	156	130	22–23	2	16–18/16	3/1
6	*Song shu* 宋書	Shen Yue 沈約	488 CE	420–479	60	100	19–22	4	11–13/11	3/1
7	*Nan Qi shu* 南齊書	Xiao Zixian 蕭子顯	c. 520	479–502	24	59	11	1	--	--
8	*Liang shu* 梁書	Yao Silian 姚思廉	636	502–557	56	56	--	--	--	--
9	*Chen shu* 陳書	Yao Silian 姚思廉	636	557–589	33	36	--	--	--	--
10	*Wei shu* 魏書	Wei Shou 魏收	555	386–550	165	124	109	1	107–108	2/1
11	*Bei Qi shu* 北齊書	Li Baiyao 李百藥	636	550–577	28	50	--	--	--	--
12	*Zhou shu* 周書	Linghu Defen 令狐德棻 et al.	636	557–581	25	50	--	--	--	--
13	*Sui shu* 隋書	Wei Zheng 魏徵 et al.	636	581–618	38	85	13–15	3	16–18/16	3/1
14	*Nan shi* 南史	Li Yanshou 李延壽	659	420–589	170	80	--	--	--	--
15	*Bei shi* 北史	Li Yanshou 李延壽	c. 659	386–618	233	100	--	--	--	--
16	*Jiu Tang shu* 舊唐書	Liu Xu 劉昫 et al.	c. 930	618–907	290	200	28–31	4	--	--
17	*Xin Tang shu* 新唐書	Ouyang Xiu 歐陽修 et al.	1060	618–907	290	225	11–22/ 11–12	12/2	--	--
18	*Jiu Wudai shi* 舊五代史	Xue Juzheng 薛居正 et al.	964	907–960	54	150	144–145	2	--	--
19	*Xin Wudai shi* 新五代史	Ouyang Xiu 歐陽修	1053	907–960	54	74	--	--	--	--
20	*Song shi* 宋史	Toqto'a 脫脫 et al.	1346	960–1279	320	496	126–142	17	68–84/68	17/1
21	*Liao shi* 遼史	Toqto'a 脫脫 et al.	1345	907–1125	219	116	54	1	--	--
22	*Jin shi* 金史	Toqto'a 脫脫 et al.	1345	1115–1234	120	135	39–40	2	--	--
23	*Yuan shi* 元史	Song Lian 宋濂 et al.	1345	1271–1368	99	210	67–71	5	--	--
24	*Ming shi* 明史	Zhang Tingyu 張廷玉 et al.	1739	1368–1644	277	332	61–63	3	--	--
25	*Xin Yuan shi* 新元史	Ke Shaomin 柯劭忞 et al.	1920	1271–1368	99	257	58–61	4	--	--
26	*Qing shi gao* 清史稿	Zhao Erxun 趙爾巽 et al.	1928	1616–1912	296	529	94–101	8	--	--

the Fung Ping Shan Library holds, contains the second half of the "Yue zhi" 樂志 ("Monograph on Music," Fig. 2.13). Close investigation of the entire *juan* in the Fung Ping Shan Library copy does not reveal that any pages have been added by Ming dynasty efforts to repair it, so its pages can all be regarded as original, which means that its woodblocks were sent to the Nanjing Imperial College before any such repairs might have been contemplated; this consistency and completeness is a particularly unusual and interesting feature of the book.[16] Another distinctive characteristic is that some (and only some) of its pages are made up of two faces joined together to create the requisite book dimensions. At the front of each volume is the stamp of the "Dun Fu Book Chamber" 敦復書室 of the collector Luo Yuanjue 羅原覺 (1891–1965).[17]

Jiu Tang shu 舊唐書 (*The Old Official History of the Tang Dynasty*, Table 2.1) is one of two equivalent books for the Tang dynasty and is composed of two hundred *juan*. It was written during the Later Jin period (907–979) before being superseded by Song Qi 宋祁 (998–1061) and Ouyang Xiu's 歐陽修 (1007–1072) rival *Xin Tang shu* 新唐書 (*The New Official History of the Tang Dynasty*, Table 2.1) in 1060.[18] Following the model of *Records of the Grand Historian*, the monograph section of *The Old Official History of the Tang Dynasty* begins with two separate monographs on ritual and music. The "Monograph on Music" occupies four lengthy *juan*, numbered 28 to 31. Its first *juan* offers a chronological account of court music and unfolds into two parts: the first focuses on music performed at the imperial ancestral shine and the second on music performed on festive occasions. Up until the end of the Kaiyuan 開元 era (713–741), both accounts are extremely detailed but deteriorate and become fragmented thereafter. Similar stylistic variation can be found in *juan* 29, which details repertoires and instruments, and *juan* 30–31, which quote the lyrics of hymns and dances. The reason behind this strikingly uneven density of information is that the primary sources for the monograph were (1) a pre-existing scholastic work entitled *Taiyueling biji* 太樂令壁記 (*The Wall Inscription for the Director of the Imperial Music Office*) by Liu Kuang 劉貺 (act. 726), and (2) an authoritative repertory of song texts compiled by Wei Tao 韋縚, Minister of the Court of Imperial Sacrifices, in 737.[19]

Wen Renquan 聞人詮, a student of the neo-Confucianist idealist and philosopher Wang Yangming 王陽明 (1472–1529), is responsible for the copy of *The Old Official History of the Tang Dynasty*, whose page is reproduced here (Fig. 2.14). In 1535, in private libraries in Suzhou, Wen discovered several incomplete copies of the earliest Southern Song printed edition (published by the Tea and Salt Monopoly Office of eastern Liangzhe province 兩浙東路茶鹽司 at Shaoxing in the early Shaoxing 紹興 era, 1131–1162) and revived interest in it.[20] In 1538, Wen issued his own facsimile edition. Its typeface is notable for its small size and the upright and vigorous quality of the script employed, imitating that of the Song dynasty Zhejiang original (Fig. 2.15).

By the Song dynasty, the accumulated official histories of the various dynasties had expanded to seventeen items, some more than one thousand *juan* in length. So as to make this amount of material digestible, Lü Zuqian 呂祖謙 (1137–1181) wrote a shortened and redacted version entitled *Shiqi shi xiangjie* 十七史詳節 (*An Abridgement of the Seventeen Official Histories*). In his version of *Sui shu* 隋書 (*The Official History of the Sui Dynasty*), both

16. Ozaki Yasushi suggests that this edition was published in Jiangsu or Zhejiang during the Yuan dynasty, see Ozaki Yasushi, *Seishi Sōgen-ban no kenkyū*, 367–380. A photograph of another copy of the same edition in the collection of Peking Library can be found in Kuraishi Takeshiro 倉石武四郎, *Jiujing shuying* 舊京書影 (Beijing: Renmin wenxue chubanshe, 2011), 275–277.

17. Another important item in the Fung Ping Shan Library from Luo's collection is an (arguably) Yuan dynasty reprint of the Southern Song dynasty revised edition (1266) of Zhu Mu's 祝穆 *Fangyu lansheng* 方與勝覽 (*Newly Edited Geographical Encyclopedia*). The Fung Ping Shan Library acquired this book via Fong Shu-chuen's 方樹泉 (1899–1987) philanthropic foundation The Fong Shu-fok Hall 方樹福堂.

18. For detailed discussion on the compilation of *The Old Official History of the Tang Dynasty*, see Denis Twitchett, *The Writing of Official History under the T'ang*, 191–197.

19. Denis Twitchett, *The Writing of Official History under the T'ang*, 212–219; Denis Twitchett, "A Note on the 'Monograph on Music,' in *Chiu T'ang shu*," *Asia Major*, 3rd ser., 3.1 (1990): 51–62. See also Kishibe Shigeo 岸辺成雄, *Tōdai ongaku no rekishiteki kenkyū: Gakuseihen* 唐代音樂の歴史的研究：樂制篇 (Tokyo: Tokyo Daigaku Shuppankai, 1960–1961), vol. 2, 327–328, 345, 358–359.

20. One of the incomplete copies that Wen Renquan discovered containing all the volumes of the basic annals and monographs (including the "Monograph on Music") was in the collection of the former Grand Secretariat Wang Ao 王鏊 (1450–1524). See Wen's preface to *The Old Official History of the Tang Dynasty*. For further information on the earliest edition of this book, see Qu Yong 瞿鏞, *Tieqin tongjian lou cangshu mulu* 鐵琴銅劍樓藏書目錄 (Beijing: Zhonghua shuju, 1990), 127–132; Wang Guowei 王國維, *Liangzhe gu kanben kao* 兩浙古刊本考, in *Wang Guowei quanji* 王國維全集, ed. Xie Weiyang 謝維揚 and Fang Xinliang 房鑫亮 (Hangzhou: Zhejiang jiaoyu chubanshe, 2009), vol. 7, 109–110; Zhao Wanli, *Zhongguo banke tulu*, vol. 1, 20, and vol. 2, pl. 74; and Ozaki Yasushi, *Seishi Sōgen-ban no kenkyū*, 488–494.

子夜歌者女子名子夜造此聲晉太元中琅琊王

軻之家有鬼歌子夜則子夜是此時人也

鳳将雛歌者舊曲也應璩百一詩云言是鳳将雛然則其来久矣

前漢歌者車騎将軍沈充所制

阿子及懽聞歌者穆帝升平初歌畢輙呼阿子汝聞不語在五行志後人衍其聲以為此二曲

團扇歌者中書令王珉與嫂婢有情愛好甚篤嫂捶撻婢過苦婢素善歌而珉好捉白團扇故制此歌

懊憹歌者隆安初俗聞訛謠之曲語在五行志長史

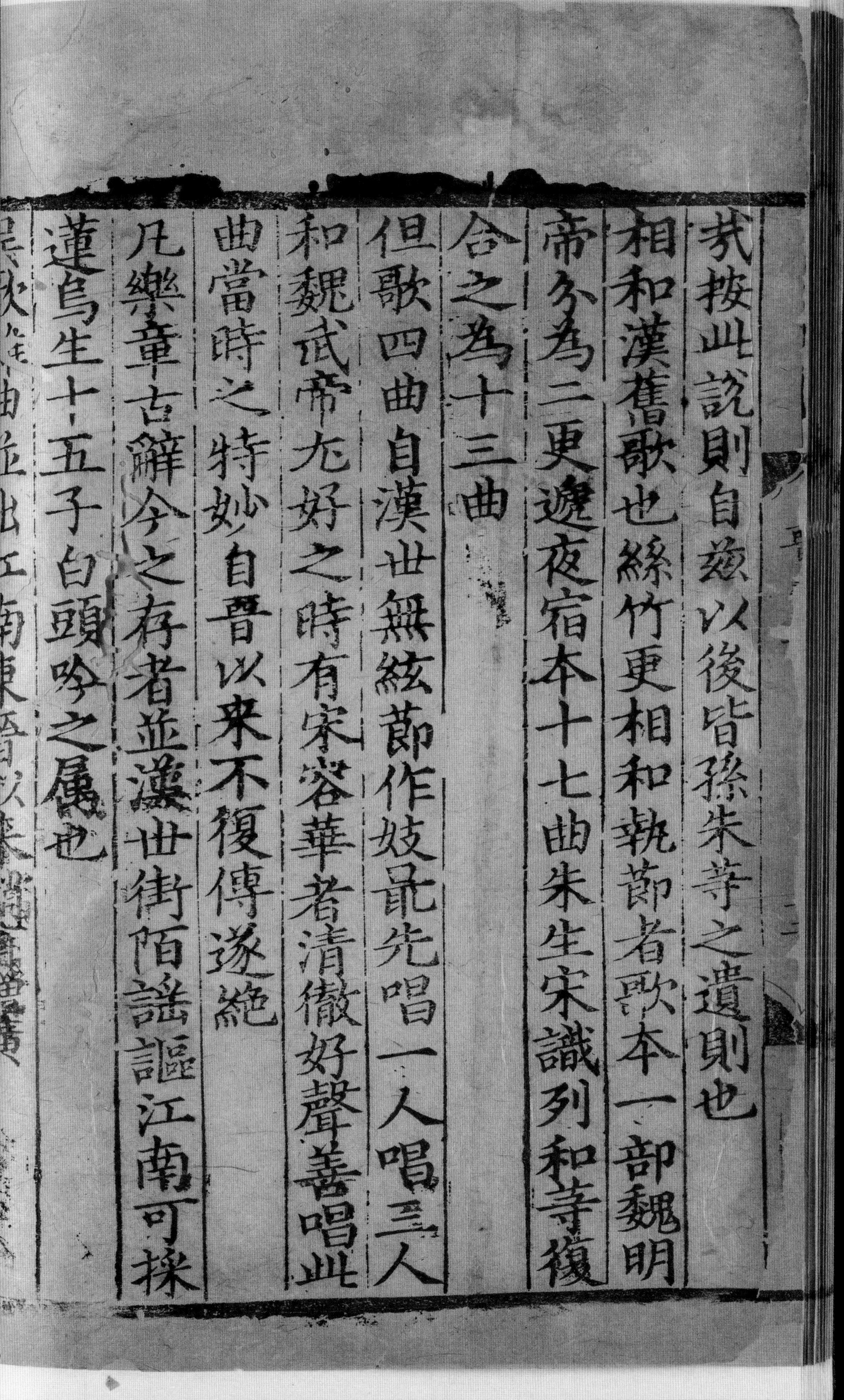

式按此說則自茲以後皆孫朱等之遺則也
相和漢舊歌也絲竹更相和執節者歌本一部魏明
帝分為二更遞夜宿本十七曲朱生宋識列和等復
合之為十三曲
但歌四曲自漢世無絃節作伎最先唱一人唱三人
和魏武帝尤好之時有宋容華者清徹好聲善唱此
曲當時之特妙自晉以來不復傳遂絕
凡樂章古辭今之存者並漢世街陌謠謳江南可採
蓮烏生十五子白頭吟之屬也

Fig. 2.13: *Jin shu* (*The Official History of the Jin Dynasty*), "Yue zhi" ("Monograph on Music"), *juan* 23, fols. 22v–23r.
Author: Fang Xuanling (579–648).
Date: 1271–1368.
Woodblock: 22.4 × 17.4 cm.
Fung Ping Shan Library.

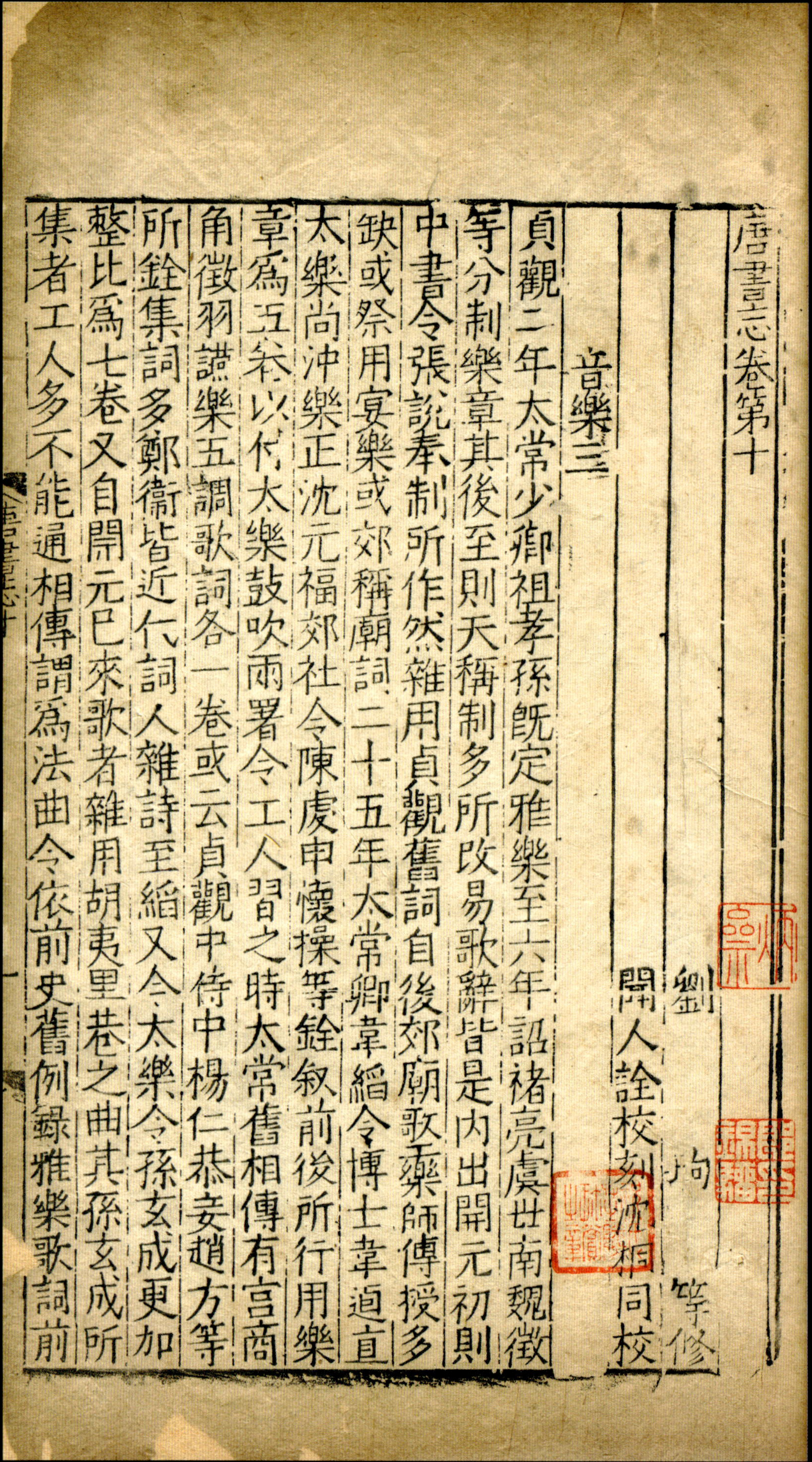

唐書志卷第十

劉昫等修

聞人詮校刻　沈桐同校

音樂三

貞觀二年太常少卿祖孝孫既定雅樂至六年詔褚亮虞世南魏徵等分制樂章其後至則天稱制多所改易歌辭皆是内出開元初則中書令張説奉制所作然雜用貞觀舊詞自後郊廟歌工樂師傳授多缺或祭用宴樂或郊稱廟詞二十五年太常卿韋縚令博士韋逌直太樂尚沖樂正沈元福郊社令陳虔申懷操等銓叙前後所行用樂章爲五卷以付太樂鼓吹兩署令工人習之時太常舊相傳有宫商角徵羽讌樂五調歌詞各一卷或云貞觀中侍中楊仁恭妾趙方等所銓集詞多鄭衛皆近代詞人雜詩至縚又令太樂令孫玄成更加整比爲七卷又自開元已來歌者雜用胡夷里巷之曲其孫玄成所集者工人多不能通相傳謂爲法曲今依前史舊例録雅樂歌詞前

Fig. 2.14: *Tang shu* (*The Official History of the Tang Dynasty*), "Yinyue zhi" ("Monograph on Music"), *juan* 10, fol. 1r.
Author: Liu Xu (887–946).
Date: 1538.
Woodblock: 21.5 × 14.8 cm.
Private collection.

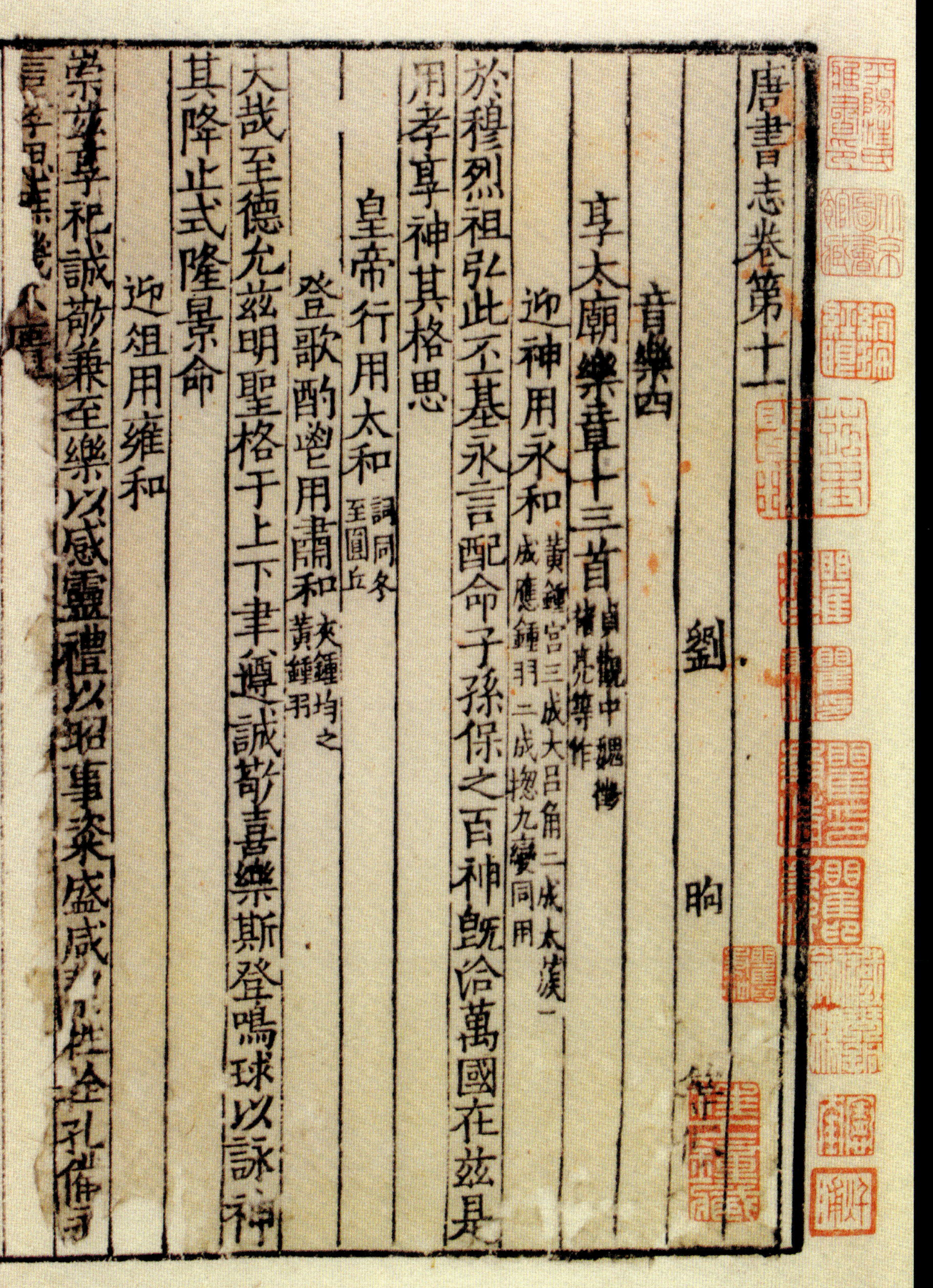

唐書志卷第十一　　劉　昫　撰

音樂四

享太廟樂章十三首 貞觀中魏徵褚亮等作

迎神用永和 黃鍾宮三成大呂角二成太蔟一成應鍾羽二成摠九變同用

於穆烈祖弘此丕基永言配命子孫保之百神既洽萬國在茲是用孝享神其格思

皇帝行用太和 詞同冬至圓丘

登歌酌鬯用肅和 夾鍾均之黃鍾羽

大哉至德允茲明聖格于上下聿遵誠敬喜樂斯登鳴球以詠神其降止式隆景命

迎俎用雍和

粢盛享祀誠敬兼至樂以感靈禮以昭事粢盛咸[illegible]牲牷孔備[illegible]

言孝思[illegible]

Fig. 2.15: *Tang shu* (*The Official History of the Tang Dynasty*), "Yinyue zhi" ("Monograph on Music"), *juan* 11, fol. 1r.
Author: Liu Xu (887–946).
Date: 1131–1162.
Woodblock: 21.7 × 15.0 cm.
Peking Library.
After Zhongguo guojia tushuguan and Zhongguo guojia guji baohu zhongxin, ed., *Di yi pi guojia zhengui guji minglu tulu* (Beijing: Guojia tushuguan chubanshe, 2008), vol. 2, 161.

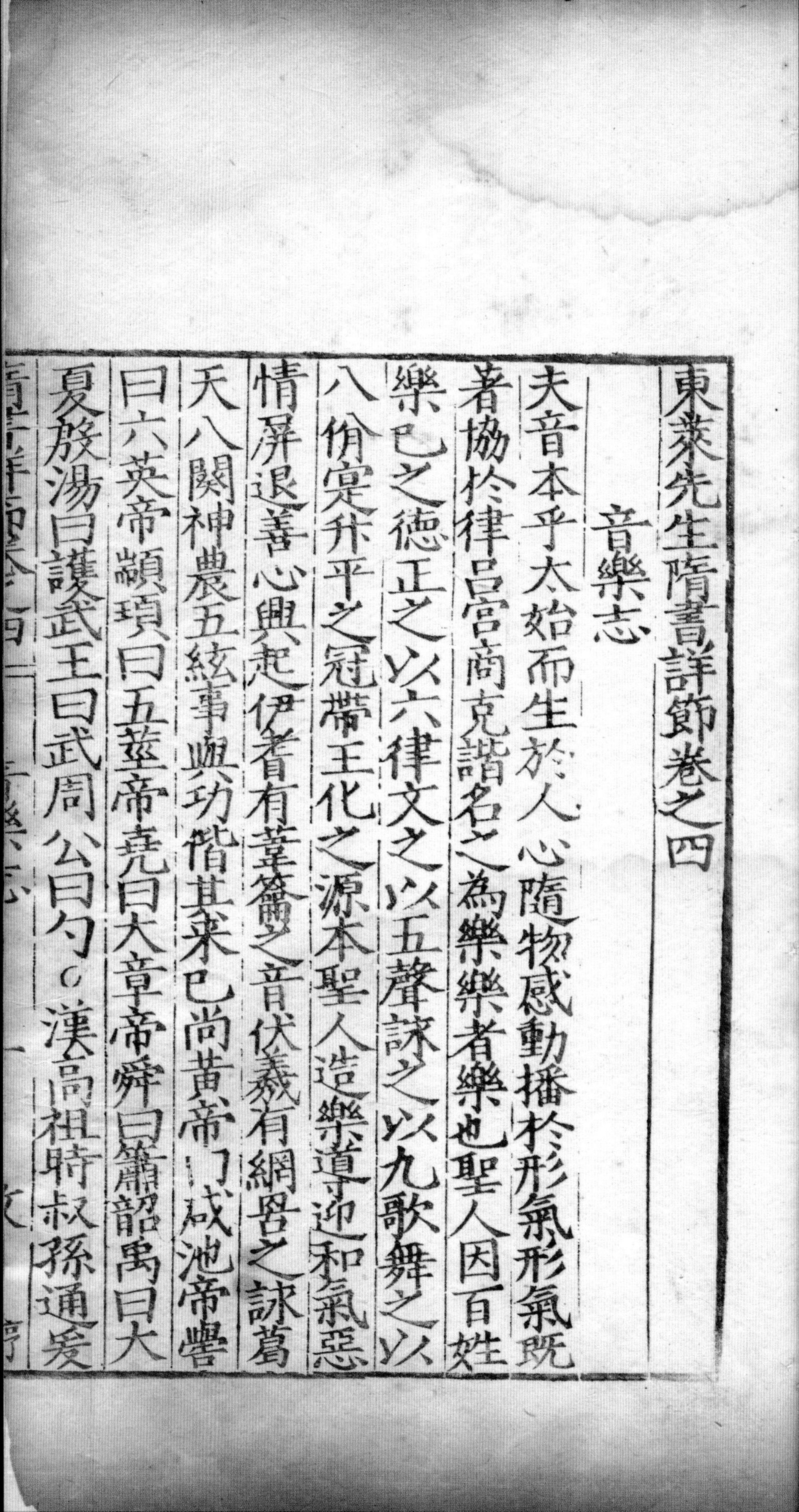

東萊先生隋書詳節卷之四

音樂志

夫音本乎太始而生於人心隨物感動播於形氣形氣既著協於律呂宮商克諧名之為樂樂者樂也聖人因百姓樂巳之德正之以六律文之以五聲詠之以九歌舞之以八佾寔升平之冠帶王化之源本聖人造樂導迎和氣惡情屏退善心興起伊耆有葦籥之音伏羲有網罟之詠葛天八闋神農五絃事與功偕其來巳尚黃帝乃咸池帝嚳曰六英帝顓頊曰五莖帝堯曰大章帝舜曰簫韶禹曰大夏殷湯曰護武王曰武周公曰勺。漢高祖時叔孫通爰

Fig. 2.16: *Sui shu xiangjie* (*An Abridgement of the Official History of the Sui Dynasty*), "Yinyue zhi" ("Monograph on Music"), *juan* 4, fol. 1r.
Editor: Lü Zuqian (1137–1181).
Date: 1521–1566.
woodblock: 19.1 × 13.7 cm.
Private collection.

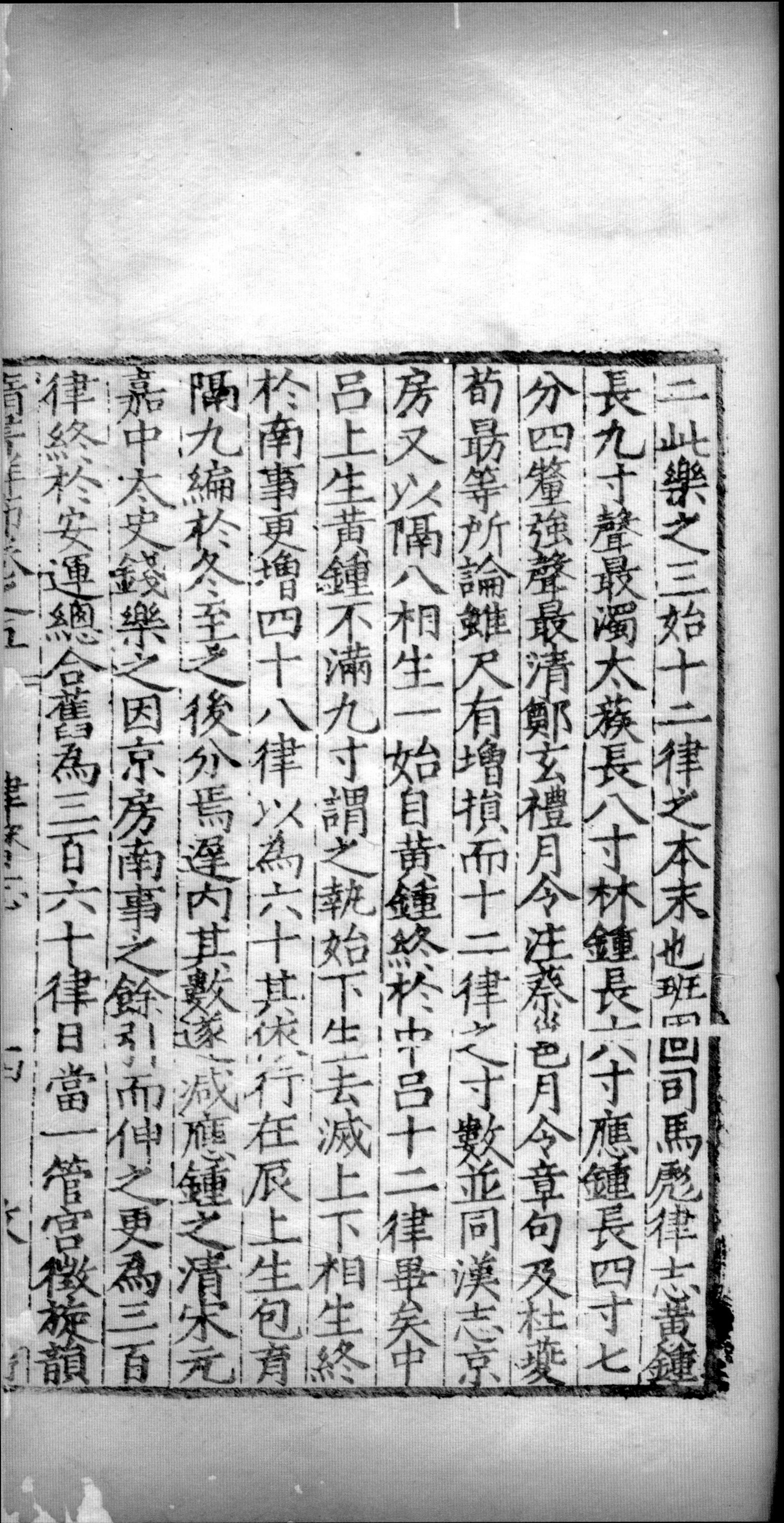

二此樂之三始十二律之本末也班固司馬彪律志黄鍾
長九寸聲最濁太蔟長八寸林鍾長六寸應鍾長四寸七
分四釐強聲最清鄭玄禮月令注蔡邕月令章句及杜夔
荀勗等所論雖尺有增損而十二律之寸數並同漢志京
房又以隔八相生一始自黄鍾終於中呂十二律畢矣中
呂上生黄鍾不滿九寸謂之執始下生去滅上下相生終
於南事更增四十八律以為六十其依行在辰上生包育
隔九編於冬至之後分焉遲內其數遂減應鍾之清宋元
嘉中太史錢樂之因京房南事之餘引而伸之更為三百
律終於安運總合舊為三百六十律日當一管宮徵旋韻

Fig. 2.17: *Sui shu xiangjie* (*An Abridgement of the Official History of the Sui Dynasty*), "Lüli zhi" ("Monograph on Pitch-Pipes and the Calendar"), *juan* 5, fol. 4r. Editor: Lü Zuqian (1137–1181). Date: 1521–1566. Woodblock: 19.6 × 13.8 cm. Private collection.

周宋公䪫鐘三 依元樣製

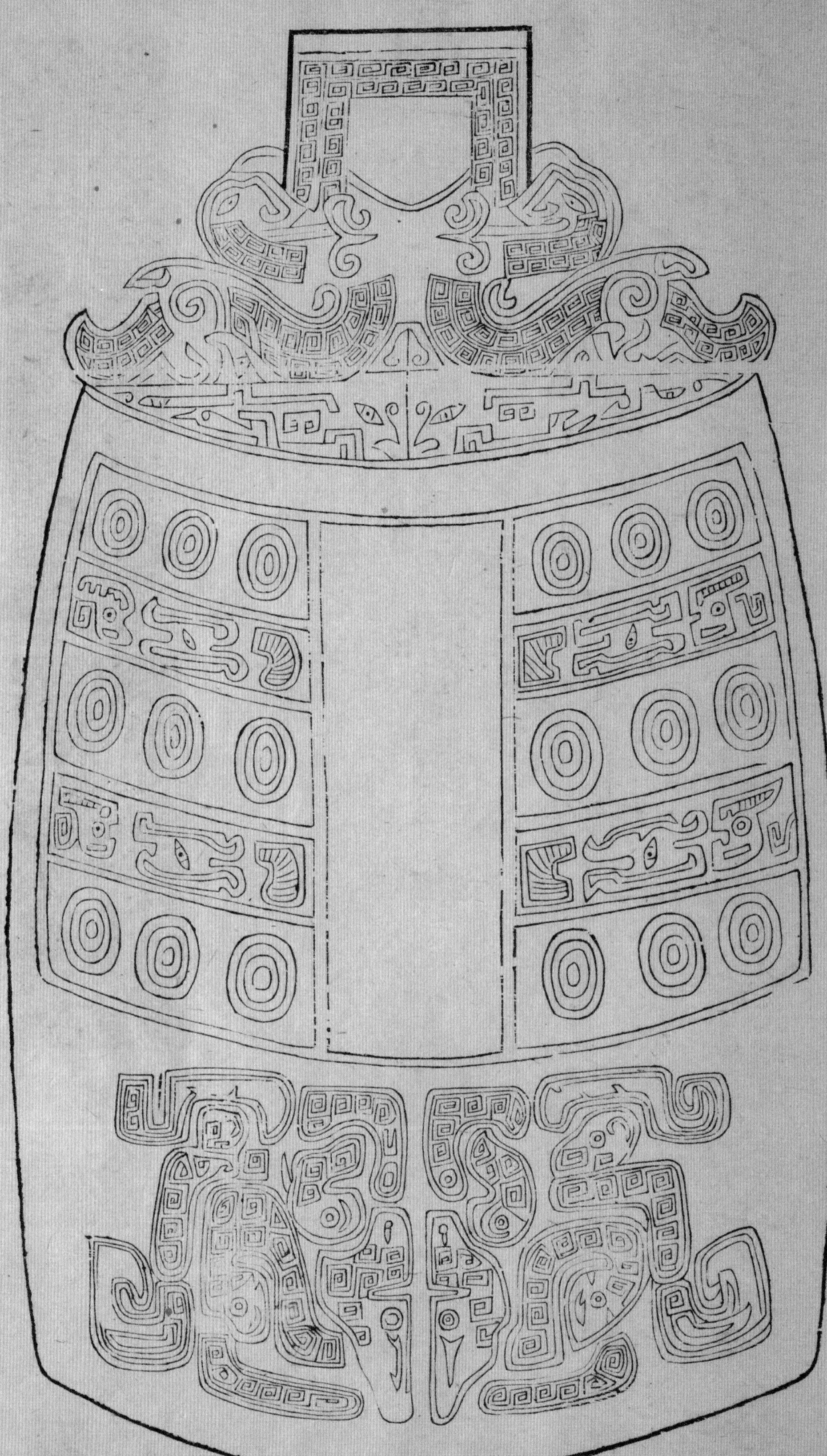

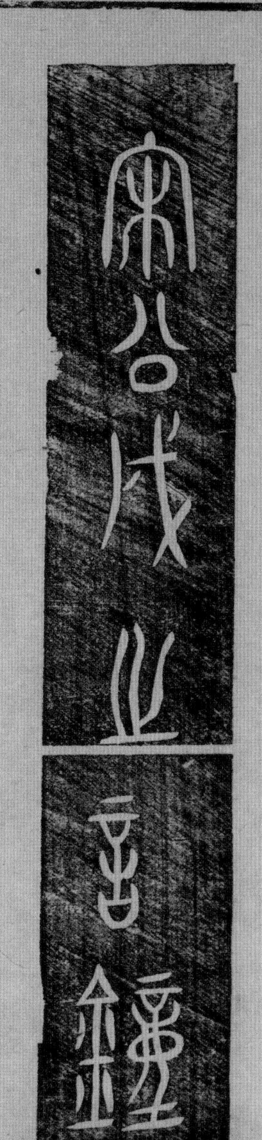

宋公成之䪫鐘

高一尺二寸八分鈕高三寸九分闊九寸三分兩舞相距九寸五分橫七寸五分兩銑相距一尺一寸三分橫九寸三分枚三十六各長五分重三十二斤銘六字

Fig. 2.18: *Xuanhe bogu tulu* (*The Xuanhe Era Illustrated Catalog of Ancient Bronzes*), *juan* 22, fols. 28v–29r, illustration of the third of a set of six chime-bells cast by Duke Cheng of Song, Zhou dynasty.
Author: Wang Fu (1079–1126).
Date: 1528.
Woodblock: 28.6 × 23.2 cm.
Fung Ping Shan Library.

宋王復齋鐘鼎款識

宋平公鐘

博古廿二法帖六皆作宋公䜌鐘有六

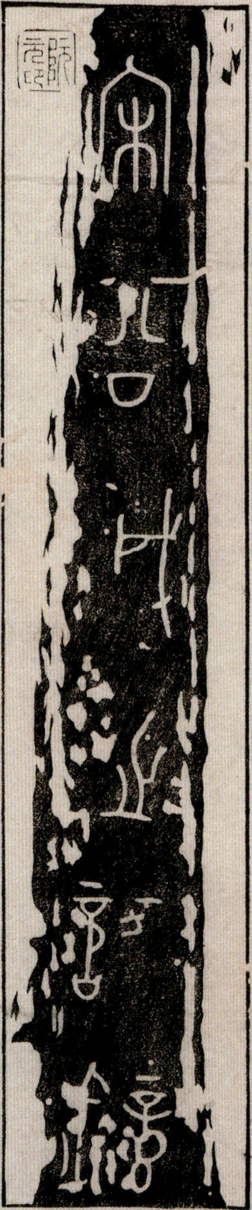

宋公成之䜌鐘

吳侃叔云左昭十年傳宋公成公羊作戌史記亦作成今觀是銘當以公羊為正是平公器也頌壺銘甲戌豐姞敦丙戌文皆作戌與此同又按左昭二十年傳公子城杜注平公子成與城同若平公名成其子不得名城也

周呆皿鼎

畢少董分盂字為二未然當作盂申鼎

積古齋藏宋拓摹刻

Fig. 2.19: *Zhong ding kuanzhi* (*Zhong Bells and Ding Tripod Inscriptions*), fol. 28v.
Author: Wang Houzhi (1131–1204).
Date: 1848.
Woodblock: 32.7 × 22.1 cm.
Fung Ping Shan Library.

the "Monograph on Music" and the "Monograph on Pitch Standards and the Calendar" survive (Figs. 2.16 and 2.17). The pages reproduced here belong to a copy of *An Abridgement of the Seventeen Official Histories* published in the Jiajing era (1522–1566) by the Shaanxi Provincial Administration Commission 陕西布政司.

Representing the Song dynasty, the book selected for discussion here is *Xuanhe bogu tulu* 宣和博古圖錄 (*The Xuanhe Era Illustrated Catalog of Ancient Bronzes*). As a product of a late Song dynasty zeitgeist for promoting the revival of ancient practices, it catalogs Emperor Huizong's 徽宗 (1082–1135, r. 1100–1126) entire collection of ancient bronzes.[21] The artifacts are divided into some twenty categories, for example, *ding* 鼎 vessels or *zun* 尊 goblets, and some of these comprise musical instruments such as bells and chimes. For each object, there is first a picture of the object, followed by the reproduction of any inscriptions on it, and then come records of its size, weight, and volume. The first edition was printed in the Zhida 至大 era (1308–1311) of the Yuan dynasty and furnished with fine illustrations of the objects in question and at their original sizes where possible. This made the book conspicuously large. Some of the illustrations are even spread across a double page, and where even this was not enough, and the size of the woodcuts needed to be reduced further, this is noted below the title for the relevant object. A popular book, it was reprinted many times in the Ming dynasty; the Fung Ping Shan Library copy is one of these editions, published in the seventh year of the Jiajing era (1528) by Jiang Yang 蔣暘 (*jinshi* degree 1521), and is the only contemporary version to retain the large size of the original.[22]

In it, *juan* 22–25 are devoted to bells, and *juan* 26–27 to chimes and other percussion, that is, *chunyu* 錞于, *duo* 鐸, *zheng* 鉦, and *nao* 鐃. In the Song dynasty at the time of writing the book, ancient bronze instruments of the Shang and Zhou dynasties had just begun to become the focus of scholarly attention,[23] and research concentrated not just on the objects themselves but also their relationship with mention of them in the Confucian canon, such as have been cited. An example of this investigative process is the Zhou dynasty Spring and Autumn period six-bell set of Duke Cheng of Song 宋公成 (*juan* 22, fols. 27v–33r, Fig. 2.18), whose provenance is made clear by inscriptions on the bells (Fig. 2.19). In the third and fourth years of the Chongning 崇寧 era (1104–1105), the Emperor Huizong had twelve sets of twenty-eight replica chime-bells made according to this pattern cast for his "historically-informed" Confucian music ensemble.[24] Although the original Zhou dynasty bells have not survived, the Emperor's research methodology has proved highly effective and many of his replicas can still be found in museums worldwide.

Moving to the Qing dynasty, the ruling class was displaced by the non-Han Manchu tribe. Undermining the intellectual achievements of the ousted Han aristocracy was essential to their political control, and in the sphere of music theory, the Ming dynasty prince Zhu Zaiyu became their target.[25] The Emperor Kangxi's 康熙 (r. 1661–1722) *Lülü zhengyi* 律吕正義 (*The Orthodox Meaning of Pitch Standards*, 1713, Fig. 2.20) in four *juan* represents the first generation of Qing contributions to this area, even advocating a division of the octave into fourteen tones (Fig. 2.21) as opposed to Zhu Zaiyu's twelve equal semitones.[26] This peculiar theory was created because, contrary to traditional approaches, Kangxi calculated the length of pitch-pipes of equal diameter via a circle of fifths without considering any end-corrections. As the result

21. Patricia Buckley Ebrey, *Accumulating Culture: The Collections of Emperor Huizong* (Seattle: University of Washington Press, 2008), 172–183.

22. Rong Geng 容庚, "Songdai jijin shuji shuping 宋代吉金書籍述評," *Xueshu yanjiu* 學術研究 (1963) 6: 88–92.

23. Yang Yuanzheng, "Musical Archaeology and the Prehistory of Chinese Music," in *The Oxford Handbook of Music in China and the Chinese Diaspora*, ed. Jonathan P. J. Stock and Yu Hui (New York: Oxford University Press), forthcoming; Yang Yuanzheng, "Finding the Key: Tuning Keys Discovered from the Imperial Collection of Emperor Huizong," *Music in Art: International Journal for Music Iconography* 40.1/2 (2015): 275–284; and Robert E. Harrist, "The Artist as Antiquarian: Li Gonglin and His Study of Early Chinese Art," *Artibus Asiae* 55.3/4 (1995): 237–280.

24. James C. Y. Watt, "Antiquarianism and Naturalism," in *Possessing the Past: Treasures from the National Palace Museum, Taipei*, ed. Wen C. Fong and James C. Y. Watt (New York: Metropolitan Museum of Art, 1996), 222–228; Joseph S. C. Lam, "Huizong's Dashengyue, a Musical Performance of Emperorship and Officialdom," in *Emperor Huizong and Late Northern Song China: The Politics of Culture and the Culture of Politics*, ed. Patricia Buckley Ebrey and Maggie Bickford (Cambridge, Mass.: Harvard University Asia Center, 2006), 395–452; and Patricia Buckley Ebrey, *Accumulating Culture: The Collections of Emperor Huizong*, 159–166.

25. Yu Siu-Wah, "Meaning and Cultural Functions of Non-Chinese Music in the Eighteenth-Century Manchu Court" (PhD diss., Harvard University, 1996).

26. Chun-Yan Tse, "Erroneous Discourses on Tuning Theories between China and the West: The Kangxi 14-tone System," *Theoria: Historical Aspects of Music Theory* 26 (2020): 7–11.

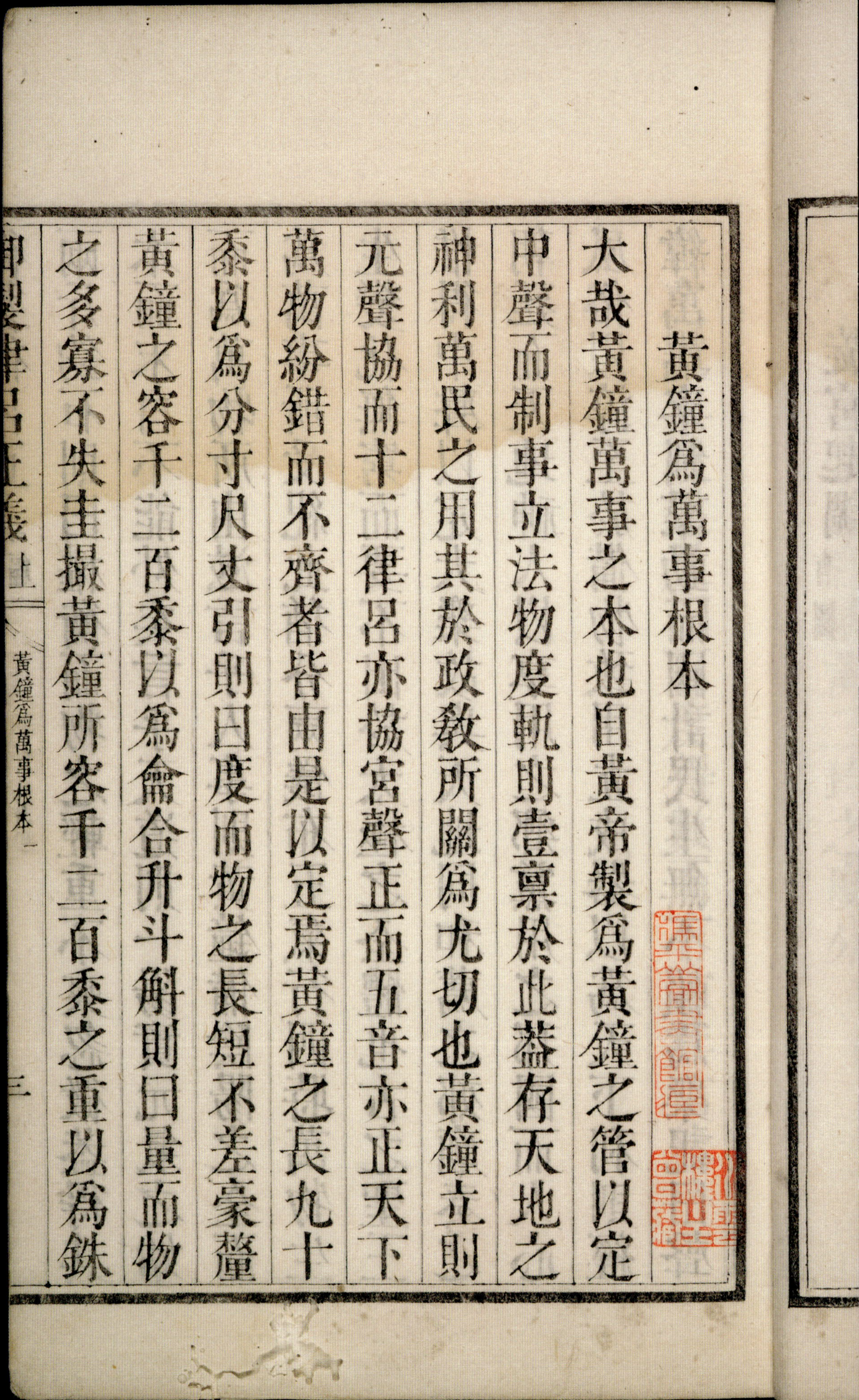

黃鐘爲萬事根本

大哉黃鐘萬事之本也自黃帝製爲黃鐘之管以定中聲而制事立法物度軌則壹稟於此葢存天地之神利萬民之用其於政教所關爲尤切也黃鐘立則元聲協而十二律呂亦協宮聲正而五音亦正天下萬物紛錯而不齊者皆由是以定焉爲黃鐘之長九十黍以爲分寸尺丈引則曰度而物之長短不差豪釐黃鐘之容千二百黍以爲龠合升斗斛則曰量而物之多寡不失圭撮黃鐘所容千二百黍之重以爲銖

Fig. 2.20: *Lülü zhengyi* (*The Orthodox Meaning of Pitch Standards*), *juan* 1, fascicle 1, fol. 3r.
Authors: Yunlu (1695–1767) et al.
Date: 1713.
Border: 21.4 × 14.8 cm.
Fung Ping Shan Library.

Fig. 2.21: *Lülü zhengyi* (*The Orthodox Meaning of Pitch Standards*), *juan* 1, fascicle 2, fol. 37v (detail).
Authors: Yunlu (1695–1767) et al.
Date: 1713.
Border: 21.4 × 14.8 cm.
Fung Ping Shan Library.

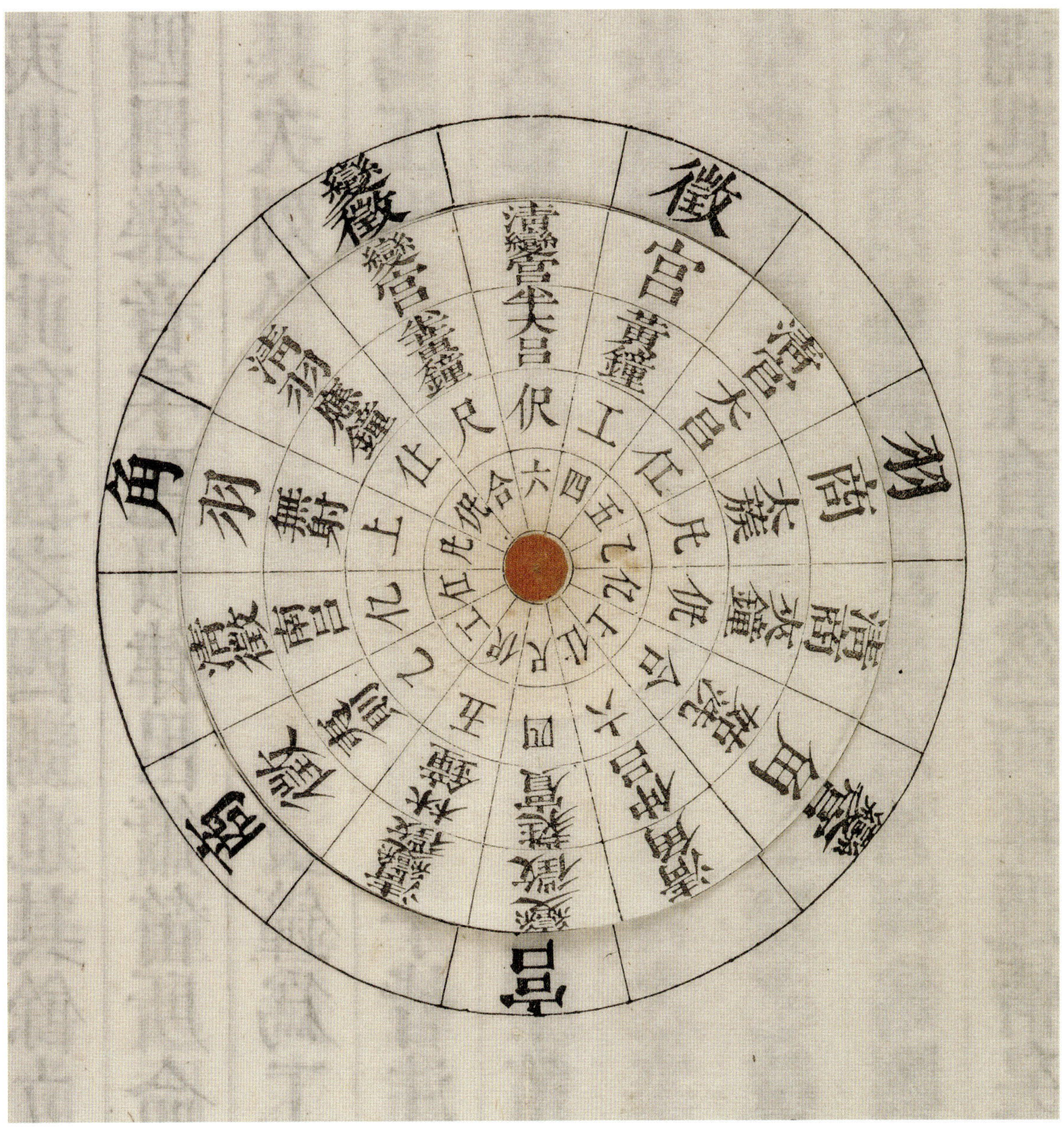

of the experimental process, the higher octave was reached only at around the fourteenth pitch above the fundamental. Therefore, the Emperor concluded there should in fact be fourteen tones within an octave, with two "semitones" between all adjacent pitches of an equidistant heptatonic scale, thus resulting in "seven-tone equal temperament."

The scholars of Kangxi's court were most likely aware of the error, but due to the intimidating political environment, they dared not speak up. There is evidence that they covertly defied their master by compressing the intervals between some adjacent tones to make the scale more conventional.[27] Their clandestine defiance was not understood by the uninformed, and Western scholars even misinterpreted the "seven-tone equal temperament" scale as a whole-tone scale. Jean-Philippe Rameau (1683–1764) reported in 1760 the use of the whole-tone scale as one of two scales used in China, and commented on it as "ordre des plus vicieux qu'on puisse imaginer."[28] Subsequently, J. A. van Aalst (1858–1914) also reported the use of a whole-tone scale in his *Chinese Music* (1884).[29] Interestingly, Joseph-Marie

27. Chun-Yan Tse, "Erroneous Discourses on Tuning Theories between China and the West: The Kangxi 14-tone System," 11.

28. Jean-Philippe Rameau, *Code de musique pratique avec de Nouvelles réflexions sur le principe sonore* (Paris: De l'Imprimerie royale, 1760), 191–192.

29. J. A. van Aalst, *Chinese Music* (Shanghai: The Inspectorate of Customs, 1884), 50.

最高聲
高聲
中聲
下聲

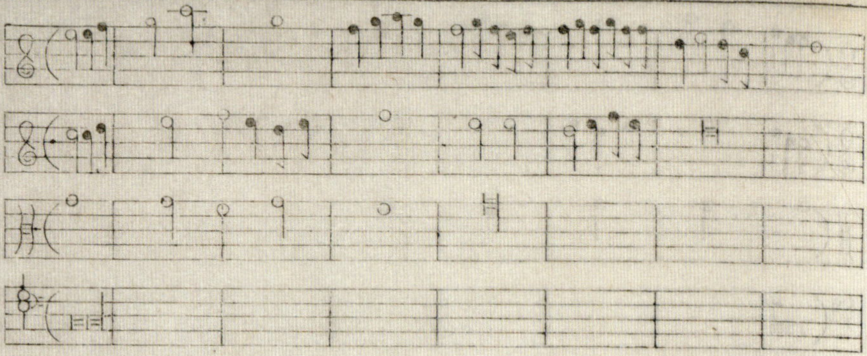

八形號配合音節

全準之紀八形號者得分奇零難於計算姑置不論其大半準之八形號所屬之音配合遲速長短之節其間自有高低上下之宜按其所宜而品第之則理一貫而諸法備焉爰設四圖分為最高聲高聲中聲下聲之四層俱以豎畫界為八分將四聲所宜之音各列於本層每層皆準八度故最下第一層止書一

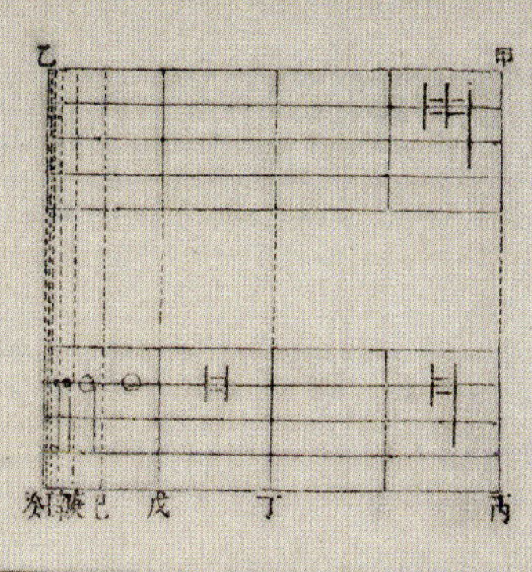

二度丁戊爲緩分準一度戊己爲中分準半度己庚爲半分準一度之四分之一庚辛爲小分準一度之八分之一辛壬爲速分準一度之十六分之一壬癸爲最速分準一度之三十二分之一此小半準之八形號得大半準之半而得分亦整齊者也

Fig. 2.22: *Lülü zhengyi* (*The Orthodox Meaning of Pitch Standards*), *juan* 5, fascicle 5, fols. 12v–13r, examples of European staff notation.
Authors: Yunlu (1695–1767) et al.
Date: 1713.
Border: 21.4 × 14.8 cm.
Fung Ping Shan Library.

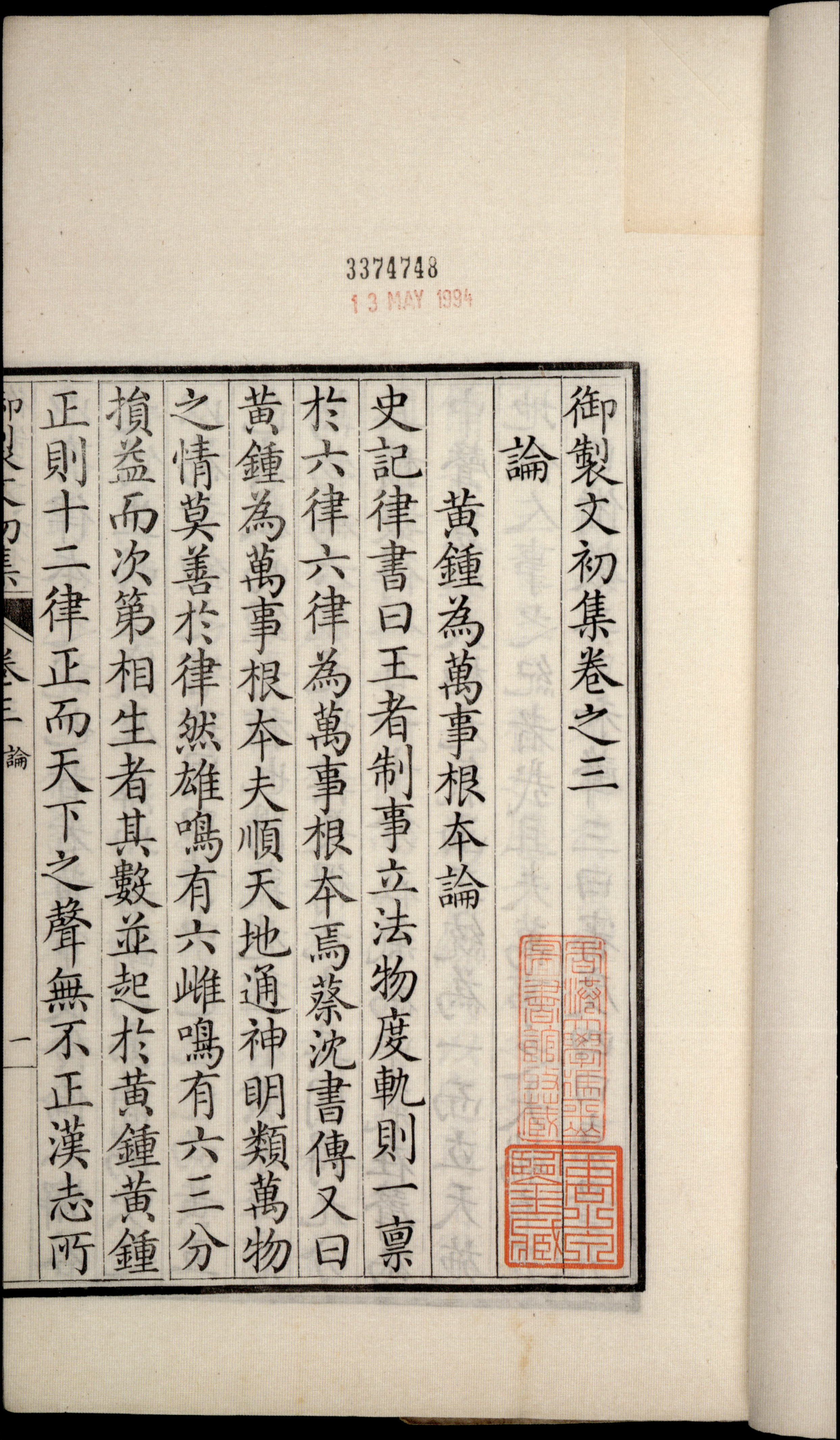

御製文初集卷之三

論

黃鍾為萬事根本論

史記律書曰王者制事立法物度軌則一稟於六律六律為萬事根本焉蔡沈書傳又曰黃鍾為萬事根本夫順天地通神明類萬物之情莫善於律然雄鳴有六雌鳴有六三分損益而次第相生者其數並起於黃鍾黃鍾正則十二律正而天下之聲無不正漢志所

Fig. 2.23: *Yuzhi wen chuji* (*The Emperor's Collected Works: The First Installment*), *juan* 3, fol. 1r.
Author: Qianlong (r. 1735–1796).
Date: 1764.
Woodblock: 20.2 × 13.9 cm.
Fung Ping Shan Library.

Amiot, who probably understood the error, chose not to discuss the system in his *Mémoire sur la Musique des Chinois* (1780), using only the works of Zhu Zaiyu as his primary theoretical sources.[30]

Appropriately, an additional fifth *juan* (Fig. 2.22) was added to *The Orthodox Meaning of Pitch Standards*, which took as its wellspring another entirely new non-Han source, that of the music of European Jesuits active in China at the time, principally Thomas Pereira 徐日昇 (1645–1708) and Theodorico Pedrini 德理格 (1671–1746).[31] In this *juan* are found details of staff notation, solmization, and the contrapuntal notions of consonance and dissonance. As was customary for Jesuits, both were extremely cultured and well-educated: more traditionally theoretical in mindset, Pereira leaned towards expertise in Renaissance counterpoint, while Pedrini was a fully-fledged harpsichordist, instrument builder and repairer, and composer in the European Baroque style, who taught music to Kangxi's three sons.

The copy of Kangxi's *Orthodox Meaning of Pitch Standards* in the Fung Ping Shan Library, which came as a donation from the former Fung Ping Shan Librarian Chen Junbao 陳君葆 (1898–1982), is not the later woodcut version printed in large quantities for broad circulation, but a limited edition using the then rare (in China) technique of movable copper type. This printing method, used at the Manchu court, was probably also imported, this time from Korea, where the practice had already been employed for several centuries.

Kangxi's grandson Qianlong 乾隆 (r. 1736–1796) went much further and in 1746 produced the second generation of Qing dynasty texts on music, an 120-*juan* expanded *Lülü zhengyi houbian* 律呂正義後編 (*Sequel to the Orthodox Meaning of Pitch Standards*). As East Asia's Louis XIV "Sun King" and roughly contemporary with him, Qianlong's goal was to be as opulent and magnificent as possible, and this text is just one example of his absolutism. In *Yuzhi wen chuji* 御製文初集 (*The Emperor's Collected Works: The First Installment*, Fig. 2.23) is a preface written by the Emperor to *The Sequel to the Orthodox Meaning of Pitch Standards* in which a single passage sums up Kangxi's gloss on the Confucian role of music:

> The fundamental meaning of ancient music was crystal clear, and only now has the lengthy debate [regarding it] arrived at a fixed ideology. Today, the principles of music have been fully established, and for the long-term future an elegant aesthetic voice is assured. And most certainly it could be said that only the sage could be so adept.
>
> 古樂之大義明，而千古有定論；今樂之至理具，而千古有正聲。誠所謂惟聖人能之者。

Illustrations of court instruments standardized during Qianlong's reign can be found in *juan* 8–9 of *Huangchao liqi tushi* 皇朝禮器圖式 (*Illustrated Regulations for Ceremonial Paraphernalia of the Imperial Qing Dynasty*). Compiled under an imperial order in 1750, this book was completed in 1759 and first published by the court in 1766 (Fig. 2.24).[32] Each instrument in it is carefully furnished with an illustration together with description of its appearance, dimensions, the materials of which it is made, the decoration it bears, the numbers of performers playing it during a particular ceremony, and its specific use. Beautiful colored manuscript copies of these illustrations, which were also prepared and gathered into albums, are now scattered in various museums and collections around the world (Fig. 2.25).

Chinese literature has traditionally been divided into four categories: Confucian classics and their commentaries; official histories and generically related material; the named works of non-Confucian philosophers and works devoted to religions, professions, and the fine arts; and the collected works of individuals or genres. So far, most of the material discussed in these first two chapters has been drawn from the first two of these categories. In the Age of Confucius, the principal role of such texts was weighted towards

30. Lam Ching Wah, "A Highlight of French Jesuit Scholarship in China: Jean-Joseph-Marie Amiot's Writings on Chinese Music," *CHIME: Journal of the European Foundation for Chinese Music Research* 16/17 (2005): 127–147.

31. François Picard, "Musik der Jesuiten im Peking der 17. und 18. Jahrhunderten," in *Der Fremde Klang: Tradition und Avantgarde in Musik Ostasiens*, ed. Hinrich Bergmeier (Hannover: Biennale Neue Musik Hannover, 1999), 93–119; François Picard, "Music (17th and 18th centuries)," in *Handbook of Christianity in China, Volume One: 635–1800*, ed. Nicolas Standaert (Leiden: Brill, 2001), 851–860; and Sheryl Chow, "A Localised Boundary Object: Seventeenth-Century Western Music in China," *Early Music History* 39 (2020): 75–113.

32. Lai Yu-chih 賴毓芝, "Tu yu li: *Hongchao liqi tushi* de chengli jiqi yingxiang 圖與禮:《皇朝禮器圖式》的成立及其影響," *Gugong xueshu jikan* 故宮學術季刊 37.2 (2020): 1–56; and Yu Hui-chun 余慧君, "Zun lü du yu wujiang: *Hongchao liqi tushi* yueqi juan yanjiu 遵律度於無疆:《皇朝禮器圖式》樂器卷研究," *Gugong xueshu jikan* 故宮學術季刊 37.3 (2020): 95–133.

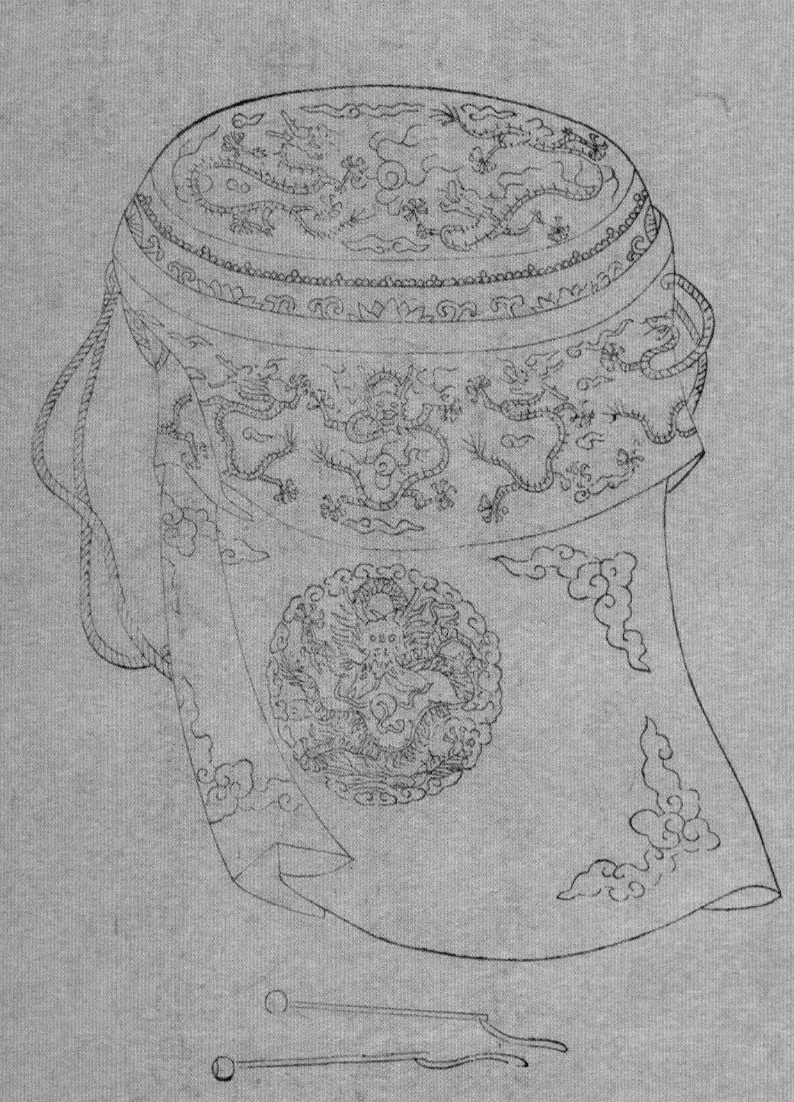

Fig. 2.24 (detail): *Huangchao liqi tushi (Illustrated Regulations for Ceremonial Paraphernalia of the Imperial Qing Dynasty)*, *juan* 9, fol

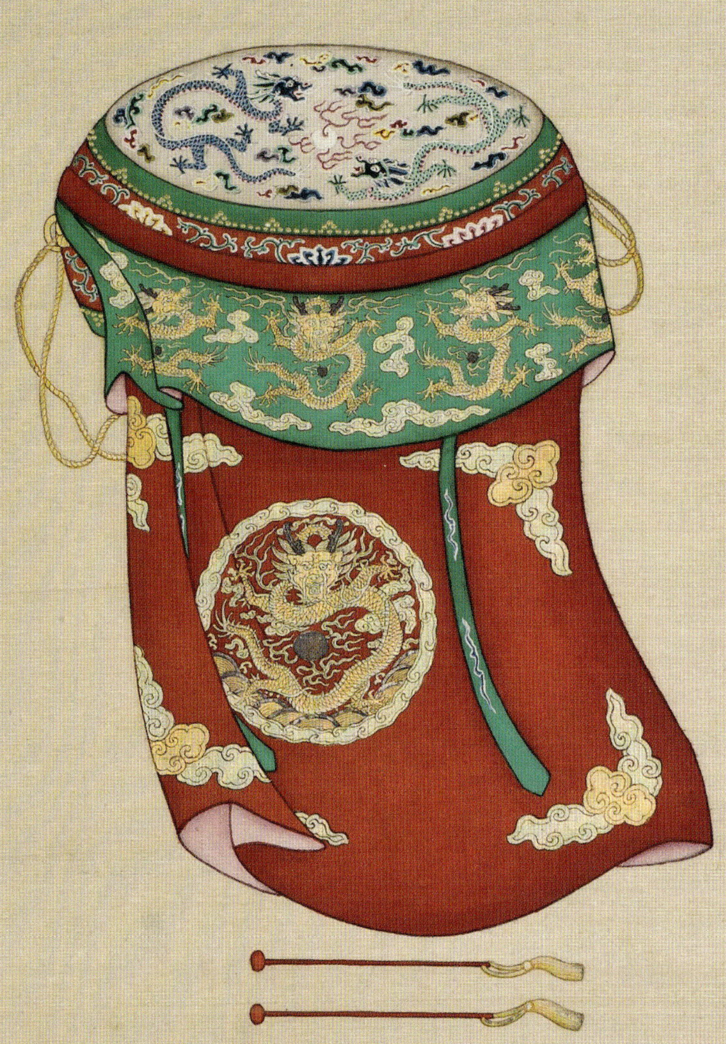

耕耤禾詞樂鼓圖

Fig. 2.25 (detail): *Huangchao liqi tushi (Illustrated Regulations for Ceremonial Paraphernalia of the Imperial Qing Dynasty)*, illustration personal cultivation, while in the later days of imperial China, the bias swung more strongly in favor of their role as an aspect of statecraft. The ruling classes were undoubtedly quick to understand the significance of Confucian texts in underpinning their political control, so early imprints of these works are comparatively numerous, as can be seen from the texts already discussed.

None of these works was produced for the purposes of entertainment. As the age of printing progressed, vernacular elements gradually encroached on this territory and began to include ever more frequent and fine illustrations, literature from outside the Confucian canon, and accounts and manuals of vernacular art. With the rise of an economically active mercantile class, a new readership sought entertainment rather than edification, as will be discussed in the third and fourth chapters.

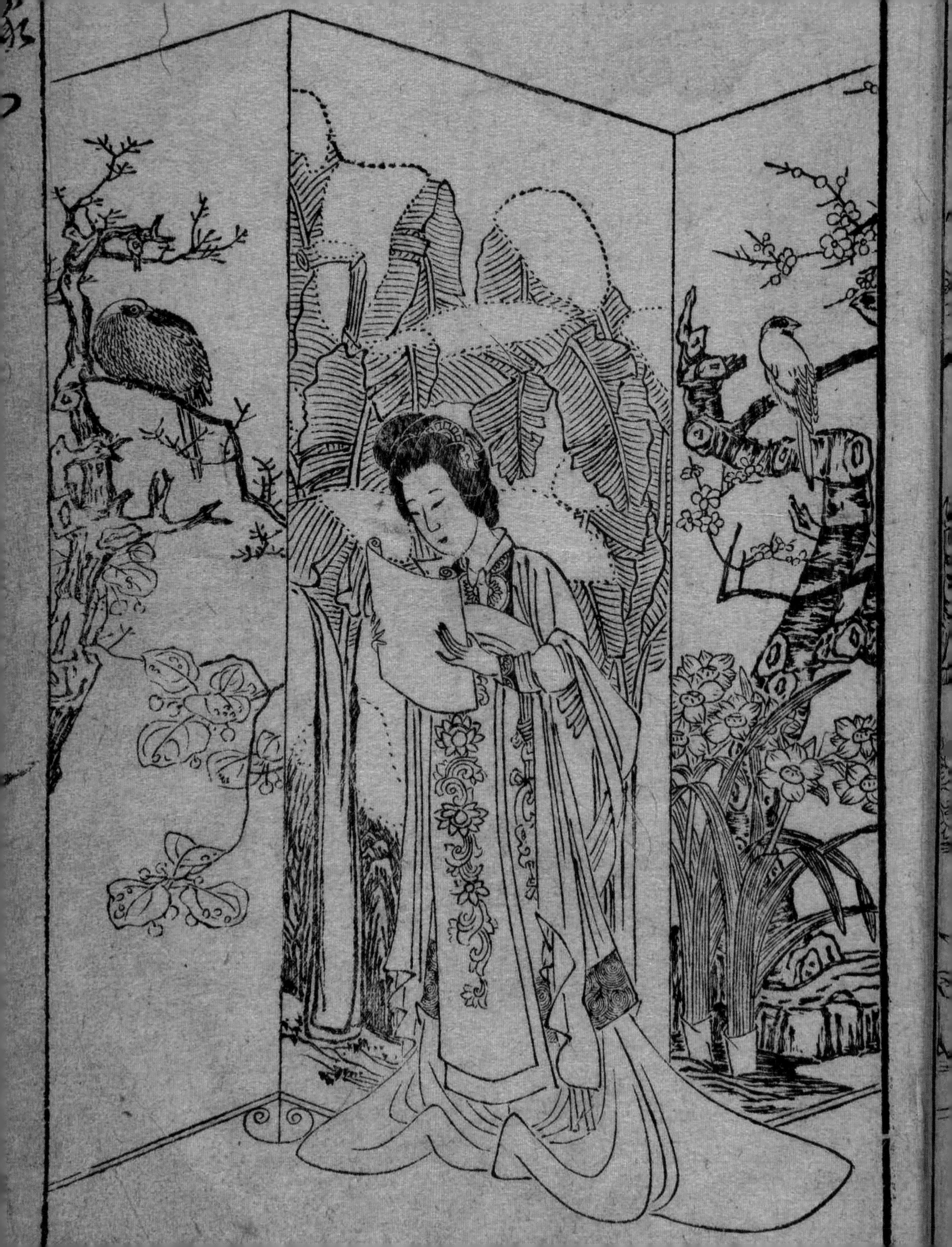

Chapter 3

Vocal Music: Opera and Song

Fong Sing Ha

On the relationship between Confucian music and its vernacular counterparts, seventeenth-century polymath Liu Xianting 劉獻廷 (1648–1695) in his *Guangyang zaji* 廣陽雜記 (*Miscellaneous Jottings of Guangyang*) remarks:

> Of the common people that I have viewed, never have I observed any that did not like singing songs or watching dramas, and these are the ordinary world's *The Book of Odes* and *The Book of Music*, and there has not yet been any that did not read novels or listen to storytelling, and these are the ordinary world's *The Book of Documents* and *The Spring and Autumn Annals*. And there has not yet been any that did not trust divining or making sacrifices to ghosts and spirits, and these are the ordinary world's *The Book of Changes* and *The Canon of Rites*. The teachings of the Six Canons have their origins in human emotions.
>
> 余觀世之小人未有不好唱歌看戲者，此性天中之《詩》與《樂》也，未有不看小說聽說書者，此性天中之《書》與《春秋》也，未有不信占卜祀鬼神者，此性天中之《易》與《禮》也。聖人六經之教原本人情。

The second part of this book focuses on two themes: vernacular song and opera (Chapter 3) and literati music (Chapter 4). The audience for opera crossed numerous social boundaries, but the principal motivation of audience members was entertainment (Fig. 3.1). This resembled *qin* music of the literati, though enjoyment of the *qin* focused more on practicing the craft rather than viewing someone else's performance. Alongside these two themes, discussion will linger on the evolution of printing technology as it developed to satisfy the demands of consumers.

Fig. 3.1: *Zhang Shenzhi xiansheng zheng bei Xixiang ji* (*The Northern Version of Romance of the Western Wing annotated by Mr. Zhang Shenzhi*), illustrations, fol. 4r, *Kui jian* (*Reading a Letter*).
Author: Wang Shifu (c. 1260–c. 1337).
Artist: Chen Hongshou (1598–1652).
Engraver: Xiang Nanzhou (c. 1615–1670).
Date: 1639.
Woodblock: 20.4 × 16.5 cm.
Peking Library (15086).

The earliest extant manuscripts of Chinese secular music genres were found in the Dunhuang 敦煌 caves and are now in the collections of the Bibliothèque Nationale de France, the British Library, and elsewhere.[1] Most are tablature for *pipa*; they are generally accompaniments to songs, written on the reverse sides of fragments of discarded Buddhist sutras and local government documents.[2] With the advent of printing in the Song dynasty, the music of these genres began to achieve the wider circulation allowed by this new technology. The first organization to embark on this journey was the Xiuneisi 脩內司 (Department of Palace Supply), which assembled available material and issued it as *Yuefu huncheng ji* 樂府混成集 (*The Music Bureau Multi-Genre Compendium*).[3] Now sadly lost, according to the literatus Zhou Mi 周密 (1232–1298) of the late Southern Song and early Yuan dynasties, it extended to more than one hundred volumes.[4] Scholar-official Wang Jide 王

1. Among these Dunhuang sources are *pipa* notation: manuscripts Paris, Bibliothèque Nationale, Pelliot chinois 3808, 3719, and 3539; dance notation: manuscript Paris, Bibliothèque Nationale, Pelliot chinois 3501; manuscripts London, the British Library, S.5643, 5613, and 785; manuscript Beijing, the National Library of China BD.10691; manuscript St. Petersburg, the Institute for Oriental Manuscripts Дx.10264; and the most recently published is manuscript Ōsaka, Kyōu Shooku 羽49; See Takeda Kagaku Shinkō Zaidan Kyōu Shooku 武田科学振興財団杏雨書屋, *Tonkō hikyū: Kyōu Shooku zō* 敦煌秘笈: 杏雨書屋蔵 (Osaka: Takeda Kagaku Shinkō Zaidan, 2009), vol. 1, 337–339.

2. Hayashi Kenzō 林謙三, *Gagaku: kogakufu no kaidoku* 雅楽: 古楽譜の解読 (Tokyo: Ongaku no tomosha, 1969), 202–234; Jao Tsong-yi and Paul Demiéville, *Airs de Touen-houang (Touen-houang k'iu): Textes à chanter des VIIIe–Xe siècles* (Paris: Éditions du Centre National de la Recherche Scientifique, 1971), 31–34, 215–219, and plates LI–LVIII; Jao Tsung-i 饒宗頤, *Dunhuang pipa pu* 敦煌琵琶譜 (Taipei: Xinwenfeng chuban gongsi, 1990); Jao Tsung-i 饒宗頤, *Dunhuang pipa pu lunwen ji* 敦煌琵琶譜論文集 (Taipei: Xinwenfeng chuban gongsi, 1991); Chen Yingshi, "A Report on Chinese Research into the Dunhuang Music Manuscripts," *Musica Asiatica* 6 (1991): 61–72; Marnix Wells, "West River Moon: Great Music of Few Notes," *CHIME: Journal of the European Foundation for Chinese Music Research* 7 (1993): 58–89; Laurence Picken, Noël Nickson, and Marnix Wells, "'West River Moon': A Song-Melody predicted by a Lute-Piece in *Piba* Tablature," *CHIME: Journal of the European Foundation for Chinese Music Research* 10/11 (1997): 172–185; and Chen Yingshi 陳應時, *Dunhuang yuepu jieyi bianzheng* 敦煌樂譜解譯辨證 (Shanghai: Shanghai yinyue xueyuan chubanshe, 2005).

3. Wang Guowei 王國維, *Liangzhe gu kanben kao* 兩浙古刊本考, in *Wang Guowei quanji* 王國維全集, ed. Xie Weiyang 謝維揚 and Fang Xinliang 房鑫亮 (Hangzhou: Zhejiang jiaoyu chubanshe, 2009), vol. 7, 18.

4. Zhou Mi 周密, *Qidong yeyu jiaozhu* 齊東野語校注 (Shanghai: Huadong shifan daxue chubanshe, 1987), 200.

此二曲為石帚自製聲律至細開慶四明續志吳毅夫和此詞於過片處國字不次均非是玉田改此曲名為紅情綠意以之賦荷花亦多疏于律本如姜詞中玉字雪字並以入作平用暗香疏景二曲或有謂押韻處全以入作去聲用者余案曲中凡三字逗皆用入聲字且審之皆叶如却渴韃次首之憶字並是至却又怨句絕妙好詞選本作又怨之字亦叶此微眇處知之者蓋鮮已

暗香疏影

乙久リ久ム一乙フ久リフリアム一么人乙フ
舊時月色算幾番照我梅邊吹笛喚起玉人不管
マ与夂ㄅ夕乙一ア久ㄌ夂フム人乙ろマアム
清寒與攀摘何遜而今漸老都忘却春風詞筆但
一乙フ乙夂リ久一ろリア　リア乙フ久フリ
怪得竹外疏花香冷入瑤席　江國正寂寂歎寄
久ク久一フリアム一乙人乙ろマ与久ㄅ夂乙
與路遙夜雪初積翠樽易泣紅萼無言耿相憶長
一ㄅ久ㄌ夂フㄥ人乙ろマアム一么フ乙夂リ
記曾攜手處千樹壓西湖寒碧又片片吹盡也幾

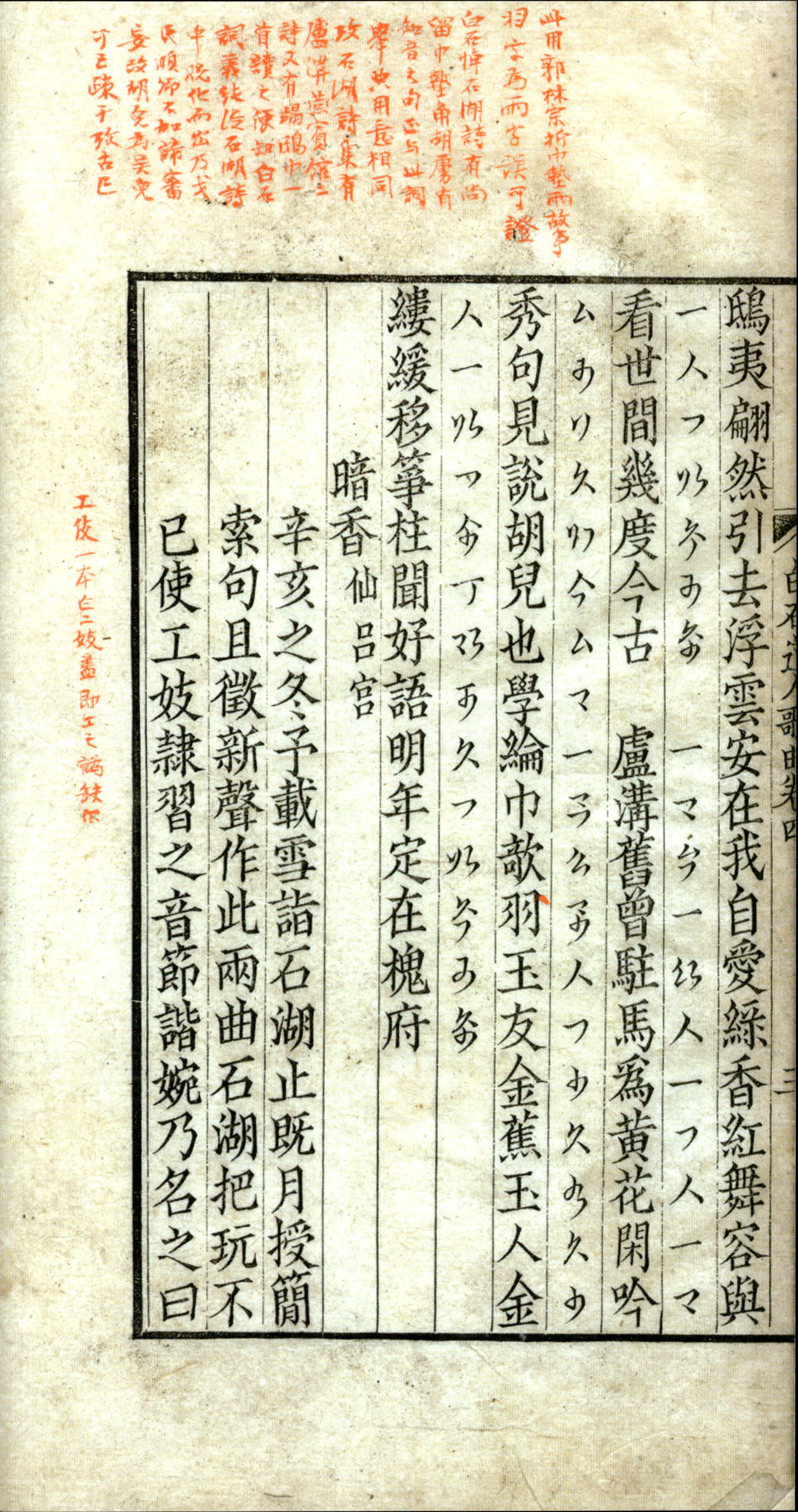

此用郭林宗折巾墊雨故事羽字爲雨字誤可證白石悼石湖詩有尚留巾墊角胡虜有知音之句正与此詞摩典用意相同攷石湖詩集有盧溝嵗宿館二詩又有蹋鵰巾一首讀之便知白石詞義然後石湖詩中脫化而出乃戈氏順卿不加諦審妄改胡兒爲吳兒可云疏于攷古巳

鷗夷翩然引去浮雲安在我自愛綠香紅舞容與看世間幾度今古　盧溝舊曾駐馬爲黃花閑吟秀句見說胡兒也學綸巾攲羽玉友金蕉玉人金縷緩移箏柱聞好語明年定在槐府

暗香　仙呂宮

辛亥之冬予載雪詣石湖止既月授簡索句且徵新聲作此兩曲石湖把玩不已使工妓隸習之音節諧婉乃名之曰

工伎一本作二妓蓋即工之譌[illegible]

Fig. 3.2: *Baishi daoren gequ* (*Songs of the Whitestone Daoist*), *juan* 4, fols. 3v–4r, *Anxian* (*Secret Fragrance*).
Author: Jiang Kui (1155–1221).
Editor: Lu Zhonghui (?–1761).
Date: 1743.
Woodblock: 18.5 × 11.8 cm.
Jiaxing City Library (812.4/5).

白石道人歌曲目錄

卷一

Fig. 3.3: *Baishi daoren gequ* (*Songs of the Whitestone Daoist*), table of contents, fol. 1r.
Author: Jiang Kui (1155–1221).
Editor: Lu Zhonghui (?–1761).
Date: 1743.
Woodblock: 18.5 × 11.8 cm.
Jiaxing City Library (812.4/5).

驥德 (c. 1540–1623) of the Ming dynasty had also caught sight of it, but the copies he viewed were already fragmentary and incomplete.[5] Given the paucity of surviving sources of musical scores, all that is left to the modern scholar from the early centuries of printing are the seventeen *ci* 詞 lyric songs for which Jiang Kui 姜夔 (1155–1221) provided notation in his *Baishi daoren gequ* 白石道人歌曲 (*Songs of the Whitestone Daoist*), first published in Shanghai in 1202. This edition also does not survive, but a copy of it made by the Yuan dynasty hermit-scholar Tao Zongyi 陶宗儀 (1316–1403) was fortuitously discovered during Qianlong's reign in the mid-Qing dynasty. The published result of editorial work on this discovery, which was issued in 1743 (Figs. 3.2 and 3.3), and the working manuscript used for this publication are discussed here.[6]

A thorough comparison between this working manuscript (Fig. 3.4) and the early modern editions published since 1743 reveals examples of textual and musical editing by the early modern collators.[7] Among these discrepancies, one that is of particular interest to Chinese music historians concerns manipulation of the stanzaic divisions of four of Jiang's seventeen songs that he furnished with musical notation, namely *Danhuangliu* 淡黄柳 (*Pale Yellow Willows*), *Changtingyuan* 長亭怨 (*Discontentment at the Long Pavilion*), *Jueshao* 角招 (*A Shao in the Jue Mode*), and *Nishang zhongxu diyi* 霓裳中序第一 (*Rainbow-Skirt: Middle Prelude, First Section*). Our discussion dwells first on *Pale Yellow Willows* and is then followed by an examination of metrical and tonal pattern:[8]

§ 1. In the desolate city, the daybreak horn
blows over the street of hanging willows
§ 2. On horseback in thin clothes
sorrowfully cold
§ 3. Having looked around, the goose yellow and tender green
are my old acquaintances from South of the River

§ 4. I am lonely and
tomorrow is again the Cold Eating Festival
§ 5. With great effort I carry wine
to younger Qiao's house
§ 6. I fear, the pear blossom
having fallen completely, all will become autumn in color
§ 7. The swallows fly back
asking where is spring?
but there is only the pool's green

§ 1. 空城曉角，吹入垂楊陌。
§ 2. 馬上單衣，寒惻惻。
§ 3. 看盡鵝黃嫩綠，都是江南舊相識。

§ 4. 正岑寂，明朝又寒食。
§ 5. 强攜酒，小橋宅。
§ 6. 怕梨花，落盡成秋色。
§ 7. 燕燕飛來，問春何在？唯有池塘自碧。

§ 1. *Kou cheng xiao jiao, chui ru chui yang mo.*
○ ○ ● ● ○ ● ○ ○ ●
△ ▲
§ 2. *Ma shang dan yi, han ce ce.*
● ● ○ ○ ○ ●●
△ ▲
§ 3. *Kan jin e huang nen lü, dou shi jiang nan jiu xiang shi.*
● ●○ ○ ● ● ○ ● ○ ○ ● ○ ●
△ ▲

§ 4. *Zheng cen ji, min zhou you han shi.*
● ○ ● ○ ○ ● ○ ●
▲ ▲
§ 5. *Qiang xie jiu, xiao qiao zhai.*
● ○ ● ● ○ ●
△ ▲
§ 6. *Pa li hua, luo jin cheng qiu se.*
●○ ○ ● ● ○ ○ ●
△ ▲
§ 7. *Yan yan fei lai, wen chun he zai? wei you chi tang zi bi.*
● ● ○ ○ ● ○ ○ ● ○ ● ○ ○ ● ●
△ △ ▲

5. Wang Jide 王驥德, *Wang Jide Qu lü* 王驥德曲律 (Changsha: Hunan renmin chubanshe, 1983), 206–208.

6. A complete facsimile of the working manuscript of the 1743 edition can be found in Yang Yuanzheng, *Plum Blossom on the Far Side of the Stream: The Renaissance of Jiang Kui's Lyric Oeuvre with Facsimiles and a New Critical Edition of the Songs of the Whitestone Daoist* (Hong Kong: Hong Kong University Press, 2019), 191–254.

7. Yang Yuanzheng, *Plum Blossom on the Far Side of the Stream*, 42–58 and 89–187.

8. With slight modifications, the English translation of the *Pale Yellow Willows* is from Yang Yuanzheng, *Plum Blossom on the Far Side of the Stream*, 43. Following conventional Chinese practice since the early modern period, tones are indicated by a system of circles: ○ for a level tone, ● for a deflected tone, and line division by an underdot ▲ for the end-rhyme. Clause division within a line is shown by △, which denotes a pause within a line. For further information on the metrical pattern of *ci*, see Glen William Baxter, "Metrical Origins of the Tz'u," *Harvard Journal of Asiatic Studies* 16.1/2 (1953): 108–145; and Shih-chuan Chen, "The Rise of the Tz'u, Reconsidered," *Journal of the American Oriental Society* 90.2 (1970): 232–242.

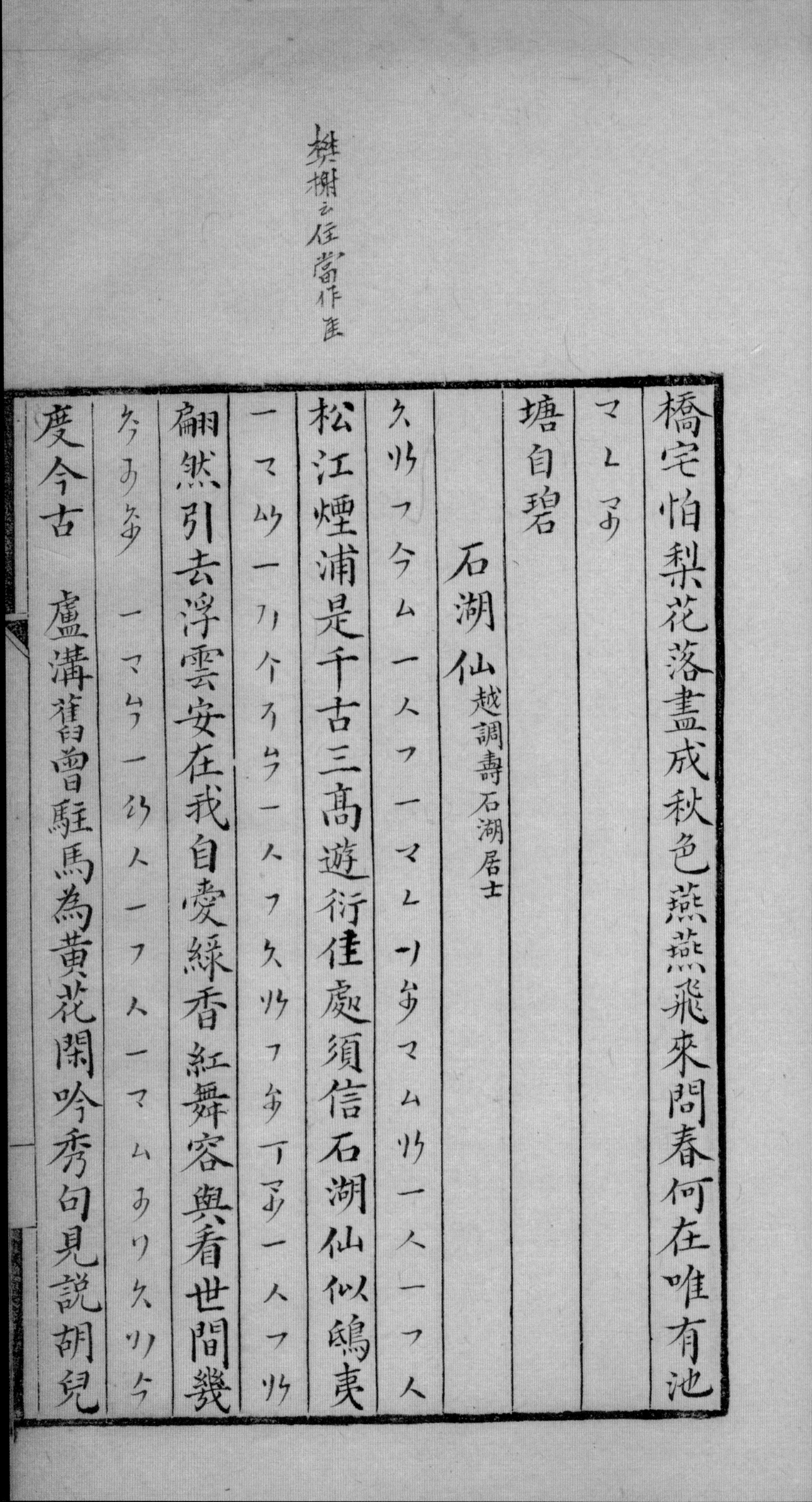

樊榭云住當作庄

橋宅怕梨花落盡成秋色燕燕飛來問春何在唯有池
塘自碧

石湖仙 越調壽石湖居士

松江煙浦是千古三高遊衍佳處須信石湖仙似鴟夷
翩然引去浮雲安在我自愛綠香紅舞容與看世間幾
度今古 盧溝舊曾駐馬為黃花閑吟秀句見說胡兒

Fig. 3.4: *Baishi daoren gequ (Songs of the Whitestone Daoist), juan 5*, fols. 2v–3r, *Danhuangliu* (*Pale Yellow Willows*).
Author: Jiang Kui (1155–1221).
Editors: Li E (1692–1752), Min Hua (1697–after 1773), and Wang Zao.
Date: c. 1736.
Border: 18.2 × 12.8 cm.
Private collection.

只

正岑寂三字語寫在上

么一ムム么ㄎフ人久人么马么马

人為主筭空有并刀難剪離愁千縷

淡黃柳 正平調近

客居合肥南城赤欄橋之西巷陌凄凉與江左異

唯柳色夾道依依可憐因度此闋以紓客懷

フ人么ㄋ刂久么一マ么フ马久ㄋ刂马ムマリマ么

空城曉角吹入垂楊陌馬上單衣寒惻惻看盡鵞黃嫩

フリ久一マム么马马么马—ㄋ人么リフ么ㄅ久ㄅ

綠都是江南舊相識正岑寂—明朝又寒食強攜酒小

刂フ人フ人刂马ㄋ今今リ久ㄅ久么リリ今リ久么

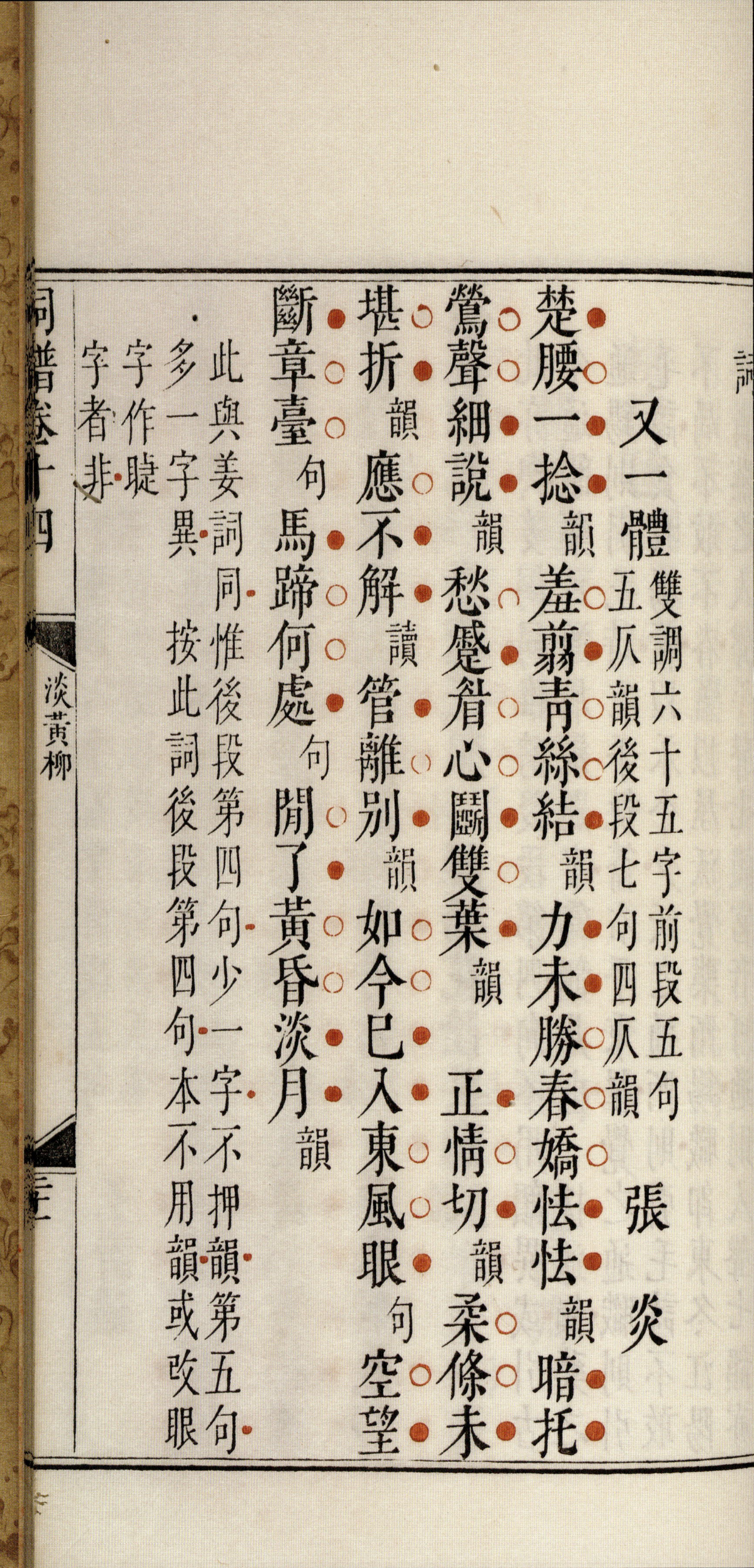

又一體　雙調六十五字前段五句五仄韻後段七句四仄韻　張炎

楚腰一捻韻羞剪青絲結韻力未勝春嬌怯怯韻暗托鶯聲細說韻愁蹙眉心鬬雙葉韻正情切韻柔條未堪折韻應不解讀管離別韻如今已入東風眼句空望斷章臺句馬蹄何處句閒了黃昏淡月韻

此與姜詞同惟後段第四句少一字不押韻第五句多一字異　按此詞後段第四句本不用韻或改眼字作睫字者非

詞譜卷十四　淡黃柳

Fig. 3.5: *Qinding Cipu (The Imperial Register of Lyric Song), juan* 14, fols. 20v–21r, metrical pattern and rhyme scheme of the tune *Pale Yellow Willows* by Jiang Kui. Compilers: Wang Yiqing (1664–1737) et al. Date: 1715. Woodblock: 19.4 × 12.3 cm. Fung Ping Shan Library.

此調僅見此詞無別首可校

淡黃柳 姜夔自度曲白石集注正平調

淡黃柳 雙調六十五字前段五句五仄韻後段七句五仄韻 姜夔

空城畫角韻吹入垂楊陌韻馬上單衣寒惻惻韻看盡鵝黃嫩綠韻都是江南舊相識韻 正岑寂韻明朝又寒食韻強攜酒讀小橋宅韻怕棃花讀落盡成秋色韻燕燕飛來句問春何在句惟有池塘自碧韻

正岑寂三字詞律移作前段結句查張炎王沂孫詞俱屬換頭今改正 此詞可平可仄卽叅下張王二

The lyrics are arranged in two stanzas, which can be further subdivided into seven strophic units. The first three strophes belong to the first stanza, each ending respectively in the rhyming words: *mo* 陌 (*mɐk*), *ce* 惻 (*ʧʰĭək*), and *shi* 識 (*ɕĭək*). The other four strophes form the second stanza, this time ending respectively in the rhyming words: *shi* 食 (*dʑĭək*), *zhai* 宅 (*ȡɐk*), *se* 色 (*ʃĭək*), and *bi* 碧 (*pĭɛk*). Each of these seven strophes can be further subdivided into one, two, or three clauses. The fourth strophe also contains an additional rhyming word *ji* 寂 (*dzĭək*), which adheres to the end of the first of its two clauses, that is, *zheng cen ji* 正岑寂. Syntactically and semantically, this three-word clause should be the opening line of the second stanza; in all the early modern editions, it is treated in this manner, however, in the working manuscript of the 1743 edition it is, rather curiously, positioned at the end of the first stanza (see Fig. 3.4, fol. 2v, col. 9).

Twenty-eight years before the publication of the 1743 edition (1715) and in the complete absence of information on the musical and melodic component, Kangxi published in red and black ink the *Qinding Cipu* 欽定詞譜 (*The Imperial Register of Lyric Song*) that listed a grand total of 826 of the metrical patterns and rhyme schemes of Song dynasty *cipai* 詞牌, a number that increases to over 2,300 when all of the different variants are considered. The Fung Ping Shan Library holds a copy of this text.[9] An authoritative publication, it too moves the clause *zheng cen ji* to the beginning of the second stanza (Fig. 3.5, fol. 20v, vol. 5).

Jiang Kui's inclusion of notational symbols affords unique possibilities for exploring the poet's original intentions. When the transitional clauses between the two stanzas of the four pieces in question are examined, an unusual phenomenon is observed: the melodic contour of the relevant clause at the transition always repeats the final notes of the first stanza: in *Pale Yellow Willows* (see Fig. 3.4, fol. 2v, col. 8), the transitional clause *zheng cen ji* 正岑寂 is sung to *si shang si* (in *gongche* notation, D-F-D),[10] and the last three characters of the first stanza *jiu xiang shi* 舊相識 are sung to *he shang si* (C-F-D); in *Discontentment at the Long Pavilion*, the transitional clause *ri mu* 日暮 is set to *shang yi* (F-E♭), as are the last two characters of the first stanza *ru ci* 如此; in *A Shao in the Jue Mode*, the transitional clause *you you* 猶有 is sung to *che yi* (G-E), as are the last two characters of the first stanza *hui shou* 回首; and in *Rainbow-Skirt: Middle Prelude, First Section*, the transitional clause *you ji* 幽寂 is sung to *liu fan* (C-B♭), as are the last two characters of the first stanza *yan se* 顏色.

Melodic repetition as precise as this is unlikely to be a coincidence. Without exception, the four problematic transitional clauses are all located at the end of the first stanza. This being the case, given the early modern collators' stance that these clauses were incorrectly positioned in the 1202 edition, the issue must be addressed: how great is the probability that this was an error? Recent research reveals that the transitional clause was in fact deliberately situated by Jiang Kui at the end of the first stanza to correspond to the musical form of the piece, and this particular musical device was called *jindou* 巾斗.[11] Just as in a somersault, by which the body tumbles 360 degrees with the feet looping over the head, the musical form *jindou* occurs when the cadential notes of a strophe immediately repeat at the

9. Jao Tsung-i 饒宗頤, Li Zhifang 李直方, and Zhang Lijuan 張麗娟, *Xianggang daxue Feng Pingshan tushuguan cang shanben shulu* 香港大學馮平山圖書館藏善本書錄, enlarged ed. (Hong Kong: Hong Kong University Press, 2003), 331. In chronological order, the seals found on it belong to: Chen Li 陳澧 (1810–1887), He Kunyu 何昆玉 (1828–1896), Liang Yuwei 梁于渭 (1840–1912), and Liang Dingfen 梁鼎芬 (1859–1919), followed by a married couple Cai Zhefu 蔡哲夫 (1879–1941) and Tan Yuese 談月色 (1891–1976), all inhabitants of Guangdong. In 1930, Cai Zhefu and Tan Yuese invited Wen You 聞宥 (1901–1985) to compose a poem and a colophon that are found at the end of the book. The poem stresses the book's importance and its scarcity in south China owing to the wet and humid climate. Due to bookworm damage, the blank margins above and below the printing block of many pages have been excised and new paper of an identical color and quality stuck on at this point, together with leaves inserted between the folded pages to give additional support. When this was done is not entirely clear, but it has been accomplished so expertly that these repairs can only be discerned with difficulty.

10. Following Rulan Chao Pian, a pitch of c' has been accepted for the Huangzhong 黃鍾, the fundamental of the modal system, rather than d', as proposed by Yang Yinliu 楊蔭瀏 and Laurence Picken. See Rulan Chao Pian, *Sonq Dynasty Musical Sources and Their Interpretation* (Cambridge, Mass.: Harvard University Press, 1967), 43–44; Yang Yinliu 楊蔭瀏 and Yin Falu 陰法魯, *Song Jiang Baishi chuangzuo gequ yanjiu* 宋姜白石創作歌曲研究 (Beijing: Yinyue chubanshe, 1957), 35; and Laurence Picken, "Secular Chinese Songs of the Twelfth Century," *Studia Musicologica Academiae Scientiarum Hungaricae* 8 (1966): 139.

11. Yang Yuanzheng, *Plum Blossom on the Far Side of the Stream: The Renaissance of Jiang Kui's Lyric Oeuvre with Facsimiles and a New Critical Edition of the Songs of the Whitestone Daoist*, 42–58; and Yang Yuanzheng, "*Jindou*: A Musical Form found in Southern Song Lyric Songs," *T'oung Pao* 101.1/3 (2015): 98–129. A complete facsimile of the working manuscript of the 1743 edition can be found in Yang's *Plum Blossom on the Far Side of the Stream*, 191–254.

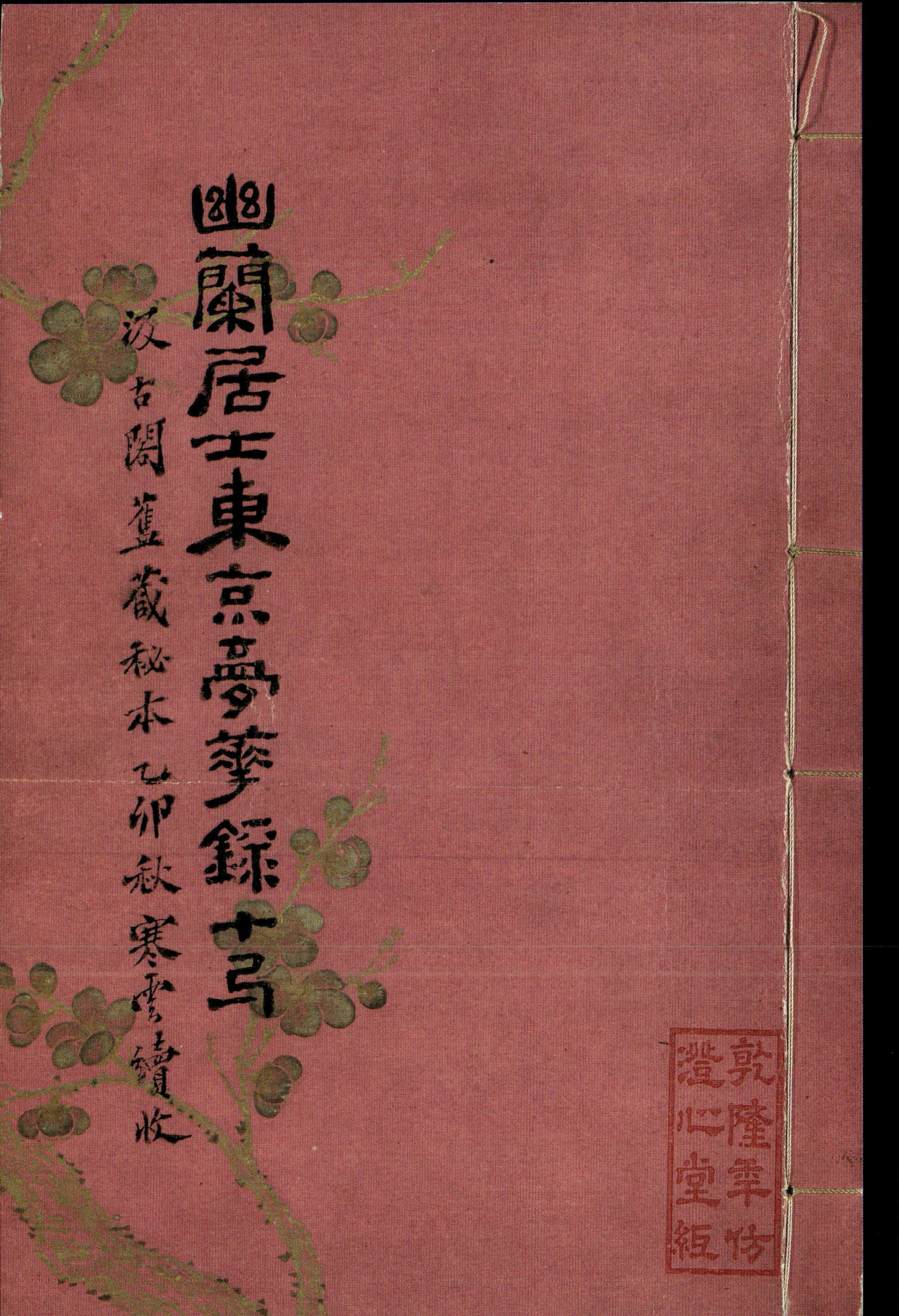

Fig. 3.6: *Dongjing menghua lu (Reminiscences of the Eastern Capital)*, book cover.
Author: Meng Yuanlao (fl. 1103–1147).
Date: 1328.
Woodblock: 22.1 × 16.3 cm.
Peking Library (08676).

情緒牢落漸入桑榆暗想當年節物風流人情和美但成悵恨近与親戚會面談及曩昔後生往往妄生不然僕恐浸久論其風俗者失於事實誠爲可惜謹省記編次成集庶幾開卷得覩當時之盛古人有夢遊華胥之國其樂無涯者僕今追念回首悵然豈非華胥之夢覺哉目之曰夢華録然以京師之浩穰及有未嘗經從處得之於人不無遺闕倘遇鄉黨宿德補綴周備不勝幸甚此録語言鄙俚不以文飾者盖欲上下通曉爾觀者幸詳焉紹興丁卯歲除日幽蘭居士孟元老序

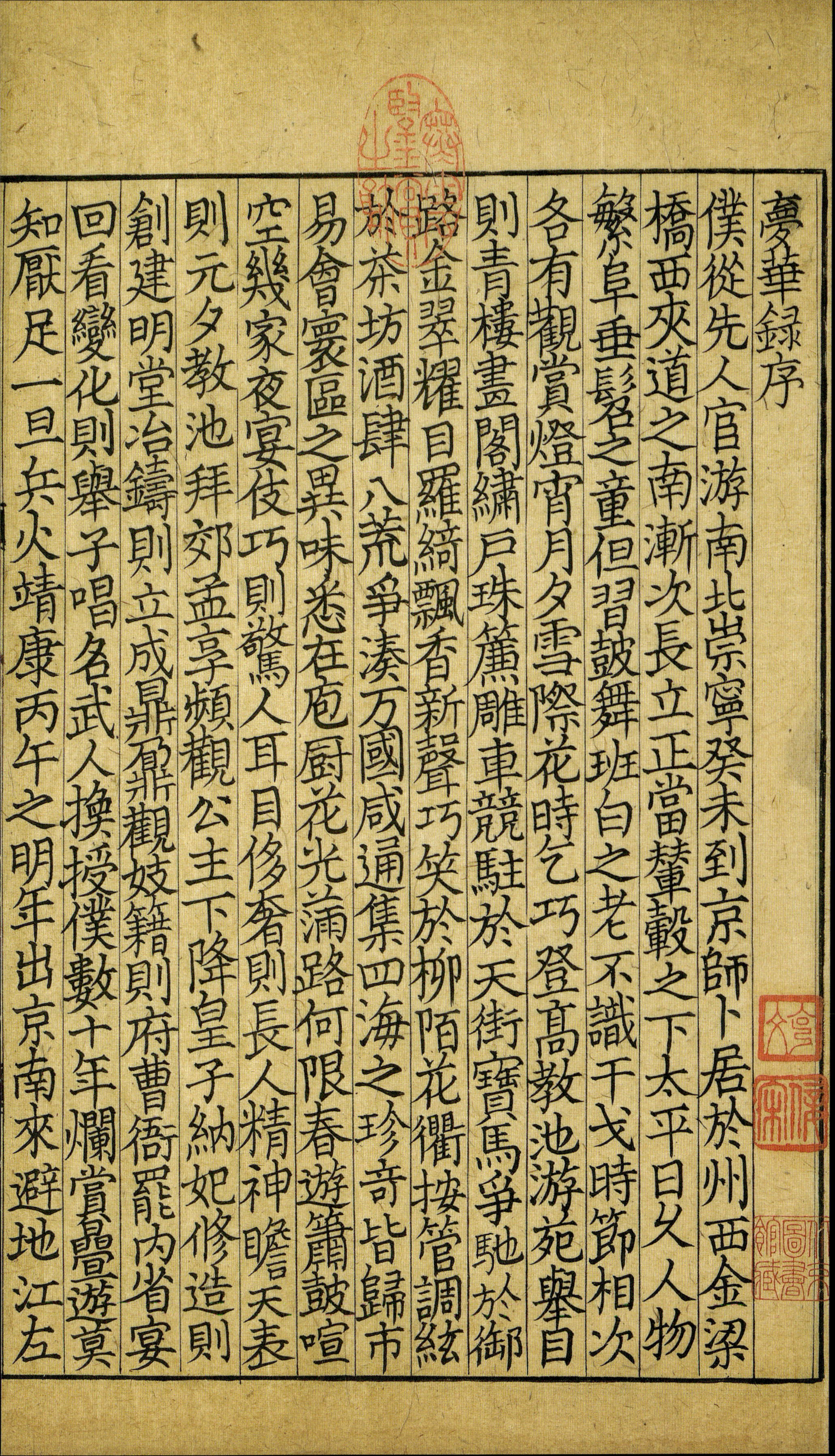

夢華録序

僕從先人宦游南北崇寧癸未到京師卜居於州西金梁橋西夾道之南漸次長立正當輦轂之下太平日久人物繁阜垂髫之童但習鼓舞班白之老不識干戈時節相次各有觀賞燈宵月夕雪際花時乞巧登高教池游苑舉目則青樓畫閣繡戸珠簾雕車競駐於天街寶馬爭馳於御路金翠耀目羅綺飄香新聲巧笑於柳陌花衢按管調絃於茶坊酒肆八荒爭湊万國咸通集四海之珍奇皆歸市易會寰區之異味悉在庖厨花光滿路何限春遊簫鼓喧空幾家夜宴伎巧則驚人耳目侈奢則長人精神瞻天表則元夕教池拜郊孟享頻觀公主下降皇子納妃修造則創建明堂冶鑄則立成鼎鼐觀妓籍則府曹衙罷内省宴回看變化則舉子唱名武人換授僕數十年爛賞疊遊莫知厭足一旦兵火靖康丙午之明年出京南來避地江左

Fig. 3.7: *Dongjing menghua lu (Reminiscences of the Eastern Capital)*, preface, fols. 1r–v.
Author: Meng Yuanlao (fl. 1103–1147).
Date: 1328.
Woodblock: 22.1 × 16.3 cm.
Peking Library (08676).

新鐫古今大雅北宮詞紀六卷目錄

閨情

黄鍾醉花陰 七套

簾捲春寒杏花雨 春情　鴛鴦浦蓮開並蒂長 春怨

雪浪銀濤大江迴 趕蘇卿　錦繡江山画圖裡 仕女郊遊

黑海愁心最難寫 抒懷　牕外芭蕉戰秋雨 同上

今歲江梅試花早 冬怨

願成雙 二套

梅腮退柳眼肥 憶別　春初透花正結 春思

正宮端正好 四套　南梁州令 一套

Fig. 3.8: *Xinjuan gujin daya nanbei gong ciji* (*Newly-Cut, Ancient and Modern, of Extreme Elegance, Northern Lyrics in the Musical Modes*), table of contents, fol. 1r.
Editor: Chen Suowen (1587–1626).
Date: 1604.
Woodblock: 21.5 × 14.1 cm.
Fung Ping Shan Library.

opening of the subsequent strophe. In these four Jiang Kui songs, the opening line of the second stanza may well have been intentionally inserted at the end of the first stanza so as to remind the performers of an approaching *jindou*. In other words, this unusual positioning is not erroneous, but a manifestation of conventional performance practice as formulated by musical processes. Memoirs of cultural life in the Northern and Southern Song capitals, such as Meng Yuanlao's 孟元老 (fl. 1103–1147) *Dongjing menghua lu* 東京夢華錄 (Figs. 3.6 and 3.7) and Wu Zimu's 吳自牧 (act. 1274) *Mengliang lu* 夢粱錄, reveal that this musical form had also been employed in the contemporary vernacular repertoire of *zhuan* 賺 vocal tunes.

The Song dynasty *ci* faded from prominence as the Yuan dynasty progressed and was partially supplanted by the *qu* 曲. A subtype of the *qu* form is the *sanqu* 散曲,[12] another fixed-rhythm genre of classical Chinese poetry or literary song and one that originated in the Jin 金 dynasty (1115–1234), though the form is more associated with the Yuan, Ming, and Qing. Like *ci*, *sanqu* words were added to pre-existing melodies, nowadays mostly lost, though their metrical patterns remain. More so than *ci*, however, their tonal patterns were modeled on tunes drawn from folksongs or other music, and in style their texts were vernacular or even humorous. The poetry of both genres could also be joined together in chains to form a suite. As a vernacular literary style, *sanqu* tend to express a counterculture of resentment at political domination by the foreign Jurchen or Mongol ruling classes. Additionally, the line between *sanqu* as a literary form and sung dramas with a narrative structure can be blurred, and many distinguished writers had a foot in both camps, for example, Ma Zhiyuan 馬致遠 (c. 1270–1330) and Guan Hanqing 關漢卿 (c. 1225–c. 1302). The popularity of music of these various genres continued into the Ming dynasty, and private publishing houses were keen to increase the accessibility of printed works by including illustrations. One such example is *Xinjuan gujin daya nanbei gong ciji* 新鐫古今大雅南北宮詞紀 (*Newly-Cut, Ancient and Modern, of Extreme Elegance, Northern and Southern Ci Lyrics in the Musical Modes*) of which the Fung Ping Shan Library possesses a copy (Fig. 3.8).[13]

This *sanqu* selection was edited by Chen Suowen 陳所聞 (c. 1553–?) and in it are works by Tang Shi 湯式, Chen Duo 陳鐸 (c. 1436–1507), and the editor himself, some of which are unique to this book. Chen Suowen, *zi* soubriquet Jinqing 藎卿 and *hao* soubriquet Luoyue daoren 蘿月道人 (The Purple Vine-Moon Daoist), was originally from Nanjing. Knowledgeable in music theory and adept at composing both *ci* and *qu*, while sojourning next to the Mochou hu 莫愁湖 (Don't Worry Lake) in Nanjing, he joined together with Wang Wenyao 王文耀, Cong Wenwei 叢文蔚 (*jinshi* degree 1568), Jin Luan 金鑾 (1494–1587), and others to form the Changgan Society 長干社, a fellowship of about forty elderly compatriots, all free-thinking and libertine, who wallowed in the delights of poetry and wine. Later in life, he lived under the protection and patronage of the salt merchant Wang Tingne 汪廷訥 (1573–1619). Eight of the eighteen dramas listed in Wang Tingne's drama anthology *Huancui tang yuefu* 環翠堂樂府 (*The Hall of the Jadeite Circlet Yuefu Repertory*) were in fact written by Chen Suowen.[14]

Newly-Cut, Ancient and Modern, of Extreme Elegance, Northern and Southern Ci Lyrics in the Musical Modes was published by the well-known printers Jizhi zhai 繼志齋 (Continued Aspirations Studio), whose owner was Chen Dalai 陳大來, and issued in the thirty-second year of the Wanli era (1604). Throughout the book, illustrations are spread across double pages; they are exquisitely fine in execution and of the first rank of specimens produced by these publishers.

The *Northern Ci Lyrics* portion was first issued in 1604 and the *Southern Ci Lyrics* in 1605, each

12. For further information about *sanqu*, see, for example, Patricia Sieber, "Rethinking the History of Early *Sanqu* Songs," *CHINOPERL: Journal of Chinese Oral and Performing Literature* 26.1 (2005): 83–98; Patricia Sieber, "Nobody's Genre, Everybody's Song: *Sanqu* Songs and the Expansion of the Literary Sphere in Yuan China," *Journal of Chinese Literature and Culture* 1.1 (2014): 29–64; Patricia Sieber, "The Protean World of *Sanqu* Songs," *Journal of Chinese Literature and Culture* 8.1 (2021): 1–11; and Wang Shi-pe, "Plays within Songs: *Sanqu* Songs from Literary Refinement (*ya*) to Popular Appeal (*su*)," *Journal of Chinese Literature and Culture* 8.2 (2021): forthcoming.

13. Jao Tsung-i 饒宗頤, *Xianggang daxue Feng Pingshan tushuguan cang shanben shulu* 香港大學馮平山圖書館藏善本書錄 (Hong Kong: Longmen shudian, 1970), 109–110; and Jao Tsung-i, Li Zhifang, and Zhang Lijuan, *Xianggang daxue Feng Pingshan tushuguan cang shanben shulu*, enlarged ed., 335–336. For transcriptions of the *sanqu* contained therein, see Zhao Jingshen 趙景深, *Nan bei gong ciji* 南北宮詞紀 (Beijing: Zhonghua shuju, 1959); and Wu Xiaoling 吳曉鈴, *Nan bei gong ciji jiaobu* 南北宮詞紀校補 (Beijing: Zhonghua shuju, 1961).

14. Zhou Hui 周暉, *Xu Jinling suoshi* 續金陵瑣事 (Beijing: Wenxue guji kanxingshe, 1955), 150. For a facsimile edition of a woodblock printing album depicting Wang Tingne's Hall of the Jadeite Circlet, see Li Pingfan 李平凡, ed., *Huancui tang yuanjing tu* 環翠堂園景圖 (Beijing: Renmin meishu chubanshe, 1981).

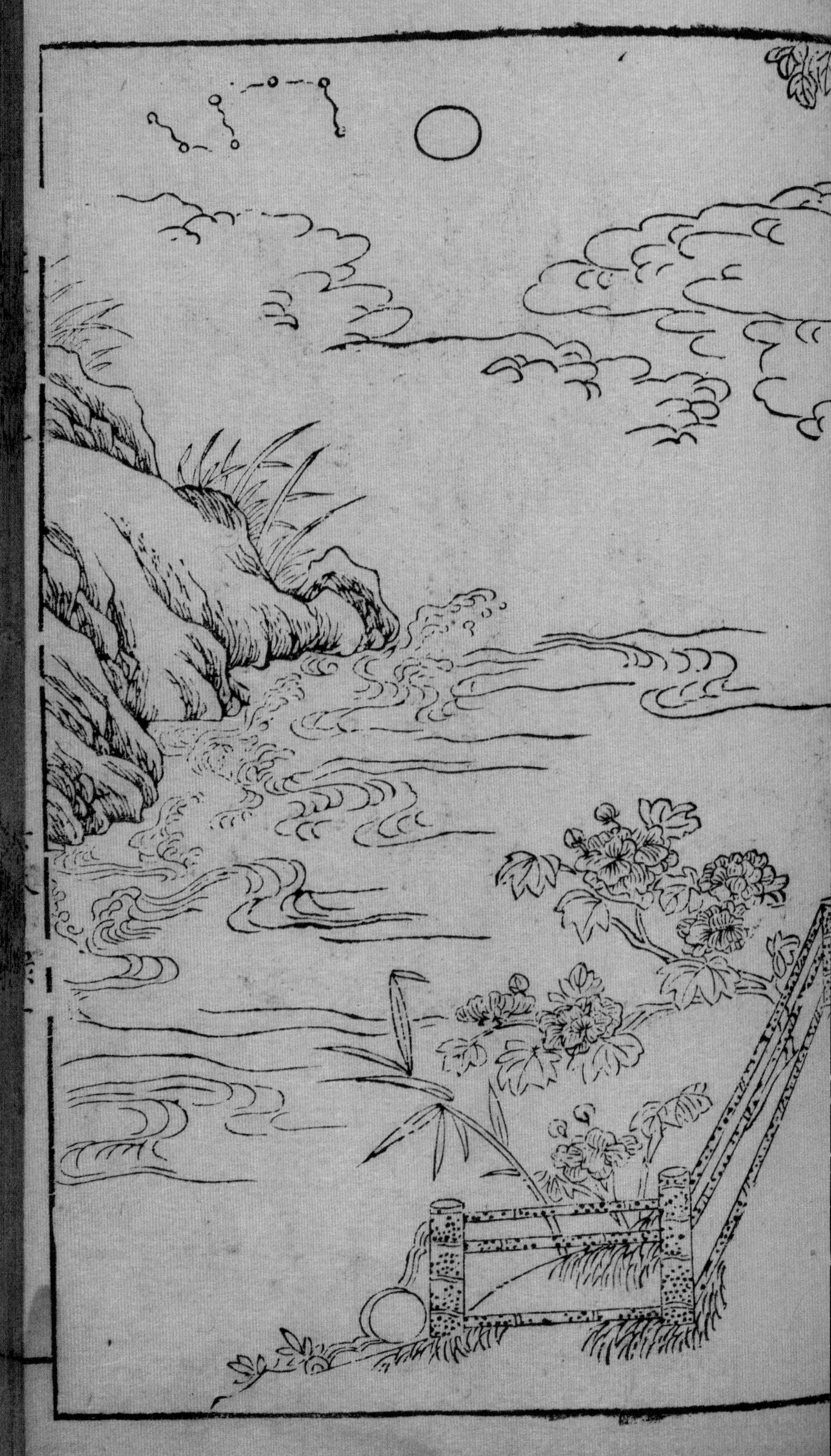

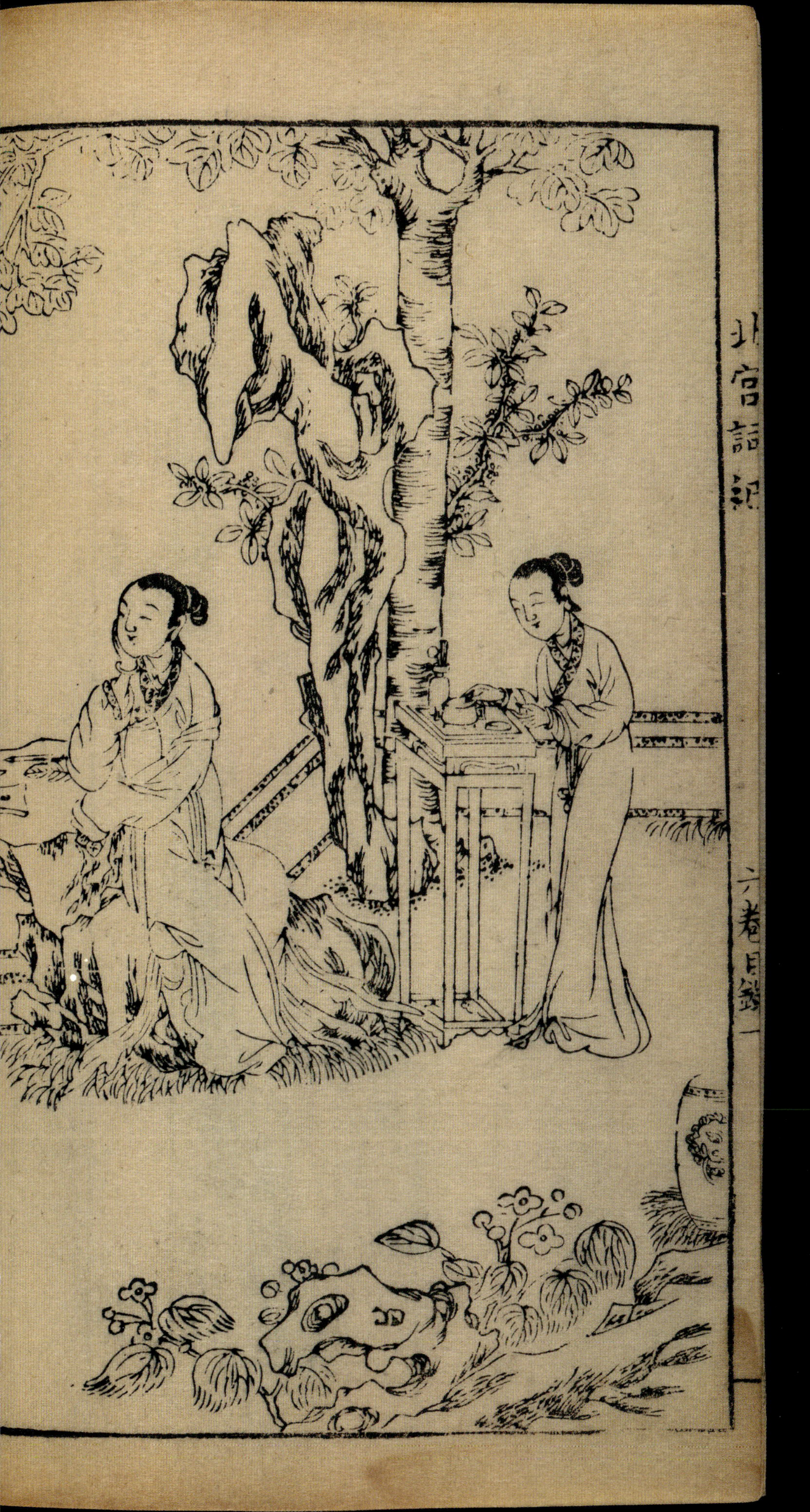

Fig. 3.9: *Xinjuan gujin daya nanbei gong ciji (Newly-Cut, Ancient and Modern, of Extreme Elegance, Northern Lyrics in the Musical Modes), juan* 6, fascicle 7, fols. 1v–2r, woodblock engraving of an opera aria.
Editor: Chen Suowen (1587–1626).
Date: 1604.
Woodblock: 21.5 × 14.1 cm.
Fung Ping Shan Library.

comprising eight volumes. On examining the Fung Ping Shan Library copy, the print quality strongly indicates that the two portions belong to impressions made at different times. In this respect, the Fung Ping Shan Library rare book catalog entry (enlarged version) is flawed, as it regards the first set of the eight volumes as containing both the northern and southern portions, and the second set of eight volumes as a duplicate,[15] whereas this is not in fact the case.

In the *Southern Ci Lyrics* section, the seal of an early nineteenth-century bibliophile Ma Guohan 馬國翰 (1794–1857) can be found, and on a page preceding the first printed folio is an anonymous handwritten collector's note that tells the story of how the book was bought and how precious it has proved to be, followed by a stamp showing it as an item in the collection of the Nanhai dujing tang 南海讀經堂 (The Hall of Reading Canonic Texts of the Southern Sea). Influenced perhaps by the collector's note, Jao Tsung-i recorded that the book is not furnished with any illustrations,[16] but in fact, in the sixth *juan* of the *Northern Ci Lyrics* portion is a woodcut spanning a double page (Fig. 3.9). The subject of this picture appears to be an aria from the celebrated *zaju* 雜劇 opera *Xixiang ji* 西廂記 (*Romance of the Western Wing*) by Yuan dynasty playwright Wang Shifu 王實甫 (c. 1260–c. 1337) called "Fenxiang baiyue" 焚香拜月 ("Burning Incense and Praying to the Moon") sung by the principal female protagonist Cui Yingying 崔鶯鶯.[17] Leaning on a stone, she and her servant Hongniang 紅娘 are situated beneath a *wutong* 梧桐 tree. Appearing distracted, she gazes out over the water, perhaps thinking of what to write with the brush and inkstone placed on the rock beside her. On her other side is an incense burner resting on a long-legged stand that is tended by her maid. Zigzagging railings divide the bank from the gently rippling waters and the cloudscape above them, in which a full moon shines resplendently; the constellation of the Big Dipper is visible immediately to its left. Carefully graded thicknesses of intricate lines and swirling patterns of water, rock, leaf, and cloud make this a fine example of the Nanjing style of woodcut illustration.

The popularity of this most celebrated of dramas, as art historian Wang Fangyu has aptly remarked, "stretched the imagination of the illustrator."[18] Its narration of the romance between the young girl Cui Yingying and the young scholar Zhang Gong 張珙 is portrayed in more than twenty different illustrated editions of the Ming and early Qing, including a beautifully designed and executed specimen in color containing twenty-one prints issued in 1640 by Min Qiji 閔齊伋 (1580–after 1661), a highly respected publishing lineage of Wuxing in Zhejiang.[19]

As an important example of early multiple-block coloring, the only surviving copy of this edition is in the collection of Cologne's Museum für Ostasiatische Kunst.[20] At the end of the sixteenth and the beginning of the seventeenth centuries, woodblock color printing technology developed to its apotheosis. The Min family and other private publishing houses in Zhejiang printed several hundred classics, illustrated novels, dramas, and medical books in two to five colors. Among members of the clan, the most celebrated was Min Qiji, who at that time, together with others, published no fewer than one hundred books. In 1581, Ling Mengchu 淩濛初 (1580–1684) printed

15. Jao Tsung-i, Li Zhifang, and Zhang Lijuan, *Xianggang daxue Feng Pingshan tushuguan cang shanben shulu*, enlarged ed., 335–336. The original bibliographical record is correct; see Jao Tsung-i, *Xianggang daxue Feng Pingshan tushuguan cang shanben shulu*, 109–110.

16. Ibid.

17. For an English translation of Wang's opera, see Stephen H. West and Wilt L. Idema, trans., *The Story of the Western Wing* (Berkeley: University of California Press, 1995). For further information about *zaju*, see Wilt L. Idema, "Why you have never read a Yuan Drama: The Transformation of *Zaju* at the Ming Court," in *Studi in onore di Lionelle Lanciotti*, ed. S. M. Carletti et al. (Naples: Dipartimento di Studi Asiatici, Istituto Universitario Orientale, 1996), 765–791.

18. Wang Fang-yu, "Book Illustration in Late Ming and Early Qing China," in *Chinese Rare Books in American Collections*, ed. Sören Edgren (New York: China Institute in America, 1984), 33.

19. Tao Xiang 陶湘, *Mingdai Wuxing Minban shumu* 明吳興閔板書目, in Tao Xiang 陶湘, *Taoshi shumu congkan* 陶氏書目叢刊 (Wujin: Taoshi, 1933), vol. 1; and Wang Rongguo 王榮國, Wang Xiaowen 王筱雯, and Wang Qingyuan 王清原, *Mingdai Min Ling ke taoyinben tulu* 明代閔淩刻套印本圖錄 (Yangzhou: Guangling shushe, 2006).

20. For a beautiful colored facsimile of the twenty-one illustrations in this album, see Edith Dittrich, ed., *Hsi-hsiang chi, Chinesische Farbholzschnitte von Min Ch'i-chi* (Köln: Museum für Ostasiatische der Stadt Köln, 1977). Fan Jingzhong suggests the album might have been published in Nanjing and not Wuxing. See Fan Jingzhong 范景中, "Taoyin ben he Min keben jiqi *Huizhen tu* 套印本和閔刻本及其《會真圖》," *Xin meishu* 新美術 (2005) 4: 77–82. For more information on multi-colored woodblock printing, see, for example, James Cahill, "The Shibui Printed Books in Chinese and Japanese Erotic Pictorial Art," *Orientations* 40.3 (2009): 43–48; and Sören Edgren, "The Bibliographic Significance of Colour-Printed Books from the Shibui Collection," *Orientations* 40.3 (2009): 30–37.

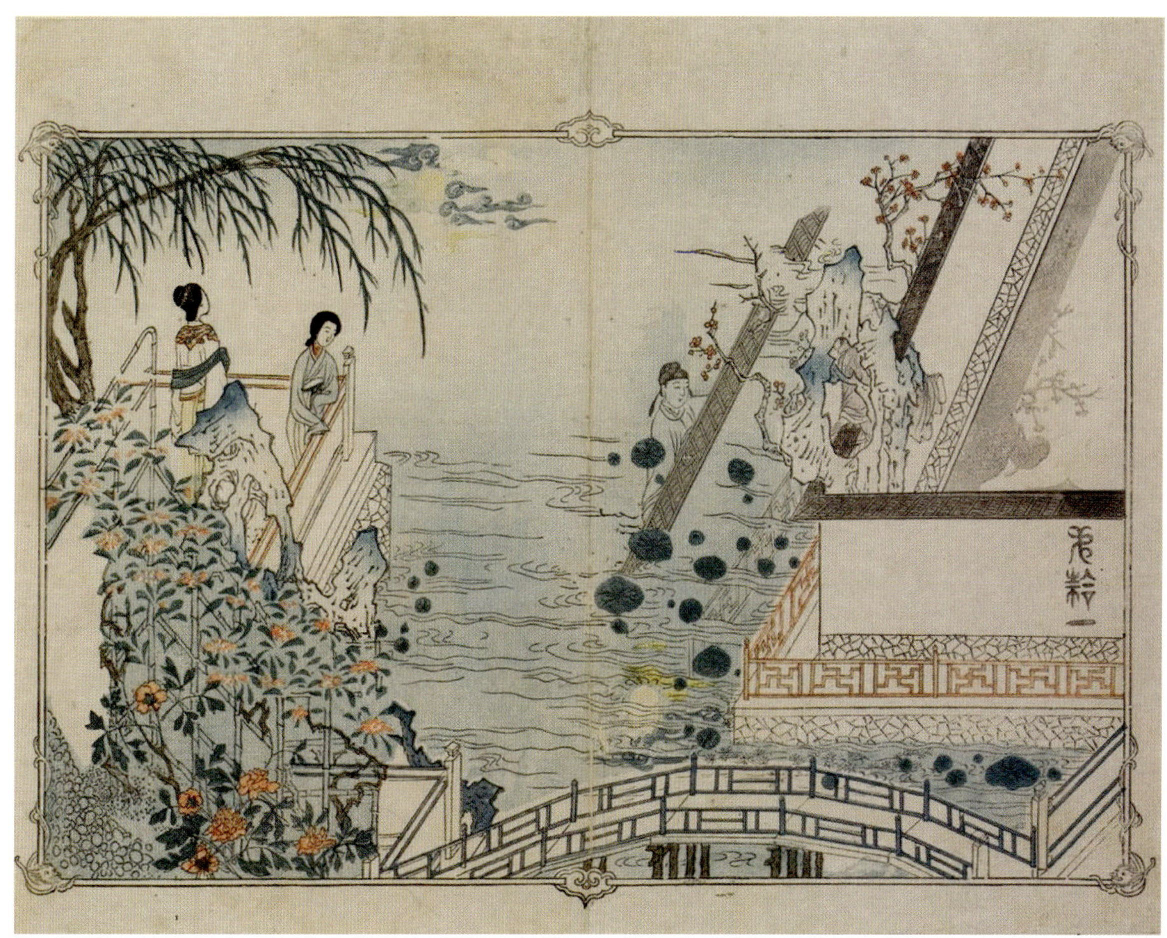

Fig. 3.10: *Xixiang ji (Romance of the Western Wing)*, album leaf 11.
Author: Wang Shifu
(c. 1260–c. 1337).
Date: 1640.
Dimensions: 25.5 × 32.2 cm.
Museum für Ostasiatische Kunst der Stadt Köln (R 62.1).

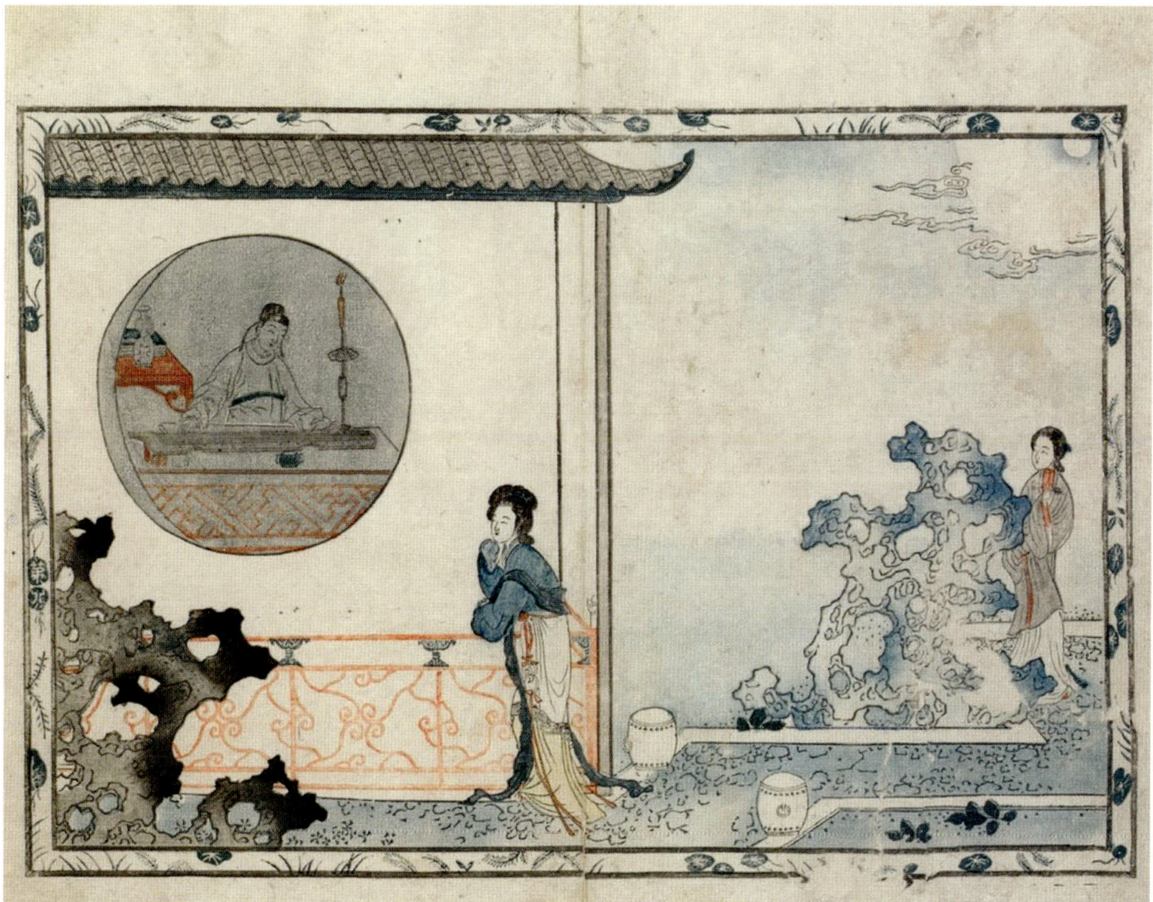

Fig. 3.11: *Xixiang ji (Romance of the Western Wing)*, album leaf 8.
Author: Wang Shifu
(c. 1260–c. 1337).
Date: 1640.
Dimensions: 25.5 × 32.2 cm.
Museum für Ostasiatische Kunst der Stadt Köln (R 62.1).

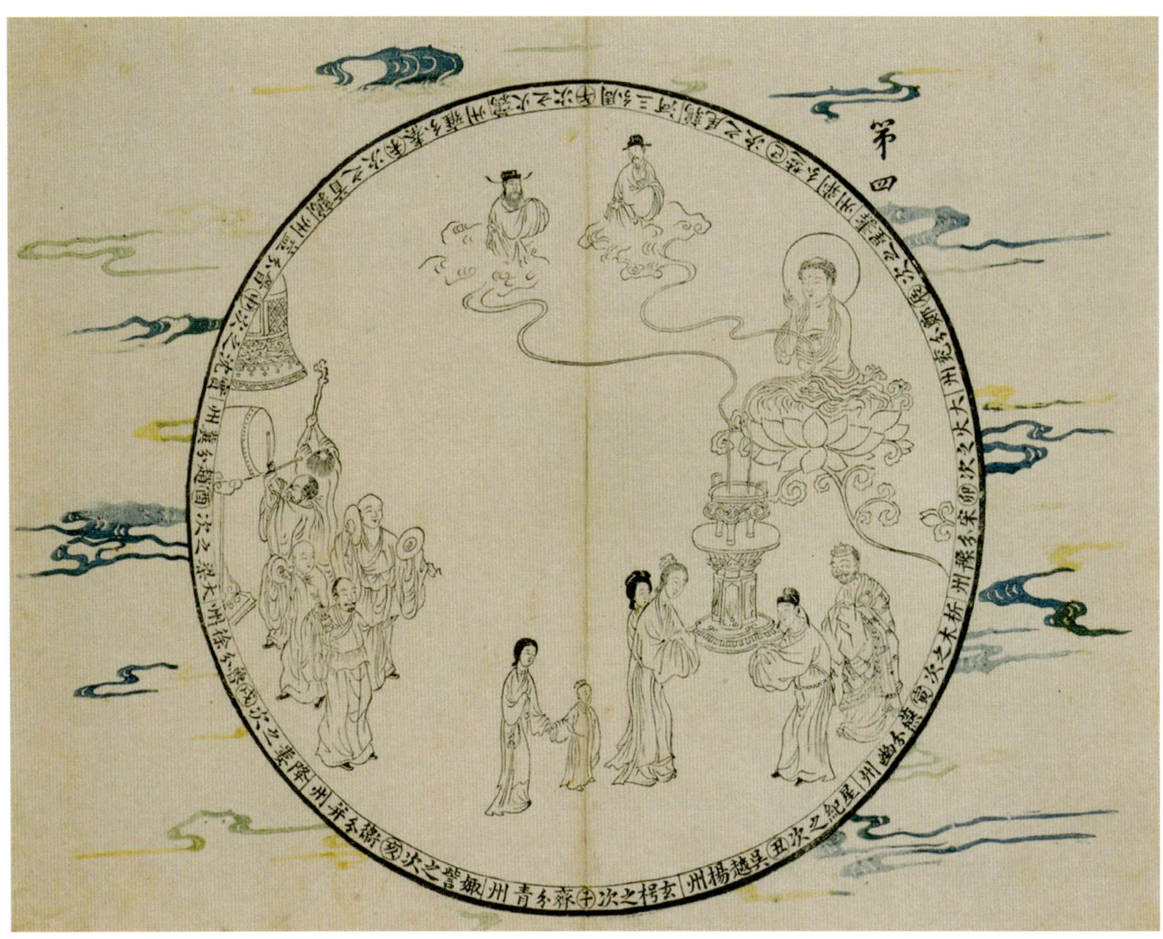

Fig. 3.12: *Xixiang ji (Romance of the Western Wing)*, album leaf 4.
Author: Wang Shifu
(c. 1260–c. 1337).
Date: 1640.
Dimensions: 25.5 × 32.2 cm.
Museum für Ostasiatische Kunst der Stadt Köln (R 62.1).

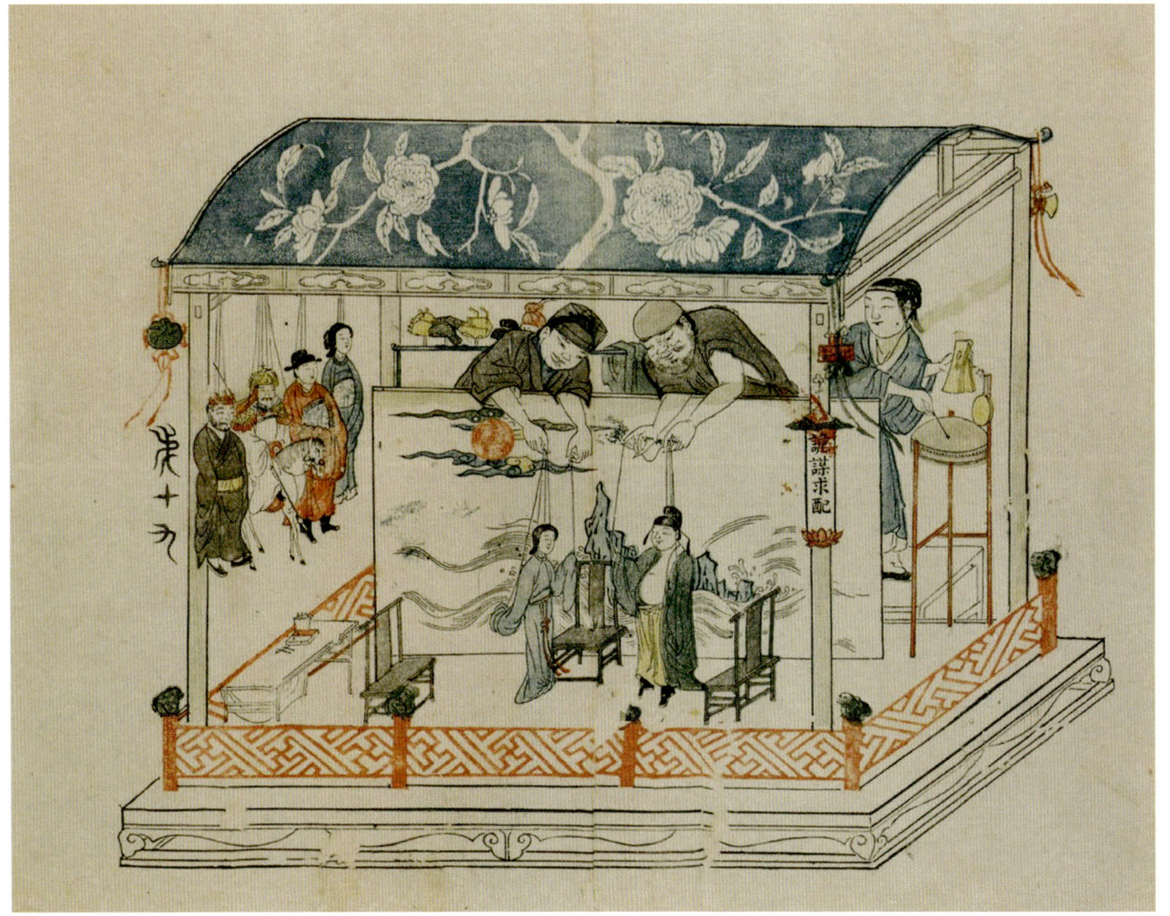

Fig. 3.13: *Xixiang ji (Romance of the Western Wing)*, album leaf 19.
Author: Wang Shifu
(c. 1260–c. 1337).
Date: 1640.
Dimensions: 25.5 × 32.2 cm.
Museum für Ostasiatische Kunst der Stadt Köln (R 62.1).

Shishuo xinyu 世説新語 (*A New Account of the Tales of the World*), a collection of fifth-century short stories in blue, red, yellow, and black. At the beginning of the seventeenth century, well-known Huizhou ink maker Cheng Dayue 程大約 (1541–1616) issued *Chengshi moyuan* 程氏墨苑 (*The Ink Garden of the Cheng Family*) in five colors in 1606. In these publications, however, solid colors in the illustrations are applied evenly, with no gradations or shadings.[21]

The coloring of the twenty-one prints of *Romance of the Western Wing* differs from these specimens. Its new technique is characterized by painting colors of varying gradations directly onto the wooden plates, so that the prints exhibit diverse shades. The most intricate composition of these coloring techniques is a scene depicting Zhang Gong climbing over a garden wall beneath a full moon to meet Yingying (Fig. 3.10). Zhang's image is reflected in the pool and his shadow is projected behind him. The depth of the courtyard is layered in winding paths, a small bridge and flowing water, a lotus pond reflecting the moon, ancient willows, strange rocks, and clusters of flowers. The scene is complex but not cluttered; it focuses on Zhang's shadow and his reflection in the water. Another fine specimen is a scene of Yingying listening to Zhang Gong's *qin* playing (Fig. 3.11).

Not only are the carving and coloring superbly executed, but so too the compositions of the pictures. Nearly half of the play's twenty scenes are illustrated in arrangements that focus on a particular *objet d'art*, with the relevant scenes painted directly onto the objects in question.[22] The initial flowering of the romance between Cui Yingying and Zhang Gong is portrayed on an opened handscroll. Another scene involving the evocation of spirits (in this case, Yingying's deceased father) is depicted around a compass (Fig. 3.12). In one scene, the two main protagonists stand on an actual stage; in another, the characters are impersonated by a group of six puppets handled by two puppeteers whose heads are poking out of a curtain (Fig. 3.13). These illustrations exemplify the finest aspects of late Ming woodblock printing, as well as the inspirational power the literature it portrayed had on the artists.

In the Ming dynasty, emanating from two places in Jiangsu—Kunshan and Suzhou—*sanqu* and related opera forms achieved a particular generic definition that has come to be known as *kunqu* 崑曲, which spread out across a wide swath of southern China. Examples of this style of opera as performed in the Qing dynasty can be found in *Shenyin jiangu lu* 審音鑒古錄 (*A Record of Examining Music and Assessing Antiquity*), of which the Fung Ping Shan Library also has a copy.

This book contains a selection of some of the most popular arias of the genre, with a total of sixty-five scenes to be found from nine operas. No precise information is given regarding the editor who made the selection, but from a preface written by Qinyin weng 琴隱翁 ("The *Qin*-Playing Old Hermit"), the intention behind assembling the anthology can be understood:

> Wanhua [zhuren] recorded the operas but did not provide musical notation; Huaiting [jushi] furnished musical notation but eliminated the dialogue in recitative; and Liweng gave a rich theoretical account but did not include the actual scenes themselves.
>
> 玩花錄劇而遺譜，懷庭譜曲而廢白，笠翁又泛論而無詞萃。[23]

Wanhua zhuren 玩花主人 was the compiler of an opera anthology *Zhui baiqiu* 綴白裘 (*Sewing together the White Fur Coat*), and although he presents many operas in his book, none is furnished with musical notation and only the lyrics are provided, so their format is similar to the librettos or synopses of later generations. Huaiting jushi's 懷庭居士 (i.e., Ye Tang 葉堂, 1724–1795) opus, *Nashu ying qupu* 納書楹曲譜 (*Musical Scores of Shelving Books*), simply includes the notation of some two hundred or more arias as instructions on how the music should be performed, but none carries stage directions or an intervening recitative. [Li] Liweng's 李笠翁 (Li Yu 李漁, 1611–1680) text

21. Tsien Tsuen-Hsuin, *Chemistry and Chemical Technology: Paper and Printing*, in Joseph Needham, ed., *Science and Civilisation in China*, vol. 5, pt. 1 (Cambridge: Cambridge University Press, 1985), 283.

22. Wang Fang-yu suggests this technique of portraying events and characters on *objets d'art* is distantly related to the fashion of painting a screen within a screen, that is, the tenth-century painter Zhou Wenju's 周文矩 (fl. 940–975) *Chongping huiqi tu* 重屏會棋圖 (*Playing Chess in front of Double Screens*). See Wang Fang-yu, "Book Illustration in Late Ming and Early Qing China," 33.

23. Wang Jishan 王纘善, ed., *Shenyin jiangu lu* 審音鑑古錄 (Beijing: Xueyuan chubanshe, 2003), vol. 1, preface, fol. 2r.

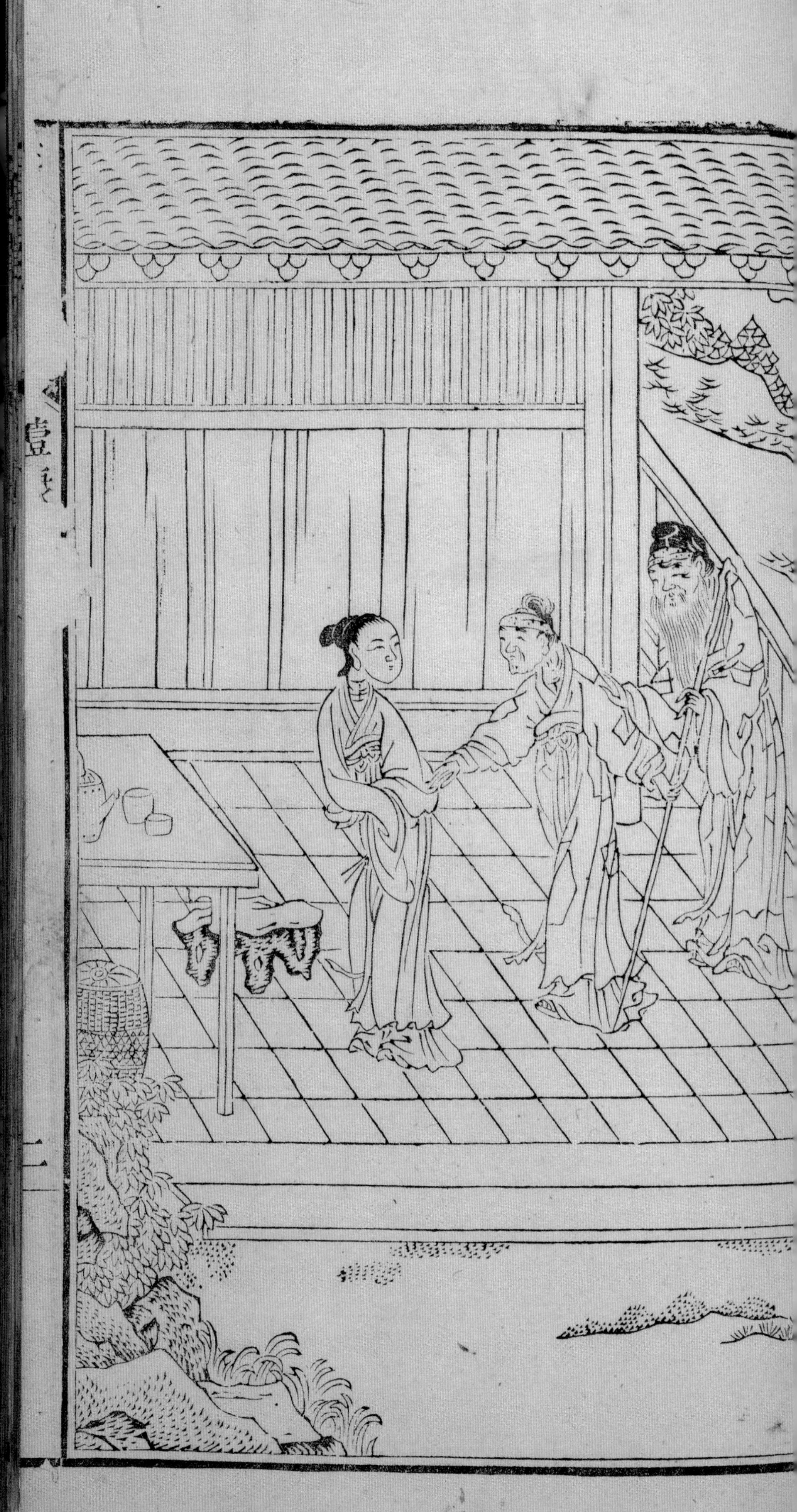

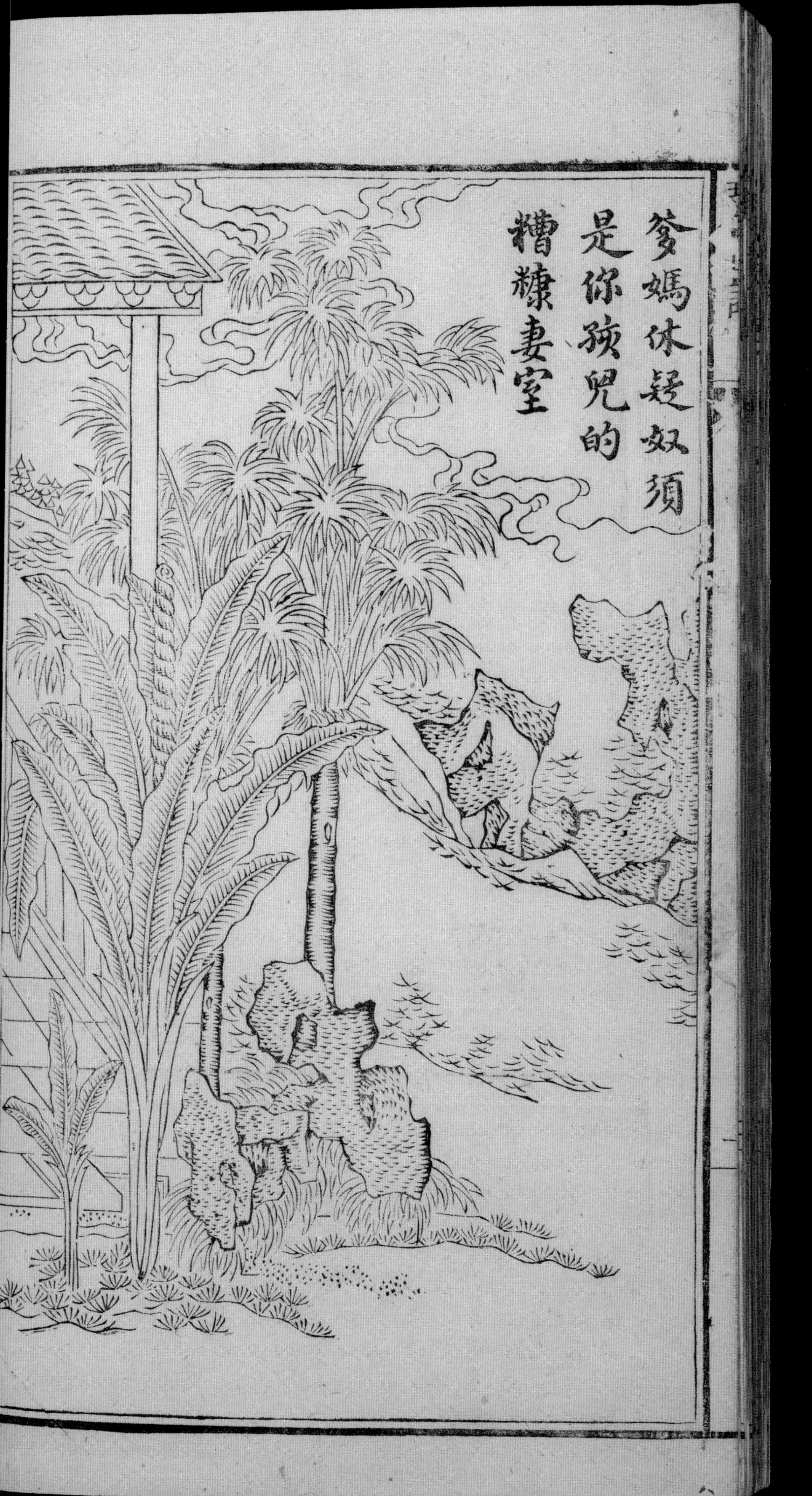

Fig. 3.14: *Shenyin jiangu lu* (*A Record of Examining Music and Assessing Antiquity*), *The Tale of the Pipa Lute*, fascicle 2, woodblock engraving of the scene "Eating Chaff."
Editor: Wang Jishan (act. 1834).
Date: before 1834.
Woodblock: 24.2 × 15.1 cm.
Fung Ping Shan Library.

is *Xianqing ouji* 閒情偶寄 (*Emotions at Leisure, an Occasional Record*), and although two sections, "words and music" and "performance practice," are included, these merely outline how the issues should be addressed rather than providing the actual words and music. Published in the mid-Qing dynasty, *A Record of Examining Music and Assessing Antiquity* was designed to remedy the defects of these three works and combine their qualities so as to provide a one-stop manual for performing *kunqu*.[24]

The scene "Yekang" 噎糠 ("Eating Chaff," Fig. 3.14) from the opera *Pipa ji* 琵琶記 (*The Tale of the Pipa Lute*) is included in the book and is one of many where comprehensive instructions on delivering different facets of the opera performance are provided, including an elaborate series of stage directions necessary for taking the plot forward as a step-by-step guide to the required movements. The drama is a love story between Cai Bojie 蔡伯喈, the main male protagonist, and Zhao Wuniang 趙五娘, his wife and the female lead. Cai Bojie departs to take the imperial examination (as is so often the case in opera plots), leaving his wife behind to care for his elderly parents while famine is stalking the land. As an act of pure altruism and filial piety, Zhao Wuniang saves all the available rice for Cai Bojie's parents and allows herself to be satisfied with the chaff. In this scene, she attempts to force herself to eat it, but with limited success. The original Yuan dynasty libretto offers only the stage directions "eat, vomit" 吃吐介, but here this has been expanded to the following:

> (On the left of the stage are positioned a table and a low stool, and on the table are placed a teapot, bowl, and chopsticks. Seated on the low stool, her left hand takes the teapot and pours the tea, and her right hand takes the chopsticks and stirs the chaff-tea mixture. Her left hand puts down the teapot, takes up the bowl, and makes a movement as if to eat. She eats again and chokes, and then with her left hand pats her chest.) "Aiya! Poor me!" (She pours the water once more and stirs, eats two mouthfuls, chokes vehemently, vomits, and weeps.)
>
> （場左設椅、矮櫈，椅上擺茶鐘、碗、筯。坐于矮櫈上，左手將鐘倒茶，右手將筯攪；左手放鐘，拿碗，作喫一口；再喫，作搶，出左手拍胸科）「哎呀，苦嗄！」（又倒水攪，喫兩口，大搶，作嘔，哭科）[25]

Not only are the relevant objects indicated, but even the hands she should use are specified. Altogether, perhaps a dozen movements are listed, as are the number of mouthfuls relevant to the context, along with the emotional impact that each gesture should convey. This recitative section is a perfect prelude to arguably the dramatic heart of the entire opera, which is the subsequent "Song of Eating Chaff."[26]

A Record of Examining Music and Assessing Antiquity describes the movements in exquisite detail, while also giving a full account of the costumes. Later in the opera, in the scene "Saosong" 掃松 ("Sweeping under the Pine," Fig. 3.15), after Cai Bojie has achieved success in the imperial examinations, he sends his subordinate Li Wang 李旺 to check on his family. Li Wang fortuitously meets Zhang Guangcai 張廣才, whom Zhao Wuniang has entrusted with the task of tending the graves of Cai Bojie's now-dead parents, while she, unaware of his success, has set off to find him. Zhang Guangcai is described as "[Sporting] a white three-pronged beard [two prongs for the mustache and one for the beard itself], a rectangular hat, a head-kerchief, and a pleated robe of pongee silk belted at the waist, while leaning on a stick and carrying a broom" 白三髯、長方巾、帕打頭，繭綢襲（褶）、裙打腰，拄杖，執帚.[27]

Issued at the end of the Jiaqing era (1795–1820), the manual *Chuandai tigang* 穿戴提綱 (*A Summary of Costumes and Props*), by the institute that performed opera for the emperor, gives an almost identical list of items to be worn by Zhang Guangcai when performing this scene, with only an additional pair of "red shoes" 紅鞋 completing his attire,[28] which attests to the influence of *A Record of Examining Music and Assessing Antiquity*.

In the scene "Shanglu" 上路 ("On the Road," Fig. 3.16) from the opera *Jingchai ji* 荊釵記 (*A Tale of the Thorn Hairpin*), an equally elaborate description of stage directions is included. The entire scene is omitted from the Yuan dynasty original and would have been improvised by the actors. Its main protagonists are the female lead Qian Yulian 錢玉蓮, her father, her stepmother, and a servant sent to accompany them. Upon learning that Qian Yulian had drowned, and concerned that her parents now had no one on whom to rely, her prospective husband steps into the breach and indicates that he will support them. He sends a subordinate to take them on a boat journey

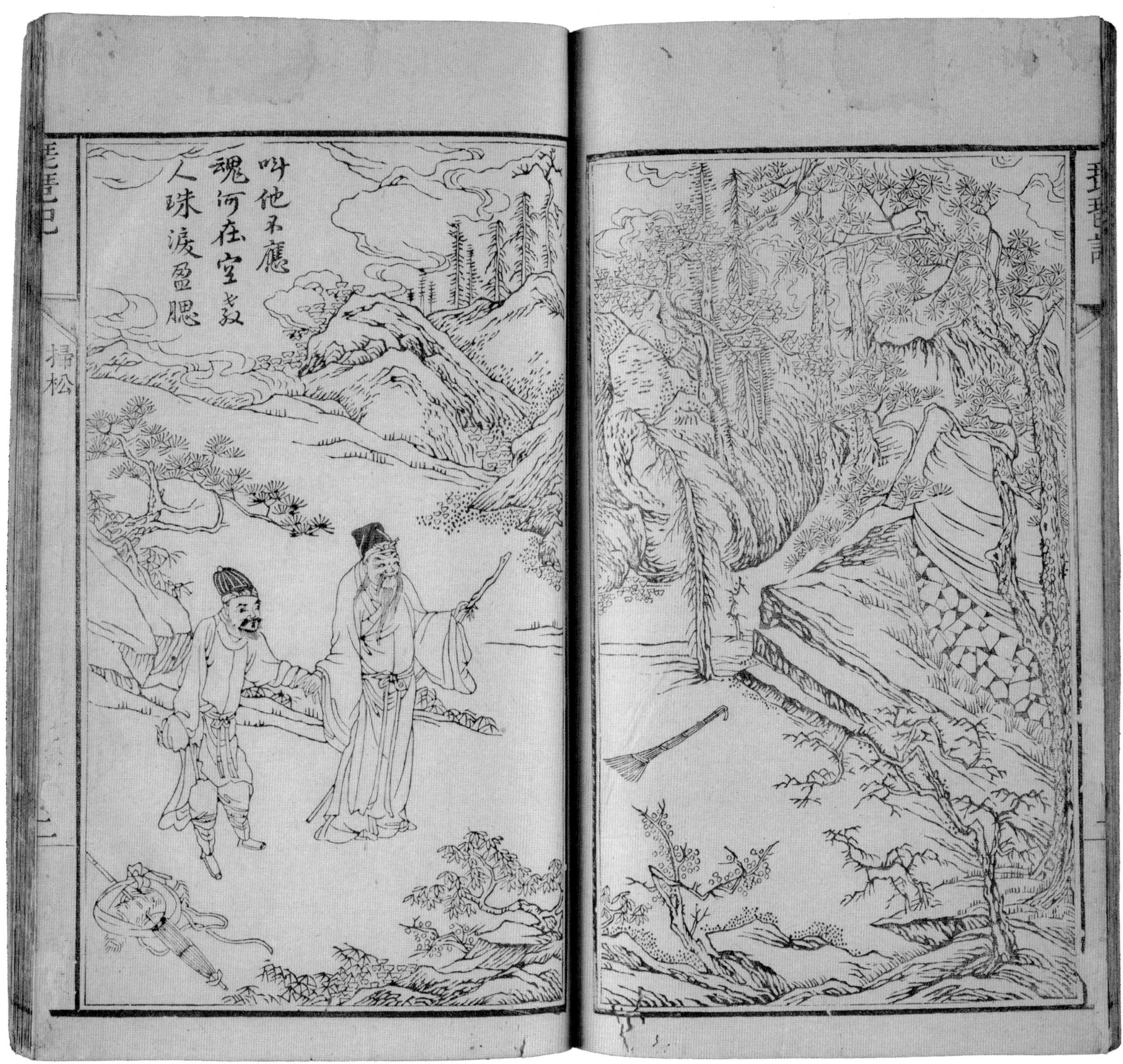

Fig. 3.15: *Shenyin jiangu lu* (*A Record of Examining Music and Assessing Antiquity*), *The Tale of the Pipa Lute*, fascicle 3, woodblock engraving of the scene "Sweeping under the Pine."
Editor: Wang Jishan (act. 1834).
Date: before 1834.
Woodblock: 24.2 × 15.1 cm.
Fung Ping Shan Library.

from Wenzhou to Ji'an to meet him. Bored of the claustrophobic atmosphere of the cabin, the elderly couple decide to leave the boat and take a walk on the bank. In this scene, very little is sung, nor is there much recitative; virtually the entire dramatic narrative is carried by actions. When the actor playing the part of Qian Yulian's father sings the phrase "The scenery on the bridge is the most splendid" 小橋景最佳, description is given of the required movements. The three characters represented here are a *wai* 外 who takes the part of an old man (Qian Yulian's father), a *mo* 末 who takes the part of a middle-aged man (the servant sent by her prospective husband), and a *fu* 副 who takes the part of her stepmother.

24. Zhu Jiajin 朱家溍, *Xiaoshan Zhu shi jiuchang mulu* 蕭山朱氏舊藏目錄 (Beijing: Gugong chubanshe, 2014), 286.

25. Wang Jishan, ed., *Shenyin jiangu lu*, vol. 1, 56.

26. Ibid., vol. 1, 56–57.

27. Ibid., vol. 1, 137.

28. Huang Ke 黃克, "*Shenyin jiangu lu*: Qianlong shiqi de kunqu yanchu shilu《審音鑒古錄》：乾隆時期的昆曲演出實錄," *Wenshi zhishi* 文史知識 (2008) 3: 130.

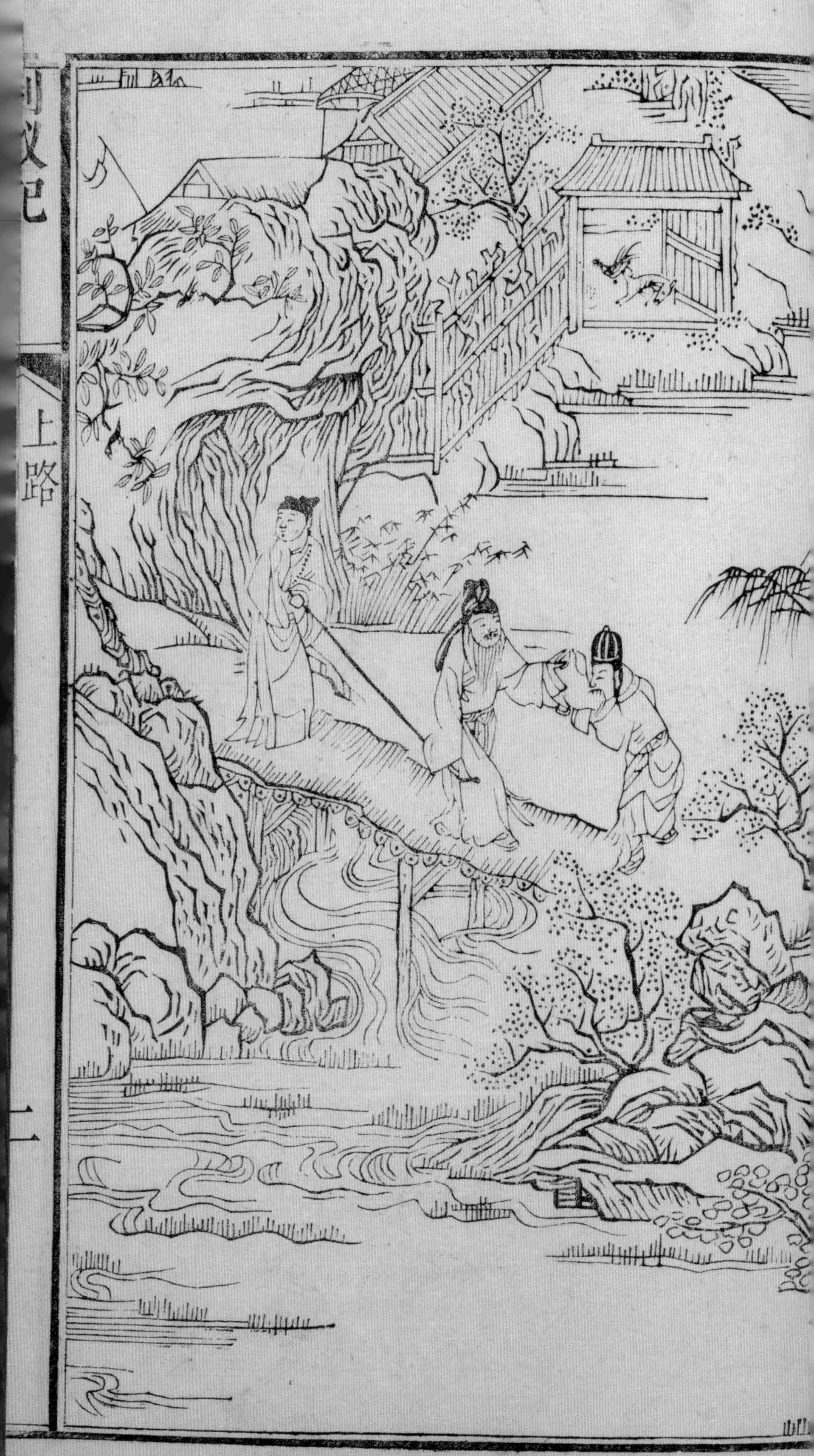
上路

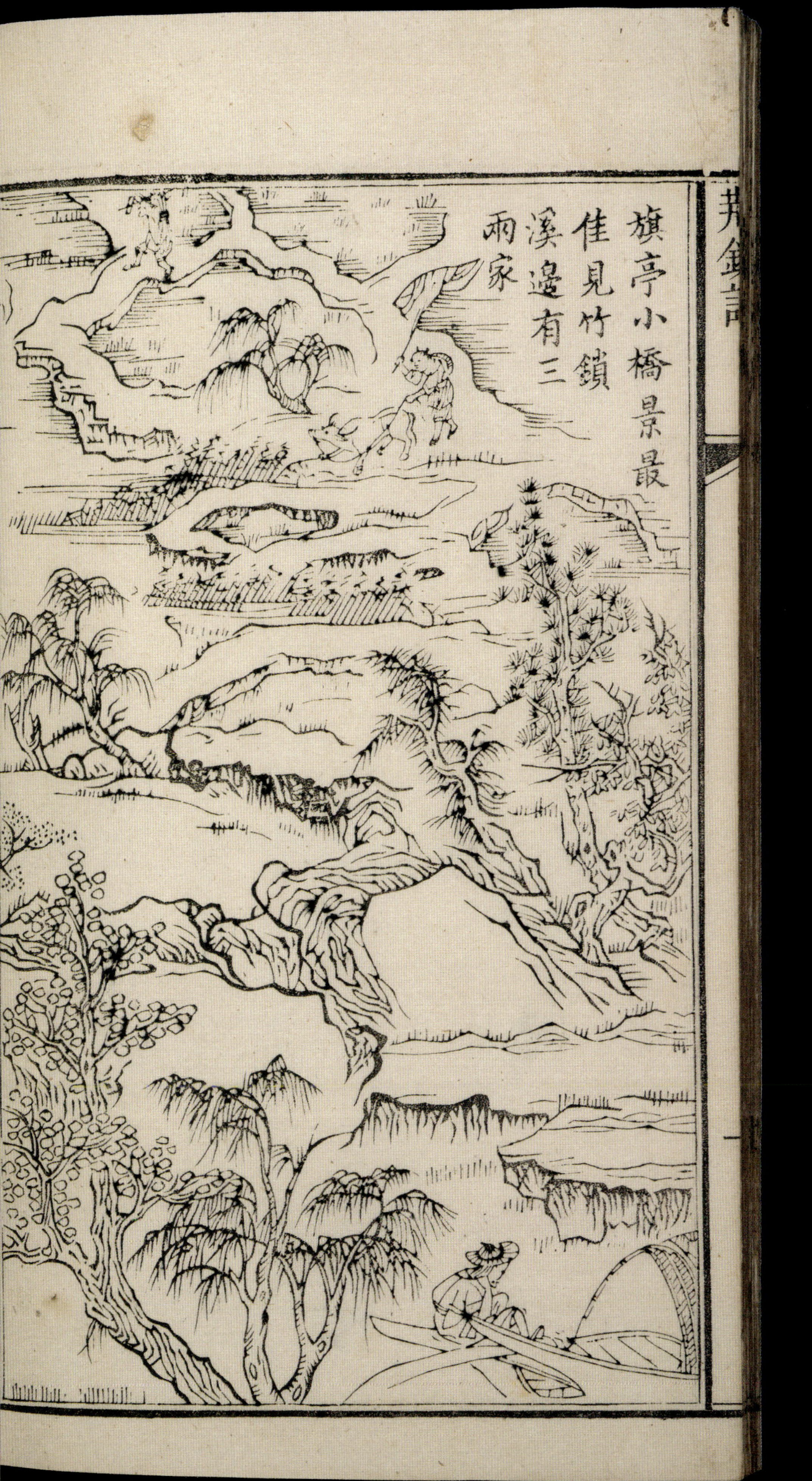

Fig. 3.16: *Shenyin jiangu lu* (*A Record of Examining Music and Assessing Antiquity*), *A Tale of the Thorn Hairpin*, fascicle 5, woodblock engraving of the scene "On the Road."
Editor: Wang Jishan (act. 1834).
Date: before 1834.
Woodblock: 24.2 × 15.1 cm.
Fung Ping Shan Library.

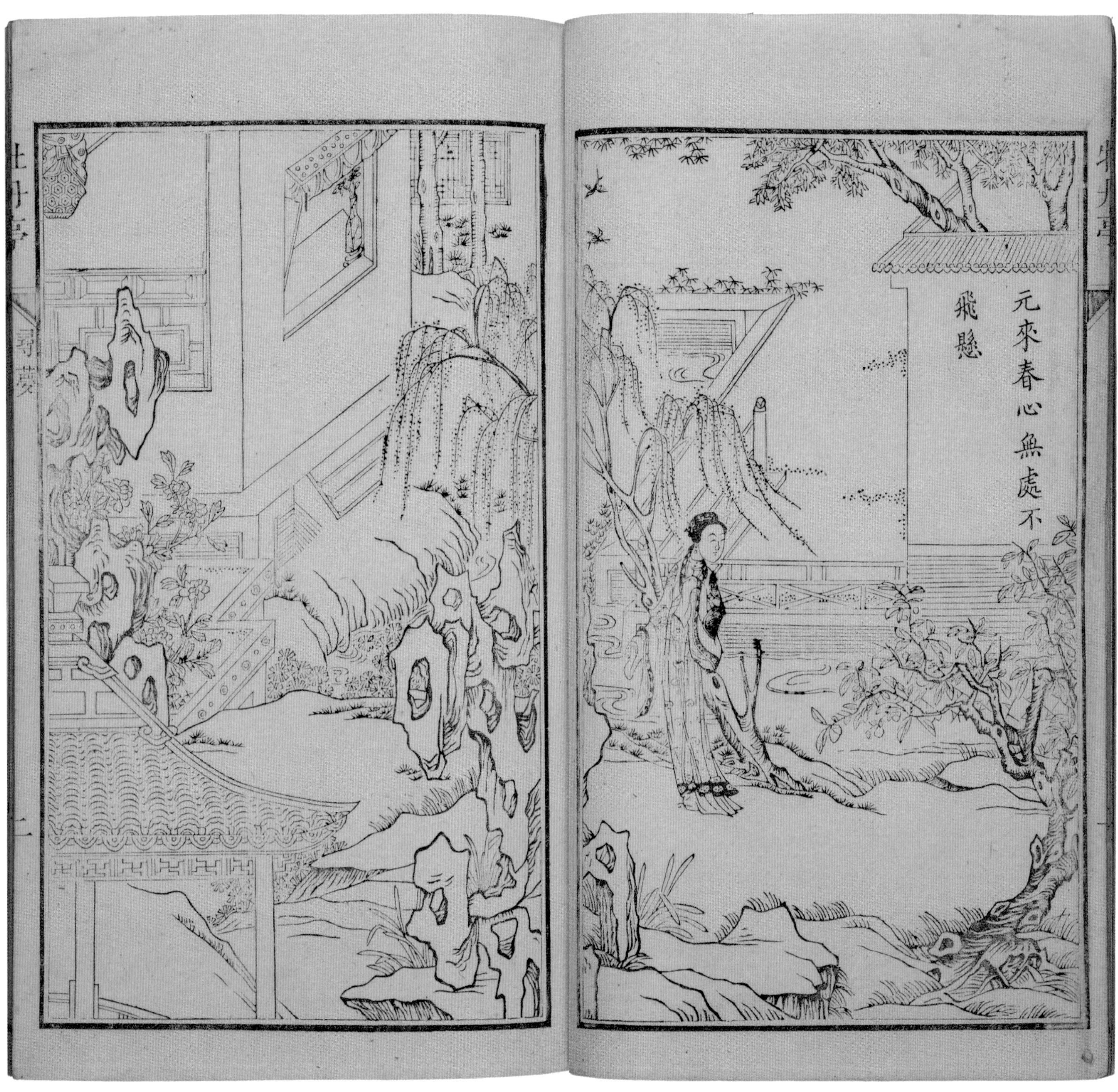

Fig. 3.17: *Shenyin jiangu lu (A Record of Examining Music and Assessing Antiquity)*, *The Peony Pavilion*, fascicle 8, woodblock engraving of the scene "Seeking a Dream." Editor: Wang Jishan (act. 1834). Date: before 1834. Woodblock: 24.2 × 15.1 cm. Fung Ping Shan Library.

The *wai* turns his body to the left. First, he lifts his stick onto the bridge. Having planted it firmly, with his left hand he lifts his robe and at the same time raises his left foot, and when the character "xiao" is sung, puts it down.
外轉身對左，先提杖於橋上戳定，後左手提衣，連左足起， 在「小」字上踏下。

The *mo* takes his right hand and supports the *wai*'s left hand; the *wai* steps onto the bridge with his right foot and stands still when he has reached the middle, his body facing towards the audience. He takes the far end of his stick and gives it to the *fu* and assumes a posture that supports her hand and guides her.
末將右手攙外左手，外即右足上橋，至中立住，身對正場；將拐尾與副作扶手而引狀。

The *fu*, seeing that the *wai* has stepped onto the bridge, becomes even more weak-footed, and

> when the character "jing" is sung, with both hands she holds the end of the stick and mounts the bridge. All face towards the audience and walk sideways as if moving along the bridge. When the character "zui" is sung, it is as if the bridge itself is moving, and all assume squatting postures. They look at each other, shake their heads, and appear frightened. They then stand up very slowly and walk sideways as if crossing the bridge. The *fu* turns her head and looks backwards again, sticking her tongue out [at the bridge], shakes her head, and then, following the *wai*, from the left corner, turns and exits.
>
> 副見外上橋，愈加足軟式，在「景」字雙手搭杖尾上橋科介。各對正場，皆要橫走。至「最」字二腔，似橋動，各蹬身式，皆照面搖首怕科；立起俱慢，橫走過橋。副回身重顧，對上伸舌搖頭，即隨外從左角轉介。[29]

According to *A Record of Examining Music and Assessing Antiquity*, this scene had originally been performed by Sun Jiugao. His elaborate movements were all essential components of the dramatic action, so in order that they would not be lost for posterity, they were all recorded 此齣乃孫九臯首劇，身段雖繁，俱係畫景，惟恐失傳，故載身段.[30] Another book, *Yangzhou huafang lu* 揚州畫舫錄 (*A Record of the Yangzhou Painted Boat*), recounts that the selfsame Sun Jiugao had at one time been a member of the Xu 徐 troupe of Yangzhou as an understudy for *wai* roles. Although his voice was considered sufficiently resonant, it was not thought to be as good as that of the principal actor Wang Danshan 王丹山, but his in-depth knowledge of opera lore was conversely regarded as superior.[31] Apparently, "at the age of more than ninety, he was still performing the Will Scene from *The Tale of the Pipa Lute* in a manner that was breathtaking."[32]

Another actor mentioned by both *A Record of Examining Music and Assessing Antiquity* and *A Record of the Yangzhou Painted Boat* is Chen Yunjiu 陳雲九. In the former book, on the score of the opera *Mudan ting* 牡丹亭 (*The Peony Pavilion*), a headnote above the top margin reads: "The melody employed for singing the character 'di' here was transmitted by Chen Yunjiu" 「地」字工尺，教習陳雲九傳."[33] In the fifth *juan* of the latter text, it is recorded that as an actor performing young male parts even into his nineties, he still overflowed with the essential spirit of these roles and exhibited a distilled perfection of technique.[34]

The traditional scholarly view is that the preface to *A Record of Examining Music and Assessing Antiquity* of 1834 is the means for dating the book, but the Fung Ping Shan Library copy does not contain this preface, and its imprint has clearly been made from freshly cut woodblocks, unlike those made from worn blocks that do contain the preface. These features likely suggest an earlier printing date, a hypothesis also supported by other indications. The preface itself is signed by someone going by the pseudonym "The *Qin*-Playing Old Hermit," who candidly admits that he was not the original creator of the woodblocks, but only responsible for obtaining and then taking them to South of the River and re-using them. His confession adds fuel to the fire and again suggests an earlier date. Regarding the illustrations, although evidently of Qing dynasty workmanship, in terms of composition and content, they can be divided into two categories: those that retain late Ming dynasty characteristics and those that are clearly Qing dynasty in style. An example of the former accompanies a scene entitled "Xunmeng" 尋夢 ("Seeking a Dream," Fig. 3.17) from *The Peony Pavilion*,[35] and the latter is represented by a scene "Chicha" 喫茶 ("Drinking Tea") from *Mingfeng ji* 鳴鳳記 (*The Tale of the Phoenix Calling*),[36] where the depiction of facial expressions and gestures is much more realistic than in the Ming dynasty predecessors and closer to conveying an impression of what the scene would have actually looked like on stage.

A Record of the Yangzhou Painted Boat, published in 1795, is an account of the author's thirty years spent in the city. As both this book and *A Record of Examining Music and Assessing Antiquity* mention Chen Yunjiu and Sun Jiuge, who were then in their nineties, a similar date or a couple of decades earlier at most is likely for the latter text. The Fung Ping Shan Library copy came into the collection on August 21, 1941, and the only earlier seal found

29. Wang Jishan, ed., *Shenyin jiangu lu*, vol. 1, 308.

30. Ibid., vol. 1, 310.

31. Li Dou 李斗, *Yangzhou huafang lu* 揚州畫舫錄 (Beijing: Zhonghua shuju, 1960), 122–123.

32. Ibid., 126.

33. Wang Jishan, ed., *Shenyin jiangu lu*, vol. 2, 597.

34. Li Dou, *Yangzhou huafang lu*, 122.

35. Wang Jishan, ed., *Shenyin jiangu lu*, vol. 2, 552–553.

36. Ibid., vol. 2, 678–679.

湖上畱止帀月主人授簡索句且徵新聲因作仙呂宮二曲石湖把玩不已使二伎隸習之音節諧婉乃命之曰暗香疎影

宋　姜夔堯章

舊時月色　韻　算幾番照我　句　梅邊吹笛

去平入入上上平去上平平平入

韻　喚起玉人　句　不管清寒與攀摘　韻　何

去上入平入上平平上平入平

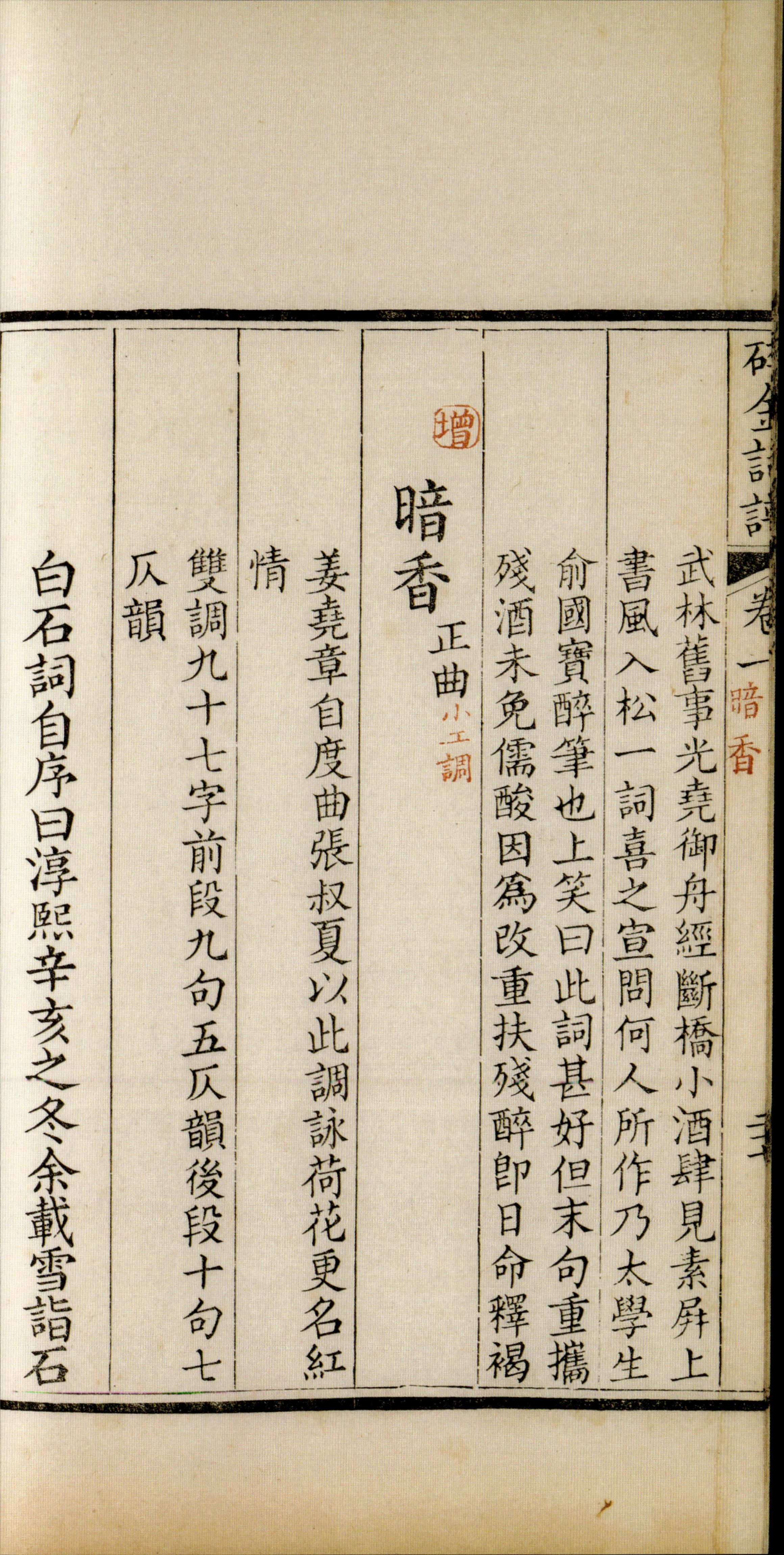

武林舊事光堯御舟經斷橋小酒肆見素屏上書風入松一詞喜之宣問何人所作乃太學生俞國寶醉筆也上笑曰此詞甚好但末句重攜殘酒未免儒酸因爲改重扶殘醉卽日命釋褐

增

暗香 正曲 小工調

姜堯章自度曲張叔夏以此調詠荷花更名紅情

雙調九十七字前段九句五仄韻後段十句七仄韻

白石詞自序曰淳熙辛亥之冬余載雪詣石

Fig. 3.18: *Suijin cipu* (*Scattered Gold: Scores of Lyric Songs*), *juan* 1, fols. 27v–28r, the reinvented *gongche* notation, metrical pattern, and rhyme scheme of the tune *Secret Fragrance* originally composed by Jiang Kui.
Author: Xie Yuanhuai (1784–1867).
Date: 1848.
Woodblock: 19.4 × 14.3 cm.
Fung Ping Shan Library.

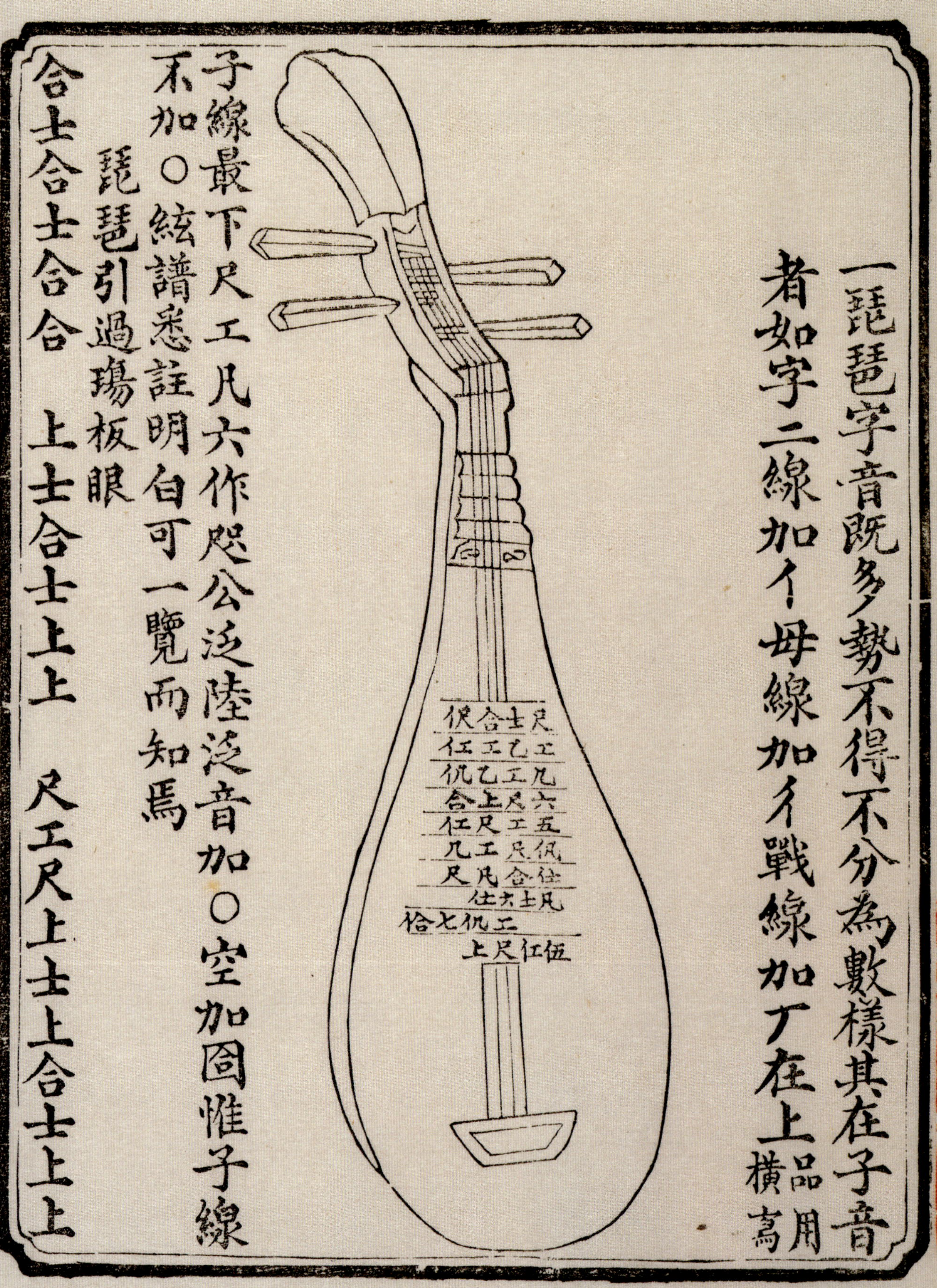

一琵琶字音既多勢不得不分為數樣其在子音者如字二線加亻母線加彳戰線加丁在上品用橫寫子線最下尺工凡六作𠯗公泛陸泛音加〇空加圓惟子線不加〇絃譜悉註明白可一覽而知焉

琵琶引過瑒板眼

合士合士合合　上上士合士上上　尺工尺上士上合士上上

on it belongs to a family surnamed Yin 尹, whose studio was Shigu tang 式穀堂 (The Edification Hall).

Given that by the late Qing dynasty *kunqu* had assumed a preeminent position, in order to restore the lost melodic component of *cipai* metrical patterns and rhyme schemes it is to *kunqu* that *Suijin cipu* 碎金詞譜 (*Scattered Gold: Scores of Lyric Songs*), published in the twenty-fourth year of the Daoguang era (1844), turned to fill the vacuum. Edited by Xie Yuanhuai 謝元淮 (1784–1867), it comprises fourteen *juan* in which are assembled 449 *cipai* metrical patterns and rhyme schemes, and 558 matching melodies, of which 173 were taken from the Qing dynasty publication *Jiugong dacheng nan bei ci gongpu* 九宮大成南北詞宮譜 (*In all the Musical Modes, Northern and Southern Ci Scores*) dated 1746. Also published with *Scattered Gold: Scores of Lyric Songs* is *Suijin xupu* 碎金續譜 (*A Sequel to Scattered Gold: Scores of Lyric Songs*) in six *juan* that contains 180 *cipai* metrical patterns and rhyme schemes and 244 matching melodies, as well as 77 large Tang and Song dynasty suites. Lacking the original melodies to add to the *ci* words, curiously, *kunqu* melodies are used to provide the musical component instead. At the end of each *juan*, the names of the musicians who participated in composing the melodies are supplied: Chen Yingxiang 陳應祥, Lu Qitang 陸啓鏜, Fan Yunkui 范雲逵, Wang Yongqing 王永慶, and others.

Several tunes originally composed by Jiang Kui, including *Secret Fragrance* and *Discontentment at the Long Pavilion*, are included in *Scattered Gold: Scores of Lyric Songs* (Fig. 3.18). In Xie's compilation, the urtext of Jiang's lyrics comes from *The Imperial Register of Lyric Song*. Down the center of each writing column, the words of the *ci* poems are printed in large type. On the right, next to each character in a smaller typeface in red ink, the note or notes sung to them are indicated; on the left, the pitch tone of the character is given in black, again in a smaller typeface. As is indicated by book seals, the Fung Ping Shan Library copy was once owned by a married couple: Wu Baojie 吳保鍇 (1886–?) and Qi Wudi 齊無棣.

The Yue ballad is a narrative song genre of the Pearl River Delta whose text was based on a combination of classical and vernacular Chinese. The Fung Ping Shan Library has a copy of the first anthology of these ballads, a collection titled *Yue'ou* 粵謳. Compiled by Zhao Ziyong 招子庸 (1786–1847) in one *juan* and printed in 1828, it contains the lyrics of 121 pieces under 97 titles.[37] The ballads are given only as texts; at the opening of the book as a helpful glossary is a list of important dialectical words in Cantonese followed by translation into Mandarin. Next is a diagram of a *pipa* with the finger positions used for *gongche* notation indicated on the frets in order to assist the reader in playing the two introductory excerpts in the same notation (Fig. 3.19).

Fig. 3.19: *Yue'ou* (*Cantonese Love Songs*), fol. 17r, a diagram explaining how to use *gongche* notation on the *pipa*.
Author: Zhao Ziyong (*juren* degree 1816).
Date: 1828.
Woodblock: 18.4 × 13.9 cm.
Fung Ping Shan Library.

Two English translations of this anthology appeared in the twentieth century. The first was by Sir Cecil Clementi 金文泰 (1875–1947), a British colonial administrator who served as Governor of Hong Kong from 1925 to 1930 (see also chapter 5) and Governor and Commander-in-Chief of the Straits Settlements from 1930 to 1934. He completed his translation when serving as a Member of the Land Court, Assistant Land Officer, and Police Magistrate in the New Territories, Hong Kong, and it was published by the Clarendon Press in 1904.[38] The second was by the linguist Peter T. Morris and issued by Hong Kong University Press in 1992.[39] Of the two translators, Clementi pays significantly more attention to the musical element of what was fundamentally a vocal genre. In the introduction to his translation, he states: "They are emphatically *songs*, not *poems*, and to a Chinaman are inseparable from the music to which they are set. It is with difficulty that a Cantonese who knows these songs well can be prevailed upon to read them in his ordinary tone of voice. He will instinctively begin to hum them over, and, unless ruthlessly prevented, he will soon burst out into song, accompanying himself, if possible, on the *phê-phâ* [*pipa*] or Chinese guitar."[40] Grounded in his musical sensitivity, Clementi not only translates the accompanying diagram of a *pipa*,[41] but also provides a six-page discussion of the musical notation employed,[42] while more strongly

37. Photography of a copy of the same edition can be found in Zhao Wanli 趙萬里, *Zhongguo banke tulu* 中國版刻圖錄 (Beijing: Wenwu chubanshe, 1961), vol. 6, plate 588. For a facsimile of the 1828 edition, see Zhao Ziyong 招子庸, *Yue'ou* 粵謳, in *Su wenxue congkan di yi ji* 俗文學叢刊第一集, ed. Yang Jialuo 楊家駱 (Taipei: Shijie shuju, 1963), vol. 6.

38. Cecil Clementi, *Cantonese Love-Songs* (Oxford: Clarendon, 1904).

39. Peter T. Morris, *Cantonese Love Songs: An English Translation of Jiu Ji-yung's Cantonese Songs of the Early 19th Century* (Hong Kong: Hong Kong University Press, 1992).

40. Cecil Clementi, *Cantonese Love-Songs*, vol. 1, 13.

41. Ibid., vol. 1, 25. Translation of this accompanying note is not included by Peter T. Morris.

42. Ibid., vol. 1, 12–17.

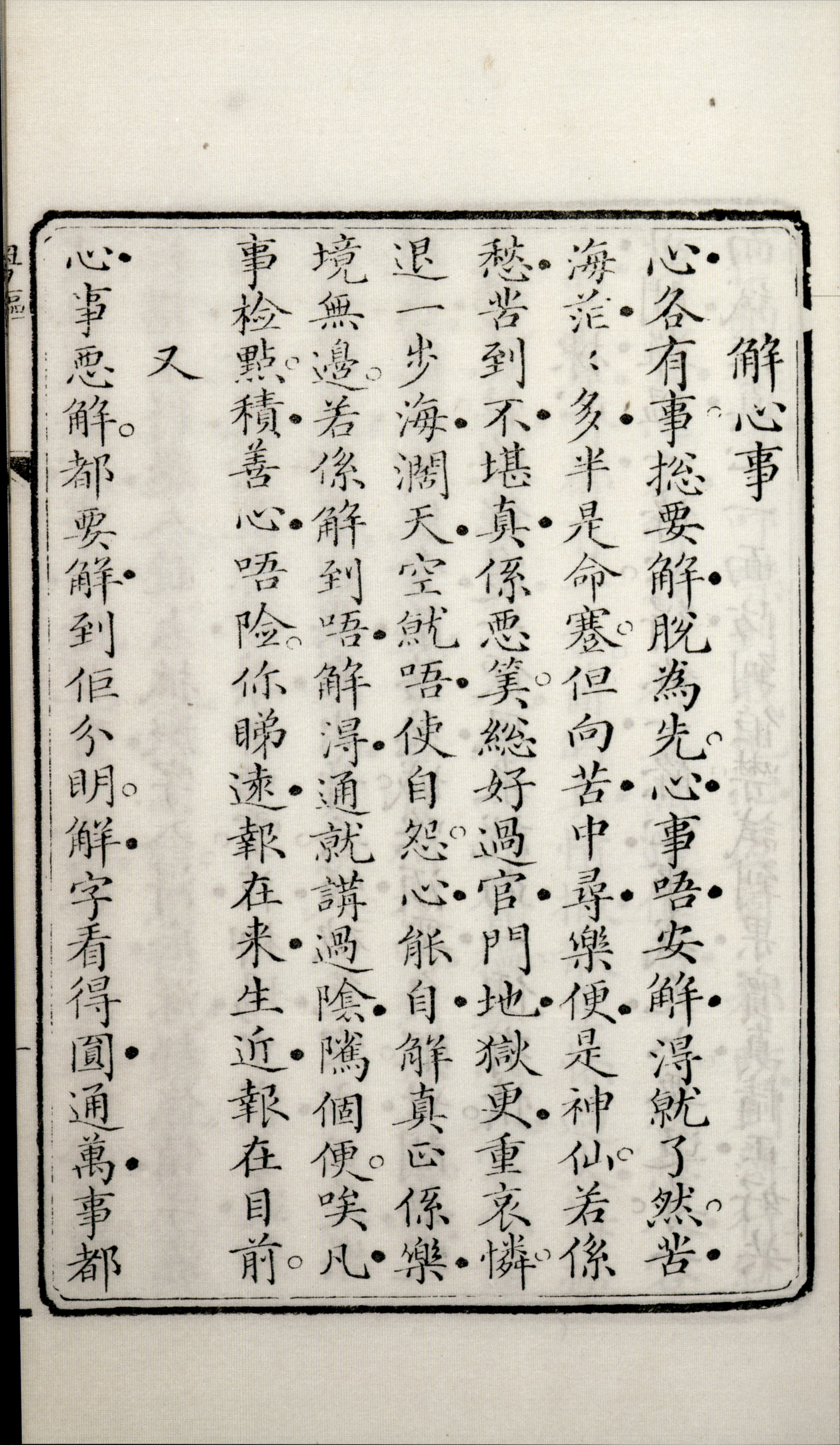

Fig. 3.20: *Yue'ou* (*Cantonese Love Songs*), fol. 17v, music notation of the two introductory excerpts (right), and *juan* 1, fol. 1r, *Quit ye the Soul's Sorrow*, first of the two parts (left).
Author: Zhao Ziyong (*juren* degree 1816).
Date: 1828.
Woodblock: 18.4 × 13.9 cm.
Fung Ping Shan Library.

解心事

心各有事。揔要解脫為先。心事唔安解得就了然。咁海茫茫多半是命蹇。但向苦中尋樂便是神仙。若係愁苦到不堪真係惡算。總好過官門地獄更重哀憐。退一步海闊天空就唔使自怨。心能自解真正係樂境無邊。若係解到唔解得通就講過陰騭個便。唉凡事檢點。積善心唔險。你睇遠報在來生近報在目前。

又

心事惡解。都要解到佢分明。解字看得圓通萬事都

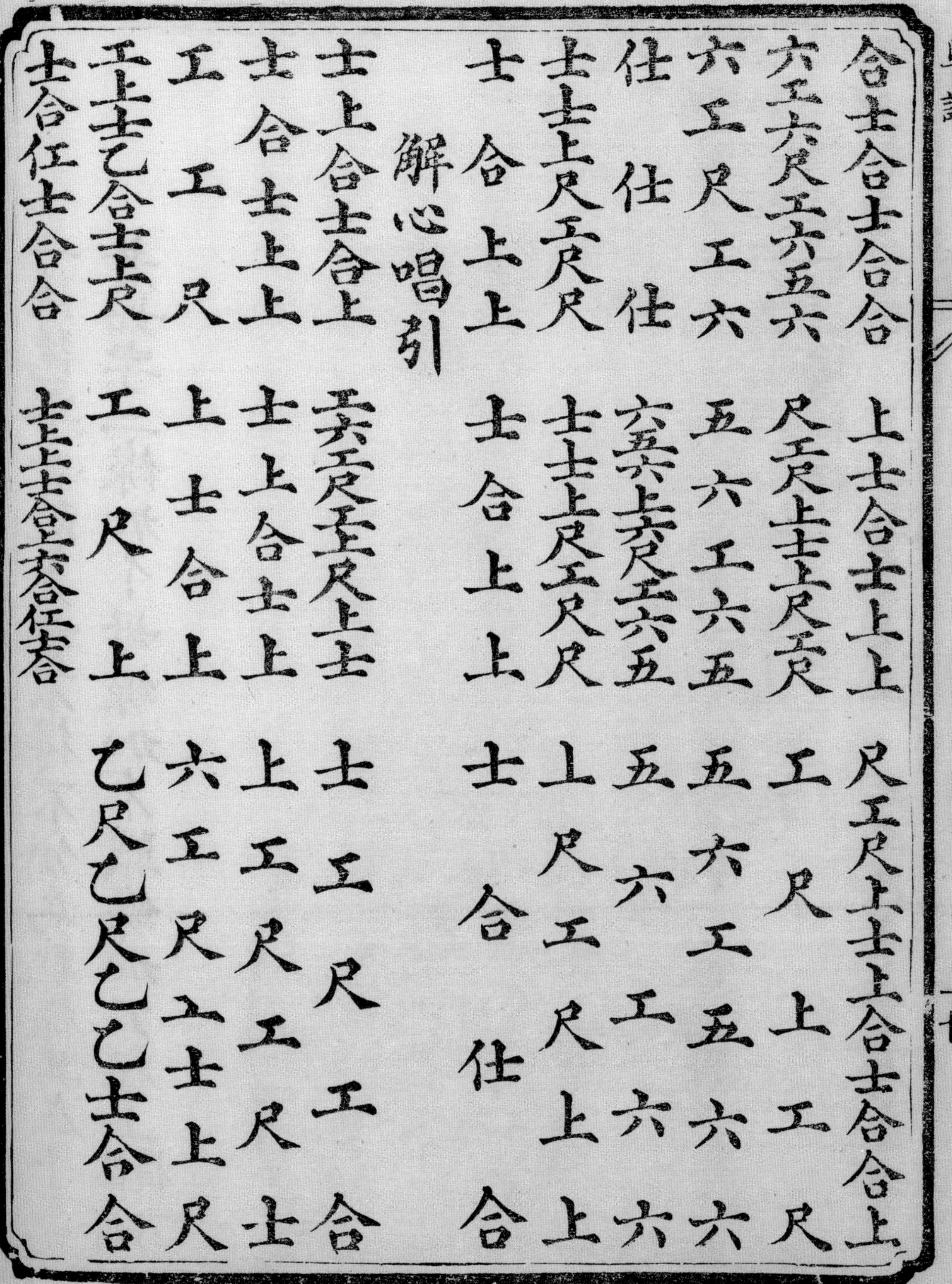

合士合士合合 上士合士上上 尺工尺上士上合士合合上
六工六尺工六五六 尺工尺上士上尺工尺 工 尺 上 工 尺
六 工 尺 工 六 五 六 工 六 五 五 六 工 五 六 六
仕 仕 仕 六五六上六尺工六五 五 六 工 六 六
士士上尺工尺尺 士士上尺工尺尺 上 尺 工 尺 上 上
士 合 上 上 士 合 上 上 士 合 仕 合

解心唱引

士上合士合上 工六尺工工尺上士 士 工 尺 工 合
士合士上上 士上合士上 上 工 尺 工 尺 士
工 工 尺 上 士 合 上 六 工 尺 上 士 上 尺
工上士乙合士上尺 工 尺 上 乙尺乙尺乙乙士合合
士合仕士合合 士上士合上六合仕士合

emphasizing the rhyme scheme. Herewith his translation of the first song in the anthology, *Jie xinshi* 解心事 (*Quit ye the Soul's Sorrow*, the first of its two parts, see Fig. 3.20):

> Each soul has its sorrow: this ye ought first to quit and cast aside.
> The soul's sorrow galls: quit it, then there is peace.
> Wide, wide is the sea of bitterness: ill-fated be more than half therein: but whoso find joy amid the bitter, theirs is an angel-spirit.
> If woe and bitterness pass beyond sufferance, then 'tis an evil shift; though better than that hell which is the judge's gate: it were more grievous far.
> Draw back but a step from your petty grief: ocean widens: heaven's void deepens: no need then to fret yourself. The soul that can quit its thrall truly is as a land of boundless joy.
> If quittance there be, but quittance be not complete, then exercise yourselves in secret charity.
> Aye! But take count of all things: the hoard of a good heart brings no hazard: Look you! Its far reward is in the life to come, its near reward is beneath your eyes.[43]
>
> 心各有事，總要解脱為先。
> 心事唔安，解得就了然。
> 苦海茫茫多數是命蹇，但向苦中尋樂便是神仙。
> 若係愁苦到不堪，真係惡算，總好過官門地獄更重哀憐。
> 退一步海闊天空就唔使自怨，心能自解，真正係樂境無邊。
> 若係解到唔解得通就講過陰騭個便。
> 唉，凡事檢點，積善心唔險，你睇遠報在來生，近報在目前。[44]

Situated at the beginning of the book, directly after notation of the instrumental prelude,[45] *Quit ye the Soul's Sorrow* is the only poem in the anthology that deals with the sorrows and anguish of society as a whole. Most of the other song lyrics portray the more sophisticated psychological experiences of Cantonese sing-song girls; for example, song LXIII *Dui chuiyang* 對垂楊 (*Facing the Weeping Willow*):

> He who is broken-hearted, fears to face the weeping willow.
> Aye, for he fears to face the charm in that pair of weeping willow eyes:
> Therefore I see him sadly lock together his eyebrows at the tip, even as I do also.
> O willow! why e'er thine own sorrow is ended, dost thou strive to tinge my mood with sadness.
> Pity thou wast planted, not in the shelter of yon fair lady's bower, but at the road-stage where men part.
> At sight of passion's farewell thine heart-strings will be wrung with woe.
> I fear that much grieving will not inure thee to this debt of loss from sight.
> Ah! thou must needs bethink thee.
> Lo! look towards Yŏng Kwán.[46]
> O willow, why in first autumn does thy colour change to yellow green?[47]
>
> 斷腸人怕對住垂楊。
> 怕對垂楊箇對媚眼一雙。
> 見佢愁鎖住眉尖，同我一樣。
> 柳呀！做乜你愁唔了，又試惹起我愁腸。
> 可惜咁好深閨唔種，種在你離亭上。
> 見一遍離情，就會碎一遍胆肝。
> 恐怕愁多捱不慣呢首相見賬。
> 唉！須要自想。
> 試睇睇吓陽關上。
> 柳呀！做乜初秋顏色，你就變了青黃。[48]

This song contains a poignant "willow" motif such as had been employed over six centuries earlier by Jiang Kui in his *Pale Yellow Willows*. According to Xia Chengtao's 夏承燾 (1900–1986) research carried out in the mid-twentieth century, *Pale Yellow Willows* was composed in remembrance of two Hefei sing-song girls by Jiang Kui when he revisited the city in his late thirties in 1191:[49] the "goose yellow and tender green" image of late spring willows in Jiang's highly-refined lyric song refers to his "old acquaintances of South of the River," i.e., these two girls. In the early nineteenth-century Cantonese vernacular love-song cited here, the willow motif again represents a sing-song girl who this time has been abandoned in early autumn by her patron and benefactor. The willow personifies the unfortunate young lady, now sadly all too familiar with the emotions of rejection and estrangement: "Pity thou wast planted, not in the shelter of yon fair lady's bower, but at the road-stage where men part." Here too, the colors yellow and green symbolize her final resting place, a destination shared by the two Hefei sing-song girls who had undoubtedly met their demise well before Jiang Kui revisited the city. Although the cultural eco-niches of the two types of vocal genres contrast sharply, the metaphorical meanings embodied in their inner depths concur, both stemming from deeply felt human emotion. No matter whether a musical setting from the august *Book of Odes* or a simple love-song from the ordinary world, they can still share the same roots. How plausible then Liu Xianting's remark quoted at the opening of this chapter!

Compared with the stern epigrams of the Confucian canon, the texts discussed in this chapter are certainly jewels scattered on a pearly strand. The most vernacular are the Yue Ballads, which represent a grassroots tradition grounded in a dialect that required translation for readers elsewhere in China to understand. At the extreme of complexity, *kunqu* opera portrays an array of emotions and narratives that encompasses the entire range of human experience. With Jiang Kui's *ci* poems, there is translucent delicacy and lightness, which have been realized in different musical terms in recurring forms by generations of musicians. Yet all this was underpinned by an immersion in deep and permanent cultural roots and ancient texts to which musicians repeatedly returned for sustenance and inspiration.

43. Cecil Clementi, *Cantonese Love-Songs*, vol. 1, 28.

44. Zhao Ziyong, *Yue'ou*, fol. 1r.

45. The *pipa* interlude and instrumental prelude of the first song *Quit ye the Soul's Sorrow* are the only music preserved in the printed edition of *Yue'ou*. Musical notation of three *Yue'ou* songs, namely *Diao Qiuxi* 吊秋喜 (Song XLVII: *Dirge for Tshau Hei*), *Xin dianfen* 心點忿 (Song XIX: *How Can My Heart Be Tranquil?*) and *Taohua shan* 桃花扇 (Song LXXXIX: *The Peach Blossom Fan*) are published in *Qinxue xinbian* 琴學新編, *Zhongxi xiange hepu* 中西絃歌合譜, and *Yue yuefu* 粵樂府 respectively. See Qiu Hechou 丘鶴儔, *Qinxue xinbian* 琴學新編 (Hong Kong: Shichang yanghuopu, 1920), 255–274; Shen Yunsheng 沈允升, *Zhongxi xiange fengqin hepu* 中西絃歌風琴合譜 (Hong Kong: Yinyue yanjiushe, 1936), 273–275; and Xu Taikong 許太空 et al., *Yue yuefu* 粵樂府 (Aomen: Tianlai lelu, 1932), 335–342. Made by Radio Television Hong Kong in the 1960s, a recording of *Taohua shan* sung by Lee Ngan-giu 李銀嬌 has survived. For a recently released compact disc of Lee's recording, see Dou Wun and Lee Ngan-giu, *Rare Recordings of Melodies from a Bygone Age* (Hong Kong: The Chinese Music Archive of the Chinese University of Hong Kong, 2011). For a transcription of Lee's singing and the flute accompaniment in staff notation, see Bell Yung, "The Scholar and the Courtesan: Love Songs on Pearl River's Flower Boats," *CHINOPERL: Journal of Chinese Oral and Performing Literature* 41 (2022): forthcoming.

46. The Yöng Kwán (i.e., Yangguan) gate is situated in the Longle 龍勒 district of Gansu province on the frontier of the Chinese heartlands and Central Asia. As it opened onto foreign regions, it is frequently used in poetry to symbolize "parting." See Cecil Clementi, *Cantonese Love-Songs*, vol. 1, 123.

47. The English translation is also rendered by Cecil Clementi. See ibid., vol. 1, 77.

48. Zhao Ziyong, *Yue'ou*, fols. 41r–v.

49. Xia Chengtao 夏承燾, *Jiang Baishi ci biannian jianjiao* 姜白石詞編年箋校 (Shanghai: Shanghai guji chubanshe, 1998), 32–36. For the interaction between Song literati and courtesans, see Beverly Bossler, "Shifting Identities: Courtesans and Literati in Song China," *Harvard Journal of Asiatic Studies* 62.1 (2002): 5–37. Interestingly, Song ambivalence toward *ci* poetry parallels a similar attitude toward intimacy with courtesans; see Chengjuan Sun, "The Hidden Blessing of being a Last Ruler: Anecdotes and the Song Dynasty Interpretation of Li Yu's (937–978) Lyrics," *Chinese Literature: Essays, Articles, Reviews* 34 (2012): 105–129.

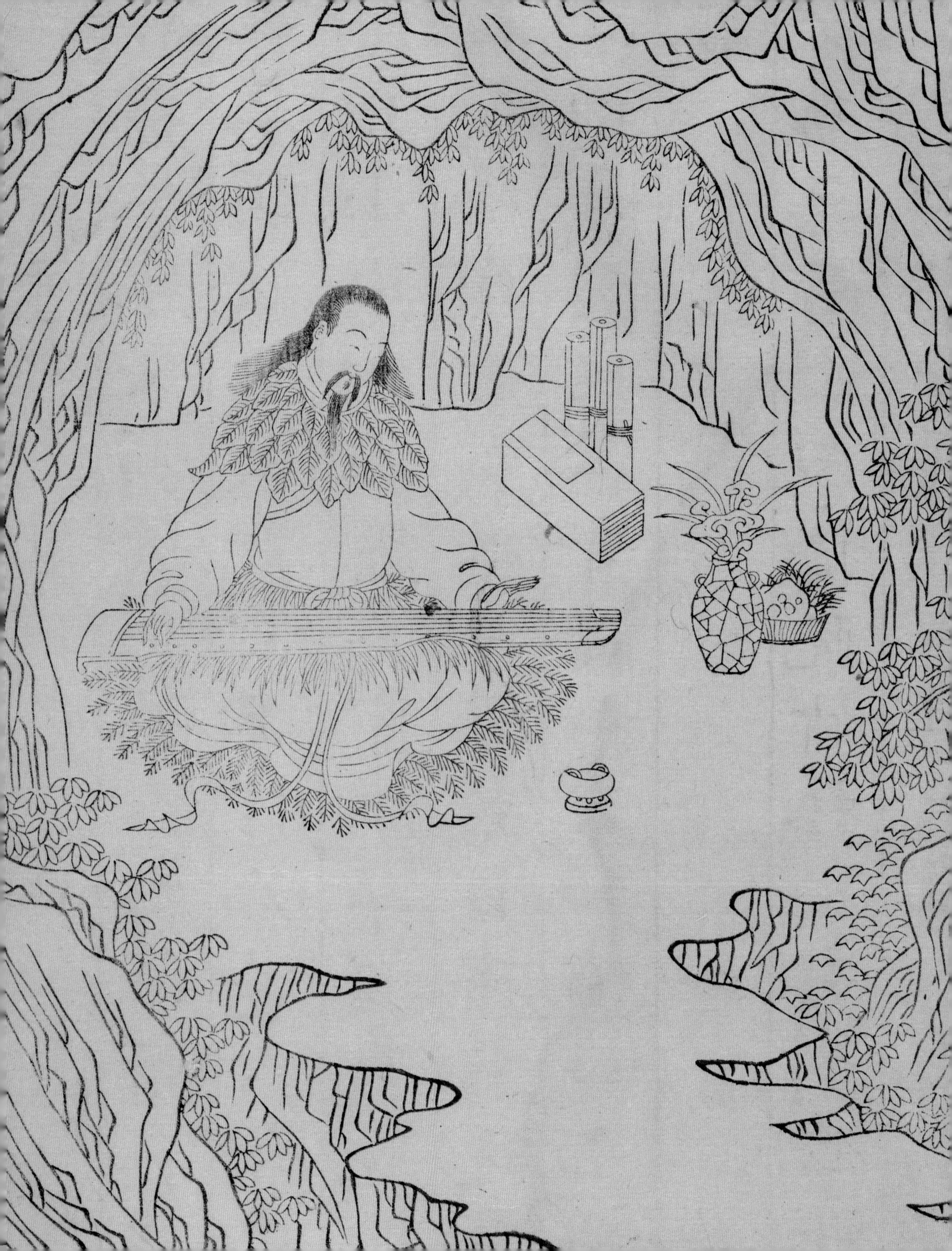

Chapter 4

Qin Music and the Literati

Yang Yuanzheng

The range of entertainments covered by the publications so far discussed is as broad as the social backgrounds of the public they served. Certain opera styles and *ci* poems (lyric songs) were sophisticated cultural gems of the literati, whereas at the opposite end of the spectrum, Yue ballads were much closer to grassroots traditions. For more than a thousand years, the instrument *par excellence* of the literati had been, of course, the *qin* 琴 (Fig. 4.1),[1] and it is to records of its repertories and performances that the investigation now turns.

Both Confucius and the Confucianists who followed had emphatically claimed the *qin* as their cultural preserve, yet subsequent to the Han dynasty, the instrument managed to break free from this straitjacket. The lynchpin in this process was literatus and *qin* practitioner Ji Kang 嵇康 (223–262), who was highly critical of Confucianism, skeptical of many of the social conventions of his time, and as such considered to be scandalous and seditious; for example, he advocated "transcending Confucianism and recognizing nature" 越名教而任自然,[2] as well as "refuting the founding Emperors Tang of the Shang dynasty and Wu of the Zhou dynasty, and looking askance at Duke Zhou and Confucius" 非湯、武而薄周、孔.[3] He married into the imperial Cao 曹 family, but when the usurping Sima 司馬 family achieved ascendency, he was sentenced to death at the age of forty, though before the punishment was carried out, he famously called for his *qin* and played his swansong *Guangling san* 廣陵散.[4]

Unlike the Confucian standpoint that regarded music as innately comprising the complete gamut of emotions, Ji Kang argued in his discourse on the nature of sound "Sheng wu ai le lun" 聲無哀樂論 ("In Music, there is no Sorrow or Joy") that the same music could engender different emotions in different people.[5] Put another way, if the Confucian view is commensurate with Plato's, then Ji Kang's has a degree of similarity to opinions expressed by the nineteenth-century supporter of Brahms' absolute music Eduard Hanslick (1825–1906). In the service of propagating his opinions, Ji Kang himself composed a well-known tract "Qin fu" 琴賦 ("Rhapsody on the *Qin*"),[6] which can be found in the eighteenth *juan* of a Ming dynasty copy in the Fung Ping Shan Library of *Liujia Wenxuan* 六家文選 (*Six Commentaries on Selections of Refined Literature*, Fig. 4.2).

Selections of Refined Literature was first compiled by Xiao Tong 蕭統 (501–531), and the Fung Ping Shan Library copy is a version by Yuan Qiong 袁褧 of Suzhou, re-cut in 1549 from a Song dynasty original. The entire text is furnished with a colophon at the end in which Yuan Qiong records the various exegetical authorities consulted and that it had been in preparation for sixteen years

Fig. 4.1: *Renjing yangqiu* (*Mirror of Morality*), *juan* 12, fols. 28v–29r, woodblock engraving of Sun Deng playing the *qin*.
Author: Wang Tingne (1573–1619).
Date: 1600.
Woodblock: 24.4 × 16.5 cm.
Fung Ping Shan Library.

1. The *qin*, a type of plucked horizontal zither, has long been considered China's preeminent musical instrument. For the complex ideology that has developed around its music, see R. H. van Gulik, *The Lore of the Chinese Lute: An Essay in Ch'in Ideology* (Tokyo: Sophia University, 1940). In this book, he calls the *qin* a "lute," rather than a "zither," in order to convey to the general reader something of the cultural significance of the instrument and its music.

2. Dai Mingyang 戴明揚, ed., *Ji Kang ji jiaozhu* 嵇康集校注 (Beijing: Renmin wenxue chubanshe, 1962), 234.

3. Ibid., 122.

4. Ibid., 444–480.

5. Ibid., 196–232. An English translation of this article can be found in Robert G. Henricks, *Philosophy and Argumentation in Third-Century China: The Essays of Hsi K'ang* (Princeton, NJ: Princeton University Press, 1983), 71–106.

6. Dai Mingyang, ed., *Ji Kang ji jiaozhu*, 82–111. For translations of the poem, see R. H. van Gulik, *Hs'i Kang and his Poetic Essay on the Lute* (Tokyo: Sophia University, 1941); Georges Goormaghtigh, *L'Art du Qin: Deux Textes d'Esthétique Musicale Chinoise* (Bruxelles: Institut Belge des Hautes Études Chinoises, 1990), 21–46; and David R. Knechtges, trans., *Wen Xuan, or Selections of Refined Literature*, vol. 3. (Princeton, NJ: Princeton University Press, 1996), 279–302. Both "In Music, there is no Sorrow or Joy" and "Rhapsody on the *Qin*" are regarded by modern scholarship as highly influential; see Jiyeon Kang, "Ji Kang's Criticism of Confucian and Naturalistic Music Theory," *Acta Musicologica* 86.2 (2014): 159–176; and Ronald Egan, "The Controversy over Music and 'Sadness' and Changing Conceptions of the *Qin* in Middle Period China," *Harvard Journal of Asiatic Studies* 57.1 (1997): 5–66.

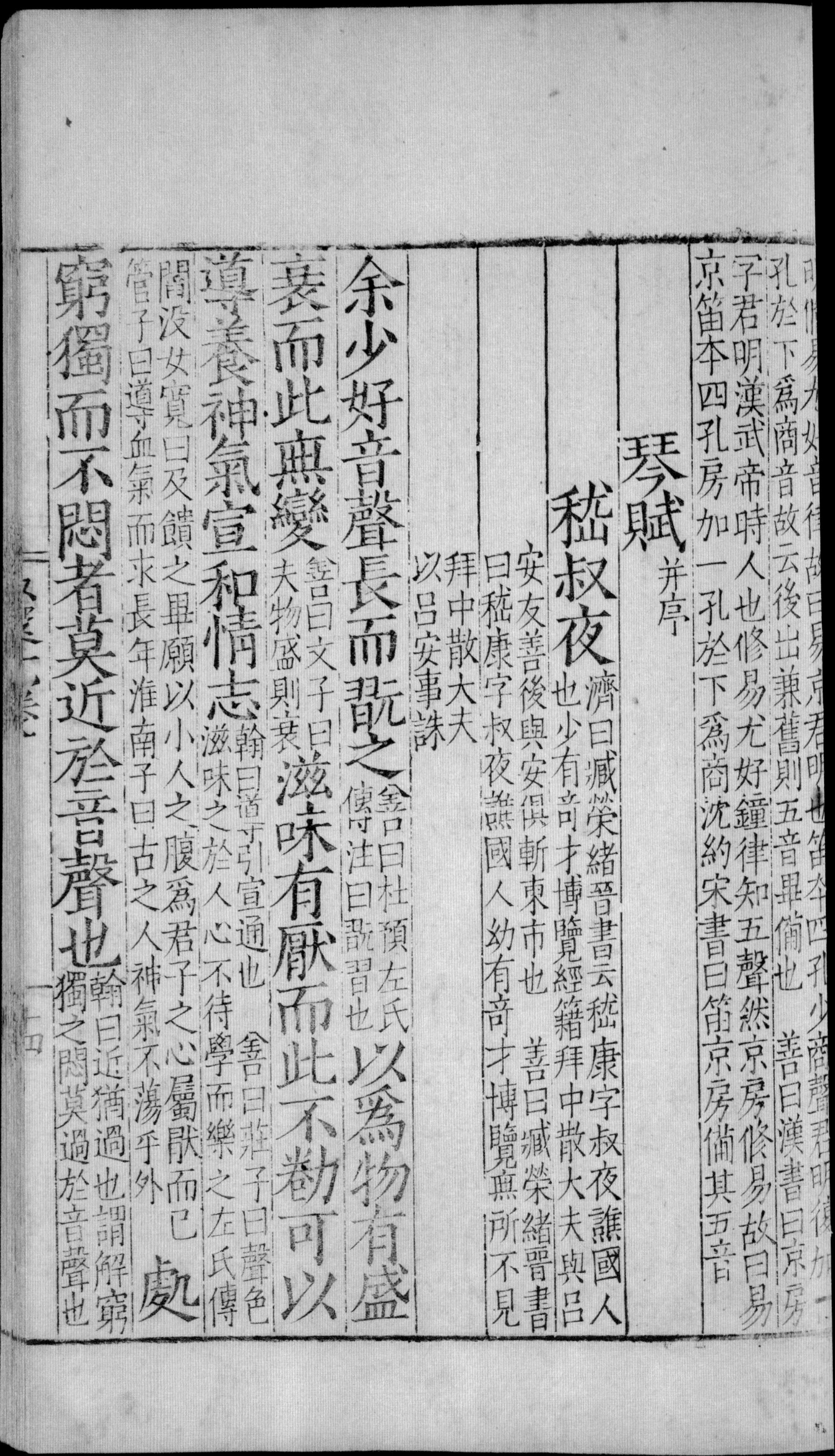

明假易加如音律故曰易京君明也笛本四孔少商聲君明倍加

孔於下為商音故云後出兼舊則五音畢備也　善曰漢書曰京房

子君明漢武帝時人也修易尤好鐘律知五聲然京房修易故曰易

京笛本四孔房加一孔於下為商沈約宋書曰笛京房備其五音

琴賦 并序

嵇叔夜 濟曰臧榮緒晉書云嵇康字叔夜譙國人也少有奇才博覽經籍拜中散大夫與呂安友善後與安俱斬東市也　善曰臧榮緒晉書曰嵇康字叔夜譙國人幼有奇才博覽無所不見拜中散大夫以呂安事誅

余少好音聲長而翫之 銑曰杜預左氏傳注曰翫習也 以為物有盛衰而此無變 銑曰文子曰夫物盛則衰 滋味有猒而此不勸可以導養神氣宣和情志 翰曰導引宣通也　善曰莊子曰聲色滋味之於人心不待學而樂之左氏傳闇沒女寬曰及饋之畢願以小人之腹為君子之心屬猒而已管子曰道之血氣而求長年淮南子曰古之人神氣不蕩乎外 處窮獨而不悶者莫近於音聲也 翰曰近猶過也謂解窮獨之悶莫過於音聲也

Fig. 4.2: *Liujia Wenxuan (Six Commentaries on Selections of Refined Literature), juan* 19, fols. 13v–14r, "Rhapsody on the *Qin*."
Editor: Xiao Tong (501–531).
Date: 1549.
Woodblock: 24.1 × 18.8 cm.
Fung Ping Shan Library.

助戚美忽而不讃悲夫向曰大漢漢朝也笛生乎大漢之朝而當時學士不識其可益助天
子之盛美輕忽而不爲讃頌之亦可悲也裨益也夫助辭也 善曰說文曰裨益也婢移切有庶士丘仲
言其所由出而不知其弘妙濟曰丘仲漢武時笛人庶士謂庶祿位也弘大也言
學者忽而不讃有丘仲言其所由出處尚亦不知其大妙矣其辭善曰尚書曰庶邦庶士風俗通曰笛武帝時丘仲所作也
曰翰曰且丘仲所言之辭也近世雙笛從羌起羌人伐竹未及
已龍鳴水中不見胡練已截善本作截竹吹之聲相似
銑曰羌西戎也起謂首作也其人伐竹未畢之間有龍鳴水中不見其身羌人旋即截竹吹之聲與龍相似也 善曰風俗通曰笛元羌出
又有羌笛與笛二器不同已謂龍也剡其上孔通洞之裁以當去簻竹瓜
使善本作便字易持良曰剡剔也上孔吹處也羌人裁截之以當馬簻使其易執持而復吹之也簻鞭也 善曰裁
笛以當簻故便而易持也簻馬策也裁或爲材易京君明識音律故本四孔加
以一君明所加孔後出是謂商聲五音畢翰曰京

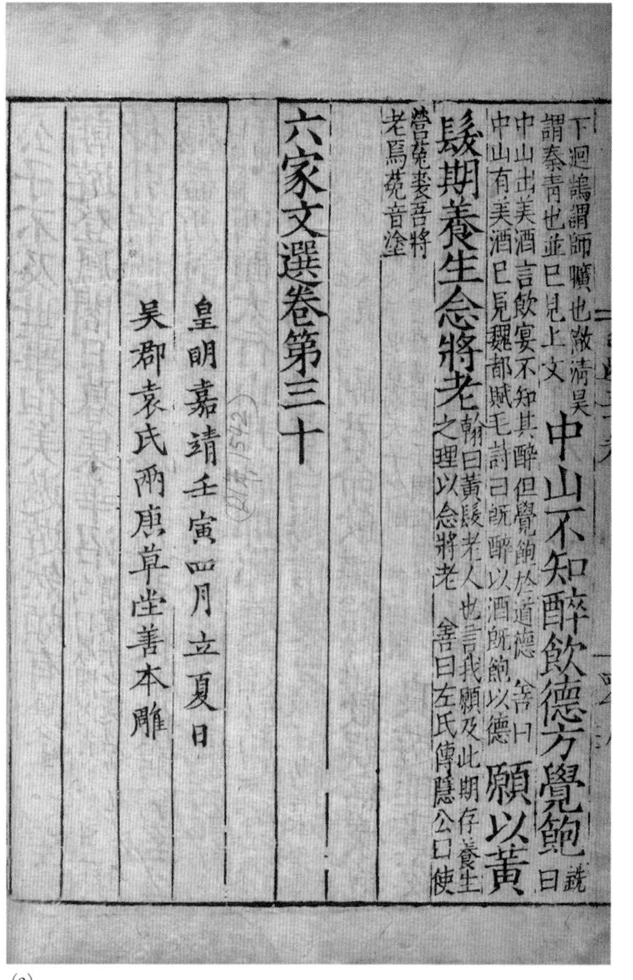
下迴鵠謂師曠也激清昊謂秦青也並已見上文中山不知醉飲德兮覺飽銑曰中山出美酒言飲宴不知其醉但覺飽於道德　翰曰中山有美酒已見魏都賦毛詩曰既醉以酒既飽以德願以黃髮期養生念將老翰曰黃髮老人也言我願及此期存養生之理以念將老　善曰左氏傳隱公曰使營菟裘吾將老焉菟音塗

六家文選卷第三十

皇明嘉靖壬寅四月立夏日
吳郡袁氏兩庚草堂善本雕

(a)

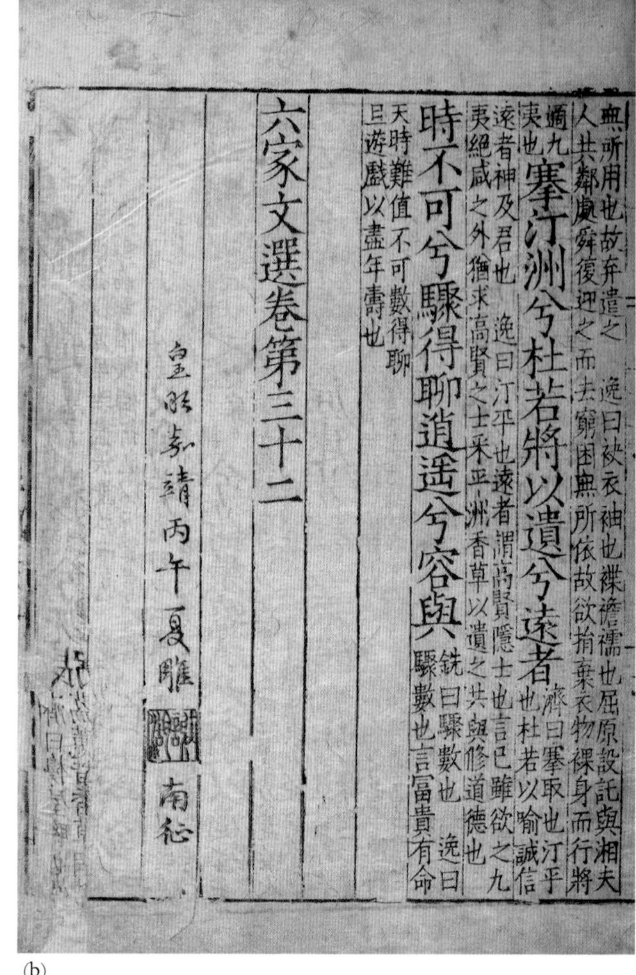
無所用也故弃遺之　逸曰袂衣袖也褋襜襦也屈原設託與湘夫人共鄰處舜復迎之而去窮困無所依故欲捐棄衣物裸身而行將適九夷也搴汀洲兮杜若將以遺兮遠者濟曰搴取也汀平也杜若以喻誠信遠者神及君也　逸曰汀平也遠者謂高賢隱士也言已雖欲之九夷絕域之外猶求高賢之士采平洲香草以遺之共與修道德也時不可兮驟得聊逍遥兮容與銑曰驟數也言富貴有命天時難值不可數得聊且遊戲以盡年壽也　逸曰驟數也

六家文選卷第三十二

皇明嘉靖丙午夏雕

南沁

(b)

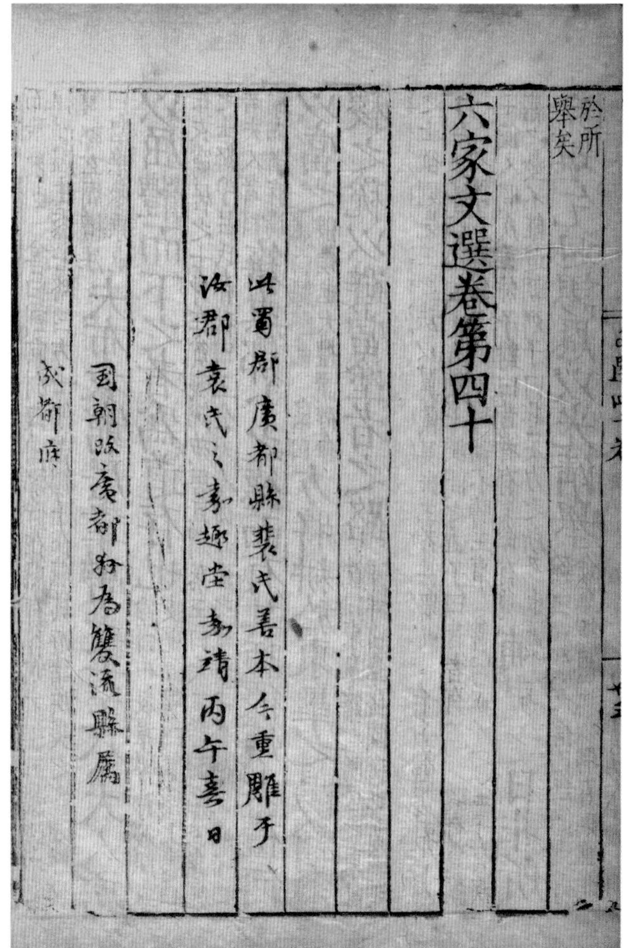
於所舉矣

六家文選卷第四十

此蜀郡廣都縣裴氏善本今重雕于
汝郡袁氏之嘉趣堂　嘉靖丙午春日
國朝改廣都為雙流縣屬
成都府

(c)

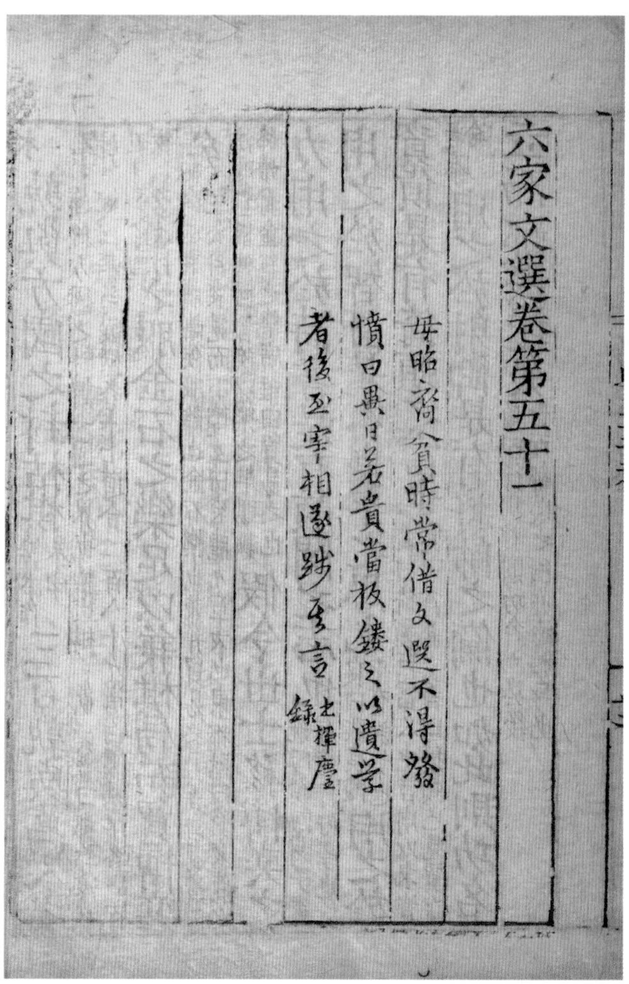
六家文選卷第五十二

毋昭裔貧時常借文選不得發
憤曰異日若貴當板鏤之以遺學
者後至宰相遂踐其言
士揮麈錄

(d)

Fig. 4.3: *Liujia Wenxuan* (*Six Commentaries on Selections of Refined Literature*), four additional colophons by Yuan Qiong at (a) *juan* 30, fol. 40v, (b) *juan* 32, fol. 28v, (c) *juan* 40, fol. 35v, and (d) *juan* 52, fol. 22v.
Editor: Xiao Tong (501–531).
Date: 1549.
Woodblock: 24.1 × 18.8 cm.
Harvard-Yenching Library (T 5236.03 4).

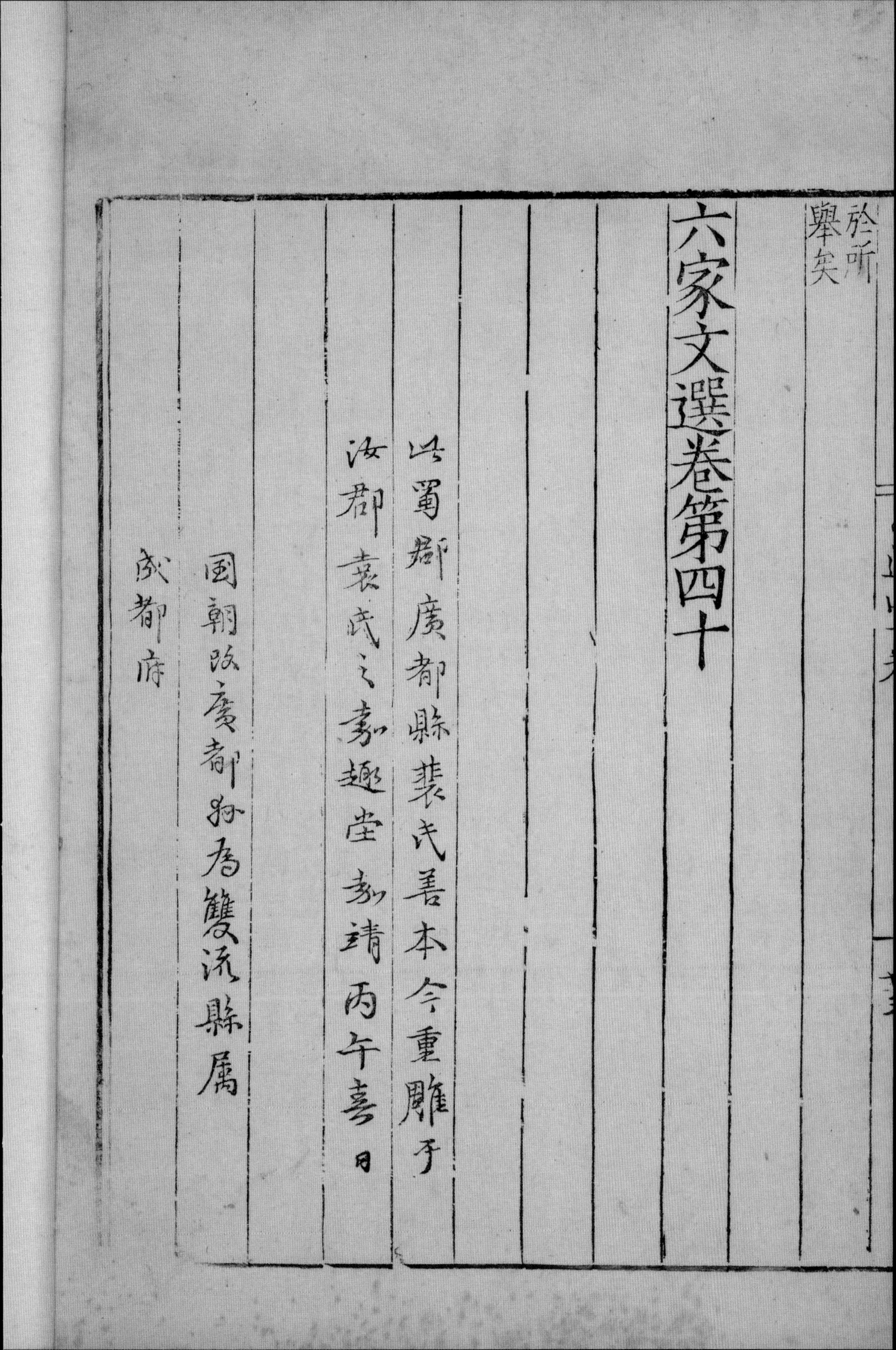

於所
舉矣

六家文選卷第四十

此蜀郡廣都縣裴氏善本今重雕于
汝郡袁氏之嘉趣堂嘉靖丙午喜日

國朝改廣都為雙流縣屬
成都府

Fig. 4.4: *Liujia Wenxuan* (*Six Commentaries on Selections of Refined Literature*), *juan* 40, fol. 35v, the additional colophon by Yuan Qiong. Editor: Xiao Tong (501–531). Date: 1549. Woodblock: 24.1 × 18.8 cm. Fung Ping Shan Library.

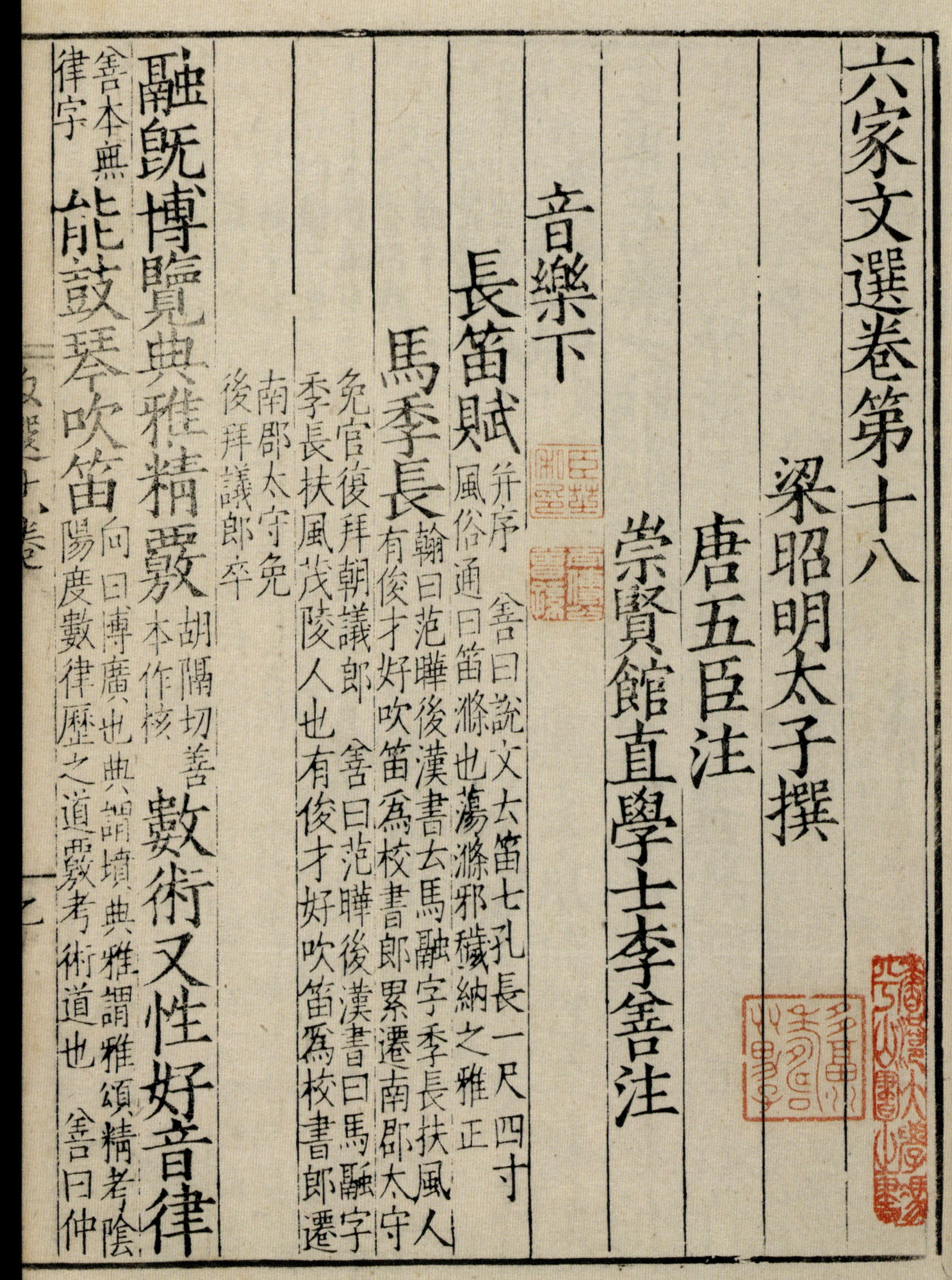

六家文選卷第十八

梁昭明太子撰

唐五臣注

崇賢館直學士李善注

音樂下

長笛賦

幷序 善曰說文云笛七孔長一尺四寸 風俗通曰笛滌也蕩滌邪穢納之雅正

馬季長 翰曰范曄後漢書云馬融字季長扶風人有後才好吹笛爲校書郎累遷南郡太守免官復拜朝議郎 善曰范曄後漢書曰馬融字季長扶風茂陵人也有後才好吹笛爲校書郎遷南郡太守免後拜議郎卒

融既博覽典雅精覈 胡隔切善本作核 數術又性好音律 善本無律字 能鼓琴吹笛 向曰博廣也典謂墳典雅謂雅頌精考陰陽度數律歷之道覈考術道也 善曰仲

(1534–1549);[7] at the end of *juan* 30 (Fig. 4.3a), 32 (Fig. 4.3b), 37, 40 (Fig. 4.3c), 41, 42, 51 (Fig. 4.3d), 52, 56, and 60, ten colophons have also been added to confirm that he had been the printer. In the Fung Ping Shan Library copy, seven of these colophons are missing, and three are at the end of *juan* 37, 40, and 41. At the end of *juan* 40 is written (Fig. 4.4):

> This is a fine edition produced in the Shu prefecture, Guangdu county, by [someone surnamed] Pei, and has been re-cut by [someone surnamed] Yuan in the Ru prefecture at the Fine Taste Hall. The *bingwu* year of the Jiajing era [1546], spring. (The current dynasty has changed the place name Guangdu to Shuangliu county in the city of Chengdu.)
>
> 此蜀郡廣都縣裴氏善本，今重雕於汝郡袁氏之嘉趣堂，嘉靖丙午春日。（國朝改廣都為雙流縣，屬成都府。）

According to Pan Chengbi 潘承弼 (1907–2004) and Gu Tinglong 顧廷龍 (1904–1998), the phenomenon of missing colophons indicates that the Fung Ping Shan Library copy is a later imprint. Both believed that the greater the number of additional colophons, the earlier the imprint.[8] In this regard, a copy kept in the Seikadō Bunko 靜嘉堂文庫 has the largest number of such additional colophons, followed by one in the Harvard-Yenching Library.[9] Close comparison between the Harvard-Yenching and Fung Ping Shan copies reveals that the former is in fact the later imprint. Jao Tsung-i 饒宗頤 (1917–2018) therefore proposed an alternative interpretation: perhaps these additional colophons were added to the wooden plates at later dates, so that the earlier the imprint, the fewer the colophons.[10]

My examination of the Fung Ping Shan copy reveals that the seven missing colophons have in fact been excised from the pages where they should be present. Of them, on *juan* 60, fol. 22v, not only has the Ming publisher Yuan Qiong's colophon been removed from columns 5–7, but the paper of the relevant area has also been carefully replaced by black ruled paper of the same type found elsewhere in the book. This gives readers the impression that the Ming publisher's colophon had never appeared.

The book itself is a fine copy, large and clearly printed. Its quality is such that it has been mistaken for the Song dynasty original. If the forgers had gone one step further, adding a colophon dated to the Song dynasty, Yuan Qiong's edition would have had the potential to be sold for a much higher price; for example, of the ten copies kept in the imperial library of the high Qing, the publisher's colophons of nine have been removed and replaced by imprints of various forged Song dynasty colophons dating to 1056, 1071, 1097–1098, 1209–1216, 1242, and 1261–1274.[11] Scholars have also reported copies bearing the imprint of forged colophons dating to 1106–1111 and 1155.[12] The only surviving fragments of the genuine Song original, of which the Yuan Qiong edition is a facsimile, are kept at the National Palace Museum in Taipei.[13] For a well-trained modern bibliographer, it is not difficult to recognize stylistic differences between the fonts employed by the Song original and its Ming facsimile. Back in the seventeenth and eighteenth centuries, however, even scholars as erudite as Zhu Yizun 朱彝尊 (1629–1709) and Peng Yuanrui 彭元瑞 (1731–1803) regarded the Ming facsimile as being of Song provenance.[14] Nearly seventy seals of a previous owner Xie Zizhi 謝紫芝 (fl. early eighteenth century, see Fig. 4.5) can be found on the Fung Ping Shan Library copy in various places, which is some measure of the importance that he ascribed

Fig. 4.5: *Liujia Wenxuan* (*Six Commentaries on Selections of Refined Literature*), *juan* 18, fol. 1r, "Rhapsodies on Music."
Editor: Xiao Tong (501–531).
Date: 1549.
Woodblock: 24.1 × 18.8 cm.
Fung Ping Shan Library.

7. Pan Chengbi 潘承弼 and Gu Tinglong 顧廷龍, *Mingdai banben tulu chubian* 明代版本圖錄初編 (Shanghai: Kaiming shudian, 1941), vol. 6, fols. 37v–38r.

8. Ibid., vol. 6, fols. 37r–38v.

9. See Shiba Rokurō 斯波六郎, *Monzen sakuin* 文選索引 (Kyoto: Kyōto daigaku jinbun kagaku kenkyūjo sakuin iinkai, 1957), vol. 1, 44–48; and Jao Tsung-i 饒宗頤, Li Zhifang 李直方, and Zhang Lijuan 張麗娟, *Xianggang daxue Feng Pingshan tushuguan cang shanben shulu* 香港大學馮平山圖書館藏善本書錄, enlarged ed. (Hong Kong: Hong Kong University Press, 2003), 280.

10. Jao Tsung-i 饒宗頤, *Xianggang daxue Feng Pingshan tushuguan cang shanben shulu* 香港大學馮平山圖書館藏善本書錄 (Hong Kong: Longmen shudian, 1970), 92.

11. Ye Dehui 葉德輝, *Shulin qinghua* 書林清話 (Beijing: Guji chubanshe, 1957), 265–266.

12. Shi Tingyong 施廷鏞, "Gugong tushu ji 故宮圖書記," *Tushuguan xue jikan* 圖書館學季刊 1.1 (1926): 54; and Zhu Yizun 朱彝尊, *Pushu ting ji* 曝書亭集 (Shanghai: Shangwu yin-shuguan, 1935), vol. 9, 839.

13. Guoli gugong bowuyuan bianji weiyuanhui 國立故宮博物院編輯委員會, ed., *Songban shu tezhan mulu* 宋版書特展目錄 (Taipei: Guoli gugong bowuyuan, 1986), 78–79.

14. Modern scholar Fu Gang has claimed that even the celebrated sixteenth-century scholar-officials Wu Kuan吳寬 (1435–1504) and Wang Ao王鏊 (1450–1524) regarded the Yuan edition as being of Song provenance. See Fu Gang 傅剛, *Wenxuan banben yanjiu* 文選版本研究 (Beijing: Beijing daxue chubanshe, 2000), 88. His assertion simply cannot be accurate as these two individuals had died decades before the publication of the Yuan edition in 1549.

碣石調幽蘭序一名倚蘭

丘公字明會稽人也梁末隱於九疑山妙絕楚調於幽
蘭一曲尤特精絕以其聲微而志遠而不堪授人以陳
禎明三年授宜都王叔明隨開皇十年於丹陽縣卒
年九十七無子傳之其聲遂簡耳

幽蘭第五

耶臥中指十上半寸許案商食指中指雙牽宮商中
指急下與構俱下十三下一寸許住末商起食指散緩半
扶宮商〻指挑商又半扶宮商縱容下無名於十三外一
寸許案〻 角於商角即作兩半扶挾挑聲 一句 緩〻起
中指當十間 案商緩〻散歷羽徵無名打商食指挑徵
一句 大指當八案商無名打商食指散挑羽無名當十一

Fig. 4.6 (opposite): The Tōkyō manuscript, cols. 1–12, preface and the beginning of section one.
Author: Qiu Ming (493–590).
Date: early seventh century.
Dimensions: 27.4 × 423.1 cm.
Tōkyō Kokuritsu Hakubutsukan (TB1393).

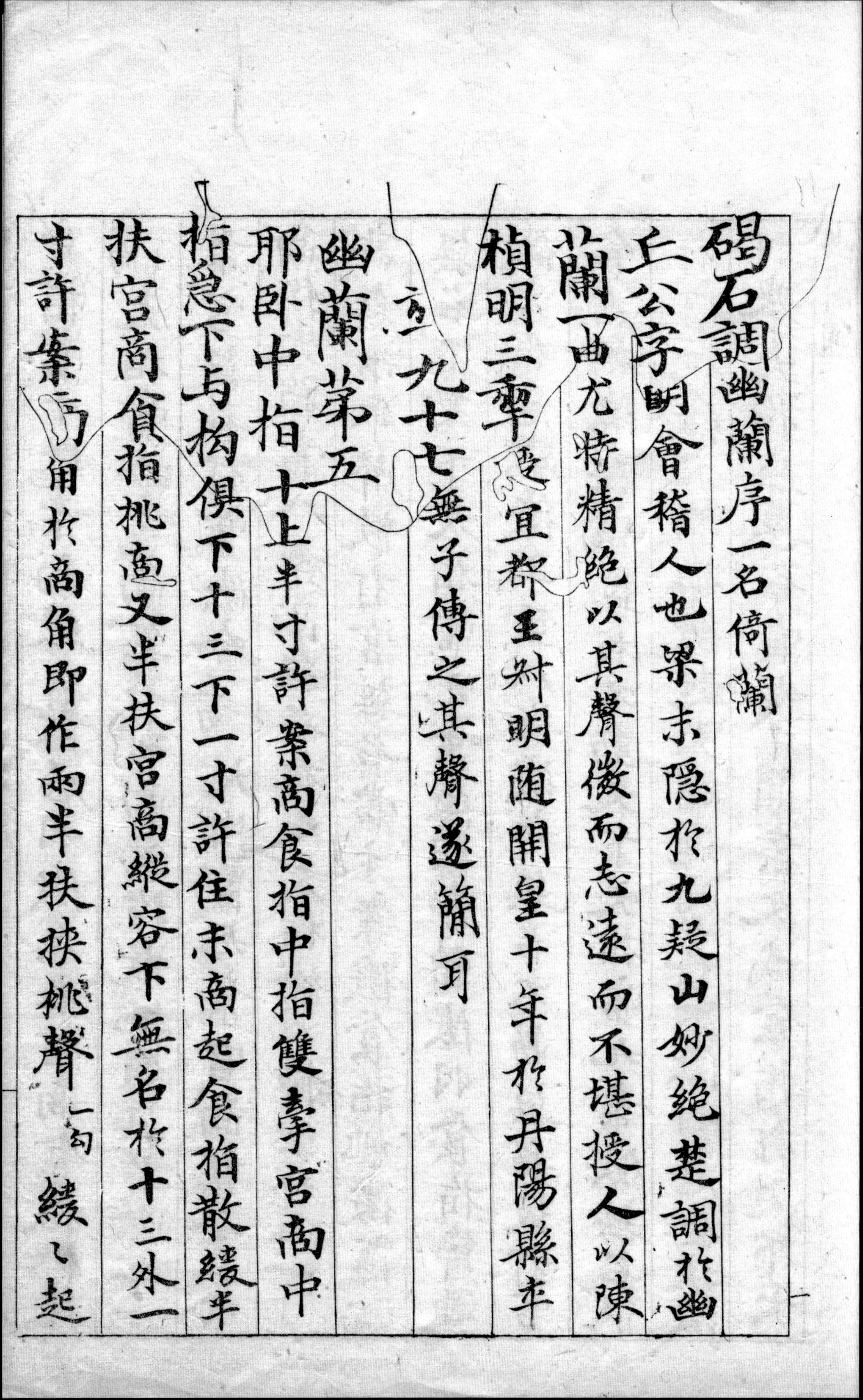

碣石調幽蘭序一名倚蘭
丘公字明會稽人也梁末隱於九疑山妙絕楚調於幽
蘭一曲尤特精絕以其聲微而志遠而不堪授人以陳
禎明三秊授宜都王叔明隨開皇十年於丹陽縣卒
年九十七無子傳之其聲遂簡耳
幽蘭第五
耶卧中指十上半寸許案商食指中指雙牽宮商中
指急下与构俱下十三下一寸許住末商起食指散緩半
扶宮商食指挑徵又半扶宮商縱容下無名於十三外一
寸許案商角於商角即作兩半扶挟挑聲一句緩緩起

Fig. 4.7: Woodcut facsimile of Kojima Hōso's tracing copy of the Tōkyō manuscript, cols. 1–10.
Editor: Li Shuchang (1837–1897).
Date: 1884.
Woodblock: 23.3 × 16.6 cm.
Private collection.

即𨉼角徵大指當十一案徵𨉼角徵大指隨𨉼

上至十縮案徵羽應羽徵前後𨉼宮徵初緩後急一句拍之

食指泛八無名打徵無名泛九食指桃武應霞泛九疾

全扶文武桃武應食指泛八無名打文手泛十九前後𨉼

羽武舉大指無名不動無名打文大指泛九於文武羽半扶疾

𨉼宮羽一句霞泛九食打羽無名打商散桃羽應無名泛十一無名舉大指無名泛九於歲角羽

打宮大指泛九桃羽應一句食指泛八無名打徵無名泛

十桃文應仍𤄊武無名泛十一食指打文無名泛十二

全扶文武即桃武應手泛十二十三前後𨉼羽武無名

當暗徵無名便打文一句暗徵逸徵是也仰泛十二却轉武文食

指仍歷至徵緩全扶角徵無名節打角疾全扶徵羽

手泛十一十二食指搴羽文仰泛十二半扶徵羽間拘

角徵手泛十十一中指搴徵羽霞泛十作前桃間拘轉

Fig. 4.8 (opposite): The Tōkyō manuscript, cols. 200–212, the end of section three and the beginning of section four, characters scraped off and replaced by a scribe in cols. 204 and 205, and continuing into the bottom margin.
Author: Qiu Ming (493–590).
Date: early seventh century.
Dimensions: 27.4 × 423.1 cm.
Tōkyō Kokuritsu Hakubutsukan (TB1393).

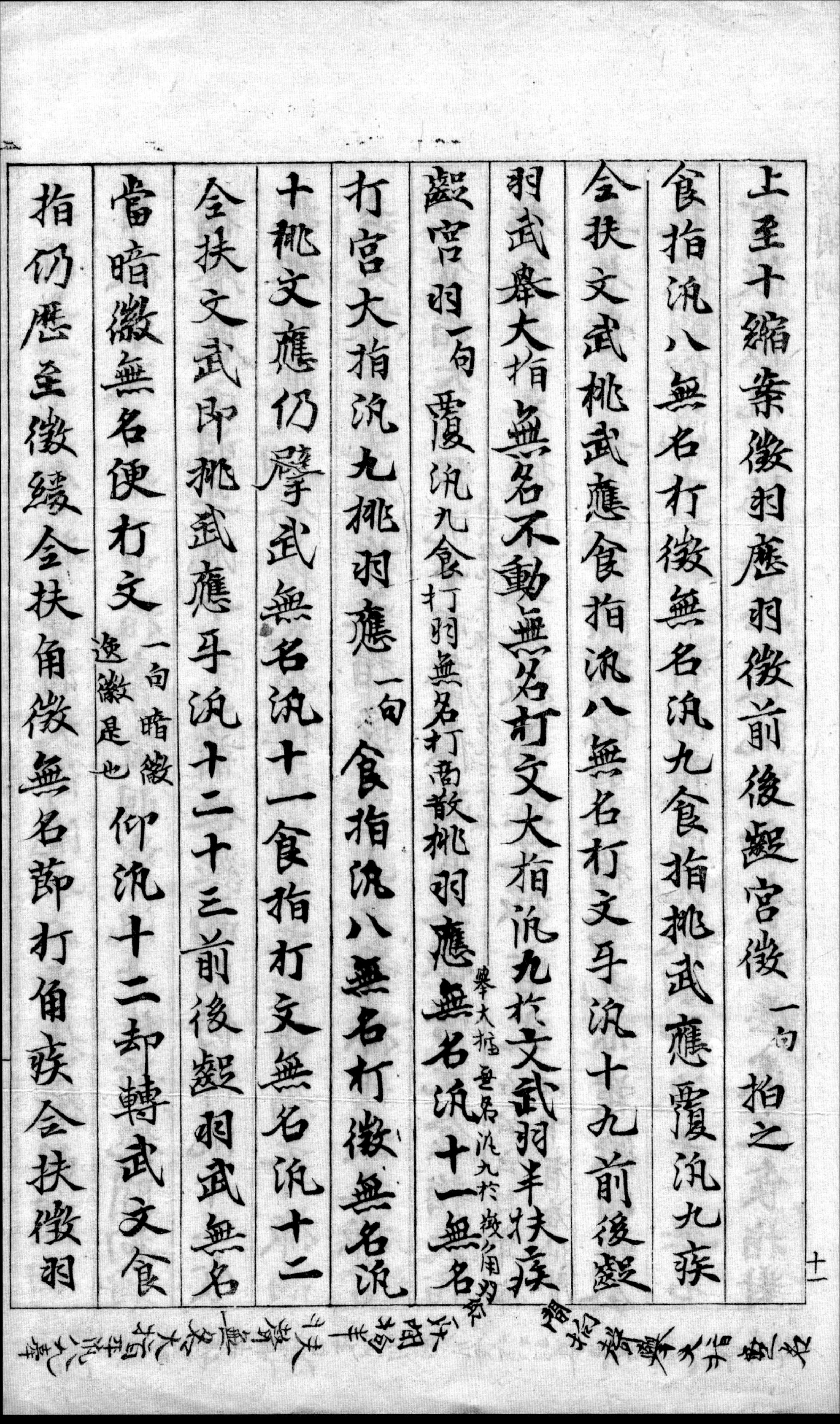

上至十縮案徽羽應羽徽前後𧽘宮徽　一句　拍之
食指泛八無名打徽無名泛九食指挑武應覆泛九疾
全扶文武桃武應食指泛八無名打文手泛十九前後𧽘
羽武舉大指無名不動無名打文大指泛九於文武羽半扶疾　舉大指無名泛九於徽角羽
𧽘宮羽一句覆泛九食打羽無名打商散挑羽應無名泛十一無名
打宮大指泛九挑羽應　一句　食指泛八無名打徽無名泛
十挑文應仍擘武無名泛十一食指打文無名泛十二
全扶文武即挑武應手泛十二十三前後𧽘羽武無名
當暗徽無名便打文　一句暗徽逸徽是也　仰泛十二却轉武文食
指仍歷至徽緩全扶角徽無名節打角疾全扶徽羽

十一

Fig. 4.9: Woodcut facsimile of Kojima Hōso's tracing copy of the Tōkyō manuscript, cols. 201–210.
Editor: Li Shuchang (1837–1897).
Date: 1884.
Woodblock: 23.3 × 16.6 cm.
Private collection.

to it. Xie Zizhi likely had also been cheated by the forger and regarded his copy as a Song edition. A notable book collector, he was a great-grandson of scholar-official Xie Sheng 謝陞 (1572–1645) of Dezhou county, Shangdong.[15] Eleven of his seals are transcribed by Jao Tsung-i[16] and another twenty by Li Zhifang 李直方 (who supplemented the former's bibliographical record), [17] though their lists are still not comprehensive.[18]

Regarding musical notation, only two manuscripts contemporary to early *qin* practice are extant:[19] one is the manuscript Tōkyō, Tōkyō Kokuritsu Hakubutsukan TB1393 (henceforth the Tōkyō manuscript, Figs. 4.6 and 4.8), currently accepted by scholarship as a seventh-century scroll and whose recto contains a notated version of the *qin* piece *Youlan* 幽蘭 (*Solitary Orchid*); the other is the manuscript Hikone, Hikone-jō Hakubutsukan V633 (henceforth the Hikone manuscript); the recto of the Hikone scroll preserves several treatises on the finger techniques of early *qin* playing (Fig. 4.10), while the verso includes sketches of a *saibara* 催馬樂 piece, Chinese verses, and three assemblages of casual drawings (Fig. 4.11).[20] As the oldest extant manuscripts of Chinese *qin* music, the Tōkyō and Hikone scrolls are essential to any exploration of musical transmission in East Asia. The *qin* notation employed by the two scrolls is *wenzipu* 文字譜 ("full ideogram notation"), the earliest method of committing *qin* musical sounds to paper and the prototype for present-day *qin* tablature. This notation system explains pitches and finger movements through prose, by which a compiler writes out which finger of the left hand is to be placed on which string in which position, thus prescribing the pitch and timbre of the sound that is produced; the right hand's fingering and method of execution are indicated so as to suggest rhythmic values and how ornamentation is to be deployed.

The Tōkyō manuscript first came to the attention of music historians when a woodcut facsimile of Kojima Hōso's 小島寶素 (1797–1847) tracing copy of it was published in 1884 (Figs. 4.7 and 4.9).[21] Evidently representing an early stage of the *qin* notational system, the Tōkyō manuscript substantially changed modern scholars' perception of early *qin* music. Many attempts at deciphering the notation involving numerous uncertainties have appeared since then, and a preliminary dating identifying the scroll as a seventh-century artifact has been suggested by musicologists and art historians.[22]

Compared with the current state of research on the Tōkyō manuscript, levels of exploration of the Hikone manuscript are even more unsatisfactory. Although several conflated copies of the Hikone manuscript compiled by the Confucian fundamentalist of the Edo period, Ogyū Sorai 荻生徂徠 (1666–1728), have been studied by modern

15. Li Shude 李樹德 et al., *Dexian zhi* 德縣志 (Taipei: Chengwen chubanshe, 1968), 290.

16. Jao Tsung-i, *Xianggang daxue Feng Pingshan tushuguan cang shanben shulu*, 93.

17. Jao Tsung-i, Li Zhifang, and Zhang Lijuan, *Xianggang daxue Feng Pingshan tushuguan cang shanben shulu*, enlarged ed., 280.

18. The other thirty-five unidentified seals read:「紫芝」，「霞綺樓章」，「樸愚猶本性」，「春草堂印」，「長吟」，「池塘春草書房」，「卷簾聽雨」，「紫芝之章」，「商隱」,「古人之義」，「東山世家」，「安德謝芝」，「多福多壽多男子」，「似倩麻姑癢處搔」，「園柳鳴禽又一時」，「步惠子亭」，「讀書雖少愛書香」，「竹巖」，「河上草廬」，「不薄今人愛古人」，「曲有微情」，「麈衣澹蕩人」，「直舉胸情」，「郵筒珍重寄相思」，「遙懷具短札」，「休息乎篇籍之囿」，「與天為徒」，「唯豪素之所擬」，「寶藏」，「皆大歡喜」，「心地似梅花」，「抱樸含真」，「意愜」，「短歌微吟」，「學然後知不足」。

19. Current usage regards "early *qin* music" as the *qin* playing practiced between the third and ninth centuries, i.e., roughly from the Southern and Northern dynasties (420–589) to the Sui and Tang dynasties (581–907).

20. The verso of the scroll as understood here is the verso of its first layer; a new backing layer has been added subsequently; for details of the physical structure of the Hikone scroll, see Yang Yuanzheng, "A Tale of Two Manuscripts: The Making and Origins of the Earliest Scrolls of *Qin* Music," *Acta Musicologica* 86.1 (2014): 32–73. Excellent introductions to the Sino-Japanese craft of scroll mounting can be found in R. H. van Gulik, *Chinese Pictorial Art as Viewed by the Connoisseur: Notes on the Means and Methods of Traditional Chinese Connoisseurship of Pictorial Art, based upon a Study of the Art of Mounting Scrolls in China and Japan* (New York: Hacker Art Books, 1981); David Helliwell, "The Repair and Binding of Old Chinese Books: Translated and Adapted for Western Conservators," *East Asian Library Journal* 8.1 (1998): 33–50; and Xiao Zhentang 蕭振棠 and Ding Yu 丁瑜, *Zhongguo guji zhuangding xiubu jishu* 中國古籍裝訂修補技術 (Beijing: Shumu wenxian chubanshe, 1980).

21. As an item in *Guyi congshu* 古逸叢書, a series of books issued with the aim of re-circulating early Chinese books that had been lost to the Chinese mainland; the facsimile was based on a tracing copy originally held in the collection of Kojima Hōso. During a sojourn in Japan from 1880 to 1884, Yang Shoujing 楊守敬 (1839–1915), a Chinese bibliophile, directed the making of the facsimile as well as its eventual publication in Tokyo in 1884, while editorship of the set of books was entrusted to Li Shuchang 黎庶昌 (1837–1896), the Chinese ambassador to Japan at the time.

22. Nakata Yūjirō 中田勇次郎, "Kessekichō yūran 碣石調幽蘭," in *Tō shōhon* 唐鈔本, ed. Osaka Shiritsu Bijutsukan 大阪市立美術館 (Kyoto: Dōhōsha, 1981), 171; Tomita Jun 富田淳, "Kessekichō yūran daigo ni tsuite 碣石調·幽蘭第五について," in *Yūran kenkyū kokusai shinpojiumu* 幽蘭研究国際シンポジウム, ed., Tōyō kingaku kenkyōjo 東洋琴学研究所 (Tokyo: Tōyō kingaku kenkyūjo, 1999), 31–32; Yang Yuanzheng, "A Tale of Two Manuscripts: The Making and Origins of the Earliest Scrolls of *Qin* Music," 32–73.

Fig. 4.10: The Hikone manuscript, recto, cols. 7–16, Chen Zhongru's treatise entitled *[Qin]yong zhifa*. Authors: Chen Zhongru (act. 519), Feng Zhibian (fl. 581–618), and Zhao Yeli (564–639). Date: Nara or Heian periods. Dimensions: 30.0 × 408.0 cm. Hikone-jō Hakubutsukan (V633).

三鏁　右頭指挑打一弦作聲

打鏁　右頭指先打一弦停仍即依三鏁法

鏁　右頭指桃打一弦无定數

全扶　右頭指中指相逐拘度二弦无名即約前弦絶餘聲

半扶　右頭指急拘度二弦中指即約前弦使絶餘聲

蠲一名分摟　假令右頭指拘羽中指即逐拘度徵羽二弦無名即抱宫令斷後聲

差馳　假令右頭指拘商中指拘宫各拘一弦度

間拘　假令右中指拘角無名拘商各拘一弦度

擽　假令右頭指擽武中指打文應

搶　假令右頭指歷徵角大指約徵致餘聲若五弦

Fig. 4.11 (opposite): The Hikone manuscript, verso, the *saibara* sketch and casual drawing (using a light sheet placed behind the manuscript).
Date: Heian or Kamakura periods.
Dimensions: 30.0 × 408.0 cm.
Hikone-jō Hakubutsukan (V633).

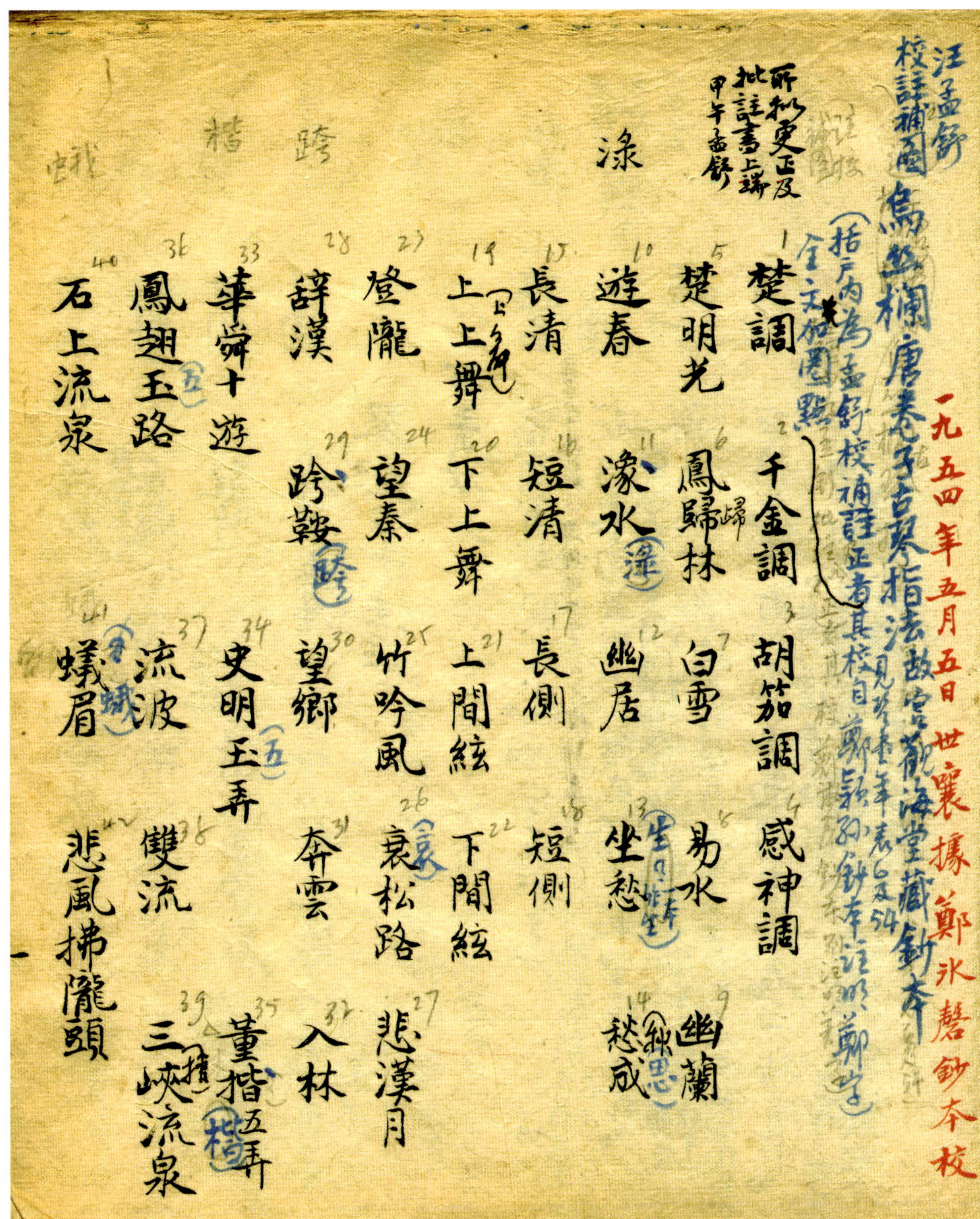

一九五四年五月五日世襄據鄭氷磬鈔本校

所私更正及批註書上端 甲午孟舒

1 楚調 2 千金調 3 胡笳調 4 感神調
5 楚明光 6 鳳歸林 7 白雪 8 易水 9 幽蘭
10 遊春 11 淥水 12 幽居 13 坐愁 14 愁成
15 長清 16 短清 17 長側 18 短側
19 上上舞 20 下上舞 21 上間絃 22 下間絃
23 登隴 24 望秦 25 竹吟風 26 哀松路 27 悲漢月
28 辞漢 29 跨鞍 30 望鄉 31 奔雲 32 入林
33 華舜十遊 34 史明五弄 35 董揩五弄
36 鳳翅五路 37 流波 38 雙流 39 三峽流泉
40 石上流泉 41 蟻眉 42 悲風拂隴頭

Fig. 4.12: The first draft of *Wusilan zhifa shi* (*A Study on the Black-Ruled Manual*), fol. 1r.
Author: Wang Mengshu (1887–1969).
Date: 1954.
Dimensions: 26.0 × 22.0 cm.
Private collection.

scholars,[23] the original itself, which had lain buried among historical documents of the Ii family for several centuries, remained unknown to modern scholarship until its existence was announced by Goshima Kuniharu, curator of historical documents at Hikone-jō Hakubutsukan, in 1994.[24]

Wang Mengshu's 汪孟舒 (1887–1969) monograph *Wusilan zhifa shi* 烏絲欄指法釋 (*A Study on the Black-Ruled Manual*), published in Beijing in 1955, is the most important twentieth-century work

23. Hayashi Kenzō 林謙三, "Kinsho sandai 琴書三題," *Tōyō ongaku kenkyū* 東洋音樂研究 (1942) 2: 235–245; Wang Mengshu 汪孟舒, *Wusilan zhifa shi* 烏絲欄指法釋, in *Guwu Wang Mengshu xiansheng qinxue yizhu* 古吳汪孟舒先生琴學遺著, ed. Yang Yuanzheng 楊元錚 (Beijing: Zhonghua shuju, 2013), vol. 1, 1–144; Cheung Sai-bung 張世彬, "Youlan pu yanjiu 幽蘭譜研究," *Journal of the Chinese University of Hong Kong* 5 (1979): 127–166; Kikkawa Yoshikazu 吉川良和, "Monobe Mokei senshi *Ushiran shihō kansu* kenkyū 物部茂卿撰次《烏絲欄指法卷子》研究," *Tōyō bunka kenkyūjo kiyō* 東洋文化研究所紀要 94 (1984): 1–66.

24. Goshima Kuniharu 五島邦治, "Iike dendai shiryō no gakusho 井伊家伝來史料の樂書," *Geinoshi kenkyū* 藝能史研究 125 (1994): 51–59.

in this field (Fig. 4.12).[25] Since Wang had based his research on two Chinese handwritten copies of Sorai's conflation prepared in the period from the 1920s to the 1940s,[26] he misinterpreted the relationship between the two scrolls. In the preface to his book, Wang states: "[The two scrolls] were originally kept as a single scroll in Japan. . . *The Black-Ruled Manual* [i.e., in Wang's imagination, the presumptive original of the Chinese treatises preserved in the Hikone manuscript], the second half of the original scroll *Youlan*, is an explanation of the playing techniques that the piece requires."[27]

Moving on to the Song dynasty, Fan Zhongyan 范仲淹 (989–1052) was a powerful statesman and neo-Confucianist who rose to the rank of Chancellor. In the field of government administration, his principal achievements were the so-called Qingli reforms 慶曆新政 that he promulgated in 1043–1045 (the Qingli era: 1041–1049) in partnership with Ouyang Xiu 歐陽修 (1007–1072). The crux of this policy was to introduce more Confucian elements into the business of government, including reforms to recruitment, higher pay for minor local officials to discourage corruption, and wider sponsorship programs to ensure that officials were drafted on the basis of their intellect and character. These policy initiatives met with resistance from conservative opponents and were rescinded by the emperor in 1045, when both Fan Zhongyan and Ouyang Xiu were accused of factionalism.

In the musical sphere, Fan Zhongyan was an enthusiastic *qin* player and fond of playing the piece *Lüshuang cao* 履霜操 (*Treading Frost*), so much so that he came to be called "Fan Lüshuang" 范履霜 ("Fan Treading Frost"). Originally, he had learnt his *qin* playing from Cui Zundu 崔遵度 (954–1020) while the latter was acting as a tutor to the prince first-in-line to inherit the imperial throne. The Fung Ping Shan Library has two copies of a Southern Song or Yuan dynasty imprint of *Fan Wenzheng gong ji* 范文正公集 (*The Literary Collection of Duke Fan Wenzheng*), issued in twenty *juan* together with a sequel *Bieji* 別集 of four *juan* and a supplement of annals *Nianpu buyi* 年譜補遺 (henceforth copies 1 and 2, Figs. 4.13 and 4.14). The text contains many instances where playing the *qin* is mentioned; for example, the poem: "Ming Yue yao" 明月謠 ("A Bright Moon Verse"); and the essays: "Yu Tang chushi shu" 與唐處士書 ("A Letter to Tang Yi"), "Tang Yi shi xu" 唐異詩序 ("A Preface to Tang Yi's Poetical Works" [themselves published in 1026]), and "Tianzhu shan Ri Guan dashi taji" 天竺山日觀大師塔記 ("An Epitaph for Master Ri Guan, the Monk of Tianzhu Mountain").

Fan Zhongyan's central ethos was to rescue the *qin* from the clutches of the literati and its role as an instrument of entertainment and return it to Confucian realms as a tool of statecraft and edification. This philosophy is expressed most succinctly in the letter to Tang Yi quoted below. The latter was a hermit and *qin* player who had not assumed the mantle of an official position, and he appears many times in Fan Zhongyan's works. In this letter, Fan states:

> I have heard that when the sages made the *qin*, they played with it the most harmonious music in the world, and through this harmonized with the world. The rationale behind carving the *qin* is most profound. After the demise of the Qin dynasty, the rites and music lost their proper order. I regret that the true meaning of *qin* playing had already been lost for a significant period of time, and those who have subsequently transmitted the tradition with skilled fingers now simply produce a beautiful sound and compete in the fluency of their technique; yet they have lost that which is greatest, and are proud of irrelevant detail, regarding playing the *qin* simply as craftsmanship.
>
> 蓋聞聖人之作琴也，鼓天下之和而和天下。斫琴之道大哉。秦祚之後，禮樂失馭。予嗟乎琴散久矣，後之傳者，妙指美聲，巧以相尚，喪其大，矜其細，人以藝觀焉。

25. For an analysis of the textual criticism employed by Wang, see Yang Yuanzheng 楊元錚, "Wang Mengshu *Wusilan zhifa shi* de jiaokanxue 汪孟舒《烏絲欄指法釋》的校勘學," *Zhongguo yinyuexue* 中國音樂學 (2009) 4: 51–54.

26. One of these was prepared by the National Library of Peking in the 1920s or '30s, the other by the Chinese musicologist Zheng Yingsun 鄭穎孫 (1893–1950) in the 1920s or the two decades following. The exemplars of these two versions are the three manuscript copies of Sorai's conflation brought from Japan to China by Yang Shoujing. After 1949, the three Japanese copies were moved from Beijing to Taipei and could not be examined by mainland Chinese scholars in the 1950s. For further information on the three Japanese exemplars, see Yang Yuanzheng 楊元錚, "*Jieshidiao youlan* yu *Qinyong zhifa* hejuan shuo bianzheng《碣石調幽蘭》與《琴用指法》合卷說辨正," in *Qinxue lunji* 琴學論集, ed. Lau Chor-wah 劉楚華 (Hong Kong: Cosmos Books, 2010), 25; Abe Ryūichi 阿部隆一, *Chugoku hōshoshi* (*zōteiban*) 中國訪書志(增訂版) (Tokyo: Kyūko shoin, 1976), 97–98.

27. See Wang Mengshu, *Wusilan zhifa shi*, 5. No evidence is furnished by Wang to support his claim of a "single scroll."

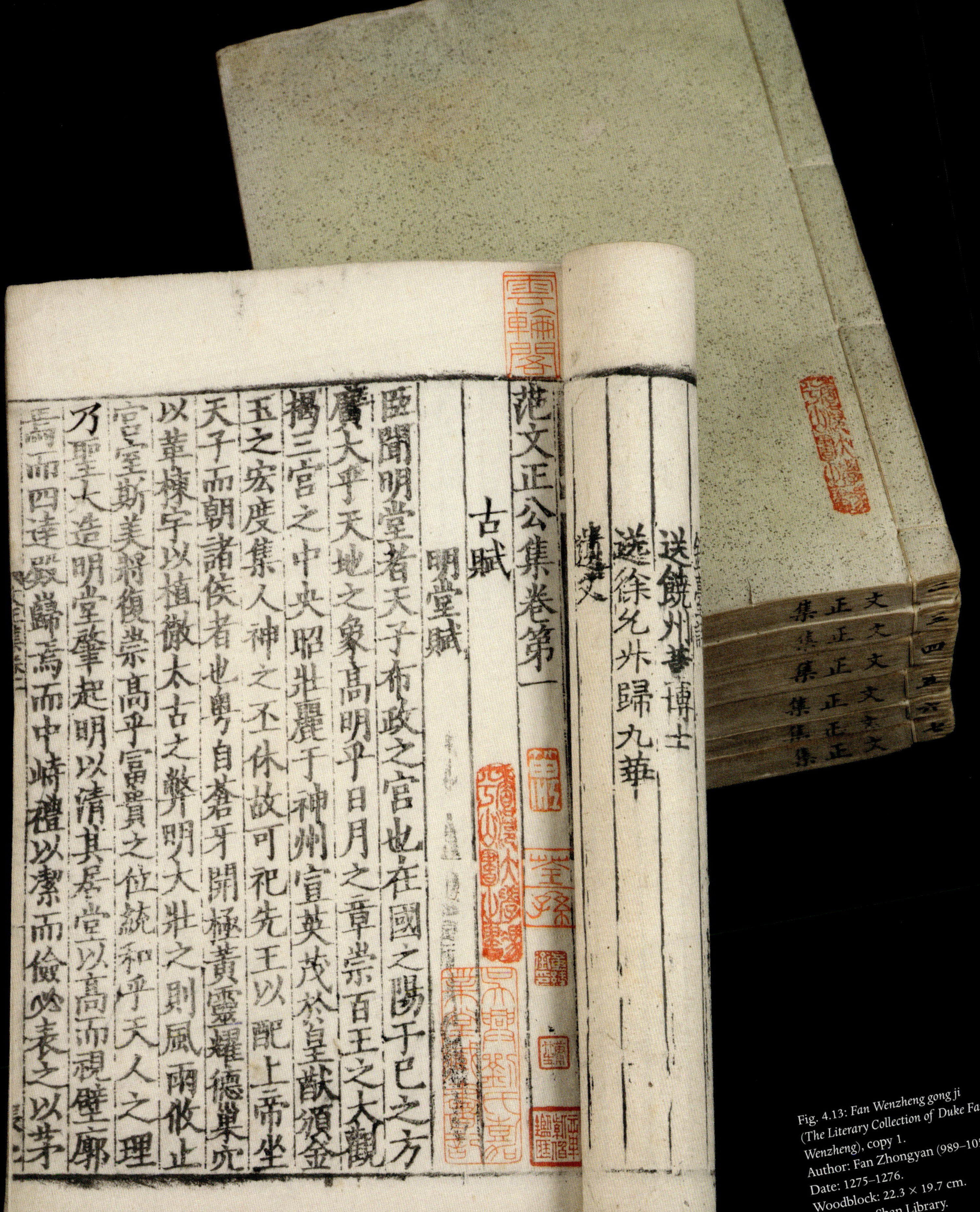

Fig. 4.13: *Fan Wenzheng gong ji* (*The Literary Collection of Duke Fan Wenzheng*), copy 1.
Author: Fan Zhongyan (989–1052).
Date: 1275–1276.
Woodblock: 22.3 × 19.7 cm.
Fung Ping Shan Library.

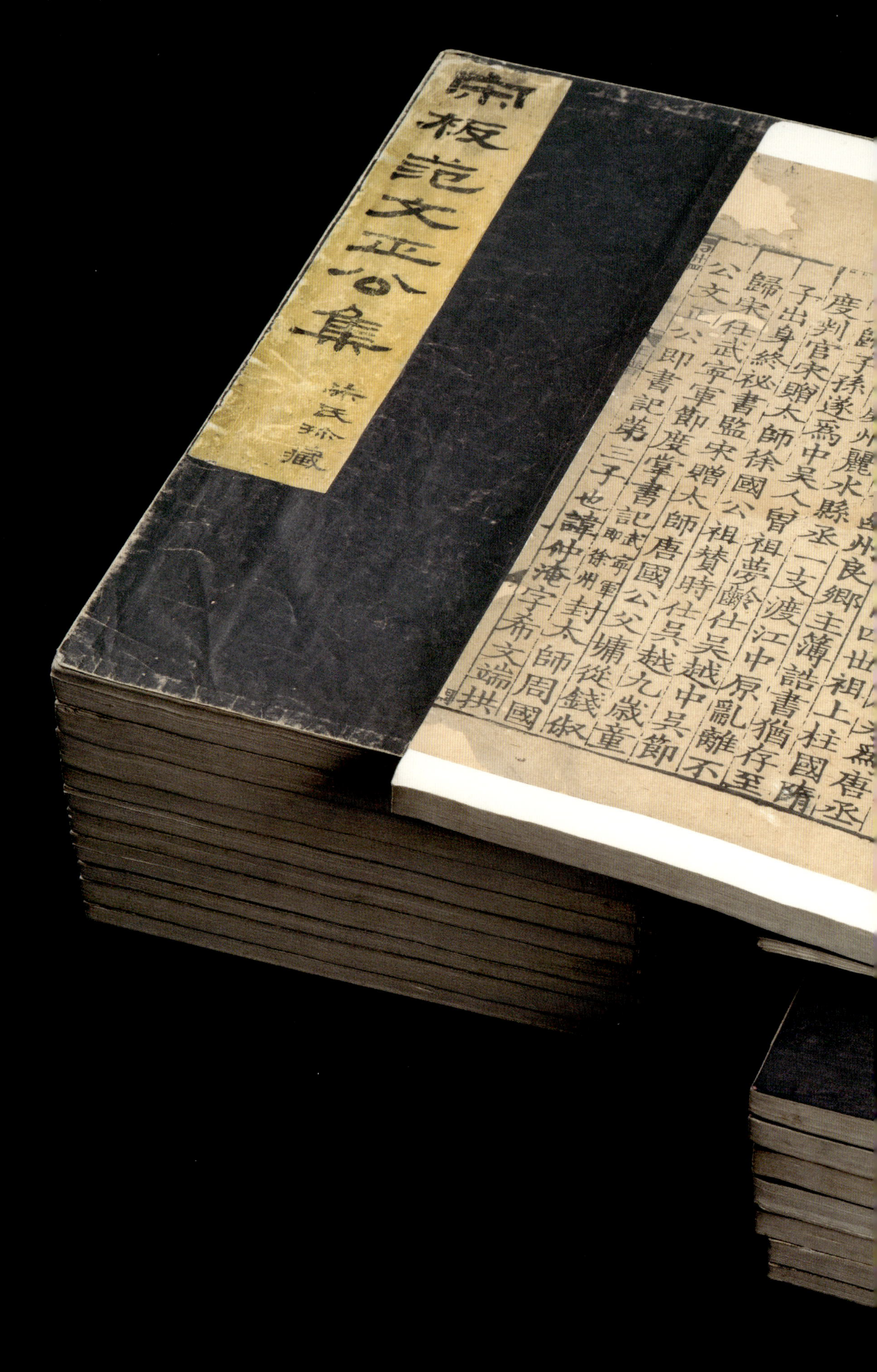
宋板范文正公集

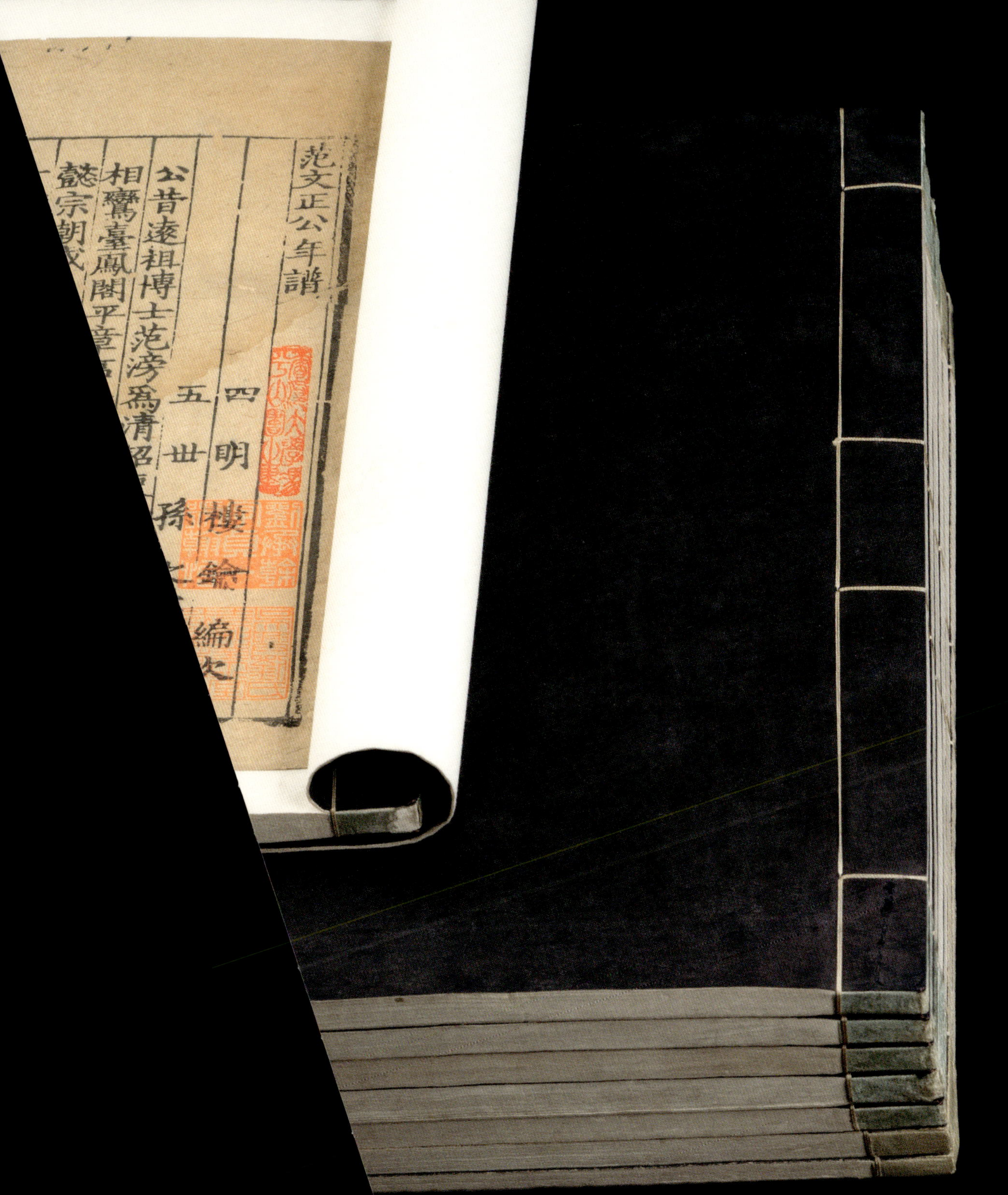

Fig. 4.14: *Fan Wenzheng gong ji (The Literary Collection of Duke Fan Wenzheng)*, copy 2.
Author: Fan Zhongyan (989–1052).
Date: 1275–1276.
Woodblock: 22.3 × 19.7 cm.
Fung Ping Shan Library.

甘棠之思乎乾道丁亥五月既望邵武俞翊

謹識

番陽郡齋州學有文正范公文集奏議歲久板多漫滅殆不可讀判府太中先生嘗謂此郡太守名德如日月之照終古不泯者在唐則顏魯公本朝則范文正公文正之集士大夫過郡者莫不欲見其可不整治乎於是委屬寮以舊京本丹陽集參校且捐公帑刊補之又得詩文三十七篇為遺集附于後其間尚有舛誤更俟後之君訪善本訂正焉淳熙丙午十二月日郡從事北海綦煥謹識

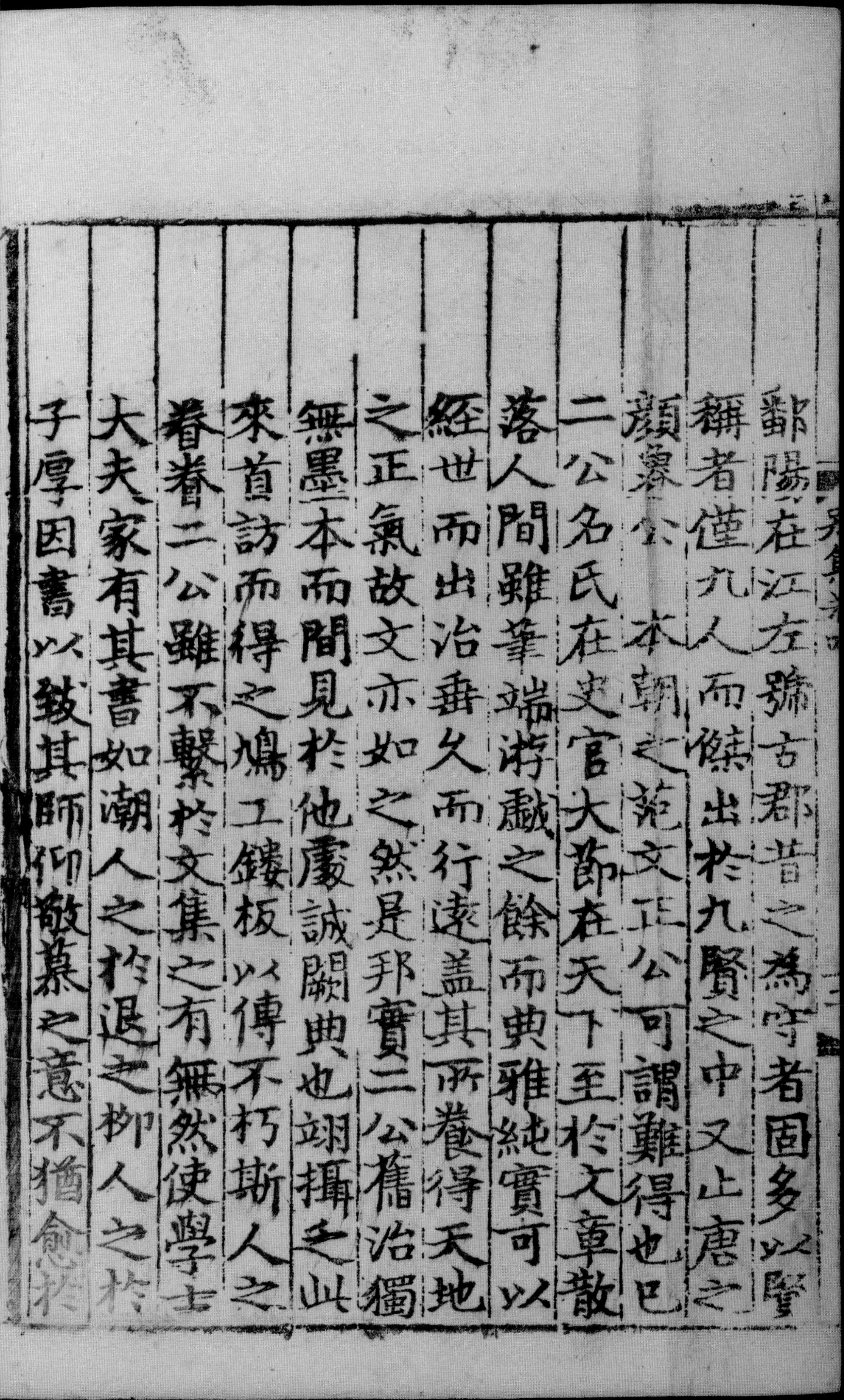

鄱陽在江左號古郡昔之為守者固多以賢
稱者僅九人而僚出於九賢之中又上唐之
顏魯公本朝之范文正公可謂難得也已
二公名氏在史官大節在天下至於文章散
落人間雖筆端游戲之餘而典雅純實可以
經世而出治垂久而行遠蓋其所養得天地
之正氣故文亦如之然是邦實二公舊治獨
無墨本而間見於他處誠闕典也翊攝之此
來首訪而得之鳩工鏤板以傳不朽斯人之
眷眷二公雖不繫於文集之有無然使學士
大夫家有其書如潮人之於退之柳人之於
子厚因書以致其師仰敬慕之意不猶愈於

Fig. 4.15: *Fan Wenzheng gong ji* (*The Literary Collection of Duke Fan Wenzheng*), copy 1, sequel *juan* 4, fols. 12v–13r, the first postscript by Yu Yu dated 1167 and the second postscript by Qi Huan dated 1186. Author: Fan Zhongyan (989–1052). Date: 1275–1276. Woodblock: 22.3 × 19.7 cm. Fung Ping Shan Library.

Copy 1 of *The Literary Collection of Duke Fan Wenzheng* had previously been regarded as being of Song dynasty provenance and was originally an item in Miao Quansun's 繆荃孫 (1844–1919) collection.[28] Originally, he had intended to sell the most precious books he owned, that is the Song and Yuan dynasty editions, to Yuan Shikai's 袁世凱 (1859–1916) second son Yuan Kewen 袁克文 (1889–1931), but Yuan Shikai's swift fall from power left his offspring without the financial resources to complete the transaction. Miao Quansun now needed another buyer, so he turned to Liu Chenggan 劉承幹 (1881–1963), and in 1916 mooted a sale of the entire set of books for 20,000 silver dollars. Negotiations dragged on until the summer of 1917, when, according to Liu Chenggan's diary, on the twentieth day of the sixth lunar month, a deal was struck at 11,000 silver dollars, though the total number of books had been reduced to just sixteen.[29]

Liu Chenggan also indicates that he regarded the set of woodblocks used to print copy 1 as latterly repaired in the *renshen* year of the Jiading 嘉定 era (1212),[30] though originally cut earlier in Jiangxi province. The bibliographical record in Liu Chenggan's library catalog, written by Wu Changshou 吳昌綬 (1867–1924), confirms his view and includes the passage:

> This book was published in Raozhou, and the woodblocks repaired in the Jiading era. . . Nowadays, the Yuan dynasty edition published by the Wintry Hall Press is already regarded as extremely scarce, still more so the edition from which it originated.
>
> 是帙為宋饒州本，乃嘉定時重修。……今元歲寒堂本已稱珍秘，况祖本耶？[31]

Other luminaries, for example, Yang Shaohe 楊紹和 (1830–1875),[32] Zhang Yuanji 張元濟 (1867–1959),[33] and Luo Zhenchang 羅振常 (1875–1942),[34] have also listed that they owned copies of the same book printed from the selfsame woodblocks. Jao Tsung-i's conclusion was that copy 1 was: "Of the Southern Song dynasty, first published in Raozhou, and printed on repaired woodblocks in the fifth year of the Jiading era (1212)."[35] Where, however, is the source for these unanimous opinions? The answer lies in three postscripts at the end of the fourth *juan* of the sequel set.

The first of these (Fig. 4.15), written by Yu Yu 俞翊 and dated to the third year of the Qiandao era (1167), discusses his admiration for Yan Zhenqing 顏真卿 (709–785) and Fan Zhongyan's moral fiber, which is why he has donated money for the purposes of printing this edition of the latter's collected works. The second, by Qi Huan 綦煥 and dated to the thirteenth year of the Chunxi 淳熙 era (1186), states:

> Boyang prefectural college has in its possession the wooden printing blocks of Fan Zhongyan's collected works and his memoranda to the emperor, but because of the length of time [that has elapsed since their initial cutting], they have already become worn, so the official Mr. Taizhong . . . has used public funds to have them re-cut.
>
> 番陽郡齋州學有文正范公《文集》、《奏議》，歲久板多漫滅，殆不可讀。判府太中先生嘗……捐公帑刊補之。

The third postscript (Fig. 4.16) indicates that the woodblocks were repaired once more in the fifth lunar month of the fifth year of the Jiading era (1212), and the names of the officials responsible together with their posts are supplied. Miao Quansun has imprinted his seal immediately after these postscripts, which gives some indication of the significance that he attributed to them.

The Japanese bibliographer Abe Ryūichi 阿部隆一 (1917–1983), on visiting the University of Hong Kong Libraries, examined both copies 1 and 2, and was able to make a link with four copies of the same book printed from the same woodblocks

28. Miao Quansun 繆荃孫, *Yifeng cangshu ji* 藝風藏書記 (Shanghai: Shanghai guji chubanshe, 2007), 138–139.

29. Liu Chenggan 劉承幹, *Qiushu zhai riji* 求恕齋日記 (Beijing: Guojia tushuguan chubanshe, 2016), vol. 5, 190; Liu Chenggan 劉承幹, *Jiaye tang cangshu riji chao* 嘉業堂藏書日記抄 (Nanjing: Fenghuang chubanshe, 2016), 319–320; and Liu Chenggan 劉承幹, *Wuxing Liushi Jiaye tang shanben shuying* 吳興劉氏嘉業堂善本書景 (Shanghai: Jiaye tang, 1929), vol. 5, fols. 4r–6v.

30. Ibid.

31. Miao Quansun 繆荃孫, Wu Changshou 吳昌綬, and Dong Kang 董康, *Jiaye tang cangshu zhi* 嘉業堂藏書志 (Shanghai: Fudan daxue chubanshe, 1997), 523–525.

32. Yang Shaohe 楊紹和, *Yingshu yulu* 楹書隅錄 (Beijing: Zhonghua shuju, 1990), 534.

33. Zhang Yuanji 張元濟, *Baoli tang Songben shulu* 寶禮堂宋本書錄 (Shanghai: Nanhai Panshi, 1939), vol. 4, fols. 13r–14r.

34. Luo Zhenchang 羅振常, *Shanbenshu suojian lu* 善本書所見錄 (Shanghai: Shangwu yinshuguan, 1958), 149.

35. Jao Tsung-i, *Xianggang daxue Feng Pingshan tushuguan cang shanben shulu*, 21.

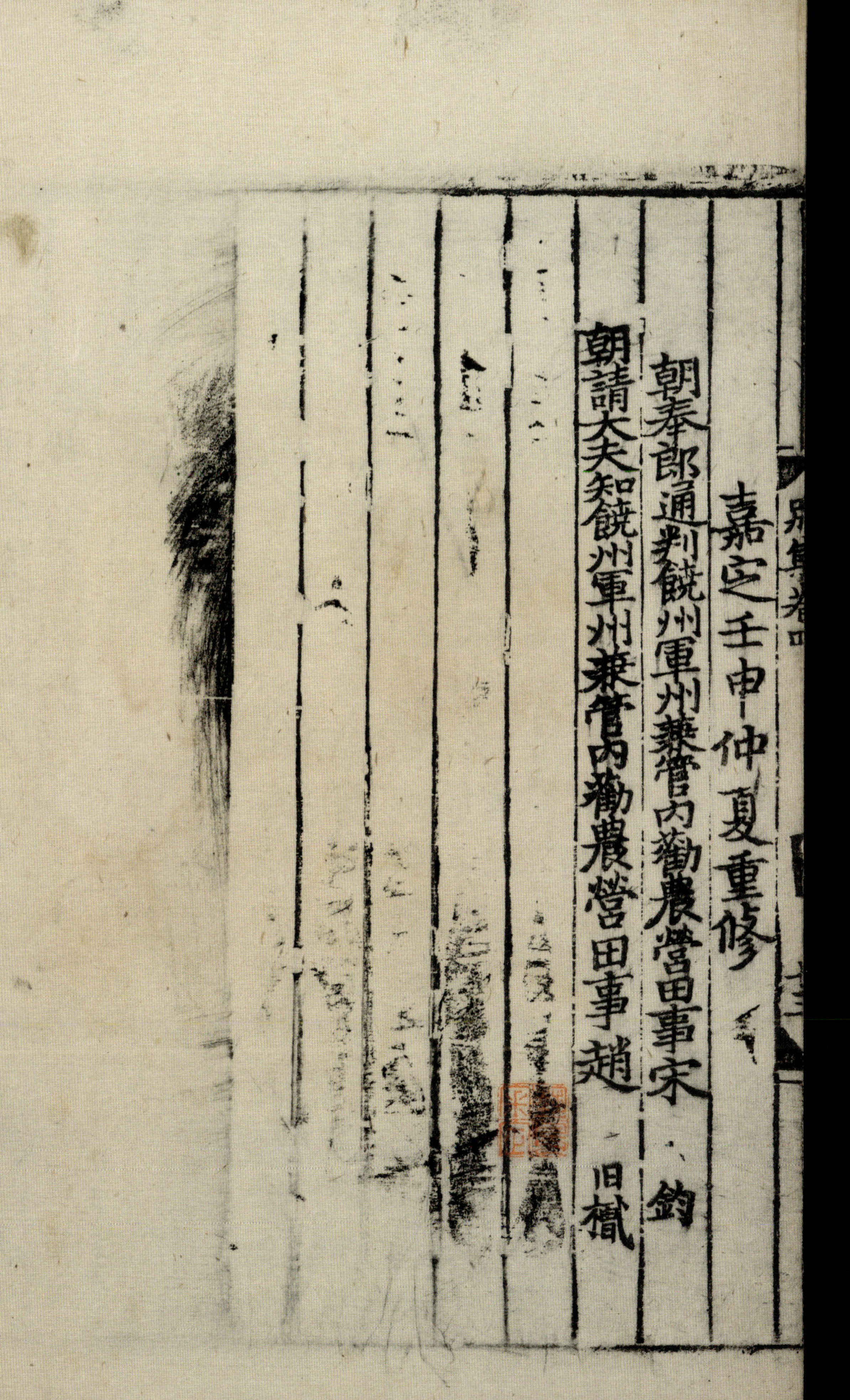

嘉定壬申仲夏重修

朝奉郎通判饒州軍州兼管內勸農營田事宋　鈞

朝請大夫知饒州軍州兼管內勸農營田事趙　旧襶

Fig. 4.16: *Fan Wenzheng gong ji* (*The Literary Collection of Duke Fan Wenzheng*), copy 1, sequel *juan* 4, fol. 13v, the third postscript dated 1212.
Author: Fan Zhongyan (989–1052).
Date: 1275–1276.
Woodblock: 22.3 × 19.7 cm.
Fung Ping Shan Library.

范文正公集敘

慶曆三年軾始總角入鄉校士有自京師來者以魯人石守道所作慶曆聖德詩示鄉先生軾從旁竊觀則能誦習其詞問先生以所頌十一人者何人也先生曰童子何用知之軾曰此天人也耶則不敢知若亦人耳何為其不可先生奇軾言盡以告之且曰韓范富歐陽此四人者人傑也時雖未盡了則已私識之矣嘉祐二年始舉進士至京師則范公沒既葬而墓碑出讀之至流涕曰吾得其為人蓋十有五年而不一見其面豈非命也歟是歲登第始見知于歐陽公因公以識韓富皆以國士待軾曰恨子不識范文正公其後三年過許

Fig. 4.17: *Fan Wenzheng gong ji* (*The Literary Collection of Duke Fan Wenzheng*), copy 1, Shu Shi's preface dated 1089, fol. 1r.
Author: Fan Zhongyan (989–1052).
Date: 1275–1276.
Border: 22.3 × 19.7 cm.
Fung Ping Shan Library.

Fig. 4.18 (opposite): *Fan Wenzheng gong ji* (*The Literary Collection of Duke Fan Wenzheng*), copy 2, Shu Shi's preface dated 1089, fol. 1r.
Author: Fan Zhongyan (989–1052).
Date: 1275–1276.
Woodblock: 22.3 × 19.7 cm.
Fung Ping Shan Library.

范文正公集叙

慶曆三年軾始總角入鄉校士有自京師來者以魯
人石守道所作慶曆
聖德詩示鄉先生軾從旁竊觀則能誦習其詞問先
生以所頌十一人者何人也先生曰童子何用知之
軾曰此天人也耶則不敢知若亦人耳何爲其不可
先生奇軾言盡以告之且曰韓范富歐陽此四人者
人傑也時雖未盡了則已私識之矣嘉祐二年始舉
進士至京師則范公沒既葬而墓碑出讀之至流涕
曰吾得其爲人蓋十有五年而不一見其面豈非命
也歟是歲登第始見知于歐陽公因公以識韓富皆
以國士待軾曰恨子不識范文正公其後三年過許

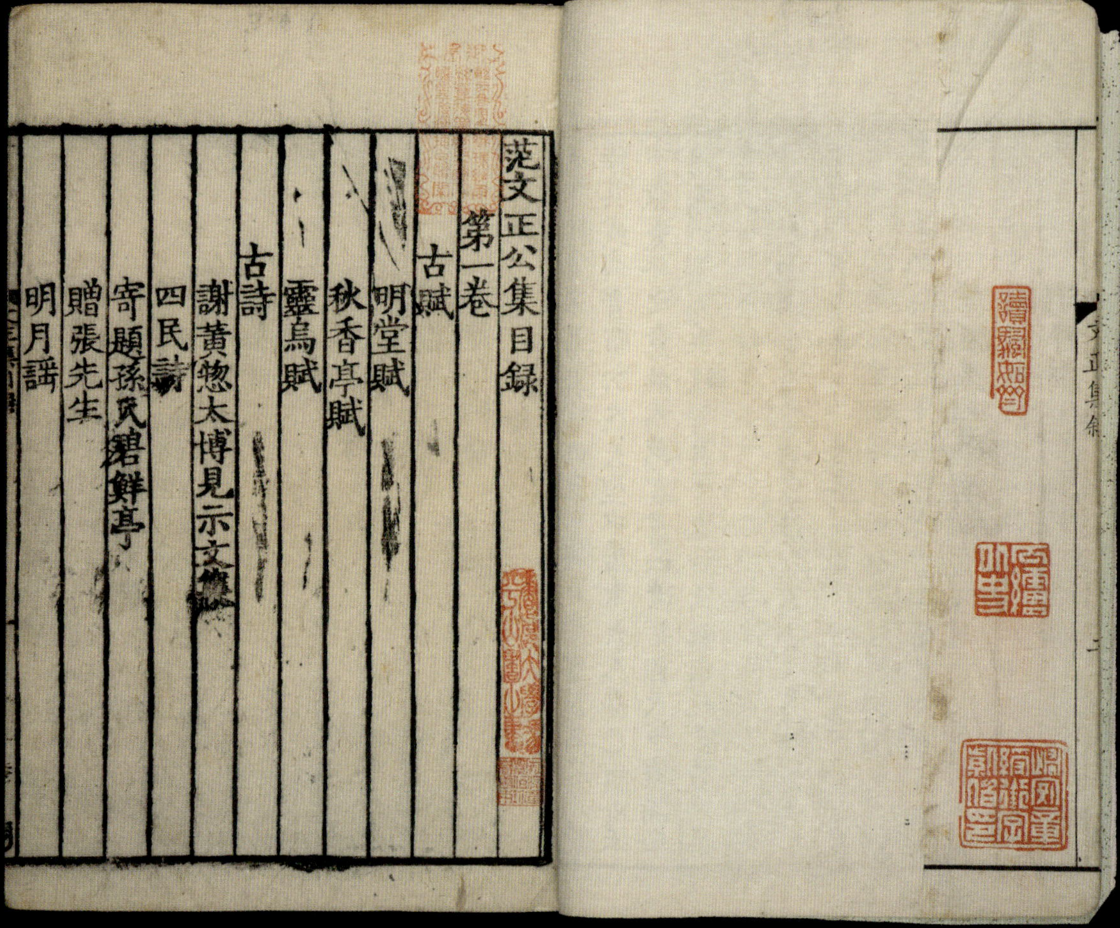

Fig. 4.19: *Fan Wenzheng gong ji* (*The Literary Collection of Duke Fan Wenzheng*), copy 1, Shu Shi's preface dated 1089, fol. 2v, and *juan* 1, fol. 1r.
Author: Fan Zhongyan (989–1052).
Date: 1275–1276.
Border: 22.3 × 19.7 cm.
Fung Ping Shan Library.

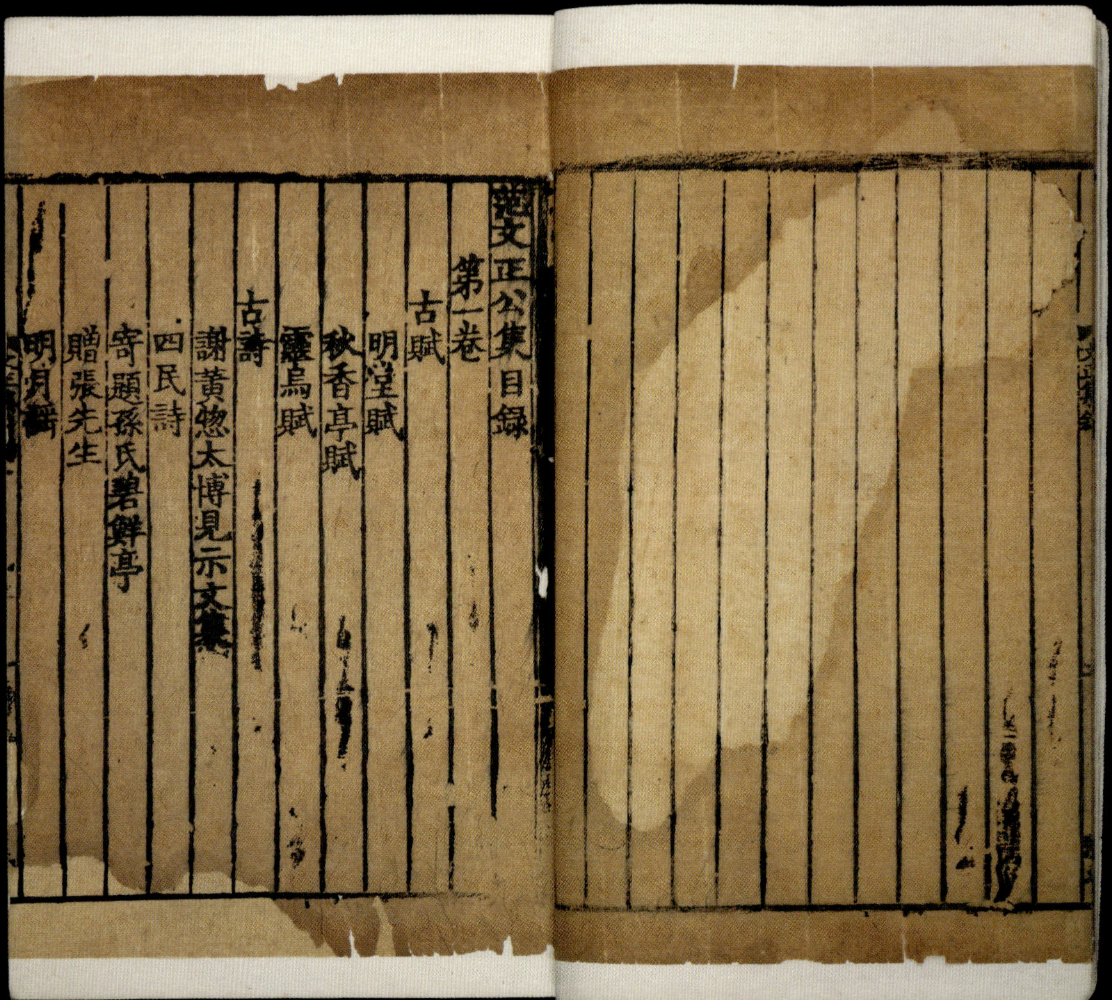

Fig. 4.20: *Fan Wenzheng gong ji* (*The Literary Collection of Duke Fan Wenzheng*), copy 2, Shu Shi's preface dated 1089, fol. 2v, and *juan* 1, fol. 1r.
Author: Fan Zhongyan (989–1052).
Date: 1275–1276.
Woodblock: 22.3 × 19.7 cm.
Fung Ping Shan Library.

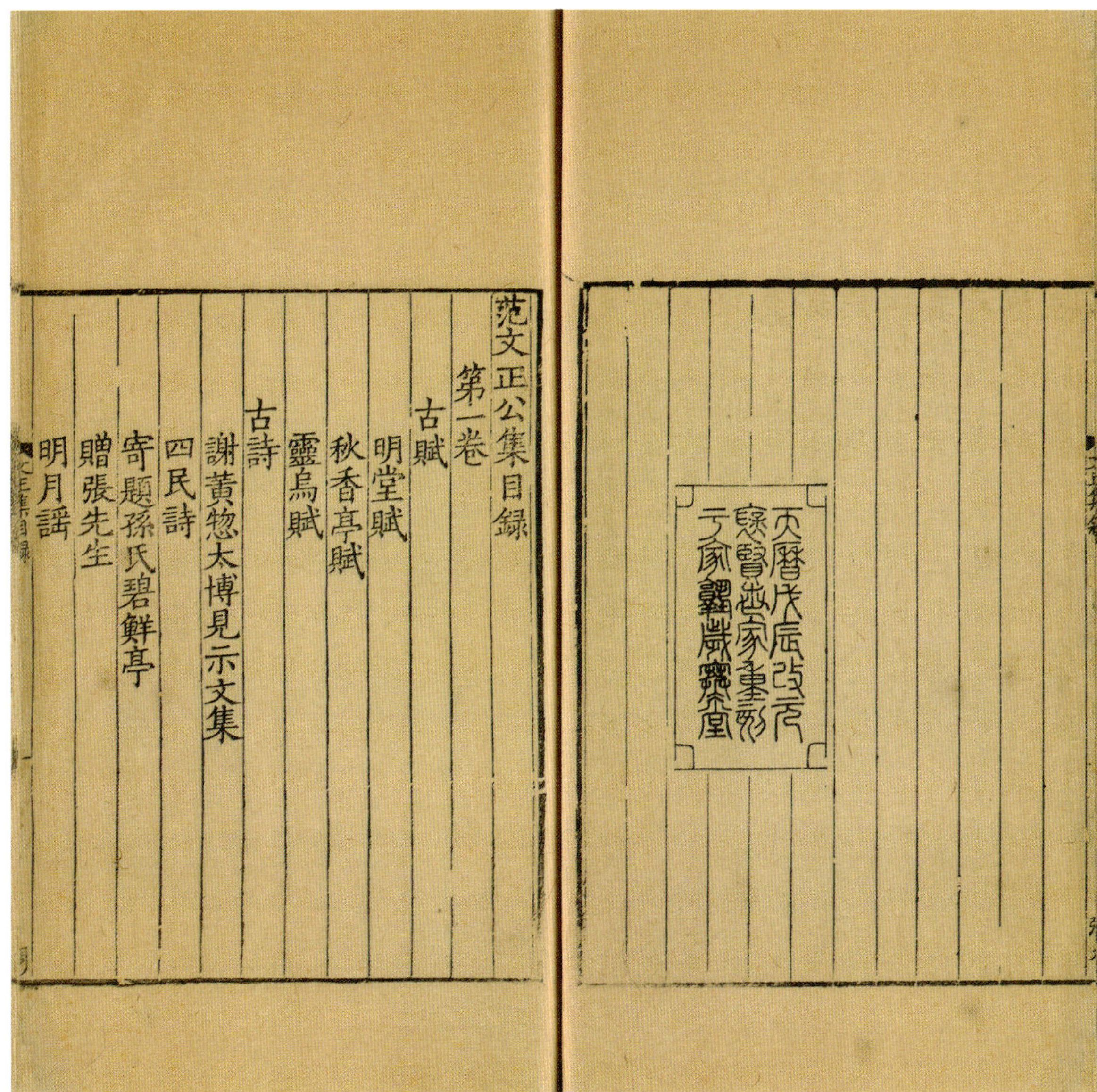

Fig. 4.21: *Fan Wenzheng gong ji* (*The Literary Collection of Duke Fan Wenzheng*), Shu Shi's preface dated 1089, fol. 2v, printer's colophon and *juan* 1, fol. 1r.
Author: Fan Zhongyan (989–1052).
Date: 1275–1276.
Woodblock: 22.3 × 19.7 cm.
National Palace Museum, Taipei
(平圖 003264-003267).

currently held in the National Central Library in Taipei and others in the National Palace Museum (also in Taipei).[36] In its complete state, the book should have a preface written by the Song poet Su Shi 蘇軾 (1037–1101) in 1089. Copy 1 has had the entire printed preface removed and replaced by a handwritten copy (Figs. 4.17 and 4.19); copy 2 retains the printed original, but on its final page is an empty space where something has been excised (Figs. 4.18 and 4.20). Of the four copies in the National Central Library, all retain the printed preface, though only two have the same empty space, and two have a printer's colophon that has not been removed. This printer's colophon can be found in a copy of the same edition in the Palace Museum in Taipei; it reads (Fig. 4.21):

> In the first year of the Tianli era (1328), descendants of His Virtuous Eminence [Fan Zhongyan] printed [this book] in his private academy, The Wintry Hall.
>
> 天曆戊辰改元褒賢世家重刻於家塾歲寒堂。[37]

If this printer's colophon had survived in the Fung Ping Shan Library copies, it would have been identical. Wu Changshou's entry in the bibliographical record in Liu Chenggan's library catalog may be correct that "the Yuan dynasty edition published by the Wintry Hall Press is already regarded as extremely scarce" but both copies in the Fung Ping Shan Library are of this provenance and are not "the edition from which

36. Abe Ryūichi, *Chugoku hōshoshi (zōteiban)*, 667.

37. See also Zhongguo guojia tushuguan 中國國家圖書館 and Zhongguo guojia guji baohu zhongxin 中國國家古籍保護中心, ed., *Di er pi guojia zhengui guji minglu tulu* 第二批國家珍貴古籍名錄圖錄 (Beijing: Guojia tushuguan chubanshe, 2010), 250.

it originated." The Chinese national rare book catalog therefore regards this imprint as "The Wintry Hall edition printed in 1328."[38]

Thorough investigation of the edition's avoidance, according to customary taboo, of the names of Song emperors reveals that not only are the last strokes of the following characters *jing* 警, *jing* 驚, *heng* 恆, *zhen* 貞, *huan* 桓, *gou* 構, *gou* 遘 normally omitted, but also in column 5, fol. 2v, *juan* 11, *xian* 陷 is replaced by *yuming* 御名 ("Emperor's name"). In this context, the emperor in question was Emperor Gong of the Song dynasty, whose personal name was Zhao Xian 趙㬎 (1271–1323, r. 1274–1276). Given that the Song court surrendered its capital Ling'an (present-day Hangzhou) to Mongolian conquerors in 1276, the woodblocks must have been cut during Zhao Xian's reign, i.e., the Deyou 德祐 era (1274–1276). If so, this edition is of late Song provenance and at least half a century older than is recorded in the national rare book catalog. The Yuan dynasty printer Wintry Hall's colophon was only added to the woodblock at a later date.

Fan Zhongyan's good friend and colleague Ouyang Xiu also played the *qin*, but the latter's view on the niche the instrument occupied, or should occupy, was at odds with Fan's and much less strictly congruent with Confucian orthodoxy. The Fung Ping Shan Library holds a copy of Ouyang Xiu's collected works, but it is a critical edition and thus titled *Ouyang Wenzhong gong wenji* 歐陽文忠公集 (*The Literary Collection of Duke Ouyang Wenzhong*); its compiler was Zeng Lu 曾魯 (1319–1372).

According to Jao Tsung-i,[39] Zeng Lu's edition was published three times in the Hongwu 洪武 era (1368–1399): pre-1371 by Cai Qi 蔡玘; in 1373, prefaced by Li Jundu 李均度; and in 1380, by Chen Fei 陳斐. In the Fung Ping Shan Library copy at the end of *juan* 24, 35 (Fig. 4.22), and 50 are found printers' colophons that make it clear that this copy belongs to the third of these imprints. Shimada Kan 島田翰 (1879–1915) was thus mistaken in his analysis of this book and seems to have regarded imprints one and three as being of a single provenance. The earliest seal of ownership on the Fung Ping Shan Library copy belongs to a Ming dynasty individual Pan Chang 潘銀 of Suzhou (dates uncertain, but a contemporary of Wen Zhengming 文徵明, 1470–1559). Later, during the transition from the Ming to the Qing dynasty, seals of the Ming dynasty loyalist Lü Liuliang 呂留良 (1629–1683) and his eldest son Lü Baozhong 呂葆中 (?–1707) were added. From the reign of Qianlong 乾隆, a seal records that it had once belonged to Yang Zuochang 楊祚昌.

When the book was received into Liu Chenggan's collection, separate bibliographic records were written by Miao Quansun and Wu Changshou. Miao Quansun writes: "Although a Ming dynasty edition, its publishing and printing quality are both extremely fine, and quite unusually, it is recorded as having been in the possession of book collectors, which is sufficient in itself to make it extremely valuable."[40] The essay relevant to *qin* playing "Song Yang Zhi xu" 送楊寘序 ("Preface Presented to Yang Zhi") is found in *juan* 42 (Fig. 4.23):

> Previously, I had suffered from depression, so I took myself away from the ordinary world and lived a life of leisure and solitude, but I could not cure myself. So, I studied how to play the *qin* from my friend Sun Daozi, learning several preludes in the *gong* mode, and after a while came to take pleasure in them, becoming unaware that I was ill at all. When someone is ill, this is caused by anxiety. The strongest medicine, despite its poisonous side effects, can alleviate the bodily symptoms of an illness, but is not as efficacious as the fineness of music that can harmonize the unbalance in one's heart. And when a heart has become balanced and the inharmonious harmonized, then, as a matter of course, the illness will be forgotten.
>
> 予嘗有幽憂之疾，退而閒居，不能治也。既而學琴於友人孫道滋，受宮聲數引，久而樂之，不知其疾之在體也。夫疾，生乎憂者也。藥之毒者，能攻其疾之聚，不若聲之至者，能和其心之所不平。心而平，不和者和，則疾之忘也宜哉。
>
> The technique of playing the *qin* is but a small matter, yet when it reaches its epitome, the tonal center is the *gong* note, and the *yu* note

38. Zhongguo guji shanben shumu bianji weiyuanhui 中國古籍善本書目編輯委員會, ed., *Zhongguo guji shanben shumu: Jibu* 中國古籍善本書目: 集部 (Shanghai: Shanghai guji chubanshe, 1998), vol. 1, 199–200.

39. Jao Tsung-i, *Xianggang daxue Feng Pingshan tushuguan cang shanben shulu*, 75–79; Jao Tsung-i, Li Zhifang, and Zhang Lijuan, *Xianggang daxue Feng Pingshan tushuguan cang shanben shulu*, enlarged ed., 211–213.

40. Miao Quansun, Wu Changshou, and Dong Kang, *Jiaye tang cangshu zhi*, 532. This book was regarded by Liu Chenggan as a Yuan edition. See Liu Chenggan, *Wuxing Liushi Jiaye tang shanben shuying*, vol. 6, fols. 14r–15v.

Fig. 4.22: *Ouyang Wenzhong gong wenji* (*The Literary Collection of Duke Ouyang Wenzhong*), *juan* 35, fol. 10v. Author: Ouyang Xiu (1007–1072). Date: 1386. Woodblock: 20.3 × 13.2 cm. Fung Ping Shan Library.

Fig. 4.23 (next spread): *Ouyang Wenzhong gong wenji* (*The Literary Collection of Duke Ouyang Wenzhong*), *juan* 42, fols. 2r–v. Author: Ouyang Xiu (1007–1072). Date: 1386. Woodblock: 20.3 × 13.2 cm. Fung Ping Shan Library.

世逢屯兮廉恥道缺中國五擅兮九州分裂朝存夕忘兮士莫守節昧者胥安兮懦夫志奪偉哉吳君兮稟全其烈世莫我知兮不妄自伐有蘊必昭兮後世而發嗚呼吳君兮寓銘斯碣

歐陽文忠公集三十五卷

旹柔兆攝提格縣人陳斐文允章校勘刊課

歐陽文忠公集卷第三十六

臨江後學曾魯得之考異

若聲之至者能和其心之所不平心而平一不和者和則疾之忘也宜哉四十五字

夫琴之爲技小矣及其至也大者爲宮細者爲羽操絃驟作忽然變之急者悽然以促緩者舒然以和如崩崖裂石高山出泉而風雨夜至也如怨夫寡婦之歎息雌雄雍雍之相鳴也其憂深思遠則舜與文王孔子之遺音也悲愁感憤則伯奇家誤作牙孤子屈原忠臣之所歎也喜怒哀樂動人心深而純古淡泊與夫堯舜三代之言語孔子之文章易之憂患家作思一作深詩之怨刺無以異其能聽之以耳應之以手取其和者道其堙鬱寫其憂思則感人之際亦有至者焉一有是不可以不學也七字

予友楊君好學有文

且多而條理不亂儒之學者莫能雜也鑒聿通於易能知太演之數又學乎陰陽地理黃帝岐伯之書其尤盡心者韻總也世一作聿本儒家子少爲浮圖入武當山往來江漢之旁十餘年不妄與人交有不可其意雖王公大人亦莫肯顧聞士有一藝雖千里必求之介然有古獨行之節所謂用心專者也宜其學必至焉耳浮圖之書行乎世者數百萬言其文字雜以夷夏讀者罕得其真往往就一有聿字而正焉鑒一無此字聿之書一作韻非獨有取於吾儒亦欲傳於其徒也

送楊寘一作送楊二一寘陶浦序

予嘗有幽憂之疾退而閒居不能治也既而學琴於友人孫道滋受宮聲數引久而樂之不知疾之在其體也

is the most subtle. Pluck the strings and the melody will change suddenly along with the emotion, and when the music is anxious, the mood will be sorrowful and urging, and when the music is slow, the mood will be relaxed and harmonious, for example, like a collapsing cliff or splitting stones, or lofty mountains spurting out spring water, or when a windy and rainy night comes; like the sighs of a resentful bachelor or a lonely widow, or male and female birds singing harmoniously together.
夫琴之為技小矣，及其至也，大者為宮，細者為羽，操絃驟作，忽然變之，急者悽然以促，緩者舒然以和，如崩崖裂石、高山出泉，而風雨夜至也。如怨夫寡婦之歎息，雌雄雍雍之相鳴也。

Its deep sorrow and profound thoughtfulness are like a remnant echo of the ancient mystical Emperor Shun, King Wen of Zhou, and Confucius himself. Its tragedy, uneasiness, lament, and resentment are sighs of the orphan Bo Qi[41] and the loyal minister Qu Yuan. Its pleasure, rage, plaintiveness, and joy can move the very depths of being. And its deep and simple tone colors are no different from the words of the ancient mystical emperors Yao and Shun and the three subsequent dynasties, Xia, Shang, and Zhou, Confucius' philosophical tracts, the desolate sadness of *The Book of Changes*, and the resentful satire of *The Book of Odes*. It can be heard by the ear and realized by the hands, and if a harmonious melody is chosen, it can expel brooding and dispel dark thoughts, and move a person's heart deeply.
其憂深思遠，則舜與文王、孔子之遺音也；悲愁感憤，則伯奇孤子、屈原忠臣之所歎也。喜怒哀樂，動人心[必]深。而純古淡泊，與夫堯舜三代之言語、孔子之文章、《易》之憂患、《詩》之怨刺無以異。其能聽之以耳，應之以手，取其和者，道其湮鬱，寫其憂[幽]思，則感人之際，亦有至者焉。

My friend, the gentleman Yang, is an enthusiastic scholar and literary man, and although he had sat the *jinshi* degree examination many times, he did not achieve his aspirations. Eventually, relying on the official positions of his ancestors, he was given the post of county magistrate in Jianpu, a small locality in the Southwest and several thousand miles away, and from that time onward, his heart has harbored a sense of injustice. Since his youth, he has suffered from numerous illnesses and medicines to treat these are scarce in the South. Local customs as far as food and drink are concerned differ greatly from what he is used to. With a body racked by illness and a heart coursing with injustice, living in a society of alien customs, how could he not be permanently dejected? Yet if he wanted to calm his heart and treat his illnesses, his *qin* playing would be of benefit. For this reason, I composed *Some Words of the Qin* in order to send him on his journey and invited [Sun] Daozi to share in the partaking of some wine, and for us to play the *qin* as a gesture of farewell.
予友楊君，好學有文，累以進士舉，不得志。反[及]從蔭調，為尉於劍浦，區區在東南數千里外。是其心固有不平者。且少又多疾，而南方少醫藥，風俗飲食異宜。以多疾之體，有不平之心，居異宜之俗，其能鬱郁以久乎？然欲平其心以養其疾，於琴亦將有得焉。故予作《琴説》以贈其行，且邀道滋酌酒，進琴以為別。

The popularity of the *qin* is abundantly reflected in the compilation and circulation of commercial publications. Many widely disseminated encyclopedias for daily use compiled from the late Middle Ages to the Ming dynasty contain a section on the *qin*. A case in point is the well-known encyclopedia *Shilin guangji* 事林廣記 (*Extensive Records of Various Things*). Compiled by a Southern Song dynasty Fujianese Chen Yuanliang 陳元靚, its Yuan dynasty Zhishun 至順 era (1330–1333) edition contains crucial information and woodcut illustrations regarding the history and construction of the *qin* and also includes musical scores. The copy shown in Fig. 4.24 came into Lord Mōri Takasue's 毛利高標 (1755–1801) private library via the Sino-Japanese book trade. A Japanese re-cut of the now-lost 1325 Chinese edition was also issued during the Genroku 元祿 period (1688–1704),[42] and the same materials on the *qin* from this encyclopedia were included in the popular Japanese miscellany *Gayū manroku* 雅遊漫錄 (1755).[43]

41. Bo Qi 伯奇 (dates uncertain), said to be a son of the Zhou dynasty Emperor Xuan Wang (?–783; r. 828–783), was orphaned and excluded from his royal inheritance by his stepmother, so he wandered in solitude in the wilderness. This story subsequently became subject matter for compositions for the *qin*.

42. For a facsimile edition of the Genroku re-cut, see Nagasawa Kikuya 長澤規矩也, ed., *Wakokubon ruisho shūsei* 和刻本類書集成 (Tokyo: Kyūko Shoin, 1976–1977), vol. 1, 171–467.

43. Ōeda Ryūhō 大枝流芳, *Gayū manroku* 雅遊漫錄 (Nagoya: Eirakuya Tōshirō, 1755), *kan* 5, fols. 1r–4r.

Fig. 4.24: *Shilin guangji* (*Extensive Records of Various Things*), supplementary *juan* 4, fol. 2v, woodcut illustration entitled "Confucius playing the *qin* at his private academy."
Compiler: Chen Yuanliang.
Date: 1330–1333.
Woodblock: 17.0 × 11.0 cm.
Naikaku Bunko, Kokuritsu Kōbunshokan (毛別60-01).

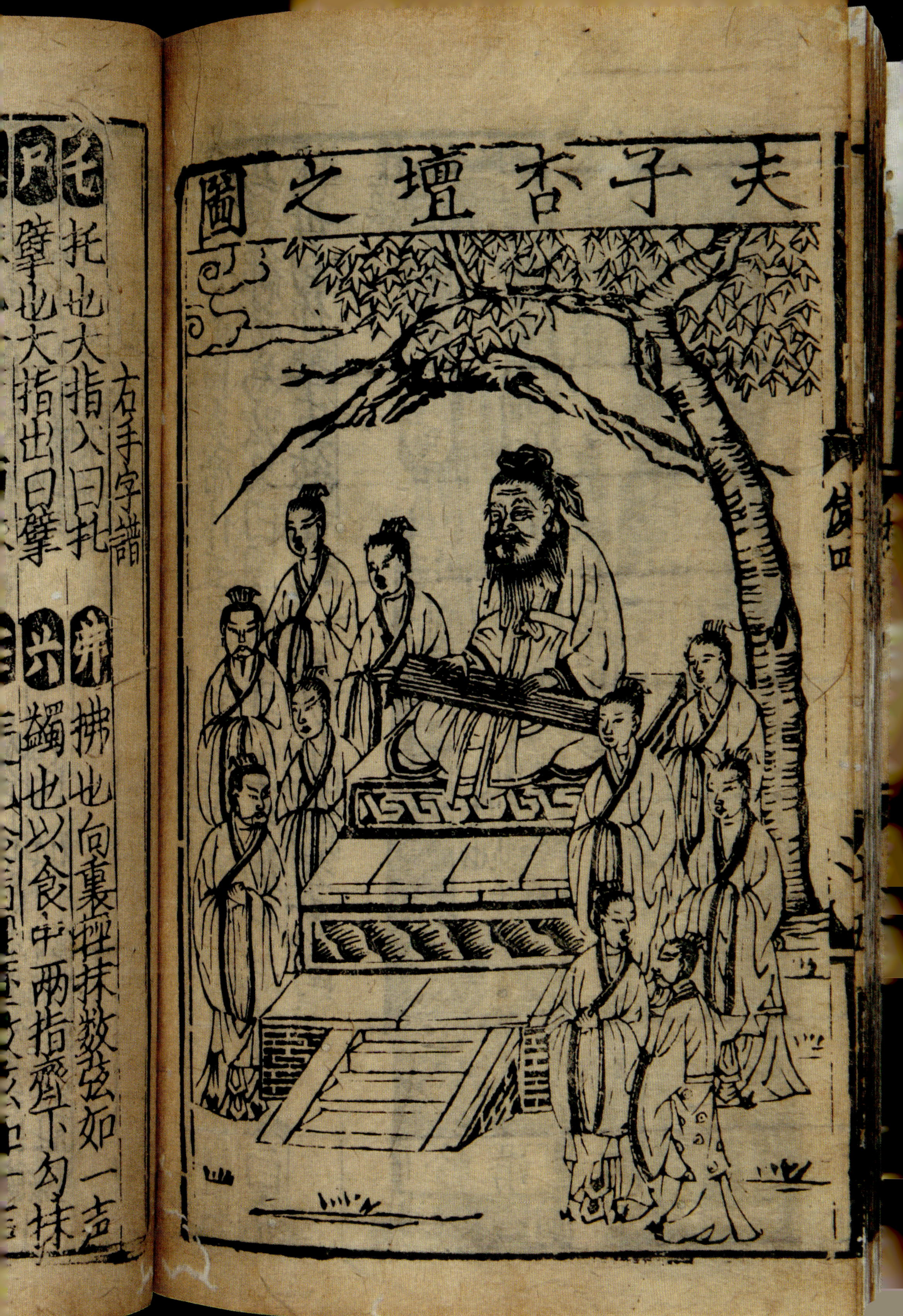

右手字譜

乇 托也大指入曰扎

尸 擘也大指出曰擘

弗 拂也向裏輕抹数弦如一声

𠔿 蠲也以食中两指齊下勾抹

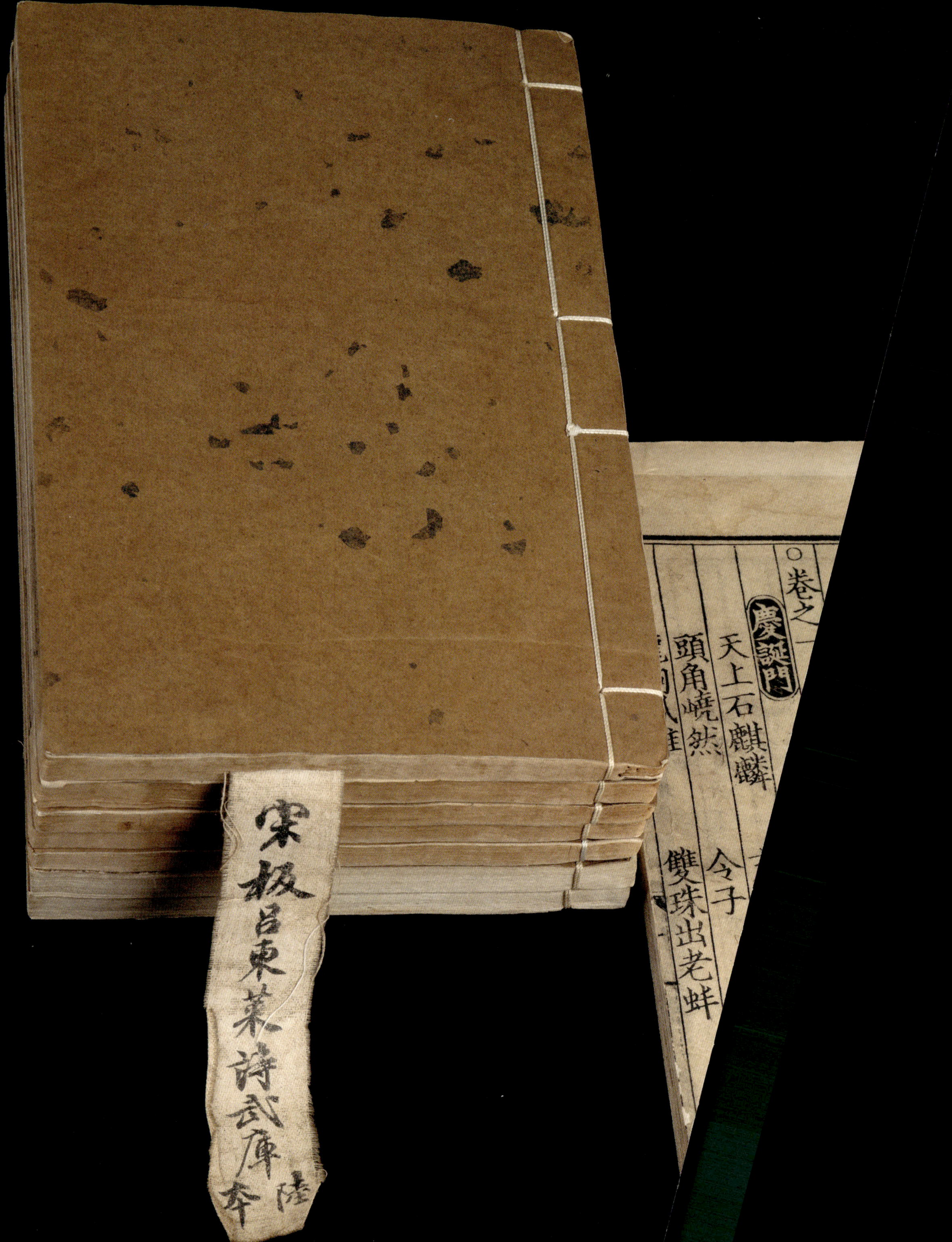
宋板呂東萊詩武庫
陸
卷之
慶誕門
天上石麒麟
頭角嶢然
令子
雙珠出老蚌

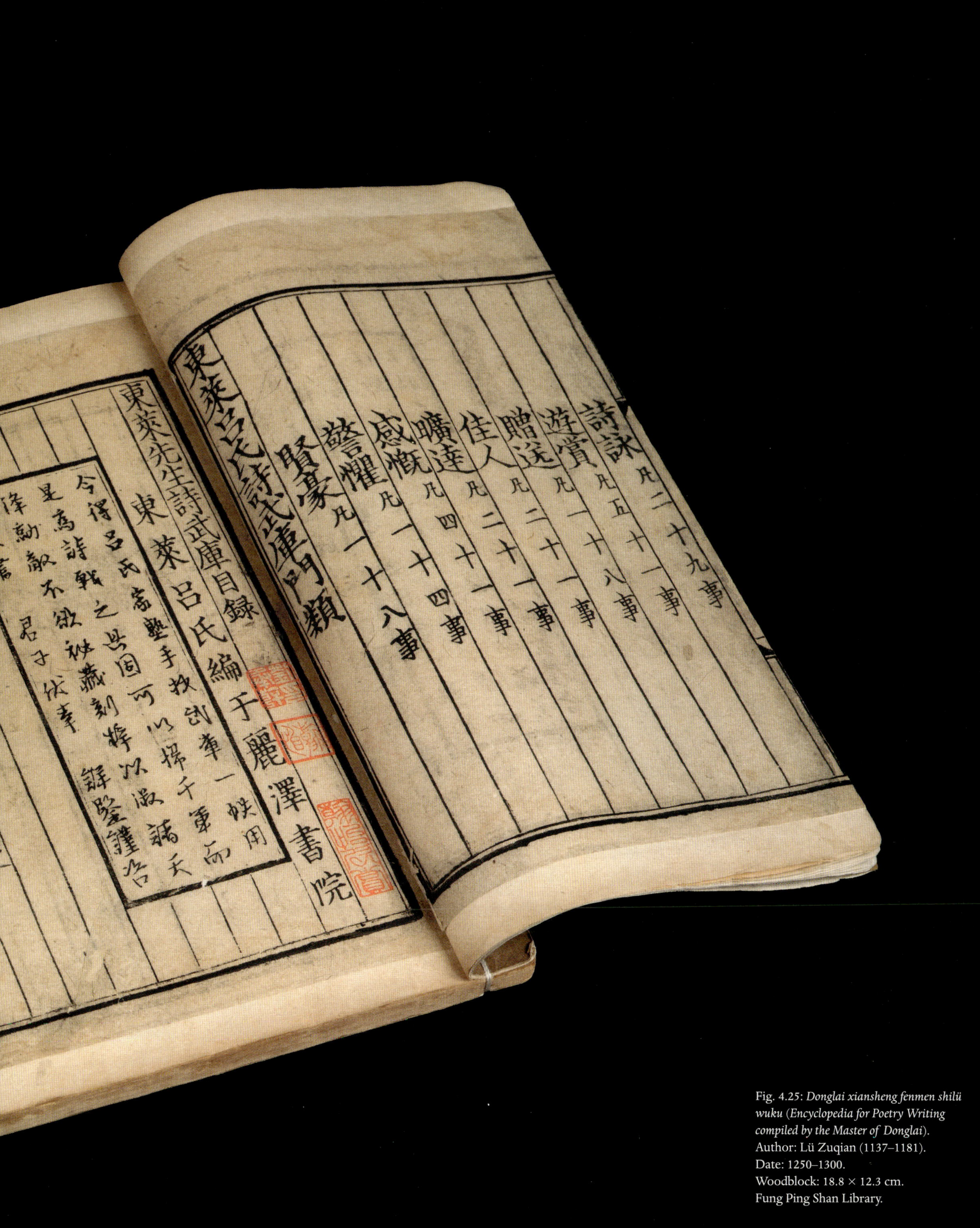

Fig. 4.25: *Donglai xiansheng fenmen shilü wuku* (*Encyclopedia for Poetry Writing compiled by the Master of Donglai*).
Author: Lü Zuqian (1137–1181).
Date: 1250–1300.
Woodblock: 18.8 × 12.3 cm.
Fung Ping Shan Library.

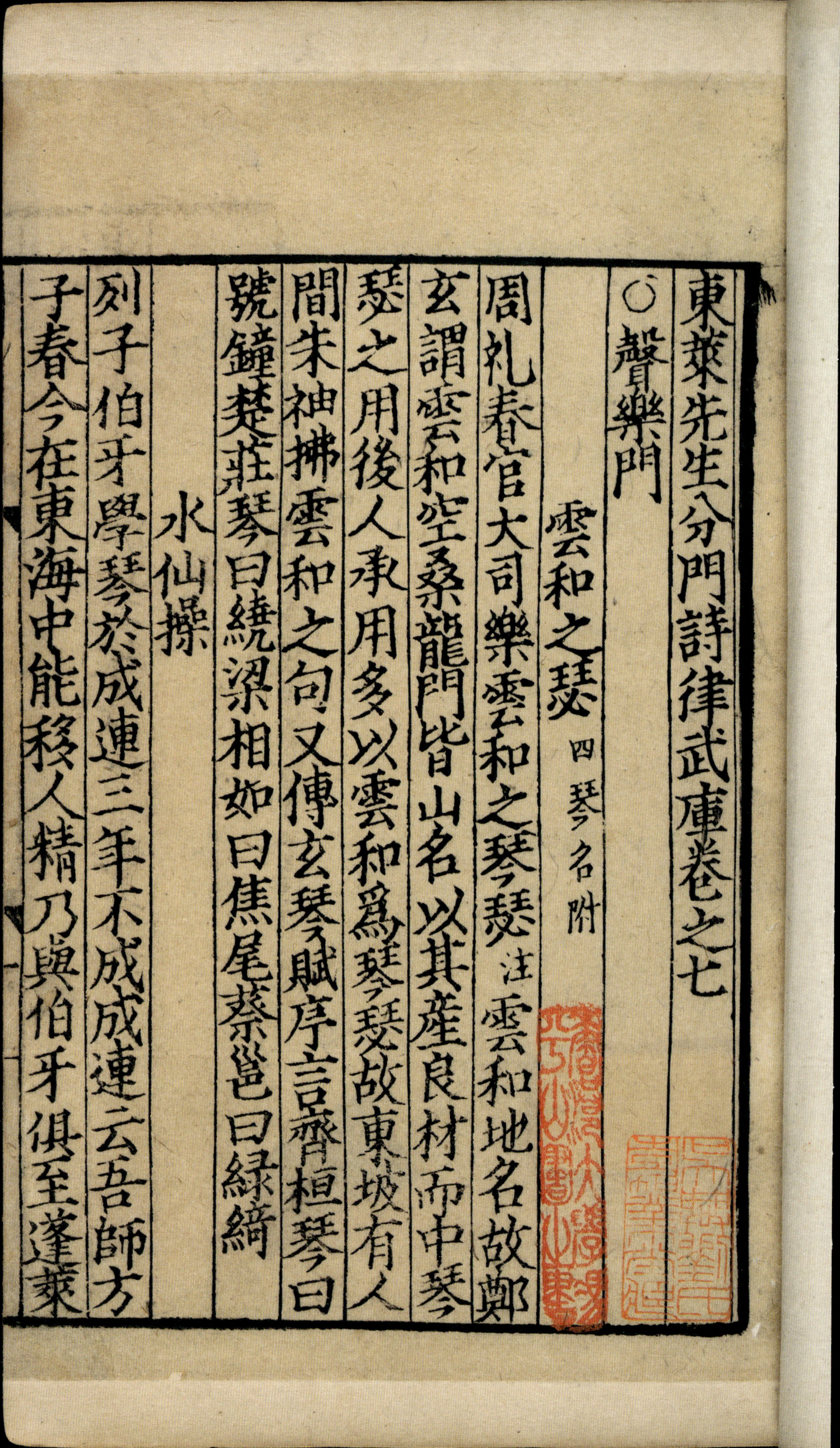

東萊先生分門詩律武庫卷之七

○聲樂門

雲和之瑟 四琴名附

周礼春官大司樂雲和之琴瑟注雲和地名故鄭玄謂雲和空桑龍門皆山名以其產良材而中琴瑟之用後人承用多以雲和爲琴瑟故東坡有人間朱袖拂雲和之句又傅玄琴賦序言齊桓琴曰號鐘楚莊琴曰繞梁相如曰焦尾蔡邕曰綠綺

水仙操

列子伯牙學琴於成連三年不成成連云吾師方子春今在東海中能移人精乃與伯牙俱至蓬萊

Fig. 4.26: *Donglai xiansheng fenmen shilü wuku* (*Encyclopedia for Poetry Writing compiled by the Master of Donglai*), *juan* 7, fol. 1r.
Author: Lü Zuqian (1137–1181).
Date: 1250–1300.
Woodblock: 18.8 × 12.3 cm.
Fung Ping Shan Library.

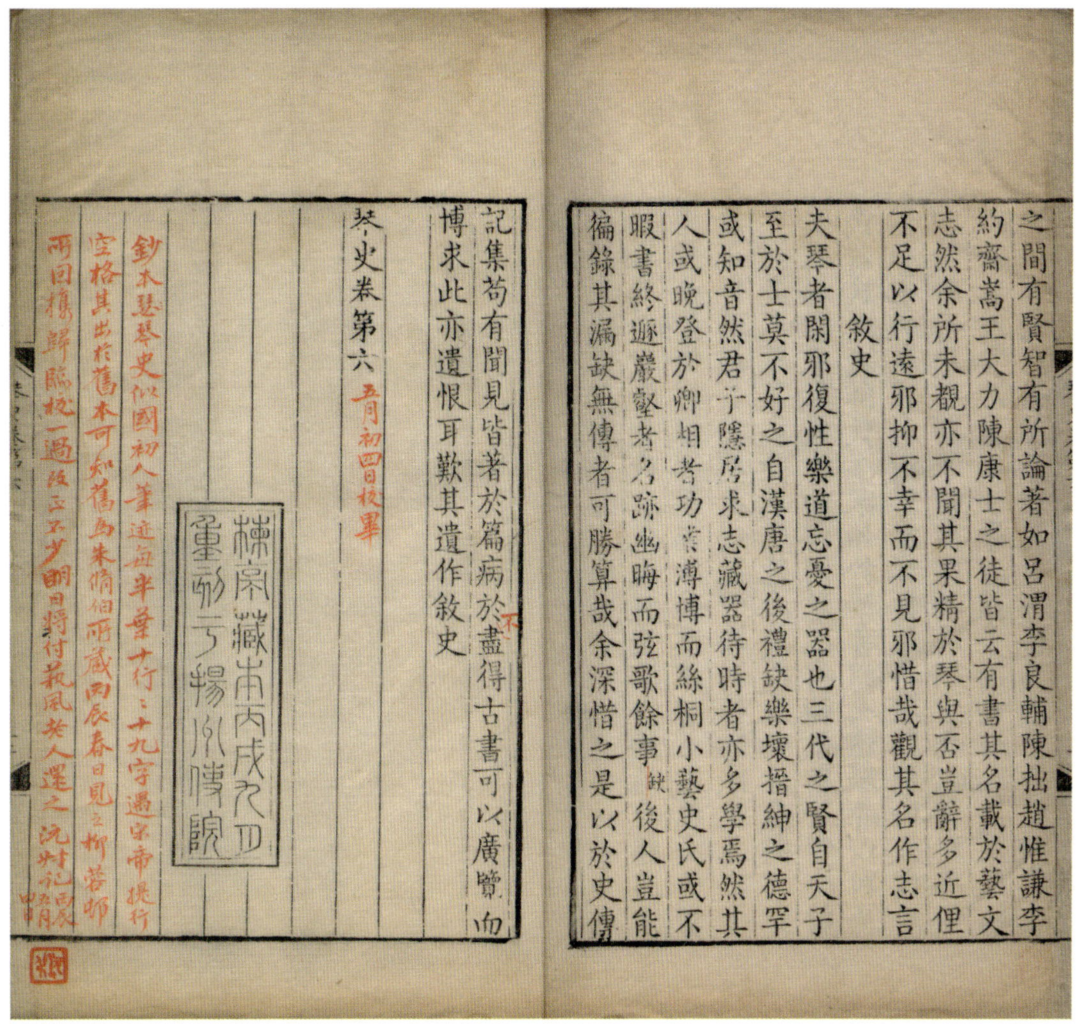
之間有賢智有所論著如呂渭李良輔陳拙趙惟謙李
約齋嵩王大力陳康士之徒皆云有書其名載於藝文
志然余所未覩亦不聞其果精於琴與否豈辭多近俚
不足以行遠邪抑不幸而不見邪惜哉觀其名作志言

敘史

夫琴者閑邪復性樂道忘憂之器也三代之賢自天子
至於士莫不好之自漢唐之後禮缺樂壞搢紳之德罕
或知音然君子隱居求志藏器待時者亦多學焉然其
人或晚登於卿相者功業溥博而絲桐小藝史氏或不
暇書終遁巖壑者名跡幽晦而弦歌餘事缺後人豈能
徧錄其漏缺無傳者可勝算哉余深惜之是以於史傳
記集苟有聞見皆著於篇病於盡得古書可以廣覽而
博求此亦遺恨耳歎其遺作敘史

琴史卷第六

Fig. 4.27: *Qin shi* (*Qin History*), *juan* 6, fols. 11v–12r.
Author: Zhu Changwen (1038–1098).
Date: 1706.
Woodblock: 16.1 × 11.6 cm.
Peking Library (00139).

Another example of widespread dissemination is the *Donglai xiansheng fenmen shilü wuku* 東萊先生分門詩律武庫 (*Encyclopedia for Poetry Writing compiled by the Master of Donglai*, Fig. 4.25), for which an attribution of authorship to the esteemed mid-Song dynasty writer and philosopher Lü Zuqian 呂祖謙 (1137–1181) has been claimed.[44] In *juan* 7 on music and sound, the legendary story of Boya 伯牙 learning the *qin* from his teacher Chenglian 成連 is recounted (Fig. 4.26). According to the publisher's colophon, the book was printed by Lize College 麗澤書院 in Wuzhou (modern Jinhua, Zhejiang). Only two copies of the Southern Song edition survive: one kept in the Fung Ping Shan Library and the other, a later imprint, in the Seikadō Bunko.[45] According to his diary, Liu Chenggan purchased his specimen on the ninth day of the third lunar month in 1915 from Wang Renquan 王仁權 via a book dealer named Qian Chengmei 錢長美.[46] Before making the deal, Liu had already visited Miao Quansun twice, on the sixth and seventh days of the month.[47] In Miao's diary, the entry for the seventh day duly records: "Hanyi 翰怡 (i.e., Liu Chenggan) came in the evening, bringing *Encyclopedia for Poetry Writing* in twenty *juan*. It is an excellent book and was printed in the Song dynasty."[48]

In 1084, with so many individuals praising the qualities of the *qin*, a book called *Qin shi* 琴史 (*Qin History*, Figs. 4.27 and 4.28) was written by Zhu Changwen 朱長文 (1038–1098) in order to bring many of the relevant strands together. The first five of its six *juan* record the biographies of 150 distinguished *qin* players, from the very earliest

44. Jao Tsung-i, *Xianggang daxue Feng Pingshan tushuguan cang shanben shulu*, 25–26.

45. Seikadō Bunko 靜嘉堂文庫, ed., *Seikadō Bunko Sō Gen han zuroku* 靜嘉堂文庫宋元版圖錄 (Tokyo: Kyūko shoin, 1992), vol.1, 167–168, and vol. 2, 47.

46. Liu Chenggan, *Qiushu zhai riji*, vol. 4, 213–216; Liu Chenggan, *Jiaye tang cangshu riji chao*, 225–227.

47. Ibid.

48. Miao Quansun 繆荃孫, *Miao Quansun quanji: Riji* 繆荃孫全集:日記 (Nanjing: Fenghuang chubanshe, 2014), vol. 3, 376.

琴史序

琴之爲器起於上皇之世後聖承承益加潤飾其材則鍾山水之靈氣其制則備律呂之殊用可以包天地萬物之聲可以考民物治亂之兆是謂八音之輿衆樂之統也自伏犧作琴而樂由此興女媧氏之笙簧朱襄氏之瑟葛天氏之八闋陰康氏之舞伊耆氏之土鼓蕢桴葦籥源源以流黄帝作咸池少皥作大淵帝嚳作六英堯之大章舜之九韶皆資琴以成樂三代之盛此爲重焉周官大司樂之奏宗廟也關雎之詩云窈

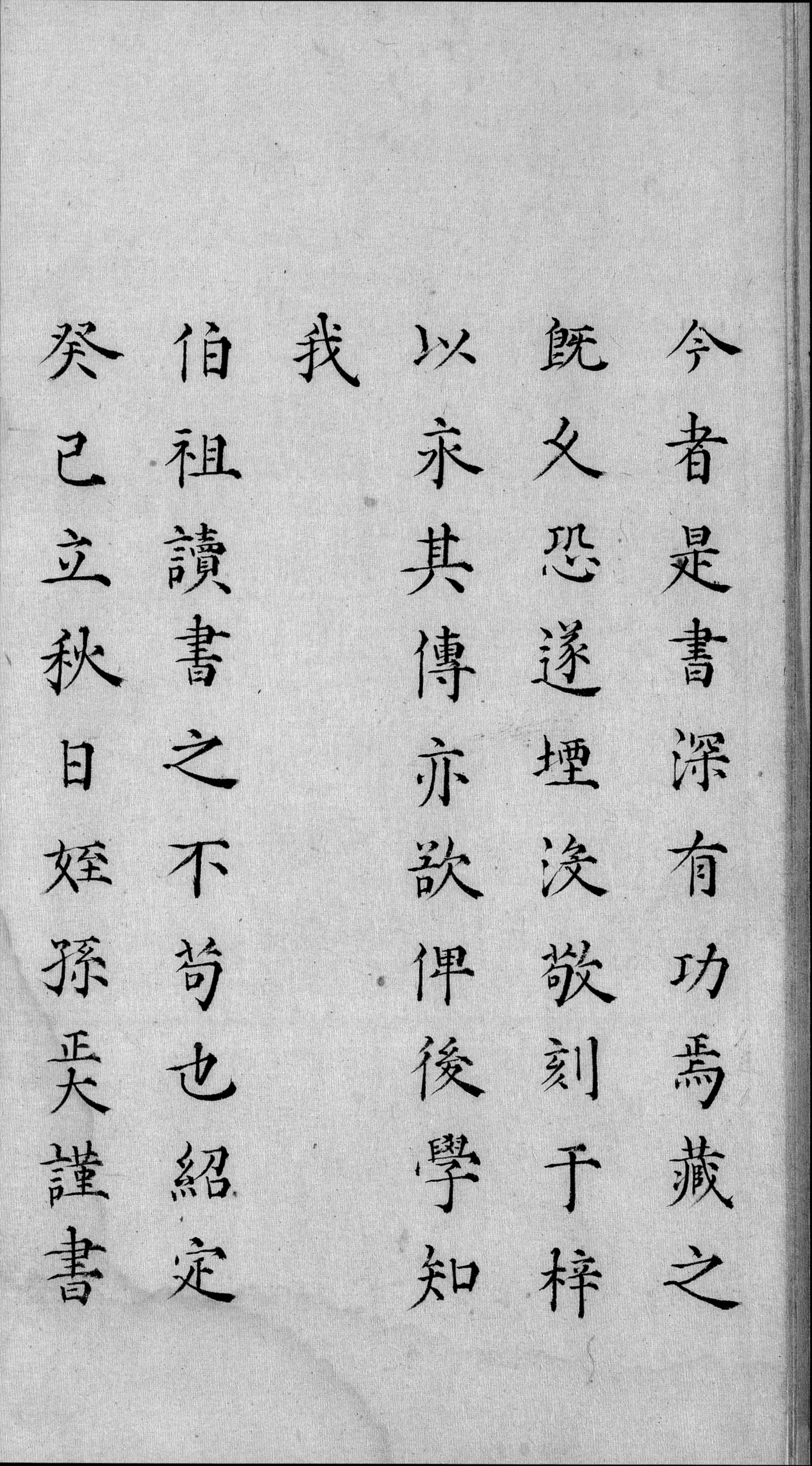

今者是書深有功焉藏之
既久恐遂堙沒敬刻于梓
以永其傳亦欲俾後學知
我
伯祖讀書之不苟也紹定
癸巳立秋日姪孫正大謹書

Fig. 4.28: *Qin shi* (*Qin History*), Zhu Zhengda's postscript dated 1233, fol. 2v (right), and Zhu Changwen's preface dated 1084, fol. 1r (left).
Author: Zhu Changwen (1038–1098).
Date: c. 1518.
Dimensions: c. 33 × c. 15 cm.
Peking Library (06870).

樂圃餘藁序

圖書五厄自古有之為人後嗣而不能明著其先德於後世是亦有所負焉

樂圃文集舊百卷家藏古今篇帙動萬計與夫數世聚族之居室宇亭榭名花古木羅建炎兵火之難吳城失守一日翦為劫灰其後獨

先生春秋通志復傳本於他郡僅有全編思玷慶孫列自幼搜訪

樂圃餘藁每得一篇必珍而藏之今裒集有年矣他未有所增益豈非詢之未廣而求之未裕歟覩 伯父都講痛心疾首之言每輒傷歎思老矣深懼異時墨渝紙

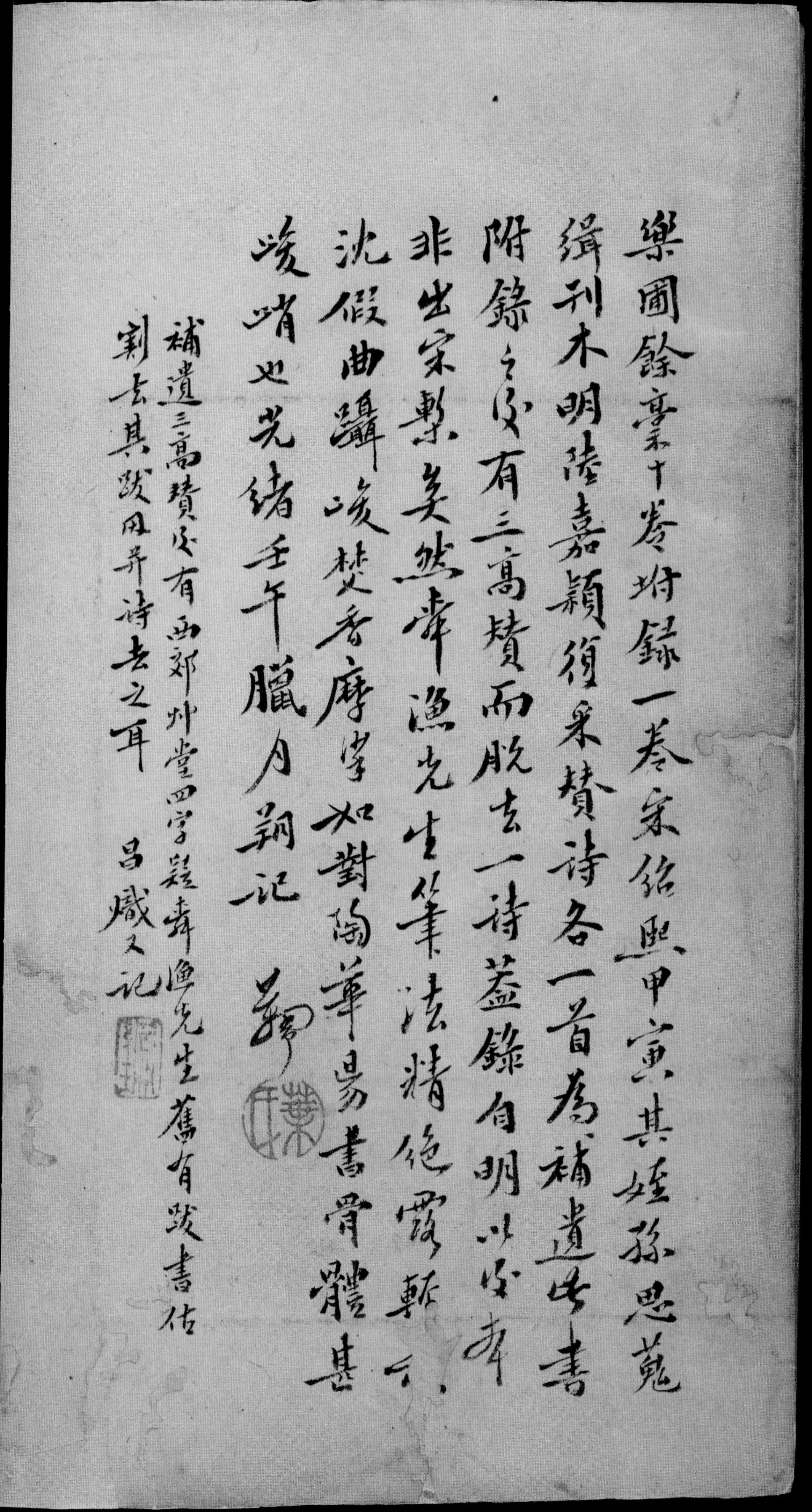

樂圃餘稾十卷坿錄一卷宋紹興甲寅其姪孫思蒐
緝刊木明陸嘉穎復采賛詩各一首為補遺坿書
附錄之後有三高賛而脫去一詩蓋錄自明以後本
非出宋槧矣然常漁先生筆法精絕霞軒之
沈假曲跋後楚香摩寫如對陶華易書骨體甚
峻峭也光緒壬午臘月朔記 鞠

補遺三高賛之有西郊草堂四字疑常漁先生舊有跋書佔
割去其跋因并詩去之耳 昌熾又記

Fig. 4.29: *Lepu yugao* (*Surplus Manuscripts of the Happiness Garden*), Ye Changchi's handwritten colophon dated 1882 (right) and Zhu Si's preface dated 1134, fol. 1r (left).
Author: Zhu Changwen (1038–1098).
Date: before 1850.
Dimensions: 23.3 × 15.1 cm.
Fung Ping Shan Library.

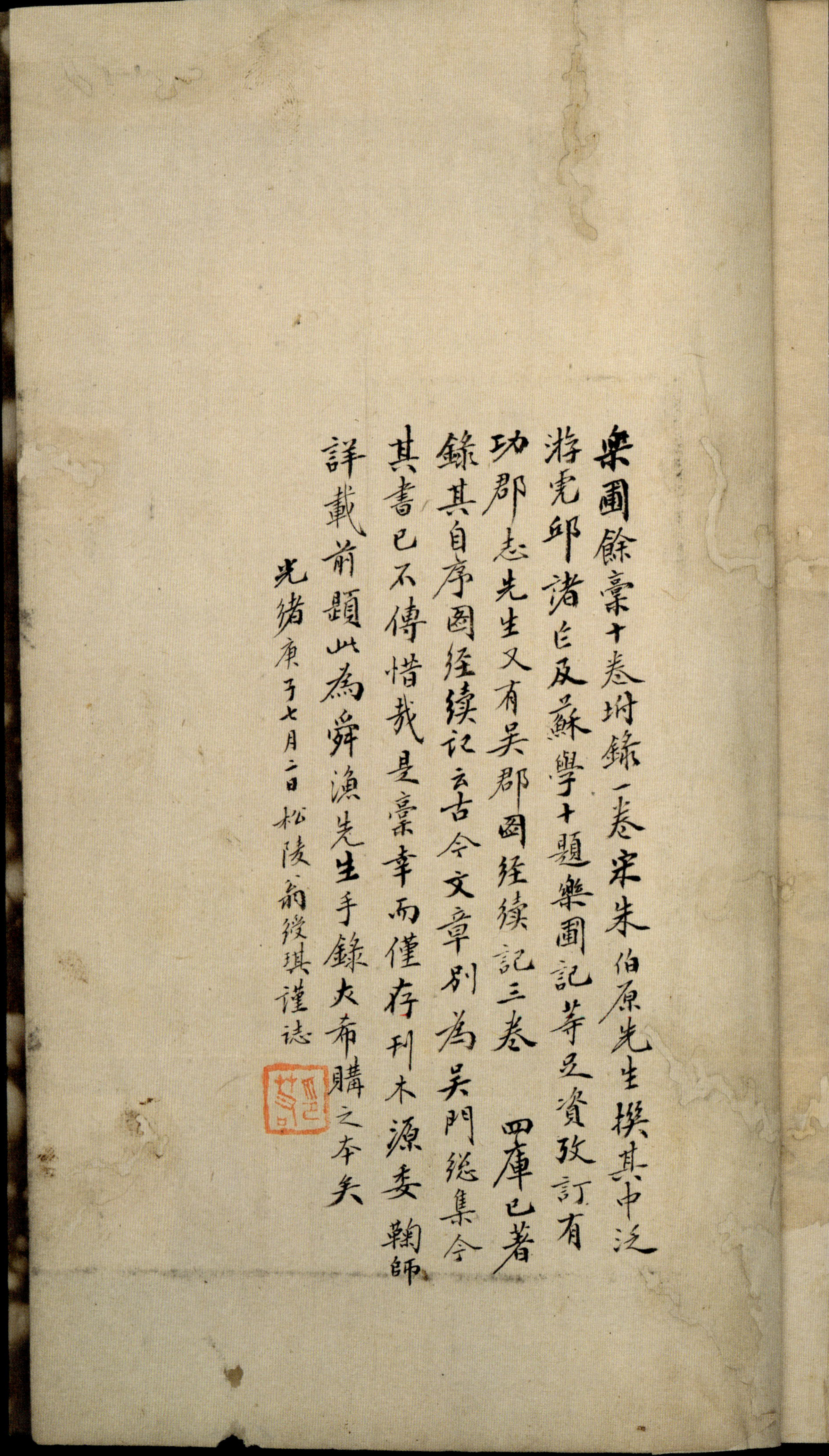

樂圃餘稾十卷坿錄一卷宋朱伯原先生撰其中泛游虎邱諸作及蘇學十題樂圃記等足資攷訂有功郡志先生又有吳郡圖經續記三卷　四庫已著錄其自序圖經續記云古今文章別為吳門總集今其書已不傳惜哉是稾幸而僅存刊木源委　鞠師詳載前題此為舜漁先生手錄大布購之本矣

光緒庚子七月二日松陵翁綬琪謹誌

Fig. 4.30: *Lepu yugao* (*Surplus Manuscripts of the Happiness Garden*), Weng Shouqi's handwritten colophon dated 1900.
Author: Zhu Changwen (1038–1098).
Date: before 1850.
Dimensions: 23.3 × 15.1 cm.
Fung Ping Shan Library.

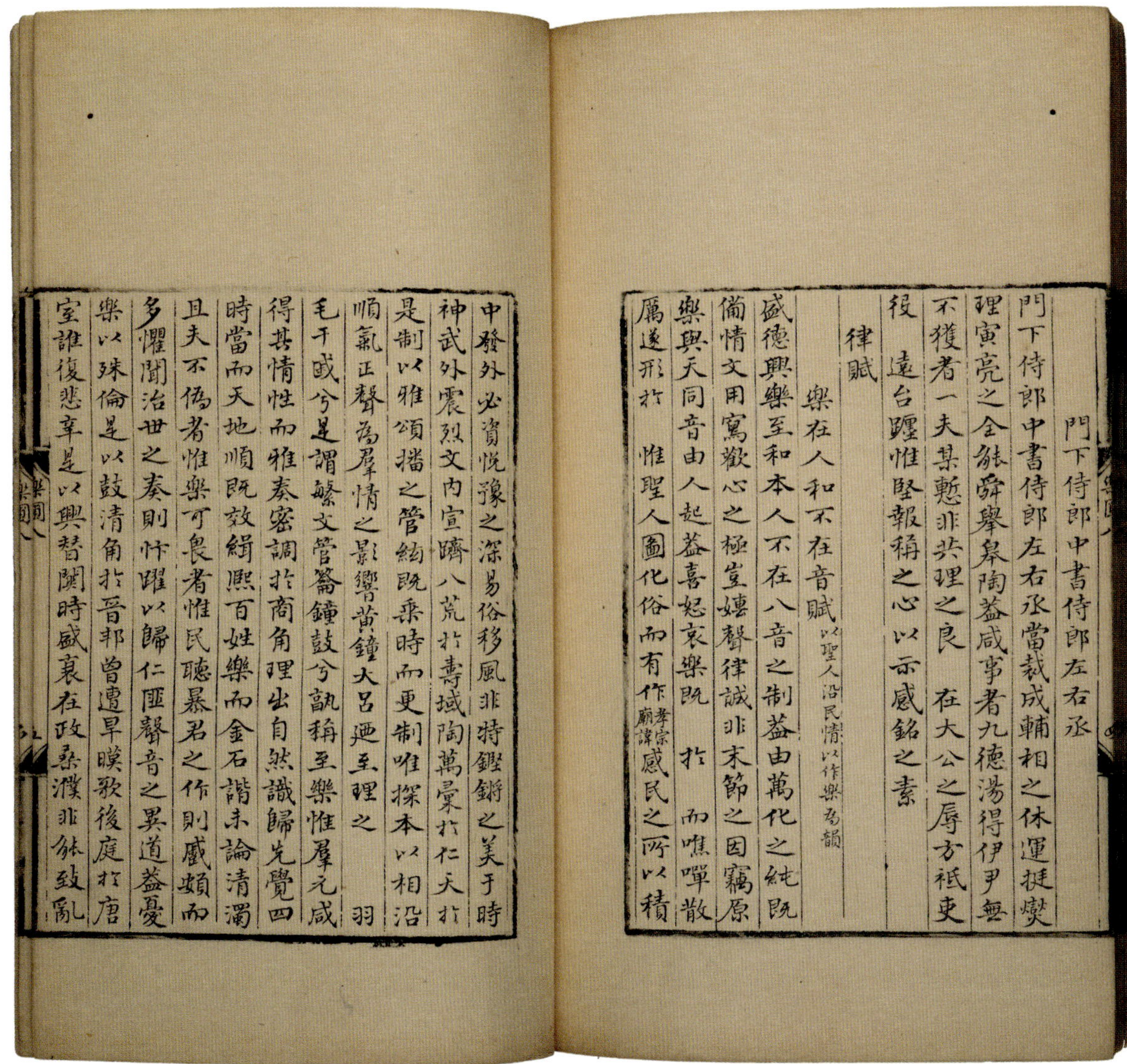

Fig. 4.31: *Lepu yugao* (*Surplus Manuscripts of the Happiness Garden*), *juan* 8, fols. 4r–5v, "The essential feature of music lies in the harmony it engenders in people and not in the sound itself." Author: Zhu Changwen (1038–1098). Date: before 1850. Border: 14.4 × 11.3 cm. Fung Ping Shan Library.

mythical representatives to the Northern Song dynasty. The sixth *juan* discusses *qin* construction, aesthetics, and theory. Zhu Changwen's text is redolent with Confucian ideology, unsurprisingly perhaps, given that he was a scion of a well-known family that had been scholar-officials for several generations. He took the imperial examinations and achieved the *jinshi* degree at such a young age that he was not immediately given an official position. At this juncture, he met with an accident while horse-riding and fractured both legs, which meant that he could no longer tread the path of an official career, so he returned to his native Suzhou and founded an academy called Lepu 樂圃 (The Happiness Garden). Although his own fate had rendered him unable to climb the bureaucratic ladder as a government official, the ethos of rectitude of this vocation remained with him, as can be perceived from a handwritten copy of his collected works in the Fung Ping Shan Library entitled *Lepu yugao* 樂圃餘稿 (*Surplus Manuscripts of the Happiness Garden,* Figs. 4.29–4.31).[49]

Seals on the opening page (Fig. 4.29) give the copyist as You Shipei 尤世培, and one of these encapsulates his work ethic: 尤世培校正手錄本 ("Proofread and hand-copied by You Shipei"), while the other records his *hao* soubriquet: "Shun Yu" 舜漁. Nearby is a seal of the first collector that reads: "At one time in the collection of Wang Langyuan [1786–?]" 曾藏汪閬源家. The seal of the second owner gives: "Jiang Fengzao [c. 1838–1908] of Suzhou, the Studio of Ten Seals of the Qin and

49. Jao Tsung-i, *Xianggang daxue Feng Pingshan tushuguan cang shanben shulu*, 182–183; Jao Tsung-i, Li Zhifang, and Zhang Lijuan, *Xianggang daxue Feng Pingshan tushuguan cang shanben shulu*, enlarged ed., 218–219.

清容居士集目録上

第一卷

賦

Han Dynasties, his locked cabinet of books" 蔣鳳藻秦漢十印齋秘篋圖書. The seal of the third owner, Jiang Biao 江標 (1860–1899), records: "Read by Jiang Jianxia" 建霞過眼. On the blank right face opposite the first handwritten page of the text proper is an evaluation by the scholar Ye Changchi, who had been invited by one of the latter two owners in 1882 to write this text. In the equivalent place at the back of the book on the blank left face opposite the last handwritten page of the text proper, a similar passage can be found, this time penned by Weng Shouqi 翁綬琪 (*juren* degree 1891) in 1900 (Fig. 4.30).

In Liu Changgan's diary on the fourteenth day of the fifth "leap" lunar month of 1914 is an entry that reads: "Someone called Zhong Songting 鍾松亭, a native of Shengze who had not previously been introduced to me, had brought books for me to look at. In their midst was an old handwritten copy of *Surplus Manuscripts of the Happiness Garden* in three volumes that had been copied by You Shipei and had once been in the collection of an official serving in Beijing by the name of Jiang Jianxia. Ye Changchi had written an evaluation that showered high praise on it, so I bought it at a price of forty silver dollars."[50]

Zhu Changwen's opinion on the role of the *qin* can be ascertained from the title to one of the *fu* 賦 poems in the book: "Yue zai renhe buzai yin" 樂在人和不在音 ("The essential feature of music lies in the harmony it engenders in people and not in the sound itself," Fig. 4.31). This aphorism expresses succinctly the quintessential truth that the Confucians took as their view of music and the relationship of music to the *qin*. Diametrically opposed to this perspective, however, are the more practical opinions of Yuan Jue 袁桷 (1266–1327) writing in the Yuan dynasty, where he supplies a much more appreciative evaluation of the *qin* aesthetic. In his book *Qingrong jushi ji* 清容居士集 (*The Literary Collection of the Hermit of Qingrong*), the seminal essay expressing his standpoint is "Qin shu zeng Huang Yiran" 琴述贈黃依然 ("Exposition on the *Qin* Presented to Huang Yiran").

Taken as a whole, *The Literary Collection of the Hermit of Qingrong* is a miscellany of literary contributions by Yuan Jue and includes poems and essays of various sorts. The Fung Ping Shan Library version is a manuscript copy in twenty volumes (Fig. 4.32), but of these, volumes thirteen and fourteen (*juan* 31–37) are written on paper of a different color and quality that is no longer white (as is the paper of the other volumes), which likely means that they joined the set at a later date.[51] Originally, the total number of *juan* was forty-three, but the insertion of the two additional volumes has increased this to fifty. Taking into account the consequent changes in *juan* numbering, subsequent to volumes thirteen and fourteen, the *juan* numbers as given at the head of each *juan* have all been overwritten in red ink with the new *juan* number. A similar process has occurred in the contents pages at the opening of the first volume.

Fig. 4.32: *Qingrong jushi ji* (*The Literary Collection of the Hermit of Qingrong*), table of contents, fol. 1r.
Author: Yuan Jue (1266–1327).
Date: before 1803.
Dimensions: 26.1 × 18.1 cm.
Fung Ping Shan Library.

On the manuscript itself, the oldest seals are those of Peng Yuanrui 彭元瑞 (1731–1803), not only a scholar-official, but also an imperial attendant, whose literary collection was housed at the Zhi shengdao zhai 知聖道齋 (Studio of Knowing the Way of Wisdom and Sagehood). His four seals reads: "The Peng Family of Nanchang" 南昌彭氏, "Ex Libris the Studio of Knowing the Way of Wisdom and Sagehood" 知聖道齋藏書, "On opening this book, read it well" 遇者善讀, and the fourth is a short homily given in poetical form (Fig. 4.32):

> If you desire to speak first-class words
> You must first have a first-class meaning
> If you desire to be a first-class person
> You must first be a first-class scholar
>
> 欲出第一等言，得有第一等意。
> 欲為第一等人，須作第一等士子。

Peng Yuanrui's seal is found on only the eighteen volumes that comprise the original format of the book, so presumably the two inserted volumes were added after it had left his collection.

The second recorded owner was Zhu Xueqin 朱學勤 (1823–1875), whose studio was called Jieyi lu 結一廬 (Building a Single Cottage). His seal reads: "The Zhu family of Tangqi; a record of the Building a Single Cottage Library" 唐栖朱氏結一廬圖書記, and is found on all twenty volumes, so the insertion of volumes thirteen and fourteen must have been either before or during the manuscript's sojourn in his collection. Liu Chenggan pops up once more as the next recorded

50. Liu Chenggan, *Qiushu zhai riji*, vol. 3, 492; Liu Chenggan, *Jiaye tang cangshu riji chao*, 172.

51. Jao Tsung-i, *Xianggang daxue Feng Pingshan tushuguan cang shanben shulu*, 187; Jao Tsung-i, Li Zhifang, and Zhang Lijuan, *Xianggang daxue Feng Pingshan tushuguan cang shanben shulu*, enlarged ed., 228–229.

客三衢毛敏仲嚴陵徐天民在門下朝夕
損益琴理刪潤別為一譜以其所居曰紫
霞名焉自渡江來譜之可攷者曰閣譜曰
江西譜閣譜由宋太宗時漸廢至皇祐間
復入祕閣今世所藏金石圖畫之精善咸
謂閣本蓋皆昔時祕閣所庋而琴有閣譜
亦此義也方閣譜行時別譜存於世良多
至大晟樂府證定益以閣譜為貴別譜復
不得入其學寖絕紹興時非入閣本者不
得待詔私相傳習媢熟整雅非有亡蹙債

州之北山不以險稱雄絕萬世朝九州以函諸夏豈峻極于天者非山之謂與在易之象曰地中有山謙不言山在地中謂有髙大之實藏于地謙之象也余嘗聞洞庭諸山跬步巖壑謝君獨取其平焉久留京師願至開平知盛世之廣洗耳目之固陋歸于故里卧游以思登東山而小魯夫豈虛言哉

琴述贈黃依然

往六十年錢塘楊司農以稚琴名于時有

Fig. 4.33: *Qingrong jushi ji* (*The Literary Collection of the Hermit of Qingrong*), *juan* 44, "Exposition on the *Qin* Presented to Huang Yiran," fols. 1v–2r.
Author: Yuan Jue (1266–1327).
Date: before 1803.
Dimensions: 26.1 × 18.1 cm.
Fung Ping Shan Library.

owner, and his diary entry gives the date of purchase as the eighteenth day of the twelfth lunar month of 1913. This time, the bookseller was Zhu Dianqing 朱甸卿, and the job lot comprised four books of which this was one, bought for a total price of ninety silver dollars.[52]

With no date given on the manuscript itself as to when it was copied, two conflicting opinions have emerged. Liu Chenggan certainly regarded it as a Ming dynasty original and the price he paid reflects this. In fact, he was not the first collector who had been offered the manuscript; the celebrated connoisseur from north China, Fu Zengxiang 傅增湘 (1872–1949), has left a record of when it appeared before him in 1912, and he too thought it was of Ming provenance, though he did not purchase it.[53] Miao Quansun concurs, and his notes in Liu Chenggan's bibliographical record read: "This [manuscript] is of the Ming dynasty; the characters are written in a simple yet delightful hand. Originally, it lacked *juan* 31–37, but these have been substituted by volumes from another old handwritten copy."[54] Jao Tsung-i's opinion is the siren voice, however, and his view is that it was penned in Peng Yuanrui's studio, which pushes its date perhaps as many as two hundred years later.[55]

Yuan Jue was not simply an amateur *qin* player; by profession he was a historian, so his prose style is logical, methodical, and analytical, and in his essay, he details important traditions of *qin* repertories, how they evolved, and under whose tutelage. The essay "Exposition on the *Qin* Presented to Huang Yiran" itself appears in the thirty-seventh *juan* (Fig. 4.33) according to the original numbering, which was overwritten as the forty-fourth *juan* once the two extra volumes had been inserted. The central purpose of his essay was to introduce the true lineage behind the *qin* anthology *Zixia dong pu* 紫霞洞譜 (*The Anthology of the Purple Cloud-Wisps Cave*) that appeared at the close of the Southern Song dynasty. Although no copies of this work survive, it comprised no less than 37 *juan* on which were notated 468 *qin* pieces and so was undoubtedly a majestic compilation. In accordance with Yuan Jue's scholarly bent, instead of simply jumping in with an account of the anthology, he begins his narrative at the start of the Southern Song dynasty with its precursors, the *Ge pu* 閣譜 (*Imperial Library Anthology*) and the *Jiangxi pu* 江西譜 (*Jiangxi Anthology*):

Sixty years ago, Yang Zan 楊瓚 [fl. thirteenth century] of Qiantang was famous as a fine appreciator of *qin* music. His guests Mao Minzhong of Sanqu and Xu Tianming of Yanling were staying at his residence. From morning to night, they wrestled with the task of editing *qin* music, and eventually by a process of excising and reworking managed to create a remarkable new anthology called *The Purple Cloud-Wisps Anthology* after the place where they were staying. And after the Song dynasty had transplanted to the region south of the Great River, those musical scores that could be investigated were either *Imperial Library Anthology* or *Jiangxi Anthology* types.

往六十年，錢塘楊司農以雅琴名于時，有客三衢毛敏仲、嚴陵徐天民在門下，朝夕損益琴理，刪潤別為一譜，以其所居曰「紫霞」名焉。自渡江來，譜之可攷者曰「閣譜」、曰「江西譜」。

Since the time of the Emperor Song Taizong [939–997, r. 967–997], *Imperial Library Anthology* scores had gradually fallen into disuse; only in the Huangyou era [1049–1054] did they once more enter the Imperial Library collection. Nowadays, all the most exquisite ancient bronzes, stele rubbings, and paintings are called Imperial Library copies, and all were formerly repository items in the Imperial Library collection. And as far as *qin* are concerned, the term "Imperial Library Anthology" also shares this original meaning. When *Imperial Library Anthology* scores were in circulation, many other types of notation could be found, but owing to the endorsement process of the Dasheng Music Bureau, it became even more the case that *Imperial Library Anthology* scores were the most important and valuable; other anthologies were no longer given the opportunity to enter into the Bureau's repertories, and so study of them gradually ceased. In the Shaoxing era [1131–1162], any player who did not use scores of the *Imperial Library Anthology* type was not permitted to perform for the emperor. In private, only those adepts in this tradition were prepared to transmit it, and its requirements were to pander, to over-practice, and to be pedantic; even if these pieces did not originally have a lifeless and stunted meaning, they now imbue a sense of nervousness. The Southern Song dynasty was small and weak, and for a hundred or more years these defects can be seen in its music.

「閣譜」由宋太宗時漸廢，至皇祐間復入秘閣。今世所藏金石圖畫之精善，咸謂「閣本」，蓋皆昔時秘閣所庋。而琴有「閣譜」亦此義也。方「閣譜」行時，別譜存於世良多，至大晟樂府證定，益以「閣譜」為貴，別譜復不得入，其學寖絕。紹興時非入「閣本」者不得待詔。私相傳習，媚熟整雅，非有亡蹙僨遽之意而兢兢然。國小而弱，百餘年間蓋可見矣。

Speaking now of the *Jiangxi Anthology*, it was grounded in the *Imperial Library Anthology*, but more detail was added: the melodies became more elaborate and impatient, and their fingering patterns embodied a completely different set of principles. Taking the majestic tragedy of *The Autumn Wind* and *The Wu Gorge*, and the loveliness of *Orchid Banks* and *Luopu* [a place name], the practitioners of *The Jiangxi Anthology* took harmoniousness and made it more resentful, and the more the music desired to proceed in a balanced manner, the more this was opposed. Therefore, poets and warriors all took pleasure in vying to admire it [the music of *The Jiangxi Anthology*], saying that if music were not like this, then it would be unworthy of the name *"qin."*

曰「江西」者，由「閣」而加詳焉，其聲繁以殺，其按抑也皆別為義例。《秋風》、《巫峽》之悲壯，《蘭皋》、《洛浦》之靚好，將和而愈怨，欲正而愈反。故凡騷人介士皆喜而爭慕之，謂不若是不足以名琴也。

In the passage that follows, Yuan Jue exposes Yang Zan's subterfuge and indicates that *The Purple Cloud-Wisps Anthology* (the Yang anthology) was not Yang's own creative contribution.

By the time the Yang anthology had become popular, the other two anthologies had gradually been discarded and were no longer used. Some said that their melodies had disappeared shortly after the demise of the Southern Song dynasty, and others said that the Yang anthology had no lineage and that was all the more reason for it not to be practiced. Alas! Yang Zan had simply hidden the achievements of earlier compilers in order to promote his own, and thus his anthology does not record the provenance of any of the music in it; and so, if it is criticized for this reason by those of the present day, nothing can be said in its defense.

方楊氏譜行時，二譜漸廢不用，或謂其聲與國亡相先後，又謂楊氏無所祖，尤不當習。噫！楊司農匿前人以自彰，故所得譜皆不著本始，其為今世所議，無可言。

I too had once practiced the Yang anthology and on numerous instances exchanged opinions on it with Xu Tianming, and it was clear that its melodies were not of a kind that Yang Zan could have created on his own, so I asked [Xu] Tianming on several occasions about this. At that time, [Xu] Tianming was of a mind only to praise the Yang anthology and was dismissive in his answers, so I did not succeed in getting to the bottom of the matter. This made me all the more suspicious, but I had no evidence as yet to present.

余嘗習司農譜，又數與徐天民還往，知其聲非司農所能意創，間以問天民。時天民誇詡猶司農也，謾對焉，終不以悉。余益深疑之而莫以據。

Later, I learnt of an anthology compiled by Zhang of Guangling and compared it with the Yang anthology. Regarding *Master Cai's Five Melodies*, Yang Zan had always said they were fine specimens that he had refined still further, yet identical pieces can be found in the Zhang anthology, so the only possibility is that Yang Zan had concealed their provenance and refused to speak of it.

後悉得廣陵張氏譜而加校焉。則《蔡氏五弄》，司農號為精加紬繹，皆張氏所載，獨楊氏隱抵不述耳。

Of the *qin* melodies currently in circulation, those of the ancient Qingshang genre are the most plentiful. Guo Maoqian [1041–1099] recorded the lyrics of the ancient Music Bureau's *qin* songs, and none are more numerous than Qingshang melodies. Du You [735–812], writing about ritual music, has said that the ancient melodies of the state of Chu and the Han dynasty were transmitted by *qin*

52. Liu Chenggan, *Qiushu zhai riji*, vol. 3, 352; Liu Chenggan, *Jiaye tang cangshu riji chao*, 140.

53. Fu Zengxiang 傅增湘, *Cangyuan qunshu jingyan lu* 藏園羣書經眼錄 (Beijing: Zhonghua shuju, 1983), 1317.

54. Miao Quansun, Wu Changshou, and Dong Kang, *Jiaye tang cangshu zhi*, 616.

55. Jao Tsung-i, *Xianggang daxue Feng Pingshan tushuguan cang shanben shulu*, 187.

> players. *Master Cai's Five Melodies* and *Four Melodies in the Chu Mode* survived until the Tang dynasty, thus the *[Master Cai's] Five Melodies* we know today are not the original compositions of Yang Zan—that much is crystal clear. So, for critics to discard them [the melodies in the Yang anthology] outright must surely be inappropriate.
>
> 今世琴調清商，號為最多，郭茂倩記古樂府琴辭，亦莫盛於清商。杜佑氏敘論雅樂，謂楚漢舊聲猶傳於琴家，《蔡氏五弄》、《楚調四弄》至唐猶存，則今所謂《五弄》非楊氏私製，明甚。議者悉去之，不可也。

Zhang Yan's anthology appeared in the early thirteenth century and certainly no later than 1207 (the date of Han Tuozhou's 韓侂冑 death), and its final coalescence was with Yang Zan and *The Purple Cloud-Wisps Anthology* in the late thirteenth century; Yuan Jue takes the reader on a detailed journey from one to the other:

> Zhang Yan of Guangling, *zi* soubriquet Xiaoweng, held an official position during the Jiatai era [1201–1204]. When he was living in Li [present-day Huzhou in Zhejiang], he had once said that the music of *The Imperial Library Anthology* was not refined melodies, and that he had managed to obtain some ancient scores from the residence of Han Tuozhou [1152–1207], and had bought others secretly in a cross-border market town. The combined collection of Zhang Yan and Prime Minister Han comprised an anthology of fifteen *juan*, and these were prepared for cutting into woodblocks for printing. At this juncture, because Zhang Yan had taken part in Han Tuozhou's unsuccessful policy bid advocating a northwards military incursion, he was dismissed. His guest, Guo Chuwang [i.e., Guo Mian 郭沔, c. 1190–1260] of Yongjia, obtained the manuscript anthology, and he in turn added some of his own melodies and pieces; however, most of these were composed according to the [ancient] melodic style of Cai Yong.
>
> 按廣陵張氏名巖，字肖翁，嘉泰間為叅預，居霅時嘗謂「閣譜」非雅聲，於韓忠獻家得古譜，復從互市密購，與韓相合定為十五卷，將鋟于梓。以預韓氏邊議罷去，其家[客]永嘉郭楚望獨得之，復別為調曲，然大抵皆依蔡氏聲為之者。
>
> When Guo Chuwang died, the manuscript was given to Liu Zhifang. The more Liu Zhifang came to be respected, the more he lost touch with his *qin*-playing roots [i.e., Zhang Yan]. Xu Tianming had once said that Yang Zan and Mao Minzhong had in their youth also practiced *The Jiangxi Anthology*. One day, after Mao Minzhong had come back from a journey through the mountains and was playing the opening to one of Guo Chuwang's melodies in the *shang* mode, Yang Zan, upon listening, was both astonished and delighted, and provided a stipend so that Xu Tianming could study with Liu Zhifang. Therefore, today's *Purple Cloud-Wisps Anthology* only acknowledges Liu and Guo and does not mention that Zhang Yan of Guangling had transmitted it. This is the self-centered cronyism of Yang Zan and his guests.
>
> 楚望死，復以授劉志芳。志芳之傳愈尊而失其祖愈遠。天民嘗言楊司農與敏仲少年時亦習「江西」，一日敏仲由山中來，始弄楚望商調，司農驚且喜，復以金帛令天民受學志芳，故今《紫霞》獨言劉、郭，而不言廣陵張氏傳授，皆楊氏與其客自私之蔽。
>
> In Zhejiang, there lived a certain Xu Li who was a contemporary of Yang Zan, and he had compiled *Mysterious Music: A Jade Anthology* in one *juan*; and because he had presented a book entitled *The Mirror of Temperament and Orthodox Qin Music Theory* to the imperial court, he was awarded an official position. His *[Master Cai's] Five Melodies* were identical to those of Yang Zan. In his later years, he had contact with Yang Zan, who greatly respected him. This is additional evidence that the melodies of the state of Chu and the Han dynasty are not original compositions of Yang Zan.
>
> 越有徐理氏，與楊同時，有《奧音玉譜》一卷，以進《律鑒琴統》入官。其《五弄》與楊氏亦無異。晚與楊交，楊亟重之，益知楚漢舊聲非楊氏所作。
>
> When I came to the Capital [modern Beijing], I saw *qin* players there whose style of playing resembled that of the Southern Song, though it was more solemn in mood and broader in tempo, like a hale and hearty distinguished elderly gentleman, but I could not tell them these sentiments. Huang Yiran is a descendent of Huang Tingjian 黃庭堅 [1045–1105] and has played his *qin* in many distinguished noble houses. I do not know him, but his love of the *qin* is as deep as mine, so I have written this

evolutionary outline in order to smooth away the puzzlements of our present-day world; and because of this, I present it to him.

余來京師見鼓琴者，與紹興所尚微近，第重緩，如寬厚長者，余不能以是説告之也。黃君依然，豫章太史之裔，以琴遊公卿，余未識之，而余之嗜琴當有同者，故書其源緒，以解夫今世之惑，而因以告之。

The first printed anthology of *qin* music appeared in 1425, sponsored by Prince Zhu Quan 朱權 (1378–1448), the seventeenth son of Zhu Yuanzhang 朱元璋 (1328–1398, r. 1368–1398), the first Ming dynasty emperor. The anthology is titled *Quxian Shenqi mipu* 臞仙神奇秘譜 (*The Emaciated Immortal's Mysterious and Secret Scores*, Figs. 4.34 and 4.35) and comprises sixty-four pieces divided into three *juan* of sixteen, twenty-seven, and twenty-one pieces respectively. Zhu Quan supplies a note to the first *juan*, titled "Masterpieces from Ancient Antiquity" 太古神品, that records: "These are pieces of ancient antiquity that contain secrets not transmitted by our forefathers." The second and third *juan* are both subsumed under the title "Masterpieces from Outside the Cloud-Wisps" 霞外神品. After its appearance in the late Southern Song dynasty, the manuscript *The Anthology of the Purple Cloud-Wisps Cave* that Yuan Jue had discussed in detail was redacted in the Yuan dynasty to *The Outside the Cloud-Wisps Qin Anthology* 霞外琴譜; the forty-eight pieces in *juan* two and three of *The Emaciated Immortal's Mysterious and Secret Scores* have their origins in this lineage.

An example of this transmission is the piece "Xiaoxiang shuiyun" 瀟湘水雲 ("The Clouds over the Rivers Xiao and Xiang") by Guo Mian (i.e., Guo Chuwang mentioned earlier by Yuan Jue), which is found in the third *juan* of *The Emaciated Immortal's Mysterious and Secret Scores*. At the opening to this piece, Zhu Quan writes:

The Emaciated Immortal says: "This piece was written by Mr. Guo Mian whose *hao* soubriquet was Chuwang. Mr. Guo was a native of Yongjia. Whenever [while in Chu territory] he wanted to look at the Jiuyi mountains, because they were blocked by clouds above the Xiao and Xiang rivers, he used [writing music about] this to express loyalty to his country. However, he also took the notion of water and clouds, and imbued his piece with it, which gives it a melodious and leisurely attractiveness, a mood of glittering water and cloudy shadows, still more so with the wind and rain in one's face, wearing a straw rain-cape and drifting on the water's surface, and the picturesqueness of a small skiff on the five lakes."

臞仙曰：「是曲也，楚望先生郭沔所制。先生永嘉人，每欲望九嶷，為瀟湘之雲所蔽，以寓惓惓之意也。然水雲之為曲，有悠揚自得之趣，水光雲影之興；更有滿頭風雨，一蓑江表，扁舟五湖之志。」

The ten sections of the piece are as follows:

Mist and rain on Dongting Lake
Over the Jiang and Han Rivers, the sky broadens, and the air is clear
Heaven's light and the clouds' shadows
Water meets Heaven's edge
Waves churn, clouds fly
A wind whips up the water's waves
Water and sky, one pure azure
On the cool river, the moon is cold
For ten thousand leagues, translucent waves
Reflections reveal ten thousand images

洞庭烟雨　　江漢舒晴
天光雲影　　水接天隅
浪捲雲飛　　風起水涌
水天一碧　　寒江月冷
萬里澄波　　影涵萬象

Reproduced in Fig. 4.34 are the third, fourth, fifth, and sixth sections of this piece, which are found in the twentieth folio of the third *juan*. Unlike the *wenzipu* preserved in the Tōkyō and Hikone manuscripts, the *qin* notation employed in this anthology is *jianzipu* 減字譜, a simplified form of ideogram notation characterized by the representation of musical sounds without indicating register or melody. Still in use today, the notation shows finger positions and the required technique for both hands. Hu Gongxuan 胡公玄, an earlier owner of this copy of *The Emaciated Immortal's Mysterious and Secret Scores*, upon discovering that his copy had two imprints of folio 20 but none of folio 21, took the errant duplicated folio and in 1955 gave it to bibliographic experts for evaluation. From this time onwards, the folio and the book itself have been separated. One expert, Luo Fubao 羅福葆 (1899–1967), on the grounds of paper quality, ink color, and the format of the page fold, determined that it belonged to a

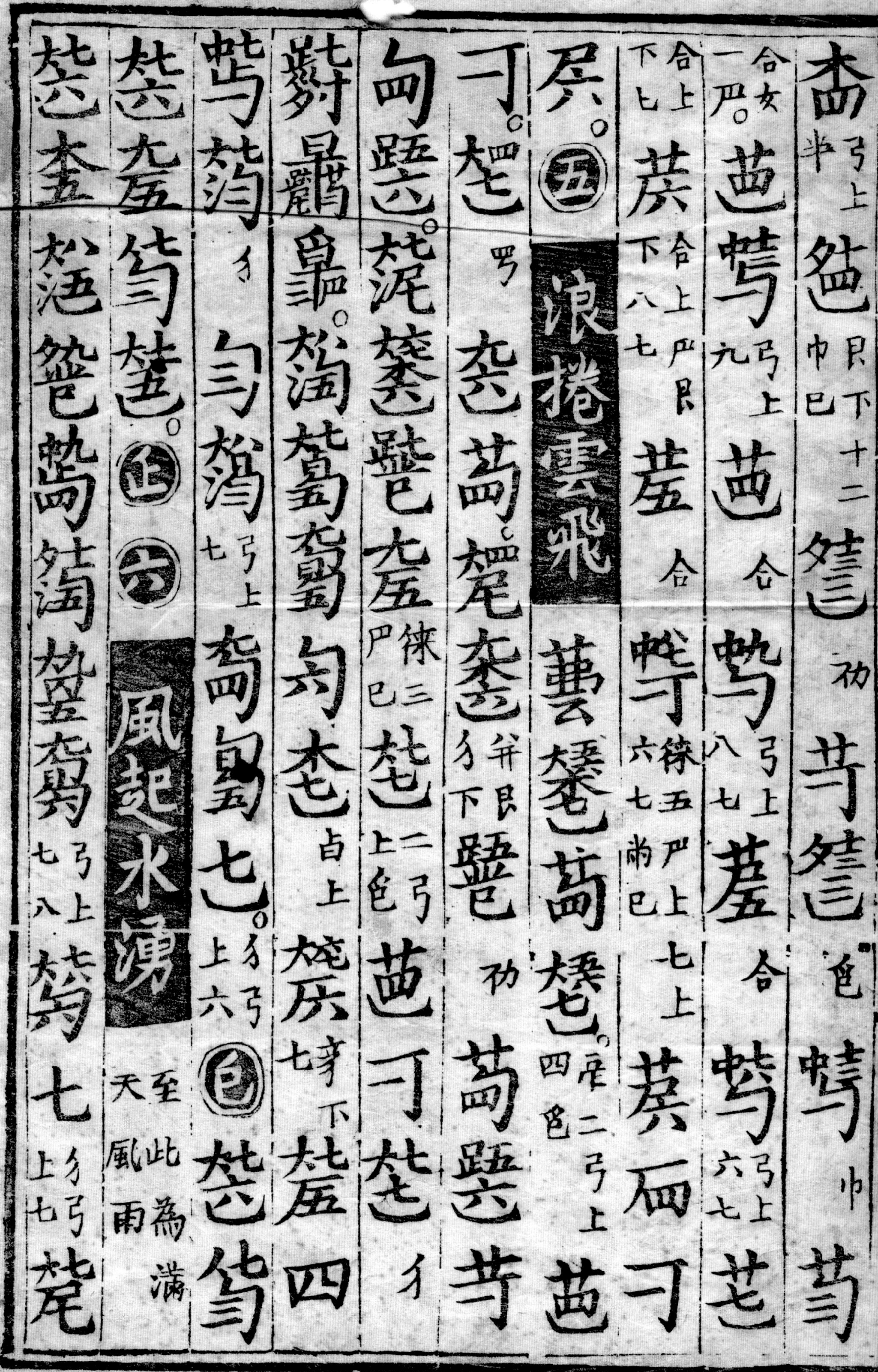

[illegible]

五

浪捲雲飛

[illegible]

六

[illegible]

七

風起水湧

至此為滿天風雨

[illegible]

[illegible] 仂 [illegible] 徐三尸 上九 [illegible]

三 [illegible] 彡 [illegible] 巾已 [illegible]

[illegible] 合女 一尸 [illegible] 弓上 九 [illegible] 合 [illegible] 弓上 七八 [illegible] 合 [illegible] 弓上六 七旳 [illegible]

[illegible] 合女 一尸 [illegible] 合上 一尸 尸女 [illegible] 下八 [illegible] 合艮 下九 [illegible] 合 [illegible]

四彡上 七旳 [illegible] 包 [illegible] 正 四 水接天陽 [illegible]

[illegible] 仂 [illegible] 二作 [illegible] 彡 [illegible] 巾 [illegible] 合

[illegible] 五 [illegible] 七 [illegible] 五 [illegible] 丏彡上 复下 [illegible] 苗女 尸 仂

[illegible] 苗女 一尸 [illegible] 苗女 一尸 [illegible] 五 [illegible] 方一 合

[illegible] 方二 合 [illegible] 弓上 七 [illegible] 四 [illegible]

[illegible] 九 艮彡 下 [illegible]

臞仙神奇秘譜序

粤自蒼精之君按五行之德以定五音乃製琴瑟始有琴焉赤精之君削桐為琴繩絲為絃而又繼其製也軒皇以遞鐘之琴會神靈於西山以歆神明之德此三聖之所為備也然琴之為物聖人製之以正心術導政事和六氣調玉燭實天地之靈器太古之神物乃中國聖人治世之音君子養修之物獨縫掖黄冠之所宜柰何俗流遺濫淫風斯竭致使

late Ming edition.[56] Another, Zhao Wanli 趙萬里 (1905–1980), using paper quality, the knife-work of the woodblock carver, and ink color, deemed that it was subsequent to a Wang Liang 汪諒 re-cut of the Jiajing 嘉靖 era (1522–1566), since it is included in an advertisement inserted into the latter's edition of *Wenxuan zhu* 文選注 (*Commentary on the Selections of Refined Literature*) published in 1523.[57] *Qin* connoisseur Zha Fuxi 查阜西 (1895–1976) even claimed that it was a copy of a reprinted edition of the Wanli 萬曆 era (1573–1620).[58] The book itself is now in the Shanghai Library, but its duplicate folio 20 is housed separately in a private collection. Writing in 2015, Guo Lixuan 郭立暄 (b. 1971) of the Shanghai Library has argued that neither Zhao nor Luo's evaluations are convincing and has postulated that the Shanghai Library and Wang Liang editions are two entirely independent re-cuts of the 1425 first edition, while also suggesting that both were issued well before 1522.[59]

In total, five copies of different printed editions of *The Emaciated Immortal's Mysterious and Secret Scores* survive. They are held at the following institutions:

1. Shanghai Library[60]
2. Naikaku Bunko, Kokuritsu Kōbunshokan, Tokyo (See Fig. 4.35)
3. National Palace Museum, Taipei[61]
4. Chinese National Academy of Arts (only *juan* 3 survives), Beijing[62]
5. Hunan Provincial Library (only *juan* 2–3 survive), Changsha

Of these five, I have examined the first three on-site. The three copies kept in Tokyo, Taipei, and Beijing are imprints of the same Wang Liang re-cut, which is believed to have been issued in approximately 1522; the one kept in Shanghai is an imprint of another reprinted edition on whose exact issue date scholarly views vary. Through comparison of the three copies kept in Shanghai, Taipei, and Changsha, a recent journal article published in 2019 has suggested that the Changsha copy is an imprint of a hitherto unknown third printed edition that contained the fewest mistakes and could thus be regarded as the earliest of the three surviving editions.[63]

Given this plethora of often conflicting data, where does the *qin* lie? With the Confucians or with those who loved music for music's sake? In fact, both viewpoints are simultaneously tenable. Many of the literati who played for their own amusement would have engaged at some level, maybe even successfully, with the imperial examination system. As strict Confucians for whom music was simply a tool of edification and statecraft, they would have naturally endorsed this perspective, yet the music they played breathes with limpid images from the natural world. It is precisely the mutual sustainability of both views as embodied in a single instrument that has formed the united contradiction at the heart of *qin* culture.

In either case, the *qin* represented a culture of the elite, but it was not the only instrument played in China, and the literati were not the empire's only inhabitants, even if they controlled most of the *qin*'s intellectual heritage. What instruments did the ordinary mortal hear and play for his or her entertainment and edification, and how have records of them survived against all odds? It is to one of these instruments, the *erhu*, and an entirely different wellspring, material in non-indigenous sources, that the discussion now turns.

Fig. 4.34 (previous spread): *Quxian Shenqi mipu* (*The Emaciated Immortal's Mysterious and Secret Scores*), *juan* 3, fols. 20r–20v.
Editor: Zhu Quan (1378–1448).
Date: Ming dynasty.
Woodblock: 22.9 × 15.8 cm.
Private collection.

Fig. 4.35: *Quxian Shenqi mipu* (*The Emaciated Immortal's Mysterious and Secret Scores*), preface, fol. 1r.
Editor: Zhu Quan (1378–1448).
Date: Ming dynasty.
Woodblock: 22.9 × 15.8 cm.
Naikaku Bunko, Kokuritsu Kōbunshokan (子65-4).

56. Zha Fuxi 查阜西, *Zha Fuxi qinxue wencui* 查阜西琴学文萃 (Hangzhou: Zhongguo meishu xueyuan chubanshe, 1995), 379–380.

57. Ibid. For Wang Liang's advertisement, see Chapter 2, Fig. 2.9.

58. Zha Fuxi, *Zha Fuxi qinxue wencui*, 579.

59. Guo Lixuan 郭立暄, *Zhongguo guji yuanke fanke yu chuyin houyin yanjiu* 中國古籍原刻翻刻與初印後印研究 (Beijing: Zhongxi shuju, 2015), vol. 1, 265, and vol. 3, 133–138.

60. For a facsimile of the Shanghai copy, see Wenhuabu wenxue yishu yanjiuyuan Yinyue yanjiusuo 文化部文學藝術研究院音樂研究所 and Beijing guqin yanjiuhui 北京古琴研究會, ed., *Qinqu jicheng* 琴曲集成 (Beijing: Zhonghua shuju, 1981), vol. 1, 95–170.

61. For a facsimile of the Taipei copy, see Zhongyang yinyue xueyuan Zhongguo yinyue yanjiusuo 中央音樂學院中國音樂研究所 and Beijing guqin yanjiuhui 北京古琴研究會, ed., *Qinqu jicheng* 琴曲集成 (Beijing: Zhonghua shuju, 1963), vol. 1, 69–144.

62. For photographs of the Beijing copy, see Yu Bing 俞冰, *Guqin shu tukao* 古琴書圖考 (Beijing: Xueyuan chubanshe, 2009), vol. 1, 5; and Anita Wong, ed., *Guyue fengliu: Zhongguo yuepu yueshu yueren* 古樂風流: 中國樂譜樂書樂人 (Hong Kong: University Museum and Art Gallery, The University of Hong Kong, 2001), 22.

63. Lü Zhuang 呂壯, "*Shenqi mipu* banben kao《神奇秘譜》版本考," *Yinyue yanjiu* 音樂研究 (2019) 6: 33–43.

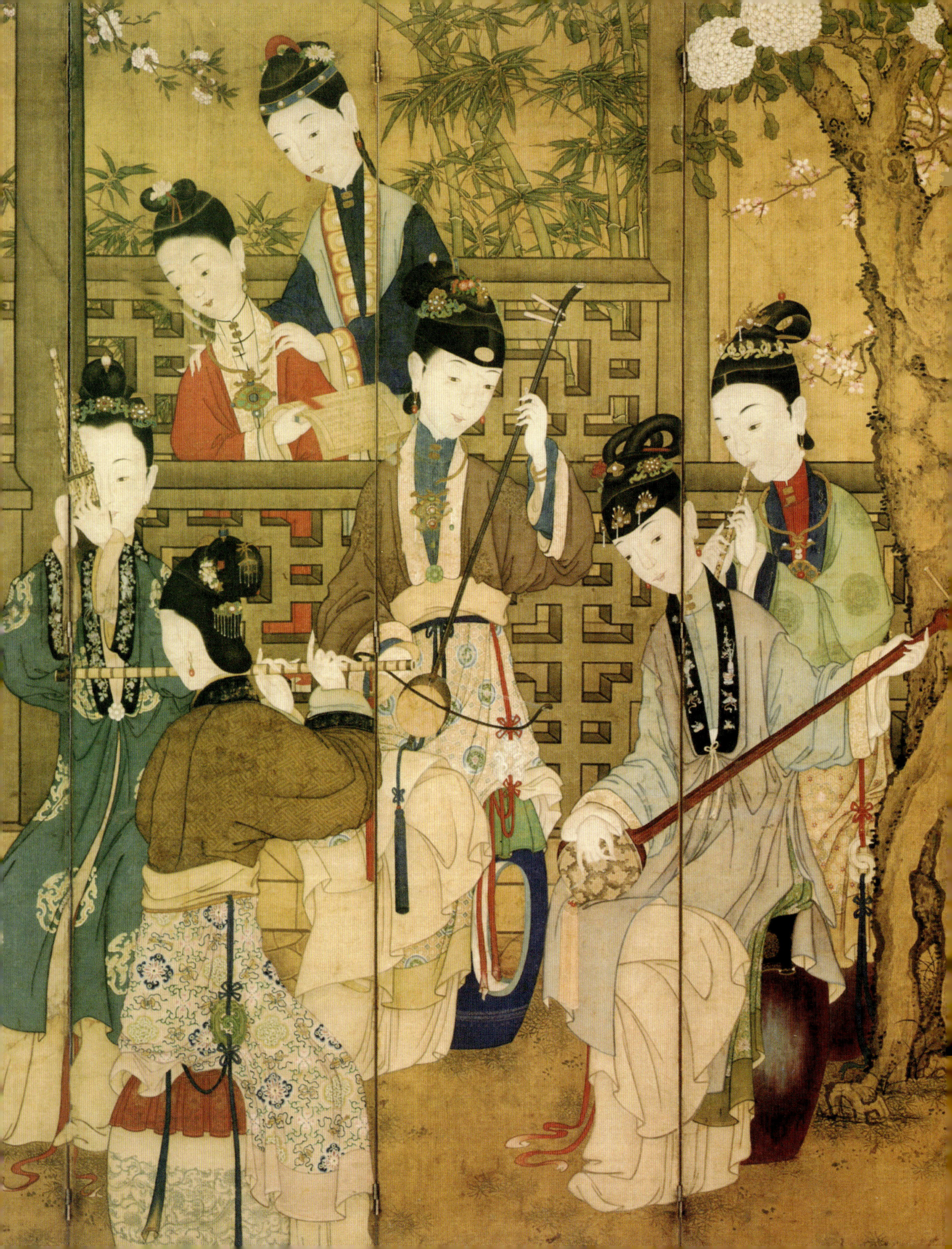

Chapter 5

Chinese Music through Western Eyes

Colin Huehns

Bowed instruments of the *erhu* 二胡 family, now known collectively as *huqin* 胡琴 (Fig. 5.1) and distinguished by placement of the bow-hair between the strings, first appeared in Chinese documents and iconography during the Song dynasty.[1] Up until the nineteenth century, information concerning their construction, playing technique, and role in instrumental formations and societal activities was comparatively scarce in indigenous sources. This could simply be because they were rare. Even so, such material as is available indicates they were associated with the rural poor, theatrical entertainers, "ladies of the entertainment industry," and beggars, and thus may have been deemed unsuitable for depictions commissioned by the ruling class or texts composed for their edification. Books in Western languages compiled and written by visitors to China, whose eyes were unsullied by such prejudices, are therefore an extremely useful supplement. This chapter concentrates on two late eighteenth-century texts in the Hong Kong University Libraries (HKUL) collection—one in French and the other English—that depict bowed Chinese instruments. Discussion will include the information that the texts provide, an assessment of their significance, and codicological details accounting for their presence in the collection:

Isadore Stanislas Helman, *Suite des Seize Estampes représentant les Conquêtes de l'Empereur de la Chine avec leur Explication*; Paris: chez Helman and chez Ponce, 1788 (ULB 769 944 H4).

George Staunton, *An Authentic Account of an Embassy from the King of Great Britain to the Emperor of China*; four copies are under the same classmark, as discussed further (U[LB] 951.074 S79 a [1797/1798]).

To give a context to this pair, four other texts in the HKUL collection are also touched on:

Giovanni Gonzalez di Mendozza, *Dell'Historia Della China*; Venice: Appresso Andrea Muschio, 1588 (U 915.1 G643a).

Jean-Baptiste Du Halde, *A Description of the Empire of China*; as will be discussed, three copies (ULB 951.3 D86 [1738/1741], and called *The General History of China* U 951 D86g [1739] and U 951 D86 [1741]).

John Barrow, *Travels in China*; London: for Cadell and W. Davies, 1806 (U 915.1075 B2).

G. T. Lay, "Musical Instruments of the Chinese," *The Chinese Repository*, vol. VIII (1839): 38–54 (US 951 C54 R4).

The modern *erhu*, the quintessential Chinese bowed instrument, is shown in Fig. 5.2. Formed of a cylindrical soundbox, often octagonal or hexagonal, it is wedged on the player's left upper thigh. Through the soundbox a spike passes that extends upwards. Two strings run from pegs at its far end that are gathered along the spike by a string loop or *qianjin* 千斤. The strings then pass over a bridge situated in the center of a python skin membrane on the front of the soundbox and a felt pad so as to absorb impurities in the tone; they are finally attached to the bottom face of a supporting wedge on which the soundbox rests. The bamboo bow is normally a straight stick slightly curved at either end and equipped with horsehair that is inserted between the two strings. It is drawn horizontally by the player's right hand with the stick resting on the soundbox. Left-hand fingertips press the strings, though there is no fingerboard. The wooden wedge on which the soundbox is mounted is a modern innovation

Fig. 5.1: Beautiful ladies playing the two-string fiddle *erhu*, the vertical end-blown flute *xiao*, the three-string lute *sanxian*, the transverse flute *dizi*, and the mouth organ *sheng* (detail).
Date: early eighteenth century.
Artist: unknown.
Dimensions: 220 × 268 cm.
After Christopher Bruckner, *Chinese Imperial Patronage: Treasures from Temples and Palaces*, vol. 2 (London: Asian Art Gallery, 2005), 62–63.

1. The Northern Song dynasty: 960–1127; the Southern Song dynasty: 1127–1279. *Yue shu* 樂書 (*The Book of Music*) by Chen Yang 陳暘 (1064–1128), *juan* 128 (folio numbers are not indicated), of which an edition published in 1347 (and perhaps an earlier one) survives, contains a picture of a *xiqin* 奚琴 that resembles a *huqin*, though no bow is depicted. The accompanying description mentions bamboo slips inserted between the strings as the means for causing them to vibrate and emit sound. This illustration is widely regarded by modern scholars as the earliest indication of *huqin* in China and its caption notes that the *xiqin* had come with the Xi 奚 people from Central Asia.

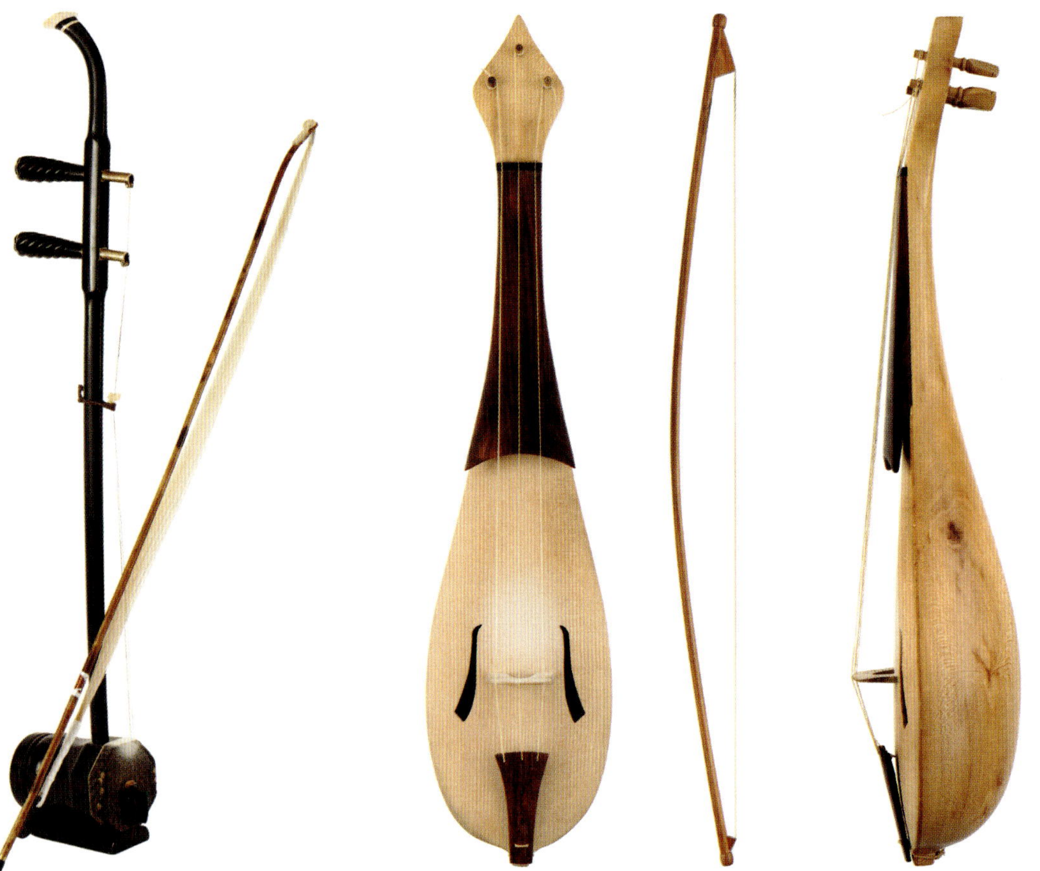

Fig. 5.2 (left): The modern *erhu*, a fine model of black rosewood from the workshop of Lü Jianhua in Beijing.

Fig. 5.3 (right): The rebec, a modern reconstructed model.

designed to weight the instrument down so that it sits more securely, and is absent on all historic specimens.

Dell'Historia Della China by Giovanni Gonzalez di Mendozza (1545–1618) is the oldest book in a Western language in the HKUL collection, and an Italian translation published in 1588 in Venice of the Spanish original of 1585. Juan González de Mendoza, his Spanish name, was an important ecclesiastical figure in the early period of Spanish rule of Latin America. He served as a bishop of several of the newly created dioceses of the region, yet apparently never set foot in China, so the sources for his information are all second-hand. Although unillustrated, his narrative reads with the freshness and vivacity of someone who has had a close experience with his subject matter, and with its Italian translation comprising 462 pages, it is a substantial text. A popular book and now commonly found in repository libraries of Europe and North America, an English translation by Robert Parke appeared soon afterwards in 1588, titled *The Historie of the great and mightie kingdome of China, and the situation thereof: Togither with the great riches, huge citties, politike gouernement, and rare inventions in the same.*[2]

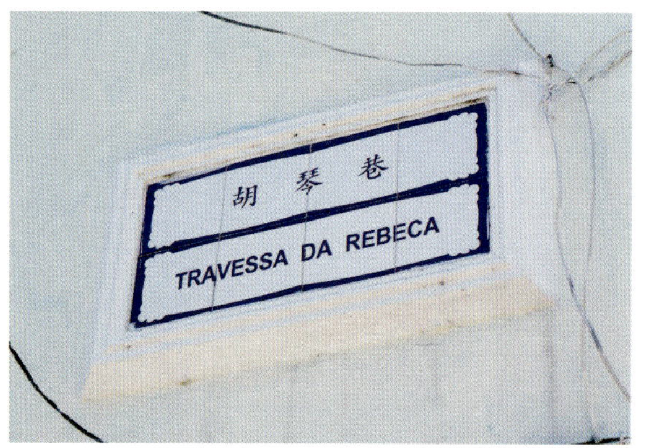

Fig. 5.4: Street name sign from the island of Taipa, Macau: Travessa da Rebeca ("Huqin xiang" or "*Huqin* Lane").

Three passages can be identified as possibly referring to bowed instruments that are found in the HKUL edition on pages 132–133 (Parke: 107–108), 250–251 (Parke: 207–208), and 266–267 (Parke: 221). Likely contenders for renderings of "*huqin*" among lists of instruments seen in Chinese ensembles described in the first two of these passages are given below for the Italian, English, and Spanish editions respectively. Particularly eye-catching is the recurrence of a term now normally rendered as "rebec."

Fig. 5.5: "A Plan of the City and Harbour of Macao" (detail). From *An Authentic Account of an Embassy from the King of Great Britain to the Emperor of China*, folio volume, plate 11.
Date: 1797.
Author: George Staunton (1737–1801).
Dimensions: 57 × 43 cm.
Hong Kong University Libraries (ULB 951.074 S79 a).

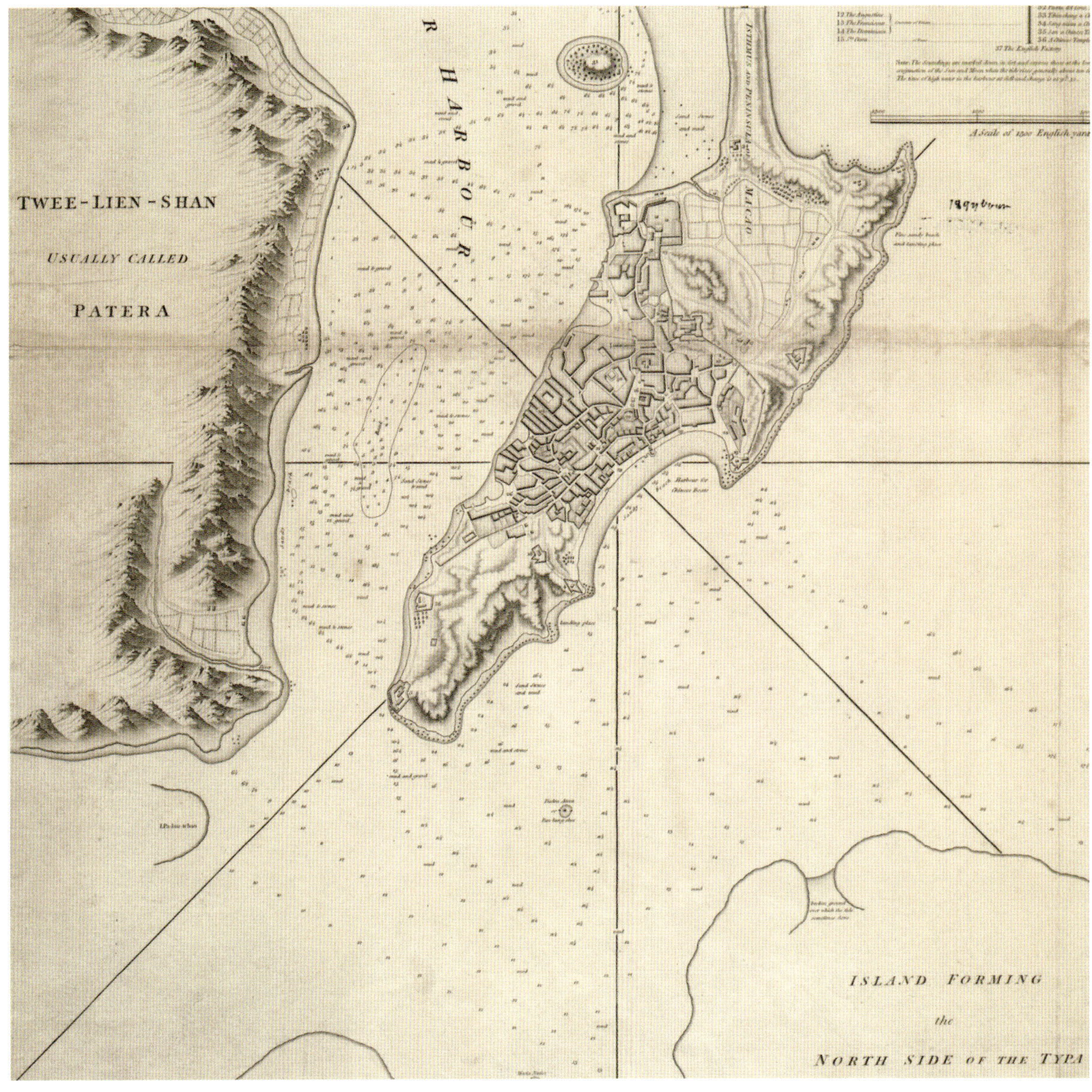

Italian	English	Spanish
first passage:		
violini	vyalles	duzaynas **raueles**
lironi	**rebukes**	
second passage:		
rebeche	**rebuckes**	**rabeles**

A plausible modern reconstruction of a Medieval or Renaissance European rebec is shown in Fig. 5.3. Especially noticeable are its three strings, pear-shaped resonating chamber, and a bow that is not inserted between the strings.

Surprising evidence supporting the hypothesis that the term "rebec" was used for *"huqin"* has unexpectedly come from an entirely different source. Several years ago, my first serious *erhu* student taking elective classes at the Royal Academy of Music, Hong Kong-born Jacqueline Leung, sent a photograph of the street name sign on the island of Taipa, Macau, that is reproduced as Fig. 5.4. It gives three Chinese characters 胡琴巷, which are translated into Portuguese (as is customary on such signs) as "Travessa da Rebeca" and could be rendered into English as *"Huqin* Lane."

"Erhu" as the name for the instrument in fact only attained currency in the last century, and before that the more generic *"huqin"* is commonly found

2. The frontispiece states that it was "Translated out of Spanish by R. Parke" and published in London "Printed by *I. Wolfe* for *Edward White*, and [copies of which] are to be sold at the little North *doore of Paules, at the signe of the Gun.* 1588." A facsimile of a Cambridge University Library copy with an accession stamp of "2 Jul 1973" has been reproduced as: *The English Experience: Its Record in Early Printed Books Published in Facsimile*, no. 522 (Amsterdam and New York: Theatrum Orbis Terrarum and Da Capo Press, 1973).

Fig. 5.6 (next spread): "The Procession of a Chinese Wedding when a Bride is brought home to her Husband." From *A Description of the Empire of China*, vol. 1, unnumbered plate opp. p. 303 (although the plate itself is labeled as opposite "p. 304," it is in fact opposite page 303).
Dates: 1738/1741.
Author: Jean-Baptiste Du Halde (1674–1743).
Artists: drawn by Antoine Humblot (?–1758), engraved by Charles Mosley (c. 1720–1756).
Dimensions: 40 × 25.5 cm.
Hong Kong University Libraries (ULB 951.3 D86).

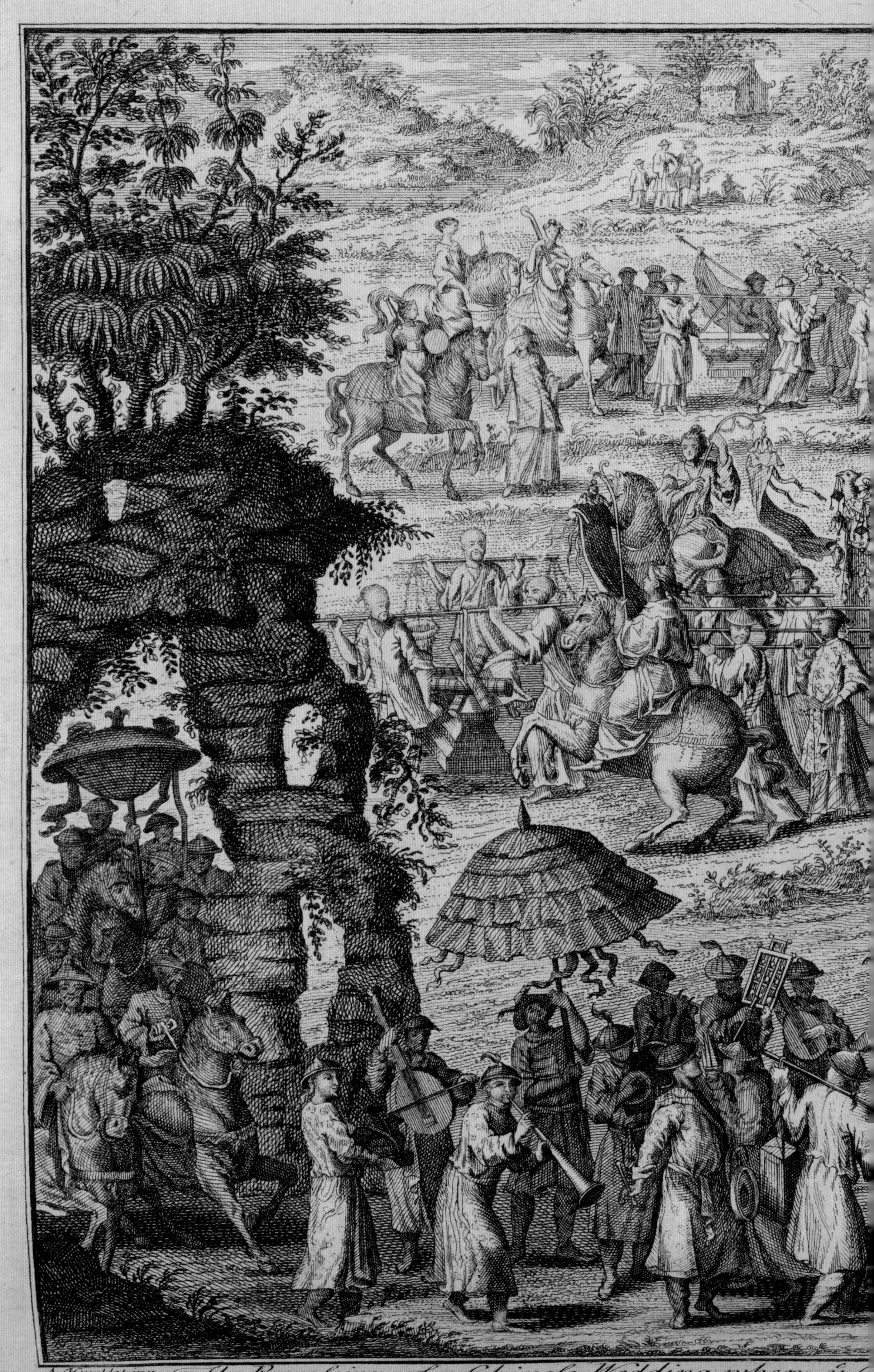

A. Humblot inv. The Procession of a Chinese Wedding when y^e

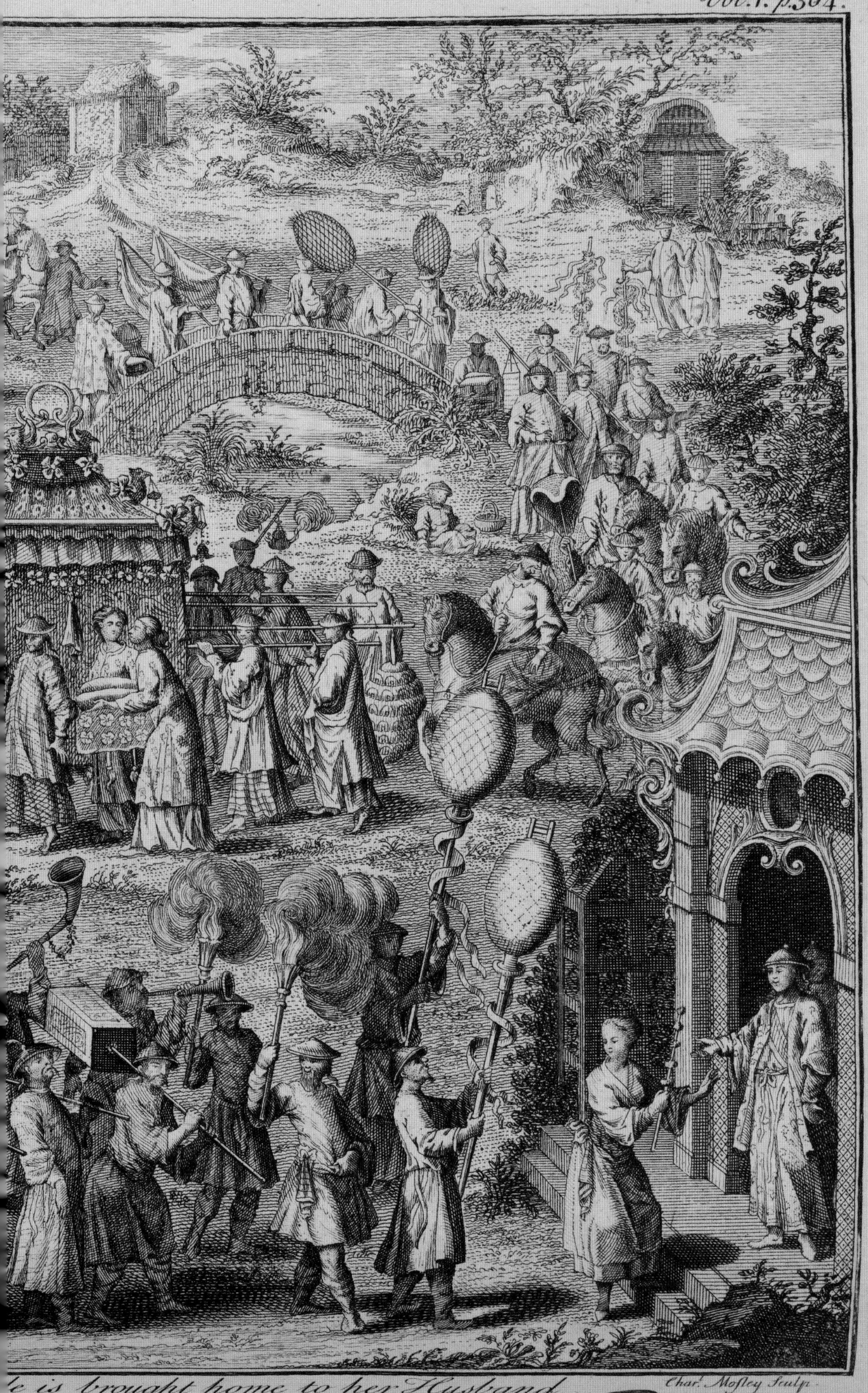

de is brought home to her Husband. — Char. Mosley Sculp.

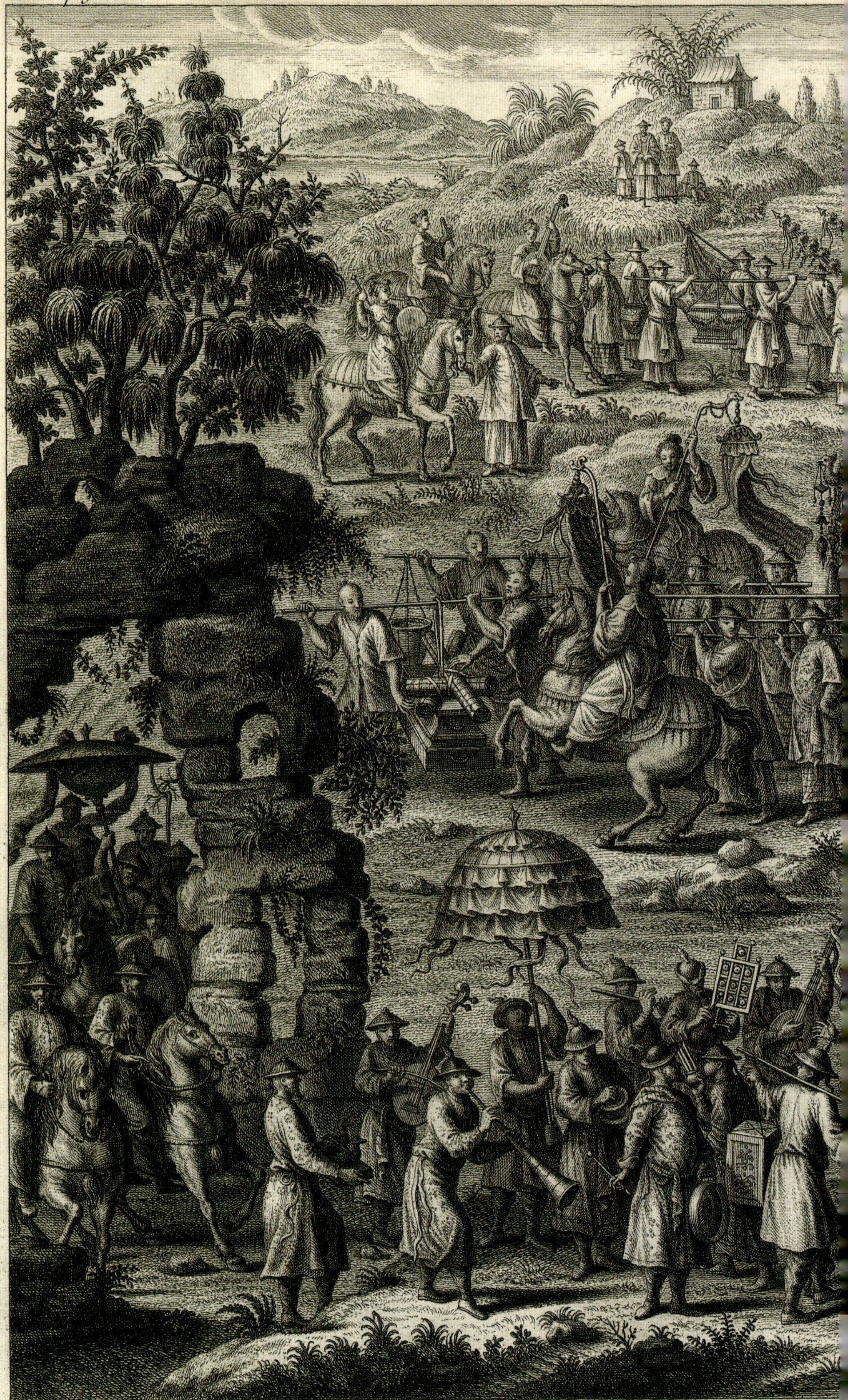

A. Humblot inv.

Nôce

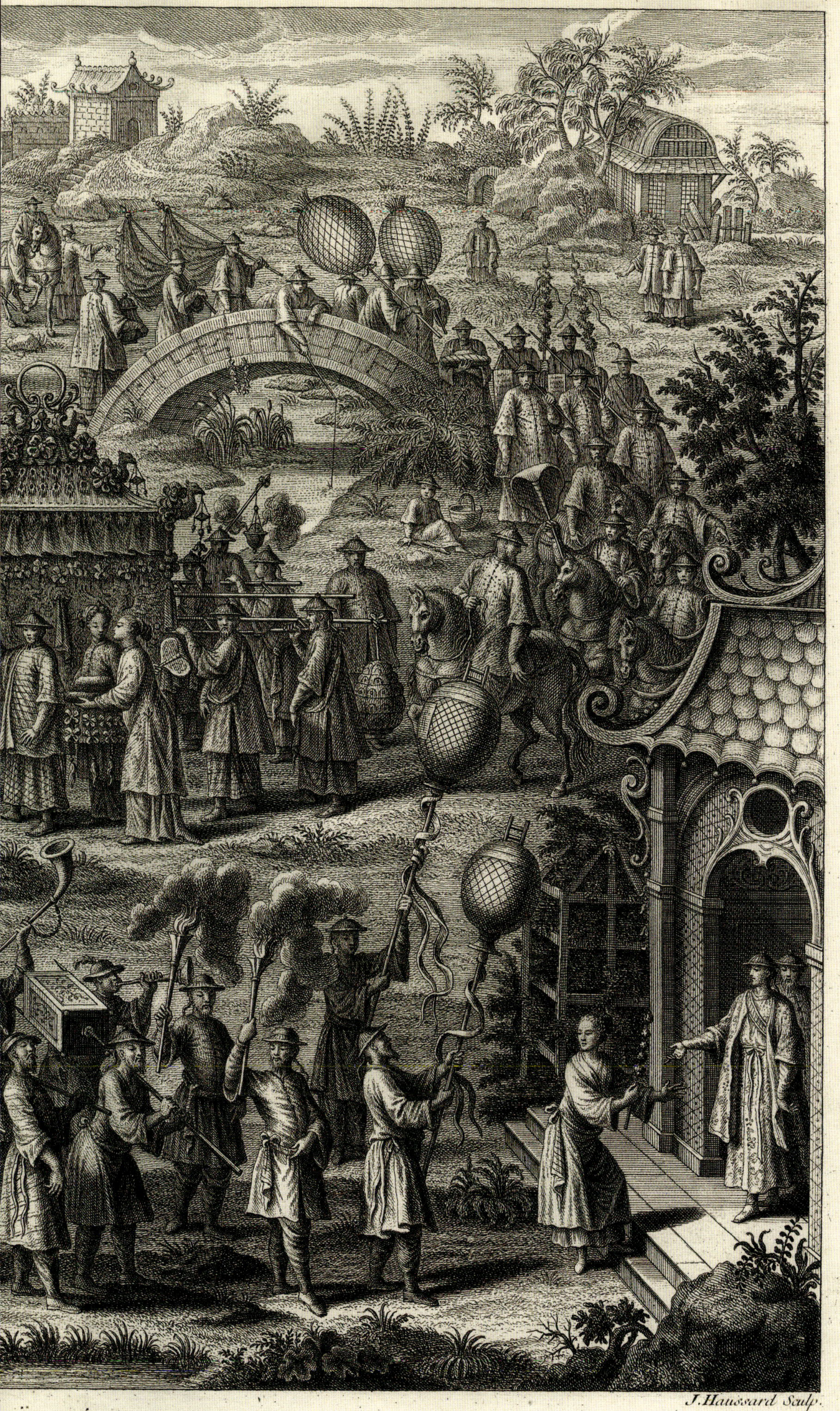

Fig. 5.7: "Nôce Chinoise." From *Description de l'Empire de la Chine et de la Tartarie Chinoise* (the original French edition), vol. 2, unnumbered plate between pages 120 and 121.
Date: 1735.
Author: Jean-Baptiste Du Halde (1674–1743).
Artists: drawn by Antoine Humblot (?–1758), engraved by Jean-Baptiste Haussard (1679 or 1680–1749).
Dimensions: 50.7 × 41 cm.
Private collection.

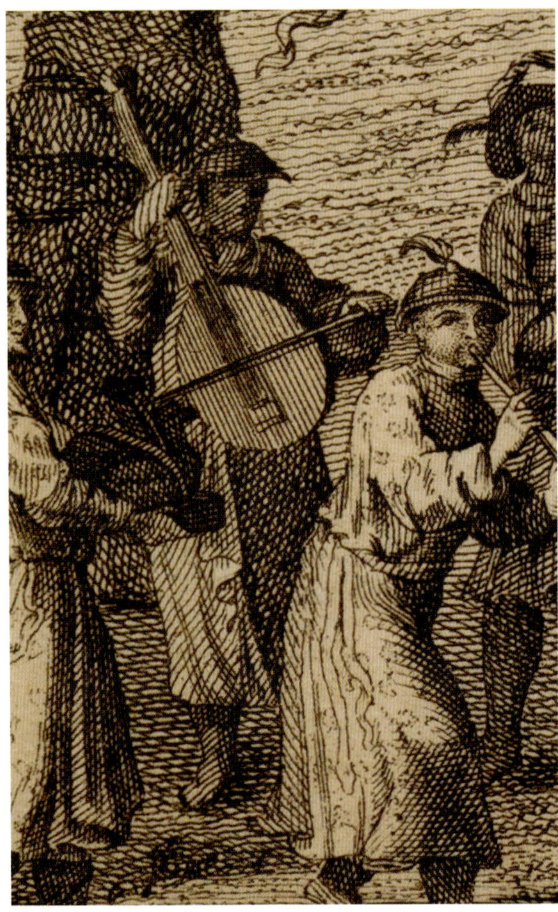

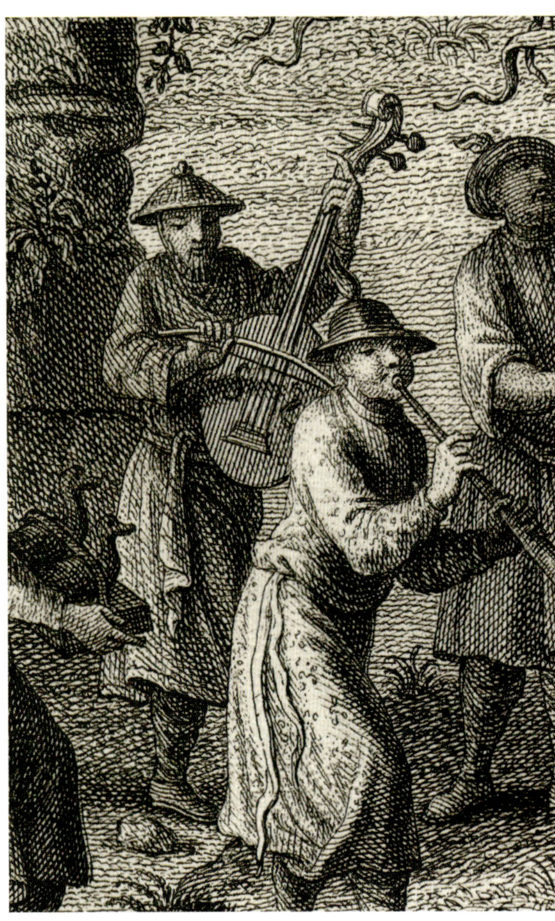

Fig. 5.8: Close-up of the *huqin* player in Fig. 5.6.

Fig. 5.9: Close-up of the *huqin* player in Fig. 5.7.

instead, though the latter term does not in itself specify which member of the family is intended. The third character of the sign 巷 (*xiang*) means "lane" in English or "*travessa*" in Portuguese. For "*huqin*," the translation into Portuguese is "*rebeca*." This choice is both intriguing and informative, given that the word "rebec" had largely disappeared from European nomenclature by the mid-seventeenth century with the demise of the instrument, superseded by the violin. Its presence here suggests that the original name for this street and its translation may be contemporary to the earliest history of Macau in the sixteenth century and the research that initiated Mendoza's text, which is why he also used the term. It is possible the obsolete term "rebeca" was once used in Macau Portuguese for "*huqin*."

In older quarters of both European and Chinese cities, streets are commonly named after the professions who lived and worked there, so perhaps the lane was once occupied by a workshop making *huqin* or well-known players (such as might have inhabited a house of ill repute). Taking the ferry to Taipa to investigate, I found the lane to be a small and sorry affair, ill-kempt and leading nowhere, but the architecture of the surrounding streets is old and vernacular Chinese in style, though probably impossible to date. Maps and histories of early Macau abound, but Taipa is not normally mentioned, and no other useful information has emerged. The maps that constitute plates 10 and 11 of George Staunton's *An Authentic Account of an Embassy from the King of Great Britain to the Emperor of China* (1797) include the island as "Typa," but do not indicate it as being inhabited (see Fig. 5.5).

Next in the chronological sequence, *A Description of the Empire of China*, first published in French in 1735 by Jean-Baptiste Du Halde (1674–1743), is an important subsequent history of China furnished with fine illustrations. Like Mendoza, Du Halde had also never visited China. In terms of the history of *huqin*, this text is of seminal importance because it likely contains the first depiction of an instrument of this type in a Western source—as is seen in Figs. 5.6, 5.7, 5.8, and 5.9—which reproduce the illustration as it occurs in the 1738/1741 large-sized English edition in the HKUL (ULB 951.3 D86; Figs. 5.6 and 5.8) and the French original (Figs. 5.7 and 5.9).

Fig. 5.10: The *erhu* bow-hold. The index finger curls around the stick, the second and third fingers press the hair to regulate its tension during performance, and the little finger hangs loose and has no function.

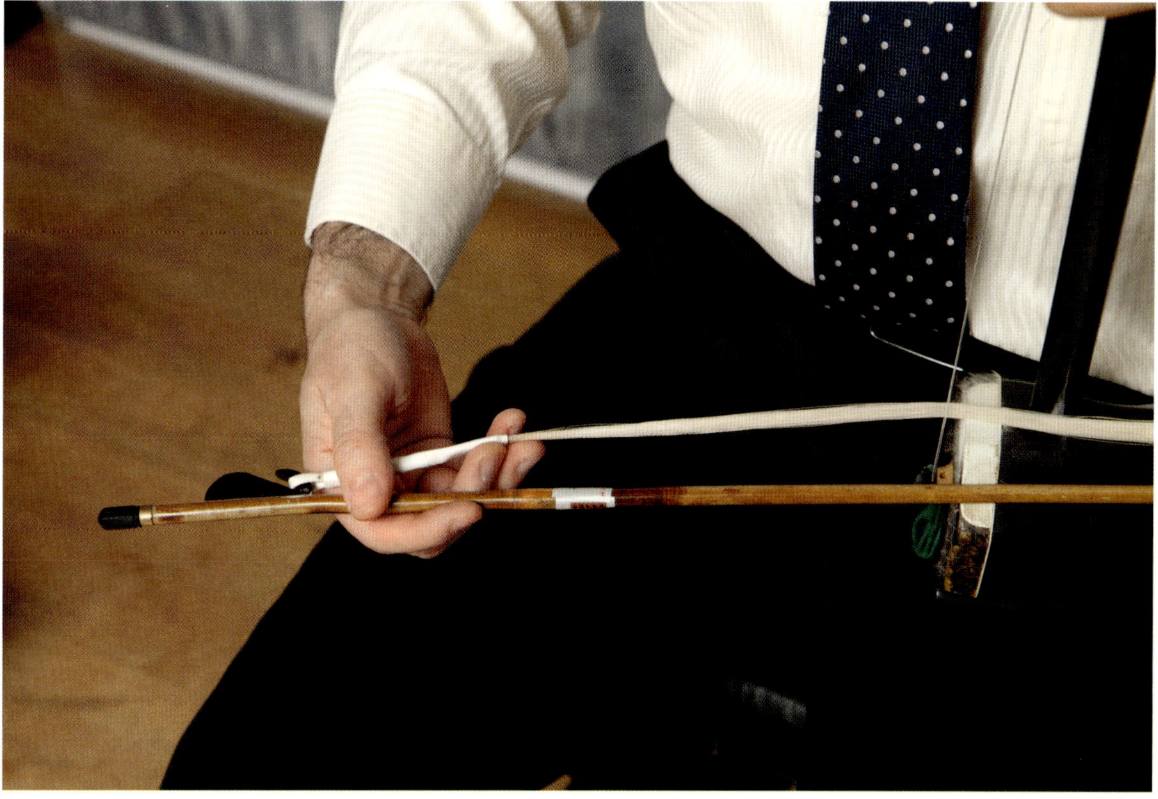

Whether this illustration actually represents a *huqin* is a moot point. The French original is a truly magnificent engraving that fills an entire double-page spread with a myriad of detailed and subtle shadings in a rollercoaster mix of Chinese custom and flagrantly European styles. Taking inspiration from generic eighteenth-century European landscape paintings, in authentic rococo fashion, the composition comprises a lengthy procession snaking like an inverted letter S from the background to foreground. Romantic foliage frames the entire image, while the horses depicted, one even leaping, are all the heavy steeds of European knights and not Mongolian ponies. Yet Chinese aspects are still present, for example, pagoda-like structures in the background, a circular arched bridge, the costumes worn by the gentlemen, and parasols. In the background, a lady mounted on a horse is plucking a stringed instrument, but the principal musical ensemble is in the foreground towards the front of the procession on the left of the picture. From left to right, the instruments are: *huqin*, *suona* 嗩吶, cymbals, side-blown flute, gong, *sheng* 笙, *yunluo* 雲鑼 bell-tree, plucked instrument, trumpet, and *suona*.

Is the bowed instrument a *huqin*? My contention is that in the context of the overall impact of the illustration, after peeling away the layers of prejudice implanted by among others "A. Humblot"[3] who drew the plate and "J. Haussard"[4] who engraved it, a *huqin* is intended, and a critical mass of the instrument's essential elements is indeed present to permit a case for this to be made. Referring to the photograph of an *erhu* in Fig. 5.2, Du Halde's specimen has the required characteristically round (or octagonal or hexagonal) soundbox and spike pointing upwards from it, albeit with the soundbox appearing disproportionately large. Crucially, there are two pegs, indicating two strings, and both pegs are on one side of the instrument rather than placed one on either side. The soundbox is correctly positioned next to the left hip, the spike held near-vertically with the left-hand fingers pressing the strings; no fingerboard, with or without frets, is suggested. Although played standing, such practice is common in historical depictions and photographs, and sometimes still found on the

3. "A. Humblot" is given as the drawer on the bottom left of the plate, that is, Antoine Humblot (?–1758). No evidence suggests he ever went to China, though it is possible; the original artist was probably a French Jesuit stationed in China at the time, of which there were many.

4. "J. Haussard" is given as the engraver on the bottom right of the plate, that is, Jean-Baptiste Haussard (1679 or 1680–1749).

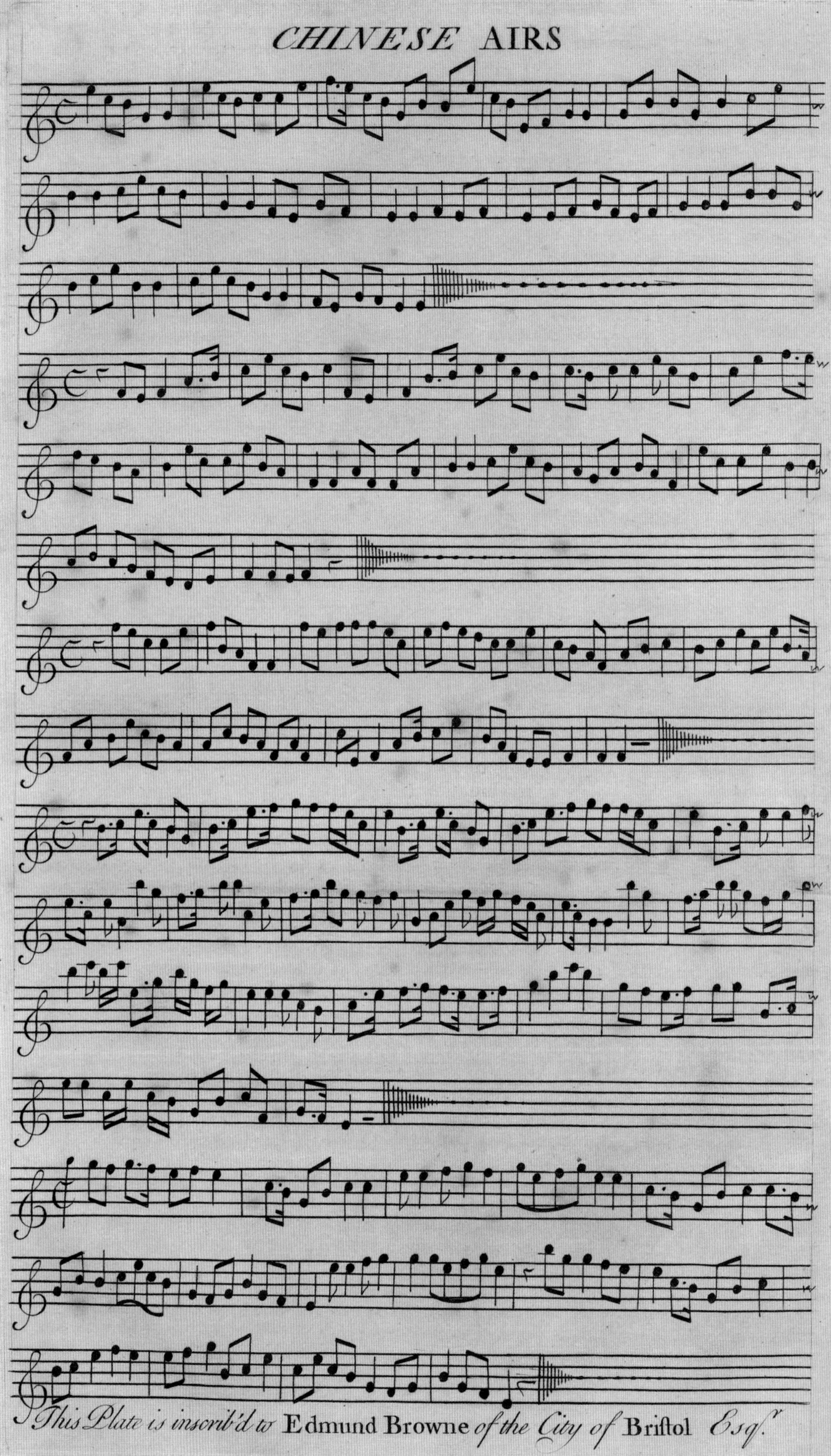
CHINESE AIRS
This Plate is inscrib'd to Edmund Browne of the City of Bristol Esq.r

Fig. 5.11: "Chinese Airs." From *A Description of the Empire of China*, vol. 2, unnumbered plate opp. p. 125.
Dates: 1738/1741.
Author: Jean-Baptiste Du Halde (1674–1743).
Artist: "This Plate is inscrib'd to Edmund Browne of the City of Bristol Esq." Edmund Browne cannot be traced.
Dimensions: 39.8 × 25.5 cm.
Hong Kong University Libraries (ULB 951.3 D86).

concert platform. Most importantly, the right elbow is held low and the forearm horizontal, as is customary with modern technique and the only possible way to play without producing a scratchy tone; by contrast, violin and cello bow-arms are now held much higher, though this is not the case when playing the viol. Notably, the bow evinces the strongly arched convex curve of surviving late eighteenth-century *huqin.*[5]

Arguing against this likelihood, the following can be cited: The two pegs are inserted into a scroll, in shape much like that of the violin, not a spike that tapers elegantly back as is normal on the *erhu*. At the other end and over the soundbox, the strings are wound onto a tailpiece, a component entirely absent on *huqin*, where traditionally they were bound to the spike as it emerged from the bottom of the instrument or on modern versions to the wedge positioned there. Largely because the soundbox is too big in Du Halde's illustration, the bow cuts the strings across it, whereas a crucial feature of *huqin* is that the bow rests on the soundbox so that it can stroke the strings at an angle such that they vibrate directly into the front plate, as this produces the most pleasing sound. Simply put: if the bow is not positioned above the soundbox, the hair cannot be between the strings and will stroke them so that they vibrate parallel to the front plate, as is the case on the violin or Mongolian fiddle (see Fig. 5.18). On *huqin*, whether the front face is python skin or a wooden plate, there are never any sound holes. The sound always emerges from the empty or latticed hole at the reverse of the instrument, yet on Fig. 5.9, there are two f-holes in the front plate, which also means it must have been made of wood. The left hand looks more like one used to play a guitar as it curls around the neck to play chords, whereas *huqin* technique requires it to be situated further forward so that the fingers can all point along the string. The right-hand bow-grip has all of the fingers over the stick, as is customary for the modern cello, whereas with *huqin*, one or more fingers (usually the second and third) pass under the stick so as to apply pressure directly to the hair and to regulate its tension in performance (see Fig. 5.10), a technique impossible with the fingers and thumb gripping the stick as is shown by Du Halde.

Sadly, the original drawings to all of those in Du Halde's book seem not to have survived.

Charles Mosley's engraved version in the 1738/1741 English translation (Figs. 5.6 and 5.8) is a reasonably faithful rendition of the French original, albeit occupying only one face of the large volume, whereas the magnificent French prototype spans the whole of two pages. Although somewhat cruder in execution, it is still finely carved, but crucially, all the players of bowed or plucked stringed instruments (including the *huqin* player) have had their bodies inverted and now bow or pluck their instruments with their left hands and finger it with their right. The round shape of the *huqin* has not been lost, however, and the bow still cuts the string perpendicularly as it should, though now right over the center of the soundbox. Some details have been omitted completely, such as the f-shaped sound-holes and scroll, though both, as has been discussed, are inauthentic to *huqin*; also, the two pegs cannot be discerned, so this defining characteristic has also been lost. In fact, the player's arms seem generically positioned in a flowing manner of playing, rather than the more cramped and convincing posture of the French original. All the other instrumentalists are present, and no other inversions have taken place.

Moving on to volume 2, in the section "Of the Skill of the *CHINESE* in the other Sciences" (pages 124–139) is an important subsection on music (pages 124–125), after those on logic and rhetoric, and before those on arithmetic, geometry, mathematics, and astronomy. It details Chinese musical instruments and practice more carefully than hitherto in non-Chinese sources, and also unprecedentedly quotes five Chinese melodies in Western staff notation that, in their pentatonicism, fluid melodic lines, and soft, graceful cadences, are recognizably Chinese (see Fig. 5.11).

Importantly in Fig. 5.11, the treble or G-clef is placed on the bottom line of the stave, making notes on this line G, a feature preserved from the French original. Unlike Chinese notation systems that often list a series of pitches, normally with no rhythmic arrangement explicit in the system, and

5. For example, *huqin* in the Edinburgh University Collection of Historic Musical Instruments nos. 435, 438, and 441. There is evidence that these instruments and others in the EUCHMI collection were themselves brought back by the British Embassy to China of 1792–1794 that is described by Staunton and Barrow in their books discussed here. Depictions of them may also be pictures 9 and 14 of Chinese album 27 in the John Rylands Library of the University of Manchester. See Colin Huehns, "Dating Old *Huqin*: New Research on Examples of pre-1949 Instruments in Three Major British Collections," *Journal of the American Musical Instrument Society* 28 (2002): 118–173.

They have the Largeness and Shape of
of a large candied Citron; they mix
er Meats which give them a good Re-
re is Corn in every part of *China*, and
n some Provinces, they generally live
ecially in the Southern Parts: They
f small Loaves, which are prepared in
in less than a Quarter of an Hour,
short; the *Europeans* bake them a lit-
terwards; they are very light, and ex-
: Also in the Province of *Chan tong*
nd of a thin Cake, which is pretty
when mixt with some sorts of Herbs
e Appetite.

se of a very simple kind of a Mill to
; it consists of a round Stone-Table,
ly like a Mill-Stone, on which they
inder to turn circularly, which by
the Corn.

most usual Drink, as I have already
s not hinder them from using Wine
y make it of a particular kind of
m that which is eaten; the Sale of
g the People; there are different
ways of making it, the following
heir Rice soke in Water, with some
which they throw in, for twenty or
they boil it, and when it is dissolved
nmediately ferments, and is covered
ike that of our new Wine; under this
Wine, which they draw off clear,
en Vessels well glazed; that which
a kind of Brandy of as strong as
sometimes stronger, and will sooner

make use of Wine at their Tables
rtain Places of great Reputation for
is in great Esteem, and the Good-
ness

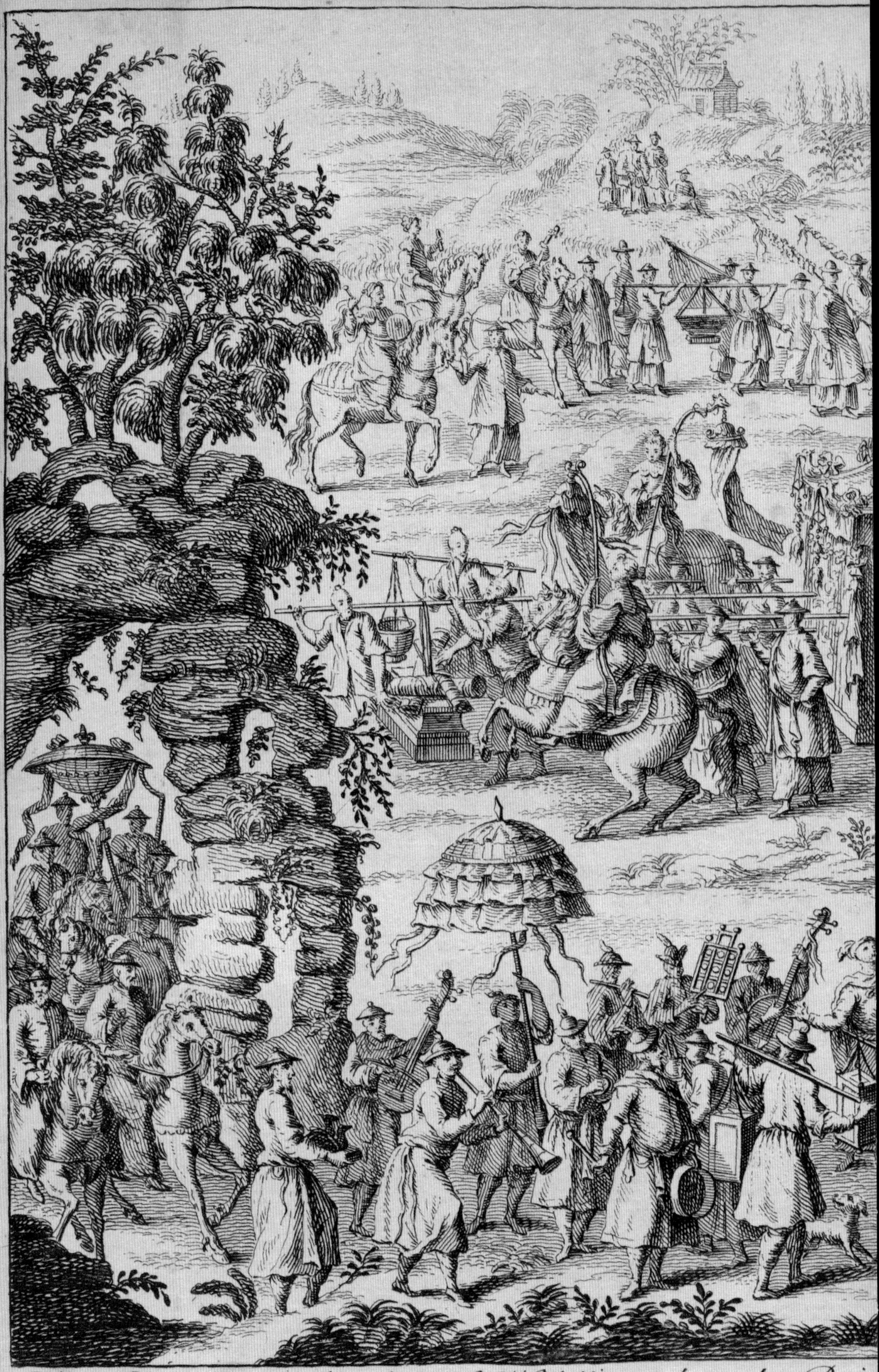

The Procession of a Chinese Wedding, when the Brid

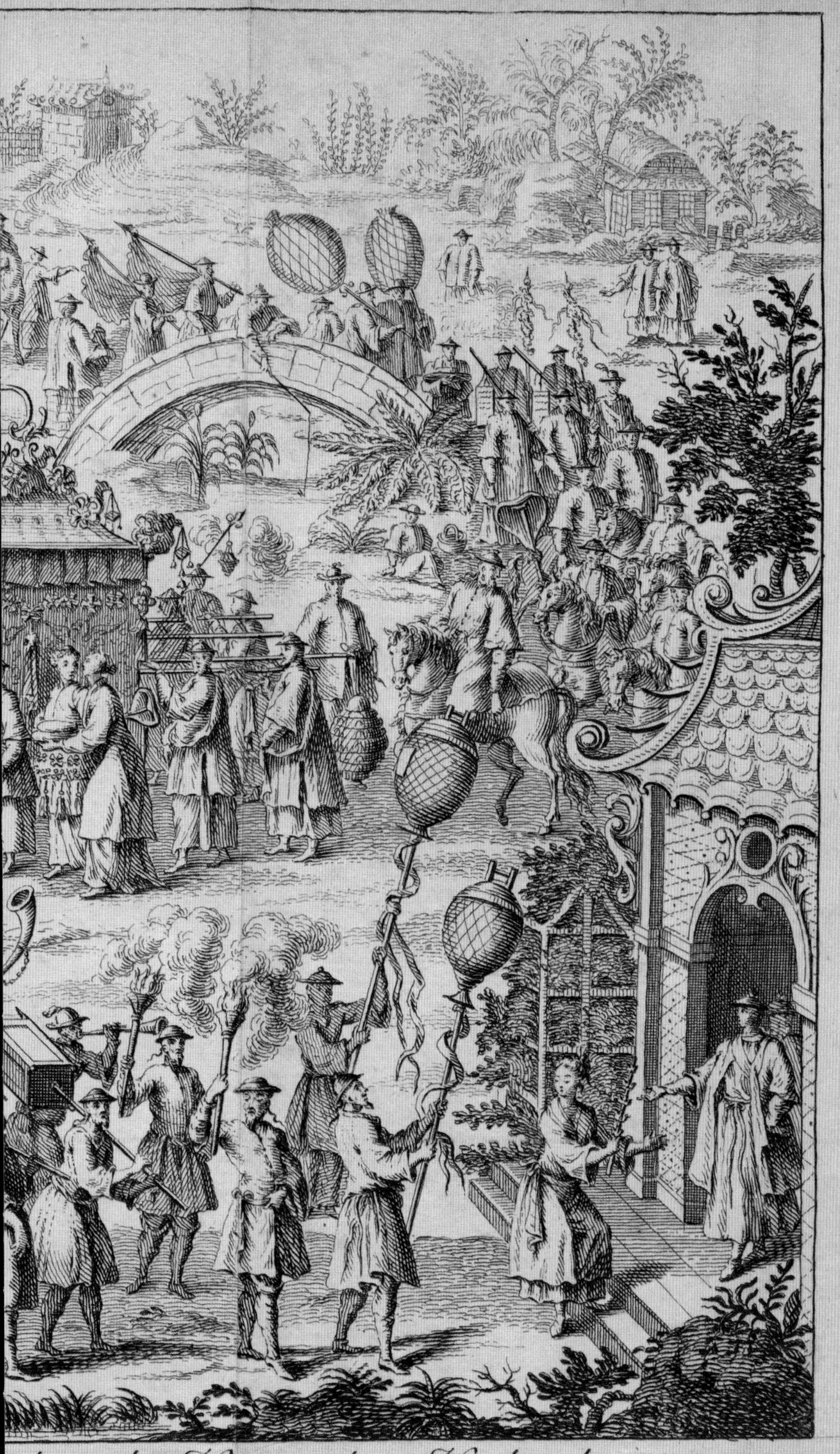

Fig. 5.12: "The Procession of a Chinese Wedding when a Bride is brought home to her Husband." From *The General History of China*, vol. II, pl. 8 opp. p. 202.
Date: 1739.
Author: Jean-Baptiste Du Halde (1674–1743).
No artists given.
Dimensions: 12.5 × 20 cm.
Hong Kong University Libraries (U 951 D86g).

CHINESE AIRS.

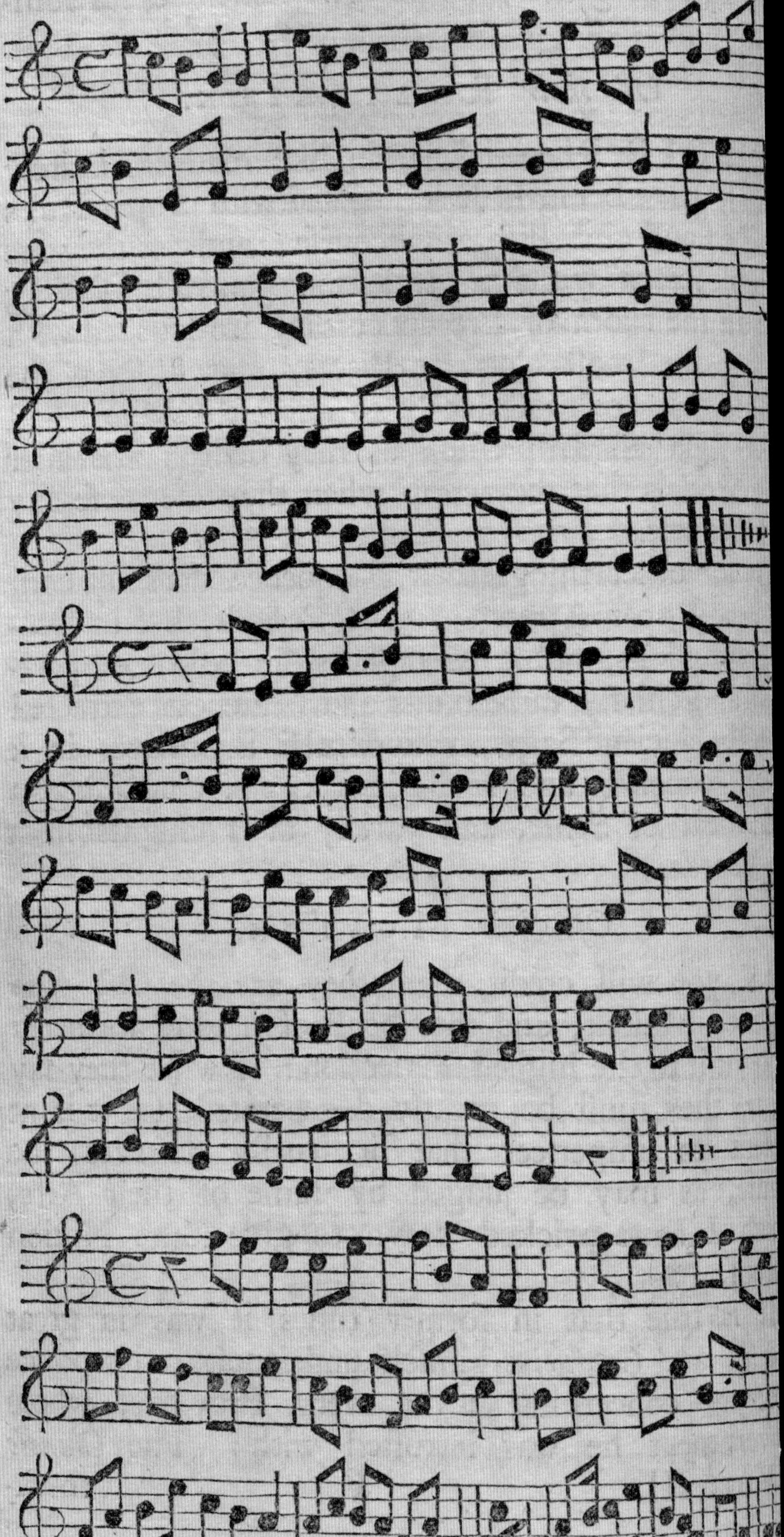

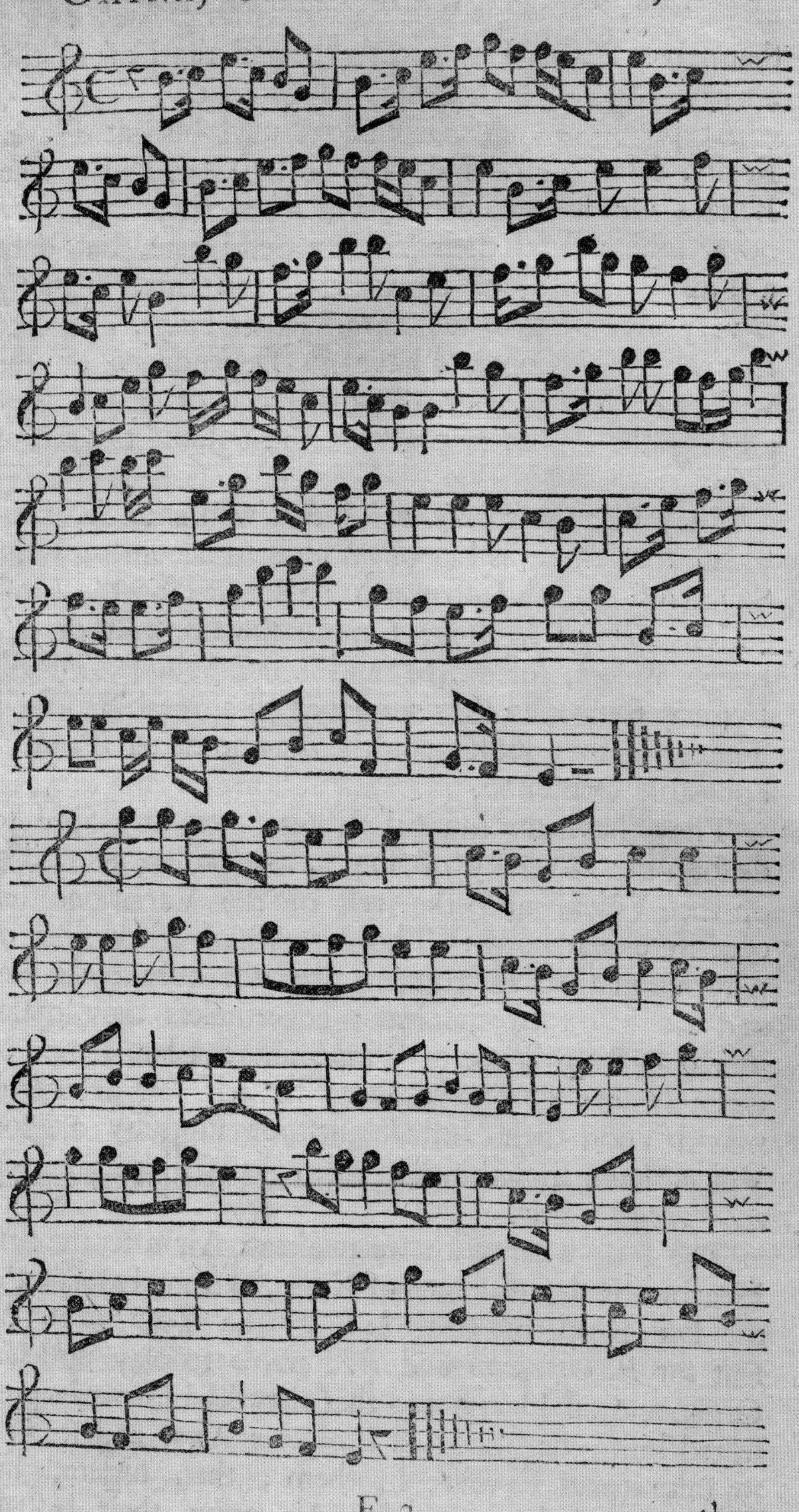

Fig. 5.13: "Chinese Airs." From *The General History of China*, vol. III, pp. 66–67.
Date: 1739.
Author: Jean-Baptiste Du Halde (1674–1743).
No artists given.
Dimensions: 12.5 × 20 cm.
Hong Kong University Libraries (U 951 D86g).

frequently not specifying octave transpositions, European staff notation details both rhythm and register effectively, and efficiently delineates the rise and fall of pitch contour visually on the page. Here, then, is a powerful record of Chinese melody in the early eighteenth century. Sadly, however, no concurrences between these five melodies and any in indigenous sources have been found. Du Halde also notes: "their Violins; each of which kinds has but three Strings, and is played upon with a Bow." "Three strings" is undoubtedly incorrect as *huqin* are normally equipped with two or four strings.

In a smaller-sized 1739 English translation of Du Halde's text held by the HKUL (U 951 D86g), titled *The General History of China*, the illustration of the wedding procession depicting the *huqin* is now a fold-out engraving (see Fig. 5.12) found between pages 202 and 203 of volume II. The players of bowed and plucked stringed instruments are no longer inverted; their instruments are held with their left hands and bowed or plucked with their right. Two pegs are clearly visible on the *huqin* as they are on the French original (Fig. 5.9), and likewise the position of the player's arms more closely resembles the posture depicted in that engraving, all of which suggests that it, and not the illustration in the 1738/1741 edition (Fig. 5.6), was the blueprint.

The musical examples are found on pages 66 and 67 of volume III and shown here as Fig. 5.13. Notably, the treble or G-clef has now been repositioned to its more usual modern placement so that the second line up is the note G. The note-heads themselves, however, remain in the same locations on the staff, which means that the semitones are all in the wrong places and the melodies are no longer in a framework plausibly anhemitonically pentatonic according to Chinese practice.

Moving into the late eighteenth century, Isadore Stanislav Helman (1743–1806 or 1809) was a distinguished French engraver who lived in Lille and Paris. His monumental *Suite des Seize Estampes représentant les Conquêtes de l'Empereur de la Chine avec leur Explication* is a set of twenty-four engravings, the first sixteen of which detail the principal events of Chinese efforts to pacify the area now known as Xinjiang in a series of campaigns of 1755–1759; the remaining eight are representations of imperial events. The latest date

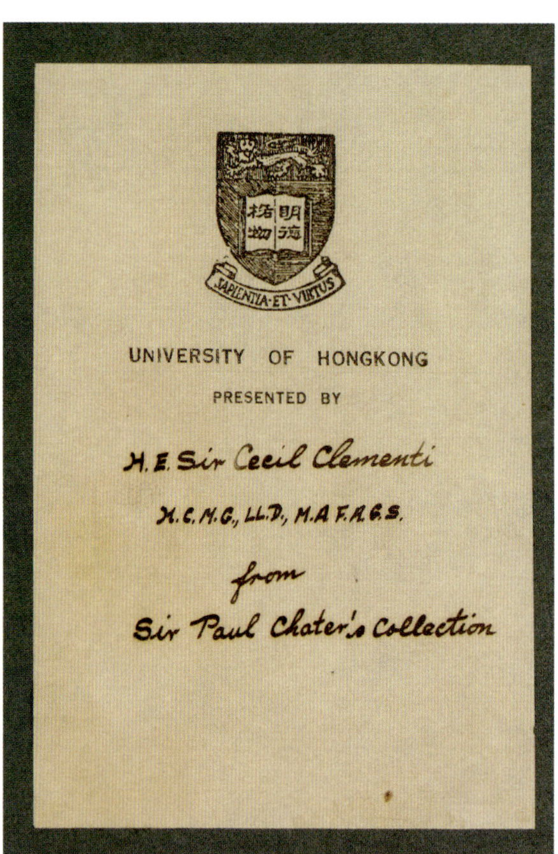

Fig. 5.14: *Suite des Seize Estampes représentant les Conquêtes de l'Empereur de la Chine avec leur Explication*, presentation label to the Hong Kong University Libraries at the opening of the book.
Date: 1784 (the book was issued in 1788).
Publisher: Isadore Stanislav Helman (1743–1806 or 1809).
Dimensions: 42 × 55 cm.
Hong Kong University Libraries (ULB 769.944 H4).

given on the illustrations themselves is 1788 (for example, no. XXIV, see Fig. 5.20), so this year can safely be taken as the date of final publication.

A large volume, the HKUL copy (U.LB 769 944 H4) probably retains its original brown leather bindings, and the title is embossed in gold down the spine. At the start of the book on the reverse of the front cover, the following label has been affixed (see Fig. 5.14):

University of Hongkong
Presented by
H[is]. E[xcellency]. Sir Cecil Clementi
K.C.M.G., Ll.D., M.A., F.R.G.S.
From
Sir Paul Chater's Collection

Sir Cecil Clementi has already been introduced in Chapter 3. A great-grandson of the celebrated keyboard player Muzio Clementi (1752–1832), he was an important British colonial administrator and fluent Chinese speaker. He served as the Governor of Hong Kong (1925–1930) and played an important role in the founding of the University of Hong Kong, writing the Latin words to the University anthem. Sir Paul Chater (1846–1926) was a businessman and collector of fine art. On his death, his collection was dispersed, but many items from it are found in the Prints and Drawings Department of the British Museum, as well as the Hong Kong Museum of Art. An accession date of June 11, 1927, for this volume's arrival into the HKUL collection is recorded on the reverse of the frontispiece. Turning over the first page, in the top right corner of the left face, virtually illegible in pencil, is written something resembling: **9/se/-**, which is most likely an abbreviation of the price requested by a dealer before it came into Sir Paul Chater's hands.

The volume contains twenty-four plates, as seems to be the case with all surviving copies of the book, for example, one held by the Department of Prints and Drawings in the British Museum.[6] The captions for plates I to XX are given in full on the frontispiece or contents page, with only slight and unimportant differences between the captions there and those on the pictures. The captions for plates XXI to XXIV are found only on the engravings, though the existence of these plates is mentioned at the bottom of the frontispiece.

The title of the volume is given on the frontispiece:

> *Suite des Seize Estampes représentant les Conquêtes de l'Empereur de la Chine avec leur Explication*
>
> (Translations into modern English are given here directly after the French originals.)
>
> *An Album of Sixteen Engravings representing the Conquests of the Emperor of China with Explanation thereof*

Following this, on the HKUL copy handwritten in black ink is "+ 8 foeuilles de Suplement" ["plus a supplement of 8 leaves"].

This phrase was perhaps penned by an early French dealer who wanted to stress that the album contained a total of twenty-four prints and that the title was misleading in this respect. In fact, this issue had already been partially addressed by a notice at the head of the page:

> AVIS, Les N^{os}. *XVIII, XIX et XX sont fait pour être rassemblés et ne former qu'une seule Estampe.*
>
> Notice: Engravings nos. XVIII, XIX, and XX are intended to be collated together and form a single engraving.

Fig. 5.15 (next spread): *Suite des Seize Estampes représentant les Conquêtes de l'Empereur de la Chine avec leur Explication*, engraving VIII.
Date: 1784 (the book was issued in 1788).
Publisher: Isadore Stanislav Helman (1743–1806 or 1809).
Artists: drawn by Ignatius Sichelbarth (1708–1780), engraved by Benoît-Louis Prévost (1735 or 1747–1804) and Isadore Stanislav Helman.
Dimensions: 42 × 55 cm.
Hong Kong University Libraries (ULB 769. 944 H4).

In the book itself, these three engravings, adhered together and folded inwards, represent a single procession.

On the frontispiece, immediately underneath is explanation of the provenance and rationale behind producing the volume:

> L'Année 30me. de son Règne l'Empereur de la Chine ***Kien-Long***, donna un Décrèt daté du 13. Juillet 1765 par lequel il ordonna qu'il seroit envoyé en France seize Dessins, des Victoires qu'il avoit remportées dans le Royaume de ***Chanagar*** et dans le Pays Mahometans voisins, pour être gravés par les plus célèbres Artistes. Ce Décrèt fut accompagné d'une Lettre de recommandation du Frere ***Joseph Castilhoni*** datée aussi de Pékin le 13. Juillet 1765 et addressée au Directeur des Arts, avec les quatre premiers Dessins: le tout fut remis à M^{r}. le Mis. de Marigny alors Directeur de l'Académie Royale de Peinture par. M^{r}. de Mery d'Arcy le 31. X^{bre}. 1766. Les autres Dessins arriverent l'Année suivante.
>
> In the thirtieth year of his reign, the Emperor of China Qianlong passed a decree dated July 13, 1765, in which he ordained that he would dispatch to France sixteen drawings of victories that he had won in the kingdom of Chanagar and the neighbouring Muslim countries in order for them to be turned into engravings by the most celebrated artists. This decree was accompanied by a letter of recommendation by Brother Joseph Castilhoni also dated in Pekin to July 13, 1765, and addressed to the Director of Arts, and included the first four drawings. All were delivered to Monsieur the Marquis of Marigny, then Director of the Royal Academy of Painting, by Monsieur de Mery d'Arcy on December 31, 1766. The other drawings will arrive the year after.
>
> La Direction générale de ces Gravures fut conftée à M. Cochin Secrétaire Historiographe de l'Académie qui employa à leur exécution huit Graveurs des plus connus en ce genre. Cet Ouvrage ne fut entièrement terminé qu'en 1774. et les Planches avec cent Exemplaires qu'on en tira furent envoyés à la Chine, il n'en fut réservé qu'un très petit nombre pour la Famille Royale et la Bibliothèque du Roi, ce qui a rendu cette suitte de la plus grande rareté.

6. Accession no.: 1877.0714.1505–1526.

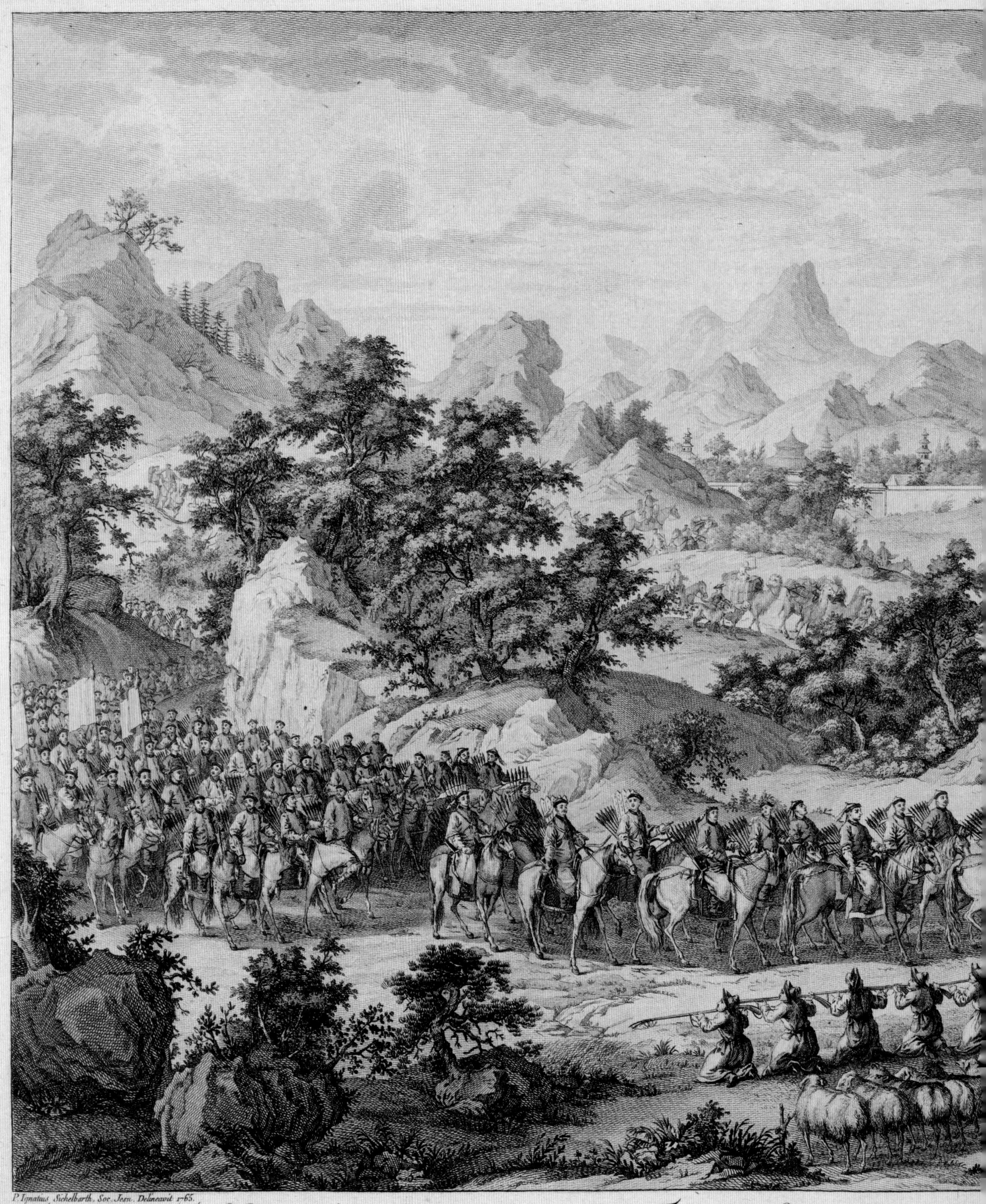

P. Ignatius Sichelbarth. Soc. Jesu. Delineavit 1765.

Fou-Té Lieutenant de Tchao-Hoei poursuit Amouv-Sana et reçoit les hommages et les Tributs de Ta-Ouan ou des hasacks que les Russes nomment C

Amouv-Sana se sauva chez les Russes, il y mourut peu-après de la petite vérole, ce qui mit fin à la mésintelligence que sa retraite avoit fait naître entre les

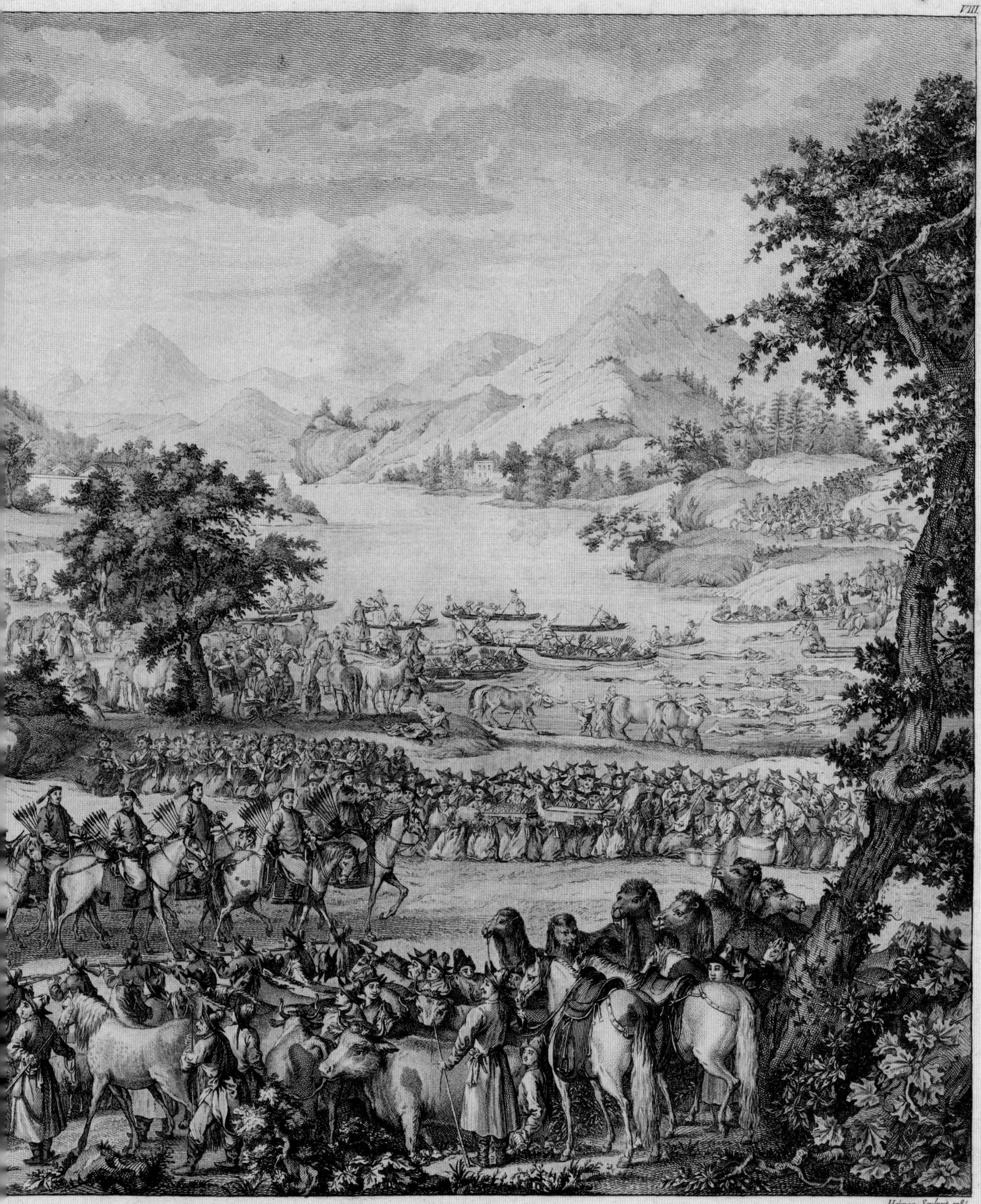

Helman, Sculpsit 1784.

x-Horda, et ceux des Pourouths des Tourgouths et de quelques autres Tartares formant en tout vingt hordes qui, jusqu'alors n'avoient en rien dépendu de l'Empereur.
virea)

The task of overseeing the engravings was entrusted to Monsieur Cochin, Secretary for Historiography at the Academy, who employed for the execution of this work eight engravers who were the most cognizant of the genre. This commission was only completed in its entirety in 1774, and the plates and a hundred examplars to accompany them dispatched to China, whilst only a very small number were retained for the Royal Family [of France] and the King's Library, which has rendered this album very rare indeed.

Ces Estampes portent 2. Pieds 9. Pouces de longueur sur 1. Pied 7. Pouces de hauteur: elles furent imprimées pour l'Empereur de la Chine et pour le Roi, sur du Papier fabriqué exprès; nommé Grand Louvois ayant 3. Pieds 4. Pouces 1/2. de longueur sur 2. Pieds 6. Pouces 1/2. de hauteur.

These engravings are 2 feet, 9 inches in length by 1 foot, 7 inches in height. They have been printed for the Emperor of China and the King on paper expressly fabricated for the purpose, called "Grand Louvois," which is 3 feet, 4-and-a-half inches in length, and 2 feet, 6-and-a-half inches in height.

Dans le distribution cy dessous, on a conservé, pour la satisfaction des curieux de ce genre, l'ordre des Noms des Missionaires Dessinateurs, et des differens Artistes qui ont concouru a l'éxécution des originaux.

In the composition of each engraving, below the illustration, have been preserved for the satisfaction of those curious as to their provenance, the names of the missionaries who drew the pictures and the different artists who collaborated with them in the execution of the original plates.

Joseph Castilhoni, normally known as Guiseppe Castiglione (1688–1766), Chinese name Lang Shining 郎世寧, was a Jesuit missionary and painter who spent most of his life in China. The Marquis of Marigny, whose name was Abel-François Poisson de Vandières (1727–1781), was an influential French nobleman and connoisseur of art and architecture. De Mery d'Arcy cannot be traced.

Plates I to XVI represent the original design of the album, that is, to celebrate the campaign and victories in Central Asia of 1755–1759, while the additional plates XVII to XXIV depict more general imperial subject matter. As given on the frontispiece, where dates are recorded, the drawings for plates I to XVI were executed in the 1760s, and four artists are cited: Jean Dionysius Attiret (plates I, XIV, and XV), Joannes Damascenus (plates II, VI, VII, XI, XII, and XIII), Joseph Castilhoni (plates III and V), and Ignatius Sichelbarth (plate VIII); plates IV, IX, X, XIV, and XVI are not ascribed artists. All four of these luminaries were Jesuit priests who had worked in China.[7] Where dates are given, these sixteen engravings were all cut between 1769 and 1774, and the craftsmen cited are: L. J. Masquelier (plate I), J. Aliamet (plates II and XV), J. P. Le Bas (plates III, V, XIV, and XVI), Augustinus de St. Aubin (plates IV and VII), François [?] Dionysius [?] Née (plate VI), B. L. Prevost (plates VIII and X), P. P. Choffard (plates IX, XI, and XIII), and N. De Launay (plate XII).[8] On the illustrations themselves, the names of these engravers have all been replaced by "Helman" and where dates are recorded, all are in the early 1780s.

On plates XVII to XXIV, which comprise the later tranche of the album, no artists are mentioned. All are given as engraved by Helman in either 1786 (XVII, XVIII, XIX, and XX) or 1788 (XXI, XXII, XXIII, and XXIV), which can be taken as the final date when the album was assembled. Plate XXI, titled "Fête Donnée aux Vieillards par l'Empereur Kien-Long" ["A Fête Given for the Aged by the Emperor Qianlong"], is specifically dated to February 14, 1785, so has a provenance some three decades later than the military campaigns relevant to the first sixteen plates.

Two of the twenty-four illustrations depict bowed instruments—VIII and XXXIV—and are reproduced here as Figs. 5.15 and 5.20, with Fig. 5.16 and Figs. 5.21 and 5.22 respectively presenting details of the ensembles of musicians in them.

The caption to engraving VIII reads:

VIIIE. ESTAMPE.

Fou-Té Lieutenant de *Tchao-Hoei* poursuit *Amour-Sana* et reçoit les hommages et les tributs de *Ta-Ouan* ou des Hasacks que les Russes nomment *Kosaccia-Horda*, et ceux des *Pourouths*, des *Tourgouths* et de quelques autres Tartares formant en tout vingt Hordes qui jusqu'alors n'avoient en rien dépendu de l'Empereur. *Amour-Sana* se sauva chez les Russes, il y

> mourut peu-après de la petite vérole ce qui mit fin à la mésintelligence que sa retraite avoit fait naitre entre les deux Empires.
>
> P. Ignatius Sichelbarth, Soc. Jesu. Delineavit 1765.
> C. N. Cochin filius, Direxit.
> B. L. Prevost, Sculpsit 1769

On the engraving itself, Prevost's name has been omitted and replaced by:

> Helman. Sculpsit, 1784.

> Engraving VIII
>
> *Fou-Té*, *Tchao-Hoei*'s chief lieutenant, in pursuit of *Amour-Sana*, receives the homage and tribute of *Ta-Ouan* or the Kazakhs that the Russians call *Kosaccia-Horda* and those of the *Pourouths* and *Tourgouths* and other Tartars that form in total twenty hordes that up until the present had never accepted the overlordship of the emperor. *Amour-Sana* had sought to escape with Russian assistance, but he died shortly afterwards of smallpox, which put an end to the discord that his retreat had engendered between the two empires.
>
> Drawn by Father Ignatius Sichelbarth of the Society of Jesus in 1765.
> Under the direction of C. N. Cochin, devout son [of the Catholic Church].
> Engraved by B. L. Prevost in 1769.

Ignatius Sichelbarth (1708–1780) was a Jesuit missionary and painter who spent most of his life in China, Charles-Nicolas Cochin (1715–1790) a prominent art critic, and Benoît-Louis Prévost (1735 or 1747–1804) a well-known engraver.

Among the kneeling assemblage in the background of the picture is a group of musicians. The apparel and especially the hats of the multitude surrounding them paying obeisance immediately suggests Central Asia and especially the northern nomadic nationalities the Kazakh and Kirghiz. Consisting of seven members, the band of instrumentalists comprises, from left to right, a bowed fiddle, a set of two small kettledrums, an end-blown flute resembling a descant recorder, a bass drum, two *suona*, and a pair of small clash cymbals. Similar ensembles of melody instruments accompanied by this pairing of drums are customary in outdoor Central Asian settings to this day. The artist has certainly observed his subject matter faithfully, and details that particularly attract the eye are the rows of pins that attach the drumskins to their resonating chambers, and the characteristic protruding perpendicular plates just below the mouthpieces of both *suona*, all of which indicate that Sichelbarth had first-hand experience of his subject matter.

Looking closely at the bowed instrument, it is pear-shaped rather like the rebec in Fig. 5.3, though it has a longer neck and fingerboard, and as the player is kneeling, it is supported on his lap. As far as can be discerned, the sound hole is circular, covered in a rosette-like lattice, and situated directly under the strings near the bridge. Four pegs are visible, so four strings implied, though only one is depicted. The player's torso is nicely erect yet leaning to one side as is typical of an instrumentalist making an effort to draw out the sound. His arms have a free and flowing appearance that suggests a high degree of expertise. Positioned over the soundbox, the bow-hair cannot be between the strings, so this is not a *huqin*. The bow itself is not quite perpendicular enough to cut the strings effectively, but otherwise, a plausible instrument and performing posture are portrayed. Even the hand shapes are keenly observed, with the first finger of the left hand reaching back to stop the string, while the second, third, and fourth extend along the strings, a deployment that resembles the *huqin* player in the French original of Du Halde's book (see Fig. 5.9). Sichelbarth's bow-arm has the low elbow required of an instrument held at the waist with the spike pointing upwards, and the bow-hold is even more accurately represented, with the index finger curled around the stick, the thumb resting on the stick, the second finger pressing the hair (the third is not visible), and the little finger hanging freely. If the third finger were to be pressing the stick too, this grip would be identical to the standard *erhu* bow-hold shown in Fig. 5.10, still more so as most players will sometimes release their third finger

7. Jean Dionysius Attiret, also known as Jean Denis Attiret, Chinese name: Wang Zhicheng 王致誠 (1702–1768); Joannes Damascenus, also known as Joannes Damascenus Salusti, Chinese name: An Deyi 安德義 (?–1781); Ignatius Sichelbarth, Chinese name: Ai Qimeng 艾啓蒙 (1708–1780).

8. Louis-Joseph Masquelier (1741–1811), Jacques Aliamet (1726–1788), Jacques-Philippe Le Bas (1707–1783), Augustin de Saint-Aubin (1736–1807), François Dionysius Née is untraceable, Benoît-Louis Prévost (1735 or 1747–1804), Pierre-Philippe Choffard (1731–1809), Nicolas De Launay (1739–1792).

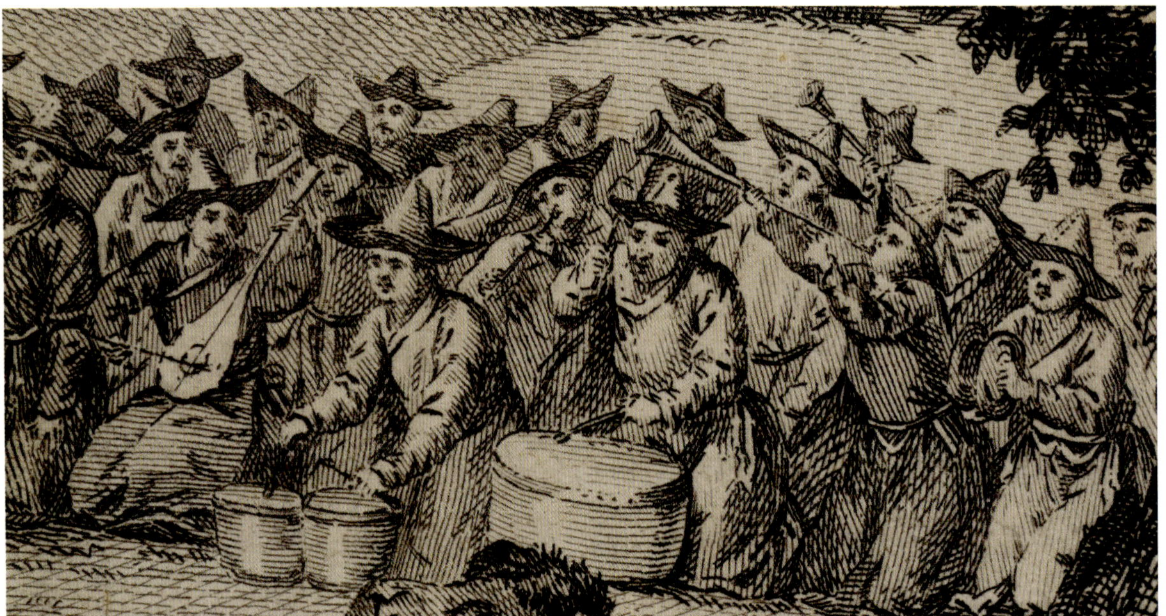

Fig. 5.16: Detail of musicians in Fig. 5.15.

from pressing the bow-hair, especially on down-bows.

A similar depiction of an ensemble of musicians is found on the roughly contemporary or slightly later export album watercolor leaf reproduced here as Fig. 5.17. It is labeled as coming from Jinchuan 金川, a Qing dynasty (1644–1911) geographical name that refers to the territory now known as northern Xinjiang. It is one leaf of a collection of twenty-four watercolors (whose accession numbers are given here), each showing a group of inhabitants of a different region of China or a neighbouring state, or various professions and activities. Of the surviving twenty-two watercolors (two are currently missing), six depict instrumentalists (marked with an asterisk below). On the bottom right corner of each picture are ink characters giving the subject of the picture. In the list below, after the accession number, these titles are recorded together with a translation in italics and information on any instruments depicted and other relevant details; in pencil, on the bottom left corner of the reverse of each picture, the same or similar titles are replicated, perhaps written by a Chinese dealer. These are given in square brackets where they differ.

1877.0714.1852 Missing
1877.0714.1853 行家相見茶客 [行家] *Tea Merchants Meeting Customers.*
1877.0714.1854 Missing
1877.0714.1855* 福建 *Fujian Province.* A pair of small clash cymbals, a small one-headed drum, a small gong, two large gongs; all accompanying an individual dancing with a staff; all those depicted are male.
1877.0714.1856 山西 *Shanxi Province.* An archer with male companions.
1877.0714.1857 杭州 *Hangzhou.* Beautiful ladies, children, and babies.
1877.0714.1858 廣東 [廣東舉(?) 子] *Guangdong Province* [*Raising a Family* or *Holder of the Juren Degree*]. Family group sitting around the dinner table; men and women.
1877.0714.1859 文官相見 *Meeting of Civil Administrators.*
1877.0714.1860 漁家 *Family of Fisherfolk.* Sewing nets.
1877.0714.1861* 陝西 *Shaanxi Province.* Six people are depicted, including a man holding clappers accompanied by a small boy, who are perhaps a storyteller and his apprentice; also, a hunter holding a long gun on which hang three dead fowls; and a beautiful lady with a little girl.
1877.0714.1862 蘇州 *Suzhou.* Two bird-sellers selling caged birds; two men, squatting, holding jars with crickets in them.
1877.0714.1863* 鳳陽 *Fengyang.* The instruments performed are a small two-headed drum, clappers, and gong; accompanying a girl dancing with a rod; the composition includes a monkey on a leash.
1877.0714.1864 北京 *Beijing.* Assemblage of eight beautiful ladies.
1877.0714.1865 習武 *Practicing with Weapons.* Archers shooting at a target, watched by onlookers; one holds a spear-like weapon, a *yue* 鉞.
1877.0714.1866 下操 *Military exercises.* Includes two mounted archers, two cannons being fired.
1877.0714.1308 皇帝出行 *The Emperor goes out on*

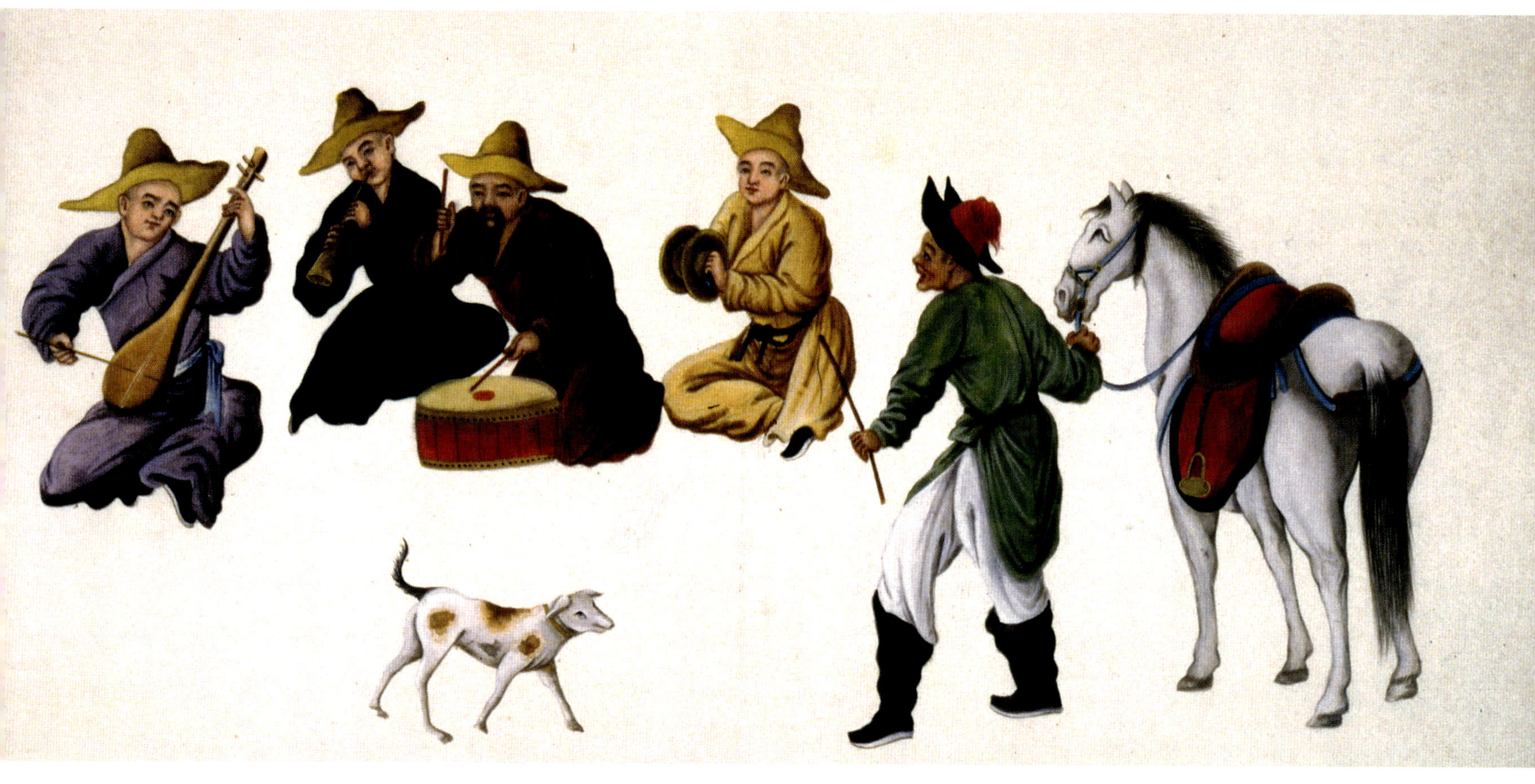

Fig. 5.17: *Jinchuan*.
Date: 1800–1831.
Artist: unknown.
Export watercolor album leaf: 48 × 36 cm.

Parade. The emperor, seated on a chair mounted on poles and held aloft by many servants; a group of literati counsellors are in attendance.
1877.0714.1309* 和尚 *Monks*. A group of seven shaven-headed monks, two playing respectively a small bell and a gong; a small boy, probably a peddler, in attendance.
1877.0714.1310 暹羅 *Siam*. Six people; five with "Indian" features and tonsured haircuts present boxes of gifts; the sixth looks "Chinese" and receives the gifts.
1877.0714.1311 回子 *Muslims*. A horse with its attendant indicates Central Asia. The two other men and two women depicted sport conical hats and hairstyles that indicate they are Muslims; one man has a beard.
1877.0714.1312* 金川 *Jinchuan*. (See below for description.)
1877.0714.1313 日本 *Japan*. Six men in kimonos and sandals, their hair in "buns" Japanese-style.
1877.0714.1314 滿州 *Manzhou*. Seven people are depicted, including three women who notably do not have bound feet. The hats worn by the men indicate they are of the Manzu race, and one man is holding a hawk.
1877.0714.1315 貓[苗]子 *People of the Miao Nationality*. Five women, some with baskets on their backs containing what appear to be tea leaves.
1877.0714.1316 廣東姑[?]女*[廣東長子] *Singsong Girls of Guangdong Province*. Four instrumentalists: *pipa* (man), *sanxian* 三弦 (woman), clappers (woman), and gong and woodblock (woman); these figures are recognizable as having been reproduced in other albums.[9]

Only four of the seven instrumentalists in the engraving are present in the watercolor: those playing the bowed fiddle, the end-blown flute, the bass drum, and the pair of clash cymbals. Of these, the flautist is blowing a *suona*. On the grounds of its date and the greater number of musicians depicted, the likelihood is that Sichelbarth's drawing and the engraving derived from it preceded the album painting, notwithstanding that it is a finer work of art with more sensitively realized facial expressions. Even so, the album painting has all the delicacy and grace of the more up-market late eighteenth- or early nineteenth-century export watercolors, and its precision of flowing contours indicates that it was executed by a Chinese hand trained initially in calligraphy.

9. Export watercolor albums often replicate pictures from other albums. See Colin Huehns, "Lovely Ladies Stroking Strings," *Music in Art: International Journal for Music Iconography* 28.1/2 (2003): 5–44.

Although the postures of the individuals depicted and the folds in their clothes are carefully molded in three dimensions—techniques learnt from Europeans—the four instrumentalists appear to be hanging in mid-air—a Chinese feature—rather than occupying a role in a unified composition as they do in Sichelbarth's masterpiece. The characteristic lack of perspective of the album leaf caused one of my students to remark acidly (and unfairly) that the dog in the foreground looked more like a cow.

The fiddle player in the export watercolor is seated cross-legged, not kneeling, and the soundbox has migrated to his right hip. This time, three pegs and only two strings are clearly visible. No sound-hole is shown on the front face, on which there is no pattern, so it is either wooden or a mammalian skin (not snakeskin). The strings are painted white, perhaps to indicate silk. No bridge is drawn, and the bow is virtually perpendicular to the strings. The left hands of both the engraving and the painting are nearly identical, though Sichelbarth's curled index finger is more convincing, and the fingers on the album leaf are not actually pressing the strings, but slightly to one side. The right-hand index finger of the album leaf instrumentalist is not curled around the bow-stick and instead presses the hair; the second and third fingers rest on the stick, and the little finger has no function and hangs in mid-air. This situation is the reverse of the *erhu* grip (Fig. 5.10) where the index finger is curled around the stick and fingers two and three press the hair, and thus an extremely unusual proposition. It is probably mistakenly drawn, but the overall lightness of touch of the fingers on the bow is a sensitive and lively representation of how an *erhu* or Central Asian fiddle bow is held. The four fingers bunched in close proximity resemble a grip when all four press the hair that can sometimes be seen in old photographs of the Mongolian horsehead fiddle in performance. For this reason, I use this technique to play my replica primitive horsehead fiddle, as is shown in Fig. 5.19.

Engraving XXIV (see Figs. 5.20, 5.21, and 5.22) depicts a much more formal Chinese context; indeed, with the emperor reciting poems to his ancestors, none could be more formal or Chinese, or indeed Confucian, even though the emperor himself was of the conquering Manzu race and not the Han majority.

XXIVE. ESTAMPE.

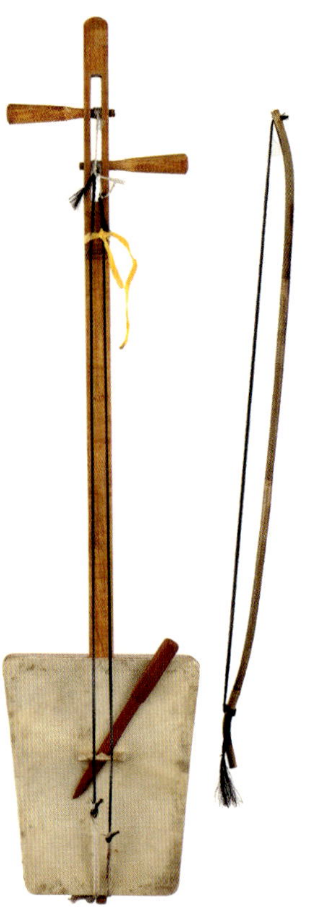

Fig. 5.18: A replica primitive horsehead fiddle from the workshop of Duan Tingjun in Hohhot.

L'EMPEREUR RECITANT DES POËMES EN L'HONEUR DE SES ANCÊTRES

La décoration de ce Monument, à peu près du même genre que celle de l'Edifice où se font les cérémonies religieuses, est cependant plus ornée tant à l'interieur qu'a l'exterieur. Les deux rangs d'Escaliers et les deux vastes Perrons qui y conduisent, sont destinés aux mêmes usages, c'est à dire à des hommages solemnels rendus par l'*Empereur* à la mémoire de ses Ancêtres, et qui sont à la Chine un des principaux devoirs du *Prince* et des Sujets. Cet Empire ne parait fondé que sur la piété filiale. Les Perrons sont revêtus du plus beau Marbre et décorés de pié-destaux portant des Symboles relatifs à l'Astronomie et aux Mathématiques, Sçiences cultivées de tems immémorial par les Chinois, et qui pourtant n'ont pas fait chez eux les progrès que cette antiquité semblerait supposer. Des Vases de Porcelaine remplis de fleurs, d'autres Vases de Bronze doré, où l'on brule continuellement des parfums, garnissent les autres pié-destaux. Tout ce Pavillon, nommé le **Tay-Ho-Tien**, est enrichi de dorures les plus precieuses et des plus rares vernis. L'*Empereur* assis sur son Thrône, et entouré des Grands de l'Empire, récite les Poëmes **Fou-Chou-Roun** et

Fig. 5.19: The bow-hold used for the primitive horsehead fiddle.

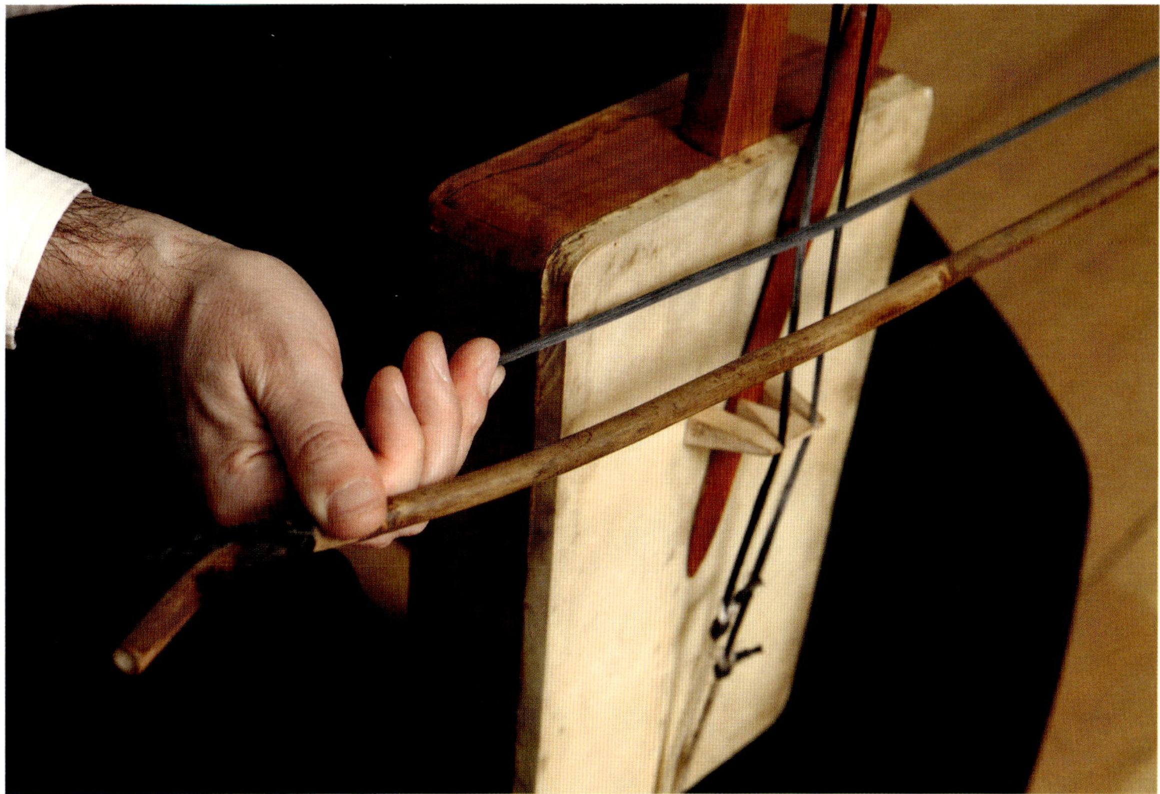

Fouki-Et-Choun. Les intervalles des lectures sont remplis par des Symphonies executées par deux troupes de Musiciens rangées aux deux côtes du Pavillon. La pompe imposante, la Majesté de cet appareil, le silence respectueux de l'Assemblée, tout concourt à donner à cette fête le caractère le plus auguste.

Helman, Sculp: 1788.

The Emperor Reciting Poems In Honor Of His Ancestors

The decoration of this building, close in style to that of an edifice where religious ceremonies take place, is nevertheless more elaborately ornamented in its interior than on its exterior. The two staircases and two vast flights of steps leading up to them are destined for the same usage, that is to say, solemn obeisances dedicated by the *Emperor* to the memory of his ancestors, which are, in China, one of the principal duties of the *Prince* and his subjects. The Empire seems to be founded only upon filial piety. The two flights of steps are clad in the finest marble and furnished with pedestals displaying astronomical and mathematical symbols, sciences cultivated from time immemorial by the Chinese, but which nevertheless do not convey to them the advancement that this antiquity is supposed to represent. Porcelain vases are filled with flowers, and other gilt bronze vases, where perfumes are ceaselessly burnt, grace the other pedestals. The pavilion, known as **Tay-Ho-Tien** [Tai he dian 太和殿 "The Hall of Supreme Harmony"], is richly adorned with gilts of the most precious and rare glaze. The *Emperor*, seated on his throne and surrounded by the Great of the Empire, recites the poems **Fou-Chou-Roun** and **Fouki-Et-Choun**.[10] Intervals in the peroration are filled by symphonies performed by two groups of musicians arranged on two sides of the pavilion. The imposing pomp, the majesty of the spectacle, and the respectful silence of those assembled, all combine to give the festival an august air.

Engraved by Helman, 1788.

Fig. 5.20 (next spread): "L'Empereur Recitant des Poëmes en l'Honeur de ses Ancêtres." *Suite des Seize Estampes représentant les Conquêtes de l'Empereur de la Chine avec leur Explication*, engraving XXIV.
Date: 1784 (the book was issued in 1788).
Publisher and engraver: Isadore Stanislav Helman (1743–1806 or 1809).
Dimensions: 42 × 55 cm.
Hong Kong University Libraries (ULB 769. 944 H4).

Zeroing in on the two groups of musicians, on the left are six individuals, but only three instruments are evident: a set of bells hung from a rack, a big bass drum, and a *guzheng* held vertically; this latter instrument is sometimes called a *yazheng* 軋箏 and

10. Discovering the original Chinese poems intended here has proved impossible.

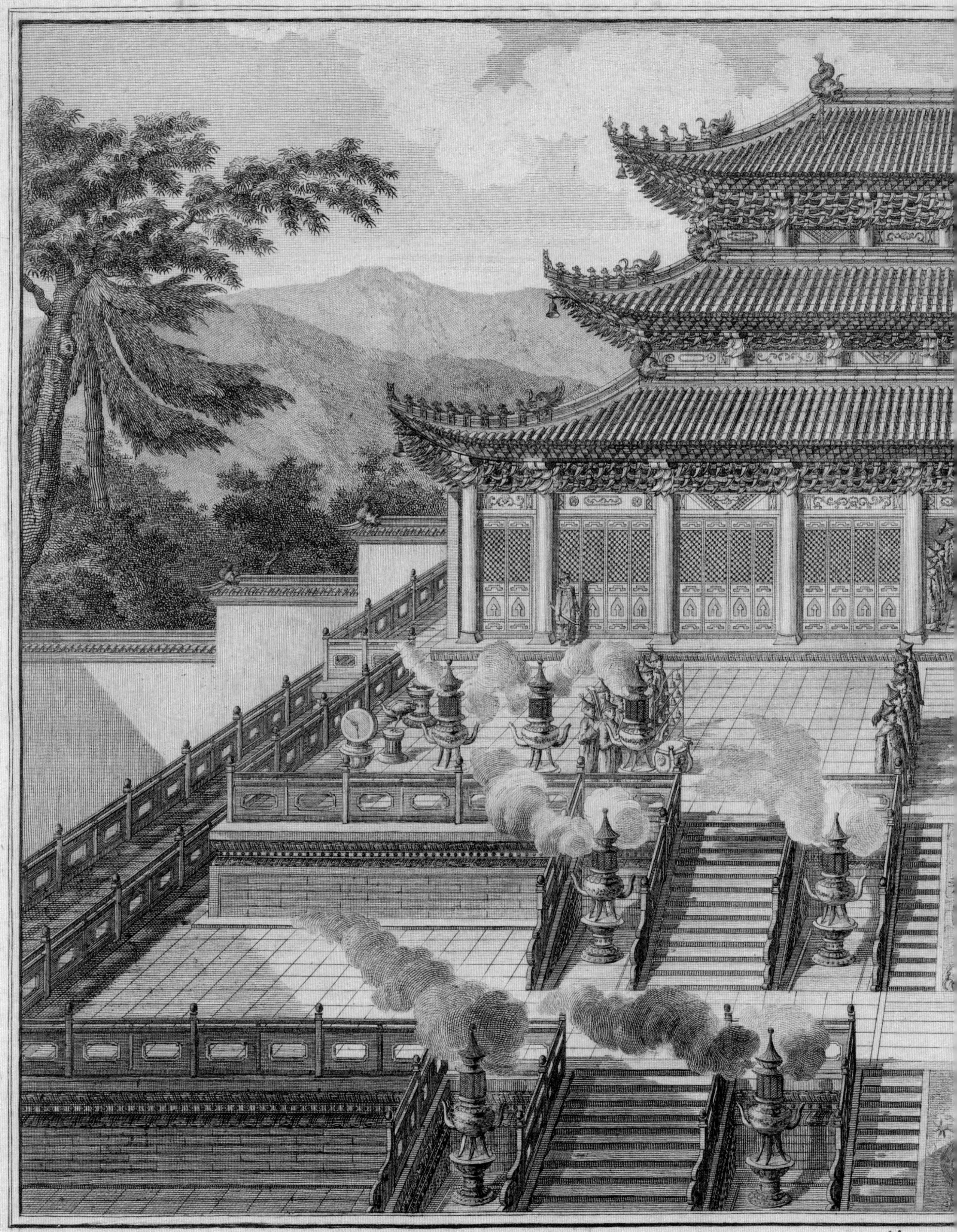

L'EMPEREUR RECITANT DES POËME[S]

La décoration de ce Monument, à peu près du même genre que celle de l'Edifice où se font les cérémonies religieus
-duisent, sont destinés aux mêmes usages, c'est à dire à des hommages solemnels rendus par l'Empereur à la mémoire a
Les Perrons sont revêtus du plus beau Marbre et décorés de pié-destaux portant des Symboles relatifs à l'Astronomie et a
antiquité semblerait supposer. Des Vases de Porcelaine remplis de fleurs, d'autres Vases de Bronze doré, où l'on brule c
les plus precieuses et des plus rares vernis. L'Empereur assis sur son Thrône, et entouré des Grands de l'Empire,
executées par deux troupes de Musiciens rangées aux deux côtés du Pavillon. La pompe imposante, la Majesté de cet app

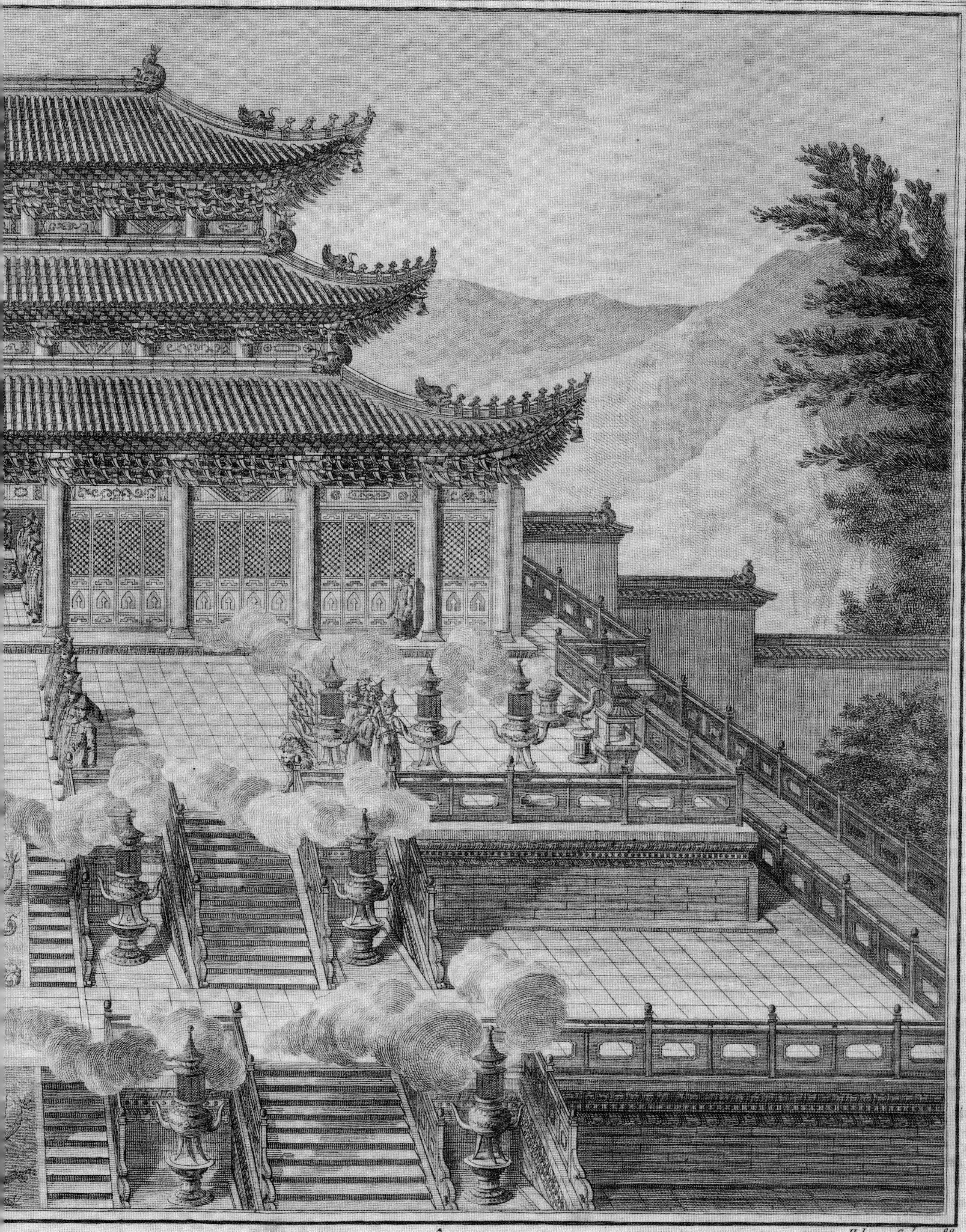

Helman, Sculp. 1788.

N L'HONEUR DE SES ANCÊTRES.

cependant plus orné tant à l'interieur qu'à l'exterieur. Les deux rangs d'Escaliers et les deux vastes Perrons qui y con-
ncêtres, et qui sont à la Chine un des principaux devoirs du Prince *et des Sujets. Cet Empire ne parait fondé que sur la piété filiale.*
hématiques, Sciences cultivées de tems immémorial par les Chinois, et qui pourtant n'ont pas fait chez eux les progrés que cette
lement des parfums, garnissent les autres pié-destaux. Tout ce Pavillon, nommé le Tay-Ho-Tien, est enrichi de dorures
s Poëmes Fou-Chou-Roun et Fouki-El-Choun. Les intervalles des lectures sont remplis par des Symphonies &
silence respectueux de l'assemblée, tout concourt à donner à cette fête le caractère le plus auguste.

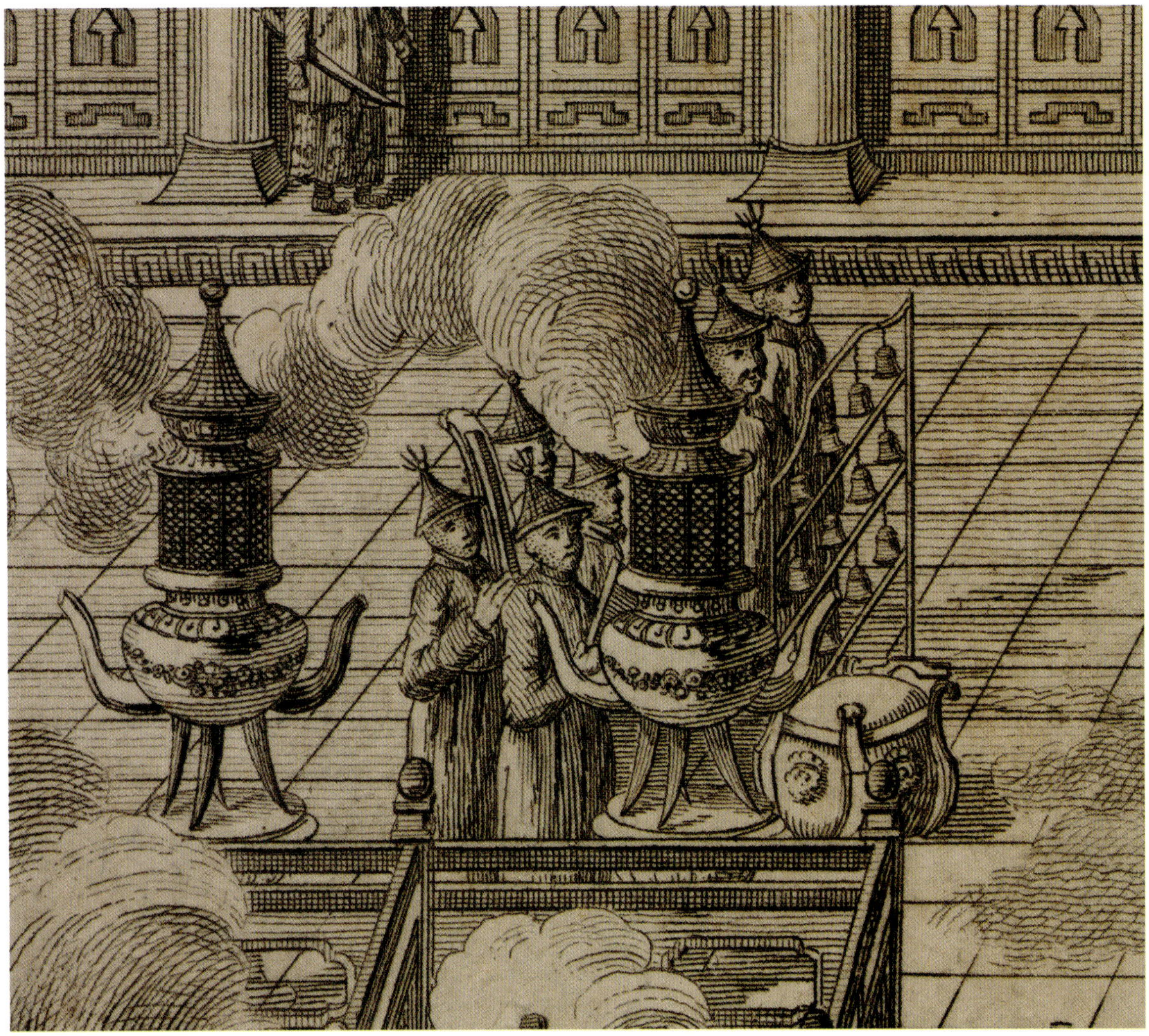

Fig. 5.21: Detail of the left group of musicians in Fig. 5.20.

is often struck with a small stick,[11] though none is visible here. Bell sets such as these must rank as the most ancient and Confucian of instruments, and thus are uniquely appropriate for ancestor worship. The group of musicians on the right comprises five people, but only two musical instruments—another set of bells hung on a rack and a hand-held fiddle clearly played with a bow. Its soundbox and vertical spike make a *huqin* or horsehead fiddle the most likely candidates, and both are equally possible. The instrument is played standing, as *huqin* can be, though no historic image survives of a horsehead fiddle played in this manner, and all modern players perform seated. As with some of the Du Halde depictions discussed earlier, this individual has also been inverted so that the instrument is held in his right hand and bowed with his left.

The soundbox is square in shape with a slight waist, and sound-holes are clearly visible on its front, the latter a feature of neither *huqin* nor historic horsehead fiddles (which were usually skin-fronted); both of these instruments have their sound-holes at the back, opposite the front face. Unlike an *erhu* soundbox, which is comparatively long and cylindrical (see Fig. 5.2), here it is shallow, as is normal for the horsehead fiddle (see Fig. 5.18). The bow passes across it, which means that the hair cannot be between the strings, as is the case with *huqin* but not the modern horsehead fiddle, though is seen in some historic photographs. Two pegs can be discerned, one on either side of the spike, a feature of the horsehead fiddle but not normally of *huqin* where the pegs are ordinarily parallel to each other, either pointing backwards or sideways. Two strings are clearly visible, as is commonly the case with *huqin* and the horsehead fiddle, though mainstream historic and modern *huqin* are sometimes equipped with four strings.

Fig. 5.22: Detail of the right group of musicians in Fig. 5.20.

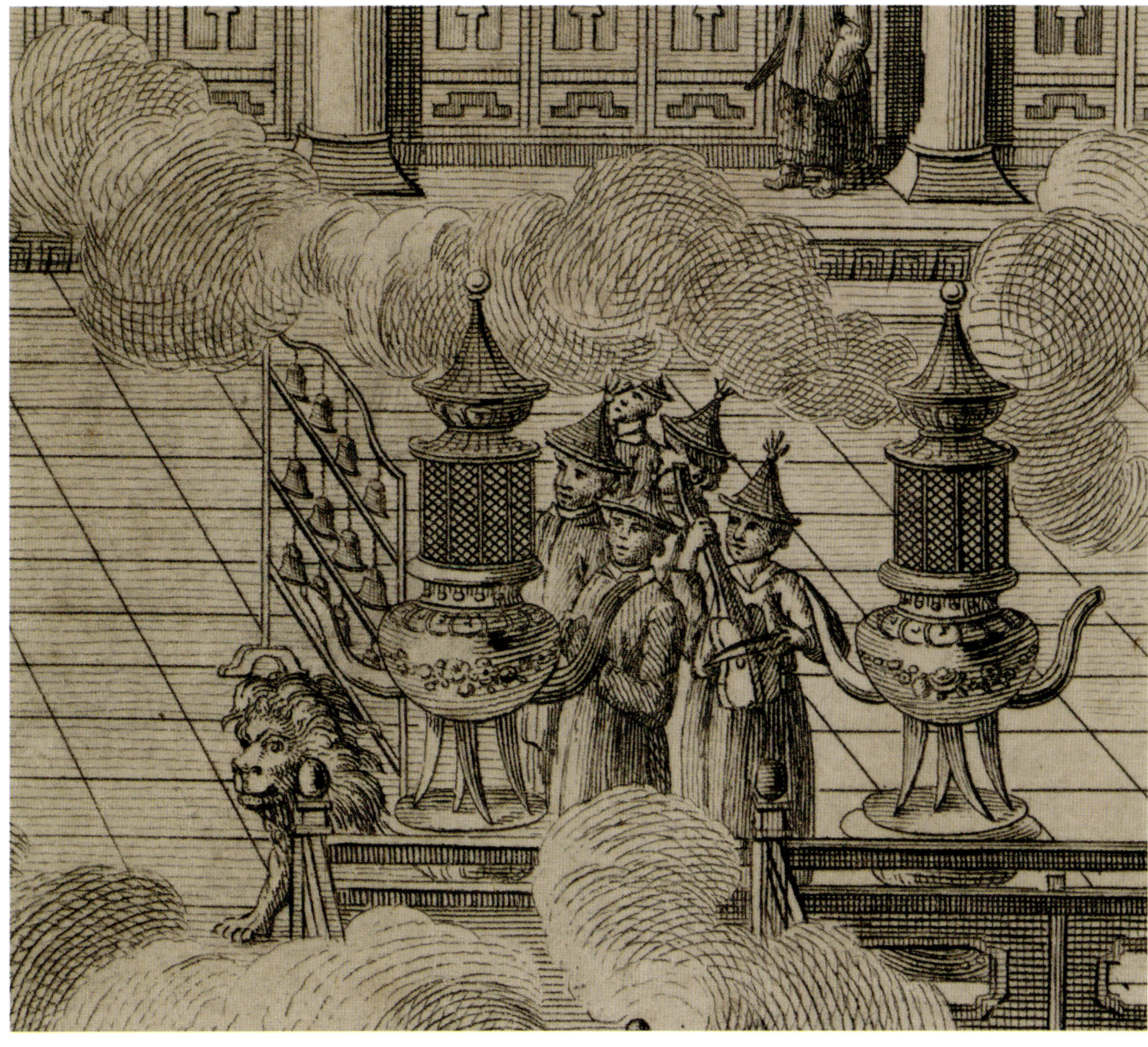

Although the image is inverted, arm positions with the bow-arm elbow held low and the fingering arm high are also perfectly plausible for both *huqin* and horsehead fiddle, and in this respect the engraver has injected a degree of flowing movement and veracity into his portrayal. By contrast, the fingers of both hands are, however, crudely rendered and unconvincing. In terms of context, paradoxically, neither horsehead fiddle nor *huqin* are likely, as neither of them is a Confucian instrument, nor are they redolent of the imperial court. Even so, Helman's engravings have proved elsewhere to be too accurate for the inclusion of either to be regarded purely as a flight of fancy, and so his representations should, to some extent, be taken on trust. If the instrument is indeed a horsehead fiddle, it would be a century earlier than any other depiction of one with a bow visible in either Chinese or European sources.

Fig. 5.23 (next spread): "A Scene of an Historical Play Exhibited on the Chinese Stage." From *An Authentic Account of an Embassy from the King of Great Britain to the Emperor of China*, folio volume, plate 30.
Date: 1797.
Author: George Staunton (1737–1801).
Artists: drawn by William Alexander (1767–1816), engraved by James Heath (1757–1834).
Dimensions: 57 × 43 cm.
Hong Kong University Libraries (ULB 951.074 S79 a).

Soon afterwards in 1792–1794, Britain sent an Embassy to China led by George Macartney, the first Earl Macartney (1737–1806). Sir George Staunton (1737–1801) was the Secretary to the Embassy and his book *An Authentic Account of an Embassy from the King of Great Britain to the Emperor of China* could be regarded as the official account of the enterprise. Four copies of Staunton's book are stored in the HKUL under the same or similar classmarks (U [LB] 951.074 S79 a):

1. A 1797 edition in three volumes, published by G. Nicol of Pall-Mall, London, with the accompanying plates comprising the third folio volume. Of the three specimens in the HKUL furnished with the plates found in the folio volume (here described as copies 1, 2, and 3), the illustrations in this copy are in the finest

11. One or possibly two *yazheng* are also depicted in engraving XXI "Fête Donnée aux Vieillards par l'Empereur Kien-long," though only one is played by being struck with a stick.

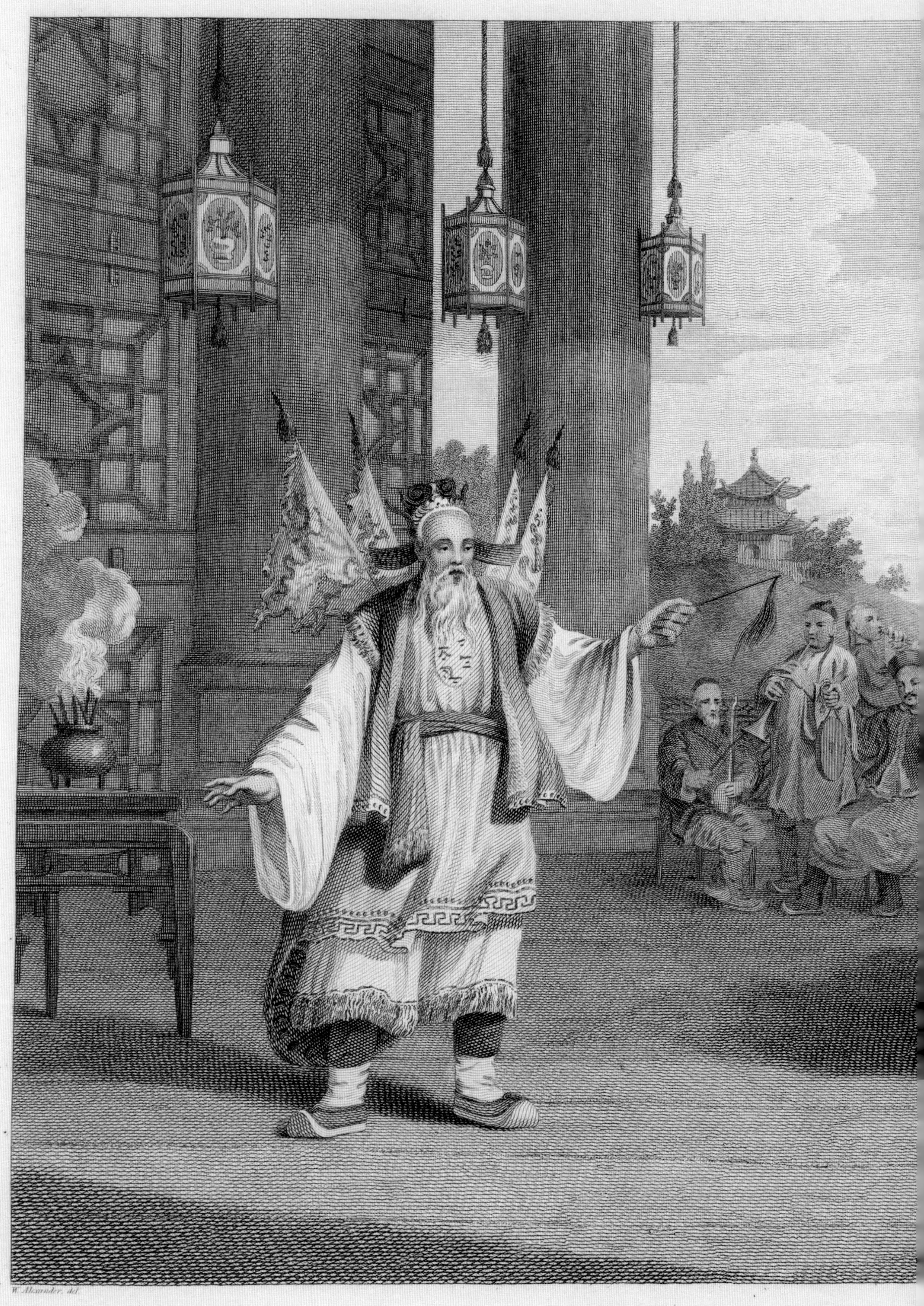

W. Alexander, del.

A SCENE in an HISTORICAL

London, Published A

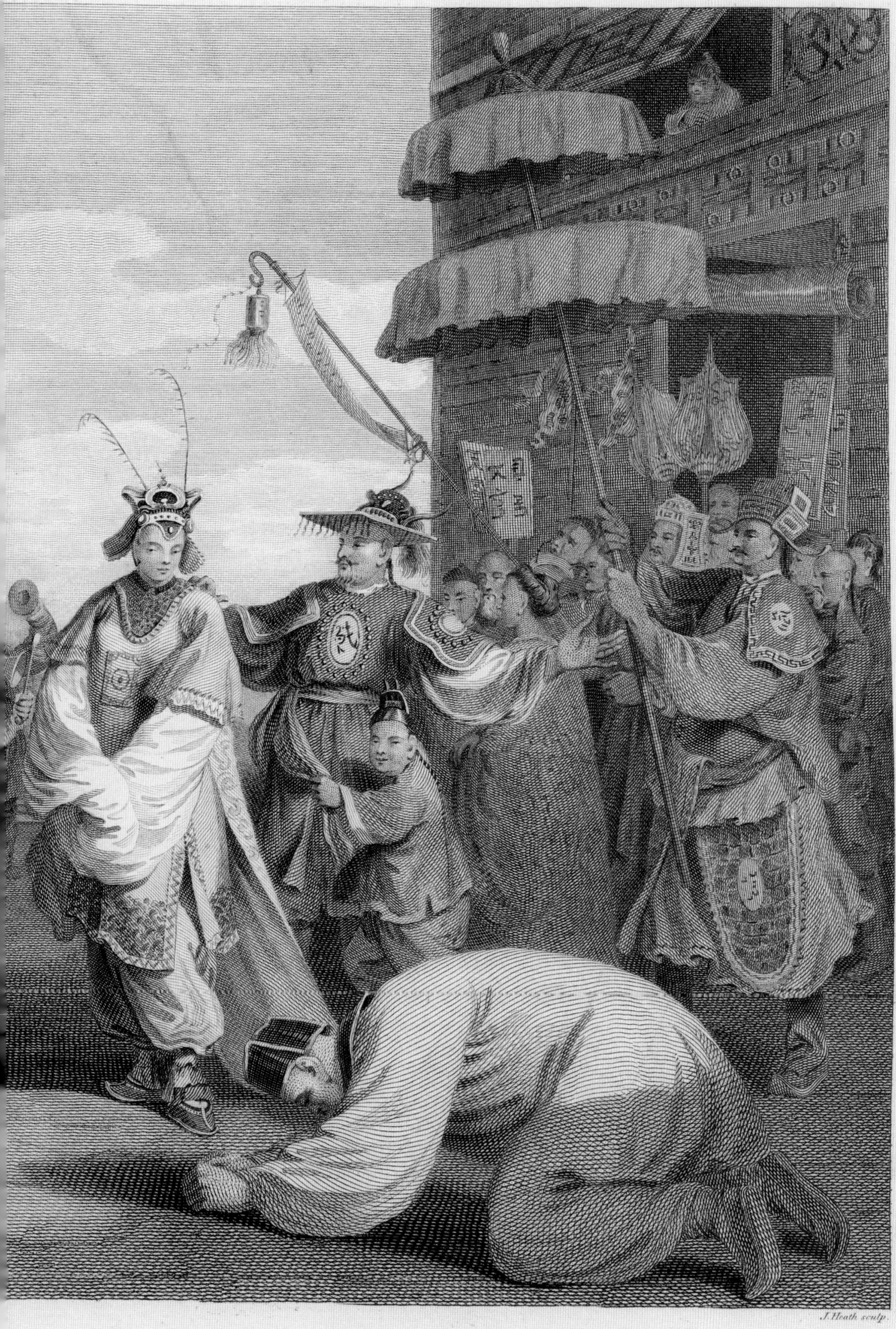

J. Heath sculp.

Y exhibited on the CHINESE STAGE.

6. by G. Nicol.

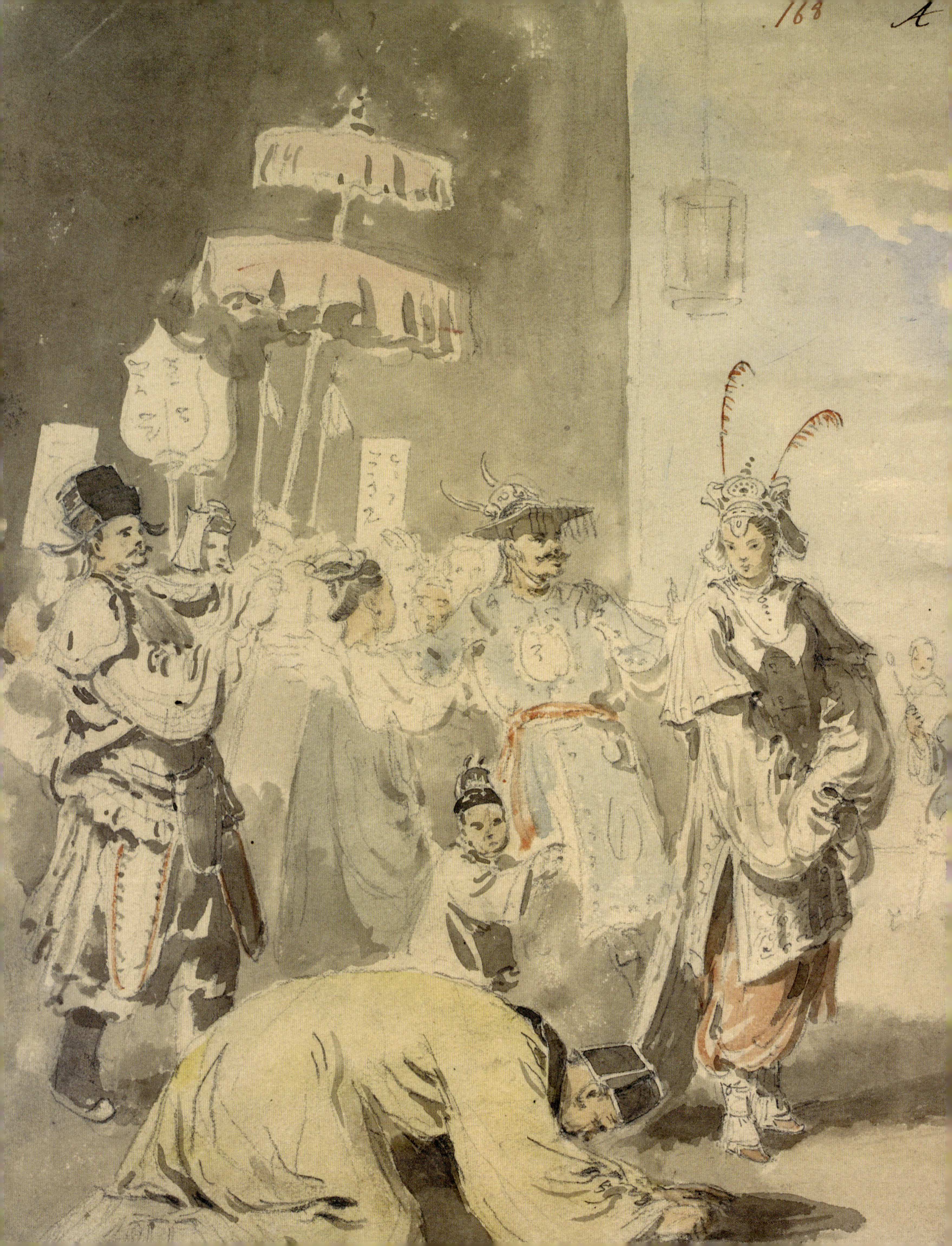

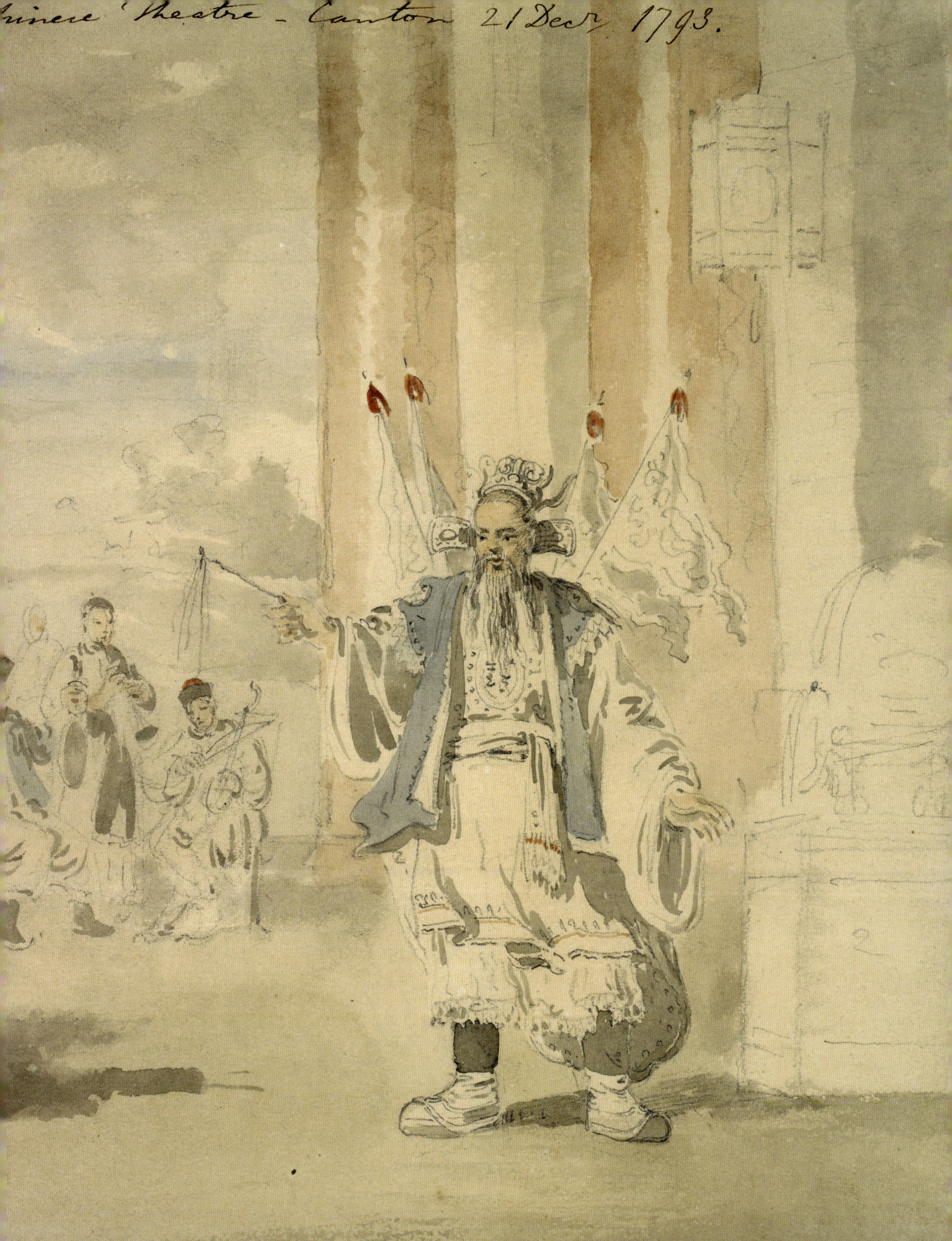
inese Theatre - Canton 21 Decr 1793.

condition. Bound in dark blue. (Henceforth copy 1.)
2. A 1798 edition in three volumes, also published by G. Nicol of Pall-Mall, London, with the accompanying plates comprising the third folio volume. Rebound in brown cloth in a more modern manner familiar from the 1960s. Confusingly, the folio volume of plates is cataloged under U.LB 951.074 S79 a, but volumes 1 and 2 are under U 951.074 S79 a, which reflects issues regarding their commonality of provenance that will be discussed below. (Henceforth copy 2.)
3. The magnificent five-volume set kept in the Fung Ping Shan Library. (Henceforth copy 3.)
4. A 1798 edition, also published by G. Nicol of Pall-Mall. Modern-bound in brown in the same style as copy 2, but much smaller in size and devoid of illustrations. It no longer carries the acronym "LB" meaning "Large Book" in its classmark, which is, thus: U 951.074 S79 a. (Henceforth copy 4.)

These four editions are now discussed in turn. HKUL also has at U 951.074 S79 h three copies of a much-abridged version of Staunton's work in one volume, published in 1797, which contains no illustrations or important references to instruments, and so is not examined here.

According to its accession stamps, like *Suite des Seize Estampes représentant les Conquêtes de l'Empereur de la Chine avec leur Explication*, copy 1 also came to the HKUL on June 11, 1927, and its provenance was also the Chater collection, but on the label at the front of the book where this is acknowledged, the information is now typed and not handwritten, and "Chater" is misspelt "Charter," though the errant "r" has been crossed out by hand. The accession notes on the reverse of the frontispiece also indicate that it was rebound on October 8, 1956, and a slipcase added on June 14, 1960. By then, Sir Paul Chater and his legacy had faded from common consciousness, and when the paper label acknowledging this provenance was redone after the rebind, a misspelling occurred. There are scant indications on the volumes themselves of the history of copy 1 before it entered the HKUL collection. Only the partially illegible words "Mr [?] Ligg [?]" scrawled in old faded black ink on the back and at the top of the first of the folded maps of the folio volume are noteworthy.

The folio volume is a magnificent monument to British engraving of the time. It is said that a contemporary British Prime Minister (it is not recorded which one) remarked that nothing had resulted from the Embassy in terms of Sino-British trade or international relations, but that a fine book was produced nonetheless. The detail and variety of shadings on the engravings are every bit as fine as Helman's efforts, though the overall effect is less romantically rococo and more static, even if for this reason more realistic and useful as a historical document. Like Helman's masterpieces, all of Staunton's engravings fill the entire page, and many of them are maps that are even larger and folded to fit in. Of the forty-four plates in his folio volume, one depicts a *huqin*, plate 30, which is reproduced here as Fig. 5.23. *An Authentic Account of an Embassy from the King of Great Britain to the Emperor of China* was evidently a popular book, and the British Library currently possesses several dozen copies of the editions with the folio volume of plates.

The caption to this illustration is found at the front of volume 1 in "A List of the Plates Contained in the Folio Volume," pages xxiii and xxiv, and it reads:

> A dramatic scene on the Chinese stage. The principal story of the piece, of which this scene represents a part, is taken from the ancient history of the country. It opens with the account of an emperor of China and his empress, who, in the midst of perfect felicity and apparent security, are surprised by a sudden revolt among their subjects. A war ensues; many battles are fought upon the stage; and at length the archrebel, a general of cavalry, characterized on the stage by a whip in his hand, overcomes his sovereign, whom he slays with his own hand. The captive empress appears in all the agonies of despair naturally resulting from the loss of her husband, as well as of her state and dignity, and indeed danger of her honour. Whilst she is uttering lamentations, and rending the skies with her complaints, the conqueror enters. Of this scene the plate is a representation. He approaches her with respect, addresses her in a gentle tone, attempts to soothe her sorrows, talks of love and adoration; and, like Richard the Third and Lady Anne in Shakspeare, in less than half an hour prevails on her to dry up her tears, to forget a dead husband, and to console herself with a living

Fig. 5.24 (previous spread): "A Chinese Theatre—Canton." Date: "21 December; 1793." Artist: William Alexander (1767–1816). Watercolor: 35.5 × 23.3 cm. © The British Library Board (Macartney Albums, WD961, picture 168).

> one. The persuasions of her own officers and attendants in favour of the general, have more weight with the lady than the supplicating priest, who, prostrate on the ground, intreats her not to marry the murderer of her husband. The piece concludes as usual with the nuptials, and a grand procession.
>
> The dresses worn by the ancient Chinese are still preserved in the drama. The band of music has its situation on the back part of the stage; there is no change of scene; and, in general, the front of the theatre is exposed to the open air.

Significantly and unprecedentedly, mention here is made of the accompanying band.

Of the forty-four plates in the folio volume, other than plate 30, only three depict musical instruments: plates 18 and 25 include trumpets, gongs, and drums, though only as ceremonial instruments; and plate 31 displays a stage on which a theatrical performance is taking place watched by a smattering of spectators; a trumpet is being played in amongst a small group of accompanying instrumentalists towards the left of the stage, and although one of the other figures with his back to the viewer could be playing a *huqin*, this cannot be said with certainty. The caption to plate 31 in the "List of Plates Contained in the Folio Volume" includes a relevant sentence: "The building on the right hand corner of the plate is a tower or fortress, and that on the left, a place for theatrical representation, which are always entirely open in front."

Perusing the forty-four plates, the artists who executed the preliminary drawings and the craftsmen who cut the engravings are given below as they appear on the illustrations, including any additional comments. Where there are blanks in the list, it is because nothing is recorded.

Plate	Artist	Engraver
1	J Barrow	B Baker
2	J Barrow	W Skelton
3	J Barrow	B Baker
4	J Barrow	B Baker, Islington
5	J Barrow	B Baker, Islington
6	J Barrow	B Baker, Islington
7		Ellis
8	H W Parish Royal Artillery	B Baker
9	J Barrow	B Baker, Islington
10	J Barrow	B Baker, Islington
11		B Baker, Islington
12		
13	S. Edwards	W. Skelton
14	W Alexander	J Landseer and T[?] Shirt[?]
15	W Alexander	J Landseer
16	W Alexander	J Caldwall
17	W Alexander	J Pass
18	W Alexander	B T Pouncy
19	W Alexander	Medland
20	W Alexander	J Dadley
21	J Barrow	J Baker
22	W Alexander	W Lowry
23	taken on the spot by H W Parish of the Royal Artillery	Joseph Baker
24	Drawn by W Alexander from a sketch by H W Parish	Medland
25	W Alexander	J Fittler
26	H W Parish of the Royal Artillery, 1793	Joseph Baker
27	Drawn by W Alexander from a sketch by H W Parish	B T Pouncy
28	W Alexander	John Hall
29	W Alexander	J Smith
30	W Alexander	J Heath
31	W Alexander	J Chapman
32	W Alexander	Wilson
33	W Alexander	W Byrne
34		Joseph Baker
35	W Alexander	B T Pouncy
36	W Alexander	William and Elizabeth Ellis
37	S Edwards	W Skelton
38	W Alexander	B T Pouncy
39	W Alexander	Wilson
40	W Alexander	W Byrne
41	W Alexander	J Landseer and T[?] Shirt[?]
42	W Alexander	T Medland
43	W Alexander	J Landseer
44		W Skelton

Certain patterns emerge readily from this list: those drawn by J Barrow are all maps; those by H W Parish, commanding officer of the military escort, have military implications; the two by S Edwards are both birds; the one by T Hickey, the official painter of the Embassy, is a formal portrait; and the remainder are by W Alexander, the official draughtsman. The list of engravers represents a veritable pantheon of contemporary English masters of the craft.[12]

As well as the folio volume of plates, twenty-nine smaller illustrations are embedded into the text. Page numbers of where these are situated are not included in the "List of the Engravings contained in the Two Quarto Volumes" at the opening of copy 1, which is confusing, given that the illustrations are not recorded in the order in which they occur in the text. These page numbers have been added for copy 2, the second edition of 1798, which is one of very few differences between the two editions; thus, the numbering of the plates given here is according to copy 2. Once more, artists are given first and engravers second, and where there are blanks in the list, it is because nothing is recorded.

Plate	Artist	Engraver[13]
1	W Alexander	Collyer [this illustration is not in the 1797 edition]
2	W Alexander	S Daniell [?]
3	W Alexander	some writing, but faded and unreadable
4	W Alexander	some writing, but faded and unreadable
5		
6	W Alexander	B T Pouncy
7		J. Baker [from] Islington
8	T Hickey	J Hall
9		
10	W Alexander	W Ellis
11	W Alexander	W Angus
12	W Alexander	[faded, but the surname reads: M*l***]
13	W Alexander	W Angus
14		
15	W Alexander	J Pass
16	W Alexander	J Pass
17	W Alexander	J Pass
18		
19	W Alexander	[faded and unreadable, but not J Pass]
20	W Alexander	W Ellis
21		T Thurston
22		
23	W Alexander	C Rivers
24	W Alexander	[faded, but the surname reads: A***]
25	W Alexander	W Angus
26		
27	[An inserted picture, no draughtsman or engraver given, and not in copy 1.]	
28	W Alexander	[faded]
29	W Alexander	

Of these, only plate 21 on page 305 of volume 2 includes musical instruments, and these are simply several drums. W Alexander is given as responsible for most of the illustrations, the only other artist recorded being T Hickey.

W Alexander is William Alexander (1767–1816), and thankfully many hundreds of the watercolors he made while traveling as the official draughtsman of the Embassy are preserved in the Macartney Albums (accession nos. WD959–961) in the Prints, Drawings, and Photographs Section of the Asian and African Department of the British Library. Two of these paintings depict *huqin*, and one is the very sketch from which the engraving reproduced in Fig. 5.23 was made. It is cataloged as no. 168 in album WD961 and reproduced here as Fig. 5.24.

Dated clearly to "21 December, 1793" and painted in "Canton" shortly before the Embassy departed from China, this watercolor is quite simply the best view available to a modern reader of a Chinese opera performance at the time. William Alexander had been trained to sketch quickly and accurately, and this picture and most of his other paintings in the Macartney Albums were executed in real time *in situ* while the events were actually unfolding. As historical documents, their value is as near to photography as it is possible to get, and as an outsider whose views were unwarped by indigenous notions of social class, Alexander simply painted what he saw, not what he wanted to see.

The theatrical performance is taking place in the foreground, and the caption to the engraving quoted above gives a full description of the scene. Unfortunately, as is also the case with Mendoza's[14] and Du Halde's[15] accounts of theatrical plots, no records survive that hint at which specific historical events are being enacted, though the stories may simply be generic and no such explanation possible. Taken as a whole, Staunton's narrative is respectful, restrained, and informed, and both it and the watercolor and engraving suggest that the Embassy took a lively interest in the entertainment provided. The comparison with Shakespeare's *Richard III*, while serving on one level simply as a useful tool for drawing an English-speaking readership into the situation depicted, on another also indicates genuine empathy on the part of the Embassy for the emotions portrayed.

Relevant to the history of *huqin*, this picture's value lies in the supporting instrumentalists in the background: a three-piece band that consists of gong, *suona*, and *huqin* players. As a record of the accompanying ensemble to an opera in Canton at the time, this is important evidence in itself. Looking first at the watercolor, as far as the *huqin* is concerned, its round body, spike, and arched bow are all clearly visible, and although its body is proportionally too large and slightly too centrally situated, instead of being wedged on the left thigh as is customary today, its spike remains vertical and correctly next to the player's ear. Even his slight lean towards his bow-hand is characteristic of the shape and posture required for a down-bow, and crossed legs such as his are commonly found in early depictions and photographs. William Alexander has done a good job, by a long way the best so far.

Even so, there are still problems, for example, the characteristic backward curve of the *huqin* tip has been replaced by a concave violin-type "scroll." The bow is also situated too high up the instrument; a satisfactory sound is only made when the stick rests on the soundbox; and it is also not perpendicular to the strings as is generally required. A slanted angle is still possible, however, if a sharp attack is needed on a down-bow, as a *huqin* bow can only be lifted from a string by moving it upwards in this manner and readying it for a swift downward strike to engage the string just above the soundbox. William Alexander's powers of observation and meticulous draughtsmanship are acute enough that he can be given the benefit of the doubt in this respect, and it can be readily assumed that this is what he actually witnessed. That said, the *huqin* faces more square-on towards the viewer than was likely, as the best and most resonant sound is made when the front face points to the side and the bow-hair catches the string at a perpendicular angle to the front plate.

When the drawing was made into the engraving, the entire picture was inverted so that the whip-wielding conquerer is now on the left and the empress and the priest kowtowing on the right. The instrumental band is still situated behind them in the same relative position. In only one aspect has the picture not been inverted: cleverly, the *huqin* player still holds his instrument with his left hand and bows with his right. Again, his neatly crossed legs add a touch of realism to his posture, but his left hand is too low on the instrument; placed right over the soundbox, the hand would not be able to depress the strings and the instrument be bowed at the same time. The bow itself is no longer so sharply convex, and he has not assumed the flowing posture of the watercolor, as if leaning about to play a down-bow, so its position high up and slanted across the strings is less convincing. A litmus test for the powers of observation of the artist and engraver is always the quality of the reproduction of Chinese characters. Both those on the drawing and engraving are plausible in design, but nonetheless illegible and clearly not written by a Chinese hand or someone who could write Chinese.

Staunton's text is itself a comprehensive and workmanlike account, and he tends to eschew emotional language and the denigration of Chinese customs. All the principal protagonists of the Embassy are recorded, for example: John Barrow in volume 1 on pages 36 and 104; Henry Parish (dates uncertain) on page 35; and Johann Christian Hiittner (*sic*) on pages 484 and 499, actually "Hüttner" (1766–1847). Pages 35–36 indicate William Alexander and Thomas Hickey (1741–1824): "There were, indeed, attached to the Embassy, a painter and a draughtsman by profession, of whose merit sufficient specimens will accompany the present publication." William Alexander is mentioned by name on page 233 of volume 2, and Thomas Hickey on page 84 of the same volume.

The theatrical performance in the text relevant to plate 30 is found in the narrative at a point when the Embassy had reached Tien-sing (Tianjin) on their way to see the emperor, whereas the date on the watercolor unequivocally places it in

12. Most are readily traceable, for example, Benjamin Baker (1766–1824), William Skelton (1763–1848), John Landseer (1769–1852), James Caldwell (1739–1822), John Pass (c. 1783–1832), William Ellis (1747–1810), Benjamin Thomas Pouncy (?–1799), Thomas Medland (c. 1765–1833), John Dadley (1767–1807), Wilson Lowry (1762–1824), James Fittler (1758–1835), John Hall (1739–1797), John Thomas Smith (1766–1833), James Heath (1757–1834), John Chapman (fl. 1792–1823), Richard Wilson (1713–1782), and William Byrne (1743–1805).

13. Traceable names include Joseph Collyer (1748–1827), William Angus (1752–1821), and John Thurston (1774–1822).

14. For example, pp. 250–251 and 266–267.

15. For example, vol. 2, p. 153, of the 1738/1741 edition.

Canton after the Embassy had returned from the capital. In fact, on reading the chapters relevant to the final Canton leg of the journey, which are towards the end of volume 2, there is no mention of any theatrical performance in Canton. The text describing the theatrical performance in Tien-sing on pages 30–32 of volume 2 reads:

> . . . a temporary theatre was erected opposite to his Excellency's yacht. The outside was adorned with a variety of brilliant and lively colours, by the proper distribution of which, and sometimes by their contrast, it is the particular object of an art among the Chinese to produce a gay and pleasing effect. The inside of the theatre was managed, in regard to decorations, with equal success; and the company of actors successively exhibited, during the whole day, several different pantomimes and historical dramas. The performers were habited in the ancient dresses of the Chinese at the period when the personages represented were supposed to have lived. The dialogue was spoken in a kind of recitative, accompanied by a variety of musical instruments; and each pause was filled up by a loud crash, in which the loo [cymbals, *luo* 鑼] bore no inconsiderable part. The band of music was placed in full view, immediately behind the stage, which was broad, but by no means deep. Each character announced, on his first entrance, what part he was about to perform, and where the scene of action lay. Unity of place was apparently preserved, for there was no change of scene during the representation of one piece. Female characters were performed by boys or eunuchs . . .

[There follows a paraphrase of the description of the scene as given in the "List of Plates Contained in the Folio Volume" quoted above, after which is:]

> . . . One of the principal scenes is represented in Plate 30 of the folio volume.

Regardless of whether the text describes a performance in Tianjin or Canton, its narrative is careful, sympathetic, and entirely believable, even down to confirmation of an observation also made by Du Halde that female roles were taken by eunuchs.[16]

Later, in Pekin[g], on pages 162–163 of the same volume, more information is given regarding the interaction between Chinese and European musicians:

> . . . others allured by curiosity, and not a few by the European band of music, which formed a concert every evening in the Embassador's apartments. Among these visitors was the chief director of the Emperor's orchestra, who constantly attended, and was so much pleased with some of the instruments that he desired leave to take drawings of them. He declined accepting them as presents; but sent for painters, who spread the floor with sheets of large paper, and, having placed the clarionets, flutes, bassoons, and French horns upon them, traced with their pencils the figures of the instruments, measuring all the apertures, and noting the minutest particulars; and when this operation was completed, they wrote down their remarks, and delivered them to their employer, who said it was his intention to have similar instruments made by Chinese workmen, and to fit to them a scale of his own. A few Chinese had already, it seems, adopted the European violin; but it was not yet in common use. An instrument of their own, bearing a resemblance to it in form, had two strings only. Some Chinese have likewise learned to note their music upon ruled paper.

The emperor's birthday, as is described on page 255, was celebrated by formal music of a much more Confucian type based on the ubiquitous bell sets, such as are depicted in Helman's engravings (Figs. 5.20, 5.21, and 5.22). The ceremony outlined by Staunton took place at the emperor's summer retreat in Zhe-hol (modern Chengde).

> In the mean time the celebration of the Emperor's anniversary, the seventeenth of September, had taken place. To this ceremony, as to the former, the Embassador and his suite were called before the rising of the sun . . . The princes, tributaries, embassadors, great officers of state, and principal mandarines, were assembled in a vast hall; and upon particular notice, were introduced into an inner building, bearing, at least, the semblance of a temple. It was chiefly furnished with great instruments of music, among which were sets of cylindrical bells, suspended in a line from ornamented frames of wood, and gradually diminishing in size from one extremity to the other, and also triangular pieces of metal arranged in the same order as the bells. To the sound of these instruments, a slow and solemn hymn was sung by eunuchs, who had such a command over their voices, as to resemble the effect of the

musical glasses at a distance. The performers were directed in gliding from one tone to another, by the striking of a shrill and sonorous cymbal; and the judges of music among the gentlemen of the Embassy were much pleased with their execution.

This ceremony recalls ancient equivalents described in the poetry compilation *The Book of Odes* (*Shijing* 詩經), said to have been edited by Confucius (551–479 BCE); for example, poem 274 (out of the 305 in the anthology) "Subduing Powerful Adversaries" ("Zhijing" 執競), one of the odes in the section "Lesser Songs of the Court" ("Xiao Ya" 小雅). Staunton is quite clear, however, that a "hymn" was sung over the bell-centered orchestra, while ancient texts rarely indicate singing combined with this ensemble.

Subduing Powerful Adversaries

Able to subdue powerful adversaries, Wu Wang, the Military Emperor[17]
Powerful were his valiant deeds
The illustrious Zhou emperors Cheng Wang[18] and Kang Wang[19]
Even God praises them
Since that time, emperors Cheng Wang and Kang Wang
Their empire straddles the four quarters of the world
Perceptive and sagacious, their enquiries illuminating
Bells and drums in harmonious symphony "huang-huang"
Stone chimes and bamboo pipes in resonant concord "qiang-qiang"
Let joy descend in plenty
Let joy descend in richness
In deportment and manners, diligent and circumspect
Satiated by fine wine, replete with fine victuals
Let happiness and good fortune come as recompense

執競

執競武王，無競維烈。
不顯成康，上帝是皇。
自彼成康，奄有四方。
斤斤其明，鐘鼓喤喤。
磬筦將將，降福穰穰。
降福簡簡，威儀反反。
既醉既飽，福祿來反。

A few pages later (262–263), describing entertainments laid on while the Embassy

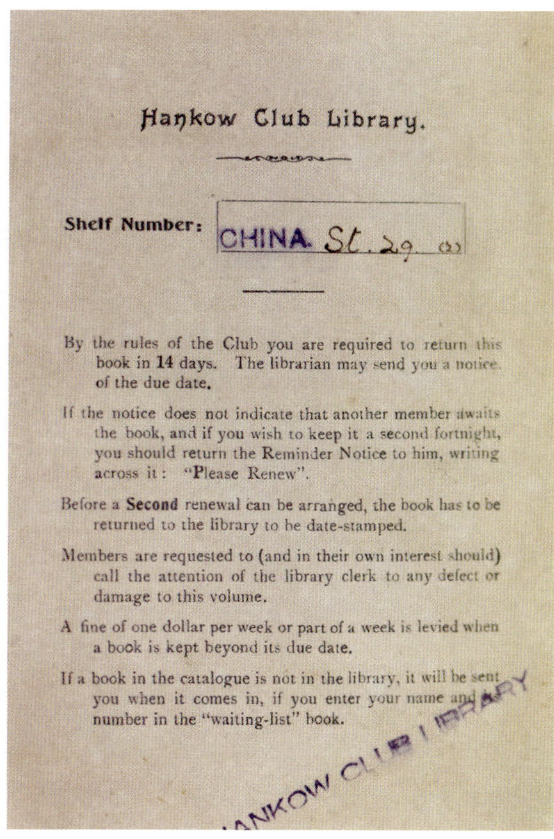
Hankow Club Library.

Shelf Number: CHINA. St. 29 (2)

By the rules of the Club you are required to return this book in **14** days. The librarian may send you a notice of the due date.

If the notice does not indicate that another member awaits the book, and if you wish to keep it a second fortnight, you should return the Reminder Notice to him, writing across it: "Please Renew".

Before a **Second** renewal can be arranged, the book has to be returned to the library to be date-stamped.

Members are requested to (and in their own interest should) call the attention of the library clerk to any defect or damage to this volume.

A fine of one dollar per week or part of a week is levied when a book is kept beyond its due date.

If a book in the catalogue is not in the library, it will be sent you when it comes in, if you enter your name and number in the "waiting-list" book.

Fig. 5.25: *An Authentic Account of an Embassy from the King of Great Britain to the Emperor of China*, vol. 2, Hankow Club Library accession sticker found at the front of the volume.
Date: 1797.
Author: George Staunton (1737–1801).
Hong Kong University Libraries (ULB 951.074 S79 a).

sojourned in Zhe-hol, Staunton quotes Hüttner as observing the anhemitonic, pentatonic, monodic heterophony of Chinese music:

> Several of them [inhabitants of the different districts of the Emperor's wide domains] danced in a pleasing manner, and with graceful attitudes. There was some singing, and a vast variety of musical instruments. The musicians affected mostly slow and plaintive airs, not unlike those of the Highlanders of Scotland; which they played in exact and measured time. To Mr. Hüttner, a good judge of music, it appeared, that "their gammut was such as Europeans would call imperfect, their keys being inconsistent; that is, wandering from flats to sharps, and inversely; except when directed by a bell struck to sound the proper notes. Mr. Hüttner farther observed, that the Chinese, in playing on instruments, discovered no knowledge of semi-tones, nor did they seem to have any idea of counterpoint, or parts in

16. See vol. 2, p. 343, of the 1738/1741 edition.

17. Wu Wang 武王 (?–1046 BCE, r. 1046–1043 BCE), the first Zhou dynasty emperor.

18. Cheng Wang 成王 (?–1021 BCE, r. 1042–1021 BCE), Zhou dynasty emperor; successor to Wu Wang.

19. Kang Wang 康王 (?–996 BCE, r. 1020–996 BCE), Zhou dynasty emperor; successor to Cheng Wang.

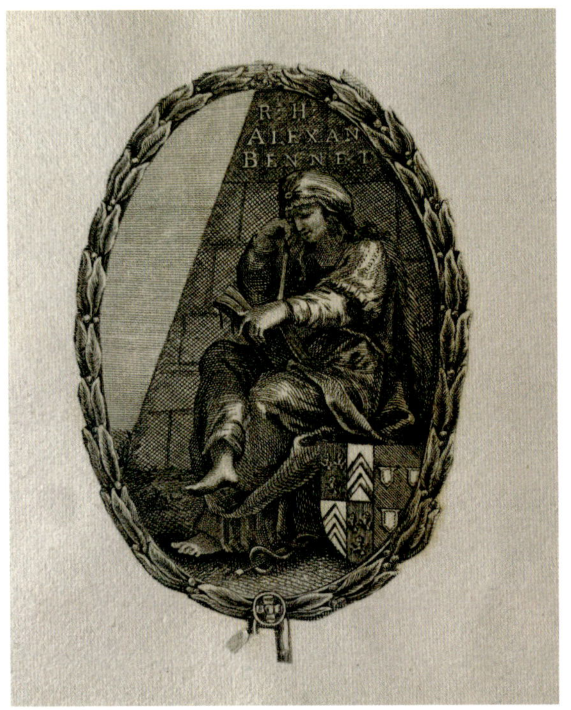

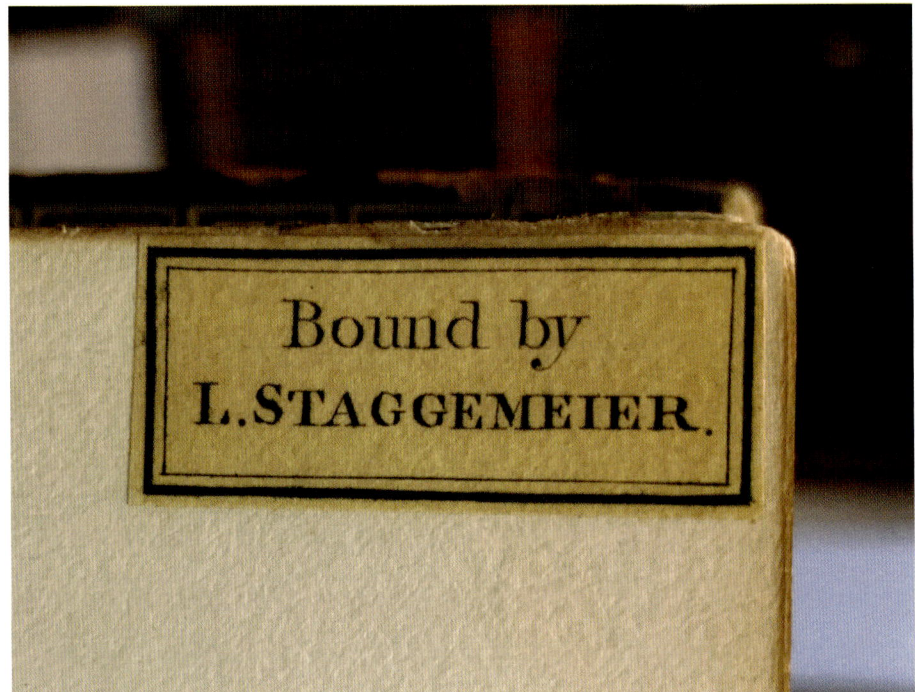

Fig. 5.26 (left): *An Authentic Account of an Embassy from the King of Great Britain to the Emperor of China*, vol. 1, bookplate of R. H. Alexander Bennet (1743–1814 or ?1771–1818) on the second page opening.
Date: 1798.
Author: George Staunton (1737–1801).
Bookplate size: 9.5 × 6.4 cm.
Fung Ping Shan Library (ULB 951.074 S79 a).

Fig. 5.27 (right): *An Authentic Account of an Embassy from the King of Great Britain to the Emperor of China*, vol. 1, binder's label on the first page opening.
Date: 1798.
Author: George Staunton (1737–1801).
Label size: 1.4 × 3.1 cm; Fung Ping Shan Library (ULB 951.074 S79 a).

> music. There was always one melody, however great the number of performers; tho, in a few instances, some of the instruments played in the lower octave, while the rest continued in the upper; and thus approached to harmony."

Copies 1 and 2, including all the plates, are virtually identical so "reprint" might be a better term. Even so, the frontispiece indicates that copy 2 is "the second edition" and "corrected." As with many historic books in the HKUL, it found its way into the collection on March 21, 1933, via the Hankow Club Library, first presented to the Club by Rev. B Upward as is indicated by a stamp at the opening of both volumes of text. Its HCL accession no. is 2755 and the date, May 21, 1924, is given in its customary place at the end of the printed text, that is, page 518 of volume 1 and 626 of volume 2. HCL items are usually furnished with a fine sticker of library regulations before the first page of the book, and although it is absent from volume 1, one of these can be found at the start of volume 2 (see Fig. 5.25).

The only immediately noticeable difference between copy 2 and copy 1 is the addition to both volumes 1 and 2 of fine portraits on the left faces opposite the frontispieces. Although absent from copy 1, they are mentioned in the "List of Engravings" so must have once been there. In volume 1 of copy 2, the Emperor Qianlong is depicted; underneath the illustration, a caption reads:

乾隆大皇帝
Tchien Lung Ta Whuang Tee
[Qianlong Da Huangdi]
[Qianlong, the Great Emperor]

The Chinese is accurately written (a rare occurrence in early Western books on China) but not by a Chinese hand. On the right side, directly under the engraving is: "Collyer sculp[r]. Engraver to her Majesty." Opposite the Frontispiece in volume 2, the Qianlong picture has been replaced by one of "His Excellency the Earl of Macartney," given as "painted by T Hickey" and "Eng[d] by J Hall Eng[r] to his Majesty."

The likelihood is that the folio volume of copy 2 did not originally belong to the other two and that they were united during their sojourn in the Hankow Club Library. In it, on the first page of the book proper after the insertion of more recent binding pages, in the top right and near the corner, is written in black ink "John Sheffield 1869." This untraceable gentleman's name is absent from volumes 1 and 2. In handwriting different to that of the equivalent place in volume 1, the folio volume is given as being presented to the Club by a different person on a different date: "R. R. Hynd Esq" in "1920." At the bottom of the last page of the folio volume, the accession no. and date are also different: "1763" and "Jan 1—1921." The HKUL accession date, however, remains the same: March 21, 1933, and the rebinding of all three volumes in

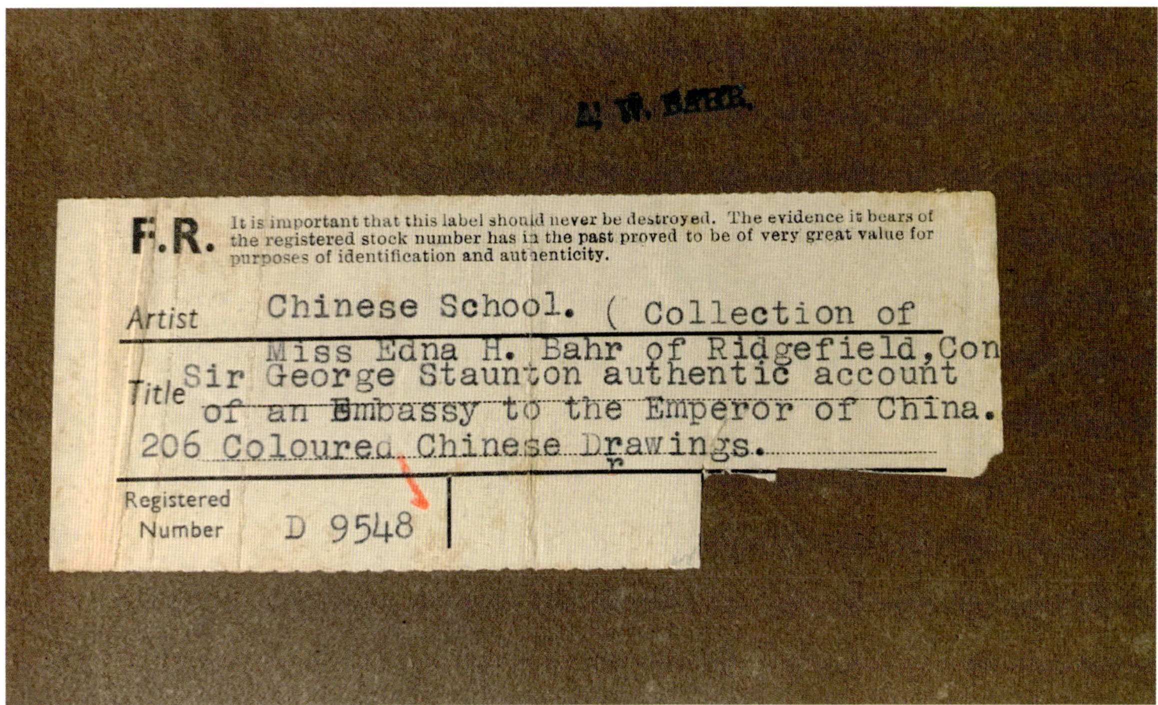

Fig. 5.28: *An Authentic Account of an Embassy from the King of Great Britain to the Emperor of China*, vol. 1, Frost and Reed label and imprinted stamp of A. W. Bahr on the first page opening.
Date: 1798.
Author: George Staunton (1737–1801).
Fung Ping Shan Library (ULB 951.074 S79 a).

the same manner confirms their assumed reunited identity, even if the folio volume is still cataloged under a different classmark and kept at another location.

One of the most prized items in the HKUL collection is a magnificent five-volume version of the 1798 edition (copy 3 here) that is now rightly kept in a safe in the Fung Ping Shan Library. Bound in heavy leather and embossed in gold, its dimensions are considerably larger than copies 1 and 2, though the typeface sizes remain the same, which means that there is a substantial margin around each page. Slightly more than two hundred export watercolors have been inserted into the text, as have the plates that are routinely gathered into the folio volume.

This copy is widely regarded as having once been the Earl of Macartney's personal copy and is undoubtedly a unique item. Macartney died in 1806 and the first record of its ownership is the bookplate of "R. H. Alexander Bennet" on the second page opening of volume 1 and in similar places in the other four volumes (see Fig. 5.26).

R. H. Alexander Bennet can refer to one of two people, father and son:

> Richard Henry Alexander Bennet (1743–1814), British landowner and Member of Parliament for Newport.

> Richard Henry Alexander Bennet (?1771–1818), British naval captain and Member of Parliament for Launceston.

Probably the oldest mark on the book is a small paper label stuck to the top right corner of the first page opening of the first volume that reads: "Bound by L. STAGGEMEIER" (see Fig. 5.27). L. Staggemeier ran a bookbinding business intermittently between 1794 and 1817 on Villiers Street, the Strand, London.

The book itself entered the HKUL collection on February 5, 1959, via the dealers Frost and Reed Ltd, 10 Clare Street, Bristol, England, whose label is found at the top left of the first page opening of volume 1 (see Fig. 5.28). This label gives the owner as: "Miss Edna H. Bahr of Ridgefield, Con." In various places on the first page openings of all five volumes can be found a tiny blue imprinted stamp of A[bel] W[illiam] Bahr (1877–1957), who was a collector of orientalia (see Fig. 5.28). On his death, Edna H. Bahr sold and dispersed his collection.

There are no other interesting marginalia, marks, or seals—who would dare besmirch such a splendid item! On the bottom right corner of the last page opening of all volumes, however, something seems to have been removed or torn off; might this have been an indication of the likely first owner, the Earl Macartney?

Fig. 5.29 (next spread): *Travels in China*, unnumbered plate between pages 314 and 315.
Date: 1806.
Author: John Barrow (1764–1848).
Dimensions: 27.8 × 22.8 cm.
Hong Kong University Libraries (U 915.1075 B2).

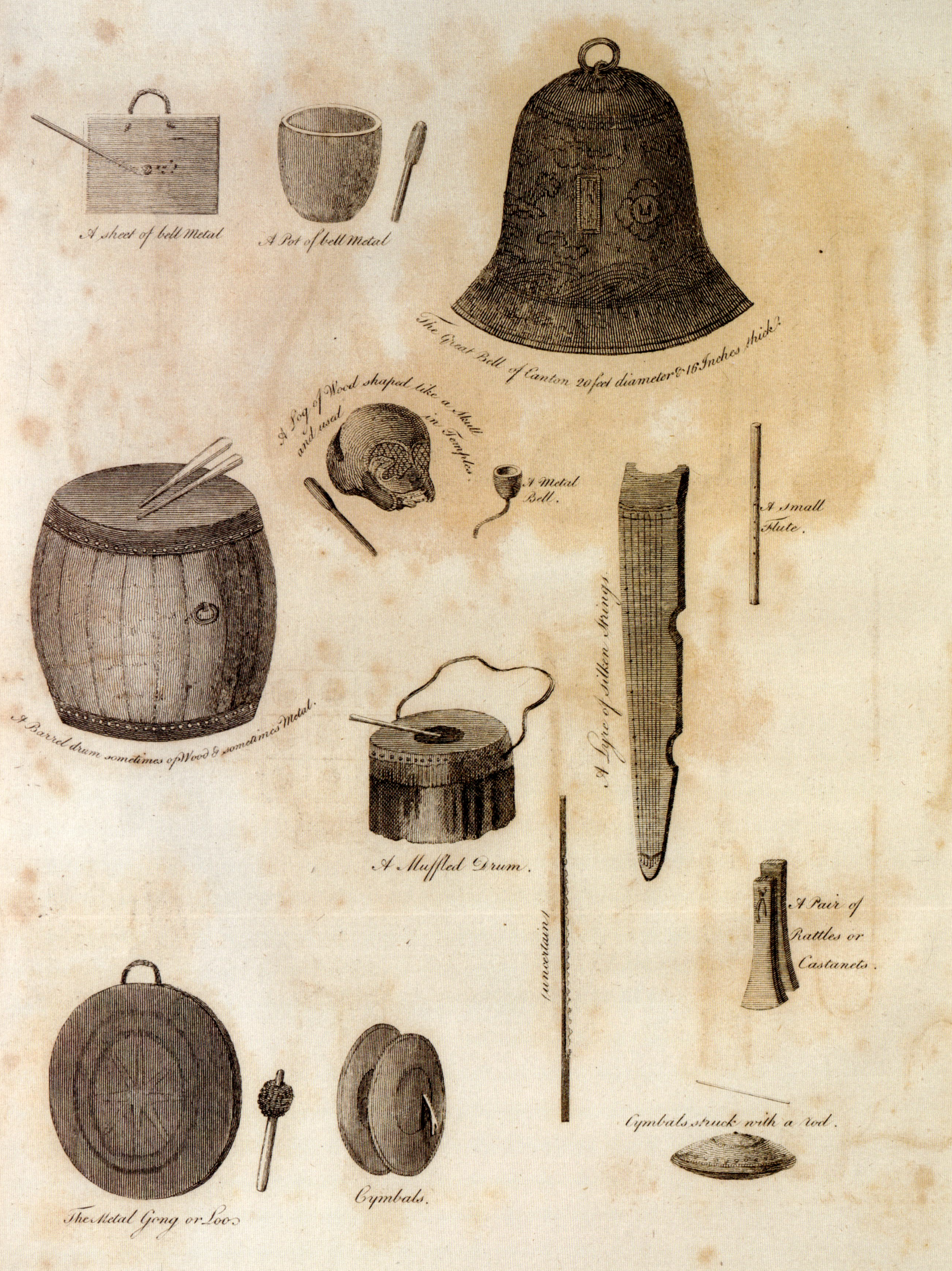
A sheet of bell Metal
A Pot of bell Metal
The Great Bell of Canton 20 feet diameter & 16 Inches thick.
A Log of Wood shaped like a Skull and used in Temples.
A Metal Bell.
A Small Flute.
A Barrel drum sometimes of Wood & sometimes Metal.
A Lyre of silken Strings
A Muffled Drum.
(uncertain)
A Pair of Rattles or Castanets.
Cymbals struck with a rod.
The Metal Gong or Loo
Cymbals.

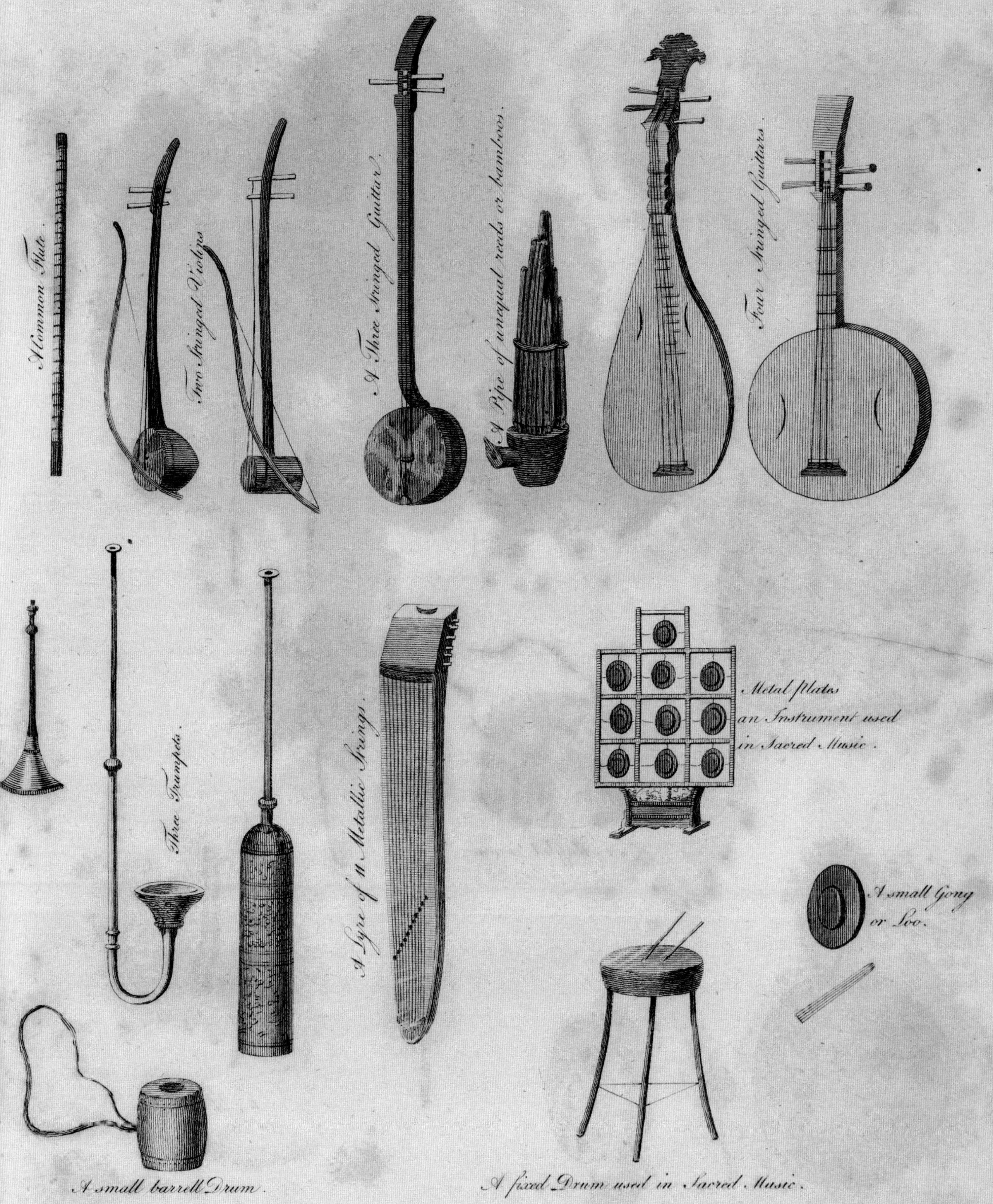
Hemmon Flute.
Two Stringed Violins
A Three Stringed Guittar.
A Pipe of unequal reeds or bamboos.
Four Stringed Guittars.
Three Trumpets.
A Lyre of 11 Metallic Strings.
Metal plates
an Instrument used
in Sacred Music.
A small Gong
or Loo.
A small barrell Drum.
A fixed Drum used in Sacred Music.
Neele, sc. Strand

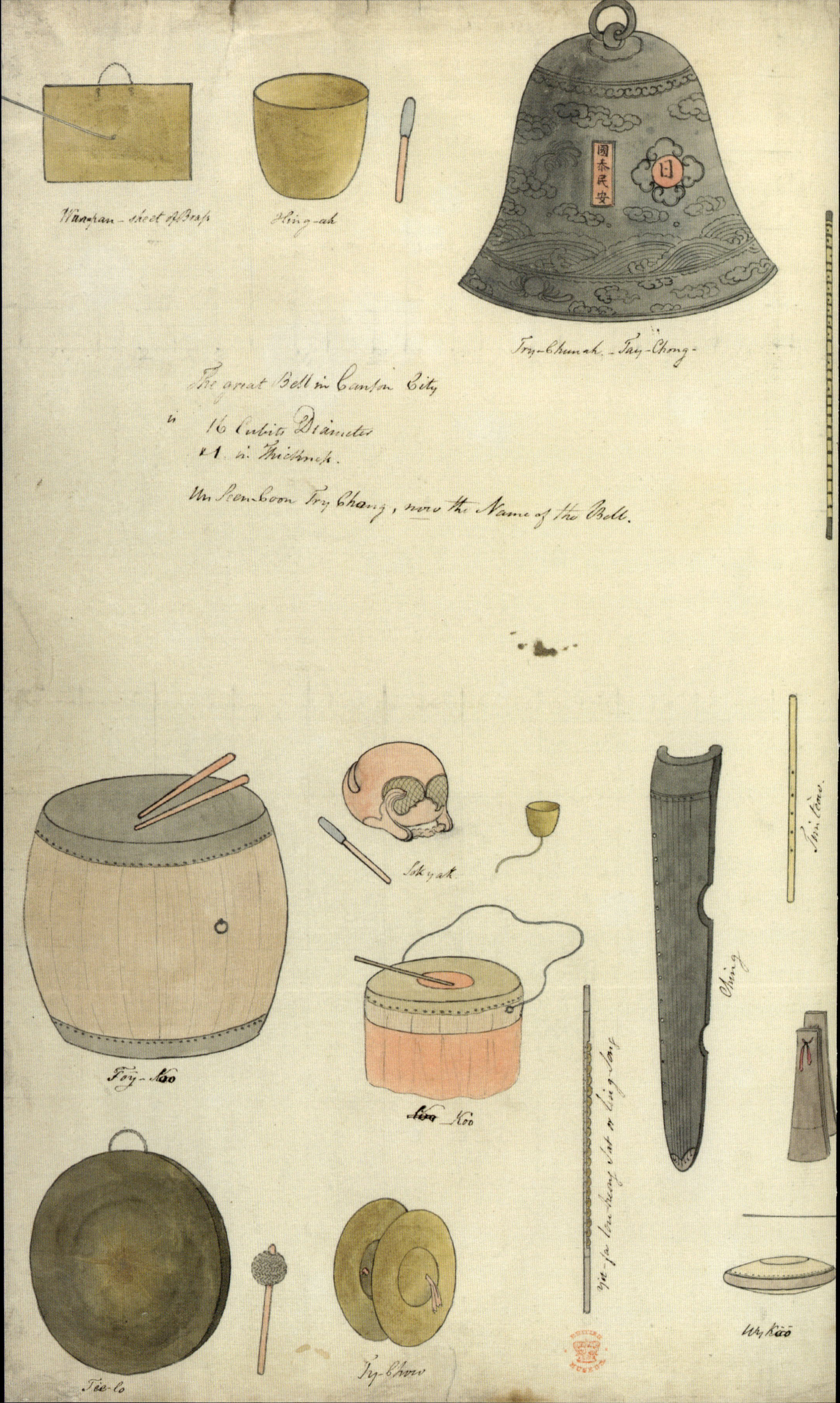

Wanpan - sheet of Brass

Hing-ah

國泰民安

日

Try-Chunah - Tay-Chong -

The great Bell in Canton City

is 16 Cubits Diameter
& 1 in Thickness.

Un Seem Coon Try Chang, now the Name of the Bell.

Sok-yak

Ching

Foy-Koo

Koo

Tée-lo

Ty-Chow

Wy-Koo

Fig. 5.30: British Library, Add. Ms. 33931, fols. 12v–13r.
Date: 1792–1794.
Artist: William Alexander (1767–1816).

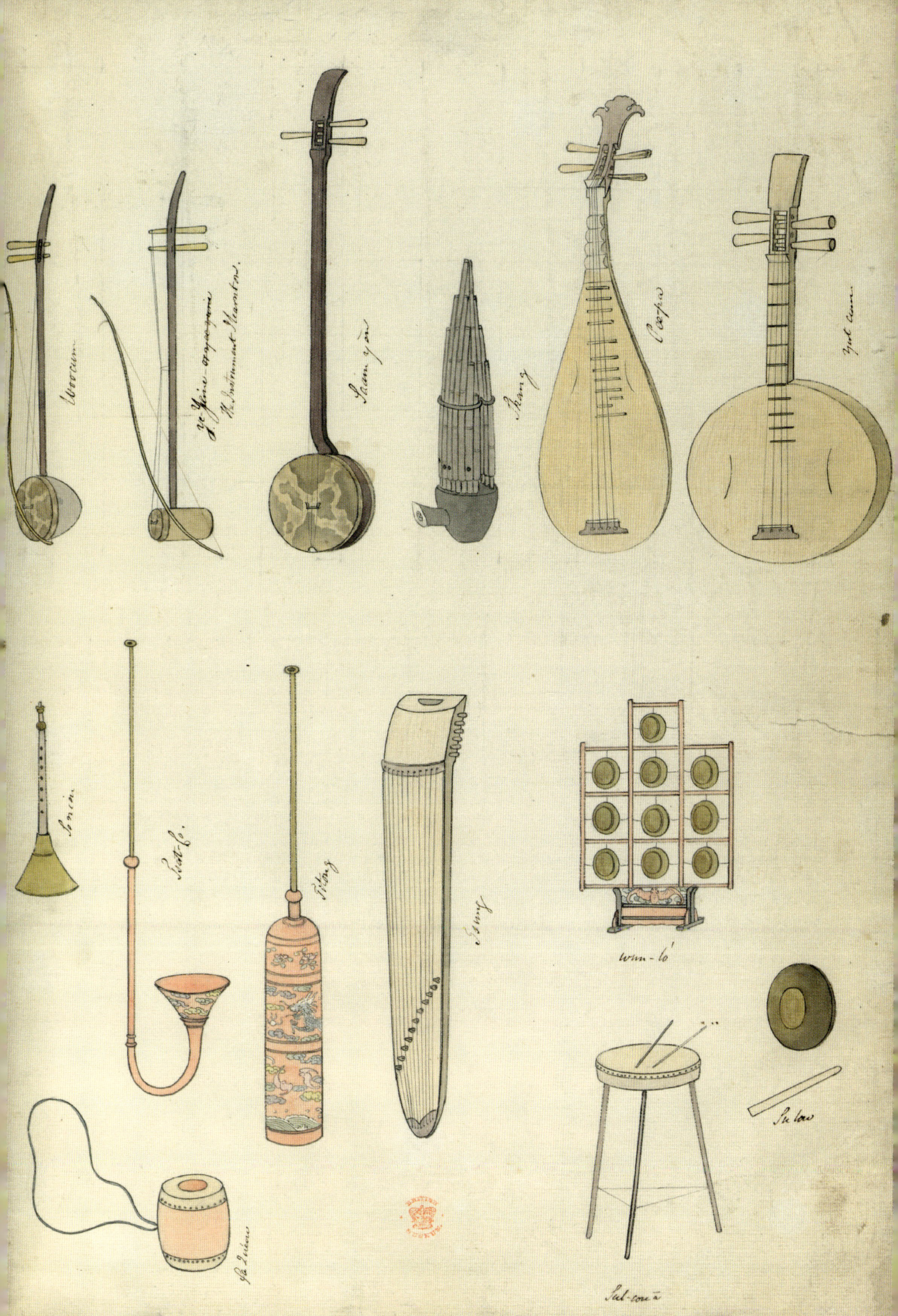
wun-lo'
Su low
Sul-coua

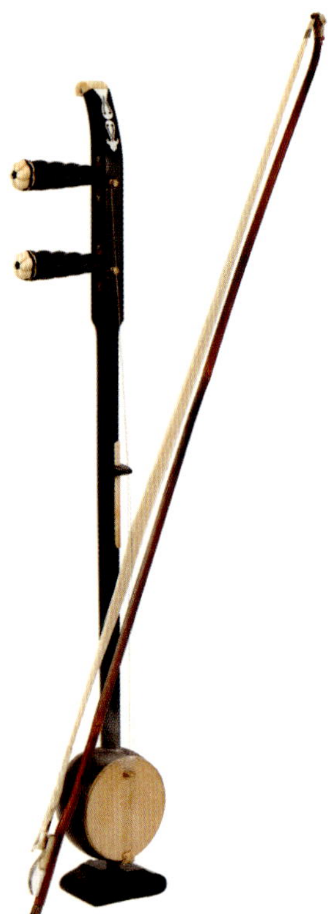

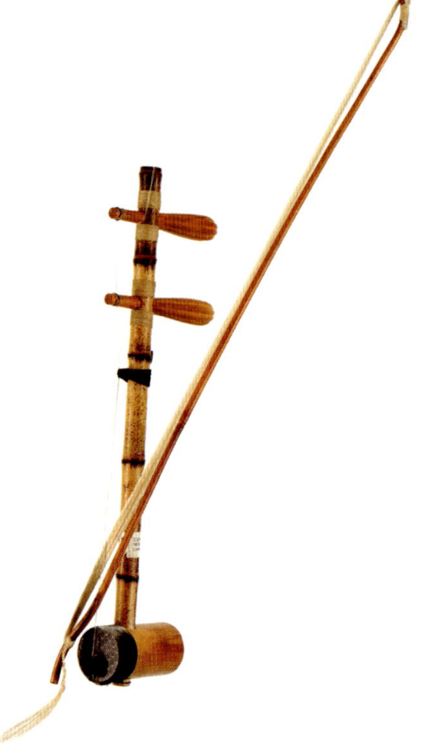

Fig. 5.31 (left): A fine modern mid-voiced *banhu* from the workshop of Lü Jianhua in Beijing.

Fig. 5.32 (right): A fine example of a *jinghu*.

Fittingly, it is Macartney's portrait that replaces Qianlong's on the left face opposite the frontispiece of volume 1. A fresh portrait of Qianlong is positioned here for volume 2, and the Qianlong engraving familiar from copy 2 now occupies the equivalent place in volume 3. Volume 1 of copy 2 is spread across volumes 1 and 2 of copy 3 (volume 2 of copy 3 starts at page 249), and volume 2 of copy 2 is divided across volumes 3, 4, and 5 of copy 3 (the first page of text of volume 4 is 281, that of volume 5, page 485). Broadly speaking, the export watercolors are interleaved at appropriate places in the text, for example, a series depicting plants where botany is mentioned. After the "Table of Contents" in volume 1 come the maps, that is, plates 1–4 and 6–11; then four additional diagrams of island elevations; then plate 5 is inserted; and finally the "List of the Plates Contained in the Folio Volume."

In most cases, the surrounding text bears little relation to the plates inserted, so their independent collection into the folio volume is much more appropriate: plate 18 is inserted between pages 386 and 387 in volume 4; plate 25 between pages 228 and 229 in volume 3; and plate 30 (the one that depicts the Chinese theatrical performance) between pages 32 and 33 in volume 3, where, as given earlier, the text mentions the opera performance that took place in Tianjin. Plate 31 is inserted between pages 488 and 489 in volume 5; although this time the surrounding text does fit the illustration (its principal subject matter is the bastinado of offenders), it does not mention the performance on the stage in the background.

Copy 4 in three small volumes, all bound in modern brown cloth, is devoid of plates, though the text is identical but broken up into chapters in a slightly different manner. It also came into the HKUL collection from the Hankow Club Library on March 21, 1933; the HCL customary sticker at the start of the book gives the classmark as "China St[aunton].29 (2);" the accession no. is 1762 and date, January 1, 1921. Curiously, though, towards the top of the first page of the original book itself and above the HCL sticker is the identifying code "15935 R" written in pencil, a number redolent of the India Office Library classification system and whose collection is now in the British Library. "10/6" is written in pencil in the top right corner, that is ten shillings and sixpence, which was probably a dealer's asking price.

John Barrow (1764–1848), the author of *Travels in China*, was, as given at the front of his book, "Late Private Secretary to the Earl of Macartney, and one of his suite as Ambassador from the King of Great Britain to the Emperor of China." Sadly, unlike Staunton, his text is unnecessarily patronizing in tone, as is particularly evident when discussing music in a section found on pages 313–323. This passage is, however, accompanied by a fine illustration (see Fig. 5.29).

Quasi-scientific in its organological categorization, all instruments of the Chinese pantheon are present on the diagrammatic engraving, with one notable exception, the *yangqin* 揚琴, which may well still have been rare at the time.[20] This plate is, furthermore, the first Western depiction of *huqin* that splits the generic prototype into its two principal variants: the cylindrical *erhu*-shape (see Fig. 5.2), generally faced with python skin, and the rounded *banhu*-shape (see Fig. 5.31), usually furnished with a wooden plate attached to a coconut shell instead.

Barrow's engraving was made (or plagiarized) from a drawing now found in British Library Add. Ms. 33931, fols. 12v and 13r (see Fig. 5.30).[21] Next to the depictions of *huqin* in this drawing is the humbling phrase: "The Instrument I learnt on." On pages 316–317, Barrow also quotes the well-known melody "Moo-Lee-Wha" (茉莉花 "Molihua" or "Jasmine Flowers") in staff notation together with a translation of the text (see Fig. 5.33).

By comparison, G. T. Lay's article "Musical Instruments of the Chinese" in *The Chinese Repository*, vol. VIII (May 1839), is ground-breaking for its more knowledgeable narrative of Chinese instruments. Relevant to *huqin*, his hands-on description seems to match most closely the modern *jinghu* 京胡 (see Fig. 5.32) rather than the *erhu*:

> The *urh heën*. The two stringed fiddle . . . The rebeck of the Chinese. This is in outline merely a stick of bamboo passing through a hollow cylinder of the same material. This cylinder is between four and five inches long, and answers the purpose of a sounding-board. One end is open, the other is shut, and covered over with a piece of snake's skin. Upon the surface thus covered by the snake's skin, stands a minute bridge, over which two strings are led, and then are made fast to the end of the projection of the bamboo stick or stem, after it has passed through the cylinder.
>
> The stem, about eighteen inches long, is provided with two pegs at the upper end, which serve to tighten and relax the strings in tuning. The strings are drawn towards the stem by a loop; by shifting this, the pitch is varied, and the purpose of a nut in our violin answered. The bow is in all its original simplicity, being a staff of bamboo, with its ends drawn towards each other by a small bundle of horsehair. The strings are usually tuned as fifths to each other, as is practiced in our violin. The hairs of the bow are fastened upon it after passing between the strings, and as they are very close, it requires no little practice to keep them clear of one while drawn over the other.
>
> As it is a very cheap instrument, it is in the hands of a great many learners, who fill up the vacuity of their leisure moments by grating the strings of this scrannel coagmentation of silk and wood. In better hands, however, its notes though shrill and piercing, are by no means contemptible, and I have sometimes seen a musician upon the stage apply the bow with so much address, that I have wished him the use of a better instrument . . .
>
> Since the above was written, I have since seen a rebeck of larger size and better workmanship. Its tone was low and plaintive, and therefore served well enough to soften the shrill sounds of the *urh heën* just described, to which it was played as an accompaniment. It seemed to be made of the swan che wood, as it was of a dark color . . .

Starting with the modern *erhu* and Mendoza's rebec, we have come full circle. Lay's "rebeck of larger size and better workmanship" with a "low and plaintive" tone and made from "darker wood" is more redolent of the rosewood *erhu* of Fig. 5.2.

Fig. 5.33 (next spread): "Moo-Lee-Wha" ("Molihua" or "Jasmine Flowers"). From *Travels in China*, pp. 316–317.
Date: 1806.
Author: John Barrow (1764–1848).
Dimensions: 26.5 × 22.7 cm.
Hong Kong University Library (U 915.1075 B2).

20. The Macartney Albums include one representation of the *yangqin*: WD961, picture 65, so it would be surprising if Barrow had not encountered it.

21. British Library Add. Ms. 33931 is another treasure trove of watercolors whose provenance is the 1792–1794 Embassy and comprises some thirty-seven illustrations, including the watercolors used for the island elevations inserted into copy 3 of Staunton's text. Its dedicatory preface, handwritten in black ink, reads: "This Collection of Original Drawings was made by Alexander; and by Mr. Barrow (afterward Sir John Barrow Bart.) and by Capn. Parish R[oyal] A[rtillery] is to be sent to the British Museum, at my death. [signed] John Barrow 25th, February, 1857." [This "John Barrow" is presumably a son or grandson of the John Barrow who wrote *Travels in China*.] Then is written: "Presented 3rd November 1890."

China. I have therefore given it in its unadorned ſtate, as ſung and played by the Chineſe, together with the words of the firſt ſtanza, and their literal tranſlation.

MOO-LEE-WHA.

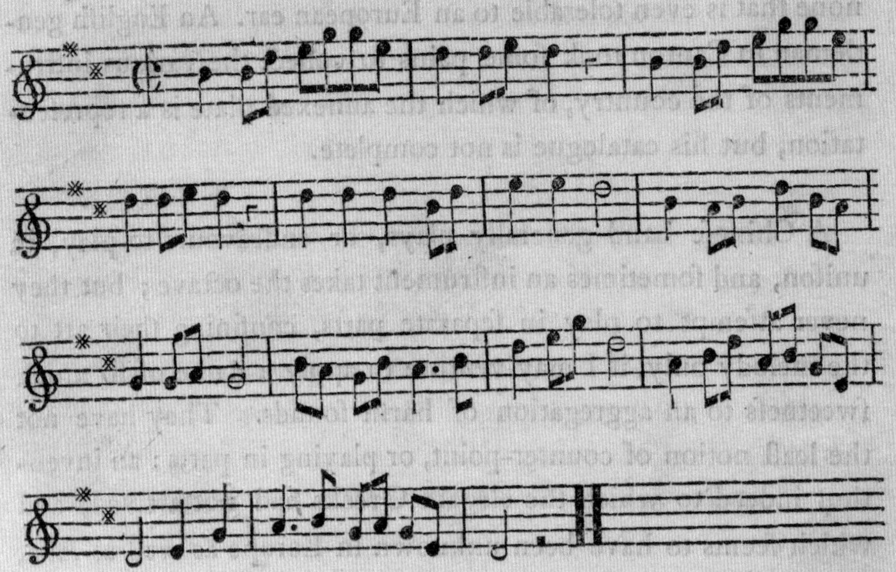

Moo-lee-wha.

I.

1 2 3 4 5
Hau ye-to ſien wha,
6 7 8 9 10 11 12 13
Yeu tchau yeu jie lo tſai go kia
14 15 16 17 18 19
Go pun tai, poo tchoo mun
20 21 22 23 24 25
Twee tcho ſien wha ul lo.

II.

II.

Hau[1] ye[2] to[3] Moo[4]-lee[5] wha[6]
Man[7] yuen[8] wha[9] kai[10] ſoy[11] poo[12] quee[13] ta[14]
Go[15] pun[16] tai[17] tſai[18] ye[19] ta[20]
Tai[21] you[22] kung[23] kan[24] wha[25] jin[26] ma[27].

Literal Tranſlation.

I.

How delightful[1] this[2] branch[3] of freſh[4] flowers[5]
One[6] morning[7] one[8] day[9] it was dropped[10] in[11] my[12] houſe[13]
I[14] the owner[15] will wear[16] it not[17] out[18] of doors[19]
But[20] I will[21] hold the freſh[22] flower[23] and[24] be happy[25].

II.

How delightful[1] this[2] branch[3] of the *Moo[4]-lee[5]* flower[6]
In the[7] full plot[8] of flowers[9] blowing[10] freely[11] none[12] excels[13] it[14]
I[15] the owner[16] will wear[17] this[18] gathered[19] branch[20]
Wear[21] it yet[22] fear[23], the flower[25] ſeen[24], men[25] will envy[27].

I have thought it not amiſs to ſubjoin a few other airs of the popular kind, which were written by the ſame gentleman at Canton, who made the drawings of their muſical inſtruments.

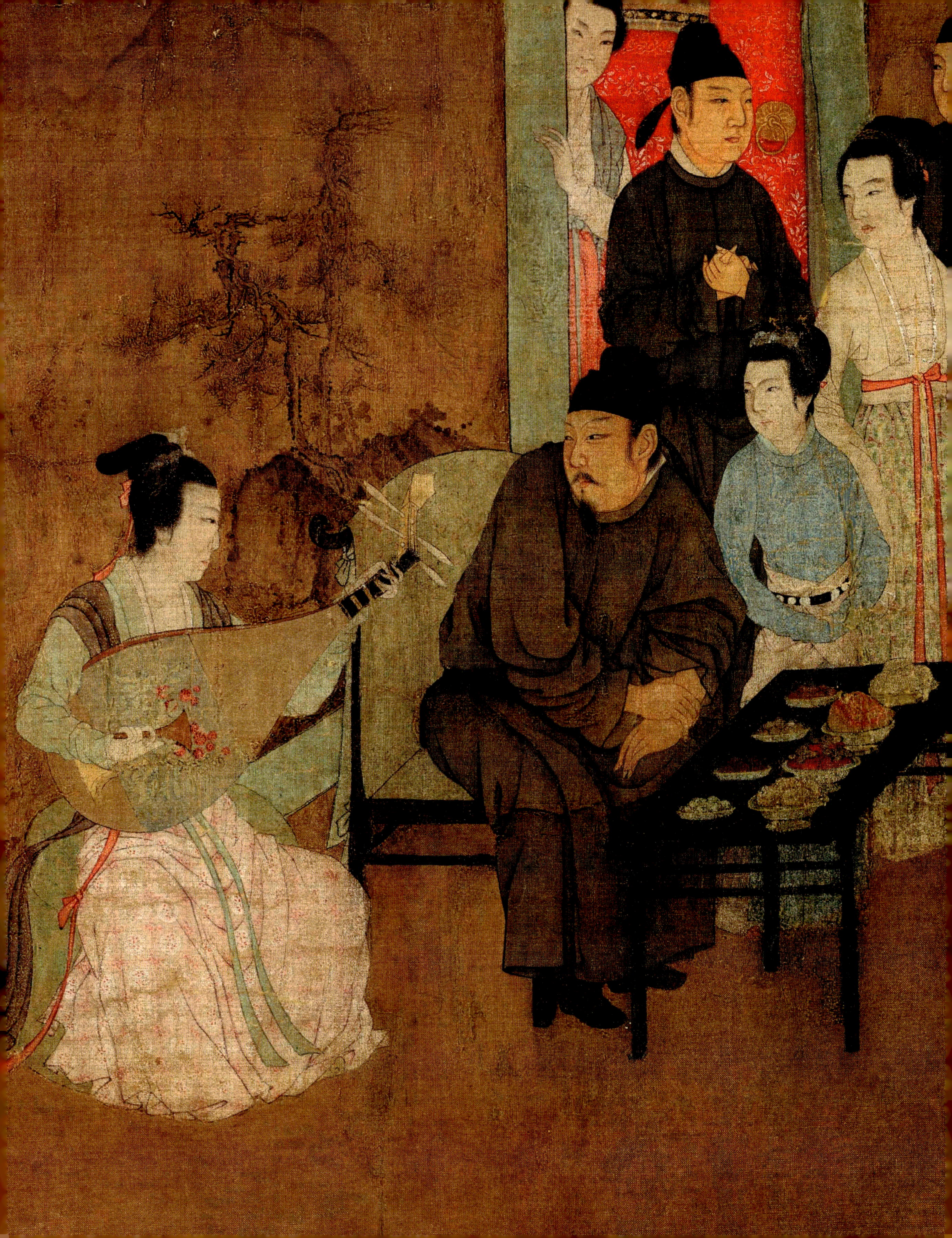

List of Tables and Figures

Fig. 5.5: "A Plan of the City and Harbour of Macao" (detail). From *An Authentic Account of an Embassy from the King of Great Britain to the Emperor of China*, folio volume, plate 11; date: 1797; author: George Staunton (1737–1801); dimensions: 57 × 43 cm; Hong Kong University Libraries (ULB 951.074 S79 a). Photograph by William Furniss.

Fig. 5.6: "The Procession of a Chinese Wedding when a Bride is brought home to her Husband." From *A Description of the Empire of China*, vol. 1, unnumbered plate opp. p. 303 (although the plate itself is labeled as opposite "p. 304," it is in fact opposite page 303); dates: 1738 / 1741; author: Jean-Baptiste Du Halde (1674–1743); artists: drawn by Antoine Humblot (?–1758), engraved by Charles Mosley (c. 1720–1756); dimensions: 40 × 25.5 cm; Hong Kong University Libraries (ULB 951.3 D86). Photograph by William Furniss.

Fig. 5.7: "Nôce Chinoise." From *Description de l'Empire de la Chine et de la Tartarie Chinoise* (the original French edition), vol. 2, unnumbered plate between pages 120 and 121; date: 1735; author: Jean-Baptiste Du Halde (1674–1743); artists: drawn by Antoine Humblot (?–1758), engraved by Jean-Baptiste Haussard (1679 or 1680–1749); dimensions: 50.7 × 41 cm; private collection.

Fig. 5.8: Close-up of the *huqin* player in Fig. 5.6.

Fig. 5.9: Close-up of the *huqin* player in Fig. 5.7.

Fig. 5.10: The *erhu* bow-hold. The index finger curls around the stick, the second and third fingers press the hair to regulate its tension during performance, and the little finger hangs loose and has no function.

Fig. 5.11: "Chinese Airs." From *A Description of the Empire of China*, vol. 2, unnumbered plate opp. p. 125; dates: 1738 / 1741; author: Jean-Baptiste Du Halde (1674–1743); artist: "This Plate is inscrib'd to Edmund Browne of the City of Bristol Esq." Edmund Browne cannot be traced; dimensions: 39.8 × 25.5 cm; Hong Kong University Libraries (ULB 951.3 D86). Photograph by William Furniss.

Fig. 5.12: "The Procession of a Chinese Wedding when a Bride is brought home to her Husband." From *The General History of China*, vol. II, pl. 8 opp. p. 202; date: 1739; author: Jean-Baptiste Du Halde (1674–1743); no artists given; dimensions: 12.5 × 20.0 cm; Hong Kong University Libraries (U 951 D86g). Photograph by William Furniss.

Fig. 5.13: "Chinese Airs." From *The General History of China*, vol. III, pp. 66–67; date: 1739; author: Jean-Baptiste Du Halde (1674–1743); no artists given; dimensions: 12.5 × 20.0 cm; Hong Kong University Libraries (U 951 D86g). Photograph by William Furniss.

Fig. 5.14: *Suite des Seize Estampes représentant les Conquêtes de l'Empereur de la Chine avec leur Explication*, presentation label to the Hong Kong University Libraries at the opening of the book; date: 1784 (the book was issued in 1788); publisher: Isadore Stanislav Helman (1743–1806 or 1809); dimensions: 42 × 55 cm; Hong Kong University Libraries (ULB 769.944 H4).

Fig. 5.15: *Suite des Seize Estampes représentant les Conquêtes de l'Empereur de la Chine avec leur Explication*, engraving VIII; date: 1784 (the book was issued in 1788); publisher: Isadore Stanislav Helman (1743–1806 or 1809); artists: drawn by Ignatius Sichelbarth (1708–1780), engraved by Benoît-Louis Prévost (1735 or 1747–1804) and Isadore Stanislav Helman; dimensions: 42 × 55 cm; Hong Kong University Libraries (ULB 769. 944 H4). Photograph by William Furniss.

Fig. 5.16: Detail of musicians in Fig. 5.15.

Fig. 5.17: *Jinchuan*; date: 1800–1831; artist: unknown; export watercolor album leaf: 48 × 36 cm; © The Trustees of the British Museum (1877.0714.1312).

Fig. 5.18: A replica primitive horsehead fiddle from the workshop of Duan Tingjun in Hohhot.

Fig. 5.19: The bow-hold used for the primitive horsehead fiddle.

Fig. 5.20: "L'Empereur Recitant des Poëmes en l'Honeur de ses Ancêtres." *Suite des Seize Estampes représentant les Conquêtes de l'Empereur de la Chine avec leur Explication*, engraving XXIV; date: 1784 (the book was issued in 1788); publisher and engraver: Isadore Stanislav Helman (1743–1806 or 1809); dimensions: 42 × 55 cm; Hong Kong University Libraries (ULB 769. 944 H4). Photograph by William Furniss.

Fig. 5.21: Detail of the left group of musicians in Figure 5.20.

Fig. 5.22: Detail of the right group of musicians in Figure 5.20.

Fig. 5.23: "A Scene of an Historical Play Exhibited on the Chinese Stage." From *An Authentic Account of an Embassy from the King of Great Britain to the Emperor of China*, folio volume, plate 30; date: 1797; author: George Staunton (1737–1801); artists: drawn by William Alexander (1767–1816), engraved by James Heath (1757–1834); dimensions: 57 × 43 cm; Hong Kong University Libraries (ULB 951.074 S79 a). Photograph by William Furniss.

Fig. 5.24: "A Chinese Theatre—Canton;" date: "21 December; 1793;" artist: William Alexander (1767–1816); watercolor: 35.5 × 23.3 cm; © The British Library Board (Macartney Albums, WD961, picture 168).

Fig. 5.25: *An Authentic Account of an Embassy from the King of Great Britain to the Emperor of China*, vol. 2, Hankow Club Library accession sticker found at the front of the volume; date: 1797; author: George Staunton (1737–1801); Hong Kong University Libraries (ULB 951.074 S79 a).

Fig. 5.26: *An Authentic Account of an Embassy from the King of Great Britain to the Emperor of China*, vol. 1, bookplate of R. H. Alexander Bennet (1743–1814 or ?1771–1818) on the second page opening; date: 1798; author: George Staunton (1737–1801); bookplate size: 9.5 × 6.4 cm; Fung Ping Shan Library (ULB 951.074 S79 a).

Fig. 5.27: *An Authentic Account of an Embassy from the King of Great Britain to the Emperor of China*, vol. 1, binder's label on the first page opening; date: 1798; author: George Staunton (1737–1801); label size: 1.4 × 3.1 cm; Fung Ping Shan Library (ULB 951.074 S79 a).

Fig. 5.28: *An Authentic Account of an Embassy from the King of Great Britain to the Emperor of China*, vol. 1, Frost and Reed label and imprinted stamp of A. W. Bahr on the first page opening; date: 1798; author: George Staunton (1737–1801); Fung Ping Shan Library (ULB 951.074 S79 a).

Fig. 5.29: *Travels in China*, unnumbered plate between pages 314 and 315; date: 1806; author: John Barrow (1764–1848); dimensions: 27.8 × 22.8 cm; Hong Kong University Libraries (U 915.1075 B2). Photograph by William Furniss.

Fig. 5.30: British Library, Add. Ms. 33931, fols. 12v–13r; date: 1792–1794; artist: William Alexander (1767–1816); © The British Library Board (Add. Ms. 33931).

Fig. 5.31: A fine modern mid-voiced *banhu* from the workshop of Lü Jianhua in Beijing.

Fig. 5.32: A fine example of a *jinghu*.

Fig. 5.33: "Moo-Lee-Wha" ("Molihua" or "Jasmine Flowers"). From *Travels in China*, pp. 316–317; date: 1806; author: John Barrow (1764–1848); dimensions: 26.5 × 22.7 cm; Hong Kong University Libraries (U 915.1075 B2). Photograph by William Furniss.

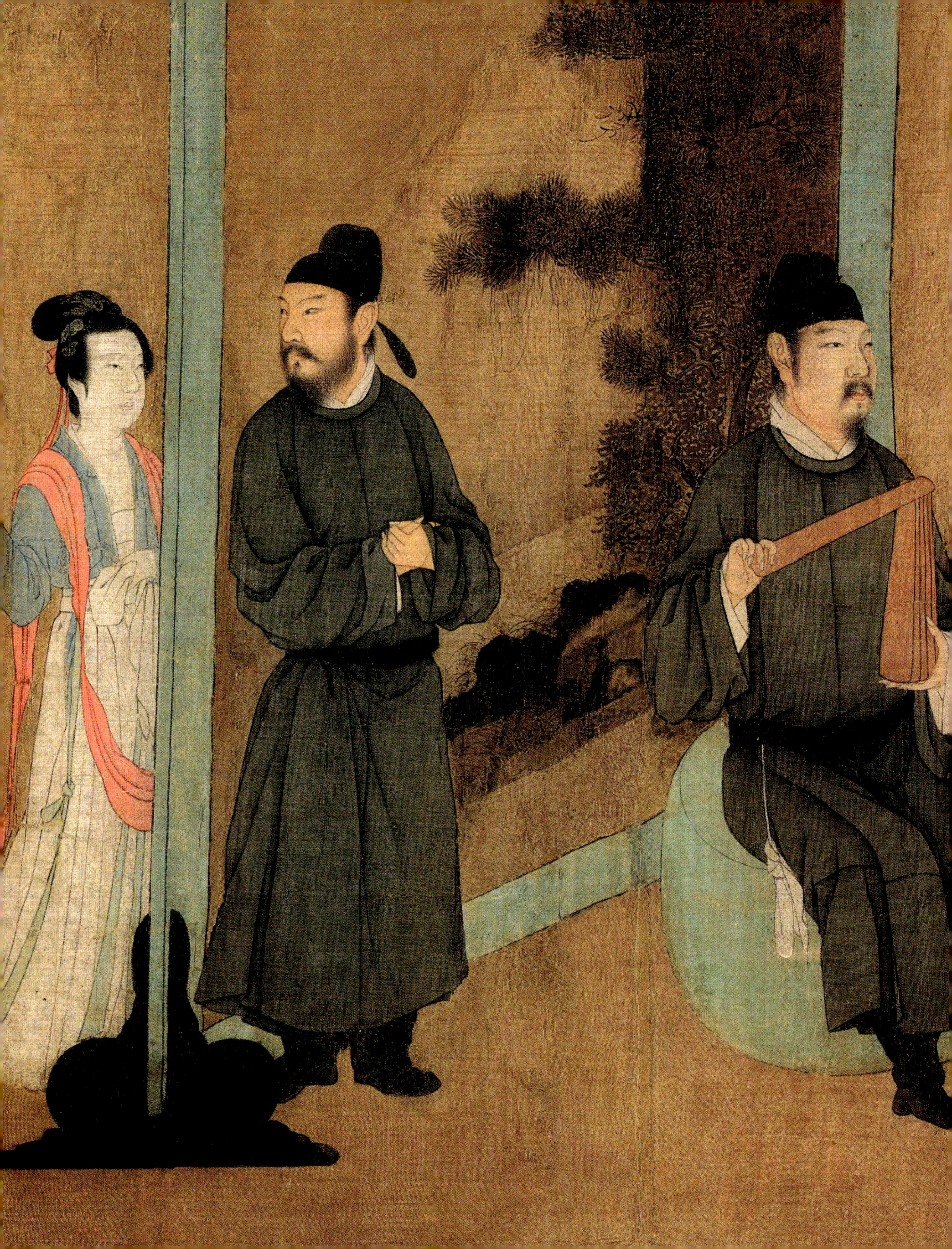

Glossary of Chinese Characters

Abe Ryūichi 阿部隆一 (1917–1983)
Amiot, Joseph-Marie 錢德明 (1718–1793)
Ao Jigong 敖繼公 (act. 1301)
Ashikaga Gakkō 足立學校
Attiret, Jean Dionysius 王致誠 (1702–1768)

ba 跋
Baishi daoren gequ 白石道人歌曲
Ban Gu 班固 (32–92)
Bei 邶
Bieji 別集
Bin 豳
Bo Qi 伯奇
Boya 伯牙

Cai Bojie 蔡伯喈
Cai Qi 蔡玘
Cai Shen 蔡沈 (1167–1230)
Cai Yuanding 蔡元定 (1135–1198)
Cao 曹
Castiglione, Guiseppe 郎世寧 (1688–1766)
Chaisang 柴桑
Changgan she 長干社
Changtingyuan 長亭怨
Chao Gongwu 晁公武 (c. 1105–1180)
Chao Yuezhi 晁說之 (1059–1129)
Chen 陳
Chen Dalai 陳大來
Chen Duo 陳鐸 (c. 1436–1507)
Chen Fei 陳斐
Chen Fengwu 陳鳳梧 (1475–1541)
Chen Fuliang 陳傅良 (1137–1203)
Chen Junbao 陳君葆 (1898–1982)
Chen Suowen 陳所聞 (c. 1553–?)
Chen Yang 陳暘 (1064–1128)
Chen Yingxiang 陳應祥
Chen Yuanliang 陳元靚
Chen Yunjiu 陳雲九
Chen Zhensun 陳振孫 (1179–1262)
Cheng Dayue 程大約 (1541–1616)
Cheng Tang 成湯 (c. 1675–1646 BCE)
Cheng Wang 成王, King (Zhou, r. 1042–1021 BCE)
Chenglian 成連
Chengshi moyuan 程氏墨苑
"Chicha" 喫茶

Chongning 崇寧, Era (Song, 1102–1106)
Chongwen zongmu 崇文總目
Chuandai tigang 穿戴提綱
chuiwan 捶丸
Chunqiu 春秋
Chunqiu Zuoshi zhuan zhushu 春秋左氏傳注疏
Chunxi 淳熙, Era (Song, 1174–1189)
chunyu 錞于
Chunyu lou 春雨樓, *see* Shen Cai
Chunyu lou ji 春雨樓集
Chuwang 楚望, *see* Guo Mian
ci 詞
cipai 詞牌
Clementi, Cecil 金文泰 (1875–1947)
Cong Wenwei 叢文蔚 (*jinshi* degree 1568)
Cui Yingying 崔鶯鶯
Cui Zundu 崔遵度 (954–1020)
cun 寸

Da Wu 大武
Da Xia 大夏
"Da Ya" 大雅
Dade 大德, Era (Yuan, 1297–1307)
Dai Sheng 戴聖 (fl. first century)
daimyō 大名
Damascenus, Joannes 安德義 (?–1781)
Danhuangliu 淡黃柳
Deyou 德祐, Era (Song, 1274–1276)
ding 鼎
Dong Kang 董康 (1867–1947)
Dong Zhongshu 董仲舒 (c. 198–c. 107 BCE)
Dongjing menghua lu 東京夢華錄
Donglai xiansheng fenmen shilü wuku 東萊先生分門詩律武庫
Du You 杜佑 (735–812)
Du Yu 杜預 (222–285)
Dui chuiyang 對垂楊
Dun Fu shushi 敦復書室
Dunhuang 敦煌
duo 鐸

erhu 二胡

Fan Lüshuang 范履霜, *see* Fan Zhongyan
Fan Wenzheng gong ji 范文正公集
Fan Yunkui 范雲逵

Fan Zhongyan 范仲淹 (989–1052)
Fang Ruiyi 方濬益 (?–1899)
Fang Xuanling 房玄齡 (579–648)
"Fenxiang baiyue" 焚香拜月
fu 副
fu 賦
Fu shiyin Chunqiu Zuo zhuan zhushu 附釋音春秋左傳注疏
Fu shiyin Mao shi zhushu 附釋音毛詩注疏
Fu shiyin Shang shu zhushu 附釋音尚書注疏
Fu Zengxiang 傅增湘 (1872–1949)
Fung Ping Shan 馮平山 (1860–1931)

Gayū manroku 雅遊漫錄
Ge pu 閣譜
Genroku 元祿, Era (Tokugawa, 1688–1704)
gong 宮
gongche 工尺
Gongyang Gao 公羊高 (act. Warring States Period)
Goshima Kuniharu 五島邦治
Gu Tinglong 顧廷龍 (1904–1998)
Guan Hanqing 關漢卿 (c. 1225–c. 1302)
Guangling san 廣陵散
Guangyang zaji 廣陽雜記
Guliang Chi 穀梁赤 (act. Warring States Period)
"Guo Feng" 國風
Guo Lixuan 郭立暄 (b. 1971)
Guo Maoqian 郭茂倩 (1041–1099)
Guo Mian 郭沔 (c. 1190–1260)

Han shu 漢書
Han Tuozhou 韓侂冑 (1152–1207)
hanlin 翰林
Hanyi 翰怡, *see* Liu Chenggan
hao 號
Hongniang 紅娘
Hongping 虹屏, *see* Shen Cai
Hongwu 洪武, Era (Ming, 1368–1399)
Hou Han shu 後漢書
Hu Gongxuan 胡公玄
Huaiting jushi 懷庭居士, *see* Ye Tang
Huancui tang yuefu 環翠堂樂府
Huang Pilie 黃丕烈 (1763–1825)
Huang Qing 黃慶
Huang Shanfu 黃善夫
Huang Tingjian 黃庭堅 (1045–1105)
Huang Yiran 黃依然
Huangchao liqi tushi 皇朝禮器圖式
Huangyou 皇祐, Era (Song, 1049–1054)
Huizong 徽宗, Empror (Song, r. 1100–1126)
huqin 胡琴
Huqin xiang 胡琴巷

Jao Tsung-i 饒宗頤 (1917–2018)
Ji Kang 嵇康 (223–262)
Ji Zha 季札 (576–484 BCE)
Jia Gongyan 賈公彥 (fl. 651–655)
Jiabin 嘉賓, *see* Zhu Hongyi
Jiading 嘉定, Era (Song, 1208–1224)
Jiajing 嘉靖, Era (Ming, 1522–1566)
jian 簡
"Jian shuo" 簡說
Jiang Biao 江標 (1860–1899)
Jiang Fengzao 蔣鳳藻 (c. 1838–1908)
Jiang Kui 姜夔 (1155–1221)
Jiang Yang 蔣暘 (*jinshi* degree 1521)
Jiangxi pu 江西譜
Jianxia 建霞, *see* Jiang Biao
jianzipu 減字譜
Jiao Hong 焦竑 (1540–1620)
Jiatai 嘉泰, Era (Song, 1201–1204)
Jiaye tang 嘉業堂
Jie xinshi 解心事
Jiegu lu 羯鼓錄
Jieyi lu 結一廬
Jin Luan 金鑾 (1494–1587)
Jin shu 晉書
Jinchuan 金川
jindou 巾斗
jing 經
Jing Du 井度 (act. 1141)
Jingchai ji 荊釵記
Jingde 景德, Era (Song, 1004–1007)
Jingdian shiwen 經典釋文
jinghu 京胡
"Jingji zhi" 經籍志
Jinqing 藎卿, *see* Chen Suowen
jinshi 進士
Jiu Tang shu 舊唐書
Jiugong dacheng nan bei ci gongpu 九宮大成南北詞宮譜
Jizhi zhai 繼志齋, *see* Chen Dalai
juan 卷
jue 角
Jueshao 角招
Junzhai dushu zhi 郡齋讀書志
juren 舉人

kai 楷
Kaiyuan 開元, Era (Tang, 713–741)
Kang Wang 康王, King (Zhou, r. 1020–996 BCE)
Kangjie 康節, *see* Shao Yong
Kangxi 康熙, Emperor (Qing, r. 1661–1722)
Ke Weixiong 柯維熊 (*jinshi* degree 1517)
Kojima Hōso 小島寶素 (1797–1847)
Kong Yingda 孔穎達 (574–648)
Kōson 篁村, *see* Shimada Shigenori
Kuai 鄶
Kuaixue zhai 快雪齋, *see* Lu Xuan
Kui 夔
kunqu 崑曲

Lantian 藍田
Lepu 樂圃
Lepu yugao 樂圃餘稿
Li ji 禮記
Li Jundu 李均度
Li Mengzhe 李孟悊
Li Wang 李旺
Li Yangong 李言恭 (1541–1599)
Li Yu 李漁 (1611–1680)
Li Yuanyang 李元陽 (1497–1580)
Li Yuanzhi 李元植
Li Zhifang 李直方
Lianghuai Jiangdong zhuanyun si 兩淮江東轉運司
Liangzhe donglu cha yan si 兩浙東路茶鹽司
Ling Mengchu 凌濛初 (1580–1684)
Lingxing xiaowu pu 靈星小舞譜
Liu Ao 劉驁, Emperor (Han, r. 33–7 BCE)
Liu Che 劉徹, Emperor (Han, r. 141–87 BCE)
Liu Chenggan 劉承幹 (1881–1963)
Liu De 劉德 (160–129 BCE)
Liu Heng 劉恒, Emperor (Han, r. 180–157 BCE)
Liu Jin 劉瑾 (c. 1245–c. 1315)
Liu Kuang 劉貺 (act. 726)
Liu Xiang 劉向 (77–6 BCE)
Liu Xianting 劉獻廷 (1648–1695)
Liu Xin 劉歆 (46 BCE–23 CE)
Liu Xu 劉昫 (887–946)
Liu Xun 劉詢, Emperor (Han, r. 74–48 BCE)
Liu Zhifang 劉志芳
Liujia Wenxuan 六家文選
"Liuyi lüe" 六藝略
Liweng 笠翁, *see* Li Yu
"Liyue zhi" 禮樂志
Lize shuyuan 麗澤書院
Long De 龍德
Longle 龍勒
Lu 魯
Lu Bing 陸炳 (1510–1560)
Lu Deming 陸德明 (556–627)
Lu Hang 陸沆
Lu Jiuyuan 陸九淵 (1139–1192)
Lu Qitang 陸啓鏜
Lu Xianggong 魯襄公 (575–542 BCE, r. 572–542 BCE)
Lu Xinyuan 陸心源 (1838–1894)
Lu Xuan 陸烜 (1737–1799)
Lu Zhuan 陸僎
lü 律
Lü Baozhong 呂葆中 (?–1707)
Lü Liuliang 呂留良 (1629–1683)
"Lüli zhi" 律曆志
Lülü chengshu 律呂成書
Lülü xinshu 律呂新書
Lülü zhengyi 律呂正義
Lülü zhengyi houbian 律呂正義後編
Lüshuang cao 履霜操
luo 鑼
Luo Fubao 羅福葆 (1899–1967)
Luo Yuanjue 羅原覺 (1891–1965)
Luo Zhenchang 羅振常 (1875–1942)
Luoyue daoren 蘿月道人, *see* Chen Suowen

Ma Duanlin 馬端臨 (1254–1323)
Ma Guohan 馬國翰 (1794–1857)
Ma Tingluan 馬廷鸞 (1222–1289)
Ma Zhiyuan 馬致遠 (c. 1270–1330)
Mao Jin 毛晉 (1599–1659)
Mao Minzhong 毛敏仲
Meigu 梅谷, *see* Lu Xuan
Meigu oubi 梅谷偶筆
Meigu shishi 梅谷侍史, *see* Shen Cai
Meigu shizhong shu 梅谷十種書
Meng Yuanlao 孟元老 (fl. 1103–1147)
Mengliang lu 夢梁錄
Mengying ci 夢影詞
Miao Quansun 繆荃孫 (1844–1919)
Min Qiji 閔齊伋 (1580–after 1661)
"Ming Yue yao" 明月謠
Mingfeng ji 鳴鳳記
mo 末
Mochou hu 莫愁湖
"Moo-Lee-Wha" 茉莉花
Mōri Takanaka 毛利高翰 (1795–1852)
Mōri Takasue 毛利高標 (1755–1801)
Mudan ting 牡丹亭

Nagasawa Kikuya 長澤規矩也 (1902–1980)
Nanhai dujing tang 南海讀經堂
nanyong ben 南雍本
nao 鐃
Nashu ying qupu 納書楹曲譜
Nianpu buyi 年譜補遺
Nishang zhongxu diyi 霓裳中序第一

Ogyū Sorai 荻生徂徠 (1666–1728)
Ouyang Wenzhong gong wenji 歐陽文忠公集
Ouyang Xiu 歐陽修 (1007–1072)

Pan Chang 潘鋹
Pan Chengbi 潘承弼 (1907–2004)
"Pan Geng" 盤庚
Pedrini, Theodorico 德理格 (1671–1746)
Peizhan 沛霑, *see* Shao Enduo
Peng Sunyu 彭孫遹 (1631–1700)
Peng Yuanrui 彭元瑞 (1731–1803)
Peng Zhenyin 彭貞隱
Pereira, Thomas 徐日昇 (1645–1708)
Pinghong nüshi 屏虹女史, *see* Shen Cai
pipa 琵琶
Pipa ji 琵琶記

Qi 齊
Qi Huan 綦焕
Qi Jin zhai 奇晉齋, *see* Lu Xuan
Qi Taigong 齊太公 (c. 1128–c. 1015 BCE)
Qi Wudi 齊無棣
Qian Chengmei 錢長美
Qian Yulian 錢玉蓮
qianjin 千斤
Qianlong 乾隆, Emperor (Qing, r. 1735–1796)
Qilüe 七略
qin 琴
Qin 秦
"Qin fu" 琴賦
Qin se pu 琴瑟譜
Qin shi 琴史
"Qin shi" 秦誓
"Qin shu zeng Huang Yiran" 琴述贈黃依然
Qin shuo 琴説
Qin zhi 琴旨
Qinding Cipu 欽定詞譜
Qingli 慶曆, Era (Song, 1041–1049)
Qingrong jushi ji 清容居士集
Qingyao shanren 青要山人, *see* Shen Cai
Qingyuan 慶元, Era (Song, 1195–1200)
Qinyin weng 琴隱翁
"Qixiu sanli zha" 乞修三禮劄
qu 曲
Qu Yuan 屈原 (c. 343–c. 278)
Quxian Shenqi mipu 臞仙神奇秘譜 (1425)

ruan 阮
Ruigua tang 瑞瓜堂

Sadahiko 彥楨, *see* Shimada Kan
saibara 催馬樂
Saiki Bunko 佐伯文庫
sanqu 散曲
sanxian 三弦
"Saosong" 掃松
se 瑟
Seikadō Bunko 靜嘉堂文庫
Sepu houlu 瑟譜後錄
Shaanxi buzheng si 陝西布政司
shang 商
Shang shu 尚書
Shang shu yi 尚書義
"Shanglu" 上路
Shao Enduo 邵恩多 (fl. late eighteenth and early nineteenth centuries)
Shao Yong 邵雍 (1011–1077)
Shaowu jiucheng yuebu 韶舞九成樂補
Shaoxing 紹興, Era (Song, 1131–1162)
shejian 射箭
Shen Cai 沈彩 (c. 1748–?)
Shen Yue 沈約 (441–513)
sheng 笙
"Sheng wu ai le lun" 聲無哀樂論
Sheng Xuanhuai 盛宣懷 (1844–1916)
Shenqi mipu 神奇秘譜, see *Quxian Shenqi mipu*
Shenyin jiangu lu 審音鑒古錄
Shi ji 史記
Shi jing 詩經
Shi Zhong 師中
Shigu tang 式穀堂
Shilin guangji 事林廣記
Shimada Kan 島田翰 (1879–1915)
Shimada Shigenori 島田重禮 (1838–1898)
Shiqi shi xiangjie 十七史詳節
Shishuo xinyu 世說新語
shōgun 將軍
Shōhei-zaka Gakumonjo 昌平坂學問所
shuanglu 雙陸
Shun 舜
"Shun dian" 舜典
Shun Yu 舜漁, *see* You Shipei
shupu 樗蒲
Sichelbarth, Ignatius 艾啓蒙 (1708–1780)
Siku quanshu zongmu 四庫全書總目
Sima Qian 司馬遷 (c. 145–c. 86 BCE)
Sishu zhangju jizhu 四書章句集注
"Song" 頌
Song Qi 宋祁 (998–1061)
"Song Yang Zhi xu" 送楊寘序
Songgong Cheng 宋公成
Su Shi 蘇軾 (1037–1101)
Sui shu 隋書
Suihan tang 歲寒堂
Suijin cipu 碎金詞譜
Suijin xupu 碎金續譜
Sun Daozi 孫道滋
Sun Jiugao 孫九皋
suona 嗩吶

Taigu yiyin 太古遺音
Taiyueling biji 太樂令壁記
Taizong 太宗, Emperor (Song, r. 967–997)
Taizong 太宗, Emperor (Tang, r. 626–649)
Takezoe Shinichiro 竹添進一郎 (1842–1917)
Tang 唐
Tang Shi 湯式
"Tang Yi shi xu" 唐異詩序
Tao Tang 陶唐
Tao Yuanming 陶淵明 (365–427)
Tao Zongyi 陶宗儀 (1316–1403)
Tianli 天曆, Era (Song, 1328–1330)
"Tianzhu shan Ri Guan dashi taji" 天竺山日觀大師塔記
Tiebao 鐵保 (1752–1824)
tiqin 提琴
Tokugawa Ienari 德川家齊 (1773–1841)
touhu 投壺

wai 外
Wang Ao 王鏊 (1450–1524)
Wang Danshan 王丹山
Wang Haoran 汪浩然 (fl. Ming dynasty)
Wang Houzhi 王厚之 (1131–1204)
Wang Jide 王驥德 (?–1623)
Wang Jishan 王繼善 (act. 1834)
Wang Langyuan 汪閬源 (1786–?)
Wang Liang 汪諒
Wang Mang 王莽 (45 BCE–23 CE)
Wang Mengshu 汪孟舒 (1887–1969)
Wang Renquan 王仁權
Wang Shifu 王實甫 (c. 1260–c. 1337)
Wang Tan 王坦 (fl. eighteenth century)
Wang Tingne 汪廷訥 (1573–1619)
Wang Wei 王維 (699–759)
Wang Wensheng 汪文盛 (?–1543)
Wang Wenyao 王文耀
Wang Xisheng 王錫生
Wang Yangming 王陽明 (1472–1529)
Wang Yaochen 王堯臣 (1003–1058)
Wang Yongqing 王永慶
Wang Yu 王禹
Wanhua zhuren 玩花主人
Wanli 萬曆, Era (Ming, 1573–1620)
Wei 衛
Wei 魏
Wei Kangshu 衛康叔 (act. 1042 BCE)
Wei Tao 韋縚
Wei Ti 衛湜 (act. 1226)
Wei Wugong 衛武公 (852–758 BCE)
weiqi 圍棋
Wen Renquan 聞人詮
Wen Wang 文王, King (Zhou, r. 1100–1050 BCE)
Wen Zhengming 文徵明 (1470–1559)
Weng Shouqi 翁綬琪 (*juren* degree 1891)
Wenxian tongkao 文獻通考
Wenxuan zhu 文選注
wenzipu 文字譜
Wu 吳
Wu Baojie 吳保鍇 (1886–?)
Wu Changshou 吳昌綬 (1867–1924)
Wu Tang 吳棠 (1813–1876)
Wu Wang 武王, King (Zhou, r. 1046–1043 BCE)
Wu Zimu 吳自牧 (act. 1274)
Wusilan zhifa shi 烏絲欄指法釋
wutong 梧桐

Xi 奚
Xia 夏
Xia Chengtao 夏承燾 (1900–1986)
"Xian you yi de" 咸有一德
Xiangyin shiyue pu 鄉飲詩樂譜
Xianqing ouji 閒情偶寄
Xiao Tong 蕭統 (501–531)
"Xiao Ya" 小雅
Xiaoweng 肖翁, *see* Zhang Yan
"Xiaoxiang shuiyun" 瀟湘水雲
"Xibo kan li" 西伯戡黎
Xie Sheng 謝陞 (1572–1645)
Xie Yuanhuai 謝元淮 (1784–1867)
Xie Zixiang 謝子祥 (fl. late thirteenth century)
Xie Zizhi 謝紫芝 (fl. early eighteenth century)
Xin Tang shu 新唐書
Xing Bing 邢昺 (932–1010)
Xinjuan gujin daya nanbei gong ciji 新鐫古今大雅南北宮詞紀
Xiong Penglai 熊朋來 (fl. thirteenth century)
xiqin 奚琴
xiucai 秀才
Xiuneisi 脩內司
Xixiang ji 西廂記
Xixue jiyan 習學記言
Xu 胥
Xu Li 徐理
Xu Tianming 徐天民
Xuanhe bogu tulu 宣和博古圖錄
"Xunmeng" 尋夢
Xushan canqie 胥山蠶妾, *see* Shen Cai

ya 雅
Yan Zhenqing 顏真卿 (709–785)
Yang Fu 楊復 (act. 1228)
Yang Shaohe 楊紹和 (1830–1875)
Yang Zan 楊瓚 (fl. thirteenth century)
Yang Zuochang 楊祚昌
Yangguan 陽關
yangqin 揚琴
Yangzhou huafang lu 揚州畫舫錄
Yanosuke Iwasaki 岩崎彌之助 (1851–1908)
Yao 堯
"Yao dian" 堯典
Yao Zhenzong 姚振宗
yazheng 軋箏
Ye Changchi 葉昌熾 (1849–1917)
Ye Shi 葉適 (1150–1223)
Ye Shulian 葉樹廉 (1619–1685)
Ye Tang 葉堂 (1724–1795)
"Yekang" 噎糠
Yi li 儀禮
Yi li jishuo 儀禮集說
Yi li shu 儀禮疏
Yi li tu 儀禮圖
Yi li zhu shu 儀禮註疏
Yin 尹
Ying Jia 應檟 (1493–1553)
"Yinyue zhi" 音樂志
"Yiwen zhi" 藝文志
Yong 鄘
Yongle dadian 永樂大典
You Shipei 尤世培

Youlan 幽蘭
yu 羽
Yu 禹
Yu Gong 虞公
"Yu Tang chushi shu" 與唐處士書
Yu Yu 俞翊
Yu Zai 余載 (fl. 1328–1330)
Yu zhai 愚齋, *see* Sheng Xuanhuai
Yuan Jue 袁桷 (1266–1327)
Yuan Kewen 袁克文 (1889–1931)
Yuan Qiong 袁褧
Yuan Shikai 袁世凱 (1859–1916)
"Yue ji" 樂記
Yue jing 樂經
"Yue ming" 說命
"Yue shu" 樂書
Yue shu 樂書
"Yue zai renhe buzai yin" 樂在人和不在音
"Yue zhi" 樂志
Yuefu huncheng ji 樂府混成集
Yuefu zalu 樂府雜錄
yuegong 樂工
Yuelü quanshu 樂律全書
Yue'ou 粵謳
yuezheng 樂正
yuming 御名
Yunlu 允祿 (1695–1767)
yunluo 雲鑼
Yuqian 玉嵌, *see* Peng Zhenyin
Yuzhi wen chuji 御製文初集

zaju 雜劇
Zeng Lu 曾魯 (1319–1372)
Zha Fuxi 查阜西 (1895–1976)
Zhang Gong 張珙
Zhang Guangcai 張廣才
Zhang Shuping 張叔平 (1898–1970)
Zhang Yan 張巖
Zhang Yuanji 張元濟 (1867–1959)
Zhao Ding 趙定
Zhao Wanli 趙萬里 (1905–1980)
Zhao Wuniang 趙五娘
Zhao Xian 趙㬎, Emperor (Song, r. 1274–1276)
Zhao Yansu 趙彥肅 (1148–1196)
Zhao Ziyong 招子庸 (1786–1847)
zheng 箏
zheng 鉦
Zheng 鄭
Zheng Xuan 鄭玄 (127–200)
Zheng Yin 鄭寅 (d. 1237)
Zheng Zhenduo 鄭振鐸 (1898–1958)
zhi 徵
Zhi shengdao zhai 知聖道齋
Zhida 至大, Era (Yuan, 1308–1311)
"Zhijing" 執競
Zhishun 至順, Era (Yuan, 1330–1333)
Zhizhai shulu jieti 直齋書錄解題
Zhong Songting 鍾松亭
Zhou 周
Zhou li 周禮
Zhou Mi 周密 (1232–1298)
Zhou Xingji 周行己 (*jinshi* degree 1091)
Zhou Xingyi 周星詒 (1833–1904)
Zhu Changwen 朱長文 (1038–1098)
Zhu Dianqing 朱甸卿
Zhu Hongyi 朱鴻儀 (1902–1973)
Zhu Quan 朱權 (1378–1448)
Zhu Shao 朱韶, *see* Zhu Hongyi
Zhu Xi 朱熹 (1130–1200)
Zhu Xueqin 朱學勤 (1823–1875)
Zhu Yizun 朱彝尊 (1629–1709)
Zhu Yuanzhang 朱元璋, Emperor (Ming, r. 1368–1398)
Zhu Zaiyu 朱載堉 (1536–1611)
zhuan 賺
Zhui baiqiu 綴白裘
zi 字
Zijin 子晉, *see* Mao Jin
Zijing 子敬, *see* Zheng Yin
Zixia dong pu 紫霞洞譜
zun 尊
Zuo Qiuming 左丘明 (556–452 BCE)
Zuo zhuan 左傳

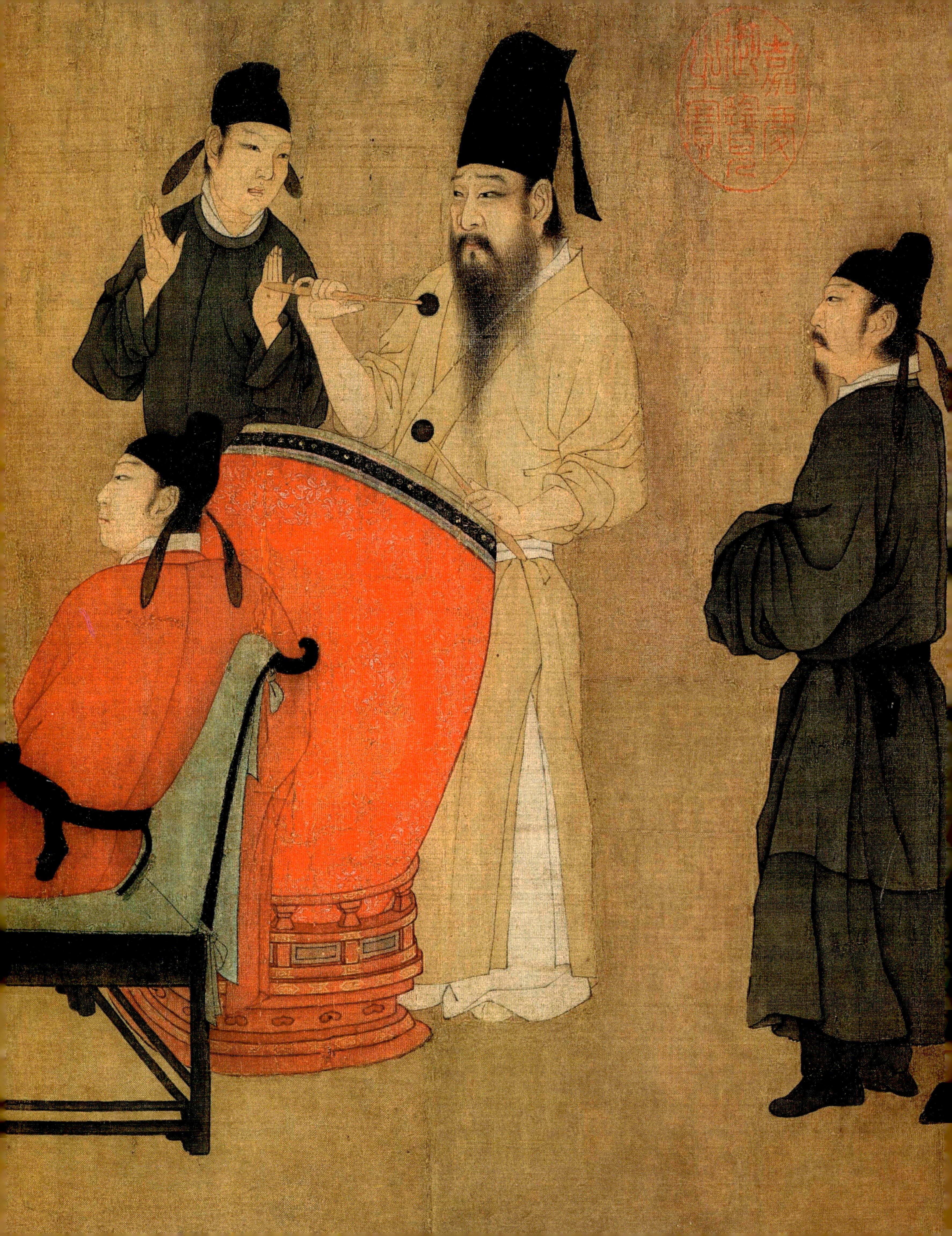

Bibliography

Aalst, J. A. van. *Chinese Music*. Shanghai: The Inspectorate of Customs, 1884.

Abe Ryūichi 阿部隆一. *Chugoku hōshoshi (zōteiban)* 中國訪書志（增訂版）. Tokyo: Kyūko shoin, 1976.

Amiot, Joseph-Marie. *Mémoire sur la Musique des Chinois, tant anciens que modernes*. In *Mémoires concernant l'histoire, les arts, les sciences, les moeurs, les usages des Chinois*, edited by Charles Batteux and Louis Georges Oudard Feudrix de Bréquigny, vol. 6, 1–254. Paris: Nyon, 1776–1814.

Amiot, Joseph-Marie. *Mémoire sur la Musique des Chinois, tant anciens que modernes*, edited by Philipp-Joseph Roussier. Paris: Nyon, 1779.

Ban Gu 班固. *Han shu* 漢書, 12 vols. Beijing: Zhonghua shuju, 1962.

Barrow, John. *Travels in China*. London: for Cadell and W. Davies, 1806.

Baxter, Glen William. "Metrical Origins of the *Tz'u*." *Harvard Journal of Asiatic Studies* 16.1 / 2 (1953): 108–145.

Bol, Peter K. *"This Culture of Ours": Intellectual Transitions in T'ang and Sung China*. Stanford: Stanford University Press, 1992.

Boltz, William G. "*I-li*." In *Early Chinese Texts: A Bibliographical Guide*, edited by Michael Loewe, 234–244. Berkeley: Society for the Study of Early China, 1993.

Bossler, Beverly. "Shifting Identities: Courtesans and Literati in Song China." *Harvard Journal of Asiatic Studies* 62.1 (2002): 5–37.

Brokaw, Cynthia and Kai-wing Chow. *Printing and Book Culture in Late Imperial China*. Berkeley and Los Angeles: University of California Press, 2005.

Brokaw, Cynthia. *Commerce in Culture: The Sibao Book Trade in the Qing and Republican Periods*. Cambridge, Mass.: Harvard University Asia Center, 2007.

Bruckner, Christopher. *Chinese Imperial Patronage: Treasures from Temples and Palaces*, vol. 2. London: Asian Art Gallery, 2005.

Cahill, James. "The Shibui Printed Books in Chinese and Japanese Erotic Pictorial Art." *Orientations* 40.3 (2009): 43–48.

Carter, Stewart. "The Editor from Hell: Information and Misinformation on Chinese Music in Late Eighteenth-Century France." In *Music in Eighteenth-Century Culture*, edited by Mary Sue Morrow, 23–47. Ann Arbor: Steglein Publishing, 2016.

Carter, Thomas and L. C. Goodrich. *The Invention of Printing in China and its Spread Westward*. New York: Ronald Press, 1955.

Chao Gongwu 晁公武. *Junzhai dushu zhi jiaozheng* 郡齋讀書志校證, 2 vols. Shanghai: Shanghai guji chubanshe, 1990.

Chartier, Roger. "Music in Print." In *Music and the Cultures of Print*, edited by Kate van Orden, 325–341. New York: Garland Publishing, 2000.

Chen Fukang 陳福康. "Zheng Zhenduo *Qiushu riji* yigao 鄭振鐸《求書日錄》佚稿." *Wenxian* 文獻 (2005) 1: 169–190.

Chen Yingshi 陳應時. *Dunhuang yuepu jieyi bianzheng* 敦煌樂譜解譯辨證. Shanghai: Shanghai yinyue xueyuan chubanshe, 2005.

Chen Yingshi. "A Report on Chinese Research into the Dunhuang Music Manuscripts." *Musica Asiatica* 6 (1991): 61–72.

Chen Zhensun 陳振孫. *Zhizhai shulu jieti* 直齋書錄解題. Shanghai: Shanghai guji chubanshe, 1987.

Chen, Shih-chuan. "The Rise of the *Tz'u*, Reconsidered." *Journal of the American Oriental Society* 90.2 (1970): 232–242.

Cherniak, Susan. "Book Culture and Textual Transmission in Song China." *Harvard Journal of Asiatic Studies* 54.1 (1994): 5–125.

Cheung Sai-bung 張世彬. "Youlan pu yanjiu 幽蘭譜研究." *Journal of the Chinese University of Hong Kong* 5 (1979): 127–166.

Chia, Lucille. "The Uses of Print in Ming Dynasty China: A Very Brief Survey." In *Books in Numbers*, edited by Wilt L. Idema, 143–196. Cambridge, Mass.: Harvard-Yenching Library, Harvard University, 2007.

Chia, Lucille. *Printing for Profit: The Commercial Publishers of Jianyang, Fujian (11th–17th Centuries)*, Harvard-Yenching Institute Monograph Series No. 56. Cambridge, Mass.: Harvard University Asia Center, 2002.

Cho, Gene Jinsiong. *The Discovery of Musical Equal Temperament in China and Europe in the Sixteenth Century*. Lewiston, NY: Edwin Mellen Press, 2003.

Chow, Kai-wing. *Publishing, Culture, and Power in Early Modern China*. Stanford: Stanford University Press, 2004.

Chow, Sheryl. "A Localised Boundary Object: Seventeenth-Century Western Music in China." *Early Music History* 39 (2020): 75–113.

Clementi, Cecil. *Cantonese Love-Songs*, 2 vols. Oxford: Clarendon, 1904.

Cook, Scott. "'Yue Ji' 樂記 — Record of Music: Introduction, Translation, Notes, and Commentary." *Asian Music* 26.2 (1995): 1–96.

Dai Mingyang 戴明揚, ed. *Ji Kang ji jiaozhu* 嵇康集校注. Beijing: Renmin wenxue chubanshe, 1962.

Dittrich, Edith ed. *Hsi-hsiang chi, Chinesische Farbholzschnitte von Min Ch'i-chi*. Köln: Museum für Ostasiatische der Stadt Köln, 1977.

Dou Wun and Lee Ngan-giu. *Rare Recordings of Melodies from a Bygone Age*. Hong Kong: The Chinese Music Archive of the Chinese University of Hong Kong, 2011.

Du Halde, Jean-Baptiste. *A Description of the Empire of China*. London: T. Gardner for Edward Cave, 1738/1741.

Du Halde, Jean-Baptiste. *The General History of China*. London, 1739/1741.

Du Halde, Jean-Baptiste. *Description géographique, historique, chronologique, politique, et physique de l'empire de la Chine et de la Tartarie chinoise.* Paris: P. G. Lemercier, 1735.

Ebrey, Patricia Buckley. *Accumulating Culture: The Collections of Emperor Huizong*. Seattle: University of Washington Press, 2008.

Edgren, Sören. "Southern Song Printing at Hangzhou." *Museum of Far Eastern Antiquities Bulletin* 61 (1989): 1–212.

Edgren, Sören. "The Bibliographic Significance of Colour-Printed Books from the Shibui Collection." *Orientations* 40.3 (2009): 30–37.

Edgren, Sören. *Chinese Rare Books in American Collections*. New York: China Institute in America, 1984.

Egan, Ronald. "The Controversy over Music and 'Sadness' and Changing Conceptions of the *Qin* in Middle Period China." *Harvard Journal of Asiatic Studies* 57.1 (1997): 5–66.

Fan Jingzhong 范景中. "Taoyin ben he Min keben jiqi *Huizhen tu* 套印本和閔刻本及其《會真圖》." *Xin meishu* 新美術 (2005) 4: 77–82.

Fong, Grace S. *Herself an Author: Gender, Agency, and Writing in Late Imperial China*. Honolulu: University of Hawai'i Press, 2008.

Fong, Grace, Emily Goedde, Jeanne Larsen, Geoffrey Waters, and Michael Farman. *Jade Mirror: Women Poets of China*. Buffalo, New York: White Pine, 2013.

Fu Gang 傅剛. *Wenxuan banben yanjiu* 文選版本研究. Beijing: Beijing daxue chubanshe, 2000.

Fu Zengxiang 傅增湘. *Cangyuan qunshu jingyan lu* 藏園羣書經眼錄, 5 vols. Beijing: Zhonghua shuju, 1983.

Gonzalez de Mendoça, Joan. *Historia de las cosas mas notables ritos y costumbres del gran reyno dela China.* Rome, 1585.

González de Mendoza, Juan. *The Historie of the great and mightie kingdome of China, and the situation thereof.* In *The English Experience: Its Record in Early Printed Books Published in Facsimile*, no. 522. Amsterdam and New York: Theatrum Orbis Terrarum and Da Capo Press, 1973.

Gonzalez di Mendozza, Giovanni. *Dell'Historia della China*. Venice: Appresso Andrea Muschio, 1588.

Goormaghtigh, Georges. *L'Art du Qin: Deux Textes d'Esthétique Musicale Chinoise*. Bruxelles: Institut Belge des Hautes Études Chinoises, 1990.

Goshima Kuniharu 五島邦治, "Iike dendai shiryō no gakusho 井伊家伝来史料の楽書." *Geinoshi kenkyū* 藝能史研究 125 (1994): 51–59.

Gulik, R. H. van. *The Lore of the Chinese Lute: An Essay in Ch'in Ideology*. Tokyo: Sophia University, 1940.

Gulik, R. H. van. *Hs'i Kang and his Poetic Essay on the Lute*. Tokyo: Sophia University, 1941.

Gulik, R. H. van. *Chinese Pictorial Art as Viewed by the Connoisseur: Notes on the Means and Methods of Traditional Chinese Connoisseurship of Pictorial Art, based upon a Study of the Art of Mounting Scrolls in China and Japan*. New York: Hacker Art Books, 1981.

Guo Lixuan 郭立暄. *Zhongguo guji yuanke fanke yu chuyin houyin yanjiu* 中國古籍原刻翻刻與初印後印研究, 3 vols. Beijing: Zhongxi shuju, 2015.

Guojia tushuguan 國家圖書館. *Guojia tushuguan shanben shuzhi chugao: Jingbu* 國家圖書館善本書志初稿：經部. Taipei: Guojia tushuguan, 1996.

Guoli Beiping tushuguan 國立北平圖書館, ed. *Guoli Beiping tushuguan xiqu yinyue zhanlanhui mulu* 國立北平圖書館戲曲音樂展覽會目錄. Beiping: Guoli Beiping tushuguan, 1934.

Guoli gugong bowuyuan bianji weiyuanhui 國立故宮博物院編輯委員會, ed. *Songban shu tezhan mulu* 宋版書特展目錄. Taipei: Guoli gugong bowuyuan, 1986.

Guoli zhongyang tushuguan 國立中央圖書館. *Guoli zhongyang tushuguan Jin Yuan ben tulu* 國立中央圖書館金元本圖錄. Taipei: Zhonghua congshu bianshen weiyuanhui, 1961.

Guoli zhongyang tushuguan 國立中央圖書館. *Guoli zhongyang tushuguan shanben shumu* 國立中央圖書館善本書目, enlarged ed., 4 vols. Taipei: Guoli zhongyang tushuguan, 1967.

Guoli zhongyang tushuguan 國立中央圖書館. *Guoli zhongyang tushuguan songben tulu* 國立中央圖書館宋本圖錄. Taipei: Zhonghua congshu weiyuanhui, 1958.

Guy, R. Kent. *The Emperor's Four Treasuries: Scholars and the State in the Late Ch'ien-Lung Period.* Cambridge, Mass.: Council on East Asian Studies, Harvard University, 1987.

Harrist, Robert E. "The Artist as Antiquarian: Li Gonglin and His Study of Early Chinese Art." *Artibus Asiae* 55.3/4 (1995): 237–280.

Hayashi Kenzō 林謙三. *Gagaku: kogakufu no kaidoku* 雅楽：古楽譜の解読. Tokyo: Ongaku no tomosha, 1969.

Hayashi Kenzō 林謙三. "Kinsho sandai 琴書三題." *Tōyō ongaku kenkyū* 東洋音樂研究 (1942) 2: 235–245.

Helliwell, David. "The Repair and Binding of Old Chinese Books: Translated and Adapted for Western Conservators." *East Asian Library Journal* 8.1 (1998): 33–50.

Helman, Isadore Stanislas. *Suite des Seize Estampes représentant les Conquêtes de l'Empereur de la Chine avec leur Explication*. Paris: chez Helman and chez Ponce, 1788.

Henricks, Robert G. *Philosophy and Argumentation in Third-Century China: The Essays of Hsi K'ang*. Princeton, NJ: Princeton University Press, 1983.

Hervouet, Yves ed. *A Sung Bibliography*. Hong Kong: Chinese University Press, 1978.

Hou Wailu 侯外廬. *Zhongguo sixiang tongshi* 中國思想通史, vol. 4, pt. 2. Beijing: Renmin chubanshe, 1960.

Huang Ke 黃克. "*Shenyin jiangu lu*: Qianlong shiqi de kunqu yanchu shilu《審音鑒古錄》：乾隆時期的昆曲演出實錄." *Wenshi zhishi* 文史知識 (2008) 3: 128–133.

Huang Zongxi 黃宗羲 et al. *Song Yuan xue'an* 宋元學案. Beijing: Zhonghua shuju, 1986.

Huehns, Colin. "Dating Old *Huqin*: New Research on Examples of pre-1949 Instruments in Three Major British Collections." *Journal of the American Musical Instrument Society* 28 (2002): 118–173.

Huehns, Colin. "Lovely Ladies Stroking Strings." *Music in Art: International Journal for Music Iconography* 28.1/2 (2003): 5–44.

Idema, Wilt L. "Why you have never read a Yuan Drama: The Transformation of *Zaju* at the Ming Court." In *Studi in onore di Lionelle Lanciotti*, edited by S. M. Carletti et al., 765–791. Naples: Dipartimento di Studi Asiatici, Istituto Universitario Orientale, 1996.

Inoue Susumu 井上進. *Chūgoku shuppan bunka shi* 中国出版文化史. Nagoya: Nagoya University Press, 2002.

Jao Tsong-yi and Paul Demiéville. *Airs de Touen-houang (Touen-houang k'iu): Textes à chanter des VIIIe-Xe siècles*. Paris: Éditions du Centre National de la Recherche Scientifique, 1971.

Jao Tsung-i 饒宗頤, Li Zhifang 李直方, and Zhang Lijuan 張麗娟. *Xianggang daxue Feng Pingshan tushuguan cang shanben shulu* 香港大學馮平山圖書館藏善本書錄, enlarged ed. Hong Kong: Hong Kong University Press, 2003.

Jao Tsung-i 饒宗頤. *Dunhuang pipa pu lunwen ji* 敦煌琵琶譜論文集. Taipei: Xinwenfeng chuban gongsi, 1991.

Jao Tsung-i 饒宗頤. *Dunhuang pipa pu* 敦煌琵琶譜. Taipei: Xinwenfeng chuban gongsi, 1990.

Jao Tsung-i 饒宗頤. *Xianggang daxue Feng Pingshan tushuguan cang shanben shulu* 香港大學馮平山圖書館藏善本書錄. Hong Kong: Longmen shudian, 1970.

Ji Yun 紀昀 et al. *Siku quanshu zongmu* 四庫全書總目, 2 vols. Beijing: Zhonghua shuju, 1965.

Kang, Jiyeon. "Ji Kang's Criticism of Confucian and Naturalistic Music Theory." *Acta Musicologica* 86.2 (2014): 159–176.

Kaufmann, Walter. *Musical References in the Chinese Classics.* Detroit: Information Coordinators, 1976.

Kawada Higuma 河田羆. *Seikadō hisekishi* 靜嘉堂祕籍志, 25 vols. Tokyo: Seikadō, 1917–1919.

Kern, Martin. "A Note on the Authenticity and Ideology of *Shih-Chi* 24, 'The Book on Music'." *Journal of the American Oriental Society* 119.4 (1999): 673–677.

Kikkawa Yoshikazu 吉川良和. "Monobe Mokei senshi *Ushiran shihō kansu* kenkyū 物部茂卿撰次《烏絲欄指法卷子》研究." *Tōyō bunka kenkyūjo kiyō* 東洋文化研究所紀要 94 (1984): 1–66.

Kishibe Shigeo 岸辺成雄. *Tōdai ongaku no rekishiteki kenkyū: Gakuseihen* 唐代音楽の歴史的研究：楽制篇, 2 vols. Tokyo: Tokyo Daigaku Shuppankai, 1960–1961.

Knechtges, David R. trans. *Wen Xuan, or Selections of Refined Literature*, vol. 3. Princeton, NJ: Princeton University Press, 1996.

Kuraishi Takeshiro 倉石武四郎. *Jiujing shuying* 舊京書影. Beijing: Renmin wenxue chubanshe, 2011.

Kuttner, Fritz A. "Prince Chu Tsai-Yü's Life and Work: A Re-Evaluation of His Contribution to Equal Temperament Theory." *Ethnomusicology* 19.2 (1975): 163–206.

Lai Yu-chih 賴毓芝. "Tu yu li: *Hongchao liqi tushi* de chengli jiqi yingxiang 圖與禮:《皇朝禮器圖式》的成立及其影響." *Gugong xueshu jikan* 故宮學術季刊 37.2 (2020): 1–56.

Lam Ching Wah. "A Highlight of French Jesuit Scholarship in China: Jean-Joseph-Marie Amiot's Writings on Chinese Music." *CHIME: Journal of the European Foundation for Chinese Music Research* 16/17 (2005): 127–147.

Lam, Joseph S. C. "Huizong's Dashengyue, a Musical Performance of Emperorship and Officialdom." In *Emperor Huizong and Late Northern Song China: The Politics of Culture and the Culture of Politics*, edited by Patricia Buckley Ebrey and Maggie Bickford, 395–452. Cambridge, Mass.: Harvard University Asia Center, 2006.

Lay, G. T., "Musical Instruments of the Chinese," *The Chinese Repository*, vol. VIII (1839): 38–54.

Lee, Thomas H. C. *Government Education and Examinations in Sung China*. Hong Kong: Chinese University Press, 1985.

Lenoir, Yves and Nicolas Standaert, eds. *Les Danses rituelles chinoises d'après Joseph-Marie Amiot: Aux sources de l'ethnochorégraphie*. Namur: Éditions Lessius and Presses Univérsitaires de Namur, 2005.

Li Dou 李斗. *Yangzhou huafang lu* 揚州畫舫錄. Beijing: Zhonghua shuju, 1960.

Li Guangdi 李光地. *Guyuejing zhuan* 古樂經傳. Taipei: Shangwu yinshuguan, 1980.

Li Kaisheng 李開升. "*Yi li zhu shu* Chen Fengwu ben, Wang Wensheng ben bukao《儀禮注疏》陳鳳梧本、汪文盛本補考." *Wenshi* 文史 (2015) 2: 277–280.

Li Pingfan 李平凡, ed. *Huancui tang yuanjing tu* 環翠堂園景圖. Beijing: Renmin meishu chubanshe, 1981.

Li Shude 李樹德 et al. *Dexian zhi* 德縣志. Taipei: Chengwen chubanshe, 1968.

Liao Mingfei 廖明飛. "*Yi li* zhu shu heke kao《儀禮》注疏合刻考." *Wenshi* 文史 (2014) 1: 185–207.

Liu Chenggan 劉承幹. *Jiaye tang cangshu riji chao* 嘉業堂藏書日記抄, 2 vols. Nanjing: Fenghuang chubanshe, 2016.

Liu Chenggan 劉承幹. *Qiushu zhai riji* 求恕齋日記, 18 vols. Beijing: Guojia tushuguan chubanshe, 2016.

Liu Chenggan 劉承幹. *Wuxing Liushi Jiaye tang shanben shuying* 吳興劉氏嘉業堂善本書景, 6 vols. Shanghai: Jiaye tang, 1929.

Liu Chenggan 劉承幹. "Renwu rangshu jishi 壬午讓書紀事." *Lishi wenxian* (di ba ji) 歷史文獻（第八輯）, edited by Shanghai tushuguan lishi wenxian yanjiusuo 上海圖書館歷史文獻研究所, 241–271. Shanghai: Shanghai guji chubanshe, 2004.

Liu Fu 劉復. "Shier denglü de famingzhe Zhu Zaiyu 十二等律的發明者朱載堉." In *Qingzhu Cai Yuanpei xiansheng liushiwu sui lunwenji* 慶祝蔡元培先生六十五歲論文集, 279–310. Beiping: Guoli zhongyang yanjiuyuan, 1933.

Liu Xiang 劉向, and Liu Xin 劉歆. *Qilüe bielu yiwen* 七略別錄佚文. Aomen: Aomen daxue, 2007.

Liu Xu 劉昫. *Jiu Tang shu* 舊唐書, 16 vols. Beijing: Zhonghua shuju, 1975.

Loewe, Michael. *Dong Zhongshu, a "Confucian" Heritage and the Chunqiu Fanlu*. Leiden: Brill, 2011.

Loon, Piet van der. *Taoist Books in the Libraries of the Sung Period: A Critical Study and Index*. London: Ithaca, 1984.

Lu Xinyuan 陸心源. *Bisong lou cangshu zhi* 皕宋樓藏書志. Beijing: Zhonghua shuju, 1990.

Lu Xuan 陸烜. *Meigu oubi* 梅谷偶筆. In *Meigu shizhong shu* 梅谷十種書 by Lu Xuan 陸烜. Pinghu: Lushi, 1766–1768.

Lu Xuan 陸烜. *Mengying ci* 夢影詞. In *Meigu shizhong shu* 梅谷十種書 by Lu Xuan 陸烜. Pinghu: Lushi, 1766–1768.

Lu Xuan 陸烜. *Shang shu yi* 尚書義. Manuscript copy prepared by Shen Cai 沈彩, Fung Ping Shan Library (善 093.2 / 74).

Lü Zhuang 呂壯. "*Shenqi mipu* banben kao 神奇秘譜版本考." *Yinyue yanjiu* 音樂研究 (2019) 6: 33–43.

Lu Zugu 陸祖穀. *Zhejiang shengli tushuguan shanben shumu tizhi* 浙江省立圖書館善本書目題識. Hangzhou: Zhejiang shengli tushuguan, 1932.

Luo Zhenchang 羅振常. *Shanbenshu suojian lu* 善本書所見錄. Shanghai: Shangwu yinshuguan, 1958.

McDermott, Joseph. *A Social History of the Chinese Book: Books and Literati Culture in Late Imperial China*. Hong Kong: Hong Kong University Press, 2006.

Meyer-Fong, Tobie. "The Printed World: Books, Publishing Culture, and Society in Late Imperial China." *The Journal of Asian Studies* 66.3 (2007): 787–817.

Miao Quansun 繆荃孫, *Miao Quansun quanji: Riji* 繆荃孫全集: 日記, 4 vols. Nanjing: Fenghuang chubanshe, 2014.

Miao Quansun 繆荃孫, Wu Changshou 吳昌綬, and Dong Kang 董康. *Jiaye tang cangshu zhi* 嘉業堂藏書志. Shanghai: Fudan daxue chubanshe, 1997.

Miao Quansun 繆荃孫. *Yifeng cangshu ji* 藝風藏書記. Shanghai: Shanghai guji chubanshe, 2007.

Mo Boji 莫伯驥. *Wushiwanjuan lou qunshu bawen* 五十萬卷樓群書跋文, 7 vols. Guangzhou: s.n., 1947.

Morris, Peter T. *Cantonese Love Songs: An English Translation of Jiu Ji-yung's Cantonese songs of the Early 19th Century*. Hong Kong: Hong Kong University Press, 1992.

Mote, Frederick W. and Hung-lam Chu. *Calligraphy and the East Asian Book*. Boston: Shambhala, 1989.

Nagasawa Kikuya 長澤規矩也, ed. *Ashikaga Gakkō zenpon zuroku* 足利學校善本圖錄. Ashikaga: Ashika Gagakkō Iseki Toshokan Kōenkai, 1973.

Nagasawa Kikuya 長澤規矩也, ed. *Wakokubon ruisho shūsei* 和刻本類書集成, 6 vols. Tokyo: Kyūko shoin, 1976–1977.

Nagasawa Kikuya 長澤規矩也. *Jūsankyō chūso eifu* 十三經注疏影譜. Tokyo: Nihon Shoshi Gakkai, 1934.

Nagasawa Kikuya 長澤規矩也. *Nagasawa Kikuya chosakushū* 長澤規矩也著作集, vol. 1. Tokyo: Kyūko Shoin, 1982.

Nagasawa Kikuya 長澤規矩也. *Shoshigaku ronkō* 書誌學論考. Tokyo: Shōundō shoten, 1937.

Nakata Yūjirō 中田勇次郎. "Kessekichō yūran 碣石調幽蘭." In *Tō shōhon* 唐鈔本, edited by Osaka Shiritsu Bijutsukan 大阪市立美術館, 171. Kyoto: Dōhōsha, 1981.

Ōba Osamu 大庭脩, ed. *Hakusai shomoku* 舶載書目. Suita: Kansai daigaku tōzai gakujutsu kenkyūjo, 1972.

Ōba Osamu 大庭脩. *Edo jidai ni okeru tōsen mochiwatarisho no kenkyū* 江戶時代における唐船持渡書の研究. Suita: Kansai daigaku shuppanbu, 1967.

Ōeda Ryūhō 大枝流芳. *Gayū manroku* 雅遊漫錄. Nagoya: Eirakuya Tōshirō, 1755.

Ōki Yasushi 大木康. *Minmatsu Kōnan no shuppan bunka* 明末江南の出版文化. Tokyo: Kenbun shuppan, 2004.

Orden, Kate van. *Materialities: Books, Readers, and the Chanson in Sixteenth-Century Europe*. New York: Oxford University Press, 2015.

Orden, Kate van. *Music, Authorship, and the Book in the First Century of Print*. Berkeley: University of California Press, 2014.

Ouyang Xiu 歐陽修. *Ouyang Xiu ji biannian jianzhu* 歐陽修集編年箋注, 8 vols. Chengdu: Bashu shushe, 2007.

Ouyang Xiu 歐陽修. *Ouyang Xiu quanji* 歐陽修全集, 2 vols. Beijing: Zhongguo shudian, 1986.

Ozaki Yasushi 尾崎康. *Seishi Sōgen-ban no kenkyū* 正史宋元版の研究. Tokyo: Kyūko shoin, 1989.

Pan Chengbi 潘承弼, and Gu Tinglong 顧廷龍. *Mingdai banben tulu chubian* 明代版本圖錄初編, 12 vols. Shanghai: Kaiming shudian, 1941.

Pi Xirui 皮錫瑞. *Jingxue tonglun* 經學通論, 4 vols. Shanghai: Shangwu yinshuguan, 1930.

Pian, Rulan Chao. *Sonq Dynasty Musical Sources and Their Interpretation*. Cambridge, Mass.: Harvard University Press, 1967.

Picard, François. "Music (17th and 18th centuries)." In *Handbook of Christianity in China, Volume One: 635–1800*, edited by Nicolas Standaert, 851–860. Leiden: Brill, 2001.

Picard, François. "Musik der Jesuiten im Peking der 17. und 18. Jahrhunderten." In *Der Fremde Klang: Tradition und Avantgarde in Musik Ostasiens*, edited by Hinrich Bergmeier, 93–119. Hannover: Biennale Neue Musik Hannover, 1999.

Picken, Laurence, Noël Nickson, and Marnix Wells. "'West River Moon': A Song-Melody predicted by a Lute-Piece in *Piba* Tablature." *CHIME: Journal of the European Foundation for Chinese Music Research* 10/11 (1997): 172–185.

Picken, Laurence. "Secular Chinese Songs of the Twelfth Century." *Studia Musicologica Academiae Scientiarum Hungaricae* 8 (1966): 125–172.

Picken, Laurence. "Twelve Ritual Melodies of the T'ang Dynasty." In *Studia memoriae Belae Bartók sacra*, edited by Benjámin Rajeczky and Lajos Vargyas, 147–173. Budapest: Aedes Academiae Scientiarum Hungaricae, 1956.

Qian Tong 錢侗. *Chongwen zongmu jishi* 崇文總目輯釋. In *Xuxiu siku quanshu* 續修四庫全書, edited by Xuxiu siku quanshu bianzuan weiyuanhui 續修四庫全書編纂委員會, vol. 916. Shanghai: Shanghai guji chubanshe, 1995.

Qiu Hechou 丘鶴儔. *Qinxue xinbian* 琴學新編. Hong Kong: Shichang yanghuopu, 1920.

Qiu Qiongsun 丘瓊蓀. *Lidai yue zhi lü zhi jiaoshi* 歷代樂志律志校釋, vol. 1. Beijing: Zhonghua shuju 1964.

Qu Yong 瞿鏞. *Tieqin tongjian lou cangshu mulu* 鐵琴銅劍樓藏書目錄. Beijing: Zhonghua shuju, 1990.

Rameau, Jean-Philippe. *Code de musique pratique avec de Nouvelles réflexions sur le principe sonore*. Paris: De l'Imprimerie royale, 1760.

Reed, Christopher. *Gutenberg in Shanghai: Chinese Print Capitalism, 1876–1937*. Honolulu: University of Hawai'i Press, 2004.

Robinson, Kenneth and Joseph Needham. "Sound (Acoustics)." In *Science and Civilisation in China*, vol. 4, pt. 1, edited by Joseph Needham, 126–228. Cambridge: Cambridge University Press, 1962.

Rong Geng 容庚. "Songdai jijin shuji shuping 宋代吉金書籍述評." *Xueshu yanjiu* 學術研究 (1963) 6: 81–97.

Seikadō Bunko 靜嘉堂文庫, ed. *Seikadō Bunko Sō Gen han zuroku* 靜嘉堂文庫宋元版圖錄, 2 vols. Tokyo: Kyūko shoin, 1992.

Shao Yichen 邵懿辰. *Lijing tonglun* 禮經通論. In *Qing jingjie* 清經解, edited by Ruan Yuan 阮元 and Wang Xianqian 王先謙, vol. 13. Nanjing: Fenghuang chubanshe, 2005.

Shen Cai 沈彩. *Chunyu lou gao* 春雨樓稾. Shanghai: Tanyin lu, 1924.

Shen Cai 沈彩. *Chunyu lou ji* 春雨樓集. In *Qingdai shi wen ji huibian* 清代詩文集彙编, edited by Qingdai shi wen ji huibian bianzuan weiyuanhui 清代詩文集彙編編纂委員會, vol. 379, 1–64. Shanghai: Shanghai guji chubanshe, 2010.

Shen Cai 沈彩. *Chunyu lou ji* 春雨樓集. In *Jiangnan nüxing bieji san bian* 江南女性別集三編, edited by Hu Xiaoming 胡曉明 and Peng Guozhong 彭國忠, vol. 1, 1–115. Hefei: Huangshan shushe, 2011.

Shen Yunsheng 沈允升. *Zhongxi xiange fengqin hepu* 中西絃歌風琴合譜. Hong Kong: Yinyue yanjiushe, 1936.

Shi Tingyong 施廷鏞. "Gugong tushu ji 故宮圖書記." *Tushuguan xue jikan* 圖書館學季刊 1.1 (1926): 53–59.

Shiba Rokurō 斯波六郎. *Monzen sakuin* 文選索引, 4 vols. Kyoto: Kyōtō daigaku jinbun kagaku kenkyūjo sakuin iinkai, 1957.

Shimada Kan 島田翰. *Kobun kyūsho kō; tsuketari Kokon shokoku* 古文舊書考；附古今書刻, 4 vols. Tokyo: Min'yūsha, 1905.

Sieber, Patricia. "Nobody's Genre, Everybody's Song: *Sanqu* Songs and the Expansion of the Literary Sphere in Yuan China." *Journal of Chinese Literature and Culture* 1.1 (2014): 29–64.

Sieber, Patricia. "Rethinking the History of Early *Sanqu* Songs." *CHINOPERL: Journal of Chinese Oral and Performing Literature* 26.1 (2005): 83–98.

Sieber, Patricia. "The Protean World of *Sanqu* Songs." *Journal of Chinese Literature and Culture* 8.1 (2021): 1–11.

Staunton, George. *An Authentic Account of an Embassy from the King of Great Britain to the Emperor of China*. London: G. Nicol of Pall-Mall, 1797 and 1798.

Su Bai 宿白. *Hanwen foji mulu* 漢文佛籍目錄. Beijing: Wenwu chubanshe, 2009.

Sun, Chengjuan. "The Hidden Blessing of being a Last Ruler: Anecdotes and the Song Dynasty Interpretation of Li Yu's (937–978) Lyrics." *Chinese Literature: Essays, Articles, Reviews* 34 (2012): 105–129.

Takeda Kagaku Shinkō Zaidan Kyōu Shooku 武田科学振興財團杏雨書屋. Tonkō hikyū: Kyōu Shooku zō 敦煌秘笈：杏雨書屋藏, 10 vols. Osaka: Takeda Kagaku Shinkō Zaidan, 2009.

Takezoe Kōkō 竹添光鴻. *Sa shi kaisen* 左氏會箋, 2 vols. Tokyo: Fuzanbō, 1911.

Tao Xiang 陶湘. *Mingdai Wuxing Minban shumu* 明吳興閔板書目. In Tao Xiang 陶湘, *Taoshi shumu congkan* 陶氏書目叢刊, vol. 1. Wujin: Taoshi, 1933.

Tchen, Ysia. *La musique chinoise en France au XVIIIe siècle*. Paris: Publications orientalistes de France, 1974.

Tomita Jun 富田淳. "Kessekichō yūran daigo ni tsuite 幽蘭研究国際シンポジウム." In *Yūran kenkyū kokusai shinpojiumu* 幽蘭研究国際シンポジウム, edited by Tōyō kingaku kenkyūjo 東洋琴学研究所, 31–32. Tokyo: Tōyō kingaku kenkyūjo, 1999.

Tse, Chun-Yan. "Erroneous Discourses on Tuning Theories between China and the West: The Kangxi 14-tone System." *Theoria: Historical Aspects of Music Theory* 26 (2020): 5–24.

Tsien Tsuen-Hsuin. *Written on Bamboo and Silk*. Chicago: University of Chicago Press, 2004.

Tsien Tsuen-Hsuin. *Chemistry and Chemical Technology: Paper and Printing*. In *Science and Civilisation in China*, edited by Joseph Needham, vol. 5, pt. 1, Cambridge: Cambridge University Press, 1985.

Twitchett, Denis. "A Note on the 'Monograph on Music,' in *Chiu T'ang shu*." *Asia Major*, 3rd ser., 3.1 (1990): 51–62.

Twitchett, Denis. *The Writing of Official History under the T'ang*. Cambridge: Cambridge University Press, 1992.

Wang Chung-min. *A Descriptive Catalog of Rare Chinese Books in the Library of Congress*. Washington DC: Library of Congress, 1957.

Wang Fang-yu. "Book Illustration in Late Ming and Early Qing China." In *Chinese Rare Books in American Collections*, edited by Sören Edgren, 31–43. New York: China Institute in America, 1984.

Wang Guowei 王國維. *Liangzhe gu kanben kao* 兩浙古刊本考. In *Wang Guowei quanji* 王國維全集, edited by Xie Weiyang 謝維揚 and Fang Xinliang 房鑫亮, vol. 7, 1–192. Hangzhou: Zhejiang jiaoyu chubanshe, 2009.

Wang Guowei 王國維. *Wudai liang Song jianben kao* 五代兩宋監本考. In *Wang Guowei quanji* 王國維全集, edited by Xie Weiyang 謝維揚 and Fang Xinliang 房鑫亮, vol. 7, 193–306. Hangzhou: Zhejiang jiaoyu chubanshe, 2009.

Wang Jide 王驥德. *Wang Jide Qu lü* 王驥德曲律. Changsha: Hunan renmin chubanshe, 1983.

Wang Jilie 王季烈, ed. *Ye Changchi Yuandu lu rijichao* 葉昌熾緣督廬日記鈔. Shanghai: Yinyinlu, 1933.

Wang Jishan 王繼善, ed. *Shenyin jiangu lu* 審音鑑古錄, 2 vols. Beijing: Xueyuan chubanshe, 2003.

Wang Mengshu 汪孟舒. *Wusilan zhifa shi* 烏絲欄指法釋. In *Guwu Wang Mengshu xiansheng qinxue yizhu* 古吳汪孟舒先生琴學遺著, edited by Yang Yuanzheng 楊元錚, vol. 1, 1–144. Beijing: Zhonghua shuju, 2013.

Wang Rongguo 王榮國, Wang Xiaowen 王筱雯, and Wang Qingyuan 王清原. *Mingdai Min Ling ke taoyinben tulu* 明代閔淩刻套印本圖錄. Yangzhou: Guangling shushe, 2006.

Wang Shixiang 王世襄, ed. *Zhongguo gudai yinyue shumu chugao* 中國古代音樂書目初稿. Beijing: Yinyue chubanshe, 1961.

Wang Tan 王坦. *Qin zhi* 琴旨. In *Siku quanshu zhenben 5 ji* 四庫全書珍本五集, edited by Zhongyang tushuguan choubeichu 中央圖書館籌備處, vol. 59. Taipei: Taiwan shangwu yinshuguan, 1974.

Wang Tan 王坦. *Qin zhi* 琴旨. S.l.: Su tang, 1746.

Wang Wenjin 王文進. *Wenlu tang fangshu ji* 文祿堂訪書記. Beiping: Wenlu tang, 1942.

Wang Zhongmin 王重民. *Zhongguo muluxue shi luncong* 中國目錄學史論叢. Beijing: Zhonghua shuju, 1984.

Wang Zhongmin 王重民. *Zhongguo shanbenshu tiyao* 中國善本書提要. Shanghai: Shanghai guji chubanshe, 1983.

Wang, Shi-pe. "Plays within Songs: *Sanqu* Songs from Literary Refinement (*ya*) to Popular Appeal (*su*)." *Journal of Chinese Literature and Culture* 8.2 (2021): forthcoming.

Watt, James C. Y. "Antiquarianism and Naturalism." In *Possessing the Past: Treasures from the National Palace Museum, Taipei*, edited by Wen C. Fong and James C. Y. Watt, 219–256. New York: Metropolitan Museum of Art, 1996.

Wells, Marnix. "West River Moon: Great Music of Few Notes." *CHIME: Journal of the European Foundation for Chinese Music Research* 7 (1993): 58–89.

Wenhuabu wenxue yishu yanjiuyuan Yinyue yanjiusuo 文化部文學藝術研究院音樂研究所 and Beijing guqin yanjiuhui 北京古琴研究會, ed. *Qinqu jicheng* 琴曲集成, vol. 1. Beijing: Zhonghua shuju, 1981.

West, Stephen H. and Wilt L. Idema, trans. *The Story of the Western Wing*. Berkeley: University of California Press, 1995.

Widmer, Ellen. "The Huanduzhai of Hangzhou and Suzhou: A Study in Seventeenth-Century Publishing." *Harvard Journal of Asiatic Studies* 56.1 (1996): 77–122.

Wong, Anita, ed. *Guyue fengliu: Zhongguo yuepu yueshu yueren* 古樂風流：中國樂譜樂書樂人. Hong Kong: University Museum and Art Gallery, The University of Hong Kong, 2001.

Woo, Shingkwan. "The Ceremonial Music of Zhu Zaiyu." PhD diss., Rutgers, The State University of New Jersey, 2017.

Wu Ge 吳格. "Wuxing Liushi Jiaye tang cangshu jusan kaolue 吳興劉氏嘉業堂藏書聚散考略." *Shumu jikan* 書目季刊 37.4 (2004): 17–44.

Wu Xiaoling 吳曉鈴. *Nan bei gong ciji jiaobu* 南北宮詞紀校補. Beijing: Zhonghua shuju, 1961.

Wu, K. T. "Ming Printing and Printers." *Harvard Journal of Asiatic Studies* 7.3 (1943): 203–260.

Xia Chengtao 夏承燾. *Jiang Baishi ci biannian jianjiao* 姜白石詞編年箋校. Shanghai: Shanghai guji chubanshe, 1998.

Xiao Zhentang 蕭振棠 and Ding Yu 丁瑜. *Zhongguo guji zhuangding xiubu jishu* 中國古籍裝訂修補技術. Beijing: Shumu wenxian chubanshe, 1980.

Xu Taikong 許太空 et al. *Yue yuefu* 粵樂府. Aomen: Tianlai lelu, 1932.

Yang Shaohe 楊紹和. *Yingshu yulu* 楹書隅錄. Beijing: Zhonghua shuju, 1990.

Yang Yinliu 楊蔭瀏 and Yin Falu 陰法魯. *Song Jiang Baishi chuangzuo gequ yanjiu* 宋姜白石創作歌曲研究. Beijing: Yinyue chubanshe, 1957.

Yang Yinliu 楊蔭瀏. "Pingjun lü suanjie 平均律算解." *Yenching Journal of Chinese Studies* 燕京學報 21 (1937): 2–60.

Yang Yuanzheng 楊元錚 and Yang Jun 楊軍. "Haihun hou mu chutu de qixian qin yu Xihan qinzhi 海昏侯墓出土的七弦琴與西漢琴制." *Wenwu* 文物 (2022): forthcoming.

Yang Yuanzheng 楊元錚. "*Jieshidiao youlan* yu *Qinyong zhifa* hejuanshuo bianzheng《碣石調幽蘭》與《琴用指法》合卷説辨正." In *Qinxue lunji* 琴學論集, edited by Lau Chor-wah 劉楚華, 15–30 and color plates 1–6. Hong Kong: Cosmos Books, 2010.

Yang Yuanzheng 楊元錚. "Wang Mengshu *Wusilan zhifa shi* de jiaokanxue 汪孟舒《烏絲欄指法釋》的校勘學." *Zhongguo yinyuexue* 中國音樂學 (2009) 4: 51–54.

Yang Yuanzheng. "A Tale of Two Manuscripts: The Making and Origins of the Earliest Scrolls of Qin Music." *Acta Musicologica* 86.1 (2014): 32–73.

Yang Yuanzheng. "Finding the Key: Tuning Keys Discovered from the Imperial Collection of Emperor Huizong." *Music in Art: International Journal for Music Iconography* 40.1/2 (2015): 275–284

Yang Yuanzheng. "*Jindou*: A Musical Form found in Southern Song Lyric Songs." *T'oung Pao* 101.1/3 (2015): 98–129.

Yang Yuanzheng. *Music in Print: Selections from the Fung Ping Shan Library and Western Rare Book Collection*. Hong Kong: University of Hong Kong Libraries, 2021.

Yang Yuanzheng. "Musical Archaeology and the Prehistory of Chinese Music." *The Oxford Handbook of Music in China and the Chinese Diaspora*, forthcoming, edited by Jonathan P. J. Stock and Yu Hui. New York: Oxford University Press.

Yang Yuanzheng. *Plum Blossom on the Far Side of the Stream: The Renaissance of Jiang Kui's Lyric Oeuvre with Facsimiles and a New Critical Edition of the Songs of the Whitestone Daoist*. Hong Kong: Hong Kong University Press, 2019.

Yang Zhishui 揚之水. *Zhima tongjian* 脂麻通鑒. Shenyang: Liaoning jiaoyu chubanshe, 1995.

Yao Zhenzong 姚振宗. *Sui shu jingji zhi kaozheng* 隋書經籍志考證. In *Xuxiu siku quanshu* 續修四庫全書, edited by Xuxiu siku quanshu bianzuan weiyuanhui 續修四庫全書編纂委員會, vol. 915. Shanghai: Shanghai guji chubanshe, 1995.

Ye Changchi 葉昌熾. *Yuandu lu riji* 緣督廬日記. Taipei: Taiwan xuesheng shuju, 1964.

Ye Dehui 葉德輝. *Shulin qinghua* 書林清話. Beijing: Guji chubanshe, 1957.

Ye Shi 葉適. *Xixue jiyan xumu* 習學記言序目, 2 vols. Beijing: Zhonghua shuju, 1977.

Yu Bing 俞冰. *Guqin shu tukao* 古琴書圖考, 2 vols. Beijing: Xueyuan chubanshe, 2009.

Yu Hui-chun 余慧君. "Zun lü du yu wujiang: *Hongchao liqi tushi* yueqi juan yanjiu 遵律度於無疆：《皇朝禮器圖式》樂器卷研究." *Gugong xueshu jikan* 故宮學術季刊 37.3 (2020): 95–133.

Yuan Tongli 袁同禮. "Zhongguo yinyue shu juyao 中國音樂書舉要." *Zhonghua tushuguan xiehui huibao* 中華圖書館協會會報 3.4 (1928): 6–17.

Yung, Bell. "The Scholar and the Courtesan: Love Songs on Pearl River's Flower Boats." *CHINOPERL: Journal of Chinese Oral and Performing Literature* 41 (2022): forthcoming.

Yu, Siu-Wah. "Meaning and Cultural Functions of Non-Chinese Music in the Eighteenth-Century Manchu Court." PhD diss., Harvard University, 1996.

Zha Fuxi 查阜西. *Zha Fuxi qinxue wencui* 查阜西琴学文萃. Hangzhou: Zhongguo meishu xueyuan chubanshe, 1995.

Zhang Shunhui 張舜徽. *Han shu yiwen zhi tongshi* 漢書藝文志通釋. Wuhan: Hubei jiaoyu chubanshe, 1990.

Zhang Yuanji 張元濟. *Baoli tang Songben shulu* 寶禮堂宋本書錄, 4 vols. Shanghai: Nanhai Panshi, 1939.

Zhao Jingshen 趙景深. *Nan bei gong ciji* 南北宮詞紀, 4 vols. Beijing: Zhonghua shuju, 1959.

Zhao Wanli 趙萬里. *Zhongguo banke tulu* 中國版刻圖錄, 8 vols. Beijing: Wenwu chubanshe, 1961.

Zhao Ziyong 招子庸. *Yue'ou* 粵謳. In *Su wenxue congkan di yi ji* 俗文學叢刊第一集, edited by Yang Jialuo 楊家駱, vol. 6. Taipei: Shijie shuju, 1963.

Zhongguo guji shanben shumu bianji weiyuanhui 中國古籍善本書目編輯委員會, ed. *Zhongguo guji shanben shumu: Jibu* 中國古籍善本書目：集部, 3 vols. Shanghai: Shanghai guji chubanshe, 1998.

Zhongguo guji shanben shumu bianji weiyuanhui 中國古籍善本書目編輯委員會, ed. *Zhongguo guji shanben shumu* 中國古籍善本書目, 9 vols. Shanghai: Shanghai guji chubanshe, 1986–1996.

Zhongguo guji zongmu bianzuan weiyuanhui 中國古籍總目編纂委員會, ed. *Zhongguo guji zongmu* 中國古籍總目, 26 vols. Beijing and Shanghai: Zhonghua shuju and Shanghai guji chubanshe, 2009.

Zhongguo guojia tushuguan 中國國家圖書館 and Zhongguo guojia guji baohu zhongxin 中國國家古籍保護中心, ed. *Di er pi guojia zhengui guji minglu tulu* 第二批國家珍貴古籍名錄圖錄, 10 vols. Beijing: Guojia tushuguan chubanshe, 2010.

Zhongguo guojia tushuguan 中國國家圖書館 and Zhongguo guojia guji baohu zhongxin 中國國家古籍保護中心, ed. *Di yi pi guojia zhengui guji minglu tulu* 第一批國家珍貴古籍名錄圖錄, 8 vols. Beijing: Guojia tushuguan chubanshe, 2008.

Zhongguo yishu yanjiuyuan yinyue yanjiusuo ziliaoshi 中國藝朮研究院音樂研究所資料室. *Zhongguo yinyue shupuzhi* 中國音樂書譜志. Beijing: Renmin yinyue chubanshe, 1994.

Zhongyang yinyue xueyuan minzu yinyue yanjiusuo 中央音樂學院民族音樂研究所, ed. *Zhongguo yinyue shiliao chenlieshi shuoming* 中國音樂史料陳列室說明. Beijing: Zhongyang yinyue xueyuan minzu yinyue yanjiusuo, 1956.

Zhongyang yinyue xueyuan Zhongguo yinyue yanjiusuo 中央音樂學院中國音樂研究所 and Beijing guqin yanjiuhui 北京古琴研究會, ed. *Qinqu jicheng* 琴曲集成, vol. 1. Beijing: Zhonghua shuju, 1963.

Zhou Hui 周暉. *Xu Jinling suoshi* 續金陵瑣事. Beijing: Wenxue guji kanxingshe, 1955.

Zhou Mi 周密. *Qidong yeyu jiaozhu* 齊東野語校注. Shanghai: Huadong shifan daxue chubanshe, 1987.

Zhou Qingyun 周慶雲, ed. *Qinshu bielu* 琴書別錄. Shanghai: Mengpo shi, 1914.

Zhou Qingyun 周慶雲, ed. *Qinshu cunmu* 琴書存目. Shanghai: Mengpo shi, 1914.

Zhou Xiaoying 周小英. "Nüxing huaxue zhuzuo de di yi bu shu *Chunyu lou shuhua mu* (shang) 女性畫學著作的第一部書《春雨樓書畫目》(上)." *Xin meishu* 新美術 (2009) 6: 42–53.

Zhou Zimei 周子美. *Jiaye tang chaojiaoben mulu* 嘉業堂鈔校本目錄. Shanghai: Huadong shifan daxue chubanshe, 1986.

Zhu Jiajin 朱家溍. *Xiaoshan Zhu shi jiuchang mulu* 蕭山朱氏舊藏目錄. Beijing: Gugong chubanshe, 2014.

Zhu Xi 朱熹. *Zhuzi yulei* 朱子語類, 8 vols. Beijing: Zhonghua shuju, 1986.

Zhu Yizun 朱彝尊. *Pushu ting ji* 曝書亭集, 14 vols. Shanghai: Shangwu yinshuguan, 1935.

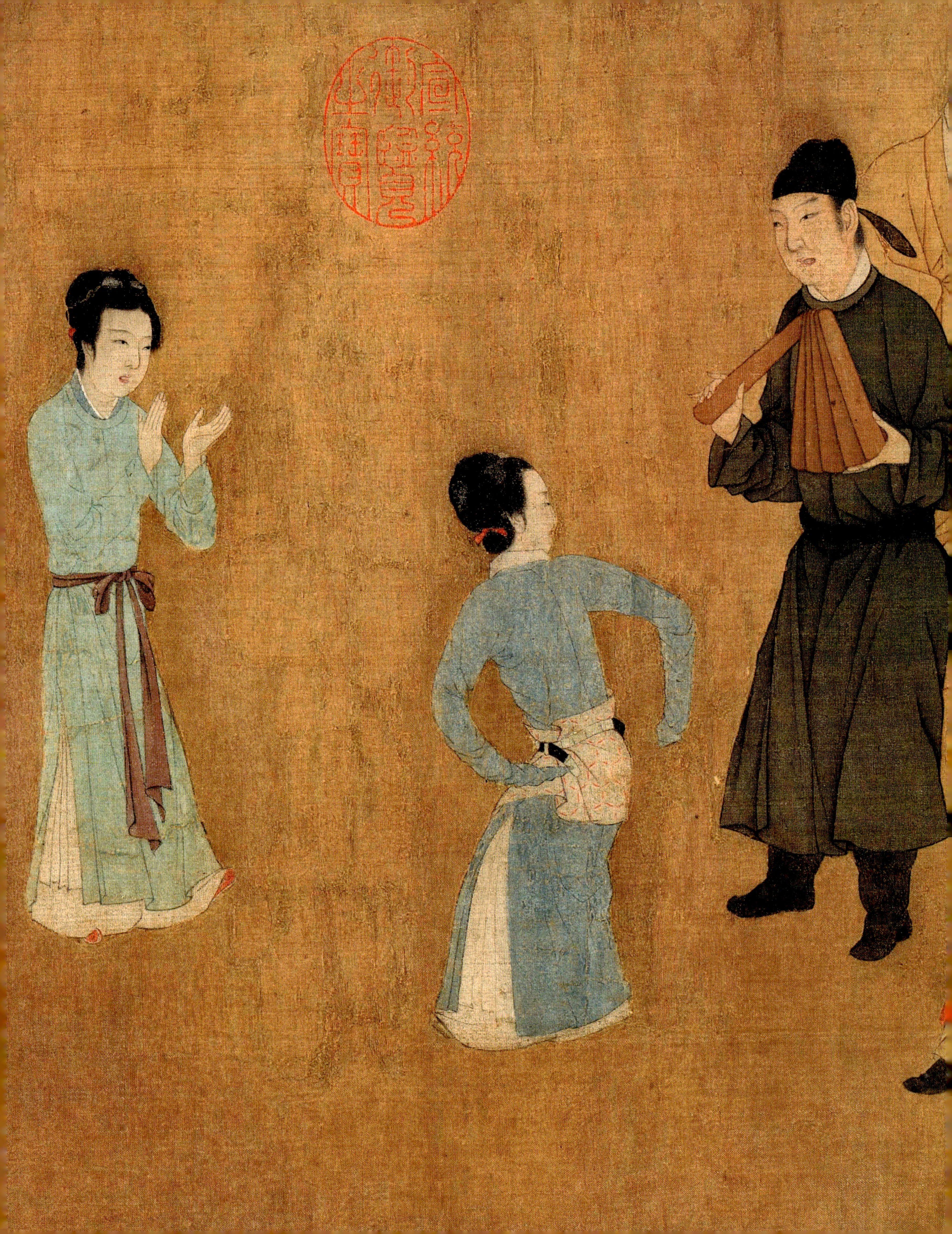

Index

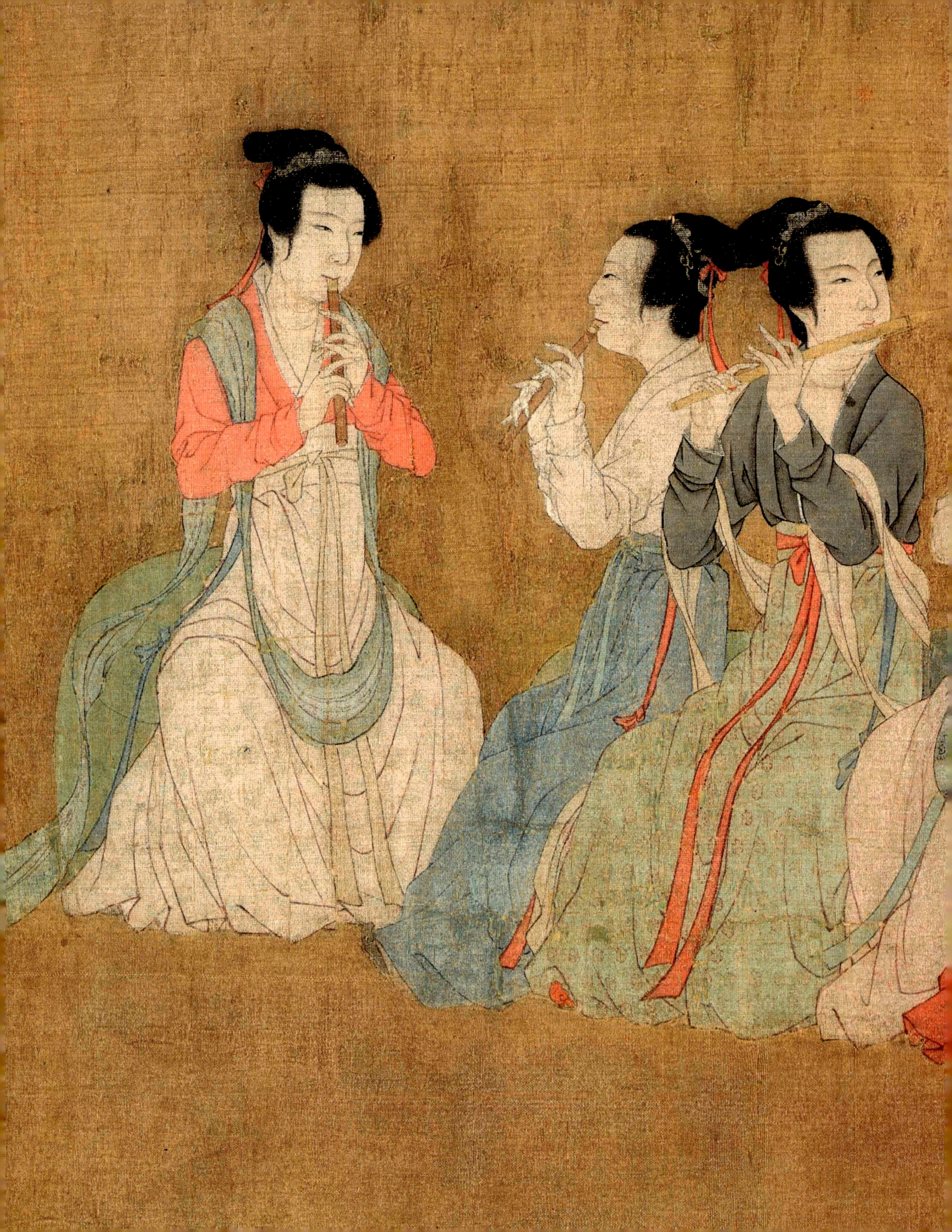

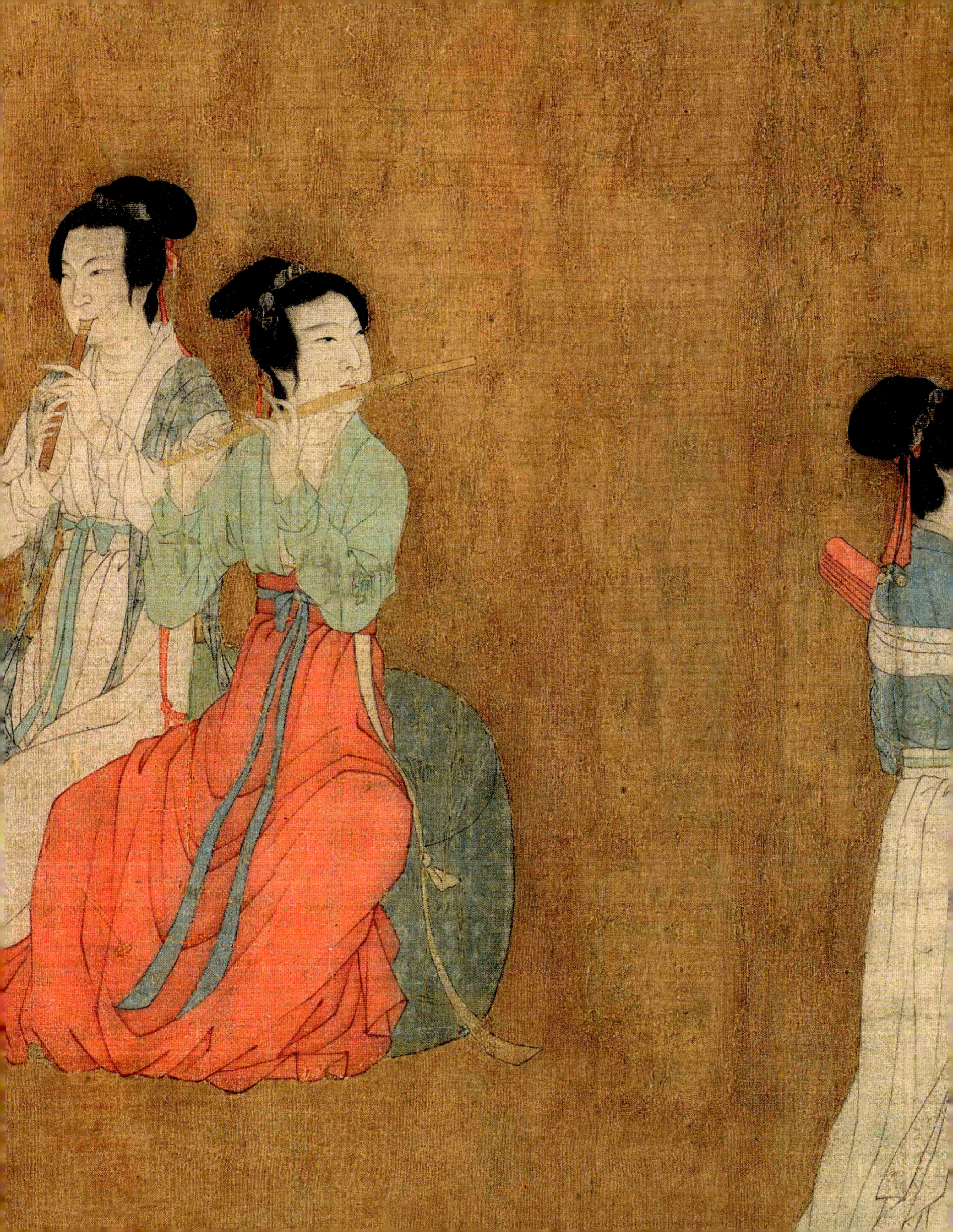

Published by
Hong Kong University Press
The University of Hong Kong
Pokfulam Road
Hong Kong
https://hkupress.hku.hk

Authors: Yang Yuanzheng, Fong Sing Ha, and Colin Huehns
Editor: Yang Yuanzheng
Copy-editing and proofreading by: Christopher Mattison
Designer: Stephy Tsui
Typeset in: Dante MT Std, MSung HK, and Goudy Old Style
Paper: GardaPat 13 Klassica 150 g/m²

Supported by

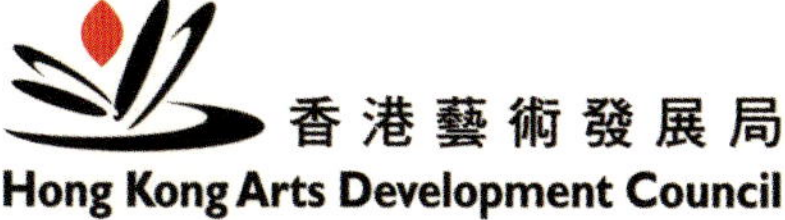

Hong Kong Arts Development Council fully supports freedom of artistic expression. The views and opinions expressed in this project do not represent the stand of the Council.

This publication has also been generously supported by the T. H. Chan Publication Fund.

ISBN 978-988-8805-66-2 (*Hardback*)

British Library Cataloguing-in-Publication Data
A catalogue record for this book is available from the British Library.

10 9 8 7 6 5 4 3 2 1
Printed and bound by Hang Tai Printing Co., Ltd. in Hong Kong, China

Jacket:
Musical notation of the *qin* piece *Solitary Orchid* (details), preserved in a facsimile made in 1884 of Kojima Hōso's (1797–1847) tracing copy of the manuscript Tōkyō, Tōkyō Kokuritsu Hakubutsukan TB1393. Edited by Li Shuchang (1837–1897). Woodblock-printed book, ink on paper; block size: 23.3 × 16.6 cm. Private collection.

Pages iv–v, vi, viii, and xii:
Procession of Daoist Immortals Paying Homage to the Primordial Spirit (details), Northern Song dynasty (960–1127). Attributed to Wu Zongyuan (d. 1050). Handscroll, ink on silk; whole scroll: 57.8 cm × 789.5 cm. C. C. Wang family collection, New York.

Pages 258, 260, 270, 278, 288, and 300–301:
The Night Revels of Han Xizai (details), twelfth century. Copy after Gu Hongzong (937–975). Handscroll, ink and color on silk; whole painting: 28.7 cm × 335.5 cm. Palace Museum, Beijing.